Melanie Klein i

In this book Claudia Frank discusses how Melanie Klein began to develop her psychoanalysis of children. *Melanie Klein in Berlin: Her First Psychoanalyses of Children* offers a detailed comparative analysis of both published and unpublished material from the Melanie Klein Archive.

By using previously unpublished studies, Frank demonstrates how Klein enriched the concept of negative transference and laid the basis for the innovations in both technique and theory that eventually led not only to changes in child analysis, but also to changes in the analysis of adults. Frank also uncovers the influence that this had on Klein's later theories of the paranoid-schizoid and depressive positions, and on her understanding of psychotic anxieties.

The first seven chapters of the book provide an explanation of the essence of Klein's approach to child psychoanalysis covering topics including:

- the inevitability and usefulness of negative transference
- development of play
- early conscious and unconscious phantasies

Part Two provides a translation of Klein's unpublished notes on the treatments of four of the children she analysed in Berlin: 7-year-old Grete, 2-year-old Rita, 7-year-old Inge and 6-year-old Erna.

Melanie Klein in Berlin is the first text to make extensive use of Klein's unpublished papers, clinical notes, diaries and manuscripts. It will appeal to anyone involved in child psychoanalysis and the development of Melanie Klein's thinking.

Claudia Frank is a psychoanalyst in private practice in Stuttgart. She is a training analyst of the DPV, a constituent society of the

International Psychoanalytical Association. Until 2001 she was Chair of Psychoanalysis, Psychotherapy and Psychosomatics in the Department for Psychoanalysis, Psychotherapy and Psychosomatics of the University in Tübingen. She has published papers on the technique, theory and history of psychoanalysis, as well as on applied psychoanalysis. She is co-editor of the *Jahrbuch der Psychoanalyse*.

THE NEW LIBRARY OF PSYCHOANALYSIS
General Editor   Dana Birksted-Breen

The New Library of Psychoanalysis was launched in 1987 in association with the Institute of Psychoanalysis, London. It took over from the International Psychoanalytical Library, which published many of the early translations of the works of Freud and the writings of most of the leading British and Continental psychoanalysts.

The purpose of the New Library of Psychoanalysis is to facilitate a greater and more widespread appreciation of psychoanalysis and to provide a forum for increasing mutual understanding between psychoanalysts and those working in other disciplines such as the social sciences, medicine, philosophy, history, linguistics, literature and the arts. It aims to represent different trends both in British psychoanalysis and in psychoanalysis generally. The New Library of Psychoanalysis is well placed to make available to the English-speaking world psychoanalytic writings from other European countries and to increase the interchange of ideas between British and American psychoanalysts.

The Institute, together with the British Psychoanalytical Society, runs a low-fee psychoanalytic clinic, organizes lectures and scientific events concerned with psychoanalysis and publishes the *International Journal of Psychoanalysis*. It also runs the only UK training course in psychoanalysis which leads to membership of the International Psychoanalytical Association – the body that preserves internationally agreed standards of training, of professional entry, and of professional ethics and practice for psychoanalysis as initiated and developed by Sigmund Freud. Distinguished members of the Institute have included Michael Balint, Wilfred Bion, Ronald Fairbairn, Anna Freud, Ernest Jones, Melanie Klein, John Rickman, and Donald Winnicott.

Previous General Editors include David Tuckett, Elizabeth Spillius and Susan Budd. Previous and current Members of the Advisory Board include Christopher Bollas, Ronald Britton, Catalina Bronstein, Donald Campbell, Sara Flanders, Stephen Grosz, John Keene, Eglé Laufer, Juliet Mitchell, Michael Parsons, Rosine Jozef Perelberg, David Taylor and Mary Target, and Richard Rusbridger, who is now Assistant Editor.

ALSO IN THIS SERIES

Feeling the Words: Neuropsychoanalytic Understanding of Memory and the Unconscious Mauro Mancia

Projected Shadows: Psychoanalytic Reflections on the Representation of Loss in European Cinema Edited by Andrea Sabbadini

Encounters with Melanie Klein: Selected Papers of Elizabeth Spillius Elizabeth Spillius. Edited by Priscilla Roth and Richard Rusbridger

Constructions and the Analytic Field: History, Scenes and Destiny Domenico Chianese

Yesterday, Today and Tomorrow Hanna Segal

Psychoanalysis Comparable and Incomparable: The Evolution of a Method to Describe and Compare Psychoanalytic Approaches David Tuckett *et al.*

Time, Space and Phantasy Rosine Jozef Perelberg

Rediscovering Psychoanalysis: Thinking and Dreaming, Learning and Forgetting Thomas H. Ogden

Mind Works: Technique and Creativity in Psychoanalysis Antonino Ferro

Doubt, Conviction and the Analytic Process: Selected Papers of Michael Feldman Michael Feldman. Edited by Betty Joseph

Melanie Klein in Berlin: Her First Psychoanalysis of Children Claudia Frank. Edited by Elizabeth Spillius

TITLES IN THE NEW LIBRARY OF PSYCHOANALYSIS
TEACHING SERIES

Reading Freud: A Chronological Exploration of Freud's Writings Jean-Michel Quinodoz

Listening to Hanna Segal: Her Contribution to Psychoanalysis Jean-Michel Quinodoz

THE NEW LIBRARY OF PSYCHOANALYSIS

General Editor: Dana Birksted-Breen

Melanie Klein in Berlin

Her First Psychoanalyses of Children

Claudia Frank

Edited and with a Preface by Elizabeth Spillius
Translated by Sophie Leighton and Sue Young

Routledge
Taylor & Francis Group

LONDON AND NEW YORK

First published 2009
by Routledge
27 Church Road, Hove, East Sussex, BN3 2FA

Simultaneously published in the USA and Canada
by Routledge
270 Madison Avenue, New York, NY 10016

Routledge is an imprint of the Taylor & Francis Group, an Informa business

Copyright © 2009 frommann-holzboog Verlag · Eckhart Holzboog 1999

First published under the title: Melanie Kleins erste Kinderanalysen

English Translation (Chapters 2–11) copyright © Sophie Leighton 2009

Typeset in Bembo by RefineCatch Limited, Bungay, Suffolk
Printed and bound in Great Britain by TJ International Ltd, Padstow, Cornwall

Paperback cover design by Sandra Heath
Cover drawings by 'Erna', one of Melanie Klein's young patients

British Library Cataloguing in Publication Data
A catalogue record for this book is available from the British Library

Library of Congress Cataloging-in-Publication Data
Frank, Claudia, 1956–
[Melanie Kleins erste Kinderanalysen. English]
Melanie Klein in Berlin : her first psychoanalyses of children / Claudia Frank ;
edited and with a Preface by Elizabeth Spillius ; translated by Sophie Leighton
and Sue Young.
p. cm.
Includes bibliographical references and index.
1. Klein, Melanie.   2. Child analysis.   I. Spillius, Elizabeth Bott, 1924–
II. Title.
RJ504.2.F69613 2009
618.92′8917092—dc22
2008046757

ISBN: 978–0–415–48497–8 (hbk)
ISBN: 978–0–415–48498–5 (pbk)

Contents

Contents

Preface

Elizabeth Spillius

In this remarkable book, first published in German in 1999, Claudia Frank shows Melanie Klein energetically starting to develop her version of a new branch of psychoanalysis: the psychoanalysis of children. Claudia might have based her book solely on Klein's published papers, but circumstances arose that led her to explore the Melanie Klein Archive in London and thus to write the first book which makes extensive use of this unique collection of Klein's unpublished papers, clinical notes, clinical diaries and other manuscripts.

At the time Claudia first encountered the Melanie Klein Archive, its existence in the Wellcome Library for the History of Medicine had been known for some years, but none of Klein's English colleagues had as yet been interested enough in archival research to explore its potentialities. Heinz Weiss, from the Julius-Maximillian University in Würzburg, and a guest member of the British Psychoanalytical Society, became aware of the Archive when he was working at the Tavistock Clinic in London in 1992. Soon afterwards he began to organise a psychoanalytic conference at Würzburg in 1994 and used the opportunity to ask Claudia to join him in making a link to the 'First German Conference of Psychoanalysis', which had taken place at Würzburg seventy years earlier, in 1924. At this first Würzburg conference Melanie Klein had given a paper called 'From the analysis of an obsessional neurosis in a six-year-old girl'. This was 'Erna', Klein's difficult 6-year-old patient who became particularly important in the development of Klein's ideas about child analysis. Having found the original version of Klein's Würzburg paper in the Archive, Claudia made a close study of it, which she and Heinz Weiss

xi

published in 1996 as 'The origins of disquieting discoveries by Melanie Klein: the possible significance of the case of Erna' (Frank and Weiss, 1996a). This was followed by an article by Claudia in 1999 in the first issue of the journal *Psychoanalysis and History* and then by her book *Melanie Kleins erste Kinderanalysen: Die Entdeckung des Kindes als Object sui generis von Heilen und Forschen*, which, with some changes in the arrangement and content of the early chapters because of the different background of child analysis in English-speaking countries, has now been translated into the present English version.

Claudia first visited the Klein Archive in 1994 and was captured – a victim of archival research. In the next three years she visited London and the Klein Archive more than twenty times, usually for long weekends, much of which was spent reading, photocopying and transcribing Klein's mainly handwritten notes and papers, a time-consuming but absorbing task once one has succumbed to the lure of archival research. Klein's handwriting, though not as difficult as Freud's, is difficult enough to leave one exhausted at the end of a day deciphering it.

Claudia began by reading the clinical material on the children and mulling over which would be the best ones to describe in detail. Then she used the rather incomplete records of the Berlin Polyclinic, combined with Klein's own notes in the Archive, to work out how many child and adolescent patients Klein had treated in Berlin (twenty-two), and with what sort of frequency and duration. She found that patients were seen three times a week at the Polyclinic and usually six times a week once Klein moved her practice to her own home in 1922.

Parts of the present book are not easy reading, especially the detailed translations of Klein's clinical notes, which are in a sort of shorthand. Claudia decided to keep the translation as literal and as close to the original as possible. The way Klein wrote her notes, with one short line underneath the other, is followed in the first seven chapters of the book, but in Part Two, which gives the full clinical notes for each child, the lines are separated only by forward slashes. Otherwise the book would have been totally unwieldy in size and weight.

I hope I have given some idea of the dedication Claudia needed simply to get the material available in a form that could be read and reread in order to grasp what Klein was trying to accomplish and to think about it conceptually. In the first seven chapters of her book Claudia explains the essence of Klein's approach to child analysis, including her interest in the topic as an end in itself rather than only as a means of providing proof of the correctness of Freud's deductions about children drawn from work with adults. She describes the essential discoveries and ideas of this early period of Klein's work: not only the inevitability but also the usefulness of the negative transference; the development of the play technique; the children's early and ferocious conscious and unconscious phantasies and their corresponding development of a cruel and persecuting superego; the link between inhibited development and conscious and unconscious phantasies; ideas about the development of neurosis, especially obsessional neurosis.

Claudia outlines briefly the history of child analysis and Klein's place in it, including a brief account of the disagreements between Klein and Anna Freud in the 1920s. She then describes the reasons for her choice of the child patients whom she discusses in detail: 'Grete' (one of Klein's first child patients); 'Rita' (the youngest); 'Inge' (the child with whom the 'play technique' was first developed as a method rather than a random experience); a bit on 'Ernst', who, unlike many of the other children, maintained a positive transference throughout his treatment with Klein; and finally 'Erna', the child who was most helpful in getting Klein to understand the negative transference, the need for obsessional defences, and the immense importance of 'the drive for knowledge', so strong not only in Erna but also in Klein herself.

Claudia describes Klein's encounters with 'Felix', the 13-year-old boy whom she describes as Klein's first 'real' patient, in spite of Klein's attributing that role to her son Erich ('Fritz'). On the basis of archival material, Claudia effectively disposes of Phyllis Grosskurth's (1986) assertion that Klein analysed not only her younger son Erich but also her older son Hans and her daughter Melitta.

By comparing Klein's clinical notes with her published and unpublished papers, Claudia shows how Klein enriched the concept of negative transference and laid the basis for innovations in technique and theory that led eventually to changes in adult as well as child analysis, to Klein's later theories of the depressive and paranoid-schizoid positions, and to new approaches to the understanding of psychotic as well as neurotic experience.

This book is the work of a true scholar, and we all have much reason to thank Claudia for making us aware of the results of her meticulous comparison of Klein's published papers, her unpublished papers and her clinical treatment notes. There is another sort of pleasure, however, in archival research: a personal, intimate feeling that one 'knows' the subjects of one's research in a special way: their strengths, their weaknesses, the things that intrigue them, the occasional appearance of a bill for wine in among the notes on theory, a theatre programme, a reminder to come to a meeting, a sad letter from a colleague. One of the strangest and most endearing things to emerge from Claudia's research is Klein's naïvety: she assumed at first that she could get her child patients to lie down on the couch and free associate in the way that adult patients were instructed to do in the early 1920s.

Claudia is not Klein's biographer, and she does not use this sort of information directly, but one has the feeling throughout this book of her respect and admiration for Klein, especially for what she describes as Klein's special gift for making emotional contact with children, for her honesty with the children and her carefulness in recording clinical data even when she did not fully understand them. Above all, Klein had an immense 'drive to know'. She respected that same sort of drive in the children, and we are compelled to an equal respect for it in Claudia.

PART ONE

1

Introduction[1]

> my work with both children and adults, and my contributions to
> psycho-analytic theory as a whole, derive ultimately from the play
> technique evolved with young children. . . . the insight I gained
> into early development, into unconscious processes, and into the
> nature of the interpretations by which the unconscious can be
> approached, has been of far-reaching influence on the work I have
> done with older children and adults.
>
> (Klein, 1955, WMK III,[2] p. 122)

The technique of child analysis that Melanie Klein developed was the
beginning of a psychoanalytic revolution and gradually led her to
changes and development not only of a new technique but also of
new theories. In this book I describe my research into the very early
period of Klein's work in which she developed the play technique
and the most basic of her new insights into early development. I
discuss the development of her method of child analysis through
examining the clinical case notes of four of her early child analyses in
Berlin, which I compare with her unpublished manuscripts and later
published papers on these same four children.

Klein's attitude towards children and child analysis was very different from that of the other pioneers of child analysis. She was not
primarily interested, as they were, only in showing that the pre-
existing psychoanalytic ideas about infantile sexuality which had been

1 Chapter 1 was translated by Sue Young.
2 *The Writings of Melanie Klein, Volumes I–IV* will be referred to as WMK I–IV.

discovered in the analysis of adults were also to be found in children. She *did* believe this, and indeed it was her starting point, and she soon found much supporting evidence for it. But she found additional and somewhat contradictory evidence as well, and this she stated in a straightforward manner and gradually proceeded to base new ideas and theories upon it.

Very briefly, the most important discoveries and ideas of this early period were as follows. First, the view that negative transference was an inevitable part of the analytic situation and that understanding and interpreting it could greatly increase access to the child's unconscious mind and could help to give the child increased and constructive understanding of him- or herself. Second, in about 1923 Klein began to use small toys as a standard part of the setting of child analysis, and came to consider that the play of children could be regarded as equivalent to the free association of adults. Third, she perceived that in their play small children expressed very ferocious phantasies which were accompanied by acute anxiety. This led her to the idea of an early and very persecutory superego, and, slightly later, to the idea that the Oedipus complex began much earlier than Freud had thought. Fourth, she developed the view that, similarly, anxiety-arousing and difficult phantasies lay at the heart of intellectual inhibition. Finally, in this early period she developed new ideas about childhood neurosis and especially about obsessional neurosis. This early work, as Klein says in the passage quoted above, had immense influence on her later work with both children and adults and on the development of still further ideas.

For the most part – like Freud in his discussion of Little Hans's analysis – Klein believed that children would be helped, not harmed, by knowing the truth about themselves and their unconscious mind. At the beginning, when she was doubtful, Karl Abraham reassured her and she pressed on. She also treated children with great respect, assuming that they were just as willing as adults, if not more so, to face their anxieties and cope with their resistances.

I think it is also evident from her clinical notes as well as her papers that she had a remarkable capacity to make emotional contact with children. She was quick to make associations and symbolic links, a capacity that enabled her to reach an imaginative understanding of a child's play and speech as expressing their phantasies and their dilemmas about their parents, the primal scene, their Oedipus situation, their siblings, their struggles with love and hate. Indeed, she was sometimes accused of making implausible 'symbolic' and 'deep' interpretations and she was quick to reply that she did so only when she had several congruent bits of evidence, and in any case she was careful to observe the effect of these interpretations on the child's anxiety and subsequent play and on his understanding of himself. She might have pointed out (but did not) that many of Freud's interpretations were equally symbolic and deep.

In most schools of analysis we have become more cautious about these intuitive leaps, but they were an important part of Klein's creative and courageous approach in the early years which are the subject matter of this book, and which, in turn, led to Klein's later work and so have eventually contributed to current trends in psychoanalysis.

1.1 'Vergisst alle Träume' [Forgets all dreams]: Melanie Klein's clinical starting point in 1921

'Forgets all dreams'. This was the first note Melanie Klein made on 'Felix', the boy I shall call her 'first child patient'. She began this first analysis at the Berliner Psychoanalytische Poliklinik at the beginning of February 1921, having moved to Berlin from Budapest (or rather Ružomberok) at the start of the year. Felix was a 13-year-old boy who was an important figure in her early papers (Klein, 1923a, 1923b, 1925). When Melanie Klein began her handwritten records of the therapy with 'Forgets all dreams', she was stressing that her patient's attitude towards dreams was a crucial element of the material that interested her (and us) analytically. This initial note suggests that she agreed with Freud in seeing an understanding of dreams as 'the royal road'. At the same time, with 'forgetting', she was recording her perception of her patient's resistance. Let us remember that in Chapter 7 of *The Interpretation of Dreams*, Freud stated *inter alia* that 'it shows that there was no lack of a hostile [i.e. resistant] purpose at work in the forgetting of the dream' (Freud, 1900, *Standard Edition* (*S.E.*) 5, p. 513). The perception of resistance, of hostility, of a form of negative transference is recorded in this statement – the first note of what was to become a major theme in Klein's early work.

My thesis is that this initial note by Klein, 'Forgets all dreams', contains the essence of two factors crucial to the development of what was later to become known as Kleinian psychoanalysis: the assumption that contemporary psychoanalytic theory and technique could be applied to the analysis of children, and the perception of negative transference as a challenge to psychoanalytic understanding. What does this mean? When Melanie Klein began her clinical activities, it was only natural that she should make use of the established method with its associated theoretical views. Thus she did not start out with the conviction that she would have to develop a new method, but employed in working with children and adolescents the psychoanalytic method developed for adults. She took over the usual setting used for adults, including at first the use of the couch, she interpreted the Oedipus complex as formulated at the time for adult patients, and so forth.

In my view, despite all the errors that the application of this method involved, it enabled her to learn from experience. She was able to take seriously inconsistencies between her findings and those of contemporary psychoanalytic theory and technique, and gradually she added to and revised the latter. Her opportunity and her originality lay in her conviction that children could be analysed in basically the same way as adults. At first, as I have implied above, she took this very literally, in that when she began her work at the Psychoanalytische Poliklinik in Berlin in 1921, she offered children the couch, asked them what they associated with material as it arose, and interested herself in dreams and memories of early childhood. In adopting this approach, she was going down a different path from the one usually followed when one had professional dealings with children, which in some way or other involved educating them. If the specific form of the analytical approach she initially adopted was not appropriate for children, if to some extent they accordingly rejected it, nevertheless from the outset she acted within an analytical framework. As we shall see, this enabled her gradually to develop a more adequate approach. Thus even if to some extent Melanie Klein did children an injustice when she saw their rejection of the setting that was inappropriate for them only as an expression of their negative transference, their fears and hostility, her point of access – seeing the rejection as resistance that needed to be understood in analytical terms – opened up the way to working analytically with the child without making over-hasty concessions to the child's external reality, which can so quickly close down reflection on unconscious meanings.

My beginning with 'Forgets all dreams' as exemplifying Klein's starting point could give rise to a misunderstanding. It might seem that the first thing Klein did was to ask her patients about dreams.

Although we cannot be certain about this, I consider it unlikely, since her notes on the other four patients in 1921 do not begin in the same way. Indeed, some of them do not contain the word 'dream' at all. There is a later comment in the treatment notes to the effect that Felix's mother was considering returning to her analysis with Simmel. It is possible that she had explained analysis to her son in advance by mentioning dreams, among other things. As far as we can judge, Klein assigned a significant role to dreams in the clinical situation without overemphasising the point. Hence if in practice dreams did not play an outstanding part in these early therapies in quantitative terms, they had probably been crucial to Melanie Klein's initial personal interest in psychoanalysis.

We learn from her unpublished autobiography of 1959 that Freud's work *On Dreams* (1901a) represented her first encounter with psychoanalysis:

> While living in Budapest, I had become deeply interested in Psychoanalysis. I remember that the first book of Freud that I read was a small book on dreams and, when I read it, I knew that was it – that was what I was aiming at, at least during these years when I was very keen to find what would satisfy me intellectually and emotionally. I went into analysis with Ferenczi [. . .] and he very much encouraged my idea of devoting myself to analysis, particularly child analysis, for which he said I had a particular talent.

Against this background it is hardly surprising that Freud's theory of dreams was of crucial importance to Klein's conceptualisation of the analysis of play, which she was to develop in Berlin in subsequent years. In her first lecture in London, 'Die psychologischen Grundlagen der psychoanalytischen Technik' ['The psychological foundations of psychoanalytic technique'], in 1925, she expressed this as follows:

> The child expresses his phantasies, wishes and actual experiences in a symbolic way through play [. . .]. In doing so, he makes use of the same language that we know from dreams, which after all also originates from the infantile inner life. It is reasonable that when an understanding of this language originating from infantile inner life is of such importance in adult analysis, one of the fundamental requirements of child analysis is to take account of it. It is an archaic mode of expression, one that we know to be phylogenetically

7

acquired, which the child uses, and we can understand it fully only if we approach it in the way Freud has taught us to approach the language of dreams. Symbolism is only a part of it; if we wish to understand the language of play correctly in relation to the child's whole behaviour during the analytic session, we must take into consideration the mechanisms we know from the dream work – displacement, condensation, reworking to make something representable (of which symbolism is again only a part), secondary revision and all the methods of representation employed in the dream.

(Klein (1925i), unpublished manuscript)

The aim of the present study is to portray the developments in Klein's technique and theories in her crucial early years, 1921–1926, on the basis of hitherto unpublished records of her analyses in Berlin in 1921–1926 and of unpublished manuscripts that can be consulted at the Wellcome Library for the History of Medicine in London,[3] together with her publications. To some extent, the notes on Melanie Klein's early analyses enable us to draw up a kind of biography of the work of these early years. In my view this material, despite its great diversity, constitutes a sort of counterpart to the Freud/Fließ correspondence, which gives us an insight into the crucial years of Freud's initial discoveries. In Freud's correspondence we can experience with Freud his discovery of the Oedipus complex, we can share in the origin of the interpretation of dreams, and we can follow the various stages of the maturing, rejection and development of many other theoretical and technical matters. Unfortunately we do not have a comparable correspondence between Melanie Klein and a friend, reporting on work with patients, reflections and developing theories alongside news of herself and family life. On the other hand, in her case we have direct evidence of her initial clinical experiences in the form of primarily handwritten notes on her first analyses (for a detailed description, see Chapter 2). The material available to us in Melanie Klein's own hand allows us to follow the development of her technique through to analysis of play, as well as her theoretical innovations as they suggested themselves to her in the clinical situation. She learned from her little patients about their sadistic phantasies and

---

3 I should like to take this opportunity of thanking the Melanie Klein Trust once again for allowing me unrestricted access to the documents available.

analysed their meaning. She observed anxieties about a punishing internal entity in a girl as young as 2¾ years old and conceived of an early superego at that time. She took her small patients' Oedipal phantasies and games seriously and described the pre-genital Oedipus complex. She discovered the attitude of girls to their own genitals. We find precursors of the differentiation between systems of anxiety and defence, which she was later to describe as the 'paranoid-schizoid position' and the 'depressive position'. However, it was to be a long time before she developed these nuclei of a new conceptualisation that did not emerge at the outset but followed in the course of her endeavours to understand her clinical experiences.[4]

To illustrate this, let us return to the analysis of Felix. I have described how I saw Klein's recording of the 'forgetting' as her perception of resistance on her patient's part, but in what follows when one reads through her notes this 'forgetting' no longer seems to play a part. In the second line of her notes, we read 'only knows one from earlier'. Klein then gives an account of the dream, mentions the occasion when it occurred and lists Felix's associations. Preoccupation with this dream played a major part from then onwards. This was also the only dream from Felix's analysis that Klein was to publish. In 'The rôle of the school in the libidinal development of the child' (1923a), we find:

> *He was on the road to school and met his piano mistress. The school house was on fire and the branches of the trees on the roadside were burnt off, but the trunks were left standing. He walked through the burning building with his music mistress and they came out unhurt, etc.*
>
> (Klein, 1923a, WMK I, p. 60)

In the publication, she adds that only later was the full interpretation of this dream achieved, when the analysis had shown the significance of the school as mother and of the teacher and headmaster as father. We can follow in the notes the way in which she interprets Felix's jealousy of his father in the context of his Oedipal desires in relation to his mother. What she notices in this early period is the libidinal

---

4 One constantly hears that Klein 'put her own' concepts 'onto' her patients, the children, but it can be seen that at the outset it was above all Oedipal desires and anxieties as discussed and described by Freud that lay at the heart of her thinking and interpretation, and that she did not start out with her own 'Kleinian' ideas.

meaning of the road to school, the school, the teacher, etc. She also notes down the material that cannot be directly understood by this means, but at first she seems unable to stay on this track. Only three pages further on, another dream appears, on 14 February 1921:

> Was playing football in the school playground
> with 6–7 boys, which is not allowed,
> so punishment (had) already (been)
> threatened several times. He is
> caught by the person supervising them,
> taken to the form teacher – he threatens
> will be kept in, will be bottom
> of the class – will be taken to
> the headmaster. He wakes at this point
> feeling anxious.

Here, in contrast to the first dream, no associations by Felix or possible interpretations by Klein are given. There is a great deal about castration in what follows, but it would seem that there is something Klein has been unable to catch hold of. It can be assumed that this is why she began a second notebook headed 'Dreams'. Here she makes a second note of Felix's first dream, and notes down Felix's phantasy about a '*sexual attack on a woman*'. In what follows, however, she does not pursue her original intention of noting down dreams, but instead adds further treatment notes. We now know from Klein's later publication on Felix, 'A contribution to the psychogenesis of tics' (1925), that this analysis was repeatedly interrupted and that there were two situations that were difficult for Klein, in which, contrary to her 'usual custom', she imposed prohibitions. Once she felt that she 'had' to put a stop to a relation between Felix and a school-fellow, which had led to mutual masturbation; in a later situation she forbade him to continue a relationship with a girl, again because she felt that such prohibition was the only way of making the continuation of the analysis possible (1925, WMK I, pp. 112ff.).[5]

In my opinion this beginning shows that Klein perceived anxiety and hostility from the outset and that this also appeared to have had an impact on her, but at first it was not possible for her to investigate this

---

5 Unfortunately the treatment notes still extant are incomplete, and these two situations are not documented in them.

further. From the manifest course of the analysis, this was also not directly necessary in the first instance, since Felix brought sufficient material of his own accord. Later on, it probably led to complications, and in 1925 Klein tells us of her problems in dealing with the negative transference. She informs us that when under pressure she took refuge in direct prohibitions, something she does not otherwise advocate. However, she does not regard the problems as a reason to propose a general change in technique. A reading of Klein's treatment notes of Felix shows that, in terms of Klein's starting position in 1921, she appears to perceive anxieties and hostility, but does not yet understand them adequately. One point that gradually enabled her to achieve a deeper understanding of negative transference might be associated with the fact that she was very much aware of her own problems in this respect. She was dissatisfied with her own analysis with Sándor Ferenczi in Budapest, since no negative transference had been analysed in it (cf. also Segal, 1979, p. 32), and this was probably at least one of the reasons for her approaching Abraham in Berlin with a request for a second analysis.

1.2 Melanie Klein's first case before 1921? Was Erich/'Fritz' her first analytic case, and did Klein analyse her other children?

When I cite February 1921 as marking the commencement of Klein's clinical activity with children and adolescents, many readers will wish to point out that in 'The psycho-analytic play technique: its history and significance' (1955), Melanie Klein writes that she began treating her first case in 1919: 'My first patient was a five-year-old boy. I referred to him under the name "Fritz" in my earliest published papers' (1955, WMK III, p. 122). She attaches great importance to this analysis: 'The conviction gained in this analysis strongly influenced the whole course of my analytic work' (1955, WMK III, p. 123). She says that her interest was concentrated on his anxieties and the defence mechanisms directed against them, and that this analysis marked the start of the psychoanalytic play technique. In this context, she was guided by two principles of psychoanalysis going back to Freud, namely, 'that the exploration of the unconscious is the main task of psycho-analytic procedure, and that the analysis of the transference is the means of achieving this aim' (1955, WMK III, p. 123).

11

It has always been known in German-speaking countries that Fritz was Klein's younger son Erich (born in 1914). In 1920 she had published 'Der Familienroman in statu nascendi' ['The family romance in statu nascendi'], in which she still speaks of her son Erich. In 'The development of a child' (1921), in which she returns to the same material, she speaks of 'Fritz' – we know from her letter to Ferenczi that she felt it to be necessary, in view of the more intimate details in the material, to conceal her son's identity.[6] It is certain that this first case, the analysis of her younger son Erich, had great significance for Klein, although we cannot know all the details. (I shall mention conjectures later on.) On the basis of the documentation available, however, I am not certain how accurate the view she expressed in 1955 was. In my opinion her comment in the 1948 preface to *The Psycho-Analysis of Children* was more accurate, according to which she developed the play technique in 1922 and 1923, that is, three to four years later. I believe that previously she had understood and interpreted all material, dreams, phantasies, behaviour, etc., and also of course play, as an expression of unconscious phantasies. However, only with Inge (1923) did she develop the actual play technique, as we shall see later.

The documentation available also shows that only gradually did she recognise the crucial importance of anxiety. Her treatment of the 2¾-year-old Rita in 1923 was probably an important milestone in this context. Klein certainly talked to Karl Abraham about this child – he mentions this in a letter of 7 October 1923 to Freud. Of course it is not impossible that she also – as she writes in 1955 – sought advice from Karl Abraham about Fritz/Erich, but I believe it to be more likely that this event related to Rita and later also to Erna. With regard to the importance of the unconscious, Melanie Klein herself comments in 'The development of a child' that following her presentation of 'Der Familienroman in statu nascendi', Dr Anton von Freund argued that her observations and classifications were certainly analytical, but not her interpretations, as she had taken only the conscious and not also the unconscious questions into consideration (1921,

---

6 The relevant letter has been preserved and is in the Klein Archive at the Wellcome Library for the History and Understanding of Medicine. Ruth Cycon (1995) refers to it in her note on 'Der Familienroman in statu nascendi' in '*Melanie Klein. Gesammelte Schriften. Band I, Teil 1*' (p. 2); Grosskurth (1986) reproduced it in his biography of Melanie Klein (English edition, p. 91).

WMK I, p. 30). I believe that it was this objection that led her actually to analyse her son, and that prior to this what was involved was an enlightened upbringing in which she answered her son's conscious questions truthfully.

How much of the situation with Erich can we reconstruct on the basis of the unpublished documents? We know from the date of the presentation of 'Der Familienroman in statu nascendi' (July 1919) that this phase of 'enlightened upbringing' of Erich, in which she answered his questions truthfully, must have occurred before July 1919, although the Melanie Klein Trust has no documents covering this point. We know from 'The development of a child' that there followed a period that Klein characterised as 'upbringing with analytic features' (1921, WMK I, p. 44). During this period she gave Erich the 'remaining information that had so far been withheld from him' (1921, WMK I p. 30), encouraged him to express his phantasies and only occasionally interpreted them (p. 32). The following passage from 'The development of a child' on the conclusion for the time being of this phase described in the second part of the document, is also included in the notes, which means that the timing can be confirmed:

After this period of approximately six weeks' renewed observation, with the associated analysis, chiefly of the anxiety-dreams, the anxiety entirely disappeared. Sleep and going to sleep were once more impeccable. Play and sociability left nothing to be desired. Along with the anxiety there had been a mild phobia of street children. Its foundation in fact was that street boys had repeatedly threatened and annoyed him. He showed fear of crossing the street by himself and could not be persuaded to do so. Owing to the intervention of a recent journey I could not analyse this phobia. Apart from this, however, the child made an excellent impression; when I had occasion to see him again a few months later this impression was strengthened. In the meantime he had lost his phobia in the following way, as he himself informed me. Soon after my departure he first of all ran across the street with his eyes shut. Then he ran across with his head turned away, and finally he walked across quite quietly. On the other hand, he showed (probably as a result of this attempt at self-cure – he assured me proudly that now he was afraid of nothing!) a decided disinclination for analysis and also an aversion to telling stories and to listening to fairy-tales; this

13

was the only point, however, on which an unfavourable change had occurred.

(1921, WMK I, p. 44)

On the basis of the documents in the Klein Archive, this event can now be dated to spring 1920. The first notebook on Erich still extant is labelled 'Notebook 3' on the cover; the notes begin in the middle of a sentence, and they cover the period from March to June 1920. It is apparent from the notes that Melanie Klein was away in Budapest from the middle of March to the end of May. Prior to her departure, Erich reacted with sadness to the imminent separation and expressed a *'wish for something to be brought back from Budapest'*, as Melanie Klein records. In her absence, her daughter Melitta then summarises his behaviour – including his disobedience. In her first entry following her return, on 15 June, Klein comes back to the phobia of street children quoted above: *'Shortly after my departure he discarded the last part of the anxiety he was still showing when I left, the phobia of street children.'* She goes on to describe the same stages as in the published version.

In 'The development of a child' (1921, WMK I, p. 44) Klein notes, despite the generally satisfactory result, that 'The display of so active a resistance to analysis, and the unwillingness to listen to fairy-tales seem to me in themselves to render it probable that his further upbringing will afford occasion for analytic measures from time to time' (1921, WMK I, p. 44). We then learn in 'Early analysis' (1923b) that he had a relapse and inhibitions and reluctance again arose, so that she again began to analyse him, when he was nearly 7 years old (1923b, WMK I, p. 94). She now saw an opportunity to take the analysis deep enough. I assume that Klein began this 'very deep' analysis at the beginning of 1921, when she had moved to Berlin. In 'Early analysis', she also mentions that his new delight in roaming about and all his other interests had lasted for some time, but after several months had been succeeded by the old dislike of going for a walk. Since this delight in roaming about is recorded in the third book of treatment notes in the period after her return from Budapest at the end of May 1920, and the publication then begins by mentioning the way to school (1923b, WMK I, p. 94), and the next notebook shows that Erich began school on moving to Berlin, this conclusion is very probable. It cannot be directly proved from the documents, since the next notebook to have been preserved is 'Notebook 7', which contains notes on the last ten days of March and the first seven days of

14

April 1921. The remaining three notebooks on Erich still extant contain notes covering the periods from the beginning of June to the end of August 1921 and the beginning of October to the middle of December 1921. The contents relate partly to Erich's phantasies and questions and Melanie Klein's interpretations, and in part consist of various observations, remarks, etc., ranging from his performance at school and eating habits and his remarks about the young woman who looked after him to his attacks of jealousy of his siblings. During the shared holidays in Sweden in the summer of 1921, in particular, it was again Melitta who from time to time recorded Erich's behaviour.

Erich himself probably called the analysis '*Sprechen*' [talking]. Klein asked him for his ideas about his phantasies and asked him about his dreams, although he sometimes resisted this, saying that a school-fellow's mother did not ask *him* about dreams. The question of the significance of this 'talking' to Erich must remain open – to some extent one has the impression that he had sufficient understanding to ask for it, directly or indirectly, when he feared that he had fallen behind his siblings. Klein also mentioned this in 1921:

> The child has a natural impulse to use the analysis also as a means to pleasure. At night when he should go to sleep he will state that an idea that must be discussed at once has occurred to him.
>
> (1921, WMK I, p. 50)

It is difficult to make out what may have led Klein to carry out a kind of analysis with her son – although this was not unusual among analysts at that time – and to interpret his ideas about his dreams and phantasies as various elements of the Oedipus complex. Some of her wording suggests a degree of disquiet – as for example when she cites, with regard to von Freund's objection, quoted earlier, her opinion at that time ('it sufficed to deal with conscious questions so long as there was no convincing reason to the contrary' (1921, WMK I, p. 30). The wording 'only occasional cautious interpretations' (p. 32) may also refer to this. Similarly oriented comments are also found in the notes in the Archive – for example, on 1 August 1921, when she notes that she is recommencing analysis as his learning has deteriorated to such an extent that in a dictation that was not difficult he made thirty-two mistakes. Here, for example, she adds: '*but I am not making interpretations*'. The reference to Freud can also be understood in this sense, when she says that he expressly mentions 'that no harm but only good accrued to Little Hans from becoming fully conscious of his Oedipus complex' (1921, WMK I, p. 51). When it is a question of analysing one's own children, it is only natural for constant references to be made to Little Hans's analysis by his own father, and to the fact that there are several other relevant examples at that time. The question still remains of what could have led Klein herself to take this action. To what extent may she also have felt put under pressure by von Freund's comment that her interpretations were 'not analytical'? To what extent did a tendency to compensate for her earlier spells of depression and her concern over the divorce and the various moves play a part – triggered by signs of less than optimal development, which is how she probably understood Erich's reluctance to play and to learn?

Although this 'analysis' of her son was obviously important to Klein, I believe that from an analytical viewpoint, it was not possible for her to make new discoveries within this framework. She needed a defined setting in the narrower sense of the term in order genuinely to be able to see children as subjects of analytic treatment and research, which is why I have described Felix's analysis as the first. Why, then, does Klein herself, including in her autobiographical notes of 1959, for example, ascribe such key significance to her 'first case' in the development of her theory and technique, something which (in so far as this can be verified) appears to have only very limited application in the form she asserts? The conjectures that can be made on the basis of the documents can do no more than hint at the relevant points. I should like to suggest a hypothesis. In her (unpublished) autobiographical notes, Klein writes *inter alia*: 'My interest in children's minds goes back a very long way. I remember that, even as a child of eight or nine, I was interested in watching younger children.' Elsewhere we learn that her next older sister, Sidonie, when she was that same age, 8 or 9, turned to Melanie. At 4 or 5, Melanie, the youngest child, was made to feel very unsure of herself by the way in which her older siblings treated her ('the older ones had a knack of teasing me').

> I was wildly keen on knowledge, deeply ambitious and very hurt by their being so superior to me. Sidonie, lying in bed, took pity on me, and she taught me the principles of counting and of reading, which I picked up very quickly. [. . .] I still have a feeling of gratitude to her for satisfying my mental needs, all the greater because

I think she was very ill at the time. She died when I was about 4½ and I have a feeling that I never entirely got over the feeling of grief for her death.

My conjecture is that Klein may have identified with Sidonie when she began to be interested in children when she herself reached the age – 8 or 9 – at which Sidonie had looked after her. She then turned to her younger son when he was around the age she herself had been, 4 or 5, when she suffered Sidonie's death. It is worth considering to what extent infantile feelings of triumph and guilt may have become topical in the context of her analysis with Ferenczi.[7] To what extent was the analysis of her son important because it was associated with the analysis of her own 'inhibitions', spells of depression, while von Freund's reference to the significance of the unconscious dynamic may possibly have played a crucial part, and anxiety and unconscious phantasies may actually have been key elements in this process.

Nevertheless, there is no doubt that Klein herself thought her work with Erich was crucial to the evolution of her ideas and technique. In her treatment of Erich she began, as Likierman has described (Likierman, 2001, pp. 24–43), to combine the ideas of Freud on sexual curiosity as the basis of the desire to know and the ideas of Ferenczi on the growth of the child's mind from omnipotence to a sense of reality (Freud, 1905a; Ferenczi, 1913a). Klein also encountered considerable resistance in Erich to her attempts at sexual enlightenment, which perhaps helped her to understand and take for granted the negative transference of the child patients she began to treat when she arrived in Berlin. Paradoxically, as emphasised by Likierman, this work with Klein's own child appears to have played a crucial role in leading Klein to conclude that the psychoanalytic function as a method of treatment and research should be separated from parental and educational functions (Likierman, 2001, pp. 39–42).

Considering the question of whether Klein may have analysed other children between Erich and Felix, the Archive contains no documentation of such possible analyses. Since Klein had to leave

---

7 Klein impressively describes the working through of such feelings in 1940 when she explains in barely disguised fashion her grieving process following the death of her son Hans (cf. also Steiner, 1993). Possible wishes for the death of her beloved brother Emanuel, who died in 1902, may have played an important part in her understanding of the role of feelings of triumph and of guilt in the process of mourning. See also Grosskurth (1986, pp. 251f.).

Budapest in the autumn of 1919 because of the political situation, and spent the period until the end of 1920 in Ružomberok with her children, with some interruptions, I regard it as unlikely that she carried out other child analyses during this period.

Lastly, however, in this context, I must consider the claim that Melanie Klein analysed not only her son Erich, but also her son Hans and her daughter Melitta. Grosskurth argues very strongly in favour of this:

> However, her two key cases (not mentioned in *The Psycho-Analysis of Children*) were her own sons, 'Fritz' and 'Felix' (Erich and Hans), to whom more space is devoted than to any other children in *Love, Guilt and Reparation and Other Works, 1921–1945*. A seventeen-year-old girl, Lisa (a protagonist in 'The Development of a Child'), to whom less attention is paid than to the boys, is also omitted from *The Psycho-Analysis of Children*. This appears to be Melitta. One can only speculate that these cases were omitted from the 1932 volume lest awkward questions be raised about the advisability of a mother's analyzing her own children.
>
> The identity of Erich is certain, and the ages and information about the other children accord too closely to Hans and Melitta to be coincidental. Extensive case notes on Erich and Melitta still survive. Fritz's brother, 'Felix', appears at the age of thirteen (that is, in 1920, the year they spent in Ružomberok).
>
> (Grosskurth, 1986, pp. 95–96)

In a footnote she adds:

> 'Inhibitions and Difficulties of Puberty' (1922) would seem to be based on her observations of Hans. 'Fritz' might very well be the same child as 'Ernst' in 'The Role of the School in the Libidinal Development of the Child' (1923) and 'Grete' could be Melitta.
>
> (Grosskurth, 1986, p. 96, fn.)

She adds that Eric Clyne did not comment on the fact that his siblings were also analysed by their mother,[8] but without taking this as a reason to investigate her claim more carefully.

---

8 Erich Klein was advised by Susan Isaacs' husband to change his name to Eric Clyne in 1937, when he was living in the United States (Grosskurth, 1986, p. 239).

To begin with Melitta: no notes exist on a possible analysis of Melitta. There is a notebook that has the name 'Melitta' on the cover – but when opened, it is found to contain treatment notes on the analysis of a 6-year-old boy on whom Klein published under the pseudonym 'Ernst' (Klein, 1923b). The first line of the first page contains the words 'six years old' following Ernst's forename and surname. It continues: 'begun 2.11.1923. Suffers from anxiety'. Contrary to what Grosskurth says, 'Lisa', a candidate for the identity of Melitta, plays no part in 'The development of a child', in which she does not appear. The patients on whom Klein published under the pseudonyms 'Lisa' and 'Grete' can be identified with patients for whom treatment notes exist in the Archive, on the basis of corresponding materials. It is certain that neither of these girls is Melitta.

Nor are there any notes on Hans. The patient on whom Klein published under the pseudonym 'Felix' can be clearly identified with a patient in the Archive. Like the two patients named above, he is recorded there under his real name, the home circumstances are completely different, and it can be said with certainty that it is not Hans. By chance, Felix too has a brother seven years younger – it must be assumed that such coincidences actually occur.[9]

---

9 Grosskurth believes that she can prove Klein's 'guilt' in the following passage.

> At one point, for example, she forbade Felix to see a girl older than himself because of the identification he was making with the phantasy of his mother as prostitute. 'The transference', she says, 'proved strong enough for me to impose a temporary break in this relation'; yet she unwittingly gives away their real relationship: 'This object choice served the purpose of a flight from the phantasies and wishes directed towards me (*sic*), and which only at this stage came more fully to the fore in the analysis. It could now be seen that the turning away from the originally loved but forbidden mother had participated in the strengthening of the homosexual attitude and the phantasies about the dreaded castrating mother'.

(Grosskurth, 1986, pp. 98–99)

Here, Grosskurth appears to underestimate the power of transference and obviously takes the image of the castrating mother literally – instead of being able to read it as a description of the transference situation assumed by Klein. If one takes the main publication on Felix (Klein, 1925) as a basis, both the details of the setting (three times a week, many interruptions, overall duration 3¼ years – according to the documentation, three years and five months) and the anamnestic details of the surgery at the age of 3 and the nasal examination at 11 are to be found in the documentation on 'Felix'. There is the detail of a brother seven years younger and also material on his passion for playing football. On 5 January 1922 – this too corresponds with the information (p. 108) that some time after the commencement of analysis, there was an increase in the frequency of the tic – there is

As I have already mentioned, the patient with the pseudonym 'Ernst' can also be identified in the documentation. He was treated in 1923 and 1924 and cannot possibly be Erich. Melanie Klein published on Erich himself in 1920 under his own name and later under the pseudonym 'Fritz'. The notes on him, which are in the Archive, talk of Erich, in the same way that Melitta, Hans and other family members who are mentioned in connection with particular events appear under their real names.

1.3 The beginnings of child analysis

If we look at the history of psychoanalysis, what is the context of these early clinical experiences of Klein's? There has been little research into the history of child analysis, and virtually no systematic research into the beginnings of child analysis. The only monograph in existence is *A History of Child Psychoanalysis* by Claudine and Pierre Geissmann (1998).[10] In the first part, they present the precursors of child analysis in the first two decades of the twentieth century. The protagonists of this early period will be described briefly here, to show the background to Melanie Klein's development.

Beginning with Sigmund Freud, C. and P. Geissmann set out the stages he went through: first his neurological interest in children, then his abandonment of seduction theory, then to his acceptance of infantile sexuality, and in the process they make several references to the considerable psychic resistance Freud must have had to overcome in himself. They say that in accepting infantile sexuality he was attacking humanity's image of the 'innocent child', which is why he asked his students to observe children in order to have more evidence avail-

---

a detailed description of the three phases of the tic, as in the 1925 publication (p. 109). At this point Klein also writes that a few months prior to the analysis the tic had first appeared on the occasion of the following precipitating factor: 'Felix had clandestinely witnessed sexual intercourse between his parents' (1925, p. 108). We learn from the notes that each time the precipitating factor was the father's being together with his mistress.

In the secondary literature on Melanie Klein, it is sometimes assumed that Felix was actually Hans. This results in misleading conclusions such as those in the publication 'Melanie Mell by herself', by Maria Torok, Barbo Sylwan and Adele Covello (1998).

10 Many other authors have touched on this period, and a relatively detailed survey can also be found, *inter alia*, in Hamann (1993) and Rehm (1968).

able. To some extent, this was the precipitating factor for the 'Analysis of a phobia in a five-year-old boy', which is often referred to in the literature as the first child analysis. Those who responded to Freud's call included Max Graf, who observed the development of his son Herbert ('Little Hans') from the age of 3 in 1906.[11] In 1908, Herbert developed his well-known phobia of horses. Analysis was then carried out with the father as analyst and Freud as supervisor. In Freud's eyes, the analysis of Little Hans differed from adult analyses in a number of respects. With regard to the interdependence of treatment and research that he formulated in adult analysis, when it came to the child, and here specifically Little Hans, he stated that nothing fundamentally new had emerged from this analysis, that is, that here the research aspect was not involved (Freud, 1909a, *S.E.* 10, p. 147). Freud even sees the second aspect, treatment by means of the analytic method, as not usually applicable to a child. He thought that analysis had only been successful in the case of Little Hans because the father was able to take on the treatment.

> It was only because the authority of a father and of a physician were united in a single person, and because in him both affectionate care and scientific interest were combined, that it was possible in this one instance to apply the method to a use to which it would not otherwise have lent itself.
>
> (Freud, 1909a, *S.E.* 10, p. 5)

How does Freud justify what seems to us today this very dubious feature of the setting, having the father as analyst? Freud writes: 'No one else, in my opinion, could possibly have prevailed on the child to make any such avowals', which assumes that a child opens up only to a trusted person such as his father. We can perhaps see this as meaning that Freud thought a child's negative transference could not have been analysed if the analyst had been a stranger.

C. G. Jung also responded to the call for additional material about children and informed Freud of his observations on his daughter Agathlie. In 'Psychic conflicts in a child', Jung describes the observations of a 'father who was acquainted with psychoanalysis . . .

---

11 Cf. in this context Freud's (1907b) 'Zur sexuellen Aufklärung der Kinder' [The sexual enlightenment of children].

concerning his little daughter, then four years old' (Jung, 1954, p. 8). The questions the child asked when her brother was born and the way she handled information from her parents are described. There are references to parallels with Little Hans, and the dreams of little 'Anna', as Agathlie is referred to in the publication, are used as a means of understanding her development. Jung himself carried out no further child analyses, but had them carried out by women such as Maria Moltzer. Publication of such an analysis in 'A case of neurosis in a child' (Jung, 1961) sees laziness rather than the Oedipal problem as the primary influence, indicating that Jung's concept of the child's mind is fundamentally different from that of Freud.

Influenced by reading the analysis of Little Hans, on 7 April 1909 Karl Abraham also informs Freud of observations on his daughter Hilda.

Another observation on our little girl, who is aged 2 years 4 months. On two occasions I had to give her a glycerine enema. Since then she has told me every day that she does *not* want another injection, but she says this without real affect, and on most occasions, even with a rather arch smile. So obviously she wants to get the injection. Apart from this, she does not show any other anal-erotic tendencies.

(Freud and Abraham, 2002, p. 87)

Further observations are found in the brief publication 'Some illustrations on the emotional relationship of little girls to their parents' (Abraham, 1917). In 1913, Abraham also decided to hold some analytical discussions with his daughter, as he was disturbed by her 'tendency to daydream', but he did not publish his relevant notes. Hilda Abraham (1976) published these pages later in her biography of her father. The Geissmanns point out that Abraham did not see any problem in analysing children in a similar way to adults. In his report on the 'Mental after-effects produced in a nine-year-old child by the observation of sexual intercourse between its parents', Abraham (1913a) explicitly emphasises that the reason for the restriction was that the parents had called him in 'only for one consultation'. It can also be inferred from Hilda Abraham's biography of her father that in 1917 Karl Abraham probably treated a 12-year-old boy suffering from an inhibition of learning (H. Abraham, 1976, p. 66). Since Abraham himself published nothing on this, however, we do not know to what extent he actually treated this boy and possibly other children and adolescents analytically. C. and P. Geissmann derive from these facts the conclusion that the psychoanalysts of that time, like Abraham, saw no theoretical or practical objection to treating children by analysis. It was only later that obstacles arose (Geissmann and Geissmann, 1998, p. 36). In my view, however, the Geissmanns do not present enough evidence to justify this conclusion. Certainly by the time Klein was seeing her early cases, other analysts and the general public were uneasy about or opposed to child analyses.[12]

If we are looking at the beginnings of child analysis, Hermine Hug-Hellmuth must also, of course, be mentioned. She is described by many as the first child analyst (Nunberg and Federn, 1975, Vol. 4, p. xxi; Huber, 1980; Henningsen, 1964; Geissmann and Geissmann, 1998). Others deny her this attribution. According to Hinshelwood (1989b), for example, Hug-Hellmuth developed 'a psychoanalytically inspired form of pedagogic child instruction' (Hinshelwood, 1989b, p. 240). Peters, Anna Freud's biographer, puts it as follows:

> Hermine Hug-Hellmuth was indeed an enthusiastic follower of Freud's psychoanalysis and tried to apply information on childhood derived from psychoanalysis to her educational observations. But she cannot be defined as a child psychoanalyst. What she sought was an educational practice based on psychoanalytical principles.
>
> (Peters, 1985, p. 60)

In a book entitled *Der Fall Hermine Hug-Hellmuth* [The case of Hermine Hug-Hellmuth], which appeared in 1988, Graf-Nold explains in detail how she reaches the conclusion that all Hug-Hellmuth's work was 'a mixture of ambiguous anecdotes and opinions' (Graf-Nold, 1988, p. 266; translated quotation). Berna-Simons (1989) says that Hug-Hellmuth's conception of child psychoanalysis hardly 'differed from any of the current pedagogic reforms, except that it was supposed to include "open discussion of sexual matters" ' (Berna-Simons, 1989, p. 107; translated quotation).

In treating children, Hug-Hellmuth, like Freud in the case of Little Hans, introduced fundamental changes in the setting compared with

---

12 This attitude may have been exacerbated by the murder of Hermine Hug-Hellmuth in 1924 by her nephew (Geissmann and Geissmann, 1998, pp. 45–49), although Klein never mentions this event or the publicity surrounding it.

the principles governing the setting used for adults. I shall quote just one example, namely her change in setting involving treatment of young patients in their homes:

> Just as the first meeting between the analyst and the young patient should take place in the latter's home, so should it be with the treatment itself. The analysis must go on independently of the whims of the patient, who can very cleverly contrive to have a slight indisposition which prevents him coming, or arriving in time, or he may play truant in the analysis hour.
>
> (Hug–Hellmuth, 1921a, p. 291)

It is not the fact that the problem of resistance alluded to here would not play a major part and that it can actually even make analysis impossible that is in question here, but the fact that this approach denies the 'meaning' of resistance. It is then completely logical for contact to be determined by moments of pedagogy, if it is a matter of circumventing this resistance, curing bad habits, etc. Analytic understanding of these bad habits is lost sight of. These and other modifications led Hug-Hellmuth to what she called *heilerzieh-liche Analyse* (curative child-rearing analysis), which she expressly described as meaning that children and adolescents must not only be released from their suffering but also be given moral, aesthetic and social values. With this attitude, research in the true sense was no longer possible for her.

There are frequent references to the fact that Hug-Hellmuth's aim was to confirm Freud's theses by collecting observations (cf. e.g. Huber, 1980, p. 127), and indeed these first two decades of analytic observations and treatment of children show that the child was regarded by everybody as a subject for demonstrating what had been developed in adult analyses. We have seen that Freud was seeking evidence for his statements on infantile sexuality. Abraham too explicitly interprets child observations in this way. Influenced by the analysis of Little Hans, which he says he had read immediately, straight through, he writes in a letter to Freud on 7 April 1909 about the observation on Hilda mentioned above that: 'It is certainly very gratifying to find what we learned from adult analyses so clearly mani-fested in the child' (Freud and Abraham, 2002, p. 76). The existing literature contains little discussion of the reasons why the child could not be understood as a subject of treatment and research in its own right. Hanna Segal assumes that factors of unconscious resistance were involved (Segal, 1979, p. 36). The few lines she devotes to Klein's precursors lack any more detailed comments, however.

Fear of damaging the child appears to have played a part, as we can infer from the postscript to the analysis of Little Hans. Freud writes that great damage was predicted for the boy, because his 'innocence had been taken away' at such a tender age, and he had been the victim of psychoanalysis. We also know from Alix Strachey's report on Melanie Klein's Berlin lecture, given on 13 December 1924, that this point was discussed: 'Is the small child able to support the knowledge of its own libidinal desires, & of all the facts & emotions connected with sex? Are not these realities too crushing for its undeveloped ego?' (Meisel and Kendrick, 1986, p. 326).

A look at these early publications on child analysis appears to show that negative transference was another obstacle. Freud suggests this on the grounds mentioned earlier, and Ferenczi's description of his meeting with 'the little chanticleer' can be understood as meaning that it was not possible to take up a latent negative transference. In his paper on the little chanticleer, Ferenczi (1913b) endeavours to understand the symptoms of a 5-year-old boy. This 'brother of Little Hans' had developed an interest in cocks, hens and chickens. Ferenczi saw the boy for one meeting.

> Personal investigation of the boy yielded nothing striking or abnormal. Immediately on entering my room his attention was attracted by a small bronze mountain cock among the numerous other objects lying about; he brought it to me and asked 'will you give it to me?' I gave him some paper and a pencil and he immediately drew a cock (not unskilfully). Then I got him to tell me the story about the cock. But he was already bored and wanted to get back to his toys. Direct psycho-analytic investigation was therefore impossible, and I had to confine myself to getting the lady who was interested in the case and, being a neighbour and friend of the family, could watch him for hours at a time, to note down his curious remarks and gestures.
>
> (Ferenczi, 1913b, p. 244)

Ferenczi thus concludes that manifest boredom means the impossibility of an analytical procedure. When the boy turns away, Ferenczi seems to see it as a 'proof' of the impossibility of an analytic procedure with a child rather than a reason to regard it as an instance of negative transference. The merely descriptive report of this scene, without the analytic reflection that otherwise characterises this stimulating short paper, shows the analyst's disinclination to handle the immediate experience 'analytically' rather than the impossibility of child analysis per se (see Frank, 1999).

With regard to the schools of Anna Freud and Melanie Klein, which came into being in the 1920s, in addition to the monograph by C. and P. Geissmann, there are biographies of both protagonists (of Anna Freud by Young-Bruehl (1988) and of Melanie Klein by Grosskurth (1986)). There are also publications on individual aspects of the work of each analyst (cf. e.g. Donaldson, 1996; Viner, 1996). With regard to Melanie Klein's early work, Petot (1990) presents an attempt to describe it in terms of its theoretical systems – he speaks of a 'proto-Kleinian system' by around 1923, with Klein's 'first system' having then developed by 1932 from the application of the play technique. Aguayo (1997) has published an article on the possible significance of socio-cultural factors. Likierman (2001) analyses the development of Klein's thought in relation to the ideas of her contemporary psychoanalytic colleagues. Hanna Segal has graphically described and annotated Melanie Klein's theory and technique in books and numerous articles (see Segal, 1972, 1979). Spillius has published various developments in Kleinian thought (Spillius, 1983, 1988, 1994). Hinshelwood (1991) gives a comprehensive presentation.

1.4 The approach of the present study

The present study aims to go over the early stages of Klein's development, by means of an investigation of specimen cases. Klein treated at least twenty-two children and adolescents in Berlin, so a selection had to be made. My first decision was to restrict the investigation to her child analyses, since this was where the real innovations took place. This does not mean that she did not also make important new discoveries through her analysis of adolescents, but the boundary between adult analysis and analysis of adolescents is a fluid one, and this area did not involve the same reservations about whether analysis was feasible in principle as in the case of children. The fact that account was often not taken of the specific features of the analysis of adolescents is a separate issue.

The second decision was to investigate in detail only children on whom Klein herself had published papers, for the following reason: on the basis of the material available in her published papers, the additional insights obtained by consulting her unpublished material can be described and explained, and in this way it has been possible to develop a standardised systematic procedure for reviewing the development of her findings, her technique and her ideas.

Third, the ability clearly to identify the patients with those on whom Klein herself published and the timing of the analyses have been decisive factors, as my aim is to explain the development of her work.

On the basis of these criteria, the first child analysis selected as an example is that of Grete (treated from February 1921 to May 1922). I have also consulted the other notes and documents available from this two-year period, on five boys aged 12–13 years, in order to flesh out Klein's handling of the setting and to sketch a framework for understanding Grete's treatment.

With regard to the next stages, I decided to go back to the early cases to which Klein referred in her paper of 1955 ('The psycho-analytic play technique'), namely to the analyses of Rita (March to October 1923) and Inge (September 1923 to July 1924, and again from February 1925 to May 1926). According to the criteria set out above, Ernst would also be a possible subject for this period, as will be shown in an addendum to the presentation of Inge (Chapter 5). Ernst started his analysis with a predominantly positive transference and for the most part maintained it throughout his analysis. This generally accepting and positive attitude led to interesting material, but it did not have the sort of impact on Klein that challenged her to rethink and then to reconceptualise her technique and her theory. This is the reason why I have not discussed his analysis (February 1923 to June 1924) in more detail.

While the psychoanalytic setting was established with Inge – Inge was the child with whom Klein first began to use toys systematically as the equipment for the analysis of play (1955, WMK III) – it was important to select one of the subsequent analyses to use as an example of how a child analysis could proceed on the basis of the new technique. In accordance with Klein's own references to the insights she obtained from the individual analyses, Erna, Peter, Ruth and Trude were possible subjects here. I have selected Erna, since she is the child about whom the most material has been preserved, and hers is also the most comprehensive analysis of these years in Berlin.

27

With regard to the balance of the sexes, this selection of Grete, Rita, Inge and Erna is anything but representative of Klein's practice during the Berlin years. The developmental stages of girls, a major contribution by Melanie Klein, will, however, also become clearer as a result of this selection, although this was not the reason for my choice.

1.4.1 Method

In working out a method of analysis, I have been guided by the notion that a case history is an expression of the complex relationship between analyst and patient. Every analyst can be regarded as a sort of 'soundbox' in which the analyst's varying capacity to 'vibrate', that is, variations in his or her capacity for tolerance or in the analyst's need for defences to maintain his or her psychic balance, result in variations in which particular dynamic aspects will become most evident. Applying Marquand's idea of 'pluralising hermeneutics' (quoted in Stuhr, 1995, p. 192), it is my idea that attempts should be made to understand patient case histories in new and different ways in order to get as close as possible to intersubjective truth.

In this context, in addition to theoretical knowledge, every reader can include an analysis of their own response to the text, which can be regarded as comparable to the analyst's countertransference to the patient in a session. I would like to make it clear at this point that I am *not* using the term countertransference in the classical usage defined by Freud (1910) and by Klein herself but rather in the widened sense initiated by Paula Heimann (1950). In Freud's and Klein's 'classical' definition, countertransference is regarded as a pathological emotional response to the patient rooted in the analyst's unconscious. In the widened sense initiated by Heimann and others, countertransference refers to *all* the analyst's responses to the patient, intellectual as well as emotional, conscious as well as unconscious, insightful as well as pathological. In this broader usage, countertransference, or at least some aspects of countertransference, may be used, at least in part, as a source of information about the patient.

But if we are able to use our countertransference in the clinical situation to guide our understanding of the analysand, this takes place by way of a constant process of interaction with the patient, whereas the situation as regards existing patient case histories is more limited. As readers we remain dependent on our countertransference response to the text, and the patient history 'responds' only in so far as in the process of examining it, other aspects may strike us, changes of meaning may occur to us, and so forth, until a new understanding may possibly reveal itself. The plausibility of readers' interpretations depends on the extent to which they succeed in shedding light on important aspects of the analytic interaction described in the case history so as to reveal aspects that have not been fully understood or have not been included by the author. In other words, readers, from their outside and later perspective, may be able to make the original author's findings more coherent and more inclusive. As in the analytic process, this does not justify the claim that *the* truth has been found, only that *a* possible truth has been put forward and that corresponding perspectives have been demonstrated.

Stuhr (1995) summarises the situation by stating that as yet it has not been possible to develop an alternative research tool with the aid of which transference/countertransference processes can be conveyed in such a way that the analyst's unconscious resistance to his counter-transference can be perceived and hence reflected on and discussed by the analyst who reviews the case history. Thus if what we are concerned with are the difficulties the original analyst was unable to name as such, case histories constitute the appropriate material. Case histories offer an opportunity to study a key aspect of our analytical toolkit and to further our understanding of it. If it is a question of the possible nature of the manifestation of the analyst's resistance to countertransference, for example, we can fall back on relevant analytic knowledge: in a case presentation or in clinical notes, resistance may manifest itself in breaks, gaps, slips, stresses, dark passages, inconsistencies and the like.

In principle, one point applies to both treatment notes and case histories, namely, the fact that both show the effect of transference/countertransference processes. However, since the treatment notes are simply notes – and Melanie Klein often made them in a form of shorthand – 'countertransference reactions' are frequently less clearly discernible in them than in the revised, published case histories. With treatment notes of this kind, we cannot simply read through them and annotate them at particular points, as is possible with case histories. On the other hand, some possible countertransference reactions find expression in the original notes that are not found in the publications. Thus at certain points there are many mistakes, crossings-out, insertions, etc. Since the notes can to some extent be regarded as corresponding to a manifest dream (cf. Zwiebel, 1994), they represent a kind of raw material that comes alive only when it is interpreted. If we need the transference/countertransference situation and the patient's associations to interpret a dream, then we also need a frame of reference for interpreting the treatment notes – points of 'crystallisation' that make it possible methodically to work out the meaning of the material.

I have adopted the following procedure: I began by going through the publications containing material on the cases of the patients named, picking out particularly striking aspects. I then formulated a hypothesis about the meaning of these aspects. In the next stage, I consulted the material in unpublished manuscripts relating to the patient concerned, following the same procedure when significant deviations from the published material arose. In a third stage, I then consulted the original notes. Fundamental points of crystallisation in this procedure were:

1   A comparison of the published material with the relevant sequences in the unpublished material (where available); any deviations were identified and reflected upon.
2   The start of treatment was noted in each case, the first game, the first phantasy, etc.
3   Various points of importance in the published material were investigated in terms of the form in which they appear in the original notes.

While the relevance of points (1) and (3) to the main theme, the 'most striking aspects of the case', is obvious, point (2), 'starting points', needs some clarification. In this context, the reader's attention is drawn to relevant studies that have shown how important aspects of psychodynamics are represented in compressed form in the initial scene or interview (see, for example, Argelander, 1970; Eckstaedt, 1991; Henseler and Wegner, 1991; Hinshelwood, 1991). Riesenberg-Malcolm (1994) explains that, owing to the binding nature of the decision now taken to start analysis, in the first session of an analysis it often becomes possible to see a great deal of the patient's inner world all at once or in quick succession, which conveys vivid information about the way in which the patient relates. Diatkine (1972, p. 146) draws attention to the fact that the child's first games or drawings correspond to the adult's initial dream, being the product of the patient's unconscious phantasies at both the evolved and the regressive level.

The patient histories of Grete, Rita and Inge will be investigated by these means, and we shall learn how Klein dealt with the problems that arose in the direct interaction with the children according to the stage her technique had reached in each case. Indications of new conceptual approaches will also be noted. In Erna's case, I shall also endeavour to use the original notes to (re)construct the dynamic of the transference/countertransference in the three main phases of this analysis, in order to attempt to convey the quality of the experiences that led Klein, at first intuitively, since she consciously followed Freud's concept of the libido, to propose some changes in theory. Here too, the theme is a thesis developed from the published papers on Erna. I shall show that with her ideas on the drive for knowledge (the 'epistemophilic instinct'), Klein was giving us a guideline that she herself was unable to follow consistently, owing to problems in dealing with her own countertransference, but whose use enables us to propose a plausible model of Erna's analysis, which I have tried to construct on the basis of a comparison of the published papers, the unpublished manuscript, but, above all, of the clinical notes.

1.4.2 On publishing case notes

The question arises of the extent to which we are justified in consulting Melanie Klein's own records, in transcribing and publishing them. In my view, consultation of original case notes offers an opportunity to achieve insights that are not otherwise possible. Hence, on condition that there appears to be no serious risk of breaching patient anonymity,[13] the same reservations apply as in the case of publication of other documents (letters, diaries, etc.) not intended by the authors themselves for publication. General interest in these private documents is, then, the decisive factor. Unlike documents of other kinds, the notes do not easily reveal their meaning because of their shorthand style, so it would not be very meaningful to publish them in isolation and it would therefore also be difficult to justify this. Even

---

13 In this context, see also Fichtner (1989, p. 813), who points out with reference to the Freud letters that patient confidentiality does not lapse; also, in greater detail, see Fichtner (1994, 1997).

31

though it is certain that Klein herself never intended them to be published in this form, it can be assumed from what she says in the preface to her *Narrative of a Child Analysis* (1961) that in some respects this project would perhaps not have been entirely alien to her. She refers there to *The Psycho-Analysis of Children* (1932), in which Rita, Inge and Erna, among others, are considered in detail, saying that in it she was able to give only extracts of her observations and interpretations, and regrets in particular that she could not give an all-round picture of her technique (Klein, 1932, p. 11). Towards the end of her life, she herself returned to the treatment notes on the brief analysis of Richard carried out in 1941 since, as this child analysis was limited to four months from the outset, its scope made it possible for all ninety-three sessions to be published. She inserted notes supplementing the records of the sessions at the end of each session, and her primary aim in publishing this volume was to explain her technique in more detail than she had previously done, as she said in the preface to the posthumously published *Narrative of a Child Analysis* (Klein, 1961). As far as I know, there are very few historical studies using original notes of analyses.

One exception is the only set of Freud's notes to have been preserved, those on the 'Rat Man'. Mahony (1986) consulted them in his study *Freud and the Rat Man*. The aim of this study was to write a coherent narrative (Mahony, 1986, p. xiv). To this end, he draws on a very wide range of sources (including, in addition to Freud's publications and notes, documents relating to the patient's family and to his academic, military and professional life). With regard to the method adopted, he speaks of a 'synthesis of psychoanalytic, historical, literary and textual approaches' (p. xiv), but does not explain this in detail. As regards the practical approach he adopts in dealing with the original notes, he quite definitely seeks out 'striking aspects' and reflects on them. Hence there are parallels with my own approach. However, the difference in his intention means that a different degree of importance is attached to this process of identifying striking aspects. I should mention in passing the fact that the preservation of many of Melanie Klein's original notes (in contrast to the situation with Freud, for example) could be regarded as indicating that Klein herself did not exclude the possibility of coming back to these documents.

I believe it is appropriate for the original notes employed here to be published not only for reasons of transparency, but also to enable them to be studied further, either in order to develop further hypotheses with the aid of the same approach (owing to the over-determined nature of the material), or to obtain more information on this early period by means of approaches of other kinds.

1.5. The importance of negative transference in Klein's work with her early child patients

As we shall see, understanding the negative transference was a key issue for Klein that she regarded as central to the establishment of the analytic process and crucial to understanding the mind. It was a hotly debated matter in the publications of Anna Freud and Melanie Klein on child analysis in the 1920s (Klein, 1927a; Anna Freud, 1927a, 1927b, 1927c, 1927d).

1.5.1 Historical background to the concept of negative transference

While Freud (1915a) devotes an entire paper to a form of positive transference, transference love, nowhere does he discuss negative transference in detail. Hence the brief introduction to the concept is to some extent paradigmatic for his handling of this phenomenon. The late mention of the clinical relevance of the fact of hostile impulses originating in childhood, which must have been well known to him, and the characteristic style of the definition, are facets of what might almost be called his reluctance to discuss it:

> We must make up our minds to distinguish a 'positive' transference from a 'negative' one, the transference of affectionate feelings from that of hostile ones, and to treat the two sorts of transference to the doctor separately.
>
> (Freud, 1912a, *S.E.* 12, p. 105)

He adds that negative transference merits more detailed consideration, but that this is not possible in this context.

Other analysts in this early period also write almost nothing about negative transference. Since Abraham and Ferenczi were of importance to Melanie Klein, I should like to summarise their comments in this connection. As mentioned earlier, Melanie Klein sought a second analysis with Abraham because no negative transference had been taken up by Ferenczi. It is apparent from Ferenczi's writings, however, that he was aware of the phenomenon early on. In 1909, for example, he writes:

> The analysis is very often, however, disagreeably disturbed by motiveless hate, fear and apprehension in regard to the physician, which in the unconscious relate not to him, but to persons of whom the patient is not at the time thinking . . . finally we arrive, mostly after the overcoming of great resistances, at repressed thoughts of sexuality, violence, and apprehension that relate to the nearest relatives, especially the parents.
>
> (Ferenczi, 1909, pp. 62–63)

He also succinctly formulates the significance of negative transference as follows: 'Another analytical situation which one was also in the habit of labelling incorrectly as "resistance" is the negative transference, which, from its very nature, cannot express itself otherwise than as "resistance" and the analysis of which is the most important task of the therapeutic activity' (Ferenczi and Rank, 1925, p. 40).

And he continues:

> It is not an accident that technical mistakes occurred so frequently just in the expression of transference and resistance . . . This may also be due to subjective factors in the analyst. The narcissism of the analyst seems suited to create a particularly fruitful source of mistakes.
>
> (Ferenczi and Rank, 1925, p. 41)

This is not the right place to engage in a discussion of what made it difficult for Ferenczi actually to analyse negative transference – his comments on the 'active technique' suggest that he attempted to counter negative transference with advice, instructions and prohibitions (see especially Ferenczi, 1919, 1920, 1924).

Abraham published a paper on latent negative transference, but without employing this technical term in it.[14] In 'A particular form of neurotic resistance against the psycho-analytic method', Abraham (1919b) describes a group of patients who displayed permanent

---

14 As far as I am aware, the term 'latent negative transference' occurs for the first time in Sterba (1927).

resistance to the basic principles of psychoanalysis. They did not spontaneously state that nothing occurred to them, but talked coherently and almost continuously. Their resistance was concealed behind apparent submissiveness. These were patients who were strongly narcissistic, analysis of whom posed major problems. However, if the patient's narcissistic reticence was successfully overcome and, by the same token, positive transference was effected, the prognosis was reasonably good. The question of how Abraham specifically proceeded remains open, however. He writes only: 'I certainly have the impression that it is easier to overcome such narcissistic resistances now that I make known to these patients the nature of their resistances at the very beginning of treatment' (Abraham, 1919b, p. 311). But he does not explain what this introduction consists of.

While his 1919b paper concerned latent negative transference, Abraham's paper on 'Manifestations of the female castration complex' (1920) contains examples of manifest negative transference. However, here too there are only a few examples of how this found expression in the analysis and how Abraham dealt with it. One such vignette is outlined as follows:

> A neurotic patient in whom psycho-analysis revealed an extra-ordinary degree of narcissism one day showed the greatest resistance to treatment, and manifested many signs of defiance towards me which really referred to her deceased father. She left my consulting room in a state of violent negative transference. When she stepped into the street she caught herself saying impulsively: 'I *will not* be well until I have got a penis'. She thus expected this gift from me, as a substitute for her father, and made the effect of the treatment dependent upon receiving it.
>
> (Abraham, 1920, p. 350)

In so far as we can conclude anything about the way in which Abraham handled negative transference from this summary, it seems most likely that he traced it back to the original object (the father) relatively quickly, a feature that we shall see again in Melanie Klein's work. From the perspective of present-day Kleinian technique, this would probably be seen as a sign of the analyst's collusion with the patient to avoid discomfort in the immediate analyst–patient relationship (see also Folch and Folch, 1988). However, it should be remembered that Abraham's and Klein's usage conforms to the traditional definition and usage of the concept of transference. I should also mention at this point that naturally negative transference must always be considered against the background of the unavoidable coexistence of positive and negative transference. As Folch and Folch put it, clinical descriptions of negative or positive transference must always be understood as indicating 'the predominance of one of the two qualities both in the manifest expression and in the unconscious economy of the basic affects and drives' (Folch and Folch, 1988, p. 689; translated quotation).

1.5.2 *Melanie Klein and Anna Freud on negative transference in 1926–1927*

Against this background, perhaps it is not too surprising that negative transference is one of the specific points hotly debated by Melanie Klein and Anna Freud during 1926–1927. The first techniques of child analysis capable of being described had been developed by Melanie Klein in Berlin and Anna Freud in Vienna, and their content led to controversy between London, where Melanie Klein had settled in the meantime, and Vienna. By this time Klein had already presented and published her technique in various places. Anna Freud had explained her technique in four lectures in the winter semester of 1926–1927, distinguishing it from Klein's, and these were published shortly afterwards.[15] They in turn formed the subject of the so-called Symposium on Child-Analysis held at the British Psycho-Analytical Society in May 1927. Anna Freud's view was as follows:

> But with a child negative impulses toward the analyst – however revealing they may be in many respects – are essentially disturbing and should be dealt with analytically as soon as possible. The really fruitful work always takes place in positive attachment.
>
> (A. Freud, 1927a, p. 41)

15 By the end of 1924, Melanie Klein had developed her technique to the extent that Anna Freud, who heard Klein's relevant lecture in Vienna in December 1924, was able to choose to use it as a reference framework. It can be assumed that Anna Freud was referring to this lecture, since at that time the points of Melanie Klein's work that she picked out had not yet appeared in Klein's publications in that form.

Although she herself does not put it like this, it could be said that with respect to negative transference, which often plays a part right at the outset, Anna Freud suggested using 'tricks' to win the child over in a special 'preliminary' or 'breaking-in' phase.[16] She expressly justifies the 'preliminary' phase by saying that with children (unlike adults) the preconditions for analysis should first be established: acknowledgement of illness, confidence in analysis and the decision to undertake it (A. Freud, 1927b, pp. 11, 14). She stresses that during this period, the procedure does not yet have anything to do with 'real analysis' (1927b, p. 14). The examples cited show that she finds this 'preliminary' phase necessary if the situation is initially determined by negative transference. It is clear from the six examples she uses to illustrate the 'preliminary' phase that it does not play a major part with children who come into treatment primarily with positive transference.

As the following extract shows, Anna Freud was to some extent aware of the problems inherent in this procedure:

> The decision whether such a battle for the child is a permissible method was in this case made without difficulty; the nanny's influence was undesirable not only for the analysis but for the whole development of the child. But consider how impossible such a situation becomes when the opponent is not a comparative stranger but one of the child's parents, or when one is faced with the question whether it is worth depriving the child, in the interests of a successful analysis, of an adult's otherwise favorable and desirable influence.
> (A. Freud, 1927b, p. 17)

This suggests that she had some doubts about her procedure, in which she worked towards a split in transference, seeking to accommodate the negative aspect of transference outside the analytic situation.

When Anna Freud is confronted with negative transference in the course of the analysis despite the 'preliminary' phase, she voices her problems in dealing with it surprisingly openly – the analysis of a 6-year-old patient with an obsessional neurosis involved making it clear to her that she hated her mother, something which the patient resisted.

---

16 Later on Anna Freud revised her opinion about a 'preliminary' phase, but we cannot discuss this in more detail here (cf. A. Freud, 1974.)

Finally, confronted with these constantly recurring proofs, she gave
way, but now she wanted me to tell her why she would have such
hostile feelings for her mother whom she professed to love very
much. Here I declined to give further information, for I too was at
the end of my knowledge.

(A. Freud, 1927c, p. 33)[17]

Melanie Klein uses another incident involving this little patient as
an opportunity to make her own differing technique clear. At a particular stage this child, who before treatment had displayed inhibitions
and obsessional symptoms, became naughty and lacking in restraint at
home. Looking back, Anna Freud drew the inference that at this point
she ought to have intervened in the role of educator (A. Freud, 1927d,
pp. 62 ff.; Klein, 1927a, p. 159). Klein now describes how in a similar
case she came to the same conclusion as Anna Freud: 'the analyst must
have made a mistake'. But she immediately goes on to characterise the
crucial difference:

Only – and here is probably one of the most salient and fundamental differences in our views – I concluded that I had failed
somehow on the *analytic* side, and not on the educational. I mean
that I realized that I had failed to resolve the resistances completely
in the analytic hour and to release in its fullness the negative
transference.

(1927a, WMK I, p. 161)

---

17 The material made available by Elisabeth Young-Bruehl (1988) in her biography of Anna
    Freud makes it clear that Anna Freud also knew something about the factors in herself
    that made countertransference an obstacle. On 19 February 1926, Anna Freud writes as
    follows to Max Eitingon:

    I think sometimes that I want not only to make them [Mabbie and Bob Burlingham
    CF] healthy, but also, at the same time, to have them, or at least have something of
    them, for myself. Temporarily, of course, this desire is useful for my work, but some-
    time or another it really will disturb them, and so, on the whole, I really cannot call my
    need other than 'stupid'.

    (Young-Bruehl, 1988, p. 133)

    I believe that Young-Bruehl is right to point out that Anna Freud's own negative trans-
    ference was displaced onto Eitingon, the quasi-analyst, and that Anna Freud's own
    reluctance to express negative feelings about her father was of decisive importance in her
    emphasis on positive transference in child analysis (p. 187).

Klein contrasts Anna Freud's example with Erna,[18] her 6-year-old obsessional neurotic patient, who often displayed a marked negative transference, with

> rages which were vented on objects in my room, such as cushions, etc.; dirtying and destroying of playthings, smearing paper with water, plasticine, pencils and so forth. In all this the child gave the impression of a very considerable freedom from inhibition and seemed to take a remarkable pleasure in this often quite wild behaviour.
>
> (1927a, WMK I, p. 160)

She then explains the concepts that enabled her to seek to understand this behaviour: 'To a great extent what lay behind Erna's "lack of restraint" was anxiety and also the need for punishment which compelled her to repeat her behaviour' (p. 160).[19] Klein describes the paranoid vicious circle, in which, owing to the existence of a rigid, condemnatory superego, perception of the aggressiveness of one's own aggressive phantasies and impulses is resisted by means of further aggressive actions. (The hostility leads to fear of revenge by the objects, which in turn increases the subject's hostility.) Klein also returns to Freud's description of the unconscious sense of guilt, which seeks appeasement through getting oneself punished for aggressive actions – but with the difference that Klein establishes this too at an earlier stage than Freud.[20]

It is clear from these examples how the concept of an early, severe superego enables Melanie Klein to understand and to analyse negative transference, and how Anna Freud's different concept of the superego causes her problems in dealing with negative transference, leading her potentially to set herself against the parents on the one hand and, on the other, forcing her into non-analytic interventions. What Anna

18 Young-Bruehl (1988) points out that in 1924 Anna Freud was cautious in her assessment of Melanie Klein's theory and technique of child analysis, and that one of the decisive factors in her publication of a critical opinion was having familiarised herself with a case comparable with Erna, Melanie Klein's 6-year-old obsessional neurotic. This was the 6-year-old Adelaide Sweetzer, an American friend of the Burlingham children (Young-Bruehl, 1988, p. 165).
19 Erna's case is studied in detail in Chapter 6.
20 For a summary of the development of Melanie Klein's concept of the superego, see Chapter 7 in Hinshelwood's (1989b) *Dictionary of Kleinian Thought*.

Freud sees as the child's weak superego is in her view organically connected with the outside world, and accordingly the parents are the cause of the child's illness:

> We cannot forget that it was these same parents or guardians whose excessive demands drove the child into an excess of repression and into neurosis. The parents who are now called upon to help in the child's recovery are still the same people who let the child get ill in the first place.
>
> (A. Freud, 1927d, pp. 58–59)

Since the impulses liberated by the analysis, owing to the weak superego, would seek a direct route to gratification of an inevitably perverse sexuality, guidance from the analyst is appropriate, and for the duration of the analysis she must put herself '*in the place of the child's ego ideal*' (A. Freud, 1927d, p. 60).

If we take the published works as a basis, Klein's first explicit reference to dealing with negative transference is in the 1927 publication 'Symposium on child-analysis' (Klein, 1927a). With her alternative view of Anna Freud's example and her own summarised example (Erna), Klein conveys her own understanding of negative transference and explains why we should strive to analyse it – to liberate the capacity for love (1927a, WMK I, p. 164). However, her specific method of dealing with negative transference is not made clear in this paper.

If we go through the earlier publications looking at this aspect, we have already seen how in her analysis of Felix (see Section 1.2 above), Klein felt compelled to impose prohibitions, contrary to her usual practice. In the same publication (1925), she also reports on her analyses of Werner, 9, and Walter, 5½ – in both cases the phenomenon of negative transference and her understanding of it are clear, but she does not describe how she dealt with it in practice. This also applies to the situation with Trude, 4½, as described in 'The psychological principles of early analysis' (1926, WMK I, pp. 128–138).

1.5.3 Negative transference in Melanie Klein's lectures and unpublished manuscripts of 1925

Anna Freud's explicit reference to Klein's view on transference makes it likely that she was referring not only to Klein's publications (as mentioned earlier, the term 'negative transference' occurs for the first time in Klein's publications in her reply to Anna Freud, and there is otherwise almost no explicit discussion of the transference phenomenon in her early publications), but also to Klein's as yet unpublished lectures. I shall therefore take the liberty of digressing at this point to show how Klein handles the issue of negative transference in the mid-1920s. She specifically covered this point in her second London lecture in 1925, 'The technique of early analysis', the manuscript of which is held by the Melanie Klein Trust, so I shall quote from it here. We cannot know whether Anna Freud knew of it, or whether Melanie Klein had made similar comments on this point in her lecture in Vienna on 17 December 1924. Unfortunately no manuscript of this Vienna lecture has been preserved. However, Klein had presented a version of this lecture in Berlin four days earlier, and Alix Strachey sent a summary of it to London (Meisel and Kendrick, 1986). Once again the term 'negative transference' does not explicitly occur here, but the cases on which Klein based her discussion of this phenomenon in her London lecture of 1925 obviously also formed the basis of her 1924 lecture, in so far as it can be reconstructed from Alix Strachey's details,[21] which means that it is not impossible that Klein spoke about negative transference in Vienna as well as in Berlin and London.

After discussing in detail Peter's first two analytic sessions,[22] and

---

21 Cf. the appendix to the correspondence of James and Alix Strachey, 1924 to 1925, edited by Perry Meisel and Walter Kendrick (1986, pp. 325–329): 'Summary: Alix's report on Melanie Klein's Berlin lecture'. A 2¾-year-old child is mentioned on p. 325, and this is likely to be Rita. Klein later published on the 9-year-old boy of p. 327 under the name of Kenneth. The 4-year-old boy on p. 327 is probably Peter. The two 4-year-old girls on pp. 327 and 328 are presumably Trude and Ruth. The 6-year-old patient on pp. 328–329 is Erna. In the second lecture in 1925 Klein employs material on Peter, Rita, Trude and Ruth.

22 Peter's analysis took place from 18 February to 29 June 1924 and from 8 January 1925 to 27 April 1926. When Anna Freud refers to the fact that Klein interprets 'a deliberate collision between two cars as evidence of the child having observed sexual intercourse between the parents' (A. Freud, 1927a, pp. 37–38), she is probably referring to Peter's analysis. For example, Klein's 1925 manuscript contains the following passage from Peter's first analytic session:

> in between he took two horse-drawn carriages and bumped one into another, so that the horses' feet knocked together. He immediately said, 'I've got a new little brother called Fritz'. As he repeated the bumping together of the carriages several times, I asked him what they were doing. He answered, 'That's not nice', and stopped at once, but

material from a later extract from Peter's analysis (cf. Klein, 1932, 'The technique of early analysis', Chapter 2, WMK II, pp. 17 ff., where this material is reproduced in virtually identical form), she speaks about handling transference:

> As soon as the child has given me an insight into his complexes, whether through his play or his drawings or phantasies, or by his general behaviour, interpretations can begin. This does not contradict the well-tried rule of waiting till the transference is established before beginning to interpret, because with children the transference takes place immediately, and one is usually given positive indications of this straight away. However, if from the outset the child shows shyness, anxiety or even only lack of trust, this should be regarded as a sign of a negative transference, which makes it necessary to begin interpreting as soon as possible. This leads to a reduction in negative transference by tracing these affects back to the original situation.
> (Klein [1925ii], Technique of early analysis, manuscript, p. 8; see also the relatively unchanged wording in 1932, WMK II, p. 21)

In her next brief example, Klein clarifies the facts that make rapid interpretation of negative transference appear to her to be essential:

> This became particularly clear to me in the analysis of 2¾-year-old Rita. When the very ambivalent child felt a resistance, she at once wanted to leave the room, and I felt I had to make an interpretation immediately so as to resolve this resistance.
>
> (ibid.)[23]

The next person she mentions in this manuscript is Trude:

> In another instance I was able to see with impressive clearness the necessity of immediate interpretation. This was in the case of a

---

started again quite soon. Then he knocked two toy horses together in the same way. I now said, 'Look here, the horses are two people bumping together', and at first he answered, 'No, that's not nice', then 'Yes, that's two people bumping together'.
(Klein [1925ii], Technique of early analysis, manuscript, p. 2; see also 1932, WMK II, p. 17)

23 Rita's analysis will be studied in Chapter 4.

three-year-old girl, who came to me for a single analytic session,[24] since her treatment then had to be postponed owing to illness and external circumstances. The child was very neurotic and unusually strongly fixated upon her mother. She came into my room unwillingly and full of anxiety, and I was obliged to analyse her in a low voice with the door open. But soon she had given me an idea of the nature of her complexes. She insisted upon the flowers in a vase being removed; she threw a little toy man out of a cart into which she had previously put him and scolded him, she said that the cushions had been thrown into disorder by a dog, – she wanted a man with a high hat taken out of her picture-book. – My immediate interpretation of these utterances was able to diminish her anxiety, although naturally this was only the case at a very superficial level; but at least it meant that the little girl left me in a much more trustful mood than she had come, and said at home that she would like to come to me again.

(Klein [1925ii], Technique of early analysis, manuscript, pp. 8f.)

The interpretation is not given here, but Klein inserted it at the relevant point in her 1932 publication: 'My [. . .] interpretation [. . .] that she desired to do away with her father's penis, because it was playing havoc with her mother (as represented by the vase, the cart, the picture-book and the cushion) at once diminished her anxiety' (1932, WMK II, p. 22). A notable point here is again the – as it seems to us today – rapid retracing to the original objects, something we have already noted with Abraham.

Klein then explains how she proceeded with the very difficult Ruth, showing clearly the methods she employed to try to establish contact with the child. The contrast with the procedure adopted by Anna Freud becomes very clear. Melanie Klein too seeks positive transference in order to work, she too initially falls back on 'extra-analytic' resources in a situation of extreme initial negative transference, but she does not use 'tricks' or the like in a specific attempt to establish it. Klein's way is to try to understand the significance of the indications she is receiving from the child and to put it into words.

---

24 This first session of Trude's, the notes of which are held by the Melanie Klein Trust, took place on 24 September 1923, and she was then treated from 2 May to 10 December 1924.

The relevant passage is therefore quoted here at length (readers can again compare it with the relevant pages of the 1932 publication, Chapter 2, WMK II, pp. 26ff.):

However, the 4¼-year-old Ruth presented me with very specific problems which were new to me. She too was one of those children whose ambivalence showed itself in a very positive attitude in relation to the mother and certain individual women. However, she disliked most strangers and already at a very early age she had not been able to get used to a new nursemaid. It was also impossible to leave her on her own in a strange environment, it was extremely difficult for her to make friends with other children, and in addition to this, as well as direct anxiety and various other neurotic symptoms, the child displayed great apprehensiveness in general. In her first analytic session she absolutely refused to remain in the room with me alone, and I therefore decided to ask her teacher to be present during the analysis. I should say that this companion was an unusually well educated lady, pedagogically and psychologically aware, who also knew a great deal about psychoanalysis. Otherwise it would have been impossible to create this situation, and even in cases as unusual as this I must emphasise that I do not consider it to be appropriate and now believe that all other technical measures are to be preferred to it. In the first sessions, although the teacher was extremely tactful, remained in the background as far as possible, and intervened as little as possible, the child did play, but in the process kept turning only to the teacher, was much more affectionate with her than usual, and ignored me completely. My intention had been to establish a positive transference by extra-analytic means, to achieve the eventual possibility of working alone with the child, but all attempts, such as playing with her, encouraging her to talk, etc., were in vain. The teacher also told me that she considered my efforts to be hopeless and that I would have little chance of achieving this even if I were with her for weeks on end, let alone for an hour at a time. I therefore found myself forced to take other measures and as a result again obtained striking proof of the efficacy of interpretation as a way of reducing negative transference. The child had again devoted her attention exclusively to the teacher, then she drew a picture of a tumbler with marbles inside it. She drew a kind of lid on top of this tumbler. I asked her what the lid was for, but she would not answer me. When the teacher repeated the question, she said it was 'to prevent the marbles from rolling out'. Before this, however, Ruth had gone through the teacher's bag and then shut it tightly, so that nothing would fall out of it. She had done the same with the purse, in which she had kept the coins safe in similar fashion. Furthermore, the material she was now bringing had been quite clear to me even in her previous sessions. As I now had little to lose, I made a venture and told Ruth that the marbles, like the coins, were children in her Mummy's tummy, and that she wanted to keep them safely shut up so as not to have any more brothers and sisters.

The effect of the interpretation was astonishing – to the teacher in particular: for the first time, the little girl turned her attention to me and then began to play in a completely different way, something I already know to be typical in connection with the effect of interpretations in resolving repression. The child began to play in a way that offered an opportunity for insight into her complexes, produced ever more material following interpretations, and hence made it possible [. . .] to continue the analysis. Nevertheless, it was not possible to keep the child on her own with me in the treatment room; she reacted to that with anxiety attacks, and since as a result of the analytic work the negative transference was visibly steadily diminishing and hence being replaced by a positive one, I decided to continue the analysis in her teacher's presence. After three weeks, the teacher suddenly needed to depart on a journey, and I found myself faced with the alternatives of stopping the analysis or risking an anxiety attack and endeavouring to analyse the attack itself and thus to continue to work. With her family's consent I chose the second course. The child was brought to me and handed over to me in the corridor, and her companion went away despite the child's tears and screams. In this situation, which I found extremely painful, I again began by trying to soothe the child in a non-analytical, motherly way, as any ordinary person would. I talked to her, comforted her, tried to play with her, but all in vain. When the child saw that she was alone with me, she had followed me into the room, but once she was there she seemed completely inaccessible; she screamed, her face became very white, and she showed all the signs of a severe attack of anxiety. Meanwhile I had sat down at the toy-table and now began to play by myself, all the while describing what I was doing to the terrified child, who was sitting in a corner of the sofa. Following a sudden inspiration, I had taken as the subject of my game the material the child had brought me in the previous session. At that time the child had played in the bathroom, feeding dolls, giving them huge jugfuls of milk, etc. I now put one of these dolls down to sleep, told Ruth that I was going to give the doll something more to eat, and asked her what it should be. She interrupted her screams to answer 'milk', and I noticed that she suddenly made a movement towards her mouth with the two fingers she had a habit of sucking before going to sleep, but quickly took them away. I asked her whether she wanted to suck them and she said 'Yes, but properly'. I had recognised that she wanted to reconstitute the situation in which she went to sleep at home, so I laid her down on the chaise longue and, at her request, put a rug over her. Thereupon she put her fingers in her mouth and began to suck them. She now lay – admittedly still very pale and with her eyes closed – but she was visibly much calmer and had also stopped crying. Meanwhile I went on playing with the dolls, repeating her game of the session before. As I was giving one of the dolls a wet sponge, as Ruth had done, Ruth burst out crying again and sobbed, 'No, she mustn't have the big sponge, that's not for children, only for grown-ups'. I should note here that this last session and the previous ones had produced a lot of material in connection with the child's castration wishes, her envy of her mother, and especially also her phantasy of stealing the mother's children. When following her protest about the big sponge I made an interpretation for her, always beginning by using the doll to make things clear, she became ever calmer, then opened her eyes, and was happy for me to push the table on which I was playing up to the chaise longue and continue my game and my interpretations close beside her. She gradually sat up, watched the course of the play with lively interest, and even began to take an active part in it herself. In the process I established that she would actually allow me to repeat to her that the doll had wanted to steal the mother's children and she had wanted to castrate her father. Soon, however, I went over to repeating the interpretation I had given for the doll but applying it to her own person and thus to re-establishing the analytical situation in its entirety. When she was collected at the end of the session, to her companion's amazement she was happy and cheerful and said goodbye to me in a friendly and even affectionate way. At the beginning of the next session, when her companion left her, she again showed

some anxiety, but she did not have another actual anxiety attack or
burst into tears.

(Klein [1925ii], Technique of early analysis,
manuscript, pp. 15 ff.)[25]

In her fourth London lecture of 1925, Klein mentions other
'*technical devices*' for getting the analysis started if the usual procedure
fails — such as beginning to play herself when with a small child, or
giving a bigger child a stimulus-word, for example in the form of a
brief fairy-tale. In a somewhat attenuated form, these devices are
similar to Anna Freud's preliminary phase. But Klein goes on to tell
her audience why she has rejected such devices:

> *I found one of the forms I used in the early days of my practice, namely
> telling the child something from my own childhood, not to be advisable,
> since although this very personal form of story telling is capable of establish-
> ing transference, among other things, more quickly, the analytic situation can
> easily shift, and we may pay for this at a later stage of the analysis.*

(Klein [1925iv], manuscript, p. 22)

In the sixth London lecture, she again stresses the crucial significance
of anxiety and a sense of guilt, the resolution of which through interpretation is '*the fundamental factor in establishing and consolidating positive
transference*' (Klein [1925vi], manuscript, p. 9).

The material in the manuscripts helps to clarify the manner in
which Klein dealt with negative transference, and her references to it
indicate an evolution – which was, of course, not yet completed at this
stage – in Klein's technique and in her handling of negative transference in the years 1921–1925. The references to this evolution remain
selective, however, so that even with the aid of the manuscripts we
cannot obtain a clearer picture of the aspect of it that interests us here.

In the chapters that follow I offer a detailed comparative analysis
of Klein's published papers, unpublished manuscripts and clinical
notes on four of the children she analysed in Berlin: 7-year-old Grete,
2¾-year-old Rita, 7-year-old Inge and 6-year-old Erna. In this presentation I hope to offer a more intensive insight into Klein's practice
during these formative years.

---

25 Ruth was treated from 16 September 1924 to 7 April 1925 and from 3 April to 3 July 1926.

2

Melanie Klein's psychoanalytic clinical work in Berlin

No attempt has hitherto been made to construct from the existing documents an approximate idea of the scope of Klein's psychoanalytic experiences with children and adolescents in Berlin. Instead, the mainly rather cursory references to this subject comprise inaccurate or simply incorrect statements concerning Klein's practice in Berlin. The latter range from the claim that Klein had hardly any practical experience (Biermann, 1968, p. 44) to the statement that Klein treated 'mostly the children of colleagues' (Grosskurth, 1986, p. 101), and Grosskurth's demonstrably incorrect thesis that the treatments of the children referred to as Ernst, Felix, Lisa and Grete in her published work were in fact treatments of her own children. The inaccuracies include Petot's statement that 'in 1922 . . . she began work at the Polyclinic' (Petot, 1990, p. 9), when she actually began in February 1921, and his assumption that Rita had daily sessions (p. 107), whereas in fact Klein generally saw Rita three times weekly in the first few months (March to August), visiting Rita almost daily only in the final month of treatment. Hughes' statement that 'initially the analyses had taken place in the child's own nursery' (Hughes, 1989, p. 67) applies only to Rita's analysis in 1923, because in 1921 Klein began her treatments at the Polyclinic. Petot's statement that Egon's analysis 'was conducted between 1927 and 1928' (1990, p. 212) within the London period is also wrong – it took place earlier in Berlin – as is the time to which he provisionally allocates Klein's 'encounter with infantile psychosis' (Petot, 1990, p. 211). Similarly, Hinshelwood's 'Chronology' of the treatment technique, specifying for example '1921 – Using toys and play' (Hinshelwood, 1989b, p. 9), appears questionable.

48

I shall outline the beginning of Klein's work in the Berlin Polyclinic immediately following her move to Germany in 1921, summarising the specialised work of the Polyclinic in so far as this can be ascertained from the publications in order to explain the background to Klein's child analyses.[1] The second section provides a list – only a minimal one is possible at this stage – of the children and adolescents whom Klein treated in Berlin, in so far as this can be reconstructed from the diary and original notes. In order to make clear the importance of the Berlin years, all the children and adolescents who appeared in Klein's published work are grouped together, with an indication of which treatments are known to have taken place in Berlin.

2.1 The Berlin Psychoanalytic Polyclinic

The Berlin Polyclinic opened in 1920;[2] Eitingon reported on its activities in 1922, 1924 and 1925. The first report on the Berlin Psychoanalytic Polyclinic, published in 1922 in the *Internationale Zeitschrift für Psychoanalyse* (*IZP*) and in 1923 in the *International Journal of Psychoanalysis* (*IJP*), states that there was not only a permanent Polyclinic staff, joined in 1922 by 'Fräulein Schott for children's analysis',[3] but also that there were association members who undertook individual cases for analysis, in particular Dr Liebermann and Dr Böhm; the report adds that 'other members gradually followed their example, Dr. C. Müller, Dr. I Müller, Frau Dr. Horney, and later

---

1 A more detailed description of the Berlin Psychoanalytic Institute is provided in Oberborbeck's (1994) 'Kinderanalyse im Umfeld des Berliner Psychoanalytischen Instituts 1920–1933' (Child analysis in the milieu of the Berlin Psychoanalytic Institute 1920–1933). His observations on Melanie Klein are imprecise – he states, for example, that Klein had already begun analysis with Abraham in 1921 (p. 75). His comment as to 'how little has been known about Melanie Klein's Berlin years until now' (p. 91) is undoubtedly correct; however, his work does nothing to alter this. It is also important to consider the cultural background of the Berlin Polyclinic that has been outlined by several authors, such as De Clerck (1994). In 1999, Danto gave a portrait of the Berlin Polyclinic.

2 It remains unclear what became of the plan mentioned to Freud by Abraham on 13 March 1920 – 'For the distant future there is a project to start a special department for the treatment of nervous *children*. I should like to train a woman doctor particularly for this' (Freud and Abraham, 2002, p. 418). It is possible that he regarded Melanie Klein as having partly implemented this project.

3 Ada Schott, later Müller-Braunschweig's second wife, had undergone training with Hermine Hug-Hellmuth (Oberborbeck, 1994, p. 73).

Frau Dr. M. Klein, who most readily agreed to come to Berlin from Budapest' (1923, *IJP* 4, p. 256; 1922, *IZP* 8, p. 508). The published statistics reveal that twenty-three child consultations (of 305 consultations in total) took place between March 1920 and June 1922, which led to seven children subsequently undergoing treatment.[4] A 'case list' of patients was drawn up, stating each patient's initials, sex, profession (in the case of adults), age, diagnosis, treatment duration and outcome; this list appears in the German report but not in the English one. The 1921–1922 period with which we are concerned here contains five treatment cases: since one of these patients whose age is given as 7 years is said to have a clerical profession, we can only make use of the remaining four sets of information. Two of these cases can certainly be ascribed to Melanie Klein because there are notes available that she made from memory on the sessions: first, a 12-year-old schoolboy W. G.,[5] diagnosed with kleptomania, whose treatment duration is given as five and a half months, with the outcome as 'cured'; second, a 9-year-old schoolgirl K. G.,[6] diagnosed with a stutter, who after a nine-month treatment had 'fundamentally improved'. For both these patients, there are also still outpatient files from the Polyclinic. These show that W. G.'s treatment lasted from 14 March to 10 December; the five-and-a-half month treatment duration is obtained by deducting the holiday period. For K. G. only one page still exists, on which April and May are entered; since after the 21 May 'End' is recorded, this must refer to 1922, since it is clear from Klein's treatment notes that K. G.'s treatment began at the end of February 1921. This also tells us that Klein was conducting cases in the Polyclinic in 1921 and that from January 1922 she was continuing the treatments at her place of residence. In the 1922 report mentioned above, Eitingon complains that 'The five rooms for treatment in the Polyclinic are already proving inadequate' (1923, *IJP* 4, p. 257; 1922, *IZP* 8, p. 508), which may explain why Klein continued the treatments at her own home.

A third patient of the four cases under consideration at the Polyclinic may also be attributable to Melanie Klein: the 13-year-old schoolboy H. B., with a 'neurotic character', who was 'fundamentally improved'

---

4 All patients up to the age of 14 years (inclusive) were classified as children.

5 Klein did not publish any work about him, so as with all such patients I shall refer to him only anonymously; he is called 'patient A' in the list (Section 2.2).

6 In Klein's published work she was called Grete (cf. Chapter 3), the name that I shall continue to use here.

after a nine-and-a-half-month treatment. The year given for this treatment is 1922, but on the basis of the period of the report (up till June 1922) this cannot be reconciled with a nine-and-a-half-month treatment duration, so this may in fact refer to the 13-year-old schoolboy,[7] whom Klein saw from February 1921. For this patient there exist two outpatient files, according to which he had approximately 225 sessions between 6 February 1921 and 13 November 1923. Klein's diaries show that she treated him until July 1924.

Outpatient files from the Polyclinic are available in the Melanie Klein Archive for two other patients who have evidently not been included in the above-mentioned case list. It is unclear whether they are counted in the consultations – certainly with one case it is explicitly noted: '*Attempted analysis Mrs Klein*'. The view taken of the indications in each case was the responsibility of the Polyclinic's Director, as Eitingon states: 'I took over the work of consultation entirely' (1923, *IJP* 4, p. 262; 1922, *IZP* 8, p. 510). The outpatient file indicates one case of a 13-year-old boy (Melanie Klein in later published work called him a 12-year-old boy: 1923, WMK I, p. 181) whose analysis began in April 1921, for whom 'stayed away' is recorded both at the middle and at the end of April and for the first two-thirds of May; the final session is marked with a cross on 9 June, which is followed by the entry 'long vacation'. On the reverse side of the outpatient files under the heading 'Case history and diagnosis' it states:

> Brought from the youth office in Wilmersdorf. Petty thieving (broke into the school cupboards led by [?] another boy) and sexual aggression towards little girls. Very difficult environment; appears to have been encouraged to steal from a very early age by a sister. Cries when asked if he knows he has done something that is not allowed. Speaks very little the first time, is visibly intimidated, despite otherwise having many characteristics of the uninhibited suburban child. Has difficulty learning, but gives no impression of being intellectually backward.

The other case concerns another 12-year-old boy, who was 'received' on 15 April 1921; his treatment began on 24 May and ended according to the outpatient files on 11 June – in the corresponding

---

7 In her published work, Klein called him 'Felix'.

treatment notes Klein states '24 May to 6 June'; the treatment took place because of '*Enuresis, defaecation and kleptomania*'.[8]

Eitingon's second report covering the period from June 1922 to March 1924 mentions Klein again in what is by then a longer list of voluntary workers; the statistics this time indicate 29 child consultations (of 283 consultations in total), of which 21 were converted into a treatment. However, the lack of initials in the case lists precludes any definite assignment of treatment cases to Klein. There are no out-patient files for this period among the documents held in the Melanie Klein Archive, so it remains unclear how many children Klein saw in the framework of the Polyclinic or how many were referred to her for treatment there or in her private practice. Eitingon's general comment on child analysis in 1924 is that: 'Child analysis is extremely difficult to establish, although there is a clear and steadily increasing understanding of the theoretical interest in psychoanalysis in German educational and child-welfare circles, especially in Berlin' (Eitingon, 1924, p. 230).

The report on the Ninth Congress of the International Psycho-analytical Association in Bad Homburg in September 1925 is followed by Eitingon's description of the activities in the May 1924 to August 1925 period. He writes that they have decided to wait until they have a longer period on which to report before giving a more detailed account and that 'We ourselves are only too conscious of the shortcomings in our statistics up till now' (1926, *IJP* 7, p. 139). The part that interests us here is:

> This year again the number of children who came to the clinic showed no increase; curiously enough, there has been a decrease in the seven months of this year as compared with the seven months of the same period last year. The persons attending the clinic may be roughly grouped according to age as follows: under ten years – 6; between ten and fifteen years – 10.
>
> (1926, *IJP* 7, p. 140)[9]

---

8 Both boys are referred to in Section 3.3, where Klein's procedure at the time of Grete's analysis is outlined.

9 In view of this, Oberborbeck's conclusion that many psychoanalysts after Freud were already experimenting with child analysis, accepting children for treatment, and that there was also an interest in child analysis in the Berlin Institute (1994, p. 74) appears somewhat optimistically overstated. There was certainly some interest, but how strong it was remains to be investigated. It was clearly not strong enough for any attempt to be made to keep Melanie Klein in Berlin.

The subsequent developments can be ascertained only from the extensive account in *Zehn Jahre Berliner Psychoanalytisches Institut (Poliklinik und Lehranstalt) 1920–1930* [Ten years of the Berlin Psychoanalytic Institute (polyclinic and educational establishment) 1920–1930]. Here, Fenichel's (1979) 'Statistischer Bericht über die therapeutische Tätigkeit 1920–1930' [Statistical report on therapeutic activity 1920–1930] gives the following figures in Table IV: up to 5 years: 9 consultations, 2 psychoanalytic treatments; 6–10 years: 43 consultations, 15 psychoanalytic treatments; 11–15 years: 70 consultations, 37 psychoanalytic treatments (Fenichel, 1979, p. 16). Simmel refers enthusiastically to the demand in his article 'Zur Geschichte und sozialen Bedeutung des Berliner Psychoanalytischen Instituts' [On the history and social significance of the Berlin Psychoanalytic Institute]:

Professional and marital counselling offices, school doctors and welfare workers send those placed in their care to the Psychoanalytic Polyclinic at least for consultation. Municipal youth offices, the juvenile court, and the juvenile court auxiliary staff refer their clients – young people threatened by depravity and criminality – to our Polyclinic for treatment.
(Simmel, 1993, p. 135, quoted from Simmel's selected writings)

The key term 'child analysis' – by contrast with the above-mentioned reports – is otherwise nowhere to be found. Under the heading 'Vorlesungen und Seminare über die außertherapeutische Bedeutung der Psychoanalyse' [Lectures and seminars on the extra-therapeutic significance of psychoanalysis] in Carl Müller-Braunschweig's historical overview of the nature of teaching, its organisation and administration there is only a heading 'Education':

The relationship between psychoanalysis and education and educators, in relation both to the psychoanalysis of these two entities and to the possibilities for the practical application of psychoanalysis in education and for its theoretical application in educational theory and methodology has been discussed by Bernfeld since 1926 in regular seminars with educationalists of every kind.
(Müller-Braunschweig, 1970, p. 25)

Melanie Klein is finally mentioned again in the observations made on the occasion of the 'Fifty-year commemoration of the Berlin Psychoanalytic Institute (Karl Abraham Institute)'. Bannach (1971) summarises child analysis as follows:

> Child analysis was not yet being taught at the Berlin Institute. However, there was a group of analysts who were working with children and experimenting with child analysis. Abraham had thus invited Melanie Klein to Berlin in 1921, where she worked for five years and developed her psychoanalytic play technique. Her observations on the aggressive and unrealistic nature of children's phantasies led to disputes of various kinds among the circle of colleagues, especially as most of them worked only with adults. The best-known young child analysts at the Institute at that time were the Bornstein sisters, Steff and Berta, and Ada Müller-Braunschweig. Anna Freud, who occasionally came to Berlin to see her father, gave some guest lectures at the Institute.
>
> (Bannach, 1971, p. 38)[10]

While Klein's involvement in the framework of the Berlin Poly-clinic in the first few years may be proved, it remains uncertain how far she continued with this after 1922. The form that Klein's relation-ships with Schott, and with the Bornstein sisters and Josine Müller, took and how these developed is largely unresearched – Oberborbeck is undoubtedly correct when he says that it became clear over the years that 'Ada Schott, the Bornstein sisters and Nelly Wolffheim did not subscribe to the theories that Melanie Klein was developing and felt more drawn to Anna Freud's ideas' (Oberborbeck, 1994, p. 99).[11]

---

10 When Wittenberger (1995) interprets the following sentence from Abraham's and Eitingon's circular letter of 2 June 1923 – 'The last two sessions were dropped because of a long debate about a contribution from Simmel, who wanted to prove the most compli-cated foetal memories in the material of a cathartically treated case' (quoted from Wittenberger, 1995, p. 264) – to mean that this comment appeared to indicate that 'even in Berlin there were "experiments" in early analysis even before Melanie Klein was working there' (p. 265). This strikes me as incorrect on two counts. First, the matter referred to occurred within Melanie Klein's time; second, early analyses in Klein's sense should not be confused with foetal experiences; 'early' refers to the age of the analysed patient and thus means young children. It cannot be inferred in my view from the brief description that this was a child analysis.

11 Nelly Wolffheim (1974) states in her 'Erinnerungen an Melanie Klein' [Memories of Melanie Klein], written a long time afterwards, that some of the children analysed by

At first, however, Klein seems to have occupied a position of some prominence in relation to child analysis. This also becomes clear in Alix Strachey's letters to her husband from the end of September 1924 to September 1925: 'She really is the only person who's ever regularly analysed children . . . For it is a fact that she is the only person who possesses a knowledge of the material, & *a technique*' (Meisel and Kendrick, 1986, pp. 180–181). Over a month later she writes:

> You know, my respect for her continues to grow. She's got not only vast hoards of data, but a great many ideas, all rather formless & mixed, but clearly capable of crystallizing in her mind. She's got a creative mind, and that's the main thing.
>
> (Meisel and Kendrick, 1986, p. 203)

As regards her position in the Berlin Psychoanalytic Society, it is clear that her lecture in December 1924 provoked a lively discussion. She was supported by Abraham, Böhm, Horney and Mrs Müller.

> The opposition consisted of Drs Alexander & Radó, & was purely affective & 'theoretical', since, apparently, no one knows anything about the subject outside die Melanie & a Frl. Schott who is too retiring to speak, but who agrees with her.
>
> (Meisel and Kendrick, 1986, p. 145)

2.2 Melanie Klein's young patients in Berlin

The following reconstruction of Klein's practice in Berlin is based on documents in the Melanie Klein Archive, which can be consulted

---

Klein, including Erna, were in her nursery school and Klein was repeatedly telephoning to ask after them. The sense of injury that characterises this account appears for instance in the following passage:

> It seems to be indicative, however, of her general attitude to pedagogical efforts that the nursery school was never mentioned in case descriptions of the children who attended it. It can hardly be supposed that the life in the nursery school and the relationships with the main personalities in it did not bear in any way on the analysis, that children's reactions were not noticeable in a positive or negative way or correspond to their symptoms.
>
> (Wolffheim, 1974, pp. 296f.)

at the Wellcome Library for the History of Medicine in London. For 1924 to 1926 the extant pocket diaries in which Klein entered the names of the children she was seeing form the foundation of these documents. Where applicable a comment such as 'missed' has been added to the name and, in individual instances, '2' [hours] or '1½' [hours].[12] A pocket diary also exists for 1923, but up till October only the initials of the relevant first name are given and, in fact, in one case in which there was a possibility of accidental substitution, the relevant initials of the first name and surname. From October 1923, Klein wrote out all the names in full; occasionally, she also did this before 1923, which makes all those initials decipherable. Among these is an adult female patient who until the middle of May 1923 appeared in the diary thirty-three times and was obviously still undergoing treatment with Klein in 1922, for how long cannot be reconstructed with certainty. The notes made on various subjects on a small notepad include some case material on this patient.[13]

For 1921 and 1922 there exist no corresponding pocket diaries. Here the reconstruction can be made only on the basis of the extant treatment notes, as well as with the aid of the five outpatient files from the Polyclinic mentioned earlier. How many patients Klein saw in addition to this is, of course, still uncertain – even for the names that appear for 1923–1925 the treatment notes are incomplete. We can therefore put together only a 'minimal list' of the patients Klein treated between 1921 and mid-1926 in Berlin.

Whereas it was Freud's practice 'throughout his life, after one of his works had appeared in print, to destroy all the material on which the publication was based' (1909b, *S.E.* 10, p. 253), a practice from

---

12 In particular for Inge, '1½' appears repeatedly; for the 33 sessions with Egon that had then taken place in the period from May to the beginning of July 1926, that is shortly before Klein's emigration to London, '2' hours is noted.

13 It remains unclear how many other adults Klein saw in the Berlin period. The pocket diaries mention a second woman, who was seen between 1 January and 10 January 1926 for five one-hour sessions and five two-hour sessions. Klein must have seen other adult patients: her article 'Early analysis' contains case material relating to a 'Mrs H.' (1923b, WMK I, p. 102). In 1955 Klein states:

It is possible that the understanding of the contents of psychotic anxieties and of the urgency to interpret them was brought home to me in the analysis of a paranoic schizophrenic man who came to me for one month only. In 1922 a colleague who was going on holiday asked me to take over for a month a schizophrenic patient of his.

(1955, WMK III, p. 136, fn.)

which only the notes to the 'Rat Man' escaped, Melanie Klein generally seems to have kept her notes from individual analyses. The Melanie Klein Archive now holds this material from individual analyses – varying in their extent, completeness and systematicity. It consists predominantly of handwritten notes made by Melanie Klein, ranging from highly detailed records of sessions, to notes containing only specific points, to general comments summarising the course of months in a few sentences. For some children there are German industrial standard A5 notebooks, to which I shall refer as 'treatment books' (*Behandlungsbücher*), in which at least a part of the material was recorded. At the beginning, she sometimes used the same treatment book for two patients, for example recording Grete's sessions in the first half of the book, then from the middle of the book making notes on the 12-year-old boy 'A', but inadvertently thereby repeatedly noting down material for one child in among the material for the other. In addition to this there are small notepads, in which completely different material was recorded, which also included individual case records, for example for Grete, the 12-year-old boy 'A' and Felix. This notepad also contains material relating to various patients, under specific headings such as 'writing', 'talking', 'thinking' etc., where brief reference is also made to patients for whom detailed treatment notes are missing. Furthermore, records of sessions are simply made on loose paper sheets of assorted sizes. Besides this, there are numerous children's drawings and cut-out figures on the paper sheets of various sizes, parts of which because of the thin paper on which they have been prepared are now in a fragile state of preservation. Although Klein provided patients' names and/or dates and/or associations as well as explanations for many of the drawings, there are others for which the equivalent information is missing, parts of which can now hardly, if at all, be classified. As this part of the Archive is still relatively unsorted, it was useful to piece together the material for the individual patients from the various files and classify them with the published cases as far as possible. In relation to Erna, Ruth and Trude, there is also a short note of Klein's that makes clear on which patients she published material using these names. I was able to substantiate this classification through points of correspondence between published and unpublished material. Correspondences in the material enabled further attributions to be made – in the publications there is of course only a fragment of the material recorded in the Archive; for Grete (see Chapter 3) there are only a few vignettes from the notes made from memory,[14] whereas the notes in the Archive run to well over a hundred pages.

Taking the published work as the starting-point, Melanie Klein set out what is predominantly case material on children and adolescents in her early works, most extensively in her principal work on child analysis in 1932, *The Psycho-Analysis of Children* (WMK II). This is followed by the outstanding publication on child analysis 'The case of Richard' (Klein, 1961), in which the analysis of a latency-age boy is set out session by session. In her post-1932 work, she also makes repeated reference to the children published about there and in the earlier works; only two 'new' children are now introduced, about whom only brief comments are then made.[15]

A list of the children and adolescents Klein published work on until 1932 inclusive, indicating those from the Berlin years, provides a clear illustration of the importance of this period. Correspondences in the material make it possible to classify with certainty thirteen cases as belonging to the Berlin period, and the publication date of 1925 makes it possible to add three more. Two of the cases published in 1925 – Walter and Werner – are in all probability to be attributed to specific names in the diary.[16] The classification of the 15-year-old boy who is also mentioned in 'A contribution to the psychogenesis of tics' (1925) is not certain. As Klein writes that the patient was taken away from her as a result of an improvement that set in quickly, the treatment seems to have been brief. This may suggest that it is a boy who was seen twenty-three times by Klein in 1923. In the absence of any further documents on this boy, however, this classification must remain uncertain. In a further case, that of Kurt, the duration of the analysis also suggests that this is one of those that took place in Berlin – a boy's name appears in the diary 361 times. Again, this hypothesis cannot be tested because of the lack of material.

14 Klein's 'notes from memory' were generally made shortly after the session ended.
15 See Klein (1955, WMK III, p. 129), where she gives the example of a boy who she saw only for an initial interview, as well as 'A note on depression in the schizophrenic' (1960, WMK III, p. 266), where she briefly goes into the case of a 9-year-old boy.
16 The classification is based on the following information from Klein: a footnote to Werner's analysis states that it is still in full progress and that it has been taking place for only about three months (WMK I, p. 119, n.); for Walter's case, published in the supplement, it states that treatment has so far lasted six weeks. As there is little existing material on Werner, and none at all on Walter, these classifications cannot be substantiated by correspondences in the material.

Table 2.1 lists in order of age the children and adolescents who were published about until 1932 inclusive. As far as can be determined from the publications, I state the treatment duration, the period in which Klein still heard from the children following the end of the treatment (under 'Catamnestic period') and the diagnoses, as well as the published works in which Klein mentions them. The children and adolescents who can definitely be classified within the Berlin period are indicated with 'B'.

In Table 2.2 the Berlin treatments are listed in chronological order – as far as this can be ascertained. The information given on the treatment duration is based from 1923 on the entries in the pocket diaries mentioned earlier. As diaries are not extant for 1921 and 1922, only the five outpatient files and the case documents for the individual patients can be adduced for this period. After 1923, there are periods in which there are notes on every session for individual patients, but also times where this is not the case. As for 1921 and 1922 the treatment duration can now be estimated solely on the basis of these documents, only minimal information will result.

Where I have been able to identify these patients with certainty, I refer to them with the names that Klein chose for publication; otherwise I provide names using an alphabetical letter in their order of appearance. In the final column, the situation with the material is briefly outlined (for the 9-year-old Grete, Rita, Inge, Erna and Ernst, the relevant chapters are indicated).

Concerning frequency, it can be said that in 1921 and 1922 Klein generally saw patients three times a week; in the years that followed she attempted where possible to treat patients on a daily basis, meaning six days a week.

For Klein's daily practice in 1921, it is possible to reconstruct the number of patients per day for individual periods. For example, on Tuesday 5 April she saw Grete and Felix; on Thursday 7 April, Grete; on Saturday 9 April, Grete, Felix and the 12-year-old boy (Klein, 1927b), and the same applies for 14 April etc. On Thursday 28 April, she saw Grete, Felix and patient A (for the 12-year-old boy, 'stayed away' is recorded); for Saturday 30 April, the same pattern applies.

According to the 1923 diary, Klein saw nine children in 1923, of whom five were seen at that time in parallel, up to four of whom on a single day. In 1924 she treated fourteen children in total, up to six of whom she saw on a single day. In 1925 ten patients were in treatment with her; she saw up to seven patients daily, usually six. In the first half

Table 2.1 Children and adolescents about whom material was published up until the end of 1932 (patients listed in order of age)

Name	Place of treatment	Age	Treatment duration	Catamnestic period	Diagnosis	Publications
Rita	B	2¾	83 (not completed because of emigration)	7 years	Obsessional neurosis	1926, 1929, 1932, 1936, 1945, 1955
Trude	B	3¾	82 (broken off for external reasons)		Infantile neurosis pavor nocturnus, urinary and faecal incontinence	1926, 1927a, 1932, 1955
Peter	B	3¾	278	6 years	Severe infantile neurosis	1927b, 1932, 1955
Dick		4			Inhibited development, schizophrenia	1930a
Gerald		4			Prophylactic analysis for 'a very normal boy'	1927a, 1927b, 1929
Ruth	B	4¼	190 (unfinished because of return to country of origin)	2 years	Severe infantile neurosis	1926, 1932
Kurt	?	5	450		Infantile neurosis with psychotic traits	1932

Name		Age	Treatment	Duration	Diagnosis	Dates
Franz		5	'Long-term treatment'		Severe infantile neurosis, great educational difficulties	1932
John		5			Severe infantile neurosis	1931, 1932
Unnamed boy[a]		5				1927a
Unnamed boy[a]		5				1932, 1948
Walter	B	5½	'Treatment duration to date' 6 weeks		Stereotyped movements, obsessional neurosis and incipient characterological deformation	1925
Erna	B	6	575, ended for external reasons	2½ years	Obsessional neurosis; marked paranoid traits	1926, 1927a, 1929, 1932, 1955
Günther		6			Abnormal character development; psychotic traits	1932
Ernst	B	6				1923b
Georg		6			Strong paranoid traits	1929, 1930b
Unnamed boy[b]		6			Stereotyped forms of behaviour	1930b

(Continue overleaf)

Table 2.1 Continued

Name	Place of treatment	Age	Treatment duration	Catamnestic period	Diagnosis	Publications
Grete		7	At least one month		Schizoid	1932
Inge	B	7	375	7 years	Prophylactic analysis	1932, 1955
Grete[c]	B	9			Stuttering, strong homosexual fixations	1923a, 1923b
Werner	B	9	210	5 years	Obsessional neurosis, characterological difficulties	1925, 1932
Egon	B	9½	425		Incipient schizophrenia	1932
Kenneth	B	9½	225 (discontinued for external reasons)		Abnormal character development, severe inhibitions and anxieties	1932
Ilse		12	425	2½ years	Schizoid	1932
Unnamed boy	B	12			Criminal development	1927b
Felix	B	13	370	3¼ years	Neurotic character, tic	1923a, 1923b, 1925
Ludwig		14	190	3 years	'Prophylactic analysis'	1932

Gert		14	1 year	3 years	Neurotic difficulties	1932
Bill		15	45		Neurotic difficulties	1932
Unnamed boy	B	15			Various difficulties, including tic and intense fears about his eyes	1925
Lisa	B	17				1923b

Note: The publications concerning her son Erich, who appeared from 1921 under the name of Fritz, are not recorded here.

a It is not at present possible to tell from the information (WMK III, p. 314; WMK II, p. 127 fn. 4) whether the 5-year-old boys here might be the same one, or the same as one of the boys who were published about under a name.

b It is not possible to tell from the information available (WMK I, p. 234) whether this is also one of the 6-year-old boys who was published about under a name.

c Melanie Klein published work about two patients under the name 'Grete'; the 9-year-old Grete appeared only in the 1923 publications

Table 2.2 Berlin treatments of children and adolescents in chronological order

Name	Age (where given in treatment notes)	Treatment period	Number of sessions	State of material
1. Felix	12½	1 February 1921 to 5 July 1924	290 (according to outpatient files and diaries)	Specific periods are documented in detail in several treatment books and small notepads
2. Grete		22 February 1921 to 21 May 1922	86 are documented	See Chapter 3
3. 12-year-old boy (1927b)	Given as 13 years old in the outpatient files	9 April to 9 June 1921	12 (according to outpatient files)	Seven pages in a treatment notebook, in which there are also notes on other patients
4. Patient A (male)	12	14 March to 10 December 1921	53 (according to outpatient files)	Twenty-eight sessions are documented in various treatment books and on the notepads
5. Patient B (male)	12	24 May to 11 June 1921 (according to outpatient files; Klein made summarised notes from 24 May to 6 June 1921)	8 (according to outpatient files)	Four pages on two loose sheets of paper

6. Lisa		6 January 1922 to 28 March 1923 (reference to this patient in the 1922 Grete documents; more precise detail not possible to reconstruct)	From 1923: 51 (diary) entries (of which 38 instances of '1½' and 4 of '2')	Some references on notepads under headings such as 'talking', 'constant symbols'
7. Ernst	6	2 (5?) February 1923 to 5 June 1924	118 (diary) entries (of which 6 'missed', 8 '1½')	See Chapter 5.5
8. Rita		6 March to 6 October 1923	82 (diary) entries (of which one '2')	See Chapter 4
9. Patient E (possibly the 15-year-old boy of 1925)		14 April to 6 June 1923	23	No extant documents
10. Inge	7	18 September 1923 to 5 July 1924, 3 February 1925 to 1 May 1926	In the first period 106 (diary) entries (of which 40 are '1½'); in the second period 220	See Chapter 5
11. Patient F (male)	11	8 October 1923 to 3 July 1924	90	The earliest sessions are recorded in a treatment book; further sessions appear in one of the notepads

(Continued overleaf)

Table 2.2 Continued

Name	Age *(where given in treatment notes)*	Treatment period	Number of sessions	State of material
12. Patient G (female)		16 October 1923 to 10 April 1924, 17 April to 22 December 1925	In the first period 88; in the second 105	Only occasional notes
13. Erna	6	9 January 1924 to 15 April 1926	470	See Chapter 6
14. Peter	3¾	18 February to 29 June 1924, 8 January 1925 to 27 April 1926	In the first period 89; in the second 205	A few sheets of paper on which the earliest sessions are recorded; some sessions on small notepads; drawings, cut-out figures and patterns
15. Trude	3	(One session on 24 September 1923), 2 May to 10 December 1924	74	Individual sheets of paper (the first session of 1923 is recorded on two sheets; otherwise mainly the period from the end of August to the beginning of September 1924 on several sheets)
16. Kenneth	9	22 August 1924 to 9 July 1926	255	Some pages in a treatment book, and some individual sheets of paper

17. Egon	10	2 September 1924 to 6 July 1926	442	Ten written pages in a treatment book, also an extensive collection of loose sheets of paper with drawings and corresponding annotations
18. Patient H (female)		3 September to 7 November 1924	32	No extant documents
19. Ruth		16 September 1924 to 7 April 1925, 3 April to 3 July 1926	In the first period 134; in the second 44	Few notes
20. Patient I (possibly Kurt?)		17 September 1924 to 3 July 1926	371	No extant documents
21. Werner	Nearly 9 years	17 October 1924 to 3 July 1926	188	Eight loose sheets of paper
22. Walter		13 May to 25 June 1925, 22 January to 5 July 1926	In the first period 33; in the second 99	No extant documents

of 1926, she once saw all the eight patients she was treating on one day; usually she would see between five and seven of them daily.

As regards Grosskurth's (1986) claim that Klein mainly treated the children of colleagues, the documents show that five of the children mentioned above were those of colleagues – the identity of these children is already known in the literature: Karen Horney's two daughters, Marianne (Grosskurth, 1986, pp. 104f; Rubins, 1978, p. 95; Maeder, 1989, p. 216; Sayers, 1991, p. 77) and Renate (Rubins, 1978, p. 92; Maeder, 1989, p. 217; Sayers, 1991, p. 77); Erika Happel (Friedrich, 1988, p. 196), daughter of Klara Happel; Young-Bruehl (1988, p. 260) reports on Reinhard Simmel, Ernst Simmel's son; Lockot (1985, p. 116) mentions Hilda Böhm's analysis. The qualification 'mainly' therefore needs to be revised for at least seventeen child treatments.

While this chapter provides an outline of the quantitative aspect of Klein's practice in Berlin, Chapter 3 aims to give an insight into the qualitative development of her analytic procedure and understanding, in the course of which a few of these cases will be examined in greater detail.

2.3 Klein's papers and lectures during her time in Berlin

However little may be known about Klein's child analyses, the active commitment that Klein gave to lectures and publications in the Berlin years is nevertheless apparent – in part from the reports published in the *Internationale Zeitschrift für Psychoanalyse*. This chapter will conclude with a list of these activities.

By 3 February 1921, Klein had already given a lecture to the Berlin Psychoanalytical Society on 'Child analysis', which was the subject for discussion the following week. On 19 May 1921, she gave a lecture on 'Disturbance of orientation in children'.[17] Her paper 'Eine

---

17 A footnote to 'Early analysis' (1923b, WMK I, p. 98, fn. 1) states that the paper given in May 1921 'Über die Hemmung und Entwicklung des Orientierungssinnes' [On the inhibition and development of the sense of orientation] formed part of the basis for the work. She makes a brief reference to this work in an unpublished manuscript, summarising it as an attempt to prove using some examples that these inhibitions were determined by a strong original interest against which repression was directed because it was connected with the libidinal interest in what enters and leaves the mother's body that characterises the child's sexual investigations into impregnation and birth.

Kinderentwicklung' appeared in *Imago* in 1921 ('The development of a child', WMK I, pp. 1–53).

In the form of 'Short communications', she presented 'An anecdote from Walter Scott's life' on 24 January 1922 and 'A "Sunday" neurosis in a child' on 14 February 1922.[18] On 21 February 1922, she presented a paper 'On latent anxiety',[19] a discussion of Alexander's review of 7 February, 'The castration complex and character formation'. As a further 'Short communication', she presented 'Analysis of a school composition' on 11 April 1922 and, on 2 May 1922, a paper on 'Compulsion to disguise and pseudologia'. In September 1922, Klein gave a lecture at the Seventh International Psychoanalytical Association Congress in Berlin entitled 'Infant analysis: on the development and inhibition of natural gifts',[20] of which there is a summary in the 'Report of the International Psychoanalytical Congress in Berlin. September 25–27, 1922' (1922, *IZP* 8, p. 493; 1923, *IJP* 4, pp. 374f.). Her article 'Inhibitions and difficulties in puberty' appears in *Die Neue Erziehung* ('The New Education').

Again to the Berlin Psychoanalytical Society she presented the short communication 'Notes from the analysis of a child' on 13 February 1923 and also a paper described simply as a short clinical contribution. On 10 April 1923, she presented 'The "doctor-game" played by children' and on 8 May 1923 a paper described simply as a short communication. In February 1923, having been an associate member of the Berlin Psychoanalytical Society since 1922, Klein was elected as an ordinary member. 'Zur Frühanalyse' appeared in *Imago* in 1923 ('Infant analysis', 1926, *IJP* 7, pp. 31–63) and 'Die Rolle der Schule in der libidinösen Entwicklung des Kindes' in the *Internationale Zeitschrift der Psychoanalyse* in 1923 ('The rôle of the school in the libidinal development of the child', 1924, *IJP* 5, 312–331).

At the Eighth International Psychoanalytical Association Congress in Salzburg in April 1924, Klein gave a lecture on 'The technique of

18 See the discussion of this in Chapter 3 on Grete.
19 A footnote on p. 103 in 'Zur Frühanalyse' (1923b) states that the paper given in March 1922 on 'Infantile anxiety and its significance for personality development' formed part of the basis for this work ('Early analysis'). Klein may have made a mistake about the month here because in the corresponding unpublished manuscript she noted: 'Presented in parts in February 1922 to the Berlin Psychoanalytical Society as a discussion paper to Dr. Alexander's work "Castration complex and character formation" '.
20 This lecture also forms part of the basis for 'Early analysis' (1923b) according to the footnote in the original German edition.

the analysis of young children'. Whereas here she was clearly returning to material from the analysis of the 2¾-year-old Rita (cf. summary in Congress report, 1924, *IJP* 5, p. 598), six months later at the first German meeting for psychoanalysis in Würzburg she presented the case of Erna – 'Notes from the analysis of obsessional neurosis in a six-year-old child'. Between these two presentations, on 24 June, Klein gave an explanatory commentary on children's drawings together with Ada Schott and Frau Dr Müller. On 11 November 1924, she presented a further paper to the Berlin Psychoanalytical Society on 'Manifestations of the infantile sense of guilt' and, on 13 December 1924, on 'The psychological principles of analysis in childhood', about which she also gave a lecture in Vienna a few days later, on 17 December.

On 26 February 1925, she presented a short communication on 'An analogy between children's phantasies and certain crimes'. In July, she gave six lectures in London – these formed the first chapters of *The Psycho-Analysis of Children* (WMK II).[21] The following sequence can be ascertained from the manuscripts of the Melanie Klein Trust:

1 Lecture: The psychological principles of early analysis
2 Lecture: The technique of early analysis
3 Lecture: Obsessional neurosis in a six-year-old girl
4 Lecture: The technique of child analysis in latency and puberty (in fact this lecture discusses only latency-age children)
5 Lecture (Title is missing; part of the lecture is about puberty-age children and their relationships with their parents)
6 Lecture: Indications for treatment and termination of treatment (the German version is incomplete and lacks a title).

Whether Klein gave these lectures in Switzerland is not certain. Alix Strachey writes in her letter of 12 January 1924, describing Klein's lecture project to her husband, that Klein will give the lectures in Switzerland in August (Meisel and Kendrick, 1986, p. 181).

21 Grosskurth's claim that Melanie Klein wrote up most of the cases reported in *The Psycho-Analysis of Children* (WMK II) some years later in the hindsight of the development of her theories then is contradicted as a general statement by the extant manuscripts relating to the London lectures of 1925. These lectures formed the basis for the first chapters of *The Psycho-Analysis of Children* (WMK II) and underwent some revision as a matter of course but in terms of the case material itself many passages were reproduced word-for-word.

In 1925 'Zur Genese des Tics' ('The psychogenesis of tics', WMK I) then appeared in the *Internationale Zeitschrift für Psychoanalyse*.

In 1926, she presented two more short communications in Berlin on 2 March: 'Two corresponding mistakes in a school-exercise' and 'Ideas with a five-year-old boy associated with the methods by which he was educated'. 'Die psychologischen Grundlagen der Frühanalyse' appeared in *Imago*; this was a reworking of the first London lecture of the same title – 'The psychological principles of early analysis' – which was later reworked to form the first chapter of *The Psycho-Analysis of Children* (WMK II).

This compilation, which is based until the London lectures on the information in the corresponding reports of the International Psychoanalytical Association for the years 1921–1926 as they were published in the *Internationale Zeitschrift für Psychoanalyse* is unlikely to contain all the lectures that Klein gave in these years. The Melanie Klein Trust holds further manuscripts that seem to constitute the basis for communications and lectures. Two of these manuscripts are dated – 'The theory of eternal life', April 1921, and 'A parallel between infantile and primitive ideas', 'Autumn 1921'. A paper on 'The nervous child at home and at school' is undated but on the basis of the context may well have been written during the first of her two years in Berlin. There is a further manuscript called 'A discussion paper to Mrs Horney's paper on 31 October 1925'; the corresponding Report of the International Psychoanalytical Association mentions only Horney's paper – 'Thoughts on the masculinity complex in women'.

In the Melanie Klein Archive there are also some undated documents concerning various evening sessions of an educational course – there are some points that are recorded in note form. The fact that Klein uses mainly material from Rita's case, not from Erna's, may indicate that this course took place in 1923 or the beginning of 1924. Grosskurth (1986, p. 119, fn.) refers to a course that Abraham mentioned in his letter to Freud of 7 October, which was sponsored by the Institute – as Abraham writes: 'On the "sexuality of children" for kindergarten teachers etc.' (Freud and Abraham, 2002, p. 471). Grosskurth (1986) assumes that this was a further course that took place in 1924, on the basis of Nelly Wolffheim's memoirs. These state:

Through Berta Bornstein, I met Otto Fenichel, a young analyst, and the three of us arranged to request Melanie Klein to run a course on analytic child psychology . . . The Psychoanalytical

Association made a lecture room available. Fenichel took over the publicity without having realised – only just having arrived in Berlin from Vienna – how negatively every form of advertising was resisted here. So the laboriously designed and typed signs that were displayed in the windows in the area surrounding the analytic clinic had to be removed. The first evening was nevertheless well attended, especially by outsiders. But Melanie Klein did not really have the gift – or probably the intention – of expressing what she had to say in a form that would immediately be generally understood. She used the whole register of psychoanalytic technical terms and did not refrain from talking as openly about everything as we are accustomed to doing in analytic circles. I do not really believe that she noticed how shocked some of the audience were and how others sat there with blank expressions without any real understanding of what was being discussed. Children's sexuality was still taboo at that time. As the number of participants – including from the analytic circles – declined with each lecture, the course was soon abandoned.

(Wolffheim, 1974, pp. 295f.)

As Fenichel had moved from Vienna to Berlin as early as 1922, Grosskurth's dating seems to be uncertain; in my view, this may have been the same course that was held at the end of 1923 or beginning of 1924.

3

Grete

One of Melanie Klein's very first little girl patients in Berlin

3.1 Grete in Klein's published works

We already know from 'Early analysis' (1923b, WMK I) and 'The rôle of the school in the libidinal development of the child' (1923a, WMK I) that Grete is a 9-year-old girl with a stutter and a strong homosexual fixation. Symptoms that also appear in the notes are a worm phobia and hourly micturition. The documents show that she had been living with her aunt since the age of 5. She seemed to be able to see her mother mainly in the holidays – the reason for which, like much else in Grete's history, remains unclear and uncertain. The father was drafted into the army when Grete was 3 years old; he came home on leave when she was 5 and subsequently never returned. An elder brother died. Whether this is the brother referred to in the occasional talk of a 'little brother', or whether there was another brother who was younger, cannot be established for certain. Furthermore, the case history information includes an accident in her second year, in which Grete received burns to her face from a burning object, possibly a lamp. She had stuttered since then, and undoubtedly to some extent before that as well, as her father had also done in childhood.

Melanie Klein cites the case of Grete when first illustrating the significance of speaking as genital activity. We learn that for Grete speaking and singing corresponded to male activity, and the movement of the tongue was equated to that of the penis:

She took a special delight when lying on the couch in reciting certain French sentences. She said it was 'such fun, when her voice went up and down like someone on a ladder'. Her association to this was that the ladder was set up in a snail. But would there be room for it in a snail? (A snail, however, was her name for her genitals.) The comma and the full stop, like the pause corresponding to them in speaking, meant that one had gone 'up and down' once and was beginning again. A single word stood for the penis and a sentence for the thrust of the penis in coitus and also for coitus as a whole.

(1923b, WMK I, p. 101)[1]

Klein also adduced the example of Grete to show that stuttering could be caused by the libidinal cathexis of speaking as well as of singing (1923a, WMK I, p. 62). In her general perspective and her procedural method, she follows a developing psychoanalytic tradition in drawing attention to the sexual meanings of school and learning. She also expresses herself explicitly.[2] This section on the significance of speaking as genital activity thus begins with a reference to Abraham, who had also reported on this in a case of pseudologia.[3] Klein had already referred to Abraham's 'Über eine konstitutionelle Grundlage der lokomotorischen Angst' [A constitutional basis of locomotor anxiety] at the beginning of her article 'Early analysis' (1923b, WMK I, p. 77, fn. 1). He gave examples in this paper of the way in which 'the repression of pleasurable emotions, which might "run away" with them' (Abraham, 1913b, p. 239) contributed to the development of locomotor inhibition in neurotics. In 'Über Fehlleistungen mit überkompensierender Tendenz'[4] [On parapraxes

---

1 In relation to the first idea, compare treatment notes p. 12b; for phantasy in relation to the comma compare, e.g., treatment notes p. 7d and p. 15e.
2 Specifically in relation to school, Klein starts by referring to Sadger's (1920) work 'Über Prüfungsangst und Prüfungsträume' [On examination anxiety and examination dreams], in which fear of examinations is interpreted as a form of castration anxiety (1923a, WMK I, p. 59) and the sexual symbolic meaning of desk, slate and chalk are indicated (WMK I, p. 60, fn. 1).
3 Klein is likely to be referring here to a work that according to the report Abraham presented on 25 April 1922 at the Berlin Psychoanalytical Association – 'On a case of *Pseudologia phantastica*'. To my knowledge this work has not been published.
4 Abraham may have presented this work or a part of it on 11 April 1922 under the title 'Short communications' at the Berlin Psychoanalytical Association'; the title recorded

with an overcompensating tendency], which Klein does not quote specifically, Abraham (1922) analyses a particular form of mild stutter in similar terms. In his example, stuttering acts to fulfil the infantile sexual urge to articulate tabooed words. Through the selection of syllables that are doubled, which directly counteracts this taboo tendency, satisfaction is simultaneously procured for the defence (pp. 295–7f.). He explains, for example, that in the patient's parapraxis 'potragoras' (for Protagoras), the first syllable is transformed by omission of the 'r' and stuttering-reduplicating speech into the 'Popo' that unconsciously comes to mind. In place of the dangerous omission of the 'r', an overcompensation occurs by which an additional 'r' is inserted into the second syllable (ibid). Ferenczi also makes reference to stuttering. In 'Thalassa: a theory of genitality', the Congress lecture that he presented in 1922 to which Klein refers (1923a, p. 61, fn.); on another point, he explained that the nervous disorders in vowel and consonant stuttering are to be traced psychoanalytically both to anal-erotic and to urethral-erotic sources (Ferenczi, 1934, pp. 208–9).[5]

If the purely libidinal, sexual-symbolic interpretation of stuttering strikes us as strange now, it is also remarkable and unsatisfactory within the text itself that Klein should illustrate the meaning of stuttering with an example in which Grete does not in fact stutter. The postulated connection between the libidinal cathexis of speaking and that of stuttering is certainly an easy one to construct, and it is conceivable that she chose this example for its particular vividness. Nevertheless, it remains an initial form of imprecision, for which the motivation is unclear. I shall return to this point later. It is noteworthy, too, that Klein does not explore any possible links between the memory Grete had of the accident when she was 2 years old (see p. 73) and her stuttering, which was supposed to have begun or become worse at that time.

Klein refers further to Grete in order to present her hypothesis that:

theatres and *concerts*, in fact any performance where there is something to be seen or heard, always stand for parental coitus – listening

there is 'Eine Fehlleistung (Vergreifen im Ausdruck)' [A blunder: mistaking an expression]; the corresponding material from Grete's analysis also originates from 1922.

5 Klein quotes from Ferenczi further in order to understand sexual-symbolic activities – that is, in terms of the identification that Ferenczi considered to be fundamental to such activities (1923b, WMK I, p. 85).

and watching standing for observation in fact or phantasy – while the falling curtain stands for objects which hinder observations, such as bed-clothes, the side of the bed etc. I will quote an example. Little Grete told me about a play at the theatre. At first she had been distressed at not having a good enough seat and having to be at some distance from the stage. But she made out that she saw better than the people who sat quite near the stage, for they could not see all over it. Her associations then led to the position of the children's beds, which were placed in their parents' bedroom in such a way that her younger brother slept close to his parents' bed, but the backs of the beds made it difficult for him to see them. Her bed, however, was further off and she could see theirs perfectly.

(1923b, WMK I, pp. 101–102)[6]

With this second point of reference to Grete as well, Klein is moving – without expressly referring to it in this case – into what was then little known territory. In the *Introductory Lectures to Psycho-Analysis* (1916–1917), Freud had worked out an analogical meaning of theatre in the context of a dream analysis. In this case, marrying was connected with the image of being about to go to all the plays that had previously been forbidden and being allowed to see everything.

The pleasure in looking, or curiosity, which is revealed in this was no doubt originally a sexual desire to look [scopophilia] directed towards sexual happenings and especially on to the girls' parents, and hence it became a powerful motive for urging them to an early marriage.

(Freud, 1916–1917, *S.E.* 15, p. 220)

Finally, we then learn that a strong impression had been made on Grete by a cart that she saw and heard driving into the school yard.

6 There is much mention in the treatment notes of visits to the theatre in which Grete feels hindered in taking full advantage of the opportunity, partly because of the interference caused by her sessions with Klein. There are also many references to the fact that, unlike some of her friends, she cannot sit in expensive seats. The scene to which Klein is obviously referring here reads, however, as follows in the treatment notes (p. 22e): Grete had said how happy she was to have a cheaper seat, that in the more expensive ones they had to strain their necks. Klein interprets that she (conscious memory) had her bed near her parents', her brother's elsewhere, so that she could watch the coitus more easily and feel triumphant about this. This is Klein's last entry before the Easter holidays in 1922.

Another time she related about a cart with sweetmeats, none of which she ventured to buy, as her schoolmistress came by just then. She described these sweetmeats as a kind of wadding, as something that interested her extremely, but about which she did not venture to find out. Both these carts proved to be screen-memories of her infantile observations of coitus, and the indefinable sugar-wadding[7] to be the semen.

(1923a, WMK I, p. 62)[8]

Immediately afterwards we learn that: 'Grete sang first voice in the school choir; the *schoolmistress* came quite close to her seat and looked straight into her mouth. At this Grete felt an irresistible need to hug and kiss the teacher' (WMK I, p. 62).[9]

In the section on 'Writing', Klein falls back on the example of Grete once again:

Nine-year-old Grete associated with the curve of the letter 'u' the curve in which she saw little boys urinate. She had a special preference for drawing beautiful scrolls that proved in her case to be parts of the male genitals . . . Grete admired very much a friend who could hold her pen like a grown-up person, quite erect between her second and third fingers, and could also make the curve of the 'u' backwards.

(WMK I, p. 66)[10]

A final example from Grete is used in relation to the 'libidinal significance of grammar': 'In reference to the analysis of sentences Grete spoke of an actual dismembering and dissection of a roast rabbit. Roast rabbit, which she had enjoyed eating until disgust at it supervened, represented the mother's breasts and genitals' (WMK I,

---

7 Translator's note: *Zuckerwatte*, rendered here as 'sugar-wadding', can also refer to candy floss.
8 Cf. treatment notes pp. 15b, 16b.
9 Cf. treatment notes from 9 May 1922: 'loves the new nature study and singing teacher – kisses her with head bowed and listens to her' (pp. 4f.).
10 On a small notepad under the heading 'Writing', the following note appears after the patient's name: 'Friend: who writes like an adult, holds the pen straight between two fingers – writes the curve of the letter "u" backwards'. A bit further on: 'On the curve of the letter "u": the large curve that boys make when urinating in the street'.

p. 71). This is a vivid description of a sadistic phantasy, and the transference meaning seems obvious – it is not difficult to understand the mother here as a reference to the analyst; it remains unclear, however, exactly how this phantasy was understood.

Klein also uses the example of Grete, among others, to illustrate how all behaviour and experience, as well as symptoms and phantasies, in everyday life is determined by unconscious phantasies involving sexuality (cf. WMK I, Explanatory notes, p. 421; Petot, 1990, pp. 56ff.), so that Klein interprets everything predominantly in terms of sexual symbolism. To the strangeness mentioned earlier – of the lack of reference to any analysis of a stuttering incident in order to explain it – a further irritating point of omission is now added: the 'homosexual fixatedness' itself is not actually discussed. It might be expected that Klein would make some reference to Freud here, either confirming his experiences or refuting them. In 'A case of paranoia running counter to the psycho-analytic theory of the disease' (Freud, *S.E.* 14, 1915b, p. 268), he had indicated the power of the 'mother complex'. In this case, he interpreted a paranoid delusion as a defence against homosexuality. In 'The psychogenesis of a case of homosexuality in a woman', Freud writes:

> The number of successes achieved by psychoanalytic treatment of the various forms of homosexuality, which incidentally are manifold, is indeed not very striking. As a rule the homosexual is not able to give up the object which provides him with pleasure . . . It is only where the homosexual fixation has not yet become strong enough, or where there are considerable rudiments and vestiges of a heterosexual object of choice . . . that one may make a more favourable prognosis for psychoanalytic therapy.
>
> (Freud, 1920a, *S.E.* 18, p. 151)

Grete's analysis would thus have provided a possible means of shedding more light on what was then the relatively unresearched field of homosexuality, and it is worth asking why Klein did not embark on this in the Grete case. With Felix, for example, she added a footnote to 'The rôle of the school in the libidinal development of the child' in which she discussed the genesis of his homosexual wish (1923a, WMK I, p. 61, fn. 2).

I shall now formulate a preliminary hypothesis on the basis of these two striking aspects mentioned in the published material on Grete:

it seems highly probable that 'stuttering', as well as 'homosexual fixation', led to countertransferential factors that made any precise consideration of them difficult. Considering the two scenes mentioned with the teacher, in which the transference allusions are strongly evident, the projection of a restrictive object hindering orientation and exploration seems to have played a significant role. In the first scene, Grete does not dare to be guided by her own wish – the exploration of the sugar-wadding seems to her to signify a crime against the teacher. Corresponding impulses are therefore connected with a persecutory sense of guilt. In light of this, the second scene with the teacher, in which Grete feels an irresistible need to hug and kiss her, acquires a new significance as a manic attempt at reparation. In 1932, Klein emphasised 'the part played by the girl's restitutive tendencies in consolidating her homosexual position' (1932, WMK II, p. 218).[11]

The published material on Grete therefore seems to suggest that Klein had difficulty with the facets of the object relationship in the transference that related to homosexuality, in particular with the hostile enactments that she also mentions throughout (cf. the dissection of the roast rabbit). A desire to publish on the subject of Grete may have been a dynamic that was not fully comprehensible to Klein at this stage. Incompletely understood situations of negative transference evidently provided a stimulus for Klein to find a more satisfactory understanding in corresponding treatments even long after they were concluded, as is very clear for example with Rita. Klein does not, however, return explicitly to the case of Grete in her later writings.

How far does the unpublished material on Grete lend support to the hypothesis I have formulated?

3.2 Grete in the unpublished manuscripts

The Melanie Klein Archive includes an unpublished manuscript called 'Infantile anxiety and its significance for personality development',[12] which refers to Grete. This manuscript was presented in parts

---

11 The scene in the treatment notes in which Grete scornfully reports the incident in which the teacher's false teeth fell out when she sniffed (p. 7) seems to reinforce the hypothesis formulated above.

12 This is one of the texts that forms the basis of Klein's (1923b) publication, 'Early analysis'.

to the Berlin Psychoanalytical Association meeting of 7 February 1922, where it formed a supplementary paper to Dr Alexander's work, 'The castration complex and character-formation' ('Infantile anxiety . . .' manuscript, p. 1). The title's explicit reference to anxiety suggests a clarification of the themes with which we are concerned here. The work in question is primarily a discussion of Fritz and Felix, but on page 11 Klein refers to the patient we are interested in here without mentioning Grete by name:

> In the analysis of a nine-year-old girl with a strong homosexual fixation I found I could identify in the variety of the positions and movements with which she played the ball game a similar determination to that which became apparent in specific sports activities with Fritz. As can frequently be observed in general, the little girl developed a particular skilfulness at catching back the ball from a different position, for example backwards, that she had thrown into the air or against a wall. 1). To her, as well, the ball games signified coitus – with an actively homosexual determination – and playing alone signified the masturbation that she strove to avoid in reality.[13]

Although Klein returns again to other material here, she interprets it entirely in the sense already indicated above. The interesting keyword – homosexual – recurs without any more detailed information being given. With the term 'actively homosexual', she makes use of Freud's distinction according to which 'the active inverts exhibit masculine characteristics . . . and look for femininity in their sexual objects' (cf. Freud, 1905a, *S.E.* VII, p. 145).

Thus far it is a matter for speculation exactly what form the content of a possible later work on Grete would have taken. The report states on 14 February 1922 under the heading 'Short communications' that one text presented by Klein was 'A "Sunday" neurosis in a child' (1922, *IJP* 3, p. 321). As the relevant manuscript does not exist, I cannot substantiate my supposition that this may be a communication from the treatment of Grete that was taking place at the time but I nevertheless consider this to be highly probable. The treatment notes state, for example, on 9 February 1922, that Grete first mentioned the

13 Cf. treatment notes, such as p. 10b.

headaches that she had regularly on 'Saturday to Sunday and Monday', headaches that did not stop when she went to bed. To Saturday [*Sonnabend*] and Sunday she associated 'sun'. When Klein asked her about sun-rays, Grete agreed that they were so long and sharp. Grete added that the sun-rays seemed so hot that they could kill you; she had forgotten the word 'sun-stroke'. She said that Monday had to come from the moon and then drew a sickle shape in the air. Klein finally interpreted the sun as the dead father, who had sexual intercourse with her through the rays, of which the headaches were an expression. On 6 February Klein again gave a detailed interpretation of pregnancy through direct sunlight, whereby in this session 'sun' is understood both as father and as mother ('with a pipi'), thus appearing to be heterosexually and homosexually determined.[14] It is conceivable that in her 'Short communication' on 14 February 1922, some of Klein's discussion related to Grete's passive homosexual tendencies, for she had spoken a week earlier about her active homosexual aspects in the above-mentioned supplementary paper to Alexander's.

In the title of her presentation Klein returns to a theme addressed by Ferenczi in his 1919 paper 'Sunday neuroses', which had then been complemented by Abraham in the same year with 'Observations concerning Ferenczi's paper on "Sunday neuroses"' (1919a). Both understood this symptomatology ultimately as the expression of the neurotically determined incapacity to enjoy life, something that for many people comes most strongly to the fore on Sundays. Klein may have later worked out the concomitant Oedipal phantasies with Grete.

3.3 Grete in Klein's treatment notes

Grete's treatment notes are contained in various German industrial standard A5 notebooks ('treatment books'), notepads and on

---

14 Klein does not consider the possible connection of the headaches with conditions in the setting, in which Grete mentions headaches for the first time. Grete had missed the previous session – it remains unclear whether this was because of the strike that had led to her walking to the Saturday session on 4 February – and reports that her headaches had fortunately now disappeared, while she was reading a story as she waited. The next session – for no stated reason – is, unusually, a Monday, in which Grete replies to an enquiry that she has no headaches. Here a further possible connection is not worked out, in that she did not have to wait so long for the next session and that she may therefore not have had to contend with so many aggressive phantasies.

individual loose sheets of paper, which can be found in several files in the Melanie Klein Archive:

The earliest notes appear in the second half of the remainder of an A5 notebook (the cover is missing), the first half of which is devoted to some observations and then mainly to the treatment notes for the '12-year-old boy' (cf. Chapter 2). The notes on Grete are headed 'started 22 February'; then there are entries of notes until 26 April 1921 (cf. pp. 1–13).

1   The notes continue in the first half of a treatment book, from the middle of which there are notes on boy A (for the 3 and 10 May sessions, it is now noted next to Grete 'Recorded by mistake under boy A'). There are notes from 28 April to 21 September 1921 (cf. p. 1b to p. 23b).

2   One treatment book begins with notes on Grete, continues with notes on boy A, then returns to Grete. There are notes from 24 September to 29 October 1921 and two lines on 12 November 1921 (cf. p. 1c to p. 35c).

3   There is a small notepad that includes notes on Grete, boy A and Felix. For Grete the notes run from 8 November to 10 December 1921 (cf. p. 1d to p. 14d).

4   Again the first half of the book is devoted to Grete, the second to Felix. Notes run from 13 December 1921 to 16 February 1922 (cf. p. 1d to 30d).

5   On another notepad there are a few more notes on Grete. These relate to 25 February to 7 March 1922 (cf. p. 1e).

6   On individual sheets of paper that have clearly come loose from a treatment book and been stapled together, there are notes from 9 March to 24 April 1922 (cf. p. 1e to p. 25e).

7   A further notepad contains notes including some on Grete from 24 April to 16 May 1922 (cf. p. 1f to p. 7f).

8   Various: notes under the heading 'Writing' on a notepad; a single sheet of paper; an outpatient file (cf. Chapter 2) from the Polyclinic.

To consider Grete's treatment, it is necessary first to outline what form Klein's setting took at this early stage, so that any further striking aspects of Grete's treatment will also be more easily comprehensible. Treatment notes of varying extent for Grete and four other patients from 1921 form the basis for this outline. In terms of the external framework, Klein saw all the patients in 1921 at the Polyclinic (cf. Chapter 2). From Grete's documents it emerges that the treatment continued until the end of 1921 in the Polyclinic;[15] for the others such explicit references are missing. Concerning frequency, we can conclude from the periods for which documents exist for several consecutive weeks, in which Klein seems to have regularly kept records, that she generally seems to have sought to have three times weekly sessions (for example, with Grete on Tuesday, Thursday and Saturday), but that postponements were also a regular occurrence and sometimes only two weekly sessions took place, even occasionally only one.

Otherwise, it is clear from the documents that Klein preferred the 'classical' setting. She offered children and adolescents the couch, explaining the principle in order to persuade them to collaborate with her.[16] Throughout the treatment notes, Klein's questions refer to ideas about the material that has arisen, as well as to the behaviour that comes to constitute psychoanalytic technique. She directs her interest to dreams and early memories. Klein's interventions will be more closely examined in the case of Grete. In general terms, it can be suggested that she constantly diagnosed resistances and interpreted them, as well as symptoms and phantasies, in terms of unconscious wishes (oedipal wishes, as well as wishes directed towards the fulfilment of component drives – voyeurism, exhibitionism . . .) and the concomitant anxiety (especially castration anxiety).

Her offer of the couch to children and adolescents is explicitly mentioned in the treatment notes of four of the five patients in 1921, because it gave rise to anxiety and also refusal (on those occasions). With the other patient, Felix, there is no explicit mention of the couch, probably because it did not lead to a reaction that could have been seen as resistance and thus it did not need to be analysed. The

15 It is recorded for 15 January that Grete asked Klein whether she would now never go to the Polyclinic or would only come to see Klein at her flat.
16 With Grete, for example, this can be concluded from an early comment in which Klein explains that her claim that there was something unconscious was confirmed for Grete by a plausible interpretation and that thereafter she showed an awakening intellectual interest, bringing ideas 'more readily'. Later on, also, in February 1922, a further intervention is recorded with Grete that tends in this direction: Klein substantiates unconscious thoughts through the example of thoughts that 'the other Grete does not allow' but which, like bad children who are made to stand in the corner, continue to clamour for attention.

beginning of Felix's treatment is recorded as occurring on 1 February 1921; the first notes appear from 5 February. As I have described in Chapter 1, the introduction to these notes reads '*Forgets all dreams; knows only one from a while ago*'. He then told this dream from two years earlier, described the circumstances surrounding it and continued with phantasies etc. (cf. Chapter 1). Although the couch is not explicitly mentioned here either, it can easily be imagined that he associated to this in a setting that was analogous to an adult analysis.

Klein generally seems to have suggested use of the couch in the first session. The notes for the 12-year-old boy state:

> In the first session let him lie down. Impracticable – so leave it. 14 April let him lie down again, brings rather freer ideas: – goes to [a] dead cousin's grave, waters the flowers. Likes being [in the] graveyard, and likes going to mother['s] grave, waters it, then flowers grow. Was glad the sister was delayed – her watering superfluous. He watered it alone.

He said he did not like being alone in the graveyard – it was so unpleasant. He was also suspected of wanting to steal flowers. For 20 April the notes state: 'Was aggressive towards aunt'. He remembered rages from his childhood. Then he missed two sessions. On 24 April: 'Violent resistance to lying down. Then does so – but continual silence'. Afterwards they discussed his fear of the doctor, whom he had to visit because of some growths that needed to be removed. He was afraid that the doctor might even cut his tongue by mistake. It is then partly about his castration anxiety and his bad conscience about masturbation. Klein also recorded, however, that he admitted to having been afraid of her as well, fearing that she might injure him in some way.

With boy B the notes state, for example: 'Second session lay down. Frightened reaction. Silence. Admits to fear. Afraid of electrification, might electrify him because of [his] bad thoughts.'[17]

In both these cases (the 12-year-old boy and boy B) Melanie Klein manages to understand and interpret the resistance that manifests itself in relation to the couch as a component of the setting as a fear in

---

17 With boy A there is also mention of 'anxiety about lying down', which is why it turned out to be impracticable in the first session. However, the notes on the earliest sessions are so cursory that it is not apparent what happened after he lay down.

the transference of punitive and harmful interventions from her. In both cases, however, the treatment turns out to last only a few sessions. Both children were referred for treatment partly because of stealing. It is worth considering how far Klein overlooked the nature and function of the negative transference by returning to the issue of masturbation, which might have contributed to the treatment being broken off. The paranoid quality of the experience, apparent in these boys' fear of an attack by the analyst, was not fully comprehensible to Klein at this time. In 1927, Klein expressed regret at not having assembled more experiences in relation to criminality – 'this very interesting and important field of work' (WMK I, p. 181). In the light of this we shall now consider Grete's treatment notes. In the procedure outlined above, it is a striking aspect of the setting that Klein only suggested that Grete use the couch after the sixth week of treatment – this point will also be returned to later.

3.3.1

I shall examine whether the comparison of the published sequences with the corresponding ones in the treatment notes – in so far as these can be found – points to any further possible conclusions. By considering 'striking aspects' as a connecting theme, it can be recalled that Klein's description of Grete on the couch mentioned 'certain' French sentences that she enjoyed reciting. Klein suggests that these 'certain' sentences have a significance without, however, going on to work out what this might be. These sentences, as they appear in the treatment notes on p. 12b, do seem rather inconclusive at first sight: '*Le matin nous buvons – notre café ou thé – ou notre lait – à huit heures*' (in the morning we drink – our coffee or tea – or our milk – at eight o'clock). However, if we remember that this material and the accompanying associations appear in the final notes made before the summer break, this sentence seems more significant – for example, it may be that Grete had found a possible way of managing not to miss Klein. She could recite 'certain' sentences herself and had therefore ceased to turn to Melanie Klein for understanding ('milk'). As in the published passage cited above (Section 3.1), the associative connection of the 'up and down' of the voice, like the 'ladder in the snail', indicates the significance as a masturbation equivalent which, with the temporal classification obtained from the notes, points to the compensatory narcissistic atmosphere (with self-sufficiency and self-gratification). Referring back to the connections in which the meaning of the comma emerges in the treatment at the time, a further dimension of meaning opens up. In one instance, the issue of the comma is preceded by Grete's report that her aunt always asked when there was French dictation at school and whether she had managed it, which made Grete very angry (p. 7d). This relates again to the 'up and down' of the voice, and there is also a temporal connection with a break, for this is the second session after the Christmas holiday. In the other instance, Grete is ashamed at having started a sentence with a grammatical error and afraid that the aunt will be angry with her because of this proletarian and uneducated display (p. 15e). This time the up and down in the voice appears in the third to last session before the Easter break. In my judgement there is a narcissistic component to these two associations, in which every reference to 'not-having-something-oneself' (milk), and perhaps to not-being-able and not-knowing, and feeling forced to turn to others, is felt as an imposition. In this case, the annoyance about the 'proletarian' and 'uneducated' display, which could be interpreted as the expression of a compulsive needy aspect, can be understood as a part of Grete's self.

From this perspective, the issue of the conflicting descriptions of the position of Grete's and her brother's beds in the parents' bedroom in the published account and in the treatment notes (cf. Section 3.1), which emerges from the discussion of the meaning of the theatre, gains a further significance. Again, there is a possible connection with the point at which this material emerges. This is the last session before the Easter holiday in 1922, in which Grete successfully persuades Klein to tell her a funny story. The 'normal' distance seems to be reduced and the set boundaries of the analytic situation seem easy to ignore. Grete is thus able in this instance to draw Klein into her manic defence against the approaching holiday break, and the irritation that this might have provoked in Klein may have been reflected in the conflicting description mentioned above. Grete would then have been acting out in the session what is expressed in the triumphant phantasy in respect of the parents, that is, always to have them where she could see them in bed so that she could feel she had control over their actions – a means of overcoming anxiety about feelings of exclusion and abandonment.

3.3.2

In order to ascertain the importance of the striking aspects mentioned, as well as the dynamics that the omissions bring to light, I shall mainly consider (as stated in Chapter 1) the initial stage, the first phantasy that Grete communicated, and how it developed, and Klein's initial construction of the setting, as this will show some of the relevant psychodynamics more clearly.

It is interesting that instead of recording sessions relatively close to the time at which they took place, as she did with her other patients in 1921, Klein was clearly summarising them retrospectively about six weeks later. The treatment notes start as follows:

> Orig.: [in conversation][1, 18] Claims not at all afraid of
> [at night][1] once hints at fear: [creepy when alone][1] man who
> comes in the dark – wants to
> do something – then draws back
> [admits another time * earlier page][1]

The form of these lines is immediately striking. Klein is certainly still making notes using key words, but the omissions, insertions and the supplement marked with an asterisk all suggest some irritation on Klein's part, which does not appear to have been fully comprehensible to her. The first insertion 'in conversation', which from the viewpoint of the manifest content interpreted here is actually superfluous, may indicate that she perceived that Grete's way of speaking, which we might nowadays describe as 'acting in', was not consistent with the words Grete was saying. Further, the text seems to invite a completion of the first line with an addition of 'me' at the end, to make it read 'claims not at all afraid of me' – and yet this is not mentioned by Klein. Instead of this, she continues with Grete's admission of her fear of a man in the dark and with its subsequent retraction. Grete's ambivalence finds eloquent expression in this back-and-forth

18 The system of notation is explained in detail at the beginning of Part Two (pp. 241–2). Briefly, words in square brackets with a reference note (1) were written by Klein above the line of the main text, and I have assumed that they were added at some later time after the notes were first written. An asterisk indicates that some lines that are meant to come at this point are actually put at the end of the page or on another page of the notes.

movement. It seems likely that Klein sensed Grete's fear of her, a fear of 'something dark' approaching her, and that Klein was afraid that her offer of the couch might intolerably increase Grete's fear. In contrast, however, to the two treatments mentioned above (the 12-year-old boy and boy B), in which Klein was able to take up her patients' fear of her in the transference, she does not accomplish this here. Klein certainly seems to have had an intuitive under-standing of the great importance of the fear, for she places it directly at the beginning. There must, however, have been a deeply disturbing quality to this fear. Confusion may have played a part in it. Klein seems to have wanted to move on rapidly to another subject, realised this later when writing it down, and corrected it in a supplement (*) as follows:

> But another time she presents a more specific
> fear: she is tucked up, the
> man comes with a sack.
> He has a knife in his hand.
> Says she is afraid in gen. not
> at all when noise can be heard
> from the street – but is afraid when she
> hears noises in the next room.
> Then I explain to her that this is because
> people from the street might be able to help her
> whereas in the next room there might be
> the person who would like to do something to her – she
> is surprised, agrees strongly & says
> she thought that but didn't know it
> by this sees my claim (there is something Ucs
> confirmed) then also shows awakening
> intellectual interest & presents more readily
> the fear of door-handle described
> on other page.

In this supplement the fear is made 'more definite' – it relates to a man and to the next room, not to Klein. Klein also seems to want to establish in her first intervention that this is not about a fear in the here-and-now. To that extent, this first intervention to be communicated can be interpreted as an essential component of the psychodynamics of how the specific psychic setting with this patient is constructed.[19] This first interpretation seems to be directed primarily towards soothing Grete and herself. Klein does not give an interpretation here of the oedipal wishes contained in it, as would be entirely conceivable from the manifest content of the fearful phantasy that is communicated and as would be in agreement with her practice elsewhere.

Instead, in this first intervention, which is 'extra-transference', she offers Grete a form of splitting: what is bad is in the next room, what is good is in the street and also here through the analyst in the room who knows about both. Grete is surprised by this offer, then keenly accepts it, rewarding Klein by making associations 'more readily'. However, although Grete seems to speak more readily in the material that follows, the atmosphere actually seems to be more paranoid, and the unease – albeit displaced on to an impersonal object – appears to have increased.

~~Later~~ – afraid of door handle
old wood [then says][1] that woodworm
might come out of it – thus shows
phobia – earthworms
worms in general – ideas
~~when~~ it is so long, when
it rolls up, small – but you
still know then [that][1] it is big – when ask
if knows pipi – at first no:
Then admits – yes, of small boys – has also
tried to see if she could ~~m~~
~~make~~ [urinate][1] just like them – later
in session – admits has wondered why
she does not have & envy [agrees with worm-pipi correspondence].[1] Enthusing
about dog [that she very much wants][1] – describes how will care for
what would like to do with it etc.
Agrees when I say: would like

19 Franch (1996), for example, has indicated that the analytic setting is primarily a psychic one, which finds support in the material conditions. Of prime importance, however, is the analyst's ability to receive the child's communications on all levels.

to have a child. Enthuses more and more
about girl friend.

If Klein feels unable to withstand attacks on the 'door handle' to her
inner self, how can she be able to give help in dealing with the
corresponding internal objects?

On the surface, however, Klein's splitting appears to help with
analysing within known parameters; resistances are now overcome,
Grete makes certain admissions and penis envy, wishes for children
and Oedipal phantasies are addressed.

On the basis of the material, however, it seems that Grete had
unconscious guilt feelings about the irritation that she had felt and
inflicted on Melanie Klein. The following material – enthusiasm
for the dog that she very much wants and that she describes caring
for, as well as the enthusiastic talking about her girl friend with its
sexualised component – can be understood as a manic attempt at
reparation by Grete. If the dog is considered as a self-object, the
component of narcissistic withdrawal may also predominate in this
phantasy.

It is clear from a supplement on 9 April (p. 3 and p. 4 below) that
Klein also felt the dynamics working below the surface despite the
description of successful interpretive work: even about three or four
weeks earlier there had been some exceptionally good work on the
story about a little brother and little sister that Klein had told her.
Klein does not explain this in any more detail; in terms of my hypothesis, the remark makes sense in so far as it can be imagined that Grete
also understood Klein's telling of this story as an attempt to bring
back into the discussion the persecutory malevolent object that had
originally been banished by means of splitting.[20]

---

20 Klein's explanation of her views on the Grimm tales in 'The development of a child'
(1921) provides the following illustration of her aims: 'the child's latent fear, depending
upon repression, is more easily rendered manifest by their help and can then be more
thoroughly dealt with by analysis' (WMK I, p. 52). However, she did not relate this
consideration to the transference situation but stated it in general terms:

I have particularly selected listening to Grimm's tales without anxiety-manifestations
as an indication of the mental health of children, because of all the children known to
me there are only very few who do so. Probably partly from a desire to avoid this
discharge of anxiety a number of modified versions of these tales have appeared and in
modern education other less terrifying tales, ones that do not touch so much – pleasur-
ably and painfully – upon repressed complexes are preferred. I am of opinion, however,

Klein's suggestion of the couch after six weeks can now be understood on a manifest level as an indication that Klein now saw greater prospects of success in getting Grete to use the couch, because resistance and fear seemingly no longer prevailed, so that she thought she could introduce the 'ordinary' (adult) setting. It may well be, however, that on another level this suggestion of the couch had something to do with the need to bring into the open the latent negative transference, which had been made even more difficult to grasp by the first soothing intervention, in the hope that Grete's negative feelings could be dealt with in a more analytic way instead. The first part of this 'succeeds':

On 5 April after 6 wks of treatment
ask [her][1] to lie down.
Extremely violent reaction of fear & refusal.
With great difficulty admits – after
I allow her not to lie down –
to what part of the fear is
about: I would go away if she lay
on the couch – come back with a
knife – stick it into her
arm, no – her chest.

Grete reacts to Klein's suggestion with intense anxiety; she reconnects with her initial phantasy. She formulates the phantasy now manifestly in relation to Klein. At the repetition of the relevant 'request' on 9 April, there follows 'after extremely strong resistance' a more detailed description.

When she lay down I went out
came back with large

that with the assistance of analysis there is no need to avoid these tales but that they can be used directly as a standard and an expedient.

(WMK I, p. 52)

Thus, Klein may not have consciously conceptualised the use of stories as a method of addressing the negative transference, although she seems to be close to making this point in a comment on page 20b, in which she promises a story in return for several good sessions. Overall, to judge from the treatment reports, this method does not play a very important role in Grete's treatment.

91

knife. I undressed her.
Stuck the knife in chest, no —
hesitates — lower — but then admits
only her stomach. Then I turn
away from her — she is lying in
blood — one of the doctors comes and
bandages her — gets dressed & goes
home.

But this time, as well, Klein's unease seems to be intense; she proceeds by reinterpreting the material in libidinal terms: '*I interpret: — I put her to bed, undress her, as mother used to do*'. Grete concedes this after some resistance, but then insists that that is where the similarity ends, because she is afraid of Klein. Her analyst must now obviously introduce reality and get Grete to confirm to her that this is entirely incomprehensible, since she knows that Klein wishes her no harm. Klein cannot then allow the negative transference phantasy brought on to the scene to stand unchallenged. She follows Grete's sexualising defence in a sense by continuing with the 'libidinal reinterpretation':

Taking this up
I say — and there is nothing bad there. Would like
me with pipi (uncertainty whether
have — since surprised she did not)
should fetch one for me to take
& stick in hers . . . — At first
says whether then there is a hole there — then
yes as small wish comes out of it.
Agrees completely with interpretation —
says longs more for mother than father.

Although this is conceptualised beyond the transference and in a different way from it, Klein's next intervention can, however, be understood dynamically in terms of her perception that feelings of powerlessness and exclusion were being warded off by means of these phantasies.

When I say that when parents went to bed
together — she stayed alone in hers,

– longed for mother should go to her
lie down with her in bed.

However, in the immediate interaction with Grete she is only able
to continue reacting correctively with 'reality' in respect of the negative transference. Thus, for example, she replies when Grete speaks
again about her fear and quotes her cousin in this connection, who
would not undress in front of a doctor as she had to do in the examination at the Polyclinic, that she, Grete, in fact had only to speak (p. 6).
With such comments as that on the similarity between the fear of
Klein, of the mother and the man, proverbially the father, it becomes
clear that Klein fully recognises the transference constellation and is
conceptualising it for herself. She also explicitly identifies on page 9
the problem of the 'strong negative transference'. In accordance with
the technique of the time (cf. here Section 1.5), she attempts to trace
this back to the 'original objects'. Thus, for example, she asks when
Grete has been laughing again in intense amusement at the attitude of
her head and at her gaze, whether her aunt or her mother are not
sometimes funny, which Grete indignantly and aggressively rejects
(p. 9). Grete may well have experienced this intervention as a powerful penetration into relationships that were important to her, which
she was almost being called on to betray. This session was followed by
a longer gap than was usual between sessions – normally she came on
Tuesdays, Thursdays, Saturdays; this time, almost a week had elapsed
between the Thursday session on 14 and the Wednesday session on
20, in which, as Klein recorded, she 'still' demonstrated a strong negative transference. Klein addresses Grete's onset of defiance, but does
not pursue the motivation for this – the long enforced wait for the
next session, a situation with which Grete is nevertheless thoroughly
familiar in relation to her mother. Grete cries and is outraged when
Klein says that she does not want to annoy only her but also the
mother. Because the connection with the enforced waiting is missing,
this remark can be understood only as an unjustified reproach. The
material that follows leads through Oedipal phantasies back to Grete's
homosexual strivings – an impulse that we have known about in her
from the early phase.[21]

---

21 After the summer holidays in 1921 Klein recorded in a supplement: '*Right from the first
session 14/IX to analysis on the couch*' (p. 13b), but she reflects no further on this. In my
view this lack of reflection can be understood as a further sign that the deep-seated fear

It may be that Grete is reconstituting in the treatment situation the condensed dynamics of the first memory and the screen memories.

Grete[4] – only memory
of parents. She in the cot. Mother has
smashed lampshade. Father terribly
angry & shouts – wants to send mother
outside. She shouts a lot in bed until father
picks her up. Little brother
[is][1] also in [his][1] bed. No memory [of][1] father
only that he wore pince-nez. After mother
lives apart from her – longing.

The mother smashes the lampshade in this phantasy – Grete, as described above, was injured by a burning lamp. The mother or primary object therefore cannot function in this phantasy as a container for the child's destructive impulses, but seems herself to be dominated by destructive impulses. The mother seems to offer the father and – if we add to this Grete's injury – Grete also a sadistic, wounding relationship. Accordingly, Grete is now afraid of sadistic, wounding treatment from her analyst. If we interpret this memory with roles reversed as a sadistic primal-scene phantasy, it may well be that she experiences the relationship with the mother in an identification

---

that Grete felt towards her was not actually comprehensible to her at the conscious level; the form that the supplement takes seems to reconfirm that this was a point of difficulty. This first session after the summer holidays is recorded as follows:

14/IX. – Reports – summer –
all the fruit – sweets given to her
by aunt. – Regrets when she was
healthy – that she had said choc.
that she ate when ill
did not taste good. Cannot admit
reason for this regret – [then][1]
admits: so that aunt should not stop
wanting to give presents – but thinks aunt
is not like that.

With regard to her analyst the lines can be taken to mean that Grete had attributed Klein's holidays to the fact that she told her, 'I don't like the taste of the couch'. A possible thought of Grete's may have been that further interruptions could then be avoided if she lay on the couch.

with the father, who becomes angry on account of the mother's destructiveness and attempts to throw her out. Grete would in this case understand the separation from the mother as the discharge of her (bad) behaviour. Now even the father who picked her up in the phantasy has abandoned Grete in reality. If we add to this the second memory – she used to enjoy playing with the elder brother who was now dead (p. 4) – as well as the third memory – bedwetting at around the age of 5 or 6 (p. 8) – it must be inferred that Grete phantasises herself as very destructive, ultimately deadly. Against this background, Grete may be experiencing the interruptions to her analytic treatment as something that is also traceable to her destructive behaviour. On the one hand, she attempts to soothe herself – to protect herself from interruptions to relationships, as becomes clear in the analytic relationship – by withdrawing into her world with masturbation equivalents. On the other hand, she unconsciously fears an equivalent treatment from her object and thus keeps trying to seek a form of 'soothing' through manic attempts at reparation, through the sexualised relationship in which she can still experience the object as alive through the insistence on presents that are supposed to prove to her that she is still lovable.

Reviewing the striking features of the published material that formed the basis of the first hypothesis (cf. Section 3.1), it can be noted that in the initial phase considered up till now stuttering is not mentioned even in the treatment notes. The homosexual fixation is apparent in many of Grete's ideas. Klein tries to work out in the transference the libidinal component of Grete's homosexuality towards her; however, the hostile component is clearly also at work. Klein identifies the negative transference that is not at first fully apparent when it becomes unmistakably manifest in the change of setting, but the irritation seems so intense that she feels she must – without being able to understand this as such – primarily counteract it by soothing. It may be that Klein was intuitively trying to confirm Grete's defence (homosexual love also as a defence against hatred), in order thereby to increase the room for manoeuvre for Grete's ego. (Later, in 'A contribution to the psychogenesis of manic-depressive states' (1935), Klein explains how this meaning may also be attached to manic functioning as a defence against persecution by bad, destroyed objects.)

As suggested in the preliminary hypothesis (Section 3.1) a restrictive object seems at work whose destructive nature (in the sense of an ego-destructive superego)[22] becomes comprehensible on the basis of the treatment notes. The restrictive object is both at work in part ego-syntonically in Grete, attacking her analyst, and also is projected on to the teacher/analyst, so that the attack then emanates from the teacher/analyst. In each case, a potentially good link is attacked. Unconscious guilt feelings lead, on the one hand, to manic attempts at reparation through homosexual phantasies and actions, as is again portrayed more subtly in the treatment notes. On the other hand, these guilt feelings effect a withdrawal by means of masturbation equivalents that were already apparent in the published work, but whose psychodynamic meaning in relation to disappointing object relations and experiences of abandonment becomes accessible only through the treatment notes.

3.3.3

Stuttering and, next, the difficult complex of homosexuality and negative transference will now be given a detailed reconsideration in relation to the treatment notes. Stuttering appears in the treatment notes only from January 1922, from a point at which Grete's treatment is no longer taking place at the Polyclinic but at Klein's flat. When Grete asks on 15 January whether it is only she who comes to see Klein at her flat, Klein interprets this as an indication of her wish to be the favourite child and of her jealousy of the other children. Again, further possible meanings of this change of location are not pursued. On 18 January Grete mentions how nice it is that the young woman (Melanie Klein's housemaid?) reads to her. It may be that Grete also experiences the moving of the treatment to the flat as an inducement to consider some 'private' contact with Klein as only reasonable – in compensation for the three-week Christmas break – and accordingly reacts with disappointment that nothing then changes in the therapeutic relationship. Klein certainly interprets the jealousy towards other patients but not the jealousy in respect of her family.

---

22 In *Transformations* Bion writes of the 'usurpation by the super-ego of the position that should be occupied by the ego' (Bion, 1965, p. 38), when moral dimensions exert influence over a domain to which they are inappropriate.

Says wants to go home quickly –
buy more sugar in shop where saleswoman
gives her some. (When I interpret that she wants to leave me
because I don't want to give her
sugar = something white on pipi)
she says: even saleswoman
recently turned her away because wanted to buy
sugar two days running. When she
was agreeing 'yes' to interpretations
she stuttered, saying 'yes, yes, yes',
whereas otherwise in the third session
she hardly stuttered at all.

Klein writes that the stuttering reappeared when she interpreted that Grete did not get what she wanted from Klein; what is possibly also being expressed more directly now in this symptom, if not in relation to the manifest content interpreted by Klein, is the negative transference, the anger about the withholding – Klein records it as such for the first time. There are further examples of this; in my view, the connection can be seen very vividly in a stuttering incident from the 21 January session:

When I asked her, as she was crying,
where handkerchief – stuttering for the first time in
this session – said 'i i i in
muff' (p. 14d).

I consider the stuttering in this case to be an expression of her protest and her indignation that Klein did not simply give her a handkerchief, as Grete imagined she would have done with her own children, instead asking her if she had her own. In this sense, however, Klein was not able to reflect on the function of the symptom in the immediate interaction with her. Even the associations that Grete gave after this were not understood as allusions to the transference, as an indication that Grete was telling Klein how to do it 'right', by giving her a handkerchief as she herself had done with her uncle.

Assoc. to muff: also fur inside =
warm – so warm when hands are
inside: – had said about handkerchief at the beginning

of the session, that she gave her uncle
one that he can put in a small
pocket. (Interpret muff = her genitals – remember
lady's fur coat – uncle's handkerchief = father's penis
– hence stuttered when asked where handkerchief
but because wanted ~~to say~~ like this
said several times [sth. crossed out] [full[?]][1] 'i i in the'

As in the previous examples, Klein interprets the stuttering as libid-
inally determined. However, it seems likely she remained uneasy with
this interpretation of stuttering and that this explains why she did not
use either of these examples in a published work.

I shall now address the aspects of homosexuality and negative transference. Although it was striking in the published material on Grete
that the homosexuality was not further considered by Klein, the same
does not apply to the treatment notes. She repeatedly attempts to
make aspects of this clear, yet she continues to fail to grasp the
dynamic as briefly outlined above and as she went on to explicate it in
1932. What form did her attempts take at that time? In April 1921,
there is the first explicit entry on this:

Homosexuality: flight – heterosexuality, – & stratification of castration
anxiety through mother father
castration anxiety also through
urethral phantasies – the Oedipus compls.
were activated.

What Klein is formulating here within the framework of 'classical
theory' is later to play an important part in regard to early Oedipal
conflicts, in which an intensive castration anxiety results from the
belief that the mother as well as the father forbids the sadistic impulses
towards the father's penis, which is assumed to exist in the mother's
womb (cf. 1927). In 1921, Klein seems mainly to fall back on the
concepts of regression ('flight' from the heterosexuality that is bound
up with fear) and of libidinal fixation (urethral phantasies).

In this version there is also an echo of Abraham's conceptualisation.
Abraham understood homosexuality as an 'abnormal' expression of
the female castration complex. He had given a lecture on this in The
Hague in 1920, which was published in 1921 as 'Äußerungsformen

des weiblichen Kastrationskomplexes' (Manifestations of the female castration complex). According to this paper, the woman's desire to assume the male role is based on the wish to eradicate the narcissistic injury, a wish that may also be expressed in corresponding urethral phantasies. The idea that castration anxiety relates to the mother as well as to the father is not, however, elaborated in this work.

Some weeks later Klein interprets homosexuality as a form of negative Oedipus complex – if the mother provides the penis for Grete, then the father will be superfluous. With this idea, as well, Klein is drawing on established opinion. Nevertheless, in this instance the emphasis on the mother's provision of the penis is not to be found as such in Abraham, for whom it is primarily about the father, who should give the penis as a present. Klein later interprets the wish for the penis as a wish both for a means of sadistic exercise of power and for a possibility of reparation (cf. Klein, 1932). (In the material on the 'sun-rays' – cf. Section 3.2 – both aspects are present (sun-stroke and pregnancy) but they are not conceptualised as such.)

At the end of January 1922, Klein interprets homosexual contact as Grete's wish for her mother to take her back inside herself.[23]

Klein appears to have understood important components without managing at this point to conceptualise them conclusively, which is probably why she did not go on to discuss them in the published work. She still held predominantly to a libidinal model that does not, however, seem to have agreed with her experiences with Grete as recorded in the notes.

Whereas in the first six months the negative transference was demonstrated in the setting mainly in relation to the couch, after the 1921 summer holidays the denials expressed in the context of the analytic relationship are the principal clue to the negative transference. Grete suspects here that Klein could actually be giving the other patients money or chocolate. She suspects that Klein is withholding these from her because she does not love her. Klein cannot, however, work out in this example with Grete why she thinks she is not lovable.

An example from October 1921 is selected to elucidate Klein's way of dealing with Grete's complaints. Grete complains on 18 October

---

23 In a footnote to 'The rôle of the school in the libidinal development of the child', Klein (1923a) mentions that in September 1922 at the International Psychoanalytical Association Congress Ferenczi had put forward the suggestion that 'in the unconscious, return to the maternal body seems only to be possible by means of coitus' (WMK I, p. 61, fn. 4).

that she is repeatedly missing theatre productions because of the analytic sessions. On 20 October the notes state:

> 20/X. Was very
> late also otherwise clear resistance – fierce
> complaints that again my fault missed
> some fun. Mother was there wanted to
> take her somewhere, does not know where.
> Otherwise it would be another theatre production
> that I was also stopping her from going to. ~~Tells~~ [sth. crossed out]
> Then makes a verbal slip and says: because of you
> I could not go to the play &
> not to you – (instead of not to Mummy).

Klein brings out the death phantasies towards her:

> After much
> resistance admits would be happy if I
> were not there. Did not exist
> is at night, for then would not have
> known me – if had died
> – another person would be in my place.
> – With difficulty and crying, death phantasies.
> I might die of plague or lung
> disease. Might also be
> an accident. I might fall down the stairs.

Grete's slip of the tongue indicates a possible trigger for the death phantasies – the disappointment at not being able to be with Klein all the time. The extreme delay might then make Klein feel what Grete is suffering. Grete's phantasy might take the form that if Klein did not exist there would also be none of these painful experiences with her. Klein thus encounters a key moment in her understanding. The death phantasies now provoke further anxiety in Grete, which Klein does not seem to interpret, but in which she later sees a key to understanding a corresponding dynamic. If it became clear above (see Sections 3.3.1 and 3.3.2) that a latent negative transference was appearing in connection with breaks, Klein was then able to interpret Grete's ideas of wanting to smash something and in the context of the approaching Christmas holidays she interpreted it as an expression of resistance to these holidays: '*I show her alternately* ["alternately" is abbreviated] *good bad mother, and also aunt, unfulfilled early wishes*' (p. 4d).

The sessions after the Easter holidays in 1922 – the last break before the end of the treatment – will now finally be considered again in relation to the handling of the negative transference, which has the immediate effect that Grete misses the first session after the holidays. The 22 April session is noted as follows:

22/IV. Does not seem espec. happy to
see me again: repts (and, as often, boasts) about many
~~presents~~ and sweets given by
Mummy & also aunt as presents. – Asks
if now the girl who was before her
(Patient D) is no longer coming. – Immediately afterwards:
wants the session to end.

As with every holiday, this one is followed in the session immediately afterwards by Grete's first talking about the presents received. Klein does not seem at this time to understand what significance these presents hold for Grete. The deep unease caused by her sadistic impulses leads to a strong orientation towards external objects from whom she needs presents in order to feel lovable. Yet the inner doubts are not actually assuaged by this. Once again, Grete has experienced the holiday as an indication that Klein has not wanted to have anything to do with her because she is so bad.

Grete starts by demonstrating to Klein how much better she is treated by her mother and aunt; she seems to have had to ward off a sense of unease by means of this idealising phantasy. This seems to be based partly on the fact that she has not seen the patient who has otherwise always been there before her, for she immediately wishes for her own session to end. Klein is able to interpret a part of her negative transference – that she is angry with her because she does not allow her to have things – doesn't give her chocolate and so on, sees another girl she doesn't know before her. She does not, however, mention the connection with the holidays, and her interpretation of jealousy overlooks the momentary unease that might be based on the possibility that Grete had made Klein stop seeing the other girl, thus 'eliminating' her. Grete arrives very late to the next session two days later and complains of headaches. Through dark colours, to which

Grete associates mourning clothes, Klein is able indirectly to interpret her headaches as an expression of hatred towards her – but, again, she rapidly concludes with an explanation that is reminiscent of the 'sun-ray interpretation' given in February.

3.4 The significance of Grete's analysis

Although Klein is in some sense defeated by the latent negative transference and also has to mitigate the manifest negative transference by soothing, she nevertheless manages to interpret the latter to some extent and thus to make aspects of Grete's psychic reality accessible to her. These explorations of the hostile aspects nevertheless remain a rather isolated part of this analysis.

So far my considerations have focused on what was not yet possible for Klein in this early treatment because of difficulty in dealing with the countertransference, a difficulty that was compounded by the libidinal concepts current at the time. It remains to stress what Klein was able to learn in this treatment. On the basis of her methodological procedure, and its inherently investigative approach, she was able to allow herself to be guided by Grete's associations towards entirely different meanings from those that Klein herself had originally suggested.

Whereas at the beginning – following the knowledge established at the time – Klein emphasised Grete's penis envy and lack of a penis, she was quickly able to allow herself to be corrected by Grete, when Grete made it clear that it was her own genitals that she was thinking about.

> 7 April – reports excursion
> with girl friend – how they made
> shapes, – then mussels etc.
> – strong nauseous reaction to snails
> that she saw there. [Sth. crossed out] When I
> interpret to her: snail perhaps also boy's
> pipi (as she calls it – as reluctantly
> admitted in talk about worms). She
> says – no – that cannot be right.
> After all, it is not long – looks different –
> so soft – has its little house – then

agrees completely, when I interpret
her genital organs –

Phantasies concerning the snail, the clitoris, the 'passage' (p. 2b), the
'little basket' (pp. 18b ff.), the labia, recur continually. Grete was partly
expressing fear of having damaged her genital organs through masturbation (p. 8b); here, then, are also early fears concerning the intactness
of the female genitals, which Klein goes on to investigate and describe
further later.

Klein encounters sadistic phantasies in this treatment, such as that
of biting the mother etc (cf. p. 5b, p. 25c); the *'phantasy of parental coitus
– & idea that the foetuses in the mother (drinking water!) must take care!'*
(p. 16b).

Phantasies in relation to dead objects appear – for example, the
sexual intercourse with the dead father in the sky through sun-rays
(cf. Section 3.2). The identification with Heinrich that Grete presented could also be understood in this sense (p. 24c). (Cf. the story of
'The Frog King or Iron Heinrich', in which the faithful Heinrich had
been so saddened by his master's transformation into a frog that he
placed three iron bands around his heart to stop it bursting from
sorrow.)

Klein observed here the favourable influence that the analysis had
on Grete's intellectual development. Although she stated on p. 3 that
the desire to learn and ambition were not strongly evident, it is also
recorded on p. 30d that according to information from the aunt
and the teacher, 'learning and so on were thoroughly excellent'. The
narcissistic vulnerability that Klein repeatedly records in this treatment is, however, not considered in regard to its significance for
what Bion was much later to describe as 'learning from experience'
(Bion, 1962).

Although she later goes on to understand acting in through role
play, there are also precursors to this in Grete's treatment. On p. 7b
Klein speculates that Grete identifies with the mother and is punishing the dog in the same way that she has been punished.

In conclusion, it can be stated that while Klein understood important individual factors in Grete's treatment, going beyond Grete's
manifest stated sexual symbolism, and intuitively placing Grete's
statements about fear at the beginning, she was not fully able at this
time to take note of the acting in that was decisive for the meaning of
Grete's verbally communicated phantasies. She was therefore often

unable to explore the meaning of the immediate transference situation and relied rather more on the symbolic content of Grete's verbal associations, according to the theoretical framework that was current at the time. She treated Grete's associations with absolute seriousness, while also allowing herself, where appropriate, to be corrected by Grete.

4

Rita

Klein's youngest patient

4.1 Rita in Klein's published works

Whereas with Grete our starting point was the very limited amount of published material contained in the two interrelated works of 1923, with no explicit reference to the treatment situation, whether to the transference–countertransference dynamics, the external setting, the scope of the treatment or its outcome, with the 2¾-year-old Rita we are in a sense starting from the opposite position – Klein repeatedly returns to the subject of her youngest patient in the period from 1926 to 1955.

We first read about the melancholic Rita, with her various anxiety states and compulsive symptoms, in 'The psychological principles of early analysis' of 1926 (WMK I), in which Klein explains with the example of her case how very strong guilt feelings lay behind her inhibition of play that had already lasted several months, her inability to tolerate deprivations and her excessive sensitivity to pain. In 1929, she addresses part of the same material again in 'Personification in the play of children' (1929, WMK I), mainly in order to give a more detailed explanation of the roles played by the superego and the id. In *The Psycho-Analysis of Children* (1932, WMK II), she addresses the subject of Rita in several contexts. Rita's 'deepest fear', the fear of being deprived by the mother, is central to Klein's discussion. Whereas the concept of 'wish-fulfilment' plays a role in 1929 – as will be shown in an example below – in 1932 there is generally more discussion of the anxieties Rita feels because of her aggressive behaviour and phantasies about her parents. Concerning the framework of the treatment, we also learn here that there were eighty-three treatment sessions and that the analysis could not be completed because her parents emigrated. Some fundamental results had begun to be achieved: 'anxiety was lessened and her obsessive ceremonials disappeared. Her depressive symptoms, together with her inability to tolerate frustrations, were a good deal moderated' (1932, WMK II, p. 4, n.). A successful and complete transition into the latency stage is described. According to information from her mother, Rita had continued to develop well during the seven years in which the mother kept in touch with Klein after the end of the treatment (WMK II, p. 4, n.). Klein's paper 'Weaning' (1936) contains more detailed information about the difficulties in Rita's weaning and indicates that it was only after the analysis had started that Rita had been able to manage without her bottle at night.[1]

The most detailed discussion of Rita's case history appears in 'The Oedipus complex in the light of early anxieties' (1945, WMK I), where the early relationship with the parents, the development of the superego, persecutory and depressive anxiety are elaborated in detail. Finally, Klein refers again to Rita in 1955, in 'The psycho-analytic play technique: its history and significance', in particular to the first treatment session. Here we learn that Rita's treatment took place at the child's home, but that Klein realised in the course of this therapy that the home environment was interfering with the analysis (1955, WMK III, p. 124).

To summarise, then, in complete contrast to Grete, Klein's reflections concerning Rita's pathology and treatment are strikingly abundant. The scenario to which Klein most frequently and repeatedly referred – it appeared in four of the six publications on Rita – is selected here as an illustration.[2]

---

1 Compare pp. 12 and 23 of the treatment notes. On 12 April Klein records in the treatment notes: 'She suddenly wants a glass of warm milk to drink and runs down to ask for it and drinks it (Mother reports still drinking from the small bottle – unusual to ask for a cup of milk)'. On 21 April, Klein records:

> Hear from mother that she is sleeping very badly, often wakes up screaming, wants only to go to her mother – immediately completely reassured when she caresses her – says at once – good again now. When taken into her mother's bed early in morning, snuggles in there & gets bottle, then goes back to her own bed.

2 It seems at least possible that Klein was also thinking of the discussion of the sleep-ceremonial in the light of Freud's seventeenth lecture (1916–1917) – 'The sense of

One obsessional symptom which Rita developed at the age of two was a sleep-ceremonial which wasted a great deal of time. The main point of this was that she insisted on being tightly rolled up in the bed-clothes for fear that 'a mouse or a butty might come through the window and bite off her butty (genital)'. Her games revealed other determinants: the doll had always to be rolled up in the same way as Rita herself, and on one occasion an elephant was put beside its bed. This elephant was supposed to prevent the baby-doll from getting up; otherwise it would steal into the parents' bedroom and do them some harm or take something away from them. The elephant (a father-imago)[3] was intended to take over the part of hinderer. This part the introjected father had played within her since the time when, between the ages of fifteen months and two years, she had wanted to usurp her mother's place with her father, to steal from her mother the child with which she was pregnant, and to injure and castrate the parents. The reactions of rage and anxiety which followed on the punishment of the 'child' during such games showed, too, that Rita was inwardly playing both parts: that of the authorities who sit in judgement and that of the child who is punished.

(1926, WMK I, p. 132)

In 1929 Klein explicates her understanding of the role played by the elephant in more detail:

The only wish-fulfilment apparent in this game lay in the fact that the elephant succeeded for a time in preventing the 'child' from getting up. There were only two main 'characters': that of the doll, which embodied the id, and that of the deterring elephant, which represented the super-ego. The wish-fulfilment consisted in the defeat of the id by the super-ego.

(1929, WMK I, p. 202)

This understanding had certainly necessitated an implicit redefinition of Freud's concept of wish-fulfilment, in which unconscious

---

symptoms' – in which he also presented the analysis of a sleep-ceremonial in a 19-year-old female patient with obsessional neurosis.

3 In the 1925 manuscript, the elephant is considered to be both a father- and a mother-imago.

libidinal wishes are conceived as finding imaginary fulfilment in dreams, symptoms and phantasies. This attempt to conceptualise the game in classical terms seems somewhat forced.[4]

In 1932 this understanding was broadened, so that Rita's wish to be tucked up so tightly in the bedclothes was seen not only as directed at hindering the emergence and expression of aggressive tendencies towards the parents, but also as protecting her from analogous attacks by the parents, which Klein thought Rita anticipated as punishment for her own attacks. 'The attacks were to be made, for instance, by the "*Butzen*" (her father's penis), which would injure her genitals and bite off her own "*Butzen*" as a punishment for wanting to castrate him' (1932, WMK II, p. 7). In 1945, this aspect of the protection stands in the foreground:

> The main point of it was that she (and her doll as well) had to be tightly tucked up in the bed clothes, otherwise — as she said — a mouse or a 'butzen' (a word of her own) would get in through the window and bite off her own 'butzen'. The 'butzen' represented both her father's genital and her own: her father's penis would bite off her own imaginary penis just as *she* desired to castrate *him*. As I see it now, the fear of her mother attacking the 'inside' of her body also contributed to her fear of someone coming through the window. The room also represented her body and the assailant was her mother retaliating for the child's attacks on her. The obsessional need to be tucked in with such elaborate care was a defence against all these fears.
>
> (1945, WMK I, p. 402)

The initial inconsistencies, as well as the incomplete conceptualisations, have receded here, giving more satisfactory results. Klein did not formulate her dissatisfaction explicitly at first but it seems in fact to have preoccupied her until she found an adequate means of understanding it.[5]

---

4 In 1930, Freud certainly expanded this by stating that wish-fulfilments of the superego could also occur in dreams (1900, *S.E.* 5, p. 476, fn. 2), which led to his conceptualisation of punishment dreams. Even then, Klein's example fits only in part. The stabilisation of the superego could be understood as wish-fulfilment, but in Klein's brief description the motivation ultimately remains unexplained.

5 It is also worth considering how far an autistic component may also play a part in the

Although the example that I have selected here relates to the understanding of a symptom while the treatment situation remains in the background, we find that the treatment situation is also mentioned in the later published passages. These address precisely the point that we observed had been difficult for Klein in Grete's treatment – dealing with the negative transference.

Melanie Klein explicitly discusses this challenge in relation to Rita:

I was very doubtful about how to tackle this case since the analysis of so young a child was an entirely new experiment. The first session seemed to confirm my misgivings. Rita, when left alone with me in her nursery, at once showed signs of what I took to be a negative transference: she was anxious and silent and very soon asked to go out into the garden. I agreed and went with her – I may add, under the watchful eyes of her mother and aunt, who took this as a sign of failure. They were very surprised to see that Rita was quite friendly towards me when we returned to the nursery some ten to fifteen minutes later. The explanation of this change was that while we were outside I had been interpreting her negative transference (this again being against the usual practice). From a few things she said, and the fact that she was less frightened when we were in the open, I concluded that she was particularly afraid of something which I might do to her when she was alone with me in the room. I interpreted this and, referring to her night terrors, I linked her suspicion of me as a hostile stranger with her fear that a bad woman would attack her when she was by herself at night. When, a few minutes after this interpretation, I suggested that we should return to the nursery, she readily agreed.

(1955, WMK III, p. 124)

It was twenty-three years earlier that she had used this example in a more general way to demonstrate that an indication of negative

---

'tucking up' (cf. Ogden, 1989). Klein's assessment may have pointed in this direction. On p. A5 Klein interprets – when Rita wraps a doll up tightly – '*Child in mother*'. Manifestly Klein was probably thinking more of procreative phantasies, in so far as this could be derived from the context: *Child in mother: I, Frau Klein, / Am father (put doll in)*. Intuitively, however, she may have been articulating a constant need to sense a concrete 'indestructible' container around oneself.

transference 'makes it still more imperative that interpretation should begin as soon as possible' (1932, WMK II, p. 21). She adds:

> For instance, when Rita, who was a very ambivalent child, felt a resistance she at once wanted to leave the room, and I had to make an interpretation immediately so as to resolve this resistance. As soon as I had clarified for her the cause of her resistance – always carrying it back to its original object and situation – it was resolved, and she would become friendly and trustful again and continue playing, supplying in its various details a confirmation of the interpretation I had just given.
>
> (1932, WMK II, p. 21)

We are thus given a picture both of what is clearly a chronically manifest negative transference, expressed in wanting to leave the room, and of Klein's interpretive approach to it. In this context, it certainly seems remarkable that Klein comes to discuss the initial treatment session only in her last publication in 1955, thirty-two years after Rita's analysis.

The earlier (1932) reference to the problem, which had already been mentioned in the unpublished London lectures of 1925, is rather loosely schematic and generalised in nature, leaving the reader somewhat dissatisfied. An example would have helped us to gain an impression of how the treatment actually proceeded.

It is striking in this context that Klein does not use the example of Rita in the 'Symposium on child-analysis' (1927a). In this rejoinder to Anna Freud's critique, the interpretation of negative transference played an important role and a scene from the analysis of such a young girl might have been considered as providing a particularly impressive example.

If we now reconsider the striking reason that Klein gives in 1945 for choosing Rita's material in particular to explain – that it is simple and uncomplicated – a statement that already seems to be contradicted somehow by the continuing extensions of its under-standing, we can also understand Klein's frequent return to the subject of Rita as an indication that in the actual treatment situ-ation with Rita there were many things that were not at all easy. It seems that decades afterwards Klein was still seeking an adequate way of conceptualising factors that had evidently been of lasting concern.

In order to try to describe the 'difficulties' somewhat better, it may also be useful to consider the following striking aspects.

First, in 1923, Abraham wrote to Freud saying that Klein was skilfully and successfully treating a 3-year-old child who had 'basic melancholia' (Freud and Abraham, 2002). But the diagnosis 'melancholic depression' does not appear in the publications on Rita until 1932 (WMK II, p. 3). In 1926, Klein presented Rita's case with reference to the following symptoms: '*pavor nocturnus* and a dread of animals . . . very considerable inhibition in play, as well as an inability to tolerate deprivations, an excessive sensitivity to pain, and marked moodiness' (WMK I, p. 130). In 1929 she completed this list with a diagnosis of 'severe obsessional neurosis' (WMK I, p. 201) but she identified the melancholic components only in 1932, at which point little material of this kind was being presented.

Second, we learn a great deal about Rita's background – anamnesis, domestic scenes – whereas relatively little direct material from the treatment is made available to us. In 1926, there is the above-mentioned sleep-ceremonial game that Rita evidently played with her doll in the treatment. In 1929, there is also Rita's journey-game, which later in the analysis took the following form:

Rita and her toy bear (who then represented the penis) went in a train to see a good woman who was to entertain them and give them presents. At the beginning of this part of the analysis this happy ending was generally spoilt. Rita wanted to drive the train herself and get rid of the driver. He, however, either refused to go or came back and threatened her. Sometimes it was a bad woman who hindered the journey, or when they got to the end they found not a good woman but a bad one.

(1929, WMK I, p. 203)

Klein's interpretation is again striking here: 'In this game the libidinal gratification is positive and sadism does not play so prominent a part' (p. 203). The fact that Rita does not in fact attain a good object here seems not to be considered.

In 1932 Klein mentions two further examples: first, of Rita putting a triangular brick on one side and saying that it was a little woman:

She then took a 'little hammer', as she called another long-shaped brick, and hit the brick-box with it exactly in a place where it was only stuck together with paper, so that she made a hole in it. She said 'When the hammer hit hard, the little woman was *so* frightened'.

(1932, WMK II, p. 32)[6]

In addition to this, in 1932 we learn about Rita's obsessional neurotic games with the doll that consisted mainly in cleaning it and changing its clothes: 'Her own acute fear of being dirty or destroyed inside or wicked urged her to keep on cleaning her doll – who represented her own person – and changing its clothes' (WMK II, p. 109).

In 1945, she published some further important material from the treatment:

She scribbled on a piece of paper and blackened it with great vigour. Then she tore it up and threw the scraps into a glass of water which she put to her mouth as if to drink from it. At that moment she stopped and said under her breath: 'Dead woman'. This material, with the same words, was repeated on another occasion.

(1945, WMK I, p. 404)

Klein interprets the material as follows:

The piece of paper blackened, torn up and thrown into the water represented her mother destroyed by oral, anal and urethral means, and this picture of a dead mother related not only to the external mother when she was out of sight but also to the *internal* mother. Rita had to give up the rivalry with her mother in the Oedipus situation because her unconscious fear of loss of the internal and external object acted as a barrier to every desire which would increase her hatred of her mother and therefore cause her mother's death. These anxieties, derived from the oral position, underlay the marked depression which Rita developed at her mother's attempt to wean her of the last bottle . . . Her analysis revealed that the weaning represented a cruel punishment for her aggressive desires and death wishes against her mother.

(1945, WMK I, p. 404)

6 This scene appears in the treatment notes for 9 and 10 April on p. 6 and, in more detail, on p. 8.

It is interesting to note that it is only with Klein's increasing distance from the treatment that sequences are published that have contact with destroyed objects as their central theme. There is also an episode from beyond the treatment that was published only in 1945 and fits in with this pattern:

> At the beginning of her third year, Rita was out for a walk with her mother and saw a cabman beating his horses cruelly. Her mother was extremely indignant, and the little girl also expressed strong indignation. Later on in the day she surprised her mother by saying: 'When are we going out again to see the bad man beating the horses?'
>
> (WMK I, pp. 400f.)

Klein interprets this as follows:

> In her unconscious the cabman represented her father and the horses her mother, and her father was carrying out in sexual intercourse the child's sadistic phantasies directed against her mother ... Rita could neither identify herself with such a destroyed mother, nor allow herself to play in the homosexual position the rôle of the father.
>
> (WMK I, p. 401)

My hypothesis on the basis of the published material would therefore be that the transference–countertransference dynamics were in one sense determined by the melancholic mode and that Klein perhaps had difficulties in dealing with this. The negative transference might thus have borne the strong imprint of a dead object.

If we now return to the first publication on Rita in 1926 to consider aspects that may be relevant in the light of this, we find the following points: in her second year, Rita had shown 'a striking preference for her father' (1926, WMK I, p. 130). It is clear from the context that Klein understands this in connection with the early manifestation of Oedipal strivings without actually examining this 'striking' change from mother to father in any detail. Shortly afterwards, she describes Rita's 'very pronounced father-identification' (WMK I, p. 130); later on, she describes the hindering, disciplinary role of the introjected father, which is represented in play by the elephant – here Klein seems to have the classical Oedipal configuration in mind and she does not

113

explore the nature of the father identification any further. She also clearly categorises the incident that she presents as an example of Rita's hypersensitivity to reproach in the same way: 'For instance, she burst into tears when her father playfully threatened a bear in a picture-book. Here, what determined her identification with the bear was her fear of blame from her *real* father' (WMK I, p. 132).[7]

It is worth examining – with reference to the treatment notes – how far the scene with the father's playful reproach that is so vividly described, and Rita's inability to play the mother's role that is mentioned in this connection, contained allusions to the transference. Klein makes clear her belief that Rita fears both her parents because of her jealous and envious attacks on them, and it is not clear to what extent Klein felt that Rita's episodes of negative transference were an explicit expression of similar phantasies about Klein. Nor does Klein indicate what she herself felt about Rita during the treatment, whether, for example, she felt pushed into being more critical or more reassuring than a 'neutral' stance would prescribe.

4.2 Rita in the unpublished manuscripts

I shall now go on to consider the unpublished manuscripts. We do not know whether Klein had already reported on this analysis in December 1924[8] – she must have talked about Rita with Abraham at least towards the end of the treatment (cf. Letter to Freud of 7 October 1923) – but we know from Alix Strachey (Meisel and Kendrick, 1986, p. 325) that Rita was one of the subjects of her lecture to the Berlin Society on 17 December 1924, in which she cited Rita's case to show how the Oedipus complex in terms of a clear object choice could occur at a very early age. A manuscript for this could not be found in the archived material at the Wellcome

---

7 Compare treatment notes p. 3, p. 10. There are observations on this in the treatment notes from the beginning of April 1923. Here Klein comments, for example, on the striking way in which Rita 'for 16–18 months has been tyrannical in' insisting on her father repeatedly reading books with her.

8 There are differing draft versions of an 'educational course' in which there are various references to Rita. A date for these is nowhere indicated. As Erna is not yet mentioned, they could have taken place at the end of 1923 but also during 1924. Grosskurth (1986, p. 119) works from the premise that there were two public courses in child analysis, the one in 1923 (mentioned by Abraham) and another in 1924.

Library for the History of Medicine. If we follow Alix Strachey's outline, it is worth mentioning in relation to technique that Klein was still arguing at this stage that children did not suffer in the same way as adults because they adhered predominantly to the pleasure principle, which meant that the analyst had to offer a much greater incentive for pleasure.

However, there is a manuscript of Klein's supplementary paper to Karen Horney's lecture of 31 October 1925, in which she states that in the analysis of the 2¾-year-old Rita she discovered the same infantile sexual development that Horney found in the analysis of adult women. However, Klein does not discuss Rita's case material at any greater length in this context.

However, there is valuable material from Rita's case in three of the six London lectures in 1925 – these already contain all the essential scenes with Rita that appeared in the publications up to 1932 inclusive. The first unpublished lecture – 'The psychological principles of early analysis' – which is the earliest detailed document on the subject of Rita – is quoted next.

The young Rita had shown clear signs of heterosexual object choice at the age of 15 months: having, as is usually the case, preferred her mother until the beginning of her second year, she then directed more love to her father, wanting for example to be alone with him in his room and sit on his lap while leafing through books with him.[9] However, at the age of 18 months this love for her father diminished again and the love for her mother came back to the fore. This developed into an excessive fixation on the mother. However, at the same time she started to experience night terrors and fears of various animals. When she was about two years old, the little girl became much more intractable and deeply ambivalent, especially towards the mother, and she progressively became so difficult to manage that she was brought for analysis at the age of 2¾ years. At this time, there was also a complete inhibition of playing that had already lasted several months and a marked incapacity to tolerate deprivations, as well as the over-sensitivity to pain mentioned above with all its consequences, and these difficulties in managing her appeared to result from unsuccessful working

9 Here, as in the corresponding place (1926, p. 130), the tyrannical element that was mentioned in the treatment notes on p. 3 (fn. 7) is absent.

over of conflicts originating from the Oedipus complex. As so frequently, experiences had contributed to this development in her case: Rita had shared her parents' bedroom until she was almost two years old, and the effect of the coital observations that this had entailed became entirely clear in the analysis. However, it was the birth of her younger brother that had triggered the actual onset of neurosis. The difficulties that came to light soon afterwards and then constantly increased – as could be confirmed by the information from the parents – had first appeared shortly after the birth. However, this was only a further intensification of the conflicts originating from the already active Oedipus complex. There was undoubtedly a close connection between these early effects of the Oedipus complex and the neurosis; whether this is because it is neurotic children in whom the Oedipus complex sets in so early or because the children become neurotic as a result of this is difficult to determine. However, it is certainly the case that experiences such as observations of coitus and birth of siblings have a trigger effect on the neurosis, precisely because they intensify the conflicts that originate from the Oedipus complex.

What we encounter, however, with these neurotic children in particular as a cause of the above-mentioned manifestations such as the early inhibition of play, over-sensitivity to pain, anxiety, a very limited capacity to tolerate deprivations and so on, all of which can be termed entirely typical, is a very strong sense of guilt. I should now like to discuss this sense of guilt in more detail and give some examples.

With the 2¾-year-old Rita, something that the non-analytically educated father had observed was the strong sense of guilt, the remorse that followed any slight misdemeanour and the hyper-sensitivity towards her father. For example, the child burst into tears when her father jokingly threatened the bear in the picture-book. If this indicated fear of blame from the *real* father as an influence (in her clear identification with the bear), I was also able to recognise another effect that her sense of guilt was already having. Her inhibition in playing, for example, was strongly determined in part by a sense of guilt. The mother reported, for instance, that even at the age of 2½ years the child, when asked while playing with her doll, 'Are you Mummy?', would first confirm this and then react with extreme fear and withdraw this statement. This occurred repeatedly. The analysis provided the explanation for this and some other

116

strange aspects of the child's behaviour. She would incessantly play 'mother and child' internally and she swung constantly between these two identifications; in this game, however, she was, above all towards herself, an excessively strict and cruel mother, in a way that the real mother had never been.

In this role play there transpired with me a mechanism that I also encountered with the other children. For example, Rita would be a strict mother and I would be a naughty child. She would reproach me with all manner of things; for example, she came up to me with a brush explaining that my hair was untidy, suddenly asked if I had touched my bottom and then hit my hand. Afterwards she would react with anger and show a reluctance to play. This reaction, however, would appear repeatedly when the child had played the strict mother or strict teacher. The child was actually playing two roles here; similarly the role that she had assigned to me was a dual one – I was simultaneously the excessively strict mother and the child who suffered from this strictness.

One of Rita's compulsive symptoms that had developed from the age of about two years onwards was her sleep-ceremonial: she would draw her mother back for an endlessly long time, repeatedly call her back to the bed and insist on being tucked up in a particular way. The bedclothes had to be folded in on all sides so that the child was tightly tucked in. One of the multiple determinants of this symptom was the fear that a mouse, which she sometimes called a 'Butzen', would come in through the window and bite off her 'Butzen'. The equation of the mouse with her 'Butzen' clearly indicates her fear of castration. But her doll also had to be tightly tucked in, which took considerable time, and then when something turned out to be not quite right with the bedclothes, she would have to repeat the procedure, often even several times over. On one occasion, she put the elephant, which as we saw clearly shortly before was the father-imago, often also the mother-imago, alongside the tightly tucked-in doll. Rita then told the elephant to make sure that the child did not get up and when I asked about this told me that otherwise the doll would get up and steal very quietly into the parents' bedroom and do some harm there or take something away. In a journey-game that she played for a week and that occupied an entire section of her analysis, Rita – naturally in her imagination – would often climb into the car with the driver and then move him away and drive alone. She would repeatedly tell me, however, that now the driver was standing in the corner and wanted to do something. She also repeatedly played the role of the driver – of the father – herself and, as I explained earlier, her reactions there, as in the mother game, demonstrated that she simultaneously represented the child (and felt the suffering that she herself inflicted on it in the most painful way).

(Manuscript, pp. 5ff.)

While these passages were used extensively in the first chapter of *The Psycho-Analysis of Children* in 1932 (WMK II), the divergences from Chapter 1 of WMK II are interesting to note. First, the example of a direct interaction between Klein and Rita (with Klein as the naughty child touching her bottom) was never subsequently republished. Second, we find a more precise description of the inability to play mother: the denial occurs only following an initial affirmation. Third, the elephant is understood here both as father- and as mother-imago. Fourth, there is no destination for the journey-game; the good woman seems to have disappeared completely (cf. journey-game in Section 4.1). Fifth, the compulsive cleaning and dressing and undressing of the doll is not included here. This suggests that the interaction may have been partly determined by confusions – in the first example, between bottom and breast – so that all sight of the good object had temporarily been lost and the dynamics were characterised by aggressive phantasies of dirtying, denigration and destruction in a way that was difficult to understand immediately. It is conceivable that Rita's inability to play the role of mother stemmed from fear of being exposed to the murderous attacks that she carried out in phantasy towards the mother – the corresponding enactment in the treatment was probably unlikely, however, to have been perceived in this way. Also, the short duration of the treatment certainly did not allow Klein many opportunities for a full perception of Rita's enactment of her object relations in the transference situation.

In the second of the unpublished 1925 lectures – 'The technique of early analysis' – the passage on Rita's negative transference quoted above from *The Psycho-Analysis of Children* (1932, WMK II) appears almost verbatim. Furthermore, Klein refers to Rita several times again here in order to explain her method of interpretation:

Rita (aged two years and nine months) told me that the dolls had disturbed her in her sleep: they kept on saying to Hans, the underground train man (a male doll on wheels): 'Just go on driving your train up and down.' On another occasion, she put a triangular brick on one side and said: 'That's a little woman'; she then took a 'little hammer', as she called another long-shaped brick, and hit the brick-box with it just where it was only stuck together with paper, so that she made a hole in it. She said: 'When the hammer hit hard, the little woman was *so* frightened.' The male doll, running the underground train and hitting with the hammer, represented the coitus between her parents that she had witnessed till she was nearly two years old. My explanation, 'Your Daddy hit hard like that inside your Mummy with his little hammer', was for her entirely plausible.

(Manuscript, p. 26)

In 1932 Klein changed only the last sentence of this passage: 'My interpretation, "Your Daddy hit hard like that inside your Mummy with his little hammer, and you were so frightened", fitted in exactly with her way of speaking and thinking' (WMK II, p. 32).

In the sixth unpublished lecture of 1925 – 'Indications for treatment and termination of treatment' – she gives the example of Rita to show how changes in phantasies can appear in play. Klein states that at the end of Rita's analysis, the following scene took place with the 3¾-year-old Rita:[10]

She was holding her bear in her arms, which she had so often given me cause to recognise during the months of games she had played as the longed-for penis. While hugging and kissing him, and talking to him in a loving and motherly way, she said: 'Now I'm not sad any more' – having suffered from depression – 'because after all I've got such a lovely little child'. She had become able to renounce the penis, for which the child was to be a substitute, and this also found external expression in the child's parental relationships. Having turned definitely away from her father, she nevertheless at the end of the analysis, along with an unusual and

---

10 I presume that the age given here contains a typographical error, since Rita's age at the beginning of the analysis is always given as 2¾ years and the eighty-three treatment sessions reported in 1932 occur according to the Melanie Klein Archive documents in the period from March to October 1923, so Rita must have been 3¼ years old at the end of the treatment.

undoubtedly deeply ambivalent fixation on her mother, had a steady and unexaggerated tender relationship with her, while still definitely preferring her father, just as she had last done at the age of 15 months.

(Manuscript, pp. 18f.)

In 1945, Klein goes back to Rita's words here and substantiates them in the same terms although in more detail (WMK I, p. 406). She included this material in a slightly different context in 1932 (WMK II, p. 109).

In these lectures, which preceded all the publications on Rita, fundamental aspects of the dynamics are clearly identified. Along with the libidinal Oedipal impulses, the negative transference and also the depression are mentioned; the nature of this depression, however, was evidently difficult to grasp and remained to be explored.

4.3 Rita in the treatment notes

Let us now turn briefly to the material concerning the dates: from the pocket diary and the treatment notes, the dates of the eighty-three treatment sessions as reported by Klein in 1932 can be reconstructed. The records she made from memory from 6 March to 1 April 1923 are contained in a small notepad (pp. 1A–6A); the subsequent sessions until 12 May 1923 inclusive are in treatment book I (pp. 1–52). On individual sheets of paper, there are notes on sessions from June and July 1923. The second treatment book contains the records from 22 August to 21 September 1923 (pp. 1a–73a); from 22 September to 6 October there are no remaining records. Whereas before the summer holidays of 1923, Klein mainly gave sessions three times a week – generally Tuesday, Thursday and Saturday – after that period the setting is sometimes one of five to six hours a week. It is clear from the treatment notes that, as we already know from the 1955 publication, Rita's treatment took place at her home, since Rita made use of the whole house with its immediate surroundings in her treatment, as well as her own room in which it was probably intended to take place.

4.3.1

The first obvious point of comparison is between the published version of the first treatment session and the version in the treatment notes. This shows that the material quoted in 1955 does not relate to the actual first session but probably to the ninth treatment session, which is recorded in the first two pages of treatment book I. (The preceding sessions were recorded in a small notepad – the possible origin of Klein's error decades after the treatment may thus have to do with that fact, although the notes clearly demonstrate that there were previous sessions with Rita. By examining the actual first session in Section 4.3.2 of my present book, we may find some indications as to how this 'displacement' might be understood.) However, this ninth session certainly contains the first mention of Rita leaving the room, which is why it will now be examined more closely. It is the second session after a break – '*Had missed two weeks at Easter because of illness*' (p. 2). On this first session following her return after Easter, Klein noted:

R.[3]not asked after me at
all – tender contact with mother
soon back to contradiction & negative {this is the mother's
    information}.
Not very pleased to see me, but comes over.
Playing – but feel definite resistance.
Also asks me, if {Klein} soon must go.
Wants to go for a walk with mother.

Klein's consternation is almost palpable here – she is exposed to what Rita herself has suffered in the previous two weeks, when her analyst had shown by her absence that she preferred someone else. For the next day, 4 April, we find:

4/IV. We play – she plays as recently
with dolls etc. – but not a word about poo,
little stick etc. [sth. crossed out].
Changes game from one moment to next,
strong resistance. Suddenly explains
is going over to sand, little girls, I
tell her story, 'Fritz and the raisins',

she listens reluctantly, explains
emphatically she is going over to sand – I go with her & doll's pram
with doll inside – (at first also
played with bear again – more recent [sessions][1] no
longer) going for a walk.

Rita seems to be at pains here not to attack Klein, not to denigrate her by 'poo-thing' and not to deprive her by avoiding the phantasised appropriation of the penis (little stick). We could reconstruct the transference events by surmising that the rapid changes of game actually fulfilled the impulse of depriving Klein of the possibility of understanding something. Rita believes that she can ward off the revenge she fears from Klein only by leaving the room.

Klein's first intervention is to tell her a story, 'Fritz and the raisins'. What are we to make of this intervention? It could be understood as a counter-enactment. Klein is being feared as a persecutory, bad object and is now presenting herself instead as a good object ('raisins'), which does not actually have the desired effect: '*she listens reluctantly, explains /emphatically she is going over to sand*'.

If Rita's initial play can at first be understood either as an attack on Klein for having left her, or perhaps also as an expression of her wish to protect Klein from her attacks, and thus from becoming ill again and persecuting her with her absence, Klein had perhaps intuitively registered this wish and accordingly presented herself as a good, friendly object. This, however, is tantamount to a denial of Klein's illness, and it seems to heighten Rita's anxiety, because Rita might unconsciously have experienced this as a confirmation that Klein could not accept and withstand her attacks, so that Rita therefore may well have become even more concerned about attacking Klein and being attacked by her. Rita therefore had to leave the room, an expression of her feelings of claustrophobia at being confined with Klein.

The infantile self is imprisoned in the doll's pram as a kind of pleading for greater security, because it cannot become dangerous there. But soon Rita phantasises herself, together with her brother, in the parental position:

Says about doll's pram
doll inside – later would like a
cart with a small horse in which she &
Peter can then ride. Then

122

immediately tramples on stones as if would
like to crush them – says once saw
car that crushed stones.

Here a persecutory object immediately seems to arrive on the
scene; Rita would like quite literally to destroy it in the form of
trampling on the stones. It may well be that Rita wanted to crush her
own intolerable blocks of emotion inside. The 'stones' perhaps indicate that she experiences the uncomprehending object as dead. Klein
interprets:

Cart – car = member – her foot should
    do the same, would like to have {that is, Klein interpreted that
Rita wanted to crush the stones with her feet, as the car had done,
and that her foot was like a penis}.

At this interpretation that Rita also wants to have a member with
which she can crush big stones, Rita seems to feel sufficiently understood to be able to communicate directly with Klein again. Now she
fills Klein's pockets with stones. Her analyst, however, seems to raise an
objection to this – instead of interpreting it – so that Rita has to find a
new way: laughing, she now throws the stones into the drain and
expresses her disapproval of her own behaviour by claiming that a man
passing by said, 'well, well', which was what her father had said when
threatening the bear. Klein is unable to understand this as a commentary on her objection; instead, she reinforces the split between herself
and the man by suggesting that it is the father who forbids.

Interpret father who does not want
to allow sticking member in Mummy,
more resistance: 'no, no!' – Has
me lift her up & show 1 pit {sandpit}.
Had allowed me to hold
her away like this from little girls
sandpit. Goes [? sth. overwritten] home with me &
is certainly in a more positive
state of mind.

Following on from this episode, both are able to turn their interest
to a sandpit, which means that Rita can now go back home with

Klein because she has indirectly registered that Klein wants to deal with these dead, destroyed things (the stones) and because Klein has communicated with her first interpretation outside the house that she knows how desperately Rita is seeking a possible way to tolerate a disagreeable burden, in this case Klein's having been ill and absent and then coming back. It is an interesting exchange, but not the same as the one described by Klein in 1955.

It seems obvious that the time gap between the treatment in 1923 and the paper on the play technique in 1955 led Klein to consider anxiety as the most important dynamic element, and its description in words was intended to defuse the situation. It is clear, however, from these treatment notes that this was in reality a difficult process. Only in retrospect was Klein able to identify this clear dynamic. If then on these first two pages of the treatment book there is manifestly no discussion of anxiety, it seems likely – not least because of the corresponding description of 1955 – that anxiety was actually playing a major role. Through what we would perhaps now regard as projective identification, Klein became the one who was anxious, did not want to be rejected and still had to deal with the slight insult that she had received from Rita on the previous day. Klein seems to have sensed this partly as apprehension about the mother and aunt triumphing over a failing analyst. The external setting – the set-up of the analysis at the child's home – led to the requisite triumphant persecutor being located outside the dynamics of the transference–countertransference. Rita's anxiety thus disappeared at first from Klein's field of vision.

Insofar as the psychic setting requires support from the material setting, Rita's analysis contained a serious handicap through its lack of an adequate setting. The recourse to splitting seems inevitable in this context and plays a major role in the period to follow. In the next session on 6 April, Rita falls back on Klein's storytelling offer. She wants Klein to tell her more about 'Fritz and the raisins', while Rita herself describes the teddy bears, the winter and Father Christmas as bad and biting. In this context, the 'anxiety object' (p. 4) status of these is entirely obvious to Klein.

In her general description of Rita's negative transference, Klein had mentioned that Rita repeatedly wanted to leave the room. This is also the case in the treatment notes. The next example will again therefore be examined in detail. The previous session of 10/IV in the notes again ends with Rita indicating that she does not want to hear any more about the bad bear.

12/IV. Very friendly. Wants
to go into garden with me, because chicks
are there immediately refrains when I call her
into room. Looks through my bag & says about
my key: there is the blue key.
Sees matches & sits down, smokes
using my key as a cigar
first one end in mouth, then the other.

Here too, instead of interpreting Rita's anxiety about Klein herself, she makes a form of counter-offer – the handbag – presenting herself as a good and generous object. Although in one sense Klein is acting out a seduction – which Rita again goes on to connect with 'raisins' – this action is equally understandable – for Rita, in contrast to the session just quoted, is responsive to this offer – as the best available solution, given that she did not have an actual treatment room that could have taken on the appropriate function of an 'analytic space'.

Further on in the Thursday session we again find some parallels with the session of 4 April: '*Makes me build a little watch-house, then immediately knocks it down*'. Again, this concerns Rita's wish to protect the object and to know that it is being watched over, at which point the opposite impulse is rapidly expressed – she knocks the house down. She denies this bad part of her self – '*Go away, bear*'. She is now afraid of the bad breast that is supposedly harming her – '*Always pouring moo from tails – makes her – Rita so tired*'.

However, she puts stones in Klein's lap – it seems that she would like to get the 'dead' stones back as alive. When Klein does not interpret it in this way, Rita goes to fetch water from outside, then forces Klein to be the one in need – '*entreats me to drink*' (p. 12).

'*Then suddenly asks if I must go already (always a sign of resistance)*' (p. 12) – this somewhat milder form of negative transference, which puts Klein under less pressure than when Rita herself wants to run out of the room, is something that Klein is able to interpret to her as such:

Then interpret does
not like me now because I am Mummy
who does not give ~~enough~~ stool & milk. –
She suddenly wants a
glass of warm milk to drink & runs

125

down to ask for it & drinks it. (Mother
reports: still drinking from small bottle.)

Klein interprets that Rita is now rejecting Klein because she has not
received enough milk/understanding. Rita can consequently acknow-
ledge some separateness in action – she goes to her mother and instead
of still demanding a small bottle she now wants a *glass* of milk.

Klein did not initially succeed, then, in using an interpretation of
negative transference to prevent Rita from leaving the room. Here, as
in many further examples in the course of the treatment, she allowed
Rita to explore her handbag,[11] as in the comparable situations in
which Rita was very reluctant to enter the room with her at first
(cf. e.g. pp. 27, 39, 43). However, when presented with the somewhat
milder form of Rita's question as to whether Klein must go already,
which runs like a silver thread through the first part of the treatment,
Klein repeatedly succeeds in interpreting the negative transference.
There is a further example of this: Rita looks for a large triangular brick, puts it down and says that it is a big woman; she talks
incomprehensibly and laughs a lot at this (pp. 17f.). Suddenly Rita
again asks whether Klein must go already.

> I (as
> always when perceive resistance immediately
> resolve it through interpretation.) – say tall
> woman who talks like that is Mummy she
> angry with Mummy because she talked
> so incomprehensibly & [Mummy][1] laughed
> at her. She ~~says~~ Hans with the
> underground train also talks like that (but
> while making another sound
> from lutes.

Here Klein interprets what is certainly an important element, but
without perceiving the immediate affect, namely Rita's fear when she
makes fun of Klein.

There are many further examples that will not be discussed here.
But in order to show how Klein is clearly able to perceive Rita's

---

11 Klein later interpreted looking through a handbag as exploration of the mother's womb.
With Rita, Klein does not interpret Rita's handbag explorations in this way.

anxiety at the end of this treatment, let us turn to a further passage
from the final session recorded:

> Bakes new cake, but may
> only eat my own [piece].[1] – Immediately afterwards
> fierce resistance again, runs away, –
> but comes back, to get me
> to put long socks on her for garden.
> When I interpret fear mother from whom
> she has stolen sth. member hammer
> eaten whole mother – trusting
> again {after this interpretation}.

Also interesting in this context is that the comparison of publications and treatment notes reveals that sequences that appear as a game
in the publications were also acted out completely literally by Rita in
the treatment. Rita not only cleaned and dressed and undressed dolls
but also she constantly and repeatedly changed her own clothes in the
treatment sessions, as is described in the greatest detail in the period
after the summer holidays. Another point is that the journey-games
were carried out very much with Melanie Klein's involvement, in
particular when Klein as Rita was repeatedly allowed to return home.
Klein describes very vividly how resolutely Rita would play mother,
so that when changing her clothes, she:

> accepts no help. Says: 'Can't your Mummy
> do it well?' – I: 'Yes, you are like clever Mummy'.
> She: 'I am not a clever Mummy though – am a
> big Mummy'. I: 'Yes, an old' – She: 'no, not
> an old Mummy, a new one, but a big one'.

There are repeated descriptions of how difficult Rita finds it to
choose clothes, how anxious she is about it, how quickly she feels she
has got dirty, how angry she is when she has to turn to Klein for help,
and how she repeatedly forbids Klein to talk; it therefore seems
incomprehensible at first sight that Klein has not presented these vivid
passages as examples of negative transference in her publications as
well.

In the journey-games one reason that our young patient gives as
to why Klein must stay at home as Rita is that Klein is 'too stupid'

(p. 17a). It is conceivable that it might not have been possible for Klein to consider this projection of Rita's adequately in the setting that has already been described and that Klein often found herself in the position of feeling like the 'too stupid' analyst in relation to the parents.

In addition to the symptoms identified in the publications, the treatment notes show that Rita was afraid of bees (see Section 4.3.2) and also mention her 'phobia and violent screaming when her hair was washed' (p. 7). Klein interprets the latter in connection with Rita's castration anxiety (p. 33a). Rita's wish for her feeling of being 'injured in the head' to be examined could not be addressed here because she ran into a 'wall'/the parental couple in her explorations:

11/IX. Says is going to a tower.
Then: going to visit me, tower is
at my house. – Undresses doll, must
change her clothes – showing me a small
injury to arm, then to foot, –
(when interpret damage little hammer) a
small hole hidden under hair – that
she got when she ran into wall.
(Interpret head little hammer, – washing hair
– her anxiety coitus castration complex.)

4.3.2

To examine the first sessions that contain Rita's earliest play phantasies, we shall now refer to the earliest notes on Rita, in order to examine what light the condensed dynamics in these early notes can shed on why the negative transference was often difficult to address in this case.

The very first session of 6 March 1923 gives the impression that it is actually only fragments that are described:

R.[3]-6.III. Bone Huckebein
Twice 'poo' I
to climb chair

Even an approximate reconstruction of a possible course of the session at the manifest level cannot be made on the basis of this note.

It may perhaps be interpreted as an expression of Klein's state of mind; being confronted with an entirely new situation, she probably did not actually understand very much at first. In dealing with this document, it is to speculations about Klein's possible countertransference that we are directed in seeking the first beginnings of an understanding. While 'bone' already suggests the idea of a dead object, in conjunction with *Huckebein*, the unlucky raven in the story by Wilhelm Busch,[12] it can perhaps be understood as expressing Rita's fear of being captured by Klein as Huckebein was captured in the story and in such a way that Rita will ultimately find herself being destroyed because of her own impulses, just as the raven Huckebein was. The second line 'aah' could thus also be interpreted to refer to a sense of elimination and annihilation – Rita is getting rid of something or someone.

The second session is somewhat clearer; it is a relief to find human objects appearing, even in the first play phantasy:

Daddy duck, Mummy {teddy} bear – she
    is bears' Mummy then retracts [that]^1 [she Rita^2]^1
    (mother says: she Mummy, plays – [then]^1 immediately no)

The play inhibition is presented to us in detail here and as it was described in 1925 by the mother in the anamnesis: Rita first affirmed that she was the mother, then withdrew this statement in fear – this movement was omitted from all the publications. It now appears directly in the interaction with Klein. What is her reaction to this?

~~9/III.~~ I say doll child, – she
Mummy – she: no. – I threaten Suse {the doll}
she anxious: is good again
~~9/III. Peter shouts laughs~~
should not do this –

12 Wilhelm Busch was a nineteenth-century author who wrote illustrated stories for children in the form of rhyming couplets. In the story of Huckebein the raven, Huckebein is captured by the boy Fritz and taken home to Fritz's aunt. After much naughty behaviour, Huckebein tries to unravel the aunt's knitting and hangs himself in the process. The aunt says, 'Evil was his main delight; that's why he is hanging here'. Although so young, Rita knew not only the story of Huckebein but also other stories by Busch: 'Der Schnuller' (The dummy or comforter) and 'Der Affe und der Schusterjunge' (The monkey and the cobbler boy).

I call {her} scallywag – she is pleased.
– [Doll]¹ naked, goes away – hides
naughty – has her hide.

Klein does not take this to be latent negative transference as such,[13] but her crossings out and wish to move on to the next session perhaps testify to some irritation. Instead of interpreting Rita's anxiety when Klein threatens the doll, Klein is once again playful and, perhaps acting as Rita's superego, calls her a rascal. This situation recalls the one described in the anamnesis with the father's playful reproach towards the bear in the picture-book, which frightened Rita, as Klein's playful teasing does here. If the fear of a murderous attack by the mother is fundamental in Rita's world, her unease can only increase when this is not understood.

It seems likely that Rita is now both the attacking child and the punishing mother.[14] Klein's supposedly playful threatening of the doll maintains Rita's anxiety and depressive tendencies. The attendant superego that wants to see the naughty raven *Huckebein* hang, albeit in a moderated form, is acted out by Klein when she calls Rita a rascal.

The oral theme that is already discernible in the second session comes entirely to the fore in the third recorded session:

12. Ask [her]¹ where [(toy)]¹ dachshund, she eaten
it up = stomach = then immediately
no, does not [taste]¹ nice – then is out of
stomach like water [spit, mouthfuls]¹ drunk
then out of back – sticks for him
to build house. – [Busch:]¹ monkey hat is

I translate and expand this as follows: Klein asks Rita, 'Where is the dachshund in the game?' Rita answers that she has eaten him up, meaning that it is in her stomach. Then quickly she says, 'No, that is not nice'. She goes on explaining that it is out of the stomach again – the way you spit out saliva; then (it seems) she claims that it went

13 As was discussed in the previous section, this was comprehensible to Klein at that time only in its manifest form.
14 (Interpret her original ~~clock~~ crime [*Uhrverbrechen*] – she = / *doll, also mother.*) Here Klein has the situation clearly in view. Rita is both child and mother.

out of her back. 'Monkey hat' is a reference to another story by Busch in which a monkey, Fipps, put ink in a professor's hat.

The unlucky raven *Huckebein*, whose final act of ripping up the aunt's knitting results in his hanging, proves to be the striking condensation of a fundamental dynamic that is characterised by a biting 'ego-destructive superego'. The raven is probably also an image of Klein's uneasiness about always being observed by Rita's mother.

> Dummy bee [asks][1] – I [mention][1]
>   fear of bees earlier she [held][1] piece of
>   paper = bee – no, no. – I am sting.
>   Interpret stick [bee (?) should give to Aunt Emma][1] – confirms
>   Peter member

Klein now picks up fear; characteristically, it is a persecutory fear of Rita's that she registers, a fear of bees; Klein nevertheless reinterprets the sting as libidinal, something with which we are already familiar from Grete's case. Klein is perhaps thinking back to classical penis envy and thus overlooks the 'biting penis' that can probably be interpreted as interchangeable with the biting breast, as a bad part object.

The central role played by this fear in the dynamics is underlined by the fact that the first dream recorded is an anxiety dream Rita had when she was 18 months old: 'Bee, cheek stung, crying stick make opening' (p. 2A).

4.3.3

In the light of this, it is interesting to go back now to the material relating to the 'dead woman' in the treatment notes, which found its way to publication so late (1945). The situation described there, in which Rita blackened paper, tore it up, put it in a glass of water and began to drink it, murmuring 'dead woman', is not found as such in the treatment notes. In the treatment notes, the corresponding material appears only towards the end of the treatment, for the first time on 6 September:

> 6/IX. Very friendly
> again. Goes to Dodenstrasse
> to a Frau Dode. Then 'Frau tote [dead]'.

131

When I ask is that dead woman – she:
Yes she is dead – but she is not
yet buried. ~~Takes~~ Makes as if
to take shovel and spade
now I am burying you. A bit
later asks me if I am unwell
(mother had greeted me with this question
because looked bad)
Had said about Frau Dode = extremely
nice, has only 1 girl – (child)
cooks for herself. (Interpret death wishes
me, mother). Immediately afterwards wants
to urinate. Shows me underwear dirty
– (~~wet~~ rather mucky from stool)

It is evident that Rita is very disturbed by a possible indication that Klein is ill, reacting to it in a way that seems manic: initially she almost transfers Klein into a dead state, the finality of which (burial) rests with Rita herself.

It is already clear from the beginning how disturbed Rita is by the possibility of Klein being ill; whereas in the sessions immediately following Klein's absence through illness and Easter (see Section 4.3.1) she could only act out her fear, a few days later she found it possible to enquire about it (p. 5). '*First asks (never since illness) if I am ill. She was ill, had a cold*'. Because she can immediately counter it with her own illness, the guilt feelings seem to be sufficiently abated for her to be able to address this explosive theme. She is subsequently concerned in various ways with ill, damaged self-objects that must be treated by Klein.

On 12 September there is more talk about Frau Dode:

12/IX. Wants to go to
Zehlendorf. She is Mummy – dog Purzel
is father – they travel together because in
Zehlend. a lovely bowl broke V
& she wants to repair it. To a Frau
Prech ([brechen] {break}!); following the name
as usual then much that completely in-
comprehensible (Prech instead of Brech {break} like Dode instead
'Tote' (of dead person)

and further displacement then this completely incomprehensible)
Afterwards talks about her too as Frau
Dode – says that she was ill is
well again now, is very nice.

After she has first expressed her wish for reparation – she wants to repair the lovely bowl that was broken – she then talks again about the ill woman Frau Dode, who then actually appears to be already repaired – she is said to be well again and very nice. A passage from the second session on 18 September, containing a unique feature of the setting, is in some respects highly reminiscent of the published passage: she washes and ties pieces of fabric and says while doing so that Frau Dode cannot cook as well as she can. The dead woman is now being cooked, cut up and eaten by her, while she drinks dirty water (cf. p. 58a). The '*Desire to cook and changing clothes*' again points to a wish for reparation and the impossibility of this.

Rita's repeated attempts to ward off psychic reality by manic states of excitation are impressively described. An example is quoted from a scene on 13 September:

Suddenly wants
to take [dress] off & be completely naked. Shows
herself to me seductively from every side.
Runs to balcony taking a
hair-slide, a manicure stick
on balcony puts it in
genitals, pressing and masturbating
at first opens genitals to
show it – shows me that
Peter has urinated on balcony &
urinates also in another
place. After masturbating
shouts over to neighbour Frau Dr G.
to come over to see, she is naked
also to seamstress in the room
is completely transformed as in
a frenzy.

There are further scenes of this kind (cf. pp. 44a ff.).

4.4 The significance of Rita's analysis

Klein is not alone in repeatedly addressing Rita's case; there are frequent references to her in the secondary literature. The night terrors and sleep-ceremonial receive some attention here: Hinshelwood (1994, p. 55) quotes the example to demonstrate how attentive Klein was to the early superego. Segal also discusses it in these terms (1979, pp. 47f.), adding that: 'Rita phantasised not only a persecuting "*Butzen*" but also a very desirable one' (p. 50). In particular, however, the negative transference is repeatedly addressed in relation to Rita's leaving the room and Klein's interpretive approach to this (Geissmann and Geissmann, 1998, p. 124f.; Pick and Segal, 1978, p. 430; Cycon, 1995, p. 35). All these authors quote this passage in the terms explicitly outlined by Pick: 'instead of trying to soothe or distract her young patient, Klein interpreted her negative transference' (Pick and Segal, 1978, p. 430). This cannot be maintained so definitely with reference to the treatment notes – Klein made precisely these attempts (telling stories, offering her handbag and so on); she could not help but make them. I believe that the need to understand the negative components of the transference better and thus be able to interpret it was an important development in this treatment. Klein certainly managed repeatedly to interpret parts of the negative transference throughout, but at this time it was not yet possible for her – as demonstrated above – to do this in a comprehensive way.

The starting point for this should be made clear once again – Klein had until then applied adult technique to children; with the 2¾-year-old Rita this could no longer be maintained. Possibly following a suggestion by Hug-Hellmuth, she chose to use a setting that entailed treating such a young child at home, which turned out to be an impediment to the treatment. While she had already observed play ideas with her son, with Rita she was drawn to a method that was suitable for children; games and especially play-acting or 'enactment', instead of verbal associations alone, represented the main possibilities of communication. Through this kind of enactment, Klein gained fundamental insights into Rita's way of thinking and feeling. Although it may have been inevitable that the assigned roles would be acted out to some extent, this is of course all the more indispensable in these early stages – the corresponding concepts that make reflection easier were not at this point available to Klein. Her conceptualisation of enactment as role play tackles important elements but does not as yet give a comprehensive understanding of unconscious acting in.

The principal benefit that Klein derived from this treatment, then, is the seriousness with which she addresses the child's modes of expression and the challenge of dealing with them analytically. The immediate benefit lay in her discovery of an early, oppressive strict superego operating in many of Rita's play phantasies – it seems likely that the active projection of such a superego formed the experiential foundation on which Klein subsequently developed this concept. Perhaps her own apprehensions about the attitude of Rita's parents may have contributed to her understanding of Rita's strict superego.

Petot is undoubtedly right to emphasise the immense significance that Rita's analysis had for Klein when he states that this analysis marked the beginning of Kleinian analysis as we know it (Petot, 1990, p. 10). Petot concludes that it seems legitimate to suppose that the four essential elements of Klein's technique – the stress on anxiety, transference interpretation, 'deep interpretation' that goes back to the Oedipus complex and the idea that aggressive impulses lie at the root of anxiety – were acquired during Rita's analysis (Petot, 1990, p. 136). On the basis of the treatment notes, however, a certain restriction of this seems necessary, particularly with regard to transference interpretation and so-called deep interpretation. Klein's conscious technique of trying to diminish and resolve resistance by interpreting it as soon as she perceived it is repeatedly recorded in the treatment notes from the outset (cf. pp. 1, 12, 18). The very first interpretation in which this concept is presented illustrates her understanding of it: she interpreted Rita's resistance in relation to Rita's original objects. On the second occasion, in which she explicates her strategy, she presents an interpretation of negative transference (see Section 4.3.1). Although a move towards transference interpretations is noted here, transference interpretations – judging from the treatment notes where, of course, she might not have recorded every instance – nevertheless remain in the minority. Even towards the end we find such interpretations only occasionally. There is only limited discussion even of 'deep interpretations' – as is clear from the examples presented. Klein certainly interprets Oedipal impulses but this is within the framework of the classical Oedipus complex. The nature of the early Oedipus complex, with its painful mixture of acute love and hate for both parents and its emphasis on part rather than whole objects, is only gradually becoming clear to Klein, and Rita's treatment gave her important evidence of it, although Klein did not at this time work out a full conceptualisation.

However, where Petot (1990, p. 118) expresses some doubt as to whether orality was clear to Klein, in particular whether Rita's oral erotism was ever interpreted (Petot, 1990, p. 119), this suggestion can be refuted on the basis of the treatment notes. He is certainly right that she did not consistently interpret oral sadism at this stage – she nevertheless recorded information relating to it:

> When 11 months old bit
> Mother so passionately on the lips
> that caused injury

Interpretations of oral erotism in fact appear repeatedly: she mentions the mother telling her how Rita played at about 2¼ years of age at being Peter and then in the tram wanted to lie on her mother's breast and suck (p. 7). She interprets an oral procreative phantasy of Rita's – that eating a chocolate dog would lead to a child coming out (p. 7). Klein mentions for instance that Rita had put in her mouth the beak of the duck that represented the father when the air was being let out of this toy (p. 46). Klein interpreted: '*Sucking Mummy's breast, now father's hammer*'. It thus already occurs to her here that this turning towards the father's penis might stem, for instance, from a wish to have an inexhaustible breast available. The list of examples can be amplified in any number of ways.

Although in terms of content the points that Klein was already conceptualising with Grete were significantly enriched in the course of Rita's analysis,[15] in my view the particular progress that Rita's analysis made possible consisted in finding adequate concepts for understanding Rita's acting out, which represented a unique form of challenge. The necessity of interpreting Rita's behaviour as quickly as

---

15 On the theme of 'Femininity', there are many points at which Klein convincingly interprets Rita's material as showing the wish to explore the maternal space, which is explicitly formulated for example on 23 April – 'interpret mother-directed curiosity'. In the second part, the fears that emerged from a sharp rivalry with the mother – cf. 'original clock crime [Uhrverbrechen]', 11 September – come increasingly to the fore: fears concerning a genital that has been made dirty (2 September), broken (3 September), damaged (7 September).

possible was one of the direct insights that Klein gained from Rita's main form of negative transference – leaving the room. The experiences of being helplessly exposed to this at first formed a lasting incentive for becoming able to understand the situation better and accordingly being able to interpret it more completely.

5

The beginning of the play technique
Inge and, perhaps, Ernst?

5.1 Inge in Klein's published works

Whereas with Grete and Rita treatment had been sought because of specific existing symptoms, what is striking with Inge is that, while her case was described by Klein as a 'prophylactic' analysis (1932, WMK II, p. 61, fn. 1), in fact of the three children under discussion here, Inge received by far the longest course of treatment, consisting of 375 treatment sessions (WMK II, p. 61, fn. 1). This figure can be fairly accurately reconstructed from the corresponding diary entries for 1923–1926. Now Klein at this point had already argued on various occasions for the notion that all children should if possible undergo analysis in order to improve their developmental prospects. For example, she refers in 'Early analysis' to 'the necessity of analysis in early childhood as a help to all education' (1923b, WMK I, p. 105). She returned repeatedly to this idea in subsequent years, writing for example in 'The early development of conscience in the child' (1933) about a utopian situation in which child analysis – like school attendance – would form a regular component of our education:

> Then perhaps, that hostile attitude, springing from fear and suspicion, which is latent more or less strongly in each human being, and which intensifies a hundredfold in him every impulse of destruction, will give way to kindlier and more trustful feelings towards his fellow-men, and people may inhabit the world together in greater peace and good-will than they do now.
>
> (1933, WMK I, p. 257)

138

It is therefore no surprise that this aspiration should have been reflected and implemented in her endeavours.[1] What is slightly surprising is the emphasis that she places on this normality – Inge 'could be described as a normal child so far as her nature and behaviour was concerned, in spite of certain troubles whose full extent was only revealed by analysis' (1932, WMK II, p. 61). A footnote on the same page once again states that Inge 'throughout could be called a normal child' (WMK II, p. 61, fn. 1). An additional footnote in which she comments, with partial reference to Inge's analysis, on the severity that can also characterise the difficulties of the normal individual reveals an element of inconsistency in this concept of normality. She continues:

> This fact of analytic experience is borne out by observations of everyday life; for it is surprising how often people who have hitherto seemed quite normal will break down with a neurosis or commit suicide for some quite slight cause.
>
> (1932, WMK II, p. 84, fn. 1)

The phrase '*seemed* quite normal' is I think a key one here and it is a point to which we will return. Klein herself, however, continues to adhere to this characterisation of Inge as a normal child despite the significant difficulties that she describes as follows:

> Moreover, analysis first disclosed the severity of the depressions she was liable to, and it showed that behind her apparent self-confidence there was a severe sense of inferiority and a fear of failure which were responsible for her difficulties in regard to school life.
>
> (1932, WMK II, p. 61, fn. 1)

These difficulties consisted for instance of 'a severe inhibition in writing' (WMK II, p. 72, fn. 1). Finally, in the light of this it is difficult to understand why it was not initially possible to establish meaningful contact with a 'normal' child:

---

1 As a further example of a prophylactic analysis, she mentions 'a very normal and in every respect satisfactorily developed boy of four years, named Gerald' (1927b, WMK I, p. 171); the 4-year-old boy in 1927a, WMK I, pp. 157f. may well also have been Gerald. In addition, Ludwig's analysis is presented in 1932 as a case of this kind (cf. 1932, WMK II, p. 84, fn. 1).

In the case of Inge, aged seven, I was unable for several hours to find any means of approach. I kept up a conversation about her school and kindred subjects with some difficulty, and her attitude towards me was very mistrustful and reserved.

(1932, WMK II, p. 59)

It may be objected that none of this constitutes sufficient grounds for turning to Inge's case in particular here. However, there is a further important set of facts that leads me to select it. Although Inge is not mentioned by name, the 7-year-old girl to whose analysis Melanie Klein ascribes a decisive significance for the introduction of the play technique in her 1955 paper 'The psycho-analytic play technique: its history and significance' can be none other than Inge.[2] This retrospective view demonstrates the close interrelation between negative transference and the development of technique; having already indicated this in relation to the role of Rita's analysis, Klein then continues:

I made further significant observations in the psychoanalysis of a girl of seven, also in 1923. Her neurotic difficulties were apparently not serious, but her parents had for some time been concerned about her intellectual development. Although quite intelligent she did not keep up with her age group, she disliked school, and sometimes played truant. Her relation to her mother, which had been affectionate and trusting, had changed since she had started school: she had become reserved and silent. I spent a few sessions with her without achieving much contact. It had become clear that she disliked school, and from what she diffidently said about it, as well as from other remarks, I had been able to make a few interpretations which produced some material. But my impression was that I should not get much further in that way. In a session in which I again found the child unresponsive and withdrawn I left her, saying that I would return in a moment. I went into my own children's nursery, collected a few toys, cars, little figures, a few bricks, and a train, put them into a box and returned to the patient. The child, who had not taken to drawing or other activities, was interested in the small toys and at once began to play.

(1955, WMK III, p. 125)

---

2 Petot (1990, p. 122) also works from the assumption that this girl must be Inge.

This is especially interesting if we recall that there were no toys in Grete's treatment, nor in the analyses of boys at this time. Ernst had sometimes used the furnishings to play with but he had also constantly brought his own things with him ('bricks', marbles) – a subject to which we shall return in Section 5.5; Rita – because of the unusual setting at her own home – had her own toys available. With Inge, then, an essential component of the future setting for child analysis was discovered. It might be formulated that the introduction of a parameter in the context of an insufficiently understood and thus also insufficiently interpretable negative transference constituted a decisive stage in the establishment of the child analytic setting. It is thus interesting in my view to consider Inge's analysis in more detail in order to gain an idea of the psychodynamic conditions in which Klein introduced this 'toy' parameter. We shall consider both what it may have meant for this analysis and the extent to which these conditions provide further information about this technical method.

I shall start by formulating a preliminary hypothesis on the basis of the contradictory statements concerning Inge's diagnosis – a prophylactic analysis of a normal child versus a severe learning inhibition – and will then go on to examine it in more detail. The above-quoted phrase – 'seemed quite normal' – constitutes a key concept here and suggests that Inge's case might involve a pathology that we would now characterise by a term such as 'normopathy'. The thesis that this may be a specific form of 'as–if' personality disorder[3] is reinforced by Klein's contradictory statements on her view of the indications for treatment, which seem likely to have originated from her having a strange sense of hesitancy and uncertainty about Inge. Klein's descriptions are similar to Riesenberg-Malcolm's (1990, p. 388) description of how with as–if phenomena the analyst often experiences 'a curious feeling of hovering between thinking that the patient's action is voluntary or conscious or an unconscious bizarre behaviour'. With Inge, no classical neurosis would therefore have presented, which may have made it difficult for Klein to grasp the form of pathology that could be described as characterological in nature. It was only ten years after Inge's analysis that she stated that character

---

3 With her description of the 'as–if' phenomenon H. Deutsch (1942) referred to disorders in patients who give 'the inescapable impression that the individual's whole relationship to life has something about it which is lacking in genuineness and yet outwardly runs along "as if" it were complete' (Deutsch, 1942, p. 302).

analysis was no 'less important than analysis of neuroses as a therapeutic measure' (1933, WMK I, p. 256).

Let us first examine the two different versions that we have available
concerning the 'actual introduction of analysis'. The starting position
is described in identical terms in 1932 and 1955 – it is almost impossible to establish any contact with Inge. The breakthrough is then
described in 1932 as follows:

> She only became more lively as she began telling me about a poem
> which she had read at school. She thought it remarkable that long
> words should have alternated in it with short ones. A little while
> earlier she had spoken about some birds that she had seen fly into a
> garden but not out again. These observations had followed upon a
> remark she let fall to the effect that she and her girl friend had done
> as well at some game as the boys. I explained to her that she was
> occupied by a wish to know where children (the birds) really came
> from and also to understand better the sex difference between boys
> and girls (long and short words – the comparative skill of boys and
> girls) . . . Contact was established, the material she brought became
> richer, and the analysis was set going.
>
> (1932, WMK II, p. 59)

In Klein's 1955 paper, by contrast, we read as quoted above that
Inge took up the introduction of the small toys with interest.

> From this play I gathered that two of the toy figures represented
> herself and a little boy, a school-mate about whom I had heard
> before. It appeared that there was something secret about the
> behaviour of these two figures and that other toy people were
> resented as interfering or watching and were put aside. The activ-
> ities of the two toys led to catastrophes, such as their falling down
> or colliding with cars. This was repeated with signs of mounting
> anxiety. At this point I interpreted, with reference to the details of
> her play, that some sexual activity seemed to have occurred between
> herself and her friend, and that this had made her very frightened
> of being found out and therefore distrustful of other people. I
> pointed out that while playing she had become anxious and
> seemed on the point of stopping her play. I reminded her that she
> disliked school, and that this might be connected with the fear that
> the teacher would find out about the relation with her school-mate

and punish her. Above all she was frightened and therefore distrustful of her mother, and now she might feel the same way about me. The effect of this interpretation on the child was striking: her anxiety and distrust first increased, but very soon gave way to obvious relief. Her facial expression changed, and although she neither admitted nor denied what I had interpreted, she subsequently showed her agreement by producing new material and by becoming much freer in her play and speech; also her attitude towards me became much more friendly and less suspicious. Of course the negative transference, alternating with the positive one, came up again and again; but, from this session onwards, the analysis progressed well.

(1955, WMK III, p. 125)

We thus have two differing descriptions of the situation in which it became possible to interpret the initial negative transference to such an extent that it no longer completely dominated. It seems possible based on the content of the two reports that there may have been a sequence to these situations, such that initially the one described in 1932 had taken place but had not had as much impact at the time as was first supposed, and that somewhat later the introduction of the play materials enabled the actual intensification to occur. That this may have been so in reality (and that in the different contexts of the 1932 and 1955 manuscripts only one aspect was portrayed in each) does not help much further in understanding the dynamics. Let us consider the two versions again in detail – that of 1932, in which the attempt to identify an unconscious question in the verbal material presented by Inge finally succeeded, the interpretation of which enabled contact to be established – and the version of 1955, in which the introduction of the further aid of the toys was required, an aid that Inge needed in order to communicate to Klein what was preoccupying her. The interpretation of anxiety made it possible here for the analysis to continue.

Let us first try to understand the situation presented in 1932 on the basis of the information about the transference situation at the time that is provided by the transmitted material. From this viewpoint, the alternation of short and long words might also refer to Inge's interest in the nature of the contact between the 'long'/tall Klein and herself as a 'short'/small person. With the image of birds flying into a garden that she did not see fly back again, she gives us a vivid illustration of her anxiety concerning the quality of relationship with her analyst. This is reminiscent of a claustrophobic component, in her fear that by being drawn into the analysis and communicating about herself, she will be caught or even devoured by Klein. If we then add to this the idea that what concerns Inge here is a wish to do the same as the boys do or what Klein does, it seems obvious that one of the components is likely to be envy of the ability or capacities that Inge does not have available in herself. It also seems likely that she is representing a part of her terrible inner world that she fears and thus mainly projects – in this case into Klein. The anxiety would consist in the idea of being deprived of everything she takes up through envy of its essential nature and accordingly in the transference she would be afraid of the analyst appropriating from her all the things that hold import-ance for her. This would explain the fear of perceiving this part of her inner world, which represents a threat to her health. If we then assume that this construction contains something important, then Klein would have relieved Inge's fear with her interpretation in so far as she would have proved to be not a parasitic container in Bion's sense,[4] but on the contrary a container that seeks to give her words meaning, thus enabling the 'birds' to return strengthened. However, Klein does not explicitly interpret this fear and its role in the transference situation.

This is different in the 1955 version, in which the affect of fear was obviously communicated more directly to Klein and accordingly was also interpreted in the transference relationship. (Klein interprets that Inge is afraid of her mother/analyst disapproving of her interest in the boy/father.) Amplifying Klein's interpretation, we could perhaps consider a more direct reading of the play in the transference: I think the key sentence here is the one in which Klein describes how the play led both figures to catastrophe – they fell over or were run over by cars. This in my view reveals, as well as portraying the situa-tion in which Klein fetched the toys, that Inge is describing here how their previous interaction led at the time to catastrophes and non-communication. Both failed in their attempts (fell over) or were made to fail by others at that time (run over). Considered from this perspective, the interpretation indirectly picks up the fear that the futile, destructive play in which Inge has involved Klein might be

---

4 Bion writes: 'By "parasitic" I mean to represent a relationship in which one depends on another to produce a third, which is destructive of all three' (Bion, 1970, p. 95).

discovered. The fact that the interpretation became productive may well derive from this. It cannot be determined from the material transmitted to us here how far this component was decisive or instead introduced a further component into the interpretation, one that consisted in the difficult factor being sexualised and placed outside the transference, which thus suggests a split between Inge's relationship with Klein and her relationship with her friend.

If we compare these two reconstructions of the transference situation, their dynamics are similar – the first one mentioned (1932) seems to give a more detailed description of the catastrophe that is mentioned in the second (1955). This might suggest that where the attempt truly to understand the meaning of the words actually succeeded, then the play was not needed but that the play increased the possibility of obtaining a more effective, more direct access to the material and thus constituted an essential aid.

In my view, the material gives no indication as to how Inge understood the introduction of the toys – reference to the treatment notes will be required. The fact that Klein did not mention this introduction of play analysis before 1955 may be connected with the fact that Inge, with her apparent 'normality', evoked in Klein an equivalent apparently 'normal' reaction, namely to place her children's toys at this normal child's disposal. The multiple implications of this event may initially have escaped consideration.

The further material that Klein published on Inge in 1932 consists mainly of Inge's role playing, which thus provides an illustration of an important technical method in the analysis of latency-age children. In contrast to the publications on Rita, Klein also mentions here the role assigned to her by Inge, which provides a vivid illustration of specific sections of the analysis. Inge plays the role of an office manager for an extended period throughout – Klein identifies in this her wishes for masculinity. This is followed by the teacher role, with the role of the failing pupil assigned to Klein – Klein understands this to mean ultimately that: 'at a very early age, her own desire for knowledge had not been satisfied and was repressed; and this was what made the superiority of her brothers and sisters so intolerable and the lessons at school so distasteful' (1932, WMK II, p. 62).

I should now like to make a further incursion. The motivation for the repression of the early wish to know is not further explored at this point. On the basis of the above considerations – and the intervening expansion of Klein's and our knowledge – it seems likely that an intense early envy[5] was hindering Inge's learning and that the 'superiority of her brothers and sisters' also represents the superiority of her parents and of Klein in the transference. The situation of not knowing something or being unable to do something is so intolerable to Inge that she places herself in the position of being the one who knows in phantasy – office manager and teacher – and bypasses 'learning from experience' (cf. Bion, 1962). This factor is most vividly contained in the description of Inge's writing inhibition:

> Inge, who, as I have already mentioned, suffered from a severe inhibition in writing, had a burning wish to write 'quickly and beautifully' like grown-ups. The compromise between this wish and her inhibition was *scribbling*, which represented in her phantasy beautiful and skilful handwriting. Her wish if possible to excel the grown-ups in writing and her very strong ambition and curiosity, existing as they did side by side with a deep feeling that she knew nothing and could do nothing, played a great part in her failure in real life.
>
> (1932, WMK II, p. 72, fn. 1; Klein's italics in the German edition)

There is a further aspect to Inge's attempt to eliminate the difference between herself and the adults – with the 'scribbling', she also diminishes the adults'/Klein's thinking/doing/writing, depriving it of its essential nature and removing its meaning. This symptom thus simultaneously represents a result of envy and a defence against it.

Klein understands the subsequent game as a toy saleswoman,[6] as Inge's demonstration of what her mother should have given her (1932, WMK II, p. 62).

Amplifying Klein's considerations on the significance of this role play, presented here only in summarised form, I think it can also be gathered from this how Inge at various times perceives and also misrepresents her analyst, and how she tries to diminish her. It is not hard to identify Inge's projection of an inner object into a teacher who, according to Inge, understands her task as one of demonstrating her superiority, thus becoming an impermeable object (cf. Bion, 1959)

5 The significant extent to which the unpublished material from Inge's analysis suggests a dynamic of this kind will become particularly clear in Section 5.2 from the play with the stone figures.
6 Cf. treatment notes, e.g. p. 12, pp. 15ff., p. 19.

that surrounds itself with superiority. Later she describes her object as a toy salesman – mocking Klein's offer of the toy? The fact that Inge as a toy saleswoman gradually moves on to selling food may conceal an initial recognition of Klein as a nourishing (as opposed to an impermeable) object.

In summary, my thesis based on the publications can be formulated as follows: the profound 'as-if' dynamic concealed under the appearance of normality – and the learning inhibition resulting from and defending against envy – were not identified as such. Instead, Inge's negative attitude brought about the introduction of the toys as a parameter into this analysis. On the one hand, this offer avoided the difficult problem that required protracted working out and allowed Inge to act as if it were possible to play completely normally as if this disorder did not exist. (This could also be understood as an intuitively precise reaction to Inge's envy of Klein's 'children' and the attenuation of this envy.) Simultaneously, however, it represented the possibility of communicating the problem with all its specific features and its emotional implications. And, of course, it proved to be a productive technical development in child analysis more generally.

5.2 Inge in the unpublished manuscripts

There are two manuscripts of interest here. First, there is the fourth lecture, entitled 'The technique of child analysis in latency and puberty', which Klein gave in 1925 as part of her London lecture series; the other is a manuscript that is dedicated entirely to the case presentation of Inge and also originates from 1925 – it is unclear whether (and if so when and where) it was presented.

Let us first consider the London lecture, which later formed the basis for the fourth chapter of *The Psycho-Analysis of Children* (1932, WMK II). It is the discrepancies that are most interesting here: the first sessions with the corresponding difficulties do not appear: for the initial diagnosis, it states only 'the 8¼-year-old Inge, who is failing at school' (manuscript, p. 4) and there is no mention of her 'normality'.

Klein gives Inge here mainly as an example of extended role plays that had to be understood in every detail before they could be replaced with new role play. She again cites mainly the teacher, office manager and toy saleswoman games, without mentioning the subsequent selling of food in the latter. Conceptually she still attributes

147

the learning inhibition to the castration complex.[7] She adds that a range of special determinants was also at work here and explains in this connection that this case concerned

> a youngest child who contrary to all appearances had had the greatest difficulty in coming to terms with the superiority of her surroundings, found herself reliving this situation in its entirety when she went to school and repeated it through extensive failure.
>
> (Manuscript, p. 4)

To summarise, all these departures from the 1932 version can actually be attributed to the focus (role play) in which she describes Inge's analysis here: the conceptual evaluations (castration anxiety versus destiny of the wish to know) are not mutually exclusive but complementary. It seems possible that Klein herself was not entirely satisfied with the attribution of (the dynamic as she had experienced it) to castration anxiety and that she was therefore later driven to consider it in new ways. It seems that individual determinants such as the experience of the others' superiority as the youngest child did not yet really fit into a general concept. However, there are essentially no new hints from this manuscript in terms of the question posed here.

The manuscript that deals exclusively with Inge was written slightly later, as is clear from the information given on page 1: 'The nine-year-old Inge came to me for analysis when she was seven years old; this was interrupted by one fairly long and several shorter breaks. In total she had then had ... analytic sessions'.[8] The existence of a four-page manuscript entitled 'Fortsetzung der Inge-Arbeit' (Continuation of the Inge Work) mainly containing treatment notes from the beginning of November 1925, enables us to conclude that the

---

7 Cf. here also Klein's 1921 and 1923 publications; later, the defence against sadism plays a decisive role (cf. 1928 and 1930); in 1935, there is reference to the depression and hopelessness experienced in relation to damaged objects and some years later to the role of envy, which was then explored further by Bion.

8 According to the diaries, Klein treated Inge from 18 September 1923 for one month six times a week; at the end of November and beginning of December there were eight further sessions; from 3 January 1924, Klein saw Inge for two months approximately three times a week (every other day in the week), each time for 1½ hours; subsequently, until 5 July, at first more frequently for 1½ hours, then mainly for one hour. From 3 February 1925 to the end of June 1925 there were further one-hour sessions, as in the period from 8 September 1925 to 1 May 1926, with varying frequency.

actual 22-page 'Inge-Work' was drawn up before this time – from an analysis that was in progress.

We shall first mention the amplifications of the points raised above that arise from this manuscript. From the general introductory state- ment about Inge, we learn in more detail that she initially came exclusively because of one symptom. She had been suffering to an unusual extent from cold-related illnesses for which various measures including repeated stays by the seaside had proved ineffective (p. 1):

> Apart from this one symptom, no particular difficulties had come to light; the child gave the impression of being thoroughly nor- mal . . . The symptom appeared after a relatively short period to be favourably influenced by the analysis and when after a few months of analysis it had completely disappeared, the analysis came to a standstill.
>
> (Manuscript, pp. 1f.)

After a few months, however, it turned out that the analysis needed to be resumed, since the child was having difficulty and showed reluctance in learning and exhibited frequent bad moods. In the analysis, the learning inhibition symptom had expanded, with signs of an associated tendency to lying and cheating.

In relation to the beginning of treatment, Klein formulated gener- ally that children very often start an analysis in the early sessions – and then repeatedly after breaks – with specific representations that she considers are especially complex in nature (pp. 3f.):

> With Inge, situations of hospitality in play, birthday celebrations and shared visits to restaurants played a major role both at the beginning of the analysis and also repeatedly later on. With her characteristic optimism, she had begun the analysis with particular expectations and ideas of me, and expressed in her play the recur- rent hope that she would now obtain the full satisfaction that for her begins precisely with the situation of oral satisfaction.
>
> (Manuscript, p. 4)

At this point it becomes clear how the entire substance of the work is focused not on the difficulties known to us but on Inge's oral fixation, which Klein attributes to early weaning. In addition there were '*traumatic experiences in early childhood*', and it is the reconstruction of these based on the play to which the most space is devoted. Starting from the factor of the secrecy, which we already know about from 1955, Klein explains how she reached the conclusion that in her third year Inge had had the opportunity for observations of coitus between her governess and her fiancé, concerning which she had been asked to remain silent. 'This alarming experience, which clearly demonstrated to the child that which otherwise remained hidden, had far-reaching consequences for this child's sexual and characterological development' (p. 15). Klein thus sees a twofold determination here to Inge's '*pronounced castration complex*', which is responsible for her '*masculinity complex*' and her entrenching herself behind masculine grandiose phantasies, which in turn were expressed in her learning inhibition and her tendency to lying. Klein still ascribes this in part to the traumatic impact of a specific situation with the governess – later this aspect is dropped. It then became clearer how difficult Inge found it to tolerate other people's superiority, something for which of course there were repeated situations in which this was likely to be especially striking. Klein certainly seems to be able to identify this component as a problem at this point but she cannot yet conceptualise it adequately – the understanding that she sets out involves many essential points but does not entirely grasp the problem.

However, Klein also tells us in this manuscript about two important play sequences that – in the light of our contemporary knowledge – we can use to gain a more precise understanding of the transference situation.

After a long period during which she had repeatedly played the toy saleswoman and it had become clear to me that the persistent stereotyped form of representation in this game, which was in contrast to most of her play, was concealing other more difficult material, in the constant persistence with this game, I suddenly, as I was interpreting this resistance to her, came upon some material that was to take us deeper. The child was setting up a shop again. The small table and a chair were covered with cloths; this was to represent a shop in which there was a stone figure. The stone figure was herself; she had crawled under the chair and was now being seen by me. It turned out that this figure was made by a man called Mr Jumping Jack [*Herr Hampelmann*]. The identification of this jumping jack with the father became clear from various details. Soon, however, it was another stone figure that was in another room in the enormous building that she had described; it contained 40 rooms with 40 figures – the figure four corresponds here to the number of children, for Inge had three siblings. My looking without being able to see well in the semi-darkness is a reversal of the listening situation in which she could not see enough.

(Manuscript, pp. 5f.)

I think this passage can be understood as follows in terms of the transference: with her stereotyped play, Inge is indicating the stereotyped way in which she deals internally with Klein's thoughts, making them into 'stone figures', or dead objects, and that while she wants to communicate this to Klein through the play, she also wants to hide her innermost self from Klein and does not want to let Klein see clearly how she makes stones from something that could be nourishing and how Klein is denigrated as the jumping jack. In a certain sense, Inge is thus fully cooperative, allowing an insight into her inner functioning through her play.

5.3 Inge in the treatment notes

Unfortunately only relatively few sessions have been transmitted to us in the form of notes from memory concerning this long treatment consisting of 375 sessions, which including breaks lasted from 18 September 1923 to 1 May 1926. Essentially there are the sessions from 2 October to 19 October 1923 – a period in which Inge came daily for analysis except on Sundays – on thirty-seven pages in a treatment book entitled 'Inge II'.[9] It is therefore reasonable to suppose that the initial sessions – from 18 September to 1 October 1923 – were recorded in treatment book I, which however is unfortunately no longer to be found. In addition to this, there is a dream of Inge's of 20 June 1924 that is recorded on a notepad under the heading 'children's dreams' and some notes on individual sessions from October, November and December 1925 on separate sheets of paper.

Unfortunately, then, the question of particular interest here concerning the beginning of the treatment, with its difficulties and the final breakthrough, cannot be examined with the aid of the treatment

---

9 The patient's first name is used in the original.

notes. We can certainly assume that the introduction of the toys had already occurred – on 3 October 1923 a train is one item that plays a part, which Klein mentions in 1955 as one of the toys that she fetched from her children's room.

In a certain sense, the sessions that happen to have been transmitted to us nevertheless represent a stroke of luck that enables us to address within certain limits the question with which we are concerned. Klein had in fact obviously bought more small bricks after the introduction of the toys and in the first session for which we have records available it seems obvious that Inge is finding these bricks for the first time. Although the situation is not of course the same – the introduction of a newly bought toy at the beginning of a session as opposed to the first introduction of toys during a session – there are nevertheless enough analogies to allow certain conclusions to be drawn about the dynamic significance of the parameter of introduction of the toy from the situation presented here.

There is naturally continuing speculation as to whether Klein bought the bricks in order to 'stoke the fire' because the attraction of the toys that were originally introduced quickly diminished or whether she realised that the provision of toys needed to be amplified in a meaningful way by a satisfactory number of small bricks. It can be inferred from the course of the session – Inge repeatedly concludes that the toy that is actually needed (swing, ball . . .) is missing here – that at least one factor to have played a part in the purchase was Klein's response to Inge's negative transference in the form of a complaint about the toys.

Whereas in the publications there was repeated reference to Inge's 'toy saleswoman' game, the treatment documents open up a further dimension of meaning: on 2 October Klein had thus in reality acted as the 'toy purchaser', which Inge at first accepted very happily. The next day it is Inge who helps to shape the future setting by bringing a box from home to store the toys in. Two days later, we read: '*Does not want toy*'. Then on 6 October, Inge became the toy saleswoman, admitting in conversation that she had previously been a burglar (p. 12). This sequence can be interpreted as indicating both that Inge felt unconscious guilt about having initially robbed Klein in burglar-like fashion of her possibility of reflecting adequately, which was why Klein then had to introduce the toy, and also that Inge felt guilty because she quickly denigrated the offer of the toy as well. In this sense, her toy saleswoman role also signifies an attempt at reparation in which Klein was to be able to recover the corresponding items from her.

Let us now look at the first session with the new bricks in detail:

2/X. Much joy at so many bricks
(newly bought small dominoes).
– Builds. Keeps saying does not know
herself what it will be – or know
what will build at next
moment. Builds: a racecourse with
5 tracks running alongside
this [the coach-house &][1] the manor next to [that of][1] the
playground. – Builds a kind of rotunda
from small boxes, keeps saying
does not know what she is making. – Finally
above men are playing music below
the wedding room where the king
is dancing. Separate stand for wedding
coach – another wide crooked
path that leads to the wedding room.
Surprised that path so crooked
had not intended this herself.
(Interpret five paths = bodily orifices
she then counts them herself together
with me – path mother – father
noise & danced = coitus. Interpret
also making me guess = revenge
parents who made her guess everything.
Point at book curious pictures. She
agrees smiling.)
Goes to window [unfriendly][1] looks out, says watching
as workmen build a complete [?]
house. Interpret curiosity how through coitus
child is made. – Becomes very
friendly – & (when interpret rotunda very like
shape of flowers on carpet, point to ball
games etc. there). She: (happily)
we could play that again, shame
that no ball there. – 3/X.

153

Inge gladly takes up the offer of the new bricks and at once begins to play with them and build – here then is a parallel with the situation described in 1955, in which Inge also begins to play with the toys immediately. The next moment, in which Inge says repeatedly that she herself does not know what it will be, is also reminiscent of the mystery that surrounded the play in 1955. For one thing, this can be seen as a commentary on Klein's action, given that she probably also went to the shops without actually knowing what she was 'making' with the purchase in the transference–countertransference situation. On the other hand, Inge seems to take this to mean that she is offering a 'racecourse' with the toy. This could be interpreted to indicate that Inge understands the situation as a seduction into an excited shared activity in which the laborious path of working out negative feelings can be bypassed. The mystery-making and the ostensible not-knowing-herself may be related to Inge knowing at some level that Klein intended to offer the toy as an aid to understanding the negative transference and that the factor of bypassing the difficulties was not predominant.

Inge's repeated hint that she herself did not know what she was building seems to be a possible way of defending against her own curiosity about what Klein does between the sessions (triggered by the intervening purchase of the bricks) and against her impulse to penetrate this and instead to provoke something equivalent to this in her analyst, who then penetrates her with questions or insightful interpretations. Klein also seems to act this out initially with her interpretation that the five tracks represent the five bodily orifices; (also reminiscent of the remaining five sessions of the week, 2 October included) etc., but Klein then goes on to interpret this interaction: '*Interpret also making me guess = revenge/parents who made her guess everything*'. Although she – at least according to the record – had not interpreted it directly in the transference but attributed it to the parents, thus leaving the negative transference rather to one side, Klein had nevertheless identified the essential dynamic. At first Inge agrees and smiles but she then shows a negative therapeutic reaction: she turns away, is unfriendly and looks out of the window. She lets Klein know through the workmen who are building a house that Klein has achieved a contribution to the shared building of her 'psychic house', which is nevertheless something that she finds very difficult to tolerate.

For the next day, it is recorded that Inge showed resistance at home.

On the one hand, Inge brings the box for storing the toys; she also literally and ultimately gives Klein the idea that will become an important component of the future setting.[10] She thereby wants to show her appreciation to Klein but the next moment she nevertheless has to try to outdo her again with the toy of her own that she has brought – she already has all the small houses – she apparently does not need Klein for this. Nevertheless, Inge is able to gain some distance, jokingly inviting Klein to sit on the small chair above her head, so as to try then to outdo her. She uses the two small chairs to represent her unstable experience of the situation:

> Then puts 2 little chairs
> together so that with edges touching
> they can hardly stay upright
> (Interpret path into mother – coitus . . .

Although Klein sexualises the situation in her interpretation, she also addresses the difficult situation, which seems to give Inge some security:

> Then puts little chairs together
> so that pushed into each other
> they stay up.

Next, the toy train seems to symbolise the question of how the patient and analyst can remain in connection:

> I point at train, which
> was only toy asked for
> today (apart from boxes
> & bricks – held in
> the air so that hanging down – then
> asked how 1 carriage is hitched
> on to other, as two hooks. Then placed
> train next to building)

---

10 In 1955, though, Klein traces the introduction of the box back to the situation in which she first brought Inge her children's toys – in a box. Later on, every child had a drawer in which his toys were locked away.

On 4 October, Inge explicitly presents the theme of secret building:

> 4/X. Building secretly on window-sill away
> from my view. But then calls me to staircase
> to help. – Building made of boxes
> wide staircase at front [?] to which calls me over
> to help. – Side staircase, both together.

Inge is thus able here to call on Klein for help.

On 5 October Inge wants Klein to hide and to be the one to find her. The 'secrecy' that was understood with the aid of the unpublished manuscript in connection with the as-if problematic (cf. Section 5.2) appears repeatedly in the first documented section (October 1923). Inge constantly builds in secret and Klein has to guess the things that she is making.

I am selecting here an extract from a scene in which she illustrates most vividly what she wants to keep secret.

> 9/X. Brings me 1 postcard: (of train,
> 1 guard standing nearby 1 woman
> an overturned tree, prettily gift-
> wrapped. – Builds secretly from me in
> box: 1 dining room for many
> guests, 1 reception room.

Inge would like to be the one who, like Melanie Klein with her patients, can take care of and feed a lot of guests.

If we now consider the few documented sessions for the period from October to November 1925, this aspect is one that Inge explicates further. In this period, a part is played by a 'clown' that clearly personifies a part of Inge herself. His function is vividly illustrated for example in the session of 9 November.[11]

> At first wants to play funny lady, but plays funny man. Clown. Extremely cheeky. Tips bag on me again. Blames other people at

---

11 Whereas nearly all the notes from memory exist in handwritten form, the notes from the beginning to the middle of November 1925 are typed and entitled 'Männlichkeitskomplex in der Frau. Fortsetzung der Inge-Arbeit' (Masculinity complex in the woman. Continuation of the Inge-Work).

first. Then ceases all denial. Does what he wants. Is stronger than me. I am to ask him for shopping bag. At first he refuses, then sells it in exchange for brightly coloured pencils. Then steals bag from me again. Also steals from me a letter that a lady – with name clearly reminiscent of mother's – wrote to me. Then I have to complain because the clown has made large spots in the letter that 'ruined the letters with tails' . . . Then steals all the cushions from me, explaining that she needs something soft to sit on (now female genitals). Then goes with Frau X (mother) into cinema, pretending to think that she is me, Frau Wett (association with running a race [*Wettlaufen*]). Clown lives in 'Know-All Street' [*Alles-Wissenstrasse*]; they know him at the post office and give him my letters. Gets a letter with cinema tickets from Frau X, which I am to receive and goes with her without her noticing. Then again, and he sends her a forged ticket and she has to pay later. Before the cinema he is very sweet to her; afterwards he is rude & unfriendly and leaves her standing there. Has also taken money that Frau X gave to Frau Wett (governess's present in return for discretion). Frau Wett has to watch as the two of them drive away in the car, cannot help it. This continues with the clown standing between the two of them and there is nothing she can do about it.

Inge now lives as the clown in 'Know-All Street', she can pretend to be her analyst and successfully behave as if she were 'Frau Wett'. However, this configuration does not continue uninterrupted; she also plays situations from which it becomes clear that this relates to a 'forged ticket' for which she must 'pay', which means that she will not be spared for ever from 'learning from experience'.

This theme recurs throughout the following weeks; I am selecting the session from 4 December 1925.

Flat again
arranges it with curtains
cloth etc. – so that I (Frau Wett
again) have a room
next to clown – he has found ~~himself~~
3 books (of many
received on birthday &
brought to session.) Reads
from these. Var. [?] adventures

fire burns dog bites
beats stick etc. other
man climbs ladder,[12] falls & an
ogre appears etc.
Makes enormous noise
with the 3 books moans
sings disturbs. Makes me
keep coming to
complain – mocks – I
keep asking (is
very cheeky scornful direct
coarse! – Reversal of role in which
she had to watch
recognises identification 3 mountains
3 books = 3 sisters).
Has rented a shop
& deceives me & other
women by selling: sugar
that is just scraps of paper – vegetables
just scraps of paper – sausage
just scrap of paper (disgust
fatty sausage). Takes money
from me [sth. crossed out]. Cheeky – does
not give money back – police
(mostly identified with him) agree
with him – a clown may
do anything he wants (from coitus
observations: semen, stool – member –
that not the right one though –
(comfort from frightening
away and denigration). – In the night breaks
into my house tweaks
my hair – throws his cushions
on to my stomach (admits [says why][1]
initially I think – father through
castration mother obtains his
member) in night again

---

12 It seems likely that Klein meant *Leiter* (ladder) rather than *Leiber* (bodies).

robs me steals letter
& cuts hole in it.

It seems clear to me that this concerns a mocking object that thinks itself superior, behaves deceitfully, pretends scraps of paper are sugar, vegetables, sausage etc. and that it avoids nourishing material by treating it like scraps of paper while trying to demonstrate its own superiority, thus hindering its own growth.

5.4 The significance of Inge's analysis

Two important methods of future child analysis became clearer to Klein with the aid of Inge's analysis: first, the significance of role playing for latency-age children, for which she quotes mainly from Inge's case in *The Psycho-Analysis of Children* in 1932; and second, the significance of toys as a regular component rather than an incidental factor (Rita) in the child analytic setting, which she indicated in her review of 1955.

In so far as this can be reconstructed from the treatment notes that are available to us, together with the publications, the introduction of toys became necessary to set the analysis in motion, during which role playing then became of greater significance.

The introduction of toys into this analysis can be understood as Klein's wish to show Inge that she did not want the analysis to continue in the destructive, stultifying way that Inge had been pursuing up to that point. At the same time, the toys offered an arena for acting out that could be used in two ways. First, the toys gave a wider-ranging field, where necessary, for the acting out of resistance. Second, the toys gave a projective field for all aspects of the child's inner world such that these aspects could gradually become comprehensible to the analyst and could thus be interpreted. In general terms, the acting-out arena made possible by the toys enables the patient to find out how the analyst works from watching the way in which the analyst takes up the use the child makes of the acting-out arena, understands it or even does not understand it. This perception of the analyst by the child can in turn find expression in the play.

In my view, Inge gave her anxieties a vivid expression with her image of the birds that had flown into the garden but did not come back. She feared that Klein was an object that, like one of her inner objects, would catch something living and steal its essential nature. She could thus behave only very reticently towards Klein. Simultaneously at work in Inge was an inner object that rapidly rendered all Klein's efforts futile and did not allow Klein's 'birds' to fly back. In this context, Klein offered Inge things such as bricks that cannot readily disappear and thus Klein created a relational field that was not so easily destroyed. Inge was able to use them in both the terms outlined above, that is, in her acting out and in her making herself understandable. She shows how she misrepresents the facts of the matter, and yet she also shows how her misrepresentation makes it possible for Klein to identify an essential dynamic, that of revenge.

At this point the experience with Inge can perhaps be generalised: child analysis can founder because of a destructive attitude in the child that presents the self as superior and retreats from actual experiences. The provision of toys increases the possibility of understanding in the early stages the way in which this attitude operates and of interpreting this to the child.

5.5 Excursus: play and drawing in Ernst's treatment – does the play technique actually pre-date Inge (and Rita)?

5.5.1 Ernst in Klein's publications

In 'The rôle of the school in the libidinal development of the child' (1923a) – the only publication in which Klein refers to Ernst – it is striking how naturally she writes about Ernst's play in his analytic session, for example, playing that he was a mason (1923a, WMK I, p. 62), his drawing in the sessions (p. 68, p. 72) and his occasional displays of particular aggressiveness: 'As always, it set in with his tearing the cushions off my divan, and jumping with both feet upon them, and also upon the divan' (1923a, WMK I, p. 69). The scenes described are full of explicit references to the treatment situation and provide a lively insight into the sessions. Klein uses the play material here in the same way as she had approached Grete's stories and phantasies – by trying to understand it in relation to the unconscious content. The notion is one with which she has long been familiar – even in 1921 she had formulated that in the majority of cases 'unconscious phantasies are usually ventilated in play-activities' (1921, WMK I, p. 37) without this having been translated at that stage into something that could be designated as treatment technique. Although Klein understands this material, as in Grete's case, mainly in terms of sexual symbolism – the house-building phantasy as a mason represents coitus and the behaviour described with the cushions represents 'the castration of the mother and subsequently coitus with her' (p. 69), the passages that describe Grete's treatment in the same work (see Chapter 3) read entirely differently, since they contain no explicit reference to the treatment situation and demonstrate no play element. How can this discrepancy be explained? Had Klein already discovered the play technique with Ernst, whose treatment began two years after that of Grete, in February 1923 and before Inge's (and Rita's) analysis? This is the only question that will be tackled in this supplementary section. There will be no extensive investigation of the material beyond this.

In order to formulate a hypothesis about the basis for the lively impression that we receive of Ernst's analytic sessions, the first passage that refers to Ernst in this work will now be examined more closely:

> Six-year-old Ernst was shortly to start school. During the analysis-hour he played that he was a mason. In the course of the associated house-building phantasy he interrupted himself and talked about his future *profession*; he wanted to be a 'pupil', and also later to go to the technical school. To my remark that this was hardly a final profession he replied angrily that he did not want to think out a profession for himself, because his mother might not perhaps agree to it and was cross with him anyway. A little later, as he continued the house-building phantasy, he suddenly asked: 'Is it really yard school or high school (technical school)?' (*Hofschule* or *Hochschule*).
>
> These associations showed that for him to be a pupil meant to learn about coitus, but that a profession meant the carrying out of coitus. Hence in his house-building (so closely associated for him with school and 'yard' school) he was the only mason who, moreover, still required the directions of the architect and the assistance of the other masons.
>
> (1923a, WMK I, p. 62)

Although the house-building phantasy with his role as mason already seems constructive, Ernst then becomes even more explicit – he formulates fairly directly how important it is to him to become Klein's pupil, to learn from her and to experience things. When Klein does not seem to understand this, Ernst can formulate in relation to the mother that he wants to prevent Klein from being angry with him. He thus shows a predominantly positive transference that he is clearly concerned to maintain. From the further passages, it can also be gathered that he seems altogether to be very naturally concerned with reparation following aggressive phantasies and behaviour: thus a phantasy is described that depicts how he cuts off 'papa's popöchen' (his behind)[13] and then his head – 'then he suddenly tried very busily to read and showed much pleasure in doing so' (1923a, WMK I, p. 65). Even the aggressive enactment with the cushions described above is followed by a constructive activity: 'Immediately after this he began to draw' (p. 69).

This leads to the hypothesis that with Ernst the positive transference was in the foreground. Ernst seems to express himself spontaneously and naturally here, including in play, without this striking Klein as something out of the ordinary, which is why she does not address it in terms of a special theory of technique.

As far as I can judge, Ernst does not appear in any of the unpublished manuscripts; the 'Ernst' referred to in one of the London lectures is another boy.

5.5.2 Ernst in the treatment notes [14]

Ostensibly Ernst was less 'normal' than Inge, for in the treatment notes Klein writes, 'Suffers from anxiety, does not dare to switch the light on in the night, also very anxious during the day, tends to brood'.

If we consult the treatment notes concerning the mason game mentioned earlier, the above hypothesis about Ernst's positive transference is substantiated with reference to the context of the session of 4 April 1923, the record of which presents the play in more detail. We already know the external situation from Rita's case – Klein had '*cancelled the session because of illness*'. She now records on 3 April that

---

13 Translator's note: *Popöchen*, meaning 'behind' (buttocks), was misrendered as 'penis' in the original Hogarth edition of Melanie Klein's works (1923a, WMK I, p. 65).

14 The initial period is available to us from a treatment book that contains notes from 2 February to 3 May 1923. There are some loose pages with notes from June, others with notes from October and finally there is a small notepad with notes from November 1923.

Ernst was extremely upset by this, went pale and cried. He had written her an affectionate letter and had been happy when he could come back. In the meantime, he had been much more friendly to the mother – whereas previously he had been capable of screaming for hours on end if the mother could not play at dancing in the way that he wanted, this time he fell silent after a few minutes. The mother had meanwhile gone on a journey and things were much less difficult with the nursemaid, whom he did not much like. He now suggests to Klein that they play ballroom-dancing – when Klein comments that she would prefer to watch, he picks out an imaginary dancing partner. In the game, he then does not have much luck with the dancers; they all want to dance with someone else. Finally, there is an excited game in which he repeatedly stabs a knife into imaginary animals (cushions).

Thus whereas he is able to respond with concern to the cancelled session (or sessions), writing Klein an affectionate letter, Ernst reacts with excited sadistic phantasies and impulses to Klein's refusal to dance with him. He may have hoped for the fulfilment of his Oedipal wishes and now he may be defending against the disappointment with attacks on Klein's other children – as the product of her relationship not with him but with the father.

The report from the session on 4 April begins with Ernst bringing some tiles, for he wants to repair Klein's collapsing house – as the client, Klein is to give the appropriate instructions.

4/IV. Brings some ~~bricks~~
tiles [is mason][1] Wants to repair
my collapsing house [sth. illegible][1] (hole in wall being repaired).
As client I am to instruct.
[how][1] otherwise, he cannot even [sth. crossed out]
~~how~~ get inside. But then does
my house-building – I am client &
make plans – later am younger
mason – meanwhile makes me guess what
he will be one day. All guesses wrong
He: will be a pupil. (I: not a profession). He: later
will be high school (I: also still
learning – not a profession). He: 'I don't want
even to think about that, for
if I think of something for myself it is

not at all right with her (mother) & she might
get angry again'. Goes on building – meanwl.
asks: Is it high school [*Hochschule*] or yard school [*Hofschule*].
   (Interpret
house-building – parallel client = architect elder
brother carpenter-thing, young mason = yngr.
brother). Needs materials for this
(cushions = sacks) 1 sack lime – 1 sack
1 sack [earth][1]/groats for gluing
1 sack small stones. We must
laboriously bring these & he pours
or shakes them depending on contents. Also makes
me guess what else would be needed
for building.

Here I think it becomes clearer how – in reaction to the session of
3 April – Ernst wishes for an instruction from Klein as to how to
repair the damage that he has caused her. As he would like this to be
understood by Klein – and she obviously expresses nothing along
these lines spontaneously – he tries to get her to understand what his
exact concern is by making her guess what he will be one day. The
following passage we already know from the publication.

If we turn back to the beginning, there are the following notes on
the first session:

Showed sympathy
when at his mother's house I once
spoke quickly with him & let
him tell me about a town that had
many gates. Says when he hears that
he will come to me more often: 'Great, then I
can finish telling her about the
gates'. To the first session 2/II he brings
a brochure because his mother
had written on it: 'The gas man is called
Ernst'. When asked what the gas man
has to do: he must go everywhere
to Mummy & other ladies because
gas meters broken – that is because
the mummies leave the

children in dark room with gas
inside. Children put a stopper in & then
the water cannot get out. Above
is a tap – through which water comes
in – if because of the children's
plugged stopper it cannot get out, then
gas fumes stay inside & it can explode.
Interest in house-building opposite: lime
so durable when mixed with sand &
water. Great interest in furnit.

In contrast to the early treatment stages of Grete, Rita and Inge, with Ernst there was a positive transference from the outset. He approaches the 'pieces of furniture', Klein's possible ways of helping him, with great interest. In the first story he tells, he seems to be identifying as the gas man with Klein's function of repairing the damage that he has caused as a child.

If we now turn back to Klein's initial notes on the reason for the treatment – in the 1923 publication there was no hint about this – we learn that Ernst was suffering from anxiety and that he did not dare to put the light on at night. He was apparently also very anxious in the daytime, but also then funny, cheerful and trusting. He had a tendency to brood – he did not like telling stories as before, but talked with his mother about people, the world and so on. The way in which the description is given seems to suggest that the disorder was not as severe as it was with the three girls whom we have got to know up to this point. It seems likely that the initial negative transference was therefore less pronounced. Even in the description in the – incomplete – records of the sessions following the first session, Ernst's curiosity seems to be less sadistic than in the cases of the three girls.

In terms of technique, it should also be noted that with this 6-year-old, the youngest boy she had treated until then – the boys she saw until 1923 were 12- to 13-year-olds – Klein did not, as with the previous patients, make the request to establish an adult setting of using the couch. Unlike Hug-Hellmuth, however, she strives to proceed methodically here as well, inasmuch as she seeks primarily to understand and interpret the material. She tries to refrain as far as possible from active participation in the play – thus as indicated above she does not dance with Ernst. She is unable, however, at this time to give a great deal of consideration to the material in the transference;

for example, she does not interpret what her intended role in this situation might have to do with her, what function she is to fulfil and so on.

My impression is that Ernst was able in a certain sense to function constantly in accordance with the depressive position for long enough periods for him not to have really challenged Klein to reflect – either during the treatment or later on – on questions of technique and conceptualisation. The fact remains that she did not return to his case in relation either to content or technique. Although she naturally used play material in terms of associations and to that extent we can also talk of a play analysis, she did not conceptualise it in the stricter sense as a distinctive method, which would have implied a need for interpretation when children, as Ernst did on various occasions, brought their own things, did not make use of the toys Klein provided and so on. This is why I do not consider the beginning of play analysis *per se* to have occurred with Ernst.

The thesis formulated at the beginning can thus be honed to the effect that Ernst's predominantly positive transference certainly produced a livelier picture of the treatment in the publication but also in a sense hindered a reflection on the experiences in terms of their technical implications. It remains open to question to what extent a part was played in Ernst's and Klein's relationship by the fact that – in contrast to the children who like Grete had come to her through the Polyclinic – Ernst was the nephew of a colleague and furthermore was around the same age as her youngest son had been when she had analysed him.

6

Erna
The most extensive child analysis of the Berlin years

6.1 Erna in Klein's published works

Klein's treatment of Erna, whom she describes as 'very ill indeed' (1955, WMK III, p. 135), took place from January 1924 to April 1926 and was the most extensive analysis of the Berlin years.[1] Although Klein describes Erna's illness only briefly as an 'obsessional neurosis' at its first mention in 1926 (WMK I, p. 136), in the second publication where Erna is mentioned, 'Symposium on child-analysis' (1927a), Klein gives a vivid picture of her disorder:

> Erna, whose behaviour at home was unbearable and who displayed marked asocial tendencies in all her relations, suffered from great sleeplessness, excessive obsessional onanism, complete inhibition in learning, moods of deep depression, obsessive brooding, and a number of other serious symptoms.
>
> (1927a, WMK I, p. 160)

In a footnote Klein also records that 'the severe obsessional neurosis

---

1 Klein states that there were 575 sessions (1932, WMK II, p. 51). I think that there may be a typographical error here because around 470 sessions are recorded in the diary entries and also because with Rita and Inge the recorded and published numbers of sessions correspond fairly closely. Erna's case nevertheless remains Klein's most extensive analysis of the Berlin years.

masked a paranoia' (1927a, WMK I, p. 160, fn. 1). In 1932 Klein amplifies this description by referring to other obsessional activities such as 'banging her head on the pillow . . . making a rocking movement . . . obsessional thumb-sucking . . . excessive and compulsive masturbation' (1932, WMK II, p. 35). The analysis of this 6-year-old girl is likely to have been the treatment, following the establishment of the psychoanalytic setting, that posed the greatest challenge to Klein's capacity for analytic containment in the early years of her practice. By October 1924, Klein had presented an initial conceptualisation of this case history in her lecture 'From the analysis of an obsessional neurosis in a six-year-old child' at the First German Conference of Psychoanalysis in Würzburg. In the following year, Klein devoted the third of six evening lectures in London to Erna in what is likely to have been an expanded version of the Würzburg text. Using these manuscripts as a basis, Klein finally devoted the third chapter of *The Psycho-Analysis of Children* (1932, WMK II) to Erna, which is the only chapter of this work to deal exclusively with one case. Furthermore, she repeatedly refers throughout this book to the psychodynamic insights derived from Erna's case. In her review, 'The psycho-analytic play technique: its history and significance' (1955, WMK III), already frequently mentioned above, Klein identifies the various forms of stimulus that had emerged for her from Erna's analysis:

Through her analysis I learned a good deal about the specific details of such internalization [internalization of an attacked and therefore frightening mother – C. F.] and about the phantasies and impulses underlying paranoid and manic-depressive anxieties. For I came to understand the oral and anal nature of her introjection processes and the situations of internal persecution they engendered. I also became more aware of the ways in which internal persecutions influence, by means of projection, the relation to external objects. The intensity of her envy and hatred unmistakably showed its derivation from the oral-sadistic relation to her mother's breast, and was interwoven with the beginnings of her Oedipus complex. Erna's case much helped to prepare the ground for a number of conclusions . . . in particular the view that the early super-ego, built up when oral-sadistic impulses and phantasies are at their height, underlies psychosis.

(1955, WMK III, p. 135)

Erna's treatment thus brought important insights into the different facets of the early Oedipal relational world (see also Frank & Weiss, 1996a). However, the corresponding chapter in *The Psycho-Analysis of Children*, the most extensive publication on Erna, contains such a wealth of aspects of Erna's psychodynamics that it is difficult to form a picture of the main trajectories of the analysis from the many impressive scenes and Klein's understanding of them. Klein evidently took particular trouble with the presentation of this analysis. I will now return to the publications in chronological order.

Klein initially draws on Erna's case in her various publications to illustrate fundamental technical questions: in 1926, the significance of acting out in child analysis; in 1927, the technique for dealing with negative transference; and, in 1929, role play as a fundamental aspect of the expression of transference.

In 'The psychological principles of early analysis', Klein gives the example of Erna to demonstrate that '*acting* plays a prominent part' (1926, WMK I, p. 135). With Grete's analysis, which had begun three years before Erna's treatment, Klein placed the emphasis on verbal associations, as in the adult setting. Klein now formulates that:

> If we approach children with the technique appropriate to the analysis of adults we shall assuredly not succeed in penetrating to the deepest layers of the child's mental life . . . if, that is to say, we rightly understand the child's mode of expression . . . in the analysis of children we can go back to experiences and fixations which in analysing adults we can only *reconstruct*, while in children they are *directly* represented.
>
> (1926, WMK I, p. 135)

Let us turn to the example provided, which Klein introduces with the comment that Erna presented to her in the minutest detail the impressions received from her cleanliness training, which played a fundamental part in her analysis:

> Once she placed a little doll on a stone, pretended that it was defaecating and stood other dolls around it which were supposed to be admiring it. After this dramatization Erna brought the same material into a game of acting. She wanted me to be a baby in long clothes which made itself dirty, while she was the mother. The baby was a spoilt child and an object of admiration. This was

169

followed by a reaction of rage in Erna, and she played the part of a cruel teacher who knocked the child about. In this way Erna enacted before me one of the first traumata in her experience: the heavy blow her narcissism received when she imagined that the measures taken to train her meant the loss of the excessive affection bestowed on her in her infancy.

(1926, WMK I, p. 136)[2]

At first we can recognise some familiar aspects here. This is how Freud explained in the course of the 1917 lectures (1916–1917, p. 315) that the stool was considered to be a present. Abraham had said in 1921 that cleanliness training 'exposes the child's narcissism to a first severe test' (p. 373). He had indicated in this connection that if cleanliness training started too early, it took place through fear rather than for the sake of the object, which could lead to a lasting disturbance in the capacity to love. Klein is therefore correct to state that here Erna was directly enacting something that with adults had to be reconstructed. However, she appended to this the following footnote:

This training, which Erna had felt as a most cruel act of coercion, was in reality accomplished *without any harshness and so easily* that, at the age of one year, she was perfectly clean in her habits. A strong incentive was her unusually early developed ambition, which, however, caused her to face all the measures taken to train her from the very beginning as an outrage. This early ambition was the primary condition of her sensitiveness to blame and of the precocious and marked development of her sense of guilt. But it is a common thing to see these early feelings of guilt already playing a very big part in the training in cleanliness, and we can recognize in them the first beginnings of the super-ego.

(1926, WMK I, p. 136, fn. 1; my italics)

A new aspect arises here that Freud and Abraham did not describe and which Klein attempts to conceptualise as 'ambition'. The attribution of guilt feelings to this early ambition does not seem entirely

---

2 These scenes do not appear in this form in the treatment notes that have been preserved. However, individual elements that might apply in this connection appear, for example, on p. 8: 'She often plays the tender mother, thinks it does not matter at all if the child dirties herself – she should just keep changing her messy trousers and so on'.

conclusive here. This would require ambition to be defined in the sense that Erna was endeavouring to counteract the perception of the reality of her dependence in the most extensive way possible and would ultimately imply that the source of this ambition was an intolerance and hatred of reality, to which the guilt feelings could then be fairly easily attributed. A scene in which a defaecating doll is admired would then have to be understood as the representation of a narcissistic defensive phantasy. This implies that it would be only partly correct to say that the child directly represents experiences. As with adults, it is also necessary with a child to understand the significance of the scene. Klein still seems here to be adhering to (Abraham's and Freud's) notion of a pre-ambivalent stage and therefore consigns to a footnote the information that cannot really be made to fit with the idea of such a stage. Klein is still seeking to conceptualise everything in terms of the libido theory. She certainly goes on to discuss the significance of the repetition compulsion in the next section and the obvious next point of reference would therefore have been Freud's concept of the death drive, which he had introduced in 1920 partly to explain the repetition compulsion. Using the idea of the death drive would have facilitated a more complete understanding of her new observations, but at this time Klein refers back only to the factor of pleasure in connection with the repetition compulsion.[3]

Klein thus accorded an important role to acting out in this work, but it was not yet possible for her to consider the role of enactment in the transference–countertransference dynamics, which in my view contribute to the deficiencies of her conceptualisation. However, the intuitive perception of what Erna communicates in this scene seems to enter into the footnote, namely that Erna's ambition makes her experience of 'learning' in the analysis humiliating.

The second publication that addresses Erna's analysis, the 'Symposium on child-analysis' (1927a), concerns a central technical theme, namely the negative transference. Klein's understanding of Erna's apparently unrestrained aggression as based mainly on fear, as well as

---

3 Laplanche and Pontalis (1973) have indicated some points of conceptual ambiguity and have given an example in the following comment with a quotation from Freud:

it is obvious that if the place of the pleasure principle is 'to serve the death instincts' . . . then the compulsion to repeat – even understood in the most extreme sense proposed by Freud – can not be situated 'beyond the pleasure principle'.

(Laplanche and Pontalis, 1973, p. 80)

on a need for punishment (1927a, WMK I, p. 160), requires an interpretation of these connections. Klein understood acting out of the anal–sadistic drive excitations outside the analysis as an indication that she 'had failed to resolve the resistances completely in the analytic hour and to release in its fullness the negative transference' (WMK I, p. 161). In contrast to Anna Freud, she situates the error in such a case within the analytic rather than the educational domain. Clearly, as she formulates these connections, Klein makes very little connection in conceptual terms between this situation and two further findings that she communicates at this point. She writes in one sentence that Erna's personality exhibited 'the characteristic cleavage of personality into "devil and angel", "good and wicked princess" ' (WMK I, p. 160) and mentions in a footnote the fact that the obsessional neurosis concealed a paranoia (p. 160, fn. 1). Klein leaves these findings behind. She does not work out the connections between splitting, paranoia and the negative transference – the paranoid fear of Klein as a devil.

In 'Personification in the play of children' (1929), Klein explains in further detail the significance of acting out and enactment in play, which she believes to contain the foundations of the transference. She is still largely thinking here of the direct, manifest roles that the child assigns to the analyst and does not yet consider the function that each particular manifest role attribution might have or which unconscious object is given a role in which particular bit of the play. Klein uses Erna's material here to show how paranoia in the transference was represented in play. Erna often made Klein represent the child, while she became the mother or teacher who subjected the child to extraordinary tortures and humiliations. If the child was treated lovingly by someone in the play, this friendliness usually turned out to be only a pretence.

> The paranoiac traits showed in the fact that I was constantly spied on, people divined my thoughts, and the father or teacher allied themselves with the mother against me – in fact, I was always surrounded with persecutors. I myself, in the rôle of the child, had constantly to spy upon and torment the others.
>
> (1929, WMK I, pp. 199–200)

Klein perceives two principal roles at work here: those of the persecutory superego and the threatened and equally cruel id. She goes on to explain the interactions between them.[4] In a later section, she describes Erna's imperviousness to reality, which persisted for long periods: 'There seemed to be no bridge over the gulf which separated the loving and kindly mother of real life and the monstrous persecutions and humiliations which "she" inflicted on the child in play' (1929, WMK I, p. 205). What gradually became clear was how Erna would filter observations in a grotesquely distorted form into her system of subjection to persecution and threatening observation: 'For instance, she believed that intercourse between her parents . . . and all the tokens of their mutual affection were mainly prompted by her mother's wish to excite jealousy in her' (p. 206). Klein does not link even this observation to the paranoid constellations that Erna enacted in the analytic action, which could be understood to indicate that Erna experienced Klein too as someone whose main wish was to arouse her envy and jealousy.

The common feature to all these passages, from 1926, 1927 and 1929, is that Klein successfully describes new formulations in order to gain a more complete understanding of the mental dynamics that she sees in Erna's behaviour, but she is not yet able to reach a conclusive conceptualisation of them.

The abundance of material on Erna that is presented in 1932 in Chapter 3 of *The Psycho-Analysis of Children*, as well as the accompanying conceptual expositions and technical explanations, will not be reviewed in detail here. Klein discusses, for example, the typical phantasies of a girl's earliest anxiety situation, consisting of the phantasies and fears surrounding the mother's womb; she describes Erna's oral, anal and urethral–sadistic phantasies and her direct and indirect Oedipal wishes. What I have selected here is solely Klein's attempt to identify the crux of Erna's neurosis through all its various facets. Klein mentions Erna's envy several times as '*one*' and also as '*the*' central point (1932, WMK II, p. 39, p. 56). She first discusses, in connection with Erna's compulsive cravings, her oral envy, experienced in relation to the primal scene and the primal phantasies, which then had a fundamental influence on the development of her character and neurosis (WMK II, pp. 38–39). Klein furthermore understands this

---

4 When Klein further explains that the wish fulfilment in this play consists principally in 'Erna's endeavour to identify herself with the stronger party' (1929, WMK I, p. 200), she is describing on a less structured level a process that Anna Freud was later to explain as 'identification with the aggressor' (1936).

oral envy 'of the genital and oral gratifications which she supposed her parents to be enjoying during intercourse' as 'the deepest foundation' (WMK II, p. 46) of Erna's pronounced hatred. As a departure from these concluding reflections, Klein suggests that Erna's persecution mania is attributable to 'the transformations of love for the parent of the same sex into hatred, which is known as the cause of delusions of persecution' (WMK II, p. 45). Towards the end of the chapter, Klein again concludes that envy is the actual cause of Erna's neurosis. She explains the attacks on the mother's womb that are attributable to this envy, as well as the anxieties that are engendered by phantasised robbing and destruction of the mother's body.[5] She makes a connection between this earliest anxiety situation of Erna's and her extreme inhibition in learning.

> Her extraordinary sadism, which was fused with Erna's intense desire for knowledge, led – as a defence against it – to a complete inhibition of a number of activities which were based upon her desire for knowledge. *Arithmetic* and *writing* symbolized violent *sadistic* attacks upon her *mother's body* and her *father's penis*.
>
> (1932, WMK II, p. 57; my italics)

This seems to me to present a striking discrepancy between a very fundamentally conceptualised learning inhibition, bordering from the outset on the dimension that Bion (1962) later described in *Learning from Experience*, and an apparently rather literal restriction of arithmetic and writing. Whereas, as quoted above, Klein regarded envy throughout as the foundation of Erna's hatred and hence as an active attack on her capacity to learn, Klein also drops the idea of this active attack and speaks instead of a learning inhibition, which is restricted to a 'passive inhibition' deriving from guilt feelings. In the final section, Klein addresses Erna's paranoia once again, but without formulating a conceptual connection with the damage to Erna's drive for knowledge.

The impression that emerges here is that Klein was certainly able to perceive, identify and describe the paranoid element – she already writes of 'a paranoid trait' in the 1924–1925 manuscript – but that there was some kind of obstacle to her attempting to conceptualise

---

5 In 1957 Klein indicates in a footnote that she 'had not yet related Erna's envy specifically to the desire to take away and to spoil the mother's breasts, although I had come very near to these conclusions' (1957, WMK III, p. 181, fn.).

this dynamic more comprehensively. From Klein's statement that 'These anal phantasies were soon followed by fits of depression and hatred which she chiefly directed against me but which were actually aimed at her mother' (1932, WMK II, p. 45), we can also infer that Klein might have been protecting herself to a certain extent against this hatred. It should of course be remembered that this was the first analysis in which Klein found a way of allowing the expression of envy and hatred to unfold in the transference in the high-frequency analytic setting. However, I think that Klein's perception of Erna's intense drive for knowledge gave her an important key to the systematic understanding of Erna's analysis. My hypothesis is that this shaped Erna's analysis in a unique way but that Klein was working at this time with an idea of the 'inhibition' of the drive for knowledge, but not yet with an idea of an active 'attack' on this drive, which Bion was later to describe as 'minus K'. This lack hindered Klein's understanding of the connections between envy, paranoia, hatred of reality, negative transference and certain forms of acting out.

6.2 Erna in the unpublished manuscripts

The documents in the Klein Archive in London include an early manuscript of Erna's case history, the first sixteen pages of which are thought to have been presented at the above-mentioned Würzburg conference in 1924. This manuscript was expanded for the 1925 lecture in London (p. 16a–e, pp. 17–21),[6] and it has already been given detailed consideration elsewhere (Frank and Weiss, 1996a). We have been able to show that at this time Klein was still seeking to conceptualise Erna's case history in terms of Freud's libido theory, although some of the conceptual points that Klein selected, such as the 'shattering of the sexual life' (Frank and Weiss, p. 13), already

---

6 Along with this manuscript in file B25 of the Melanie Klein Archive, there is a further copy in file C40, the cover of which is headed 'Third Lecture' [III. Vortrag], indicating that this is the third London lecture. This is followed by page 1 of the above-mentioned manuscript and further essential parts of it, although this version of the manuscript is incomplete. What is most striking, however, are the many crossings out, as well as some additions, from which it remains unclear whether this is a draft of the London lecture or whether Klein subsequently revised it again for a further occasion. I will refer in what follows to the first mentioned manuscript, B25.

demonstrated that the experiences evoked in this analysis did not fit this conception. The material clearly points in many places beyond the conceptualisation in terms of libido theory. In this context, it is interesting that the factors Klein considered to be central are already mentioned here: the 'paranoid trait'; envy in connection 'with the oral wishes' during observations of coitus; unconscious hatred. Klein is already writing here, on the basis of various symptoms such as a pseudologia, about Erna's inability to tolerate reality (Manuscript, p. 16g).

However, there is a further striking feature that becomes comprehensible from the unpublished manuscripts that cannot be understood on the basis of the published material alone. This emerges from the descriptions of the improvements in Erna's condition at various points. From the publication, we know the cautious assessment of 1932: Erna's learning inhibition had been reduced but not removed. Social adaptation had been set in motion:

> Her obsessional symptoms (obsessive masturbation, thumb-sucking, rocking, etc.) which were so severe as to be partly responsible for her sleeplessness, were removed. With their cure and the material lessening of anxiety, her sleep became normal. Her attacks of depression also ceased.
>
> (1932, WMK II, p. 51)

Although these results proved to be enduring, as Klein finally discovered two and a half years after the termination of the analysis, she comments here that the unusual severity of the case meant that a much longer period of analysis would have been required to remove Erna's persistent difficulties and to ensure adequate stability (1932, WMK II, pp. 51–52).

However, the early descriptions written while the analysis was still in progress stand in clear contrast to Klein's gloomier prognosis in 1932. The first description originates from the part of the 1924–1925 lecture manuscript that was added for the London presentation, which must have been written around April 1925 and emerges from the observation that 'the treatment, excluding the breaks, has so far lasted one year'. Here it states:

> Specifically, the following changes can be ascertained in Erna. Her character and thus her relationship with those around her, in particular with her mother, have improved most strikingly. In

connection with this, she has become much more capable of social adaptation. She is now also better able to tolerate criticism and jokes; her sensitivity is substantially reduced. For several months, there has been no observable sign of melancholic depression and she herself repeatedly and spontaneously says that she feels well. She has also, however, adopted a more child-like nature and enjoys herself now in a way that is appropriate to her age, which also partly results from the removal of her tendency to brood and the disappearance of her play inhibition. The anxiety and the obsessional symptoms, in particular the compulsive masturbation and the associated sleeplessness, have completely disappeared, as have a timidity and indecisiveness that used to show in certain situations, such as in sport, play and various children's activities. In the foreground now are the persistent – albeit reduced – learning inhibition, the similarly reduced pseudologia and the ambivalence that is not yet completely resolved.

(Manuscript, p. 18)

In a postscript headed 'November 1925', we read the optimistic assessment:

Postscript seven months later: the analysis is finally concluded & has led to a complete removal of the persistent difficulties mentioned at the end of this report and to a comprehensive cure. The pseudologia and the learning inhibition are completely remedied and the child is attending school, where she is proving herself in every respect, including in her social adaptation, which incidentally is also now completely satisfactory & normal towards both the mother & those around her. The treatment duration (excluding breaks) was 18 months. The child is steadily cheerful and calm and the exaggerated emotional reactions have disappeared; the impression is one of an entirely normal child & and there are no educational difficulties. It is noticeable that she still clearly prefers the father to the mother but also has a good, stable & loving relationship with the latter. I would also like to discuss briefly [sth. crossed out] what had to be accomplished analytically in this final part of the treatment: the continued analysis of the homosexuality led to a very fundamental reduction of this & to a complete removal of the ideas of persecution that were connected with the homosexuality. This, however, produced a complete release of the direct Oedipus attitude from

177

repression; it was in flight from this that the child's homosexuality had developed so strongly, possibly with reinforcement from constitutional factors & child-care experiences.

The fact that the initial assessment that the analysis was finally concluded proved to be premature is clear from a further document, which is headed 'Erna work – Part 2', which must have been written in early 1926 (see Melanie Klein Archive, PP/KLE B25).

The material in the drawings clearly indicates the fragmentation of the personality into two parts. The opposition between the beautiful princess and the peasant girl or between the witch and the good princess etc. signifies the opposition between good and evil that she feels within her own personality, which is also repeatedly represented in games and phantasies by the alternating angel and devil figures. In the drawings, the evil principle, as for example represented by the witch, regularly and indeed increasingly clearly comes to take on particular characteristics of the good princess, who conversely takes on the other's traits, so that, as it finally turns out in individual drawings, the two opposing figures come to resemble each other. I refer in particular to the representation in which at the sound of a thunderbolt the ugly figure repeatedly turns into the beautiful one and the beautiful figure into the ugly one. In this way, the unsuccessful endeavour somehow to fuse together the two parts of her personality is expressed again. This splitting actually arose from the necessity to ward off this evil principle in herself. She is trying somehow to alienate herself from this part of the personality by this splitting and manages to do this by projecting it outwards. The witch, the peasant girl etc., which clearly signify the mother or a possible sister, emerge in this part of the analysis, which is certainly especially difficult and follows an earlier, highly laborious and thoroughgoing analysis of sadism, as the evil part of her own personality that she rejects. The mechanism of this projection is thus that she has to project the part of her personality that she cannot tolerate outwards on to someone else. By doing this, however, the other person becomes an entirely evil and sadistic figure about whom Erna feels guilty because of her projection. In her phantasy, Erna herself then becomes the victim of the external sadistic person (her mother), who persecutes her in the same way as Erna

178

had persecuted her. This is the genesis of the external female persecutor.

During the analysis, I had repeatedly wondered whether this was not such a strong constitutional homosexuality that even after the most thorough analysis an irreducible homosexual component beyond the normal scope would have to persist. This part of the analysis that I am now addressing, which gave me such a clear insight into the genesis of the strong paranoid traits existing in this child, seemed to me for a fairly long time to confirm the premise of this constitutional homosexuality. The familiar paranoid mechanism that turns the original loved one into a persecutor was confirmed here to the greatest degree. I have also already discussed earlier the phantasy that a piece of stool from her mother was penetrating her anus (cf. van Ophuijsen, 1920, on faeces as persecutor). In her play, representations of sexual satisfaction between her and the mother (the fishwife who exchanges fishes – also clearly stool – with her) were repeatedly followed by the wildest phantasies about what was being inflicted on her, for example by this fishwife or in other representations by the beloved mother in terms of frustration and persecutions.

When we had thoroughly analysed this paranoid component, however, I found that a completely different picture emerged. After this part of the analysis, which had proceeded with the aid of the above-mentioned drawings, there was actually an extensive resolution of the persecutory thoughts that were specifically expressed in a completely changed psychic picture. Although in one sense the child clearly felt some relief, we nevertheless then re-encountered difficulties that were also experienced much more strongly by those around her. She became much more difficult to treat in this stage and tormented those around her, especially the mother, much more. In the analytic sessions, her drawing, which as stated above was the strongest mode of expression in the analysis of this paranoid component, now almost completely stopped again. She now began again, as in a very much earlier stage of the analysis, to produce primitive anal representations; she shaped little sausages out of plasticine, smeared herself and me and the furniture with them, and exhibited a complete relapse into the sadism that earlier had been so greatly reduced by the analysis. The learning difficulties increased in a worrying way. A short dictation, for example, contained 20 errors; however, what made an

179

absolutely abnormal impression that exceeded everything else was the fact that some words were missing and others were completely mangled. After this long analysis and the extraordinary results that had already been achieved, which even now were certainly not generally put in doubt, I was nevertheless confronted with the question of whether I had not now reached the point beyond which I could not progress any further with the analysis. In any case, the analysis, notwithstanding its long duration at this point, appeared for the first time to be exhibiting a stage at which no progress was demonstrable and that seemingly could not be taken any further. The question as to why such a strong anal-sadistic phase had now reappeared was inexplicable to me. I saw only that in place of the earlier passive thoughts of persecution, which of course were still combined with active sadism, there now appeared exclusively sadistic phantasies directed specifically against the mother. However, when I did not allow any slack to enter the analysis, a way forward then emerged that was then also to shed light on these matters in theoretical terms.

Unfortunately the manuscript breaks off at this point and since for this period (January to April 1926) there are no treatment notes available either, this final part of the analysis remains inaccessible to us. As I discuss elsewhere, it seems possible that Klein's planned emigration to England may have been a factor in Erna's sudden deterioration.

The striking aspect that I wish to emphasise consists in Klein's initially highly optimistic assessment in respect of the rapid improvement in Erna's disorder. This could be understood as a temporary partial sharing by Klein of Erna's defence, her manic disavowal.

The second part of the Erna text, however, shows that Klein did not withdraw from the experiences in the analytic situation and that she succeeded in substantially advancing the conceptualisation of this case. She describes splitting here very clearly and formulates with the concept of the 'evil principle' the dynamic that she is later to work out in terms of Freud's concept of the death drive. It is therefore in my view another striking feature that the splitting but not her reflections on the 'evil principle' entered the relevant chapter in 1932, at a time when she was repeatedly returning to the problem of the death drive in the remaining chapters.

6.3 Erna in the treatment notes

I shall first consider the material available concerning Erna from the pocket diary to which frequent reference has been made. It can be reconstructed that Erna's analysis lasted from 9 January 1924 to 15 April 1926.[7] There are detailed handwritten notes essentially for three periods:

1. January to 31 March 1924 on the first sixty pages of the treatment book; (April with an Easter break and 'May–June' are recorded on a single page, p. 61 of the treatment book); in addition to this, there are some drawings by Erna from these weeks.

2. 15 September to 25 October 1924, which includes both the sessions from 20 to 29 September in a further section of the treatment book (p. 1a to 11a) and also, after some blank pages, the sessions from 7 October to 25 October 1924 (p. 1b to 18b); the sessions from 15 to 19 September; 30 September and 6 October appear on individual sheets; there is also a descriptive summary of the sessions from 25 October to 25 November 1924 (six pages).

3. (5 November and) 14 November 1925 to 18 December 1925. These sessions are again on individual sheets, to which corresponding drawings and cut-out figures are attached with paper-clips.[8]

Klein generally saw Erna six times a week (Monday to Saturday). This also included weeks in which Erna came 'only' four or five times weekly.

If we first compare the treatment notes with the published material, it is impressive how on the one hand entire play scenes, mainly from the earliest sessions, directly entered the 1932 publication with only minor stylistic revisions. On the other hand, it is also striking how

---

7 Nelly Wolffheim writes in her 'Erinnerungen an Melanie Klein' [Memories of Melanie Klein] that Erna was in her kindergarten and 'after previous consultation with Karl Abraham' went to Klein for analysis (Wolffheim, 1974, p. 296).

8 The 'postscript' mentioned in Section 6.2 must have been written at the beginning of November 1925; the 'Erna work – Part 2' that is also mentioned there, a few months after this period.

Erna's direct involvement of Klein in her play, which occurred from the outset, sometimes reaching violent proportions, has moved into the background of the publication by contrast with the treatment notes. Most of the scenes of this kind were omitted from the publication and for other incidents the violence of Erna's behaviour can only be imagined from what remains a general description. For example, Klein sometimes describes Erna's behaviour in general terms: 'attacks of rage and anxiety . . . partly precipitated by her meeting the child who came to me for treatment immediately before or after her' (1932, WMK II, p. 42).[9] The earliest mention in the publication of Klein's involvement by Erna occurs in the description of the roles that Erna assigned to Klein in her play. What corresponds in terms of treatment technique to the partial omission or toning down of Klein's direct involvements by Erna is the direct attribution of Erna's feelings by Klein to the original object. The above-quoted sentence about 'fits of . . . hatred which she chiefly directed against me but which were actually aimed at her mother' (1932, WMK II, p. 45) is indicative of Klein's conscious technical procedure, which in this respect is similar to that of Freud. This procedure of rapidly interpreting attitudes towards the analyst as indicating attitudes towards original objects is somewhat premature from a contemporary perspective. It also appears in this form in the treatment notes, where reconstructive interpretations clearly predominate.[10] Klein's understanding of Erna's role playing and her attempts to involve Klein certainly shows that Klein was working from the premise of an externalisation of inner conflicts, for example between the severe superego and the id. The idea that this involved prevailing actualisations of internal object relationships that for their part are certainly influenced by relationships with external objects but do not represent their exact counterparts is not really rigorously thought through at this time. This is also clear from statements such as the above-quoted one that the feelings of hatred actually relate to the mother. Accordingly, and of course we can base

---

9 Cf. here the treatment notes, pp. 20f., for example: 'Intense jealousy of Felix whom she met – whether my chair was there because he wanted it like that – why 2 chairs close together – furiously demands paper to make dirty'.

10 Klein naturally made notes in summarised form, so we cannot exclude the possibility that she gave more transference interpretations in reality than she recorded in the notes. However, I consider it likely that the evaluation that she made is in fact reflected to some extent in the notes made from memory.

this conclusion only on the treatment notes, Klein did not try for example directly to interpret Erna's acting out in the sessions in the form of excessive masturbation but instructed Erna to refrain from masturbation and instead to talk about her ideas (cf. for example p. 21, p. 25, p. 29).

However, by studying the treatment notes we can now examine how far, in spite of this model that she had taken over from Freud, Klein partly succeeded in interpreting the relevant enactments and how far these experiences formed the foundation for concepts that she developed later. When in 1932 Klein makes statements such as 'By analysing this specific transference situation it was possible to trace her attitude through earlier situations back to the earliest – to the experience of being cared for when she was an infant' (1932, WMK II, p. 49), the actual form that these situations took can be demonstrated from material in the treatment notes.

In the treatment notes it can be shown in my view how naturally the relevant relational dynamics were discussed even in the reconstructive interpretations, so that we can imagine that the interpretation could also 'take'. Equally, it is clear in some instances how this rapid attribution of Erna's feelings exclusively to her mother rather than also to Klein herself robbed Klein's interpretations of some of their transference richness.

It is my thesis that with her 'intense drive for knowledge', Erna actually challenged Klein in the here-and-now of the analytic relationship, and in her response to this challenge Klein was able to become involved to an extent that was probably hardly attained by other analysts at this time. She seems to have taken this challenge as a matter of course with a spontaneous willingness for a great deal of self-analytic work (initially certainly supported by her analysis with Abraham). She was able to formulate decisive dynamic connections to Erna, and with her intuitive clinical knowledge she was therefore probably clinically ahead of her theoretical conceptualisations. I believe that the specific quality of Erna's drive for knowledge, which was very rapidly governed by envy and hatred of reality, also stimulated parts of Klein's own character, which tended to lead her to frame interpretations in a way that diverted attention away from Klein herself and towards Erna's parents, especially her mother. As today we have available Bion's concepts of 'K' and 'minus K' as developed by O'Shaughnessy and others in relation to child analysis, we can I think reconsider Klein's idea of the significance of Erna's drive for knowledge in another light. The treatment notes allow us to see how far it can plausibly be demonstrated that 'K' constituted a connecting theme in Erna's analysis. 'K' stands here for thinking as an 'emotional experience of trying to know oneself or someone else' (O'Shaughnessy, 1981, p. 178) whereas 'minus K' stands for 'the cruel and denuding link of misunderstanding the self and others' (1981, p. 178 and p. 181).

Individual passages from each of the above periods will now be examined more closely, in order both to demonstrate the microstructure of the psychodynamics as they appear in the treatment notes and to outline the main themes as they expressed themselves at a particular time.

6.3.1 'Nose-biting, eye-salad . . .' – attacks on the object's perceptual capacity (January to March 1924)

Again serving as a connecting theme throughout the initial[11] treatment notes are the striking aspects that become apparent here as signs of Klein's irritation, as they arise both from the treatment notes themselves and in comparison with the publication.[12]

The treatment notes start as follows:

Begins 1st session: runs small carriage
towards me = fe (gaiming at genital region)
says is fetching me – continues with small
woman (figure).

In 1932 – and also in the 1924–1925 manuscript – the description begins as follows: 'Erna began her play by taking a small carriage which stood on the little table among the other toys and letting it run towards me' (1932, WMK II, p. 36; in the manuscript on p. 2 the words 'lets . . . run towards me' are underlined). The statement that follows in the original notes 'aims at genital region' is thus omitted from the two later versions and seems to be about to undergo the

---

11 A first evaluation of the beginning of Erna's analysis was presented in 1996 in *Luzifer-Amor* (Frank and Weiss, 1996a).

12 In contrast to the position with Grete, Rita, Inge, and Ernst, with Erna the beginning of the analysis exists in both published and unpublished form.

same fate at first in the treatment notes as well. In the original, 'ab' [the first part of the German word for 'fetching'] is crossed out immediately after 'fahren' ['runs towards me'], and Klein presumably had started to write 'abholen' [to fetch] before crossing out the first two letters and making the addition in brackets with a further orthographical error in the first letter (in the original German, the 'z' of '*zielt*' [aims] is written over a 'G'). Although the opening sequence in the 1932 version seems comparatively neutral, the underlining in the manuscript already points more clearly to an affectively significant component that is then described fairly graphically in the treatment notes. A sexualised transference constellation is immediately apparent, although from a modern perspective we might characterise it as a transference–countertransference constellation: Klein experiences Erna's initial impulse as a fairly literal intention to penetrate her. The establishment of the relationship that is thus described leads to the play being broken off, probably because of its associated overpowering sexual component. The 'running towards me' is enigmatic in terms of both libidinal and aggressive components. Erna is unable to remain in direct contact with Klein but continues the play with a toy figure, a small woman. Here the treatment notes and the published version agree again, but the intense start, in which the 'intense drive for knowledge'[13] was very directly expressed, has nevertheless lost much of its emotional force in the published version.

Erna explains this opening scene in the game that follows:

She climbs with man
on to a carriage – another man comes
up to carriage, runs them over – are dead
were eaten up.

In 1932 it states (the manuscript is identical in content here, only slightly different stylistically):

She declared that she had come to fetch me. But she put a toy woman in the carriage instead and added a toy man. The two loved and kissed one another and drove up and down all the time. Next a

---

13 It is open to question how far the penetration is motivated by a wish to know or instead by a wish not to know. It may also be that the differentiation is partly dependent on further responses and understandings by the analyst.

toy man in another carriage collided with them, ran over them and killed them, and then roasted and ate them up.

(1932, WMK II, p. 36)

Here too we can again infer a possible irritation on Klein's part, since she mentions the details of the dynamics – the couple's hugging and kissing – only in a postscript to the first session on page 5 of the treatment notes. Is it possible that the unease that may have precipitated this temporary forgetting arose from a demonstration that Klein thus received of how she was experienced by Erna as a form of combined parent figure that accordingly felt intolerable, so that Erna had to overcome the object, eating it up and taking it over for herself in an apparently manic way? In my view Erna also conveys in this association something of her emotional 'knowledge' of her dealings with the object: she seems to perceive the crushing and devouring aspects of her establishment of a relationship with Klein.

In the next play association, Erna communicates a further variation on how she experiences her new object, a sequence that is absent from the 1924–1925 manuscript and the publication (1932).

I am a lute-
player am run over by a man
with carriage because am in the way.

For a moment a somewhat more benign perception of a creative object (lute-player) seems to be possible. It cannot be ascertained from the documents whether this was facilitated by an appropriate comment or solely by Klein's attitude. Erna's idea of a lute-player could in any case be understood as a possible indication that Erna perceived that Klein was dealing in a different way with her 'tones' – her communications – from the way she might have been accustomed to. She may have become aware that this might provide her with new possibilities. The recognition is followed a moment later again by the elimination of this new object, which is an obstacle 'in the way'. A parapraxis on Klein's part – she returns to this scene again on page 2 and writes then of a lute-*beater* instead of a lute-*player* – gives some information as to how 'beaten' Erna actually feels in relation to a creative object.

The report on the first session in the treatment notes initially contains only these three play sequences; it is followed by material from other sessions. However, Klein returns repeatedly to the first session in the subsequent pages. The impression emerges that the attacking, 'running over' quality of the object relationship is also expressed by the form in which it is written down. Klein's interpretations disappeared at first in this summarised report in the treatment notes, bringing an aspect of the object relationship vividly to the fore, namely, that the object is to have nothing to say. Erna thus enacts very impressively how she would immediately like to 'fetch' the object in order to have it at her disposal and how intolerable it is for her to feel dependent on a separate object that she imagines in connection with another, which she therefore has to run over, roast and eat. The omission of Klein as a lute-player in the publication, like the parapraxis (of 'beater' instead of 'player'), reflects Erna's corresponding intrapsychic dynamic, which is characterised by the rapid development of a misconception. Erna was creating a transformation that Money-Kyrle (1978, p. 441) would have described as the 'turning, under the influence of hate and envy, of a good parental intercourse into its destructive opposite'.

The next sequence seems to summarise this principal dynamic in condensed form.

Another
time builds house. Man is on the
ground, catches mice, roasts he – [sth. crossed out] says
her favourite meal potato fritter –
The people burst, burn up,
house collapses.

Neither in the manuscript nor in the Erna chapter of *The Psycho-Analysis of Children* (1932) does the scene appear in this form. Elements of this play phantasy appear in the unpublished manuscript on page 3: 'A man and woman are inside a house that they are defending from a burglar; the third person, a burglar, creeps in; the house burns down, the people burst, the third person remains behind alone'. In 1932 Klein points to individual play elements in connection with Erna's aggressive phantasies, in which the excrement that has turned into explosive, dangerous material is used in an attack on the mother's womb: 'This was depicted by the burning down and destruction of the house and the "bursting" of the people inside it' (WMK II, p. 56).

It emerges from the treatment notes that the catastrophe (collapse of the house, destruction of the people) follows on from a constructive

187

impulse (building the house), although in the revised version this sequence is no longer clear and only the attacks remain. Thus the tragic situation in which Erna now finds herself in relation to her parents and her analyst no longer becomes so acutely apparent. I think one could maintain here that Erna is actually representing how she attempts with the house-building to learn to know something about her object/analyst but then she is driven to destroy the people and to focus instead on eating – 'her favourite meal'. Perhaps she thus experiences the object as unable to withstand her craving impulses ('favourite meal').

Her next play associations contain the idea that the object must be protected from such rapacious actions:

> Another time house
> is protected against burglars
> on all sides.

This is rapidly followed in the play by the attempt, literally towards Klein, to appropriate and incorporate what is desirable:

> A small man
> (again the 3rd one – who still runs over
> with carriage – but who also comes
> to visit man and woman & woman bites
> off nose in 1st session.) wants to
> [In first session she also wants to bite off my nose][1]
> creep in there.

Klein's emotional response to Erna's nose-biting attempts – surprise? Irritation? – can be inferred from the fact that she repeatedly introduces the nose-biting in the following pages as if it were new. In the manuscript (p. 4) and in 1932 she mentions the nose-biting in connection with sadistic and cannibalistic impulses (WMK II, p. 37). She later identifies the nose-biting as an attack on 'her father's penis which I was supposed to have incorporated' (p. 56). In my view the context in which this theme appears in the treatment notes further suggests that Erna was partly hoping that Klein would turn out to be a potent creative object who could help her but equally, however, as this would also be acutely intolerable, Erna wanted to deprive Klein of precisely this possibility of having a 'nose' for these connections.

The notes continue:

Stops playing (p. 1).

Whereas with the opening sequence of running a carriage towards Klein, it was possible for Erna to continue the play by turning away from Klein, with the more aggressive nose-biting interaction, which, as can be concluded from the repetitions, at first had an even more unpalatable quality for Klein, the play can only be broken off. It seems likely that Erna was now afraid of Klein's revenge. At Klein's interpretation, '*she small man who ident. Father wants mother*', Erna continues with her playing. How is this interpretation of Klein's to be understood? Klein may have been consciously thinking of Erna's castration complex and thus have concluded that Erna wanted to be equipped like the father so to be able to achieve an equivalent relationship with the mother. According to Klein's conscious conception, she would thus have interpreted Erna's unconscious indirect Oedipal wish, having removed her resistance by bringing it to her consciousness. The interpretation of the material as a wish to oust the father from his position with the mother is also the first conceptual explanation in the manuscript (p. 3) and in the publication (WMK II, p. 36). As we have seen, some elements that were clearly emotionally arousing to Klein were omitted there. If we ask ourselves why the interpretation 'took' (Erna continues with her playing) against the background of Klein's hypothesis about Erna's indirect Oedipus complex, this is perhaps related to the fact that with this interpretation Klein also picked up the constructive element in Erna's acting out, namely, her wish for a relationship with the mother. Klein would thereby have proved to Erna that she was a non-vengeful object. She introduced herself as an object that had thoughts about Erna. What is not contained in this interpretation, however, is what is presumably the immediate cause of the game being broken off, namely, Erna's anxiety.

Let us examine from Erna's recorded reaction how she may have understood the interpretation, '*she small man who ident. {identification} Father wants mother*'. Erna's association of school and teacher confirms in my view that she is able to perceive Klein as an object from whom she can learn something because Klein has reflected on her activity. However, Erna also seems to be commenting on the sexualised level of interpretation when she makes the teacher show the children how

189

to play the lute with their heads.[14] '*Then throws lute away and dances with school-girl*'. Klein adds here that she interprets Erna's head-bumping, presumably in the above-mentioned sexual sense, although she does not explicitly say so. Erna then vividly demonstrates how she is attempting to understand her object in the sense that Klein, like her, does not want to use the head to think but seeks to deploy it as the object of a perverse relationship. The crossed-out addition '*eight days long, day & night, in which terribly aggressive*' at the end of the first page of the treatment notes, which reappears (thus was priori-tised) at the end of the next quoted passage, can be understood to indicate that Erna's aggression and scorn provoked an impulse in Klein not to subject herself again to all the details of this situation during its written reconstruction – an impulse that Klein neverthe-less resisted.

> Another time schoolmaster and schoolmistress
> are with children – whom they were teaching
> how to bow etc. ~~abe~~ – at first very
> obedient & polite – then attack
> schoolmaster & schoolmistress – kill, roast them
> the children are devils & are happy
> while constantly trampling etc.
> then they are both in heaven
> the former devils are angels – 'but are
> not former devils at all, know nothing
> about them so cannot be them'. God the Father
> (formerly the man) kisses the woman (passionately)
> all well. – When schoolmaster dances with schoolgirl –
> tenderest embrace kisses – asks me
> if I allow marriage – dances to loud
> noise 8 days & nights long, with
> her. Thereby terribly aggressive & scornful. . .

Erna is again portraying how she has to trample down objects from whom she can learn, and by doing so she communicates to her analyst that she has some inkling of her own wish not to know by working

14 These scenes are described in the publication (1932, WMK II, p. 36) with a violin instead of a lute; whether this was partly on grounds of confidentiality must remain open to question.

out a manic denial in the play: 'The former devils had turned into angels, who, according to Erna's account, knew nothing about ever having been devils – indeed "they never *were* devils" ' (1932, WMK II, p. 37), as this scene appears in the publication.

Erna then seems to be afraid that this denial might elicit a scornful reaction from Klein; she is '*Thereby terribly aggressive & scornful towards me – shouts me down when I want to speak*'. Klein interprets this direct interaction: '*interpret – in order not to listen, which she had to with mother*'. Klein discusses the resistance here, albeit not entirely in the context of the analytic relationship. The next recorded play sequence can now also be understood as a psychodynamic response to Klein's interpretation, working from the premise that the process of reading is influenced by the unconsciously perceived psychodynamics: '*Another time shows how man reads a book while standing on his head (bumping his head!)*'. I think Erna again recognises here that Klein is 'reading', that she is taking up, deciphering and understanding a part of Erna's psychic reality.

On the basis of the indirect Oedipal wishes inferred by Klein it seems logical to understand the play scenes that portray a particular use of the head as phantasies that underlie the head-banging symptom, to which Klein refers three times in the first two pages of the treatment notes. If we suppose, however, that Erna did not exhibit this symptom during the sessions, for there is certainly no mention of this occurring, then the frequent references to the head are striking. In terms of my hypothesis, Klein is 'rightly' concerned with the provocative use of the head, although the element of perversion is largely being acted out by Erna and is not interpreted as such. This also reappears in the symptom descriptions in the 1924–1925 manuscript, which contains discussion of a 'bumping of the head' (p. 1), which became a 'banging of her head' in 1932 (WMK II, p. 35).

The next interpretation to be mentioned from the first session shows the juxtaposition of Klein's conscious libidinal conceptualisation of the material with the experiences, partly expressed in Klein's parapraxes, that appear to some extent to contradict it.

> Immediately in 1st session interpret her
> running over carriage – running over
> lute-beater – man with carriage who runs
> over man & woman – running over woman
> as coitus wish & coitus observation
> & imitation. Also that the fear

of robbers that stops as long as
she bumps her head – is why the
head-bump-
ing compulsive.

At first Klein interprets Oedipal wishes again. She thus picks up
Erna's enacted wish to enter into a connection with Klein, whereby
its quality in practice is specified by the parapraxis 'lute-beater'
instead of 'lute-player'. In the second part of the interpretation, Klein
focuses on the fear that Erna sometimes managed to deaden by masturbatory use of her head, her head-bumping. Klein thus understood
and interpreted a central factor of the dynamics at a very early point,
at the end of the first session.

Let us turn now to the next elaborated play scene to consider it in
psychodynamic terms as Erna's response to this interpretation:

Showed me that catkin (plant)[15]
in vase at my house so lovely – licks & kisses it wants
to bite it. Very soon (3rd session) she acts
Frau Dr Klein; interprets to me.

For the first time a loving scene, at least at first, is portrayed by Erna.
It seems that the experience of being understood by Klein turns the
analyst into a lovable kitten, which however is again subsequently
subjected to her oral-sadistic impulses.[16] If we then consider the next
sequence – '*Very soon (3rd session) she acts/Frau Dr Klein, interprets to me*'
– we find a vivid illustration of the precarious balance between Erna's
attempt to take in Klein's understanding function on the one hand,
and, on the other hand, her attempt to make a rapacious takeover of
that function in a way that denies generational difference.

Klein then explains with a further example how she interpreted
this role-reversal in the transference: '*She plays mother & child*'. This
enables Erna to externalise and thus to communicate her tormenting
conflict very vividly.

Then really plays mother
& child: I still small, not

15 Translator's note: The German word *Kätzchen* means both 'kitten' and 'catkin', the plant.
16 If we also consider the double significance of 'kitten', it seems likely that Erna also experiences her object in this way: as both 'cuddly' and swift to bite, presumably with her words.

speaking – put everything in mouth – first
thing I put in mouth: engine with
2 lamps, suck on it. (She had
much admired engine – said
2 gilded round parts
– lamps – were: so beautiful,
so red & burning. Thereby stuck
in mouth – just as when talks
about little collar, catkin – also when
woman run over by man – afterwards cooking
eating and puts man or woman in
mouth – sucks, bites.) She then constantly
says 'ugh' – I put away again put
to mouth – also carriage or man
(Then also interpret eng. with 2 lamps = mother's breasts & penis

Erna makes Klein put everything in her mouth, for which she is then accordingly condemned. Erna also shows how she feels exonerated in relation to her greedy impulses, which draw her into a vicious circle. In 1932, Klein certainly describes the corresponding play sequence (WMK II, p. 37). However, the context in which this material was extended following a transference interpretation has been omitted from the publication.

The following sequence explains in more detail how the dynamics of the transference–countertransference situation are influenced by this vicious circle.

(following her instruction). Divides up bricks
so – that she always has more than me –
overcompensation – then again too many to me
– back and forth – counts, begins compulsively
to divide up repeatedly. Forces me
to build as well. – Then makes ever bigger
garden or house – pushes at my
building, – knocks over bricks, throws down
wants to make me pick up. – Here
especially strong sadism emerges. Must
explain when silent, be silent when
want to speak. Makes me build so as
constantly to prove hers prettier, bigger. (Interpret

193

her competitive envy – house, garden
[into]¹ which puts man = body, genitals)

Erna very vividly demonstrates how she is visibly endeavouring to let Klein have enough bricks to enable her to build constructive interpretations. However, at the next moment this is precisely what becomes intolerable to her, so that she has to triumph over Klein. Klein's interpretation – '*competitive envy*' – is presumably again made with conscious reference to the Oedipal level, but probably pinpoints the enacted early Oedipal dynamic very precisely. In the subsequent image of drinking water – *in the garden makes fountain. As first from this: woman drinks.* – and Erna's subsequent actual drinking of water, Erna again seems both to recognise that she needs and wants something from Klein and at the same time to deny the value of what Klein can give her. A further central factor of the dynamic, envy, is thus seen and identified by Klein here at a very early stage.

Here there is the first indication of the defence through anality that will later be discussed in further detail.

> With building - thing talks about 'pieces' –
> that I threw around & other material
> as stool-thing. – When interpret is stool – anger
> with mother about stool-control –
> she puts brick in mouth, sucks
> & bites – says: it is even nicer now
> when is wet – more appetising. (Interpret
> at same time with stool also making wet & thereby
> putting in mouth).

The following repetition of scenes from the first session (notes, p. 5) of the treatment notes can also be understood psychodynamically as an indication that this conflict was difficult for Klein to grasp. Erna then returns to the bricks again.

> With building - things plays
> that in this built house
> man woman live, who burst, burn up
> house collapses etc. – Wants to make
> me give present, takes brick with her
> terrible despair when want to refuse

194

> interpret stool-frustration. While dividing up
> bricks etc. – recognises envious
> aggressive impulse, admits – also play-
> acts supposedly dividing equally – destroys house
> pretending 'by chance', throws
> bricks down etc.

Klein adds here: '*Overcom[ing] ego resistances*'. It is striking in this formulation that Klein is returning to a theme that Freud worked out in *Beyond the Pleasure Principle* (1920b), in which he explains the ego's resistance in the service of the pleasure principle in contrast to the repetition compulsion, which he considers to be connected with the death drive. The impression emerges that Klein is approaching connections that she is to work out later without at this time already having considered the concept of the death drive. However, Klein is clearly able to make the discovery that the interpretation of envious-aggressive impulses opens up the possibility that Erna is making use of a new medium (paper games) in the analysis and thus is able to communicate her conflict more precisely. With the paper-cutting Erna initially gives Klein a present, and this is immediately followed by the desire to force Klein to give Erna a present in return.

> Paper games – begins to cut out
> blankets – serrated, fringed. – Gives
> to me – but wants to make me give her
> 5 pfennigs for the paper. Gives me strips of
> coloured paper – 'no child
> brings me so many
> presents'. – Then asks me again what
> least pretty of the cut-out material –
> that she gives me – along with strips of black
> paper because least likes – even mentions
> great wish – this colour.

Erna goes on to explain why she must immediately then destroy her reparative impulse: she seems, and I think this is what the black paper that she least likes stands for, to come into contact for a moment with the destroyed object. She must quickly offload this on to Klein and try to deaden the perception of her terror with excited behaviour.

Thereby
tells how – while cutting out is making
minced meat – blood must then also
come out – 'trembles, should not speak
about it – because feels very ill then'. –
Then says are fringes that she cuts
in my nose – thereby repeated
~~praye~~ wish & also attempt to bite off
my nose.

The object must also be deprived of the capacity to perceive these connections. Erna turns her object into 'minced meat' and tries to bite off her analyst's nose. Erna then leaves Klein to put everything back together in some way. Klein interprets to Erna her reparative impulse, but does not articulate what is so intolerable about this to Erna herself. The significant details of this in the play are also omitted from the published material (cf. 1932, WMK II, p. 37).

Erna becomes somewhat clearer:

Wants to force me
to keep giving her lots of new paper to
[sth. crossed out] cut up while taking special
pleasure in using up for me as much
as possible to destroy. When I want to reject
compulsion – terrible despair. Forgets,
loses prepared paper from home.

Only now does Klein interpret Erna's *will for power and destruction* and thus she confronts the core of Erna's defensive phantasy through which Erna strives omnipotently to ward off her burgeoning guilt feelings. Now Erna readily brings paper

to cut up with her. – Folds, makes
'puff-star' that she can puff up – herself
recognises penis that expands.

Furthermore, Erna is able to express that she feels understood in her wish for a manic phallus and can then, as after the interpretation of the envious–aggressive impulses, express the connections in question via a new medium on a symbolically more developed level.

196

Access to the treatment notes produces only one of two drawings preserved from 16 January 1924:

Draws –
Drawings end of exercise book. Laughs
at drawing with house below
[(interpret mother dies)][1]
because woman above it. Heaven comes
– then house is scrawled
all over with black
lines.

Let us consider the drawings themselves.[17] The main focus in the drawing mentioned is on Erna, who as '*the laughing house (because mother is in heaven) that is scrawled over in black*' alone dominates the lower half of the drawing. Significantly, Erna draws this house in the triangular shape that later becomes her way of representing the crinolines, which represent for her one of the mother's attributes. Here the crinoline frames the face. Erna triumphs for a moment over the dead mother, inside whom she is situated. However, in accordance with the symmetrical logic of the unconscious (Matte-Blanco, 1988),[18] the dead mother is also simultaneously situated inside Erna, which must accordingly influence the dead/alive and inside/outside dynamic. The conflictual triangular situation appears in disavowed form in the upper part of the drawing. In heaven, the mother is surrounded by two angels; the disturbing situation is euphemistically reinterpreted by idealisation. This defence seems to collapse in the next picture: here Erna is banished to hell as a wicked girl and the triangular constellation is transformed into its persecutory counterpart, for Erna is surrounded by two devils. Laughter seems to stand for the scornful triumphant introject that previously dominated her. The crying devil may refer to a depressive object. The picture can also be understood as the representation of the perverse relationship between parts of the self, in which the needy part of Erna is cruelly dominated by an idealised destructive part of her personality. At the centre of this

17 See illustrations in Part Two, Chapter 11.
18 Matte-Blanco (1988) concisely indicates the 'logics of the mind' in terms of symmetrical and asymmetrical logic. He explains that primary-process events share the characteristic of symmetry: 'a is inside b' is the same as 'b is inside a'.

second picture, however, stands a tall figure: '*The mother (also a Chinese person) whose trousers are being pulled down by the child & whose benches or chairs the child was smashing*'. This dominating figure, which stretches from hell to the clouds, seems to be put completely out of action by the child. The mother is accompanied by a small 'devil that is comforting the mother' and there then appears '*St. Peter Clouds*', whose function remains unclear. The lack of allusion by Klein to this second drawing seems to confirm the dominance of the anal attitude in Erna, which seeks to ward off the confrontation with a damaged object.

Later on in this period the connections described above are developed further. Erna repeatedly makes it clear that she would like to learn from Klein's position and function but also how intolerable she finds it to see Klein or her mother in this position. Erna herself must therefore be '*as clever as mother*' (p. 9). It is Erna who cooks for the mother and surpasses her in everything (p. 10); Erna herself is the one who teaches and she repeatedly tries to take Klein's place in a completely literal way, by fighting her for her chair. It is no longer role play then that is taking place; the analyst is not to *play* the child but is *treated as* a child (cf. here Meltzer's explanations of this form of dynamic constellation: Meltzer, 1967, p. 19). Erna frequently has to reach for more violent forms of defence; this mainly takes the form of orgies of getting dirty and excessive masturbation. In connection with this, her attempts to destroy the analyst's perception increase. Whereas initially she still talks about wanting to take out the analyst's eyes and make an eye-salad (p. 18), a few weeks later during her scrawling she suddenly throws a pencil at Klein's eye (p. 37). In a drawing from 2 March 1924, Erna represents this connection vividly: '*Girl who does wee-wee and poo, next to her the mother, who at first had no eyes and nose*'. Just three weeks later, Erna throws a pencil at Klein again and asks if she will go blind if she hits her eye (p. 50). Finally, Erna gives Klein an understanding in a drawing from 26 March 1924 of how she experiences the eyes: they are terrifying and murderous. What Klein years later called the paranoid-schizoid mode becomes clear from these associations. Accordingly, Erna also has to deny that her analyst could have been ill (cf. p. 43), after which first Erna and then Klein were unwell for two days – '*Disbelief that or why ill*'. Erna's fear that there is something so wrong with her that she cannot be helped (cf. p. 34 of the treatment notes) may have been at the root of this dynamic.

However, Erna is repeatedly able to take an interest in her psychic reality. She raises the question as to whether masturbation is not ugly and unhealthy (p. 17); there are moments of bad conscience (e.g. p. 40) and, finally, at the end of this first period she is able to express her knowledge that this concerns phantasies in which either she or the object/mother is dead (cf. p. 59).

6.3.1.1 Appendix: phantasies of the analysis as an enveloping relationship with the 'beautiful (milk-giving) cow' as a defence against a devalued ugly relationship – May to June 1924

It remains unclear why only a few lines of descriptive summary with few drawings exist from this period. On this basis it is not possible to develop any very certain hypothesis about what was going on in this period.

'*Draws woman man child*' could be understood as Erna's attempt to contemplate her reality as a child with parents. The mention of a child here is something new; until this point, the combination '*Old woman princess bridegroom*' predominated. The material that follows shows that Erna quickly wards this perception off again with Oedipal illusions:

> woman man child – together
> are in meadow. This followed by enormous
> rage. No not together. Again
> draws charming woman & bridegroom
> child herself has husband.
> (Manuscript, p. 61)

In the next described play sequence, Erna again portrays how hard she finds it to tolerate it when the object, her analyst, eludes her control, 'goes away':

> Then
> plays, I her husband. ~~Went~~
> ~~away~~. At first affectedly tender
> – then I went away –
> not back on time, fetches police-
> man in rage: should lock up
> her husband who does not want to
> come to her 'to stick in penis'
> (Manuscript, p. 61)

Albeit in a sexualised form, Erna is able here to give clearer expression to her need for her object. Against this background, the drawings of 2 June 1924 can be understood to indicate that she is striving for a good, 'beautiful' relationship with Klein, while the ugly, devalued form of relationship is strongly apparent to her. However, the latter is attributed in the drawing to her younger 'analytic brother'. She portrays herself as completely enveloped by the beautiful cow.

6.3.2 *The first explorations of psychic reality and Erna's pathogenic object relationships become possible (September to November 1924)*

There are no records for the sessions immediately following the summer holidays; it is striking that in a drawing from 6 September 1924 – 'The breakfast table for mother and child' – there is no reference to the father, which might suggest that this concerns a continuation of the striving for an exclusive relationship between mother and Erna and between Klein and Erna. Records made from memory then appear from Monday 15 September 1924, the notes for which are so summarised that only a limited understanding of the discernible sense is possible.

> Erna 15/IX. Lining up carriages
> looks for engine – chair,
> bathroom – Washing.
> Washerwoman – I supposedly:
> clean – trousers thick
> with blood dirt!
> (Exercise book! Schoolmistress!)
> from dirt. Laundry
> fishes – [counting][1] [?] money also
> for that [sth. crossed out] – chair
> – water representation
> paper tap – sack
> t. {then?} stares sacrament
> – lake – fishes
> very cheap
> by policeman made
> expensive – policeman
> arm movements [?]

pastry cook – whipped cream
nut cake – same
water – paper [sth. illegible]

....

spit – with pencil
hitting – dirtying
[sth. illegible] sheet.
Back page: takes away – makes
pay – rage spitting [?]
hitting.

At first Erna still seems to be restraining damaging impulses by 'washing', which are nevertheless expressed in the form of dirt and spit. '*(Exercise book! Schoolmistress!)*' may indicate that the target of the attacks is her analyst's capacity for understanding. The next summarised words seem to indicate that Erna feels that the delicious food had been 'taken away' from her on Sunday. Faced with this capriciousness, she now brings into play the fish that were actually cheap but were made expensive by the policeman.

For Tuesday 16 September as well, the manifest sense can only be reconstructed in fragments.[19] However, the insertion in relation to Klein is then clear; '*I bad schoolmistress – holes paper*'. Erna may be indicating here why Klein becomes a 'bad' teacher for her, namely because of the 'holes' of the discontinuous relationship that become so starkly apparent during weekends and holidays. Erna now has Klein fall ill with 'enteritis' because of the fine soup spoilt by spit and thereby shows her analyst how, because it is interspersed with absences in this way, the 'fine' analytic food is making her ill. On the other hand, by caring for the ill person she seems to be suggesting to Klein through her own behaviour how this should be handled: by taking appropriate care, that is, through understanding, to bring about a recovery.

On the next day, the first component soon predominates again: on Wednesday 17 September 1924, Erna explains through her play how she experiences Klein as the cook who spoils the finely prepared food with spit. Erna makes it very clear that she interprets her perception

---

19 From this point onwards, these notes will no longer be inserted – for the sake of better readability. The interested reader is directed to the complete treatment notes that are published in Part Two.

that Klein associates with other people, even if this association is carried on internally in the form of thinking (Britton et al., 1989). It seems likely that Erna sees Klein's thinking as something that takes place solely in order to humiliate her. Thus having knowledge/food available becomes a powerful act; the *semolina pudding* becomes a *beating pudding*.

On Thursday Klein comments at the end: 'very little sadism'. In the middle of the week, the attacks on Klein seem to have subsided. They can simultaneously be connected with images of reparation: '*Am to make a few holes in exercise book & stick it*'. In the role play a forgiving object is accordingly able to assert itself against the humiliating and ego-destructive superego: Klein is humiliated by others in the role of the badly writing child but is excused by Erna. The subsequent ideas of Erna's play seem to indicate that the exclusion of the father and the negation of coitus are preconditions for this more positive attitude.

On Friday 19 September 1924, Klein also initially finds that the external attacks on the exercise book are 'relatively less severe'. The approaching Sunday may then reappear in the form of powerfully supplied food. Erna acts out a play in which she is being bitten by Klein. The manifestly intended meaning of the '*wild animal – ill*' connection remains unclear; it may be that Erna feels that she is being made 'wild' by her own ideas, in which she is being mistreated and that she somehow senses that this is related to her illness.

On Saturday 20 September 1924 Erna appears 'dictatorial' faced with the Sunday. She omnipotently turns everything into something good (the bad ink into good imperial ink) before again taking refuge in a game of capricious, manipulative dealings: fish are stolen, paid for with counterfeit money, and so on. Towards the end Erna seems to explain through her play why she is becoming so aggressive: she is trying to block the wash-basin and lavatory, a representation of the fact that the 'toilet-breast' (Meltzer)[20] is blocked by the absence of Sunday.

On Monday 22 September 1924 Erna begins the session with an enactment that Klein also addressed in the 1924–1925 manuscript and the 1932 publication, in which she states:

In one of Erna's games 'a performance was given by a priest' who turned on the water-tap and his partner, a woman dancer, drank

---

20 Meltzer terms the part-object nature of the relationship and the quality of being valued and needed but not loved the 'toilet-breast' (1967, p. 20f.).

from it. The child, called 'Cinderella', was only allowed to look on and had to remain absolutely quiet.

(1932, WMK II, p. 40)

It seems that Erna was trying to elucidate for Klein her experience of the separation on the Sunday. In the publication Klein continues: 'A sudden tremendous outbreak of anger on Erna's part at this point showed with what feelings of hatred her phantasies were accompanied and how badly she had succeeded in dealing with those feelings' (WMK II, p. 40). In the treatment notes, the representation of the priest is followed by *'sudden desire to play mother and child with me'*. Although Erna initially acts as a friendly child, she deliberately vomits up the semolina pudding that is forced on her. I am passing over the Oedipal phantasies, since I think that Erna's complaint recorded towards the end of the session that Klein is not helping her perhaps occurs because she experiences Klein's interpretations as well as her absences (only a few of which are recorded from these sessions) as food that is forced on her. She accordingly vomits this up again but this leaves her in a sad state that does not allow her any development. In this context, in which she seems either literally or internally to be referring back to Abraham, Klein reaches a psychodynamic understanding that she is to conceptualise years later in terms of the death drive. I think that *'Sometimes she loves, she bad'* can be understood to mean that Erna sometimes likes to be bad. Klein seems to understand this at a moment when Erna ceases to represent badness egosyntonically but instead, as we would formulate it today, seeks help for her ego-dystonic impulses.

The session of 23 September concerns a bad and a good child:

23/IX. Schoolmistress –
as pupil at first I am bad
laughed at by another schoolgirl
because of scrawling & holes in exercise book –
Then am praised by teachers again,
the other schoolgirl ~~praised~~
[humiliated][1]. (Repeatedly as with
sisters: mother who has a good &
1 bad child. Thinks praise of
better pupil is to humiliate worse one).

The 'bad child' seems to retreat into a masturbatory relationship, which may be what the amplifications of the previous day represent:

Yesterday
after phantasies mother bad treatment – exhibits – wants to make
me masturbate her genitals
(dubious experience with
little girl. – Bedroom door
locked – had undressed
alone with her – very embarrassed when mother
knocked. Although no reproach
repeatedly returned to it with
evident bad conscience

For Wednesday 24 September, it is recorded in the diary that Erna missed her session, and there is no corresponding mention in the treatment notes. It seems to me that Erna took the missed session to mean that Klein did not want to see her as a reaction to Erna's masturbatory attacks. In the Thursday session, Erna's 'heartache' in fact appears at the beginning. Klein summarises the report, initially clearly formulated, with the heading 'deep-seated depressions'. Erna now attempts in a compulsive way to reassure herself of the opposite, namely, of Klein's love. She later represents through her cutting and biting of paper into pieces how she deals internally with Klein's capacity for understanding. In contrast to the previous sessions, an interpretation of Klein's is also now recorded: '*Interpret connection guilt feelings mother – phantasies of last few days – castration & biting to pieces*'. Klein evidently relates the interpretation to the mother and the masturbation with another girl that Erna feels guilty about concealing from her mother. It must remain open to question exactly what Klein was interpreting when she recorded 'castration & biting to pieces'. Psychodynamically it could be understood to mean that Erna is trying to castrate Klein by biting her to pieces, then develops guilt feelings that she tries to ward off by masturbation or, as Klein later explains, by the 'anal mode'. Erna explains to Klein at her inter-vention that the schoolmistress, thus the analyst, is at fault: she had earlier 'not paid enough attention'. In relation to Klein, it could be amplified that this failure to pay enough attention signifies Klein having expected Erna to be absent. When Klein notes at the end of this report that at the interpretation of guilt feelings and depression, Erna thoughtfully remarks – '*perhaps don't like it in world that Daddy & Mummy do pipi-thing?*', which points to Erna's capacity for insight.

For Friday 26 September there are no notes; on Saturday 27 September, Erna first, probably because of the approaching Sunday, has to 'annex' her analyst's scarf. She then adopts a very dominating and scornful attitude in the role play:

proud, conceited king constantly
throwing out servant on her
orders & slapping his face.
New servant who is only to bring
her hat – immediately puts it on
her, she outraged, because hair
tousled, boxes ears again – dismisses.
At pleas for forgiveness, she scornfully
refuses (also still scornful towards mother [p. 7a]

With '*extreme aggression towards [the] toys*' – Erna had torn a hook out of an engine – she further seems to demonstrate how forcefully she experiences the separation. At the same time, she seems by doing this to be able to ward off painful feelings that may be emerging. On Monday 29 September, she again explains her situation through externalisation in role play. She projects her envy into Klein:

29/IX. – She child but has belt
ribbon head, represents
long hair. – I observe her
enviously – wants to make
cut hair – so
(to persuade her) have (p. 8a)
my own hair cut with intense
pain caused by hairdresser. –
She mocks me, is doing nothing.
Puts on lipstick, make-up – I
furiously complain to father – who {takes} her
side: I become very ill (p. 9a)

Erna scornfully rejects the envy-derived wishes and triumphs together with the father, who is on Erna's side and against whom the envious analyst furiously and helplessly attempts to defend herself in the role play. The consequence for Klein is:

> I become very ill
> 'illness: God has spoken
> to me' – conscience pangs
> was so bad to daughter.

Erna thus explains through this externalisation that she 'knows' about a connection between her envy and her illness. When she has Klein recover in the next part of the play, while making herself succumb to the ailment of 'mother's agitation', she seems to be taking back some of her projections and to be working out that a factor in her illness is related to the fact that she actually can 'agitate' the object/mother; she can repeatedly jolt her out of a state in which she is still able to receive Erna's violent impulses and phantasies in a form of containment. The 'killing off' of the maternal function/the analyst's capacities for understanding is later dealt with again in the framework of a school game with the exercise book: it is pierced with holes and scrawled on; she cuts it to pieces and eats it up. In a manic fashion it repeatedly has to be replaced with a 'fresh' exercise book.

The centrepiece of this session, the specific illnesses of mother and child, reappears in the 1924–1925 manuscript and in the 1932 publication. In both places, this phantasy is described as follows:

> To her older 'child' she would be most cruel, and would let it be tortured by devils in a variety of ways and often killed it in the end. That the child in this role, however, was also the mother turned into a child, was made clear by the following phantasy. Erna played at being a child that had dirtied itself, and I, as the mother, had to scold her, whereupon she became scornful and out of defiance dirtied herself more and more. In order to annoy the mother still further she vomited up the bad food I had given her. The father was then called in by the mother, but he took the child's side. Next the mother was seized with an illness called 'God has spoken to her'; then the child in turn got an illness called 'mother's agitation' and died of it, and the mother was killed by the father as a punishment. The child then came to life again and was married to the father, who kept on praising it at the expense of the mother. The mother was then brought to life again, too, but, as a punishment,

was turned into a child by the father's magic wand; and now she in turn had to suffer all the humiliation and ill-treatment to which the child herself had been subjected before.

(1932, WMK II, pp. 40–41)

Apart from some minor stylistic variations, the above text is identical with the 1924–1925 manuscript (pp. 9f.). The clarification that follows it is again almost identical in 1924 and 1932; the additional explanation that appears in the manuscript is indicated with square brackets in the following quotation:

In her numerous phantasies of this kind about a mother and a child Erna was repeating what she felt her own experiences had been [and wanted to re-experience because of masochism and guilt feelings], while on the other hand she was also expressing what she would like to do to her mother in a sadistic way if the child–mother relationship was reversed.

(1932, WMK II, p. 41; 1924–1925 manuscript, p. 10)

On the one hand, the material from the treatment notes is easily recognisable in this published version. On the other hand, it nevertheless becomes clear from the comparison, especially if we take the 1924–1925 version, how successfully on one level Erna had enacted the attack on her analyst's capacity for understanding. The connection with envy of the analyst's head, for which I think the story about the hair and the exercise book stands, does not appear in the published version, which seems to be toned down from the dynamic governed by repetition-compulsion into the libidinal concept of a masochistically derived desire to repeat an experience. The treatment notes, however, show how Erna somehow 'knows' about a connection between her envious attacks on her analyst's head and her own illness, which is both expressed in the misconceptions and originates from them.

Only with this session do the notes in the treatment book break off once again, but there are still some notes on a single sheet from the following session of 30 September 1924. Erna plays school again. With '*Fury holidays*' she may again be explicating more precisely a factor from the previous day, directly expressing, albeit displaced on to the holidays, how these breaks provoke such furious attacks, which she later demonstrates again by scrawling on, tearing up etc. ever more new school exercise books.

207

The next available record from memory originates from Monday 6 October 1924. As she does repeatedly in the subsequent weeks, Erna takes misunderstanding as her theme in this session. '*Erna – schoolmistress – I always "misunderstand write something else" – (she articulates unclearly*'. In the notes on 7 to 10 October 1924, this theme reappears – '*on her instructions I write badly*'. Finally, Erna also later requires Klein to write on tiny pieces of paper, which she then again cuts to pieces. This appears to be an attempt to bring Klein's capacity for understanding under her control, which she then attacks again in a familiar manner. The following phantasy of Erna's is then recorded:

> Is 35 years old – I, 40. Rebels
> against me in every way,
> annoys me by secretly
> getting herself a bridegroom – I only
> discover by chance. Is a famous writer
> a Dr – who has made
> her famous – by writing
> about her. Afterwards story father really
> wrote in newsp. [?] about her. Very
> famous. Most famous in world. Grandiose
> phantasies.
>
> (Manuscript, p. 1b)

It seems that to some extent Erna was taking refuge in these grandiose phantasies from the painful experience of feeling so dependent on Klein. However, it is also worth considering how far Klein's actual writing about Erna, her lecture on Erna the following weekend in Würzburg, is playing a part here. Erna is likely to have sensed that Klein was working more intensely with her. It appears that Erna was trying to ward off the unease that this generated through a wonderful turn of events. But she seems to have sensed that Klein might have been selecting her precisely because with her illness, among other things, she constituted a particular challenge. In connection with the mother's actual illness in the form of a throat infection, the thought occurs to Erna that she as a child has made the mother ill. She expresses her 'heartache', her sadness as well as her insight that she will 'never be able to live inconspicuously among people' (p. 2b). For the first time, suicidal comments are recorded in the context of Erna's depressions.

The dynamic outlined thus far also characterises the next few weeks. Klein's interpretive work is mainly concentrated here on the demonstration of 'guilt-derived anxiety'. At this time Klein had not yet drawn a distinction between depressive and persecutory guilt; the different characteristics of each must, however, have become especially clear to her with Erna. The depressive quality, for example, appears with Erna's increasing worry about having caused the object's illness. The anxiety that is later termed 'persecutory' and typical of the 'paranoid-schizoid position' becomes apparent in many places. It was interpreted for instance by Klein in the following form on 21 October 1924: '*Interpret shoots mother identific* [ation] *with father – guilt feelings – she is shot*'. The last note that we have from this period again summarises a principal trajectory of this phase of the analysis: Erna makes Klein as schoolmistress present all her recent guilt feelings and phantasies and then she reacts to them with scorn. Erna thus seeks Klein as someone who takes up her psychic world, considers and understands her guilt feelings, but she then has to distance herself again scornfully and thus she attacks Klein's envied capacity for understanding. In comparison with the first part of the analysis, during which she had to deny all possibility of an illness on the part of the object/analyst, in this second section Erna has more capacity to concern herself with illness/damage and its possible causes.

6.3.3 The 'prince hidden in the hair' as a retreat from Erna's increasing contemplation of her own 'ugliness', which manifests itself in robbing and damaging the object (November, December 1925)

For a year there are then no records for Erna's analytic sessions, and it is only for the period from November to December 1925 that notes reappear. There are certainly no further entries in the treatment book, but the notes made from memory all appear on separate sheets of paper to which the drawings made by Erna in the corresponding sessions are attached with paper-clips. The notes are essentially explanations of these drawings. Although pictures by Erna frequently appeared before this, during this period she continuously adheres to this mode of expression. Here we encounter many of the themes with which we are already familiar. Whereas previously they were mostly acted out in role play, now they receive a more insightful handling through the drawing process and the accompanying explanations.

The process of getting to know her own inner reality is now possible to a greater extent in the analyst's presence. The oscillation between the contemplation of reality and the withdrawal into a narcissistic world becomes particularly vivid in this section.

The first notes for the year 1925 are from Thursday 5 November.

{Picture} 1. Queen has short hair –
none at all – just wig
– draws flowers (genitals)
with special care – but then
covers in red, supposedly prettier
(Interpret steals & tears genitals to pieces
tears out pubic hair.)
Same with lines over face
– damage. Criticises fat
legs, left heel twisted
foot sprained – mother's
foot disease!)

In this first picture, the attack on the hair that is familiar to us from the second period is represented again: from *short hair* to *none* to *false* hair (wig). The careful formation of the genitals could be understood as an attempt at reparation, which is then however destroyed again. Klein interprets only the latter, the rapacious appropriation and damaging of the genitals. Erna seems to want to add to what Klein has said when she thereupon also disfigures the face with lines, as if she wanted to make it clear that her impulses are now expressed in a symbolised form. Instead of throwing a pencil at Klein's eye as she had done during the first part of the analysis, Erna now 'spoils' the face of the woman she has drawn. It seems possible that the reference to the mother's foot disease can also be understood in connection with the fact that Klein appears unwell and Erna might have felt that her attacks had been partly successful.

It seems that Erna is now trying to present herself as a 'beautiful' object in order to ward off guilt feelings:

2. Begins to draw
more beautiful princess. Does not
succeed, gives up.
3. Meant to be a beautiful

210

princess but finds this
not worked, legs
thin.

The disavowal and the associated splitting are no longer operating so comprehensively and the psychic reality strikes like a thunderbolt. In the sense of the archaic 'eye for an eye' morality, Erna herself is now as bald and ugly as she has made her object:

4. Thunderbolt princess
has become bald & ugly
behind only poo – reluctance
to play, depression, remorse
then school lessons

The added keywords – reluctance to play, depression, remorse – indicate that after this paralysis Erna finds a way of dealing with her 'ugly' impulses that has a depressive quality and that she is able to take a step towards integration in the form of remorse.

For the next seven sessions there are again no documents. Then there are some notes from memory available for Saturday 14 November 1925. Here too we encounter a scenario with which we are already familiar:

At first I ~~want~~ strict schoolmistress. Writes out
B., which I am to copy
badly. Associates: B lower part of bottom
& stomach; red line (she made)
cut up, bloody. + in middle body
whole person that she constructs from B
(In reverse, she strict mother, punishes
me [her] for cutting up & taking out
stomach. Reluctance
to play school, draws.

The school situation indicates among other things that Klein is again being seen as someone from whom Erna can learn emotionally. This, however, immediately reactivates her resistance, which is partly externalised in Klein: it is not a case of learning but of 'badly copying'. The 'B' seems likely to be multiply determined. Along with the

211

mentioned 'lower part of bottom' and stomach, the breasts may also still play a part. This seems to involve a denigration of the understanding that comes from the stomach (as well as the breasts), which is further clarified by the lines, which represent cutting up and so on. Again the archaic morality seems to bring about a symmetry: when Erna spoils the functioning of the object in this way, her own enjoyment of play is spoilt.

In the first drawing, she explicates her inner experience:

$1/X = 1$ beautiful girl
under spell from witch; black
hair poo'. _|_ Witch herself also under
spell so must do evil; cries
bloody tears (recognises red
body etc. bloodily cut to pieces, by
her.)

Erna makes it clear how little it seems to lie in her power (under spell) to do 'evil'. By placing the witch herself under a spell as well, Erna underlines how little she is able to do to counteract this 'witch part'. The bloody tears may represent both the suffering from this witch part and the attempt to eliminate it.

2. Witch is released = more beautiful
3. Princess is freed by
prince, who wants to marry her.
Suddenly explains will not marry
her, princess ugly, bad
& wants to cut her into pieces while
draws thick lines from other
side. On other page 8 stomach also
filled with stool.

In the second drawing, the witch part is already phantasised as rescued. If we compare this drawing with the third one of the rescued princess that follows, it is striking how unmagnificently this second drawing represents the events. With its round mouth, the face resembles that of a small child. With the third picture, Erna is drawn, according to her comment, back into a more magnificent world but the drawing also simultaneously reveals why her own longed-for rescue fails. The rescue here seems to be sought in phantasising herself into the role of the mother. She actually draws the princess again with all the mother's attributes (crinoline = belly with children) and gives herself very long hair again and so on. This rapacious activity is perceived as such by the 'princess part' in her and accordingly punished.

The following session on Monday 16 November 1925 starts with an almost direct commentary on the Sunday:

> Furious; mother had visit from Herr H
> she had to go out.

She accordingly gives Klein a '*bad mark*' for this, but she is herself afflicted by reluctance again:

> 1.) Strict schoolmistress. Crosses out my
> 'I', bad mark. Reluctant to play

As on 14 November, Erna then draws herself again as a beautiful princess:

> 2.) Beautiful princess (all the mother's attributes
> familiar from the material: crinoline =
> belly with children – ribbon immaculate.
> Female genitals – neck & heels on shoes = member – still: mother
> robbed
> hence guilt feelings later in play)

As Klein explains, the later play is governed by guilt feelings. Whereas in the third drawing the disavowal can partly still assert itself, in the fourth she has become completely ugly again, which Erna explains as part of the spell cast by the elf. Klein explains this as follows:

> c. elves. Recognises
> elf d. as woman, for whom she has forgotten
> to make arms. (Castrated
> by her, in picture 1 the mother
> deprived of attributes, from whom she wants
> to take father (3) & has sex with him ~~wants~~
> (to stretch arms) takes revenge. Picture 4.

213

Belly missing again, defaecating
~~all~~ thus child & bad! All attributes gone. Is only anxious & wishes
for father with erect penis.

Klein thus understands the elf as the castrated mother who is now
taking her revenge and wants to expose Erna as the defaecating child.

The sequence of drawings from 17 November 1925 also shows the
transition from the beautiful princess who has been given all the
mother's attributes (drawing 1) to the princess 'who looks dead'
(drawing 3). The intervening picture explains the background to
the change:

2. Princess on way to lover
(states has become ugly). Cannot
find his palace; ~~in front of~~ [in] 1 cave ugly
old man who became small
like Rumpelstiltskin. + she must release him
but
~~3.~~ as ~~she~~ draws [princess][1] realises

At first the grandiose ideas seem to be realisable with the help of a
Rumpelstiltskin figure who spins straw into gold. However, in the
mean time the grandiose ideas no longer hold – the palace is no
longer to be found. After the omnipotent phantasy is recognised
broadly in its essence – was called by its name – it collapses and
reveals its ugly aspects, namely the hindering of development. Instead
of wonderful life, the grandiose ideas lead to the death of psychic life.
Erna initially tries to protect herself from this insight with further
aggression:

II (Depression, spits, pushes at
carpet with feet (but very gent-
ly) – wants to pull scab off her lip
had spattered picture 1 with water
'tears' & wanted to destroy it) – I after
~~plays with water~~ breaking off
drawing first plays with rest of colour pencil
& water – scrawls then energetically
cleans [table][1] proves to me table, chair

were dirty. – From the beginning today
competitiveness her colours – my pencils –
writes exercise against my will
asks during drawing 1 if her yellow
(pencil) is not prettier than mine.

The cleaning action, along with the competitiveness about the colours that she and Klein are using, may be an expression of her attempt to reassure herself of her liveliness and capacity for reparation, during which she seems to be driven by doubts and a suspicion that this manic form of behaviour is turning out to be unproductive.

Klein summarises the psychodynamics of this session as follows:

During drawing of
1 intense guilt feelings – afterwards
repeatedly wants to destroy – that's why
2 ugly, 3 dead. She steals everything
from mother wants to rescue father from cave
(mother's genitals) in which evil witch
turned him into Rumpelstiltskin (castration member in coitus) –
incapacity competitiveness because of
guilt & inferiority feelings from
cleanliness anxiety & Oedipal guilt
dies herself – scab falls off
self-harm – also in that
wants to destroy 1.

Klein's literal interpretation of the Rumpelstiltskin figure seems to agree with my interpretation in the sense that no real paternal authority/third position appears to be available, so that the father as phallus, in contrast to what Birksted-Breen (1996) describes as 'penis-as-link', determines the psychic reality. As Birksted-Breen (1996) explains, the phallus refers to an object of desire (accessible to none) that promises a state of completeness from which all needs are absent, whereas the penis represents the capacity for linking and symbolisation.

In my view, Erna presents the way in which she uses the Rumpelstiltskin figure as something that belongs to her psychically in the first drawing of the following session on 18 November 1925:

~~Countess~~
1 charming princess, who carries
a small prince completely hidden
in her pretty bow:
4 years. When mother
tells her to change bows, puts him back in
carefully hidden – about green neck: 1
poor, [sth. crossed out] pestered, beaten
neck – green marks.

Erna thus constantly carries hidden within her a narcissistic phallic world, a constantly available place of retreat from the reality that is hard to tolerate. With the revelation of this phantasy, Erna also simultaneously seems to make greater use of this exciting place of retreat. The green, poor, pestered, beaten neck seems to represent the exciting aspect of this idyll.

Klein also bases the connection between the prince and the Rumpelstiltskin figure on the following phantasy:

3) ~~wedding: all p. at first.~~ [Then][1] prince
who was under a spell had been released because
she had carried him with her for so
long. He had bathed
in 1 lake, had & got rid of his things
there – 'pipi'. – Then came 1 witch
& made him small. (Rumpelstiltskin
a few days before!) – (castrated during coitus with
mother – she wanted to help father!)

In terms of the transference, we can suppose that Erna wished for her analyst to be a Rumpelstiltskin figure spinning straw into gold but instead found herself confronted with a witch who through the analysis had prevented the grandiose phantasies from supporting her any longer in the same way and she consequently feels belittled, 'made small'.

The fifth drawing concerns the fatal consequences of a rapacious and castrating interaction that is simultaneously enacted and warded off by masturbation.

18/XI.25
5. Has spat between lines – mixed

together & produces with great resistance
following story that received
as advert for cream butter (*Schabrameng*):
1. 1 little man chased by
robbers wants to go into house. At window
beautiful dead woman who cannot
or will not let him in. Masturbates (again
since long ago) during this story.
Masturbation during coitus observation. Fear
of mother who castrates father (robbers)
but gets killed herself –
explains lines in 5 as blood poo
wee-wee, *Schabrameng* (butter) – that
imagines in coitus.

On 20 November, Erna accuses the mother of having the same desires as a defence against her own guilt feelings ('about poos'), as Klein interprets it below:

1. Woman who became so fat because ate
so much & who urinates & does
poo. Grabs with hands ↓ urine &
poo. O in dress = collapsed
pipi – (fat stomach = pregnant,
yellow bow brown hair is stool &
urine.

In the second picture, Erna is also still projecting a part of the defence. It is now an 'elegantly behaved hypocritical mother' who eats up the stool, castrates the father and so on. In the third drawing, she takes back a part of the projection. We now see the 'beautiful princess' again who in the fourth picture becomes a princess of whom nothing remains but the stomach cut to pieces. Klein understands the session as follows:

(Interpret guilt feelings
because of poo – accuses 1.) mother of same
desires simultaneously theory to eat stool, produce
children – this makes her evil ugly,
good father releases her and makes good.

217

Erna then reveals a memory:

She tells of memory: (still concealed)
where in children's home (not at home)
repeatedly dirtied at night.
Defaecated in trousers when saw
another child defaecating.

On 21 November 1925, Klein comments on Erna's associations
in regard to the phantasies of damage into which Erna is gaining
increasing insight. Erna herself feels that her evil wishes are projected on to the mother. We also find here a variation of the nose-
biting theme with which we are familiar from the beginning of
Erna's analysis: the king who wants to continue looking has his nose
torn off. Klein again interprets this tearing off of the nose as the
wish to castrate the father who is to be found in coitus with the
mother. I think the theme can also be understood as an attack on
the perception of the events as they are perceived by a third/pater-
nal object.

In the next session, Monday 23 November, Erna considerably
extends her anxiety about the intactness of her female genitals. She
would never like to have children because she is afraid that they will
tear her to pieces when crawling out.

The session on 24 November 1925 is characterised by 'failures'.
Erna would like to be a beautiful princess but feels that she is ugly and
evil. Klein understands the pushing together of the second picture
(evil woman) and the third picture (evil, ugly daughter-in-law) with
the comment 'do pipi-thing'. Klein sees this as an illustration of the
development of repression resulting from sadistic wishes towards the
mother and the fear of punishment that stems from sadistic wishes and
a consequent flight into homosexuality. Here, as also for example on
4 December 1925 Klein thus understands homosexuality, in her later
terminology, as a defence against paranoia. She will return to this
clinical insight in her later development of theory. On 25 November,
this theme is continued.

On 26 November, Klein again notes Erna's recognition that it
was her own evil impulses that she previously projected into the
mother and also, we should add, was still projecting. In the first drawing, she explains that she is drawing a princess, then declares that she
is a stupid old woman. She then attributes to this figure the feeling

that life is no fun for her, and this again seems close to Erna's own experience.[21]

In the records from memory of 27 November 1925, we finally learn about Erna's first and only mentioned dream:

Frau Kloss ~~notices her bag~~ climbs
out through window. A little [red][1] man
still stands at the window. – Frau Kl. hears
noises in the flat & goes back
again. Then no longer there. Then something
is stolen at the back (in the flat). – Probably her
bag. – She herself, Erna[2], looks out
through the window & watches everything.
She says to the little man (very tenderly)
Nice little man will you
break into my house too? He: No, I
only do that to bad people. – Association:
to the window: that was modern before
through the window, was also such an
enormous one that you could go out
as with a door & only had to jump
a bit. – Little man was actually very nice

Erna also associated to the little man the following story:

Once was a very good kind king. He
was very fond of his daughter. Then he
went & stole things from people, for his
daughter's sake who ordered him to steal
very beautiful bags, gold & silver ones
(he brought them to her – analogy silver & gold dress
stolen from the cupboard) – Then
he stole a bag that was not
so beautiful & had little in it. But
he became very rich anyway & had
everything.

---

21 Cf. Klein's quotation from Erna in the third chapter of the 1932 publication, in which Erna expressed her depressions as follows: 'There's something about life I don't like' (WMK II, p. 35).

Klein's understanding is expressed in the following lines:

(Rumpelstiltskin, little cream-butter man
immediately recognises member) & her contrary request
to break into her house. – Becomes afraid
of coitus. Is punishment only for bad
people.

The dream appears here as the narcissistic place of retreat in which thieving can take place ego-syntonically and without consequences.

The increasing insight into her own ugly impulses thus conflicts with the attempt to construct for herself a guilt-free place of retreat. As Klein observed on 1 December 1925, Erna's ugly aspect repeatedly proves so intolerable to her narcissism that she rejects reality and seeks to cling to the dream.

In the records of later sessions preserved from December 1925, the factors that are indicated above in essence reappear.

In the mean time, however, Erna manages to attain a certain acceptance of her failed attempts (2 December 1925):

Wants to draw a girl; does not yet
know if will be princess. If not
this must do as well. With uncertain care
& patience repeatedly slowly
attempts heads, erases etc.
Always fails at mouth. Then
draws 1. – Herself completely satisfied
(unusual – actually not exaggerated
holds on to it: gloriously wonderful
hair etc. then anger & tearing up.)
but with calm criticism: pretty etc.
– mouth not pretty, 'then that's
exactly how it must be'.

However, the doubts about Erna's capacity for love that are mentioned by Klein on 9 December 1925 dominate the dynamics now as before.

There are no treatment notes for 1926, but, as I explained in Section 6.2, the Archive contains three further pages of unpublished notes that are headed 'Erna work – Part 2' (see pp. 178–80 above).

These pages cannot be dated with certainty but they probably originate from the period shortly before the termination of Erna's analysis in April 1926. They seem to relate both to the period outlined above for November and December 1925 and to further material of 1926. It appears clear that the constructive work in November and December 1925 was followed by a further very difficult period, for, as quoted above (p. 179), Klein says in 'Erna work – Part 2': 'She became much more difficult to treat in this stage and tormented those around her, especially the mother, much more'. Klein does not mention any possible reasons for this change in Erna's material, but it seems possible that the knowledge of Klein's departure for England may well have played some part in it. Klein ends 'Erna work – Part 2' by saying: 'However, when I did not allow any slack to enter the analysis, the way forward then emerged that was then also to shed light in theoretical terms on the matters at issue here'. It seems likely that she was thinking here of her ideas about splitting, projection and Erna's 'evil principle', although she does not explicitly say so.

6.4 The significance of Erna's analysis

6.4.1 *Erna's analysis as an important clinical experience that brought conceptual innovations*

Through Erna's analysis, the most extensive of her child analyses in Berlin, Klein became familiar with many facets of the early Oedipal world:

- Early introjective and projective mechanisms, most tangible in the transference–countertransference dynamics through Erna's attempts to force a role reversal on her analyst. Further, there is an impressive and vivid illustration of the introjective aspect in Erna's first drawing of 16 January 1924. The paranoid aspects based on projections occur throughout the material.
- Splitting: shown, for example, in the splitting into 'princess' and 'witch', devils and angels etc.
- Denial: shown clearly in the analysis. As the analysis progressed, Erna was able to reduce the denial.
- Paranoid guilt feelings, which formed the basis of an archaic morality, as evidenced, for example, in the sequence of drawings

in November 1925, in which first the object is robbed of its hair and then finally Erna herself becomes bald-headed.

- Depressive guilt feelings, which plunge her into deep despair but also generate reparative impulses: for example, the 'heartache' situations; Erna's attempts at reparation represented in this connection are, as indicated, often manic in nature.

What I have sought to demonstrate in relation to the treatment notes is how Klein 'against her will', so to speak, intuitively arrived at the clinical understanding of these aspects, which she was not able to conceptualise adequately in theoretical terms until some years later, because she was consciously seeking to understand and interpret Erna's communications within the framework of Freud's libido theory. Klein's above-mentioned early discoveries have since become well known. What it has been possible to demonstrate here is the way which they developed out of the clinical work. Erna's treatment stands here as probably the most important analysis of the later child analyses in Berlin. Instead of embarking on a discussion of these often-mentioned 'new' discoveries of Klein's, I should like to emphasise two aspects that hitherto have received less systematic consideration: the significance of child analysis both for the further development of treatment technique and for the development of a fundamental concept for understanding psychic reality: the drive for knowledge.

6.4.2 *The significance of child analysis for the further development of treatment technique, for which Erna's analysis provided significant impetus*

First, concerning resistance. Following Freud, Klein first conceptualised resistance as an expression of repressed libidinal wishes. Later, and especially through the work with Erna, she thought of resistance as expressing fears of various objects. This led to the idea of the internal object world as it is experienced in the analytic situation.

Klein's early interpretations to Erna demonstrate that she at first tried to resolve a resistance, when it appeared in the form of a reluctance to play in the analysis, through an interpretation of a repressed libidinal wish. However, the interpretation (treatment notes, p. 2) that Erna's fear of robbers that the head-banging is supposed to stop in fact maintains the fear already shows how Klein intuitively understands the resistance itself as a form of 'head-banging', which did not necessarily have to be performed in a literal sense. Her interpretation conveys how this understanding leads her towards another understanding of resistance, that is, resistance as something that results from fear of internal objects.

The study of anxiety goes on to form a central component of Klein's later work, in which she describes the early anxiety situations of girls and boys. Finally, much later, in the 1930s and 1940s, she breaks new ground by elaborating the concepts of depressive and persecutory anxiety.

Her study of resistance later develops into considerations of negative transference, which requires an exploration of which kind of anxiety towards which kind of object forms the basis of resistance and negative transference at any given time.

Second, interpretation of negative transference. Klein herself described negative transference in 1927, using the example of Erna. The treatment notes provide a more concrete insight into the experiences that Klein used to reach her understanding of negative transference. Particularly impressive here are the situations in which Klein interprets the envious–aggressive impulses (cf. Section 6.3.1) and the will for power and destruction (cf. Section 6.3.1) in such a way that Erna is able to renounce her acting out and instead to explain what has to be communicated in symbolic form by using new modes of expression.

The treatment notes also provide significant insight into how difficult it actually is to give an accurate interpretation of the negative transference. I have suggested that certain forms of latent negative transference that are acted out in the analytic relationship could not be completely understood by Klein at this time. I have indicated that I think there was some collusion between Erna's sexualisation and Klein's partly sexualised interpretations (cf. Section 6.3.1).

Third, from predominantly reconstructive interpretations to an emphasis on the immediate situation between analyst and patient as well. I have tried to show how difficulties in dealing with the negative transference and with the aspects of internal object relations that accompany it led Klein to focus more on reconstructive interpretations than on the more immediate feelings that Erna expressed towards her analyst. Klein did not take the specific focus on the immediate analyst-patient relationship very far in Erna's analysis, but her courage in facing and interpreting the sometimes disturbing content of Erna's material was important in developing her confidence in helping children (and adults) to express their thoughts and feelings as freely as possible.

Fourth, carrying further Freud's insight that 'acting' is resorted to when thoughts and feelings cannot be remembered or expressed in words. Klein's practice of child analysis represents an important further step from Freud's 'Remembering, *repeating* and working-through' (Freud, 1914b). It might be expressed by saying that in Klein's work it gradually became 'Remembering, *acting out* and working through', in which 'acting out' is the operative word for 'repeating'. This focus on action, whether described as 'action', 'acting in' or 'enactment', has become an essential component of our contemporary technique. The work of Betty Joseph is of particular importance here (Joseph, 1989). In the above-mentioned paper, Freud (1914b) had of course already identified and formulated the fundamental significance of acting out when he wrote that: 'the patient does not *remember* anything of what he has forgotten and repressed, but *acts* it out. He reproduces it not as a memory but as an action; he *repeats* it, without, of course, knowing that he is repeating it' (1914b, *S.E.* 12, p. 150). He further explained that 'the transference is itself only a piece of repetition, and that the repetition is a transference of the forgotten past not only on to the doctor but also on to all the other aspects of the current situation' (*S.E.* 12, p. 151). A few pages later, however, the following passage appears:

> He [the doctor – C. F.] is prepared for a perpetual struggle with his patient to keep in the psychical sphere all the impulses which the patient would like to direct into the motor sphere; and he celebrates it as a triumph for the treatment if he can bring it about that something that the patient wishes to discharge in action is disposed of through the work of remembering. If the attachment through transference has grown into something at all serviceable, the treatment is able to prevent the patient from executing any of the more important repetitive actions and to utilize his intention to do so *in statu nascendi* as material for the therapeutic work. One best protects the patient from injuries brought about through carrying out one of his impulses by making him promise not to take any important decisions affecting his life during the time of his treatment.
>
> (1914b, *S.E.* 12, p. 153)

When Freud[22] also writes a little later (p. 154) in the same paper that the principal method for mastering the patient's repetition compulsion and transforming it into a motivation for remembering consists in the handling of the transference, he seems a little uncertain of the effectiveness of this procedure, and I believe it is for this reason that he needs to fall back on the above-mentioned prohibitions as a standard component of technique rather than as a parameter in particular circumstances.

In her analyses of children, Klein started to develop the conceptions of transference and acting out that she formulates in 'The origins of transference' in 1952 as follows:

My conception of transference as rooted in the earliest stages of development and in deep layers of the unconscious is much wider and entails a technique by which from the whole material presented the *unconscious elements* of the transference are deduced. For instance, reports of patients about their everyday life, relations, and activities not only give an insight into the functioning of the ego, but also reveal – if we explore their unconscious content – the defences against the anxieties stirred up in the transference situation. For the patient is bound to deal with conflicts and anxieties re-experienced towards the analyst by the same methods he used in the past. That is to say, he turns away from the analyst as he attempted to turn away from his primal objects; he tries to split the relations to him, keeping him either as a good or as a bad figure: he deflects some of the feelings and attitudes experienced towards the analyst on to other people in his current life, and this is part of 'acting out'.

(1952, WMK III, pp. 55–56)[23]

---

22 It seems that Freud was here mainly considering acting out (thus beyond the analytic situation), but his observations clearly also apply to what we now term 'acting in'.

23 While Klein does not refer explicitly to Freud's 1914b paper, Ferenczi and Rank (1925), in *Entwicklungsziele der Psychoanalyse* [Developmental goals of psychoanalysis], had taken up the contradictory point in Freud that I have emphasised. They work from the premise that differing importance was attached to each of three factors mentioned in the title, in so far as remembering was represented as the actual goal of the analytic work, whereas the desire to repeat an experience was considered to be a symptom of resistance and therefore recommended as something to avoid (p. 13). It thus concerns precisely those elements that are absolutely inaccessible to memory, so that the patient is left with no other option than to reproduce them (p. 13). They derive from this the practical requirement that 'impulses towards reproduction in the analysis are not only something that we should refrain from impeding but are actually to be encouraged' (p. 14). The analyst should

Erna's analysis, as has been indicated, was an important milestone in reaching an understanding of the communicative function of acting out. The various forms of acting out (playing with figures, role plays, direct interaction with the analyst etc.) were not described by her as acting out at the outset, so that the dynamics of the analyst–patient relationship demonstrated at that time were not very systematically considered, which led to the conceptual inconsistencies I have described in Section 6.1.

The attention to the immediate 'here-and-now' was necessitated by the children's acting out. It became clearer with them than with adults that every aspect of the setting (the 'total situation', Klein, 1952; Joseph, 1985) required attention, which naturally made dealing with the negative transference a priority; this is something to which Klein's understanding of anxiety greatly contributed.[24]

6.4.3 Erna's analysis contains Klein's understanding of important components of the drive for knowledge, a fundamental concept in the comprehension of psychic reality

On the basis of Klein's publications, it is clearly her commitment to an accurate explication that forms the point of departure. It seems likely that she had the example of Ferenczi in mind, as expressed for instance in 'The cause of reserve in a child' (1913c):

The young mother of two children is inconsolable because the elder child (aged four) is so remarkably reserved; she endeavours by every means to get the child to be frank, and to gain her confidence, but all in vain. Even when her much-loved English nurse has to be sent away the child displays no emotion towards her mother. The mother begs her to be frank, she may tell her mamma

---

actively assist in this. The resistances to repetition compulsion, mainly anxiety and guilt feelings, should thus be overcome with the aid of active intervention in a form that encourages repetition. Ferenczi and Rank also seem, though in a different way from Freud, not really to trust interpretation as a method of handling the transference. Klein did not refer to this work, and it becomes clear from her own works that she did not draw this technical conclusion herself.

24 For the development of Kleinian technique up to recent times, see in particular Spillius (1983, 1988, 1994).

everything that is bothering her. 'May I really tell everything?' asks the little one. 'Of course, just ask,' answers the mother. 'Well then, tell me where do children come from!' (a striking confirmation of Freud's assumption that the evasiveness of parents towards inquisitive children can become the source of permanent affective and intellectual disturbance).

(Ferenczi, 1913c, p. 327)

After Klein had been made aware by von Freund that she was not paying heed to the unconscious in relation to the drive for knowledge, she discovered a conflict between a very strong investigative drive in the child on the one hand and an equally strong tendency to repression on the other (1921, WMK I, p. 29). It was not the externally imposed prohibition of knowledge but the individual's own resistance to knowledge that became the focus of her attention in her exploration of the 'inhibitions of the drive for knowledge'. In this approach, she is close to the attitude expressed by Abraham in 'Restrictions and transformations of scopophilia in psycho-neurotics' (Abraham, 1913c). Abraham demonstrates with various examples a persistent conflict between two parties, 'one of which would like to investigate and know the facts while the other strives to remain ignorant of them' (1913c, p. 212). He indicates that: 'The brooder unconsciously seeks to preserve his ignorance' (1913c, p. 214).

In 'The rôle of the school in the libidinal development of the child' (1923a), Klein demonstrates with numerous examples that castration anxiety plays a decisive part in play and learning inhibitions (cf. for instance 1923a, WMK I, p. 73). She cites examples in which difficulties in writing, reading and arithmetic are linked with the symbolic sexual significance of letters and numbers (cf. e.g. the significance of the letter 'i' for Ernst: 1921, WMK I, pp. 48f.). This method of understanding is reminiscent of Freud's example from *The Psychopathology of Everyday Life* (1901b), in which he studies the child's drive for knowledge:

A man of twenty-four has preserved the following picture from his fifth year. He is sitting in the garden of a summer villa, on a small chair beside his aunt, who is trying to teach him the letters of the alphabet. He is in difficulties over the difference between *m* and *n* and he asks his aunt to tell him how to know one from the other. His aunt points out to him that the *m* has a whole piece more than the *n* – the third stroke. There appeared to be no reason for challenging the trustworthiness of this childhood memory; it had, however, only acquired its meaning at a later date, when it showed itself suited to represent symbolically another of the boy's curiosities. For just as at that time he wanted to know the difference between *m* and *n*, so later he was anxious to find out the difference between boys and girls . . . He also discovered then that the difference was a similar one.

(Freud, 1901b, *S.E.* 6, p. 48)

The attempt to attribute inhibitions to coital phantasies (cf. e.g. Ernst's endeavours, in which he had to draw lines running up and down: 1923a, WMK I, p. 65) also appears in Freud, as an example from 'Delusions and dreams in Jensen's *Gradiva*' (1907a) shows: after the early unwanted realisation of the sexual processes, a young man, hardly more than a boy, had taken flight from all desires arising in him. He threw himself with particular enthusiasm into the mathematics and geometry that were taught at school, until one day his intellectual powers suddenly failed him when he was confronted with a few simple exercises. The wording of two of these exercises could still be ascertained:

'Two bodies come together, one with a speed of . . . etc.' and 'On a cylinder, the diameter of whose surface is *m*, describe a cone . . . etc.' Other people would certainly not have regarded these as very striking allusions to sexual events; but he felt that he had been betrayed by mathematics as well, and took flight from it too.

(Freud, 1907a, *S.E.* 9, p. 36)

Petot's explanation of Klein's approach, with which I entirely agree, is that she emphasises the wish to know and intellectual sublimation, and that the theory of sublimation and inhibition was the actual core of what he calls 'the proto-Kleinian system' (Petot, 1990, p. 188). His claim, however, that Klein was not referring back to any specific concept when she used the notion of the 'drive for knowledge' is not in my view well founded. Freud's concept of the 'instinct for knowledge or research' is her point of reference. When Petot (1990, p. 195) summarises by concluding that Klein's concept of the drive for knowledge is rather imprecise, I think that this applies to the concept as Klein discovered it in Freud's 1915 supplement to the

Three Essays on Sexuality. She took it up and developed it at an early stage, without however producing an entirely conclusive concept herself. It was only decades later that this was achieved by Bion and Money-Kyrle. Let us remind ourselves of Freud's definition:

> At about the same time as the sexual life of children reaches its first peak, between the ages of three and five, they also begin to show signs of the activity which may be ascribed to the instinct for knowledge or research. This instinct cannot be counted among the elementary instinctual components, nor can it be classed as exclusively belonging to sexuality. Its activity corresponds on the one hand to a sublimated manner of obtaining mastery, while on the other hand it makes use of the energy of scopophilia. Its relations to sexual life, however, are of particular importance, since we have learnt from psycho-analysis that the instinct for knowledge in children is attracted unexpectedly early and intensively to sexual problems and is in fact possibly first aroused by them.
>
> (Freud, 1905a, *S.E.* 7, p. 194)

Two pages earlier Freud had introduced the drive for mastery for the first time. He ascribes to this the origin of children's cruelty. Altogether Freud's deployment of the concept remains imprecise, but it could in my view be seen as a precursor of the death drive. In his formulation, Freud differentiates between two means of discovery: a libidinal activity dominated by scopophilia and a behaviour dominated by cruel impulses.

Klein's development of Freud's idea in 1923 took as its starting point the exploration of the libidinal component, the 'repressed interest in the mother's womb' (1923a, WMK I, p. 72). In Erna's case she was increasingly confronted with the 'mastery component' (cf. in particular the first section here) and was gradually also able to grasp this conceptually. In 1928, this becomes a case of *appropriating* the contents of the mother's body (1928, WMK I, p. 188). It concerns penetration, cutting to pieces and destruction. The drive for knowledge and the sadistic will to mastery thus appear in an early and close connection. In Freud this connection is already constructed; Klein discovers that these processes do not play a role only at the Oedipal stage, but rather set in earlier.

Also in common with Freud, Klein sees the connection between the drive for knowledge and the will to mastery as based partly in the

229

inevitability of the frustration of the desire for knowledge. Freud attributes this frustration to the fact that the child does not know about 'the fertilizing role of the semen and the existence of the female sexual orifice' (1905a, *S.E.* 7, p. 197), but Klein's experiences suggest other reasons for the child's frustration. According to her the inevitable frustration is connected with the fact that the onslaught of problems and questions occurs at a stage before they can be expressed in words (1928, WMK I, p. 188). Both Freud and Klein see the desire for knowledge as resolved by the perception of the fertile parental couple. In Freud we read that the question of the origin of children sets investigative activity in motion; for Klein, this is already understood in object-relational terms and the mother's womb constitutes the focus of interest.

It is striking that both Freud and Klein cite the cognitive aspect of the inability to know, albeit somewhat differently explained. For Klein the 'inability' to know was more accurately thought of as 'unwillingness' to know, for it became clear in her clinical work that the feelings bound up with 'knowing' constitute the cause of the unwillingness to know. With Erna Klein learned both how intolerable the breast/ capacity of her analyst was to her patient, and how envious impulses in the wake of the perception and knowledge of this breast/capacity gave rise to destructive impulses and actions in Erna. In addition Erna found her relation to the parental couple intolerable and humiliating.

Although on the one hand Klein discovered and described this exactly, she did not in fact arrive at an entirely satisfactory conception of the drive for knowledge. This would have required an even more extensive understanding of the negative transference, which could not be achieved within the conceptual terms of its rapid attribution to the original object without also linking it to the child's current relationship with the analyst.

However, the increasing analytic understanding of negative transference enabled Klein in the period under consideration here to carry out a further fundamental development of the concept, as can be illustrated from the cases that are described.

With Grete, the initial reluctance to learn that was recorded in the treatment notes, as with Ernst, was understood in terms of its libidinal components. The paranoid component that lay at the root of her learning inhibition did not become comprehensible here to Klein; she countered this form of negative transference with the 'innocuous' external reality. With Erna, this paranoid component became clearer to Klein. To a considerable extent Klein had also been able to allow herself to be guided by Grete, who confirmed Klein's conjectures of penis envy in some situations while also correcting it in others, that is, when the association was to Grete's own genitals.

Rita's play inhibition could be linked with an early, strict, oppressive superego. Since it was also only possible here to perceive and interpret the negative transference to a limited extent, the melancholic experiential quality that lay at the root of Rita's play inhibition was not as yet comprehensible to Klein. It was also in relation to the negative transference that the first beginnings of understanding became possible with Erna.

With Inge, the learning inhibition was subtler. The intolerability of not being able to do something and of being confronted with differences was as such not immediately comprehensible. This led to the introduction of the parameter of the toys, which facilitated communication but in the case of Inge the understanding of the contradictions within her wish to know remained difficult for Klein fully to understand.

A more direct understanding of the governing dynamic was made possible with Erna. From the very outset Erna impressively represented her envy and the resulting attacks, which repeatedly led to a paranoid state of mind that Erna sought to escape through headbanging and other obsessional symptoms (cf. Section 6.3.1). Although Abraham (1924, p. 430) had already amplified Freud's concept of obsessional neurosis with the idea of object-hostile tendencies, he still worked from the premise that conservative tendencies were predominant in obsessional neurosis. Klein was made aware through Erna's analysis, however, of the paranoid core of obsessional neurosis. When Klein interpreted Erna's envious–aggressive impulses, she encountered a positive change in the form of an increase in Erna's capacity for symbolisation.

Erna's analysis helped Klein to understand disturbances in the drive for knowledge in the following terms:

> The basis of this disturbance is, I have found, a repressed interest in the sexual life of its parents and also a defence against its own sexual life. This attitude, which brings about an inhibition of many sublimations, is ultimately due to anxiety and feelings of guilt belonging to a very early stage of development and arising from aggressive phantasies directed against sexual intercourse between the parents.
>
> (1932, WMK II, p. 99)

Along with the wish to know, in connection with which Erna was also able to use Klein's interpretations for psychic growth, Klein was confronted in Erna's case with a vehement wish not to know, which naturally manifested itself in corresponding attacks on Klein. Here Klein reacted in part by convincing Erna with 'additional knowledge' of the correctness of her interpretation. This countertransference reaction, which partly impeded a further development of the concept, in a sense prevented the recognition of a wish not to know as a component of psychic reality.[25] Against this background, it becomes comprehensible that Klein at this time could not as yet grasp, as she noted in 1957, the idea of the envy of the breast and the associated impulse to spoil it. However, the work with Erna certainly makes an important contribution to the discovery of these connections which are conceptualised later. With the 'evil principle' in Part 2 of the Erna text, Klein gained an insight into what she was later to define as the principle of the death drive.

When Klein later abandons the term 'drive for knowledge' [*Wisstrieb*], this is I think connected with the fact that although it contains an implicit concern with knowledge of inner and outer reality, the concept of knowledge had not been clearly defined in this conceptual sense, which meant that the 'drive for knowledge' was at risk of becoming identified entirely in terms of its literal elements. In my view, however, Klein further developed in her later works the formulation that along with love and hatred there is also a striving towards the discovery of reality. This appears, for example, in her conception that there is a rudimentary ego from the outset of life that struggles with the two drive components.

---

25 In 1924, Abraham described possible forms of what we now call –K:

> The displacement of the infantile pleasure in sucking to the intellectual sphere is of great practical significance. Curiosity and the pleasure in observing receive import-ant reinforcements from this source, and this not only in childhood, but during the subject's whole life.
>
> (Abraham, 1924, p. 404)

As he explains in more detail, 'The optimum is reached when an energetic imbibing of observations is combined with enough tenacity and ability to "digest" the collected facts, and a sufficiently strong impulse to give them back to the world' (1924, p. 405). In relation to Erna, the difficulties at the various steps of this process are vividly apparent in the material: the craving, on the one hand, which does not in fact facilitate a taking in, and enteritis on the other, which repeatedly and comprehensively prevents acquisition and digestion.

7

Conclusion

Child psychoanalysis constitutes a method of research and treatment that has proved to be of outstanding relevance for developments in psychoanalytic theory and clinical practice, particularly in the period from the 1920s to the 1940s. These developments facilitated changes in the treatment of adult patients as well. It is therefore all the more surprising that child psychoanalysis should occupy a marginal position, as is generally observable despite some regional variations, within a science in which children's phantasies and feelings form some of the central paradigms.

It was this deeply detrimental position of child analysis in current research and therapy that formed the starting-point of my work. I saw that a similar discrepancy had characterised the beginnings of psychoanalytic science, when childhood fixations and childhood sexuality played a significant role in adult analysis but systematic analysis of actual children was developed only considerably later.

Against this background, I have explored two problems: first, what analytic difficulties have contributed to child analysis developing only relatively late? Second, how did Klein, one of the founders of child analysis, manage to overcome some of these difficulties?

In addressing the question of difficulties in clinical practice there are relevant case reports on children and adolescents from the first two decades of the twentieth century, such as those of 'Little Hans' (Freud, 1909a) and 'A little chanticleer' (Ferenczi, 1913b), and Klein's published work on children. The published case histories in fact proved to be adequate for indicating fundamental problems in the analytic approach to children. However, when it comes to seeing how these

233

difficulties were overcome, the published case reports are not adequate for detailed understanding. It was only the discovery of Melanie Klein's notes from memory, existing in handwritten form among the Klein Archive documents held at the Wellcome Institute for the History of Medicine in London that has made possible the work I describe in this book. Transcripts of the notes on four of Klein's child treatments from her Berlin period, 1921–1926, are published here in English for the first time.

I found it essential to formulate a method for examining systematically Klein's reports about her young patients, whether these reports took the form of publications, of unpublished manuscripts or of Klein's relatively spontaneously written clinical notes soon after the sessions took place. What also proved to be central for this procedure was the understanding of both the case histories and the original notes as manifestations of countertransference responses. The reports and notes convey transference and countertransference processes in such a way that the unconscious countertransference resistances (which, as became clear, lie at the root of most of the difficulties in analysing children) become perceptible and thus open to consideration and discussion for the reader as he absorbs the case histories of Klein's various child patients. Although this procedure, albeit perhaps less explicitly, forms the basis of a substantial part of the secondary literature on case histories (in particular the extensive secondary literature on the histories of Freud's patients) and although it has already indirectly proved productive here, further procedures had to be developed to do justice to the richness and complexity of Klein's original clinical notes. I have tried to do this by making a series of comparisons between three types of material available for the four children – Grete, Rita, Inge and Erna – whom I present. For each child I have compared the published material, the unpublished documents in the Klein Archive and Klein's unpublished clinical notes in the Archive. In each case, I have focused on certain 'points of crystallisation' such as 'beginnings': the beginning of the analysis, the first game, the first phantasy, etc. I have also explored certain 'striking features' that Klein emphasises in publications by seeing how they are expressed in the unpublished documents and how they emerge in the clinical notes.

The present work thus also represents a special application of the psychoanalytic method in that it takes historical case reports as its subject matter. With reference to discoveries from the clinical development of psychoanalysis, to Devereux's (1967) seminal work on the application of these findings and to more recent studies in the scientific literature. I have attempted to develop a method for analysing original clinical notes.

The examination by analysts of published child case histories from the first two decades of the twentieth century shows that children served primarily as objects for demonstrating the conclusions drawn from adult analyses. I believe that what proved to be an obstacle to the actual direct analysis of children was the children's negative transference and the analysts' attitude towards it. Conscious and unconscious countertransference reactions hindered an analytic approach to the child, and this difficulty was not consciously perceived and identified as such by the respective analysts; the phenomena of countertransference and negative transference had only just been discovered at that time. I have described the contemporaneous theoretical and technical approach to the psychoanalytic study of children. The main focus here was Freud's work on Little Hans and his encouragement of Hug-Hellmuth's attempt at a 'therapeutic educational analysis'. I have described the ways in which Anna Freud and Melanie Klein took up the challenge posed by the negative transference in their early publications up to 1926–1927.

As a background to the study of Klein's individual child treatments, I have reconstructed the scope of her psychoanalytic clinical work in Berlin from 1921 to 1926. During this period, Klein treated at least twenty-two children and adolescents, as well as certainly two adult female patients. Klein herself published work on at least sixteen children and adolescents from her Berlin period. I selected the first three children I describe – Grete, Rita and Inge – on the basis of several criteria. First, I had to be sure that I could accurately identify the child described in the publications with that same child in the unpublished documents and the clinical notes. Second, I wanted to show the chronological development of Klein's theoretical ideas and her technique, especially her approach to negative transference. In addition, the second child is important because she was the youngest child (2¾) that Klein treated and the last whom she treated at the child's home. The third child, Inge, was especially important because it was during her treatment that Klein hit upon the idea of the 'play technique'.

Finally, I describe Klein's slightly later and more developed work with Erna, the most extensive child analysis of this period. I have examined Klein's original clinical notes in order to reconstruct the transference–countertransference dynamics and thus to convey something of the nature of the experiences that led Klein, intuitively at first, to make changes in existing conceptualisations.

In 1921 Klein offered all children and adolescents the adult setting (the couch, the invitation to free association), which to some extent became the point of crystallisation for the negative transference. In the treatment notes on the 9-year-old *Grete*, one of Klein's earliest child treatments (February 1921 to May 1922), the key term 'negative transference' already appears and it becomes clear that Klein understood this from the outset as a factor that needed to be addressed analytically, that is, as something that had to be understood and interpreted. However, the examination of the clinical notes reveals that Klein initially failed to analyse the latent negative transference adequately and that to some extent she had to counteract the manifest negative transference by soothing the child. At the same time one can see how Klein's conscious adherence to the analytic method with all the experiences that she encountered enabled her, notwithstanding mistakes, to learn from the children and also to develop an appropriate technique and corresponding conceptualisations in the long term. Thus Klein was able, for example, to treat seriously Grete's thoughts that phantasies related not only to the male genital but also to Grete's own female genital, which led to a first extension of Freud's concept of female development.

The next stage portrayed the treatment of the 2¾-year-old *Rita* (March to October 1923), Klein's youngest patient, whose age made it impossible to retain the adult setting. Although Rita is constantly presented in the secondary literature as an example of Klein's ability to deal interpretively with the negative transference, shown especially in Rita's leaving the room, it is not possible to maintain this view with such certainty on the basis of the treatment notes. In these situations, Klein attempted to soothe or divert her young patient. The examination of the publications on Rita led me to the hypothesis that a melancholic mode characterised the dynamics in a way that became difficult for Klein to deal with effectively in this short analysis, which can be affirmed from Klein's clinical notes. However, Klein's experiences with Rita seem to have produced in her an enduring impetus to seek an adequate understanding. The discovery of an early, oppressive and strict superego was the aspect that Klein first directly owed to Rita's analysis.

Although Klein treated Rita's spontaneous recourse to her toys seriously as the child's means of expression and interpreted this as she did Rita's verbal associations, it was not until the analysis of the 7-year-old *Inge*, which lasted from September 1923 to May 1926 including breaks, that her technique with toys developed into a regular rather than a random (Rita) component of the setting for children. In so far as this can be reconstructed from the treatment notes and publications, the introduction of toys as a parameter had become necessary in order to set the analysis in train, as Inge's sparse verbal communications did not allow a precise enough grasp of the negative transference through interpretation.

The stage-by-stage reconstruction of the most extensive child analysis of the Berlin years (the development of a viable model) made it possible for me to trace how Klein gradually fathomed the psychic reality of 6-year-old *Erna*. I have explained how Erna represented an important clinical experience for conceptual innovations – early introjective and projective mechanisms, splitting, disavowal, paranoid and depressive guilt feelings. I have described the significance of child analysis for the further development of treatment technique: from resistance (as repressed libido) to fears of (various) objects; interpretation of negative transference; from predominantly reconstructive interpretation to the emphasis on more immediate transference interpretations focusing more directly on the analyst–patient relationship; acting out as communication. Finally, I have tried to show how in these years Klein grasped important components of the drive for knowledge, a fundamental concept in the comprehension of psychic reality, which was developed further by Bion and Money-Kyrle in subsequent decades.

Although during the first two decades the child was regarded only as an object for demonstrating the conclusions drawn from adult analyses, Klein thus discovered the child as a unique object of treatment and research in his or her own right. The analytic understanding of negative transference represented a cardinal point here, which Klein developed in the early years and considered theoretically in her publications. In one respect, however, she encountered a limitation in herself in that she rapidly attributed negative transference if possible to the original objects, in accordance with the prevailing technique of the time. A contributing factor here was that she was still bound by Freud's conception of the countertransference. She thought of her own emotional responses as likely to be the product of her own pathology, so that she was not freely able to use her emotional responses as at least partly a source of information about the patient. It is nevertheless impressive how far Klein was able to discover an analytic approach to negative transference that enabled her to have analytic experiences with young children that led her towards important innovations in theory and in treatment technique, which she elaborated in the years that followed. As a consequence, a more direct way of working in adult analysis was initiated, a method which encompassed an understanding of psychotic as well as neurotic areas of experience.

I will conclude by taking a very brief further look at the contemporary situation. One can observe on the one hand that just as adult analysis has benefited through Klein from child analysis, child analysis is now benefiting from the important further developments of Klein's concepts made by Bion, Money-Kyrle, Segal, Rosenfeld, Joseph and others. On the other hand, there are reports from child and adult analysts practising in England that important stimuli can in turn arise from child analyses. Based on the research perspective alone – it should go without saying that analytic treatment should be accessible to children as to adults, when the corresponding indication exists – it is easy to imagine that child analyses offer a special means of examining what O'Shaughnessy (1998) calls a 'damaging kind of knowledge', and thus of achieving an important contribution to understanding impediments in psychic growth.

I wish to record at the end of this work that there needs to be support, decades after Klein's emigration, for efforts to (re)import child analysis and to facilitate training in child analysis in Germany. If dealing with negative transference is a critical factor here, then a correspondingly expert training analysis on the one hand and a close-meshed appropriate supervision on the other, together with a detailed theoretical curriculum, are essential requirements for the perception and consideration of negative transference and for the means of working it through.

PART TWO

Notes to this edition

For this first publication of the original notes on the analyses of Grete, Rita. Inge and Erna, the notes have been transcribed. The vast majority of these were handwritten; only the sessions with Inge of November 1925 are available in typewritten form. In order to present the most authentic possible version, the spelling, punctuation and abbreviations have been retained. Square brackets have been used to indicate when a word was either illegible or had been crossed out and could not then be deciphered. Insertions have also been put in square brackets and the reference marker 1 has been added. An oblique line is used here to indicate the end of a line in the original and a vertical line is used to indicate the end of the page. The patients' names have been replaced throughout with their pseudonym, and the following reference markers are used to indicate what appears in the original in each instance:

2   In the original, the patient's first name.
3   In the original, the first letter of the patient's first name.
4   In the original, the patient's first name and surname.
5   In the original, the patient's surname.
6   In the original, the first letter of the patient's surname.
7   In the original, the patient's first name and the first letter of the surname.
8   In the original, the patient's first name and abbreviated surname.
9   The patient's sister's name.

Where a tick appears in the original, this indicates the position to which the addition at the end of the page belongs, and this has been shown by a capital V in the transcription. The additions at the end of a page are distinguished with a horizontal line in the original; here they are indented in every instance.

With Erna the drawings that have remained visible in the reproduction have been added at the corresponding places – these all exist on loose pages. Many are in fact so pale in colour that the drawings are almost indiscernible in the reproduction.

Note on punctuation: Klein's case notes are imperfectly punctuated, with some missing or additional closing brackets and inverted commas, and this has generally been preserved to reflect their original form.

8

Treatment notes on Grete

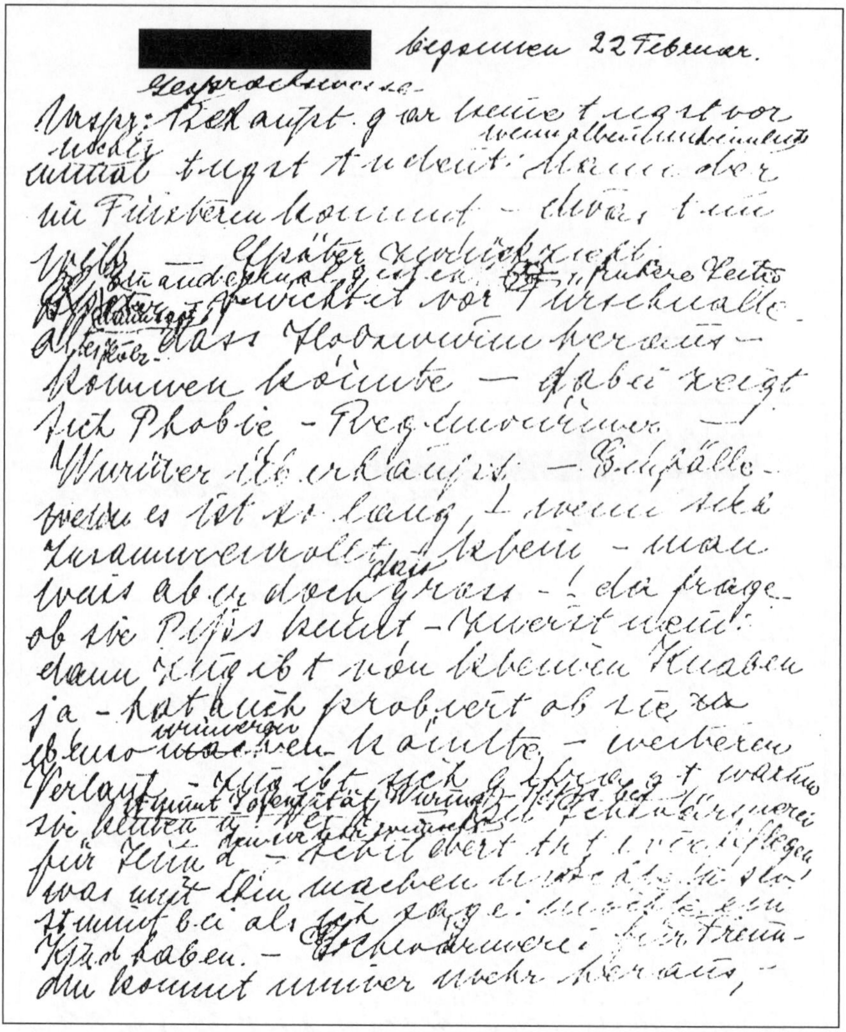
[redacted] bekommen 22 Februar.
Gesprächsweise
kommen könnte – dabei zeigt
sich Phobie
zusammen
dann zeigt
Verlauf
du kommt immer mehr heraus,

[B 3: Notebook headed 'Kindergarten & gen. observations': from the middle of the notebook, the notes relate to Grete. Melanie Klein clearly started writing on the right-hand side; insertions appear on the left-hand side, with which I shall now begin in setting out this page.]

★ Observn. on [next page][1] Grete[4] / But another time she presents a   *p. 1a*
more specific / fear: she is tucked up, the / man comes with a sack. /
He has a knife in his hand. / Says she is afraid in gen. not / at all when
noise can be heard / from the street – but is afraid when she / hears
noises in the next room. / Then I explain to her that this is because /
people from the street might be able to help her / whereas in the next
room there might be / the person who would like to do something to
her – she / is surprised, agrees strongly & says / she thought that but
didn't know it / by this sees my claim (there is something Ucs /
confirmed) then also shows awakening / intellectual interest & presents more readily / the fear of door-handle described / on other page.
Grete[4] – only memory / of parents. She in the cot. Mother has /
smashed lampshade. Father terribly / angry & shouts – wants to send
mother / outside. She shouts a lot in bed until father / picks her up.
Little brother / [is][1] also in [his][1] bed. No memory [of][1] father / only
that he wore pince-nez. After mother / lives apart from her – longing.
| Grete[4] begun 22 February / Orig.: [in conversation][1] claims not at   *p. 1*
all afraid of / [at night][1] once hints at fear: [creepy when alone][1] man
who / comes in the dark – wants to / do something – then draws
back / [admits another time ★ earlier page][1] / ~~Later~~ – afraid of door-
handle / old wood [then says][1] that woodworm / might come out of
it – thus shows / phobia – earthworms / worms in general – ideas /
~~when~~ it is so long, when / it rolls up, small – but you / still know then
[that][1] it is big – when ask / if knows pipi – at first no: / Then admits
– yes, of small boys – has also / tried to see if she could ~~m~~ / ~~make~~
[urinate][1] just like them – later / in session – admits has wondered
why / she does not have & envy [agrees with worm-pipi correspond-
ence].[1] Enthusing / about dog [that she very much wants][1] –
describes how will care for / what would like to do with it etc. /
Agrees when I say: would like / to have a child. Enthuses more and
more / about girl friend – | – does not like kissing mouth but   *p. 2*
otherwise / hugs aftern. sleeping – also / hugs with mother in her
bed, caressing / kissing – mother her neck & she mother's / neck –
also with girl friends, apply. / not genitals. Also talks about loo /

together with 2 or 3 [girls][1] then [tells that they][1] say: we / really can't bear it how / stinks = [but][1] still stay there. Says / that they pressed each other's thighs – Irmi / also showed – her brother but (when / asked) that they could not see / anything else, also that they undress naked in front of / girl friend when they sleep / together. Great significance for / her sweets oranges [(also get as presents [?])][1] chocolate / great significance elegant flat / phantasises about luxurious flat / girl friend – lavish elaborate clothes. / At this time describes theatre ~~play~~ [pieces][1] [sic] / ~~that~~ she saw – most liked story / of young girl who sells / flowers – afterwards has fiancé / then – phantasy about being / engaged – beautiful dress, how bridegroom / speaks, elegant

p. 3 man, (good colour | not too red [face][1] – black hair / eyes – then talks about wedding [reception][1]. [Sth. crossed out]. About / [marrying][1] she thinks only – that early in the morning wife / goes to man in bed, for this / is what she saw when staying at aunt's house. / On 5 April after 6 wks of treatment / ask [her][1] to lie down. / Extremely violent reaction of fear & refusal. / With great difficulty admits – after / I allow her not to lie down – / to what part of the fear is / about: I would go away if she lay / on the couch – come back with a / knife – stick it into her / arm, no – her chest. / 7 April – reports excursion / with girl friend – how they made / shapes, – then mussels etc. / – strong nauseous reaction to snails / that she saw there. [Sth. crossed out] When I /

great fun gardening – would like / to become that – [also][1] enjoyment housekpg. / duties – desire to learn, ambition [are][1] / weak – on 9 April expresses enjoyment in / learning French that had begun / at school. [Sth. crossed out] Abt. 3–4 weeks ago now / some exceptionally good work for fairy-tale

p. 4 interpret to her: snail perhaps also boy's / pipi (as she calls it – as reluctantly admitted / in talk about worms). She / says – no – that cannot be right. / After all, it is not long – looks different – / so soft – has its little house – then / agrees completely, when I interpret / her genital organs – then enthuses again about / taking ~~soft~~ teacher some little catkins (~~flowe~~ / (plants) – as forbidden / to buy nicer flowers – 9th / I repeat request for her to lie down. / Again extremely violent fearful reaction. / This time after terribly strong / resistance, more detailed descrip-/tion. –: When she lay down I went out / – came back with large / knife. I undressed her. / Stuck the knife in her chest, no – / hesitates – lower – but then admits / only her stomach. Then I turn

about the little brother & the little sister that I / told her. Likes to remember how she / used to play with older brother who died.

away from her – she is lying in / blood – one of the doctors comes *p. 5* and / bandages her – gets dressed & goes / home. I interpret: I put her / to bed, undress her, as mother / did. Then she claims does not remember / about means of identification how she / would like to do with child what she / phantasises – then admits, yes wishes / mother would like to undress her, put her to bed. / Until then she says it is similar / but – then not – then is afraid of / me – but admits herself incomprehens-/ible why is afraid – as knows I want / to do nothing bad. Taking this up / I say – and there is nothing bad there. Would like / me with pipi (uncertainty whether / have – since surprised she did not) / should fetch one for me to take / & stick in hers.) – At first / says whether then there is a hole there – then / yes as small wish comes out of it. | Agrees completely with interpretation – / says *p. 6* longs more for mother than father. / When I say that when parents went to bed / together – she stayed alone in hers, / – longed for mother should go to her / lie down with her in bed, she: but we could all 3 / have been together in bed. / When I tell her she has also / worked out this solution in her / longing – but it did not happen. / She: and what would have happened then with / my little brother? Agrees / when I said she would just have / wished – then she wants to do this / with her brother. Resistance / very much reduced, even says / she will lie down next time. / When she first [fear in this session][1] had to speak & / resistance so strong – she also says / her cousin said she would / not undress before the doctor as / she had to do in the Polyclinic / examination – & when I say / she only has to speak though – she says but that / is so similar. When I say to her simil-/arity fear of me, or mother | & fear of man, that this / likewise is only *p. 7* [?] father, she / agrees. 12 April – phantasy about king's castle / she also king's daughter, finest cloth-/es people in street looking. She also / first at school. If someone else / were there, both of them front row. / Then – that other worse clothes. Then, that not there at all. / Agrees completely with interpretation / poss. three together – even better alone / with father mother dead. Amplifies / frightening representa-tion about man, who / stabbed her with knife lower down – / thigh,

247

admits genitals. Took / her with him in sack / to his family – it was / very nice there. – 14. – Strong resist-/ance that manifests in scorn. Laughs terribly about teacher, whose false teeth / fell out while she was sniffing / which she nevertheless (with great laughter) / hardly articulated as something very / embarrassing. Then fellow pupil who

p. 8 / wets herself at school & / her shame about this (again with | great laughter) – Then spontaneously / a memory of bedwetting when / she was already older (abt. 5–6 yrs.) – That / urinates every hour. That when / needs to at night does not / dare to use potty because afraid. Of figure / that she sees as strip of light in the mirror. / Is a [sth. crossed out] stripe – under it zig-zag – thus confused. & yet a figure that could do something to her / if she sits like that facg. the window / then could do something to her from behind / if facg. away from window – from the front / something could happen. Says that / this same man is her / father again. Very strong resistance, wants / to hear no talk of this – does not want even / if she thinks like this to say / something indecent. – Says a few times / 'from behind' that is too indecent. / Much stronger resistance than Oedip. / complex recently. – Also says / fear lessens when holds on to / grandmother's bed with 1 hand / then nothing can happen to her. / Cries, would like to stop

p. 9 coming here | is very hostile. Beforehand / again with great laughter / she made fun of the attitude of my head / & my gaze – indignantly / & aggressively rejected it when I asked / if her aunt or mother not sometimes / funny. 20 Apr. Continuing strong / negative transfer-ence. When says / herself – is defiant – presents association with / mother (whom she was visiting) was defiant / & did not eat. Cries & is outraged / because I say she wants to annoy / not only me but also mother. 21. – Talks / about acquaintances who [sth. crossed out] knew / the Emperor. When lead her on to / phantasies about Emperor – phantasises about beautiful / clothes coach visits Emperor / Empress died – admits / Oedipal wishes. At first longing / 16-yr-old girl cousin went away. Tells how / early on Sunday mornings they always / get into bed together, kiss caress / tickle – (back, thighs,

p. 10 bottom) / cousin says no at first, does not | want her to get into her bed / then she furiously insults: / pig, goose – when ask how / angry she would be – if cousin / took a friend into bed / at first outraged – then admits rage. / Admits when interpret / longing & rage at mother's / rejection – since mother loved father. Then / Emperor phantasies follow. Resistance / diminished. 23/IV. Phantasises / about making pancakes in which / enthusiastically describes how likes

helping with / the [sth. crossed out] preparation & watching the / preparation. Yellowish fat in pan / into this the pancakes, which / get [bigger]¹ brown & then / sprinkled with sugar. When have her / associate [assoc.]¹ to fat in pan – small / wish [?] in potty, pancake / something red and white – does not want / to say it – finally pipi. / Reports saw it got bigger & redder / during urination. (When / asked why red and white), that this | sometimes is red & white / it all   *p. 11* depends. Bef [?] it is, it / also red down below, when it burns / it usually does burn. Then / she thinks of red and white at her uncle's / tennis club, how the men play tennis together / in white clothes. She does not care / to watch that. It is bor-/ing when you are not playing too. From this / red remind again of [rain]¹ disgust at worm / – fierce resistance. But then says / that was not true about the snail. Interpret / the 'not true'. As a child she / thought her snail would still become / a pipi like father's, which / she saw in nightshirt white / with red pipi. That boring / to watch when men do something / like that together.
26/IV. / Annoyance with shoelace when breaks / – also admits when annoyed / with girl friends would like / to box ears & hit them – but immediately / claims: never adults! / But then admits that | how   *p. 12* wanted to throw shoe at cousin's / head. Later cousin then [?] wants / her paint-box – in which there are water-colours / etc. Associates to this what / babies do in nappies. / Talks about invitation to a friend's / father's birthday – reluctance / because [friend's]¹ father's birthday does not interest / her, the friend's mother / yes. The brother died there as well. / Admits comparison with own / family in which little brother also / died. But I say to her antipaty [sic] / friend's father thus: she would like / father to be alive at her house & / mother dead.

Homosexuality: flight – heterosexua/-lity, – & stratification of castration / anxiety through mother father / castration anxiety also through / urethral phantasies – the Oedipus compls. / were activated.

[B 6: Second treatment book, which discusses Grete at the front and patient A at the back]

1921 /28/IV. – Grete² reports enjoyment / eating bread and butter in   *p. 1b* the tram by the window / so nice when keep wrapping / & unwrapping up packet in between. Also with sweets / [&]¹ other things too wraps and unwraps / packet in between, but only with things to eat –

nothing / else. When talking about largest she says / gets afraid in the street in the evening when it is / dark. Says strangely then, if / no one is there, then nothing / can happen to her. Fear of a man. / Sits down in a coach, ~~then~~ doors shut with var-/ious locks / so he cannot open. But then / the lady who last rode kept the / keys. Then the doors can be opened only by handle in usual way – pushes coachman from / behind off the box, he remains lying / on his stomach. He himself climbs [on to][1] box & / she climbs out unnoticed. / He keeps coach & then hires it out with / higher fares. Or she goes on / foot & he talks to her. Wrinkled face / not too old, otherwise he could no longer / do that, black eyes brown / hair, very red cheeks (unusually / not attractive because so flaming red) bad / black & yellow teeth. Very friend-/ly because play-acts, reminds her / of Uncle Kurt's friendli-

p. 2b ness although / he does not play-act. (When asked | if similar to him, no because it is Uncle Pince-Nez / not he who) invites her to the teatre [sic] / tells her he is fond of her and / calls her 'dear little one' (a girl friend / whom does not like very much though. / 30/IV. Talks about excursion. Had / so much fun with girl friend – they caught / fishes in shallow water – at first / smaller ones, then each a bigger one. Was amused by goggle eyes that / stared so strangely. Each dug / a channel, put water into it / & played with the fish there, gave / it cake (long, thin, full of / raisins) to eat). When asked / association to fish – strong resistance / then, when asked what / such a long narrow fish reminded her of / pipi. But claims because I / asked her like that. Fiercest resistance. Does not want / to talk about such things – cries / likes me wants to talk about / other things but not that. Interpreted / her channel (as described) as her genital / also water there, in which she wishes / for penis and also child. Then forgets / to take it out

p. 3b of there / i.e. does not want to part with it. | 3[?]/V. (mistakenly recorded for patient A) [cf. p. 18b] / 7/V. Talks about a wonderful [sth. illegible][1] ball-and-stick / big one, that received as a present, thrilled. / It has a handle on to which you / can attach a string and pull it / tight. ~~Associations: string ball-and-stick mem.~~/ It also then produces such lovely / music = associations: Reminds of her / genital – small handle clitoris. / String of hair – but only of one. / Then [?] pipi when the boys play / with it and pull to make it long. I / ask her whether the ball-and-stick do not also remind / of stool. She says yes, because / when you have eaten fruit stool / is also different colours & agrees / in lively cheerful way to the / 'music' with it, which she / laughs about and states that [it][1] more often / escapes from her Grandmamma. She mostly / has it before she has stool. / About the recent little house. She has / seen a picture in which naked women / hold leaves in place of their genitals. The / leaves of the plum-tree remind her / of this. At this I interpret / the tall tree that she described as pipi / & the [long]¹ roots that she described / as hair sticking into the earth / – as into the woman – and the roots | that are getting smaller & smaller / as children. The little green / house reminds her of the / snail's little house (that we established as / her genitals). The snail's / little house is green when the snail / comes out of the sludge, otherwise / grey. The red windows remind / her of the clitoris. She then talks / about red, it is red when it has been / rubbed – the skin around it white. / She rubs it, when she has urinated / but then confesses also in the evening & / early morning because itches. But says, she is / so furious because as soon as you / have rubbed it itches again. Reports / (resistance) that her two girl friends / when they went out in the open air showed / each other their genitals to look at / she apparently not. Completely changed / no sign of any resistance / on the contrary, extremely jolly / giggles constantly at these / things, in trusting but so strangely / affected & self-important way. When I remind / her about the teacher's false teeth / that fell out – immediately ~~gives~~ says red – white / also genitals. Tells me that / she was looking forward to session & next time / wants to bring me a bunch of lilacs: / for me – her favourite teacher & | for her aunt. 10/V. Mistakenly recorded for patient A. [Cf. p. 23b]. 12/V. Phantasises / with particular enjoyment & pass-/ion about eating cucumbers. ~~Bring~~ / How the outside tastes good & then / inside the core, that tastes good / so soft when you bite into it. / Describes in detail the appearance / of one cucumber, which was so bent / & the other so pointed at the end. / Says herself her genitals in which / the bent one the shape / of the snail – the one with pointed end / clitoris. [Small seed (sth. illegible)]¹ (Interpret: her small seed / labia wanted to suck ~~her~~ mother's / bite off, eat – at first mother's / breast with nipples [sth. crossed out]. Also / that she recently bit / into her arm & said she would like to bite / into lovely white flesh.) Then / especially her left arm, because / she prefers that one then she would wear / mother's ring. Talks about / dress – green and red occur to her / at first when you hit yourself / different-coloured bruises – then her / genitals (like a painted little house) / also white and red. With / purple also light bruises / & the plum-trees that represented / the pipi. Then she says | the leaves on the plum-tree are / the ~~bows~~ ribbons, the plum-tree / the two bows. But then

p. 4b

p. 5b

p. 6b

when / I interpreted bottom – also the 2 legs / (~~Interpret~~ When I ask about transparent / story about garment / Andersen's emperor – when it was only thought / to be garment – reality was / naked. (Interpret exhibitionism espec. / towards father – envy mother who / could show father all that. / Anal coitus, which she felt / was act of violence – therefore / also striking blows / bruises.) Agrees comp-/letely with this. 14/V. Intense happi-/ness that will be spending sev-/eral days / with mother. Speaks in gush-/ing terms about mother. Immediately / afterwards complaint that grandmother / scolded her because she was looking after / a dog in the street & she there-/fore called her 'dog-girl' at which / she is very outraged & asks if I / would do something like that. Report that she was beating / dog & you have to take care / that a 'copper' [?] does not see then. / What then did this have to do with her? Criticises / because dog's owner

p. 7b also hits its | face – this can be done at the back / after all. Tells enviously how her / friend Irma then boasted about much / smaller sweeter dog – afterwards they / quarrelled & called each other / street urchins. (Interpret behind exaggerated / love of mother: dis-satisfaction – grandmother / me, another mother sought – reproach / dog-girl: according to earlier phantasy / dog = child, also agrees that she / described putting it to bed [?] caressing it / boasting about it just like a child.) Reproach / that she wants or has / a girl a child – idents. with / mother & beats dog as she / was beaten, in which she preferred / the rear end. Jealousy that / mother (friend dog) has child she / not & inner criticisms.) / Agrees. Next association: shows / me a hole in her shoe, that / she is to get new shoes from / mother that she would so like / to throw away the old ones. That her friend / Irma has some much worse shoes still / with the whole sole coming off – that her / mother does not take enough care of / her. When asked association shoe / she does not want to say. Fiercest resis-/tance as not for long time now. / Finally – her genitals because of shape / 2 side parts & tongue. Cannot state / why so difficult to

p. 8b say? (I interpret | because of the torn damaged aspect / guilt feeling damaged because of / masturbation – mother's consolation even more damaged / by sexual intercourse with father) / (After three weeks of ab-/sence resistance such as never / appeared before – including not / turning up to session. / Then reports in many ways about pres-/ents that given on the journey. / Aunt made cakes and / gave them out – an ordinary one / a white one with yellow sprin-kled over it. / Interprets herself as stool. Says / that she ate fish

252

somewhere / with relatives. Mother so much, especially / fatty kind
– that fell ill.

[The rest of this page and the first three lines of the next page
contain material from the treatment of patient A, as Klein indicates
at the end of this section.]

Grete[2]: 21/V. & 24/V. – then from 31/V. to 9/VI. there are five ses-   *p. 9b*
sions. / Talks about poem or story / in which ghosts in the graveyard
come / back to life. Then talks about [sth. crossed out] monks / who
sinned. And says that / the monks & nuns not allowed / to meet. Asks
/ what kind of sin then? / Immediately afterwards her aunt's / sister
has a child & is not / married. Agrees with interpretation / that she
considered 'that' as a sin. / Reports about birthday of / friend to
whom she – with difficulty – gave / chocolate. Gloatingly describes /
the ball that 'Irmi' got, is / so fragile that will soon / be broken. Then
talks about / fellow pupils, also gloating / towards them. When indicate this to / her – fiercest resistance. / Another time – later reports /
Irmi's ball broken. Hers also not | very strong, if she fills it full / of air   *p. 10b*
& does not / touch for 24 hours it is all right / again. – Then agrees
interpretation / (with reference to hole in shoe) about ball / genitals –
damaged / by masturbation – gloating / mother's even more. / Before
she had also / very happily reported / that she plays with ball with her
/ head, chest, under / arm, through legs, through / etc. Tells me about
a / wedding that she attended. / About ~~weddi~~ bouquet that / aunt
sent: espec. about red / flowers whose name did not know / whose
shape she draws with [indicated four-leaf bud] / finger in the air. /
Purple flowers remind her of / plum-trees. Talks about a child /
whom met there / on stairs – was not nice / to her because thought
she would / be given the child as / company. There [she][1] also met |
[(~~I think~~ on the stairs?)][1] a man and saw his / wife. He is so tall that she   *p. 11b*
/ thought to herself that with his / long legs he could move up and
down / the stairs much better than she, she / can manage 2 or 3 he
certainly / 3–4. His wife is short & / had a black silk / dress. About
wedding bouquet / she also thinks that it had / the kind of grasses in
it that were like / grey hair. She then thinks of her / grandmother &
that / when you have grey hair / you soon have to die. / Interpret: At
wedding something / happens with genitals – coitus / (shape of
flower, plum-tree). Then / comes a child (that she met / there). The
tall man [her][1] Papa – / who can do something like that / much better

than she can because he bigger / pipi. She would be a wife to him / although she is small, if / mother, who already looked old / had died.

p. 12b Agrees / with this. | – For some time now keen / interest in French. (Only / interest among school subjects apart from / drawing & gymnastics) / – Tells how when she / is lying on the sofa, recites / sentences from Fr. class / & that is such fun / e.g. – '*Le matin nous burons / notre café ou thé / ou notre lait / à huit heures*'.[i] The associations she presents are: It / is so nice how / the voice then constantly / goes up & down. Next / associations: in the snail / you could also go up & / down on a ladder / in the part where there is room for / this. Up and down makes her think of / the hair lower down & under / the arms from the curls of which she identifies up and down. / Whether it does not go up because / that the arm is always pressing on it / like that. Then waves that also / go up and down like that / [Sth. crossed

p. 13b out] ship on top / draws the shape of the snail | in the air again. Talks / about mast & when in interpreting I / ask if that is the pipi in / the snail, she: no that / small bit (clitoris). / She says that sail / is missing. Interpret that she is lacking it, i.e. / she would like to have pipi inside. / Interpret up & down – agrees. / – First session after the holidays / 14/IX. Reports – summer / – all the fruit – sweets given to her / by aunt. – Regrets when she was / healthy – that she had said choc. / that she ate when ill / did not taste good. Cannot admit / reason for this regret – [then]¹ / admits: so that aunt should not stop / wanting to give presents – but thinks aunt / is not like that. Seeing girl friend again / new best friend, good relat-/ionship school, teacher – especially / drawing – her favourite teacher. Happy / about mother, etc. – 19/IX. School / again, learning well / aunt studying French / with her – good marks in Fr-/ench. Grade approaching. / No longer so friendly old girl friend / Irmi – talks about a shop / (Right from 1st

p. 14b session 14/IX to analysis on the couch) | that behind each other trinket-[?] / shop, confectionery – again was con-/fectionery there is a small / boy, 2-yr-old Peter – whom / Irmi noticed – when she [Grete²]¹ / only touched him, she / immediately hit ~~him~~ her. / ~~I~~ why aunt does not want / to let her go roller-skating. / Talks about car journey in / summer, the driver in front / & where the car was – so many / children in front & behind / also hung on, the / car then drove into the / yard, then the children / ~~fell on their face~~ / With the roller-skates she can / also go almost as fast / as the tram. (Interpret /

---

i In the morning we drank / our coffee or tea / or our milk /at eight o'clock.

intense love mother – aunt / teacher not so intense – Irmi / hostile – envy child – envy / mother towards little brother, remind – / envy little dog – child.) She / says – but then little brother / would also have been jealous / of her – would have | begrudged her the mother.   *p. 15b* (Interpret car – father / penis – coitus – her roller-skating / masculine wish towards aunt mother. / Much talk about fruit, sweetmeats / that received & receives as presents / espec. from aunt. ~~Has~~ 21/IX. / Again a lot about the teacher, enjoying exercises / aunt does German Fr. homework / with her. Reports about something to eat that the girls bought / from a cart in front of the school. She does not know / what it actually was – looked like / cotton-wool & when part of it was / removed, it was still like cotton wool. / The girls ate some of it – she must / also try that. V. (Interpret cart / like car – father's penis – something white that / not exactly familiar & ~~sees the~~ semen. / Noticed something of coitus, that something / went into mother – food & below ident-/ical – could not watch closely because / mother was there.) She says – whether aunt / also might have eaten something like that, with / the cart it is so strange – one moment / it is there, then gone again – then / in another street, then back again / (Interpret – penis, one moment big, then did

> She wanted to look at it more closely, / but the teacher was also there / so she could not. At the beginning of the / session complained strongly that they / espec. in her classroom and row – are not allowed to play / during the lunch break. Her teach-/er ordered this. Not other classes.

not see again (wondered where gone into). Says / that Irmi – soon no   *p. 16b* longer / allowed in the street, because will be 13 years old / no longer proper. Only goes to / the select school – asks which school more / Auguste Viktoria ~~Lyzeum~~ [school][1] or Princess Bis-/mark school where she goes. Thinks Aug. V. / is actually more – but then Princess B. is a secondary school. (Interpret Irmi – mother who walked / in street where car drove – contemptible / because of [experienced][1] coitus. She is indeed queen – but / for this she is perhaps more because more / respectable, not yet had coitus). She / confirms – tells how a car once / really drove into her school – into the / corridor – it was where the girls / drink water, ~~thus howev~~ there were also / men there, they had to take care / not to run into the car. / (~~Then~~ Explains here exactly – where steps / led where corridor was etc. / Interpret

255

association confirmn. – phantasy about / parental coitus – & idea that the / foetuses in the mother (drinking water!) / must take care! Answers yes to all this / absolutely no resistance observable.

[Page 17b contains material relating to patient A]

p. 18b [The first 11½ lines relate to the other patient] / 30.–3/V. [Relates to Grete⁴]¹. Reports about / playing ball game with 5 girl friends with large ball. Then at school / they were given the task of drawing / a plum-tree – otherwise, everything as / they wanted: She drew: a little / house ~~blue~~ green with red windows. At the front / a small garden with some grass / with a fence in front. There is a plum-/tree, with red and purple plums, underneath / a boy who is shaking it, a girl / who is holding a basket – into which plums / are falling. When asked about plums / (after fierce resistance) it / reminds her of the pipi boys have. / About tree she then says it was / a bit bent like – it reminds her / what pipi is like. (The other without / resistance) – The little basket

p. 19b makes | her think [of]¹ her own genitals. There are / drops that come out of the pipi / into the genitals – she says / small wish – she thinks a / plum-tree would completely fill it up / though. About the zig-zag roots / she says that they then become / smaller & smaller & narrower – that / the trees are supported by the / roots but also by the fence. / Grass reminds many of hair / but the zig-zag of the roots / also [of hair]¹. As very little / resistance – ask for communication about what / fear of potty meant (man from / behind – earlier phantasy / not completed). Almost without resis-/tance says – that he wanted to put / his pipi into her from behind there. – When I / explain [allow]¹ comparison stick of faeces & pleasure / in it etc. she says animatedly: There / is also some life in stool [sth. crossed out] / that is white & that is so soft when / it goes through. It becomes clear that she / never asked about this – thought that / everyone has & construes that as children. / Then she also says – that the roots / get smaller & smaller & / very tiny – interprets herself children / growing inside her. About

p. 20b plum-tree that | the lower round part where there [are]¹ still leaves on it / {reminds} her of her genitals (for which she knows / no name at all) – the plum-tree itself / is pipi. Promises from now on / [sth. crossed out] to work with / less resistance, at which I – as re-/cently promised to tell a story / in return for several good sessions. 3.V. (was mist-/akenly written / down – relates / to Grete!⁴) [Further material about the other patient follows.]

256

[Pages 21b and 22b relate back to patient A]

[The first lines again refer to the other patient.] / Grete[4] [10/V.].[1] –   *p. 23b*
Jealousy of cousin who / gets dress – she does not. Phantasises / about
dress that she would like – white / transparent, with red dots / big
purple bow at the back / green and blue pearls around her neck. /
The large bow at the back makes / Grete think of her aunt (about
whom / she had reported that she (when she / was staying there) got
into bed with the uncle / in the early morning. In this consisted in
her / opinion also opinion of / marriage). Then it occurs to her that /
the aunt gets into bed with the uncle / & that the little daughter must
/ want them both if she went / to her mummy's bed. – Then: / that
she hits etc. / a little girl whom / she is told to look after (I interpret
jealousy / of mother – because she wanted to go to father | in bed   *p. 24b*
and the beautiful clothes. / Especially also the big bow / at the back –
big bottom). Hatred / because mother treated her / badly &
capriciously. Does not / admit that, but ~~re~~ resistance / much
reduced.) [The remainder of the notebook contains material relating
to the other patient.]

[B 6: In the next treatment book some material concerning Grete
has been recorded]

When 2 years old Grete[2] accident from / burning lamp or burning   *p. 1c*
comb [?] / (unconfd.) in any case burns to her face. / Since then
stuttering – before also a bit. Father / also stuttered as child. When 3
years old / father drafted into army. When 5 yrs. old came on leave /
for 2 weeks – never returned. When / 5 years old went to aunt. /
Grete[2] & boy A[2] / Sept. 1921. / Also tells / how street sealed off for a
race / one time drove there anyway, immediately 2 coppers / sprang
forward. Whether punishment then / followed, she does not know.
(Interpret car journey / = coitus, something forbidden.) | Grete[4]   *p. 2c*
Sept. 21 / 24/IX. talks a lot about / flowers that children gave to
teacher / how she also loves them etc. / – Tells how she chose from
many essays / the one about the wood. She descs. how / dense the
trees are; and that in the / treetop bird-nest young sparrows / etc.
(When asked if likes the wood). / No, not very much, especially not
where such / dense trees – no space at all there when / you lie down
– you are pricked / by the needles (Interpret tree [trunk][1] – remind
her earlier drawing = pipi – treetop = snail (her / term for feml.

257

genitals) – tree formation / then nest – children – when lies down it pricks / = coitus.) Wants [has overwritten] ~~ma~~ to make a drawing / in which there are flowers. A flower-/shop with some steps in front, on which / pots of flowers – white – white and red / etc. Also a vase with flowers / whose shape she draws in the air / [outlined three-leafed shape]. No associations to this, strong resis-/tance. Went on a trip to / Wannsee – sat in a motor boat / & moved it with feet – it is not at / all difficult, it is very easy. Tells / how she made a mountain / there, put flowers in front of it / & wanted to put a broken / glass bowl in front

p. 3c – but it would not work | because it was broken. (Interpret – wants to have coitus / with mother instead of with father – the vase – this / shape that she earlier (flower, boat) / described as her snail = her genitals / that she wants to give teacher mother with flowers / = children). But then thinks does not go / so well – if she had / mama's [?man's] pipi hers would still grow – / boat = pipi – not difficult to move / it would go better. Mountain with flowers is / her snail, but intact glass belongs there – opening may not be / pushed through. 27/IX. Tells how she / shared the last two sugar cubes in tin / between herself & aunt. At friend I's house got / a snail with sugar on. In detl. / how got coffee & rusks there. Then / that enquired what was in the / cart that time: candy floss. V. The man first / gave some of it to taste, before he sold it. / (Interpret wants to give aunt semen – as from cart / also gets it from her (friend's mother) / but thinks would be better from father. / He gives some to taste first, before giving more but / she would like the taste). Says that she was given / an envelope with war veterans' aid coupons / at school – lost one for 5 M {Marks} – aunt does not want / to replace it – perhaps her

p. 4c mummy. Tells | how for school raffle ~~gladly~~ / received a glass as a present from aunt – from / grandmother nothing. The teacher will / certainly also not replace her lost / Marks. Pilot who threw leaflets / down from above. She and girl friend wanted / to catch them. But friend warned little / cousin not to take any – then they / would have fewer leaflets. But she still / took some. (Interpret pilot = motor boat – car / = pipi, father who brings down something white / on one. If she were mother would / allow child, even if causing disturbance. That she / certainly also disturbed parents during / coitus. V. After sugar cart thing / says how quickly & skilfully she / can crochet – how much wool / crocheted in little time – a garter / for her Grand-mamma. Laughs / about grandmother's fat / leg. Talks about girl friend who / can crochet even faster & more / skilfully. (Interpret

258

crocheting, needle in hole / also garter ~~in~~ hole = coitus / – again wish hope if she / cannot have father – so if her / pipi grows – to be able to be like father / with mother). Repts. that is borrowing / new book [sth. crossed out] to read. But not / now a long one like legends of Grk. / heroes, does not like the long / books such as I have in the box there | Only likes short stories /   *p. 5c*

[The rest of the page, like p. 6c and p. 7c, is blank; p. 8c continues with the patient 'boy A' until page 13c, then there are two blank pages; p. 16c relates back to the boy, as does p. 17c, which is followed by two blank pages, then two more pages about the boy.]

| Grete[2]: / [sth. crossed out] [8][1] / X. Repts. about trip to Wannsee   *p. 23c* with aunt. / Drank coffee, she took bowls out. / Enthuses about small dog that obeyed her / better than its owner. ~~Then complains that~~ / ~~she again~~ [sth. crossed out] ~~to the theat~~ Reports about draw-/ing & teacher (favourite). She drew 2 / brown twigs – a smaller & a larger one, & / a blue plum-tree [much praised by teacher & children][1] – Complains / that she repeatedly missed theatre / productions because of analys. session, that / with aunt's help, who wants to drive to meet / her, as the next theatre prodn. will be / later – she will actually be able to go to / the next one – but what will happen / with others. Something would always be on, when she / had a session with me. It was her cousin's / birthday, was absent, did not cele-/brate – but how could this have been, when was here. / Talks again about cart with / candy floss, that she does not get any money / for this – her friend Irmi also / highly ~~prai~~ tasted highly praised it. + If / Herr Seefeld [?] gives her money, she will buy

+ says, that she now always thinks of the cart / with candy floss whenever she sees me

at once – or – admits that she was thinking / about me again, was very   *p. 24c* disappointed / that I did not give her money at the last / session, had waited the whole time. / If I do not give her any again / ~~get~~ very angry with me, she will resolve / not to say anything more about / any thoughts – and not to be let herself be persuaded / by any encouragement & as / sign of determination / tells in detail story of / 'Poor Henry', in which the little girl / also refused to let herself be dissuaded / in any way from her wish to die for / king. Also tells me

259

about a fine lady / with white fur coat, whom she saw / get out of coach – then about eleg. lady / in car who could have driven / a bit further & did not. – / (Interpret Assoc. to drawing: brown / twigs: stool – plum-tree [him]¹ 'snail' / (Interpret: representation coitus – mother did / not allow her this – I am that when / do not allow her prodn. – if she had allowed her / like aunt – she would be good with her. Not helping to get | candy floss from cart = excluding from coitus / also not giving stool, she no longer / telling me secret thoughts = doing / = also not playing / coitus games me or mother. Dying for Henry = having coitus / (pain, representation of dying). About white / fur, assoc.: rabbit, hare, roasted / does not like. Interpret fur = hair – mother / pubic hairs (Hatred remind interpn. dress / white, red, purple bow) – hatred envy wanted / to roast and eat mother). 20/X. Was very / late also otherwise clear resistance. Fierce / complaints that again my fault missed / some fun. Mother was there wanted to / take her somewhere, does not know where. / Otherwise it would be another theatre production / that I was also stopping her from going to. Tells [sth. crossed out] / Then makes a verbal slip and says: because of you / I could not go to the play & / not to you – (instead of not to Mummy). / Tells triumphantly how Mummy gave her 1 / M for [?] candy floss. Very nice but actually / not as good as thought. Also gave / her 2 M for sweets that were very nice. / Reproaches me – I would have said / I in mother's place, she preventing her from eating | candy floss. This would be untrue. After much / resistance admits would be happy if / I were not there. Did not exist / is at night, for then would not have / known me – if had died / – another person would be in my place. / – With difficulty and crying, death phantasies. / I might die of plague or lung / disease. – Might also be / an accident. I might fall down the stairs / or out of a carousel. / There was a horse with reins there. – I might not / hold on and fall out, hurt my / arm or face or back of my head. That / the worst. Be taken to / hospital. Wound worse and worse / pains greater – only a few days / later I would die. In the arm perhaps / like the pains up and down / that she had when dog bit her. (When / asked) wound not so deep – but / some dirt got into / it, causing blood poisoning. In the / hospital doctor cared for / dressed my wound / nurse cared for me. / If fell down stairs, hurt | under the eye. Also eye [sth. crossed out] damaged / later would go blind, then die. To plague / only association worst disease. / Very strong resistance. At the beginning / claimed no wishes, now gives / reason for violent tears as

p. 25c

p. 26c

p. 27c

guilt / feelings because of death wishes. Interpret / carousel etc. – representation with coitus / damage, poss. dying (thus wanted / to die for poor Henry) – but / wishes painful death for mother. – Eye = snail / = vagina fatal damage. / 22/X. – Was very late. No resistance / as going from session to theatre. Production / in red house – grammar school. Goes / there with girl friend – friend's parents / fetch her in car. (Interpret satisfied / with mother when she also lets her go to / production. Red house – remind of drawing = / snail. Friend = mother goes with her – in / train & back.) Tells about drawing. / (i.e. cutting out.) She made a pear / a bigger & a smaller banana. Pear: / Assoc.: nose & pipi. Banana only | pipi. Tells how in drawing put / *p. 28c* banana under apple. – About apple says / reminds her of snail assoc. So beautifully red-coloured / – recently as greenish apple / so nice. Actually does not like / eating apples – when so bitter-sweet – terrible / then disgusting. Prefers pears espec. Crown / Imperial. (Interpret wish to bite into and suck out / mother's snail partly love / partly sadistic – hence disgust at apple / ~~pear pipi in~~ banana under apple / = coitus.) 25. Repts. again school / etc. (Arrived very late / as to the last few sessions) about favourite / teacher etc. – Says Frl. Stiene [?] / was not there, and instead they were / taken by school director into photographic / room – then heard lecture / about Frederick the Gr. that espec. / mentioned – how strictly Frederk. was / brought up as punishment watched / his friend die – thereafter obedient. Among / the people much loved – when children crowded | around horse – *p. 29c* he was friendly, told them: / 'Take care that my horse does not do you / any harm'. Wonders very much / about what last sentence can mean 'do you / harm' – if it bites them or? / (Interpret Frl. St. away [= mother dead] – for this director leads into / hall [father shows coitus][1] where production takes place.) / She objects – there was none – for this he / would have raised up pictures & started / machine. (Interpret leading into the hall = / that saw something of coitus – not ev-/erything – not whole hall & looked for machine [?] / Frederk. Gr. on horse = mother coitus – disturbed / or would have liked to – but fear / of horse getting angry or harming her. – / 27/X. Talks about girl friend's / forthcg. birthday she give her choc. / & vice versa. – Reports about rich girl friend / who drove 3 strs. in car; finds it too / much – it is so lovely – she would / rather have a snack in between & then drive on. / ~~tells how the G~~ Father always brings | the children *p. 30c* something like fruit etc. / – Again birthday pres. aunt / Grandmamma H. Seefeld & – I – / Thinks has little hope of getting / present from

261

me – says has my / explanation (transf. – anger not meant for me – mother / & because of another refusal / therefore only if give her pres. etc.) / – says if I had given her the 50 / Pf. {Pfennigs} – I would not have to give her / another time when she wants 1 M. / Says – really have several (analy.) children / cannot expt. me – to give presents / to them all. – Perhaps secretly give / boy who comes after her – choc. or sweets. / Take from big black bag. Cur-/ious about contents. – Perh. choc. etc. in it / that I eat alone in train. – Assoc. / choc. brown – black – hair or brown- / sml. [?] tanned children. Interpret – hair = pleasure – / children = stool – remind of worms = children / thought, showed no one because embarrassed / – Interpret choc. = stool). She

p. 31c full from it. | Choc. = thinner stool as if chilled – this / chocol. is hard – but gets softer. – / Where 1 nut in it can see near it = / brown (Interpret hard choc. = [harder]¹ stool then / comes softer – where in pieces merged / together = sees brown colour. Interpret big / black bag = my [?] [mother's]¹ rear from / which father – or brother – gave stool as present / & ate himself. – Teacher because had sexual intercourse father. / 29/X. Talks again about school – much regrets / that could not go to aunt in Friedenau. / Would have played dolls or ball there with little / girl. Even better liked production / that they had at school the day before: / ~~She p~~. Nibelungenlied. – She page-boy. Enthuses / about queen's beauty, who had her / mother's dress, white with brightly-coloured jewels / wonderful hair etc. – Then phant. / birthday, presents that will / receive. Whether will also get one from H. Seef.? / – With greatest resistce. admits curiosity / whether recently I secretly gave chocol. / to young boy – not / (H) but the one

p. 32c with attractv. / face | (patient A²). – Phantas. I give it to him – he keeps / saying no at first – for the sake of / propriety, as she would also have done / ~~when I~~ – whether she also did this / when I gave her oranges – no longer / knows. – Then takes it. Then / says takes it at once, jumps / for joy, does a bow – fierce / resistce. to further representations / what we do secretly. – Says / could convince herself as to whether I give / the boy that. Could have stayed standing / outside in waiting-rm. – then would have heard whether / I said: for your birthday I'm giving etc. / After strong resistce. admits intention / to listen – that if I opened / doors, would have denied run / quickly away. (Interpret to aunt Friedenau / ~~Une~~. to uncle in bed – wants to watch / again. – Representn. school = coitus – / admiratn. mother white skin – white / red snail etc. – but envy & hatred / (admits envy

p. 33c of girl friend) – jealousy | I secretly boy = sexual curiosity child./

Listened etc. – then on this basis / also jealsy. brother.) [Nothing written on the rest of the page, nor on p. 34c.] | 12/XI. Talks about *p. 35c* Fr. dictation – then drawing / with favourite teacher. – / [The rest of this page and the next page are blank].

[B 2: Notes then follow on a notepad that contains material including records on Grete]

8/XI: Grete,[2] – Report Sun-/day wonderful – received / choc. 5 M *p. 1D* from uncle – with / aunt & uncle constly. / ate – aftern. – / birthday wishes / [sth. crossed out] from me – sweets of / every colour – chocol. / – spec. cream truffles / semicircular – [sth. crossed out] snail / filled with something white – little seeds / on it – pipi – children's / letter-writing set – extra writing paper

10. /. Resistance. Coming to / sessions – when suits / her – bday. asked / H. Seefeld directly wish / hope – I give

[The next page contains material on the other patient, which continues on the following page]

Continues. 8/XI. Grete[2] – rubber-stamping / round date / main wish *p. 2D* or sweets

Continuation 10/XI. – to my children / yes give – they are like / sand – labia [?] pink / (brought cloud to show)

Sandman scatters / sand eyes – interpret / [sth. crossed out] four- *p. 3D* poster bed[ii] – cannot / understand name – / because so lovely white like / sky [bow] iron / pole bent attached / to the curtain, brings [?] / after – [pole][1] on which you can / pull, that does not / fall out – now / no longer needs / big bed herself. / (Coat hung up there) / Incomprehl. name / why older ones do not / have sth. like this / differences: [older ones][1] another / hairstyle – hanging hair – | ribbon, big fur *p. 4D* coat – / beautiful rings with jewels / – high heels & that / are big.

12/XI. Fr. dictation, favourite / teacher drawing – / house red with white / windows – also pink / on it – tree behind it / path in front,

ii Translator's note: The German word for 'four-poster bed' is *Himmelbett*, i.e. sky-bed.

meadow there / washes. Washerwoman. / A child goes over to the / tree – another one / comes after – is still / with washer-woman. – / Containers for washing – / over them lines / for drying washing

p. 5D   3 – if there were 5 (shows: / fingers – then would be too little / space washing, with 3 – / ~~making~~ shape like / 6 – earthworm snail / birthday – 30-year-old woman / also shapes like this from / wire covered white / as in shop (jubi-/lee, with 66.) – Pipi / 3 parts – poss. also 4th / 3 main parts – tub / shows shape potty / snail – washing
p. 6D   semen / if 5 parts not enough / space semen | 15. – Birthday – presents / – comply. satisfied nothing / about my present / – so much money choc. – / drawing washerwoman / long line washing / *un jeune soldat / pris du mal au pays* / etc. up and down / *cabane paternelle*[iii] / – because then comes / 1 comma – pipi up / down – also snail / inside – line pulled / through hole (interpret / up down from earlier
p. 7D   couch / lying) – speaking – / stuttering – scornful / poem beggars | 22. / – Arithmetic geography / singing – Seefeld birth-/day anxious [?] teacher bike / dog handlebars / calculation a =

[The rest of this page and the next 3½ pages contain material relating to the 12-year-old boy and Felix.]

p. 8D   Grete^2 24. – School at first / singing – teacher night-/cap – only missing – / room furniture doctor medicine / aunt medicine Mel. midday.

[On the same page, there follows more material about Felix, which continues on the next page and is followed by some crossed-out observations about Erich, which continue on the following page.]

p. 9D   Grete^2: 27/XI. Thought / I was not coming – unwell / tooth abscess – stomach / – doctor poisonous black / – bitter pill [howled?][1] – aunt / – Mummy stomach herpes / aunt pills – die / doctor responsibility

29/XI. [Sth. crossed out] Aunt Wilmers-/dorf Friedenau / forbidden to pick at fingers

iii   A young soldier / taken ill in the country / . . . father's shed.

[Notes follow on Felix, which continue on the next 1½ pages. These are followed by notes on the 12-year-old boy and Erich, which together with some further notes on Felix make up the next few pages.]

Grete[2] 1./ – She aunt / cousin Christm. – / I suggesting / (At first   *p. 10D* happiness Sundays / bush Mummy etc. / – holidays not to / me) to daughter – / she jewellery-box / ring, dress. / Ɨ Her Mummy gives presents / I don't. Interpret resistce. / towards holidays look at [?] / [More notes follow on the 12-year-old boy.] | 4./. [Grete][2] [1] She   *p. 11D* with girl friend / aa {poo} calculations – confirmn. friend / said does on paper / – drawing watering can / window [double][1] view [?] / etc. – Katerine / [sth. illegible] bush. – cannon / [sth. illegible] crown. Resistce. / too ~~late~~ [early][1] Mummy birthday

8/XIII. Nutcracker / beard – private conversation – / – what I say to marks / 2–3. [Do not help.][1] Defend that / not bad – complains / will not see aunt / went to theatre with friend

– cannot do grammar / go through exercise with / her does   *p. 12D* not / know past. – Interpret / speaking Fr. [aunt][1] – parsing / sentence. Irmi. I / marks for essay (etc. / – She complaint no beard / (Nutcracker) Irmi – / narrow wide / teacher already [?] old white Grandmamma / wide shoe – young / girl narrow shoe

[The next 1½ pages contain notes on Felix.]

10. /XII. – Grete[2] (late) with aunt / (visit) cream cakes etc. – / beard   *p. 13D* [sth. illegible] / Nutcracker [Nutcracker-dwarf][1] I to advise / – dream – 3 men / broom [sth. illegible] – she watches / mother red jacket [sth. illegible] / going away. Goes down / with her – terribly angry / she has done something naughty / bought bread rolls / she [sth. illegible] mother / terribly angry – she / shooting [?] pushes mother / straight between 2 [sth. illegible] / trains. – Laughs at / me talking – interpret / [Notes follow again on the 12-year-old boy and Felix.] | Grete[2] 14/XII. – ~~How~~ Very late / was fetching bread rolls. /   *p. 14D* German dictation 1–2. I / could give her present for it. 1: Up / & down. Line = diagonal – why / because better like that – above below the same / thick – finger diagonal – bowel movement / Pipi. – 2. bent – crushed / ring – stool – middle part W.C. / snail. (Interpret exercise

265

book only displacemt. [sth. illegible] / resistce. beard-thing she active / with me.) – Dream: red jacket / red so lovely lampshade / ugly blue lovely dark-blue / bull raging red – eats / butts head.

[B 6: The next treatment book begins here]

p. 1d, Grete[4] / December 1921. | December 1921 / 13/XII.21. – whether
p. 2d   & how much [analytic][1] holiday [Christm.][1] will have; – ~~rep~~ then silent / has sth. planned – espec. also visit to Mummy. – Repts. enthusly. being with Mummy. / Also gave her handkerch., received choc. from her. – She / wants to give aunt something, cousin little box of sweets. / – Resistce.: asks how much longer with me in analys. also aunt / made her ask. Again asks advice, what kind of beard should / have as Nutcracker (Christmas prod.), did not want / to ask Mummy, so that she does not spend any money. / Previously poses [?] with presents complained how / many sweets she gets that it will be / too much for her etc. – Have her analyse dream. / The 3rd of the men with black beard / a teacher whom she does not know well – does not / teach her class. – One of them (the charcoal-burner) is in front & / is holding 1 sml. outstretched broom. It may / be black o. grey. Handle red – bristles / – hairs. – Then goes over to mother, wants to / do something to her, not so very bad. – The other / two without brooms – stand near charcoal-burner. / Mother so angry because she is guilty. – Being / too angry – that you can smash / something when angry – a glass or 1 flower-/pot or 1 bowl. – But on *Polterabend*[iv] / you smash
p. 3d   sth. & are not angry. (Interpret | broom – three men with vars. hair black / grey, brown black – not exactly white / like father's pubic hairs – mother angry breaks / something – she is there = having coitus, producing / child. Remind only childhood mem. of / brok. lampshade – parents quarrelled in evening / therefore father angry, sends mother out = / in coitus mother damages father's penis. / Also wish I = mother help to get beard / = castrating father her penis – then she / man & father superfluous. Therefore asks / me where to take beard from. – Remind resis-/tance with beard-thing – because wanted to / take someone's beard.) She that is impossible, that / would get out. (When ask, but if does not / get out – she impossible. Then when say / take away ~~east.~~ father's beard). She / then it is

---

iv Translator's note: *Polterabend* is a party at the bride's parents' house on the eve of a wedding, at which crockery is smashed to bring good luck.

possible, then she would have / been more daring, he would not have reported her to the / police. (Interpret – also resistce. holidays – going away / from me = repetn. aunt took her away / from mother – because I do not give presents. She | Grete² gives pres[ents]¹ (inter-   *p. 4d* pret these) = better mother – / also wishes for father's penis from me.) She / understands everything, became / very quiet – at the beginning / of session very cheeky. – Agrees resistce. / completely disappeared. – (Show her alternly. good / bad Mummy – also aunt – unfulfilled orig. / wishes). – 15/XII. – Got 3–4 in arithmetic exerc. / altho. no mistakes, comma in the wrong / place at 13,8 inst. 138 & then comma / – counted as a mistake for her. About comma: as / with exclamation marks – when nicely / drawn so thick at the top and so thin below / – like cone of sweets that parents give / children when they first go to school. She saw / small boy whose mother had given him that. / Why does that happen? – Again about cover / for pin-cushion that will soon be embroidered / about handkerchief that aunt is buying – / how I also give something made of choc. / that is wider at the top and narrower at bottom. Does / not know its name – like pineapple [*Kienapfel*]. / Asks me to tell her name, otherwise / she cannot ask for it in shop. | Said teacher charcoal-burner forbids them to ask / Frl.   *p. 5d* Stieve [?] allows & replies. – I allow / too – no even worse – allow to ask / but do not answer. I get / 3, no: Frl. Stieve 1, charcoal-burner 1– 2, I get 2. / Says if she were a ~~strict~~ teacher, she would be / strict. – When I ask further fierce resis-/tance – until you are grown-up, you do not do that / though; – when I insisted: she would be strict / with 1 girl Dora K. who instead of / looking at the book does not pay attention – another / because she causes trouble pulls faces. / She would reprimand her (instead of making reproaches / as she now received). – Also asked a lot / when holidays from analysis begin – wish / to get away. ~~Interpret~~ about the chocolate-thing / for aunt for which has 6½ M & needs 1½ / more – which does not yet know / how will obtain – asks me the name / again. Says there is also a bow / on it. – (Interpret shape = pipi as well as comma / & cone of sweets = wish for pipi that mother / should take away from father – beard-thing & give | to her. If not give – at least give / information.   *p. 6d* Questions not answered: = are those / that she put to her mother & that her father & her / mother did not answer for her. What pipi / is called & that when it combines with bow / = snail etc. – that she did not / get answered or did not even ask. / I therefore bad Mummy because don't answer. / Also interpret, she good Mummy who gives /

presents – but would like to be strict teacher / remind hitting dog, which copper [father][1] not allowed / to see. – I dying in agonies –) / Christmas holidays 3 weeks / 13/I. – Repts. about Christmas. So nice with / Mummy. Was in 1 restaurant with her where they ate / chocol. with ice cream on top – she got 2 [bowls][1] Mummy ate / from hers. (Interpret ~~Fr. language~~ Boasts got / so much chocolate [cakes etc.][1] that already / cannot look at it. – Up until into the / night (interpret) – Says New Yr's Eve were / up late into night – raffle / she Mummy – neighbour & wife joke-/things she gave Mummy green fan |

p. 7d (Interpret) fire started there in street. / Neighbours' boys went to look. / (She was allowed but did not want to go out / in the night. Boys reported long / thick hose with which house on fire / was extinguished (Interpret also wish / for penis – also reluctance = envy in watching / parents' coitus). – 15/I. Asks whether / I never go now to Polyclinic or whether only she comes / to me at flat. (Interpret wish / to be favourite child – jealousy other / children etc.) Describes journey to me. Changing / train – another train there – easy. / Found at once. Interpret she penis, way into / me. — She repts. has done / German, French dictation. Says with feeling that / when she tells aunt she has done / Fr. dictation aunt always asks her, 'And did you manage it?' / Very annoyed about this. – Interpret writing Fr. / German = speaking – voice up & down / etc. – she also amplifies poem / to which she also had association – voice up & / down – before comma – etc. – say she Fr. / dictation = sexual intercourse, she has pipi –

p. 8d offended | because aunt asks = mistrust because of small pipi – Descs. way back: how if / she misses train – she takes / next Hohenzollern-damm / train back (Interpret staying with me). She = impat-/ient to get home because is to have bread / rolls. Phantas. rolls filled / with dripping and sausage. (Interpret snail with / pipi – her own – in it – that she receives / from aunt – only not because of this wants / to get away from me to aunt. 18/I. Says / [no][1] school because of ice. Was sledging with girl friend / & her brother; he extra sledge – she / with friend but she was uncertain, anxious, / she steered to avoid hitting rubbish / pans etc. that were around. (Interpret / she penis – has coitus with friend path mother. / – Says lovely day: sledging, going to me, to / friend to aunt. – So nice that / now comes to flat – young woman gives her / reading, so nice, to read in there. (Interpret / young woman = I – book = snail that give to her) / – She says – like school director I should also / give free time because of ice. Then she

p. 9d would go to friend | who was ill in gloomy bed & would / read to her. (Interpret flight from school to me = / from father mother who have sexual intercourse together / reading to friend = having coitus with mother). She / tells story that she read while waiting: / about idol in the temple. Temple servant stole / milk from idol [& buried statue of idol][1]. – Friend in disguise / with idol's voice accused servant. / Finally, he was beaten. – Assoc. / man in coffin who only appeared dead & / spoke from his coffin: Take care of the coffin. / Remind interpretation at time. Idol / in temple = man in coffin, bed in her / = coitus. – Servant who drinks up milk brother / father who gets stool, urine from mother / – as how she was jeals. of another / patient. – Says wants to go home quickly – / buy more sugar in shop where saleswoman / gives her some. (When I interpret that she wants to leave me / because I don't want to give her / sugar = something white on pipi) / she says: even saleswoman | recently turned her *p. 10d* away because wanted to buy / sugar two days running. – When she / was agreeing 'yes' to interpretations / she stuttered, saying 'yes, yes, yes', / whereas otherwise in the third session / she hardly stuttered at all. / When point out that stuttered then / something embarrassing = would like to say / but not allowed. When stuttering though / then actually says word even more often = / moves pipi even more. Remind / [that][1] ~~stuttering~~ was afraid [to stutter][1] when had to ask maid / Polyclinic for water = potty with / urine (according to associations). / Agrees. 19/I. Says that it was otherwise / not so good at school, only / handicraft lesson good. Then she ~~fin~~ stuffed finished pin-/cushion. And she brought it to show me. / (When she pronounces 'and' she stutters / whereas otherwise she does not stutter / for the whole session. Interpret to her that when she / wanted to show me the snail pin-cushion | at [beginning of][1] sentence ~~where~~ *p. 11d* with which she communicates / that to me she stutters, but thereby actually repeats / word a few times.) At this explanation / of the stuttering she always laughs. Says that also / has arithmetic exercise book here – going from here / to girl friend – to whom she is to explain some calculations that / she cannot do. – Uncle is going to a wedding / uncle & aunt in Friedenau travel to funeral [of their [?] father][1] / & meanwhile give their child to them about which / she is so happy. – She got 2 in arithmetic / 3 in French & 1 in calligraphy / of which she is especially proud. / Very upset because I stated that / she would also like to show me what she can do. / – Talks about picture postcards for 1 organisation that / the teacher gives out to them & that she would like to sell / cheaply to various people and also

269

to me. – Praises / how charming: 1 wood in which 1 deer roams around / – a child drinking milk from bottle / – a child on 1 cliff & sh. [?] / – also lovely bookmarks. – Upset, thinks / I do not buy it – because I have not seen it / myself & believe that children's post-
p. 12d   cards | (Interpret pin-cushion – filled with wood-wool / brown & variously coloured paper = stool / & semen – snail, mine, into which with needle / sticks her pipi. – Exercise book = snail – figures / in it stool, children – (she remembers assoc-/iation that when singing 'a a' {poo} = stool / also in arithmetic.) Wedding we made 2 / if father dies, child belongs to us. / – Wants to show me what French etc. can do = / pipi-thing, but afraid that I do not like / her child's snail = children's / postcards. Describes to me what element of sexual intercourse / they had.) She is solemn but agrees. Complains of / tiredness – that has had sessions with me for so long / just so that I know her thoughts. + / Jealousy young woman other children. – Then / it was not nice at school because teacher / did not call on her in Fr. (Interpret). She: that / so hot here in my living room. – Interpret = / wish to have coitus in my living room / with me = in me. Thus hot

    + Interpret this as reproach for lack of love / – because give words thoughts inst. / real snail.

p. 13d   21/I. – Goes from me back to friend. / To show arithmetic but it is getting so late for her. / Asks to be free for next sessions as / uncle's birthday. When agree but / suggest another day, fiercest reaction. / – Cries, if only she never had to come / to me again – year ago gave her entirely free / in a case like this. – If I do / not do it now – will come on birthday after all. / Everyone will ask where she is – aunt / will say with me – everyone think could have been given / the time free – will arrive when / everyone has already had coffee & cakes / aunt will send her to bed on time – so she will have / nothing at all. (Interpret uncle's birthday party = / party with him at which is born = coitus / with father – parents in bed = party = performance / sends her away. Tries proof of love / whether I give time free – free = sexly. free – / as I refuse bad Mummy.) Says if / she did not come on Monday, she would go to / friend to do calculations with her = show her arith-metic. (Interpret writing down arithmetic in the exercise book / she
p. 14d   shows = she does = actively homosexual | in session in which when talking I show her / I man she passive – which rejects.) Says / if she

did not come to me any more, she / would gladly receive invitations –
girl friend / Margot – also 25 children – playing party / games e.g.
Meyer family – wherever 1 family / member when called – have to
stand up on time / & turn round once. – When / so many impossible
to go on swing – when / alone take turns on swing – Margot's /
brother also there, plays no role. – / (Interpret homosex. intercourse –
friend with / elegant flat = mother – who / seeks again – but also
mother who should receive / her in her flat = into / herself.) When I
asked her, as she was crying, / where handkerchief – stuttering for the
first time in / this session – said 'i i i in / muff'. Assoc. to muff: also fur
inside = / warm – so warm when hands are / inside: – had said about
handkerchief at the beginning / of the session, that she gave her uncle
/ one that he can put in a small | pocket. (Interpret muff = her   *p. 15d*
genitals – remember / lady's fur coat – uncle's handkerchief = father's
penis / – hence stuttered when asked where handkerchief / but
because wanted ~~to say~~ like this / said several times [sth. crossed out]
[full[?]][1] 'i i in the' / 24/I. Comes altho. was given session free /
because of bday. – ~~came b~~ but hoped as / was not discussed that
another / child there & she would be sent away. / But was very
punctual. – Talks about / school outing to children's theatre performance / for which such expensive seats were / bought. 2 girl friends
take expensive / seats, she would like to but cannot. / [Sth. crossed
out] Her Mummy would certainly give it / if she knew about it.
Cannot / let her know that so quickly. Says I / would not give it to
her though – not / only because she is in treatment – / but because I
do not want to. After / resistance – because love too little / & also
don't find children's performance worthwhile. (Remind children's
post-/cards that not worthwhile to me [?] – performance | like   *p. 16d*
repeatedly coitus – that I scorn / her.) She wants to allow herself to
hope for something / from me – does not want to say / what – then I
guess: that may / go home earlier wants to buy sausage-/things with
aunt. – Spreading pieces of bread – may / stay up later. Guests only
coming / evening. (Interpret aunt = good Mummy / who allows her
to be there / at birthday party with uncle = join in with coitus / – I
bad forbid her therefore she / wants to get quickly away from me to
aunt.) / 26/I. – Says that it was lovely at uncle's / birthday party but
she was only allowed to stay up / for a while. – When she says 'But I
was only / allowed to stay up until 8.15 p.m. – she stutters at 'But'. –
Then that next day / had another visit – a lady to aunt / then she was
allowed to stay up till 8.30 p.m. – / she had paid attention & known

beforehand / on birthday of all days she was not / allowed. – Says that
p. 17d at school | she did not enjoy the drawing lesson. – Says / that today
friendly young woman who gives her book / to read was not here –
another one – / that she had no book to read / that next time she
wants to have again / otherwise she will cry – Tells me that young
woman also / studies with a boy, who does his / homework here, saw
school exercise book etc. / – Says that she was there / very punctually
– arrived at station / at last minute, she & 1 man also arrived then – /
the train went very fast. (Interpret / recently aunt good Mummy –
because / wanted to let her stay up – I bad who not did give / free
time. – As did not allow [to be][1] at bday. party / bad – saw – that when
only lady visit / Mummy alone – Papa away – she still took / her into
bed with her & caressed her – did not / go away to coitus with father.
– To me / when good Mummy came today – not satisfd. 'did not /
show book' – interpreted – jealsy. other children / quicker way to me,
p. 18d F̶ man arrived with her | coitus in me as quick & good as Mummy /
– Also interpret stuttering: 'But . . . to stay up' / wish 'to have coitus
with father to stay up with him' – hence stutters'. 28/I. Is to / go to a
theatre performance – c̶o̶m̶p̶l̶ / is pleased but is not absolutely satis-/
fied because it is only a dress rehearsal. Tickets too expensive – aunt
does not / pay so much. – At dress rehearsal / stutters. – Assoc.: a
friend's father / a general.[v] – Generals lead outside / t̶o̶ t̶h̶e̶ 'to the
quarrel' – corrects / 'to battle'. Sometimes you find / when shooting
the enemy – sometimes / you are hit. (Then remind / her father also
soldier – she: remems. / uniform – but he was / not a general.) About
dress rehearsal / she says is like the / theatre performance – and yet
not / – also the vars. kiosks are / not set up – at which [sth. illegible] /
p. 19d or refreshments. (Interpret general = father | dress rehearsal = also
being allowed to do / with father. – Interpret 'to quarrel' = her coitus
/ remind of brok. lampshade incident & that / watched coitus.) To
this fiercest resis-/tance – cries etc. says – she would / never have
done that etc. and / [really][1] watched that. – Very fiercest resis-/tance.
– Cries, says mainly – because I spoil / theatre performce. for her with
these things. / – Interpret again bad Mummy, who spoils / theatre
performce. = not allowed coitus / with father. – After interpretation
in recent sessions / always complains of tiredness – yawns / v. fiercest
resistance. – 31/I. – / Repts. about theatre performce. – that older /
fellow-pupil played a part in it. (Interpret mother) / Complains bit-

v   Translator's note: *Generalprobe* is the German word for 'dress rehearsal'.

terly that has to / come to me – envies other children who / do not have to – could go sledging meanwhile / with girl friend – this way it gets too dark / for that. – Stuttering again in last few / sessions along with stronger resistance | February 22 / now stutters even 6 or more *p. 20d* times in 1 session. / Give her concept of unconscious thoughts / mem. – through example of thoughts that / the other Grete[2] does not allow – but which like / bad children who are made to stand in the corner / continue to rumble on [understands all that].[1] – 4/II. – Missed last / session – had to walk because of / strike – shows less resistce. but stutters / much more. – Take up stutter / when talked about story of queen / in the tower [at tower][1]: about tower – that there are some on parish houses & churches – that they are / red, some also white or grey. – / Tells then how she came to me – on / foot – aunt showed way – whether she would find way / back? – [Sth. crossed out] Then names vars. streets / with tennis courts passed there etc. (Interpret / queen with tower = I [mother][1] with penis. / Wonders about way coitus – the / uncle tennis courts (remind white / red & boring to watch because cannot / join in –) = father also in | mother way = had coitus.) Agrees – / complains again tiredness. – *p. 21d* Says that fort-/unately as she was reading stories / while waiting – her headache got a bit better. – / Tells me (something not heard before) that she always / regly. Saturday – Sunday, Monday / has very bad headaches, that do not / stop when goes to bed. – At first they are / mild, increase & get worse. / Pain like stomach-ache. – ~~Then~~ / on Sat. ~~etc.~~ – Assoc. Thursday is / day of thunder. – Saturday & / Sunday must come from sun.[vi] / She loves it when the sun shines. / When she came to me [today][1] sun still shining, / now no longer. – When I ask about / sun rays – agrees that they / are so long & sharp – says yellow. / & says people can also die from them / that sun rays shine so / hot – forgotten word sun-stroke. / – About Monday – says must come from / moon. That is not hot so cold. – | Moon ~~when~~ [also like][1] sickle etc. *p. 22d* (draws / shapes in air). When asked if draws / something like banana. Agrees / (Interpret = penis). Agrees when / moon round = snail – says can / have so many shapes. – (Interpret sun / = father – he dead = also sky – rays / sexual intercourse. – Stab-wound below. Remems. stomach-ache / I with swollen cheek medic. from / doctor fatal = coitus with conception / – she headache like stomach-ache = /

---

vi Translator's note: *Donnerstag* (Thursday) takes its name from *Donner* (thunder); *Sonnabend* (Saturday) and *Sontag* (Sunday) both come from *Sonne* (sun).

impregnation. – Coitus – house / on fire that they saw neighbours' boys put out / with large hose = coitus – / fear intense heat or extreme cold / = moon. Before after & on Sunday = / holiday – special day like birthday / performance = coitus). – 6/II. – Tells / about story that read before the session / (young woman with whom were books, now cannot / stop.) | When she says in summer instead: / 'at summer'. (Stuttering better again today / also less resistce. – altogether / abt. 6–8 times.) To summer assocs. sun / that is hotter in summer because sun shines / moon cold – assocs. poem about icy / winter. Tells story of stars / that want to wander with sun. Sends / them away – because its heat would be / dangerous for them. Then they go to the moon & wander / with it. – But loves sun / & summer more, ~~aft~~ nicer then / you can wear light clothes / in winter so wrapped up: – Agrees / that stars are children – moon / when round mother, sickle father – / about sun does not know whether mother or / father. – Interpret sun both, if / mother also pipi – then sexual / intercourse just as possible. – Again descs. / pregcy. from sun-rays / interpret.

p. 23d

p. 24d When mention father probably also | [dead][1] sky thought – at first agrees / then ~~fierce~~ resistce. & affect. / Ⱡ after Zwieden [?]: longing father / that living, loving her – her shock / & buying sweets as she wished, / she could live with mother again / etc. (affect, longing father never / emerged like this before!) – As did not / want to admit coitus wishes [to herself][1] displace-/ment from below to above. – Hot father = / sun, = dangerous, sexual, – cold / winter – friendly, harmless does not / have coitus. – Interpret light white dress = / exposure – coitus. About tiredness / had again complained after 1 part of / interpretation – when asked headache – / none. + Although Monday – does not know / where that comes from. – Sunday had / slight headache only early morning in bed – Monday / also early morning in bed – not otherwise / – whereas otherwise always. –

p. 25d Before | when told me a story that was / reading before session – says she would so much / like some time to read a story / with me so that we / both read it together & also / look at pictures together. 9/II. Tells story of 'Dear little golden soul' [?] that was reading. At / my request – to me, which especially pleased her / – the large fountain the king had / made – to amuse daughter who had never / laughed. – Tall jet of oil spurted out / that messed up floor carpets everything / old woman who caught in pot – street urchin / who knocked – broke pot – woman went / after boy; she fell down, everyone laughed at her. / Associations to oil = yellow sticky – says herself / small wish. Interpret fountain father's penis. / Happiness at old woman's disgrace, that she / as child watching coitus parents – thought / urinates in mother. Said fighting – (lamp-/shade incident) hoped – wished then / to smash mother's snail – make her dirty. / Also rems. she herself was shamed / laughed at when wet herself – remind / happiness about girl friend who wet herself | at school – wish – & theref. / now laughing *p. 26d* happiness about story – because / in it mother would have disgraced herself). – Agrees. / – Ask about headaches. Monday / had no more. – Had already been having them / before coming to me perhaps for 2 or 3 / years. Strong resistce. to talking about it. / Admits never having admitted them to aunt / (the recurrence) – at most having mentioned / such a headache once (Interprets also kept / secret from me as well as fear – because uncs. felt inappropriate.) – Says when asked / does not dream. – Have associate about dream end /: reaches baker's shop with mother: / there are vars. cakes (lists them) made / – by the bakers. Must be lovely to have / own baker's shop. – When asked what / bakers use: butter, flour with water, / milk & lots of sugar with it. – / (admits liquid butter like oil – flour water / paste – stool – sugar with it – cotton-wool snow / cart = semen – that would like to receive / from father.) Is there with mother, runs out / – sits on rails – but is | not then run over by train. – After / strong resistance: is angry *p. 27d* with mother. / Ran out [of baker's shop].[1] – Rails remind her of / toy rails & train like ones small / boys have. – With real big / train important that stays on rails / because otherwise it cannot go / can run over (Interpret mother says she should take / little red jacket (remems. red white & dress etc. / = sml. penis – that raging bull has / damaged, could damage – goes with mother = / homosexuality – but can wish / heterosexual. – Presents baker receive / – then theory eating cooking in stomach – / stool comes out [sth. crossed out] not allowing child. / Wants to do it with small brother approx. / not like father's coitus). Ags. – details / but with resistance – kept long / silence. – Espec. about baker's shop, to which / 1 association = will have a week without / school. 16/II. – Ask headaches last / Sunday, but [?] only Monday when stayed | longer in bed says otherwise does *p. 28d* not know / why. – (Constantly looking at father); observation lesson, in parish / school thinks is so like geo-/graphy. – Geography = what towns & rivers are / like – does not enjoy that. – (Interpret exhibition-/ism – as with light clothes summer. / Are looked at by father. When I say has / also seen mother naked before father – says /

even if she had wanted to see / naked, would have been sent out / but admits having had bed / on side where parents' beds are.) – About early morning in / bed – ask masturbation. Then denies / touching herself – but admits by pressing / thighs together. (Interpret / phantas. with this. ~~Thus~~ on the 3 days when / phantas. during masturbation gets headaches / instead — etc.) About type of head-/ache: during stomach-aches (she / had not in fact had headaches on Monday but stomach-aches / – without being able to indicate a

p. 29d cause) there is just as | with headaches a pressing outwards. – / To pressing assocs.: pressed flower that / found in book – her white dress would be / crushed if she lay / down at my house – her legs press her / when they are so cold – her legs press / her in her shoes. (Interpret dress – remems. little red jacket / transp. dress etc. = snail, – shoe / pressed by foot = in coitus. – Head- – remems. / up & down voice = snail & pipi – that / is pressed. In stomach (eating & stool = / making child) – instead of which in head = / child – stool that wants to get out – remind / recently fear when ~~wh~~ in water pipe / there was noise from piece of dirt. Ad-/mits amusement grandmother such / noises.) – That at first Mummy sun / – interpret, also wish mother dead, father / alive (remind ~~dejectn.~~ reluctance party / friend's father's birthday.) – but / also because fear father – remind

p. 30d bull who / does not like red (red jacket) – | therefore baker's shop with mother etc. / – Ask aunt: learning etc. absolutely / excellent – stuttering that only just before / praised as so very good – worse again. / Finds spec. after sledging. – Information / (teacher letter) very favourable.

[B 2: Again on another notepad]

p. 1E G³ – 25/II. [?] Little girl / to me – headaches / arithmetic lesson Raschel Schumann / – / 26. deceitful – I & gym teacher / sun dazzling: sun warm [small [sth. illegible]]¹ / bridal carriage – little girl again / knows all 3 names Sprengers / would like to be little one / herself – sun dazzling. / [A few pages later (before this more notes on two other patients):] / G³: – 2/III. Seen exhibitionists / etc. [mad people]¹ singing cuckoo idiots / 4/III. headaches ~~Sunday~~ [Saturday]¹ / does not want to say, masturbation / through paper / 7/III. Happy aunt [&]¹ everyone away / she alone with little one – wedding / uncle – she first – I [attend]¹ latest / dark blouse – she back home / to little girl – way back narrow / bridge, she above to see train / below – [sth.

illegible] train milk bottles / interpret disturbance – wish mother's / breast.

[B 6: Individual pages from exercise book attached with paperclips]

March 1922 / 9/III. – Obsvs. that I am nicely dressed lovely / *p. 1e* patent leather shoes – pretty necklace dress etc. – that / I came with sml. boy (whom did not yet know / personly. – whether on visit – but then fol-/der with me, thinks that unlikely / phantas. Am called to patient – / rich elegant people – young girl / similar age to Hilde B. (who comes before her). / Give her session, not one like hers [a nice one].[1] We / sit together. Private lesson. / Is ill – lame in 1 leg – to school / by car but that also has other things / to do – only takes her there & back. / I give her German lesson. – Before / had me – (as a few times / now with Fr. etc. [sth illegible][1] asked whether correct) – / whether her homework was right / how to ask about main & subordinate / clause etc. (Interpret lovely private / lesson = exchanging sentences – voice up / & down etc. = ~~Sexual intercourse~~ coitus with me. / girl here passively homosexl. – castrated / bad foot.) ~~11./III. Am~~ beforehand about / way to me that can also come / over a narrow bridge – outside it | is very windy etc. (which I *p. 2e* interpret to her / as difficulties of coitus with me). / 11/III. Repts. that gymnastics was very nice. It / was gymnastics rehearsal for teacher Ceusser [?] – / she could hang and stretch out so well in / rings – knees completely straight – tips of the toes / upwards. – (Sudnly. resistce. whether I will keep / her here longer because (through my / fault) session began later) = Cries / & complains – says I should just try that / myself if I were small – had to / lie in the living-room – instead of playing a bit longer / in the sun with girl friend with ball-and-stick / when so lovely outside. / Ball-and-stick game – pretty balls that they / push fwd. with stick with the string. / At first said wants to play with friend / – friend has to decide what / if toys belong to her – otherwise / she can also decide about toys. / – Interpret (she when small in bed – perhaps fastened / into children's high chair – watched / parents' genital pleasures – wish for | mother, sun – playing ball-and-stick with friend / remind story about *p. 3e* princess dervish / cut-off beard ball = pipi mutual / ball-and-stick also stool [enjoying][1] – Mummy holds on to her / not allowed from bed – I now / bad Mummy. – Longer pause. Wish / would like to donate something / to German [children][1] collection / schools in

Poland. Teacher said / should ask everyone you [sth. overwritten] find in good / mood – but is certain though that I will / give nothing, altho. the reasons / that gave otherwise because of treatment do not / apply to that etc. – Saturday on this day / early in morning & before meal had slight headache / but now states also during / the week and more often – Friday aftern. – stuttering / noticeably better in last few sessions / 13/III.★ – Have her assoc. to cellar: – stale air / – & then story of quarrelling cobbler / & tailor – in which the cobbler wished the tailor / on to a cloud – tailor wished the cobbler / into a [deep]¹ cave — story of / the princess who found a sml. door [sth. crossed out]

~~At first~~

p. 4e made of gold, goes into a cave – there / two boys approach playing some / music – then a black man. She is frightened / but he says – used to be a white prince / with golden hair – put under spell by / witch (remind anal noises that Grandmamma / makes – also water pipe that when it was blocked / by something and noise came out – / black man – previous 'sweet prince' white cake / with yellow border = oral anal reproduction theory / poor child cellar Poland = she who was / once there & now does not get money = stool / from me) – Had remained silent almost / throughout the whole session without a sound despite much / encouragement – did not speak / until just before the end of the session – as often when / resistance strong. – (Interpret not speaking = / not releasing words = not releasing stool). Completely resolved. Resistce. – 18/III. / Missed 1 session because was / late back from an excursion. Says it was so lovely, did so much / climbing on a mountain there

> also told me about a bridge: over which they crossed to a wood / & meadow – about bridge says that saw / peacocks around there [sth. overwritten]. Also assocs. to the bridge / she crosses to come to me. – There are planks / with gaps into the water in between them. (Interpret / bridge (to me & meadow wood – remind drawing = / pipi having sexual intercourse with me).

p. 5e and sat on a tree-trunk – became / dizzy – her ball almost went into the water / nearby but some bushes stopped / it. – Asks what I did in the session / without her – if I cried? – When say / whether she was perh. anxious – very scornful – not / even thought about this – could still have / been with me on time in the end. Preferred to stay / 1 more hour with aunt in Wannsee. There / she constly. jumped 1 mountain with both feet / at the same time, so that ~~she~~ made [them]¹ completely rigid, / up and down. Counted that must have jumped / 11 ×. – Strong resistce. when asked – about / what I occupied myself with meanwl. Finally that I jumped / like her in playground opposite. – / At first alone – then my son came & jumped / with me. – (Interpret mountain climbing, fear tree-trunk / is mother's pipi – ball nearly fell in water / stopped by bushes = her pipi does not / stay in mother. – Jumping mountain aunt Grete² [good Mummy]¹ = / sexual intercourse with her. – Angry with me because Mummy / who forbids. – Jealousy of coitus father / = jumping with boy.) – Stuttering much | improving. – Only 3 or 4 times durg. the session / & also in   *p. 6e* such a way – that [each time]¹ much weaker e.g.: says / t terrible – whereas previously [approx.]¹ said / t-t-t-t terrible. – Saturday says headache / very slight – only ½ hr. while eating. / 21/III. – Talks about girl friend Jakobov. [?] who will / dance in 1 ballet theatre. Asks me / about vars. theatres, thinks that I am / very rich, go to the theatre a lot, Sundays / & when she is not there. – Very happy / invited to a theatre prod. on / Sunday – plans vars. invitations etc. in the near / future – would be nice if always / had something planned for every day. – Says spontaneously / had no headache on Sunday, on Monday / had only ½ hr. early in the morning when / after waking up she lay 'a bit longer' / in bed. ★ – When asked what she was thinking / about there: about collection for poor children / in Poland, she has collected 35 M. / – are children who less, others / espec. Jewish children large sums. / Then looked forward to Sunday

★ But on Friday she had severe headaches / all day – grandmother said / to ask me.

got theatre ticket from Irmchen's^vii mother. Gerh. / Irmi's brother   *p. 7e* does not like it – when mother / gives tickets to I's girl friends. There-/fore planned play-acting that she much / enjoys. She should come and say is going to / theatre – they will say they / too etc. – Becomes very animated at / this idea & stutters (very little / now). – Talks about theatre prod. that saw / there last year: about young

---

vii Translator's note: 'Irmchen' and 'Irmi' are diminutive forms of Irma.

woman who always sings / so beautifully alone – about her gentleman & servant / want to stop her – buy / flowers from her – finally she manages to / get them to leave her to sing in peace. / – Says would be so wonderful if you / could have something planned every day. When / she [sth. crossed out] was staying with her mother 1 week / every day: 1 day cinema, – 1 day café in which / drank cocoa – restaurant (sausage / & potato) café in which ladies performed / dances with veils. – (Interpret money [for][1] poor / children: wishes stool from mother father) / – theatre [with ladies][1] – tricking Gerhart = [going

p. 8e beh.][1] father's | back coitus mother – jumping up mountain / etc. – Singing alone – gentleman = father for-/bids = masturbation that is forbidden her – but is / allowed – makes child herself = / headache instead masturbation (that I / leave up to her.) – About singing remind how / exhibitionist a̶t̶ with idiot-singing = / had to have coitus & that she in the / session today even before singing mentioned / – suddenly sang a whole word / reprimanded herself about it. – Always / having something planned – cinema = theatre = coitus / cocoa with mother stool inst. – sausage / pipi – potato stool – (at that time [see][1] interpretation) / ladies with some veil dances = coitus / homosexl. – wants that daily = daily coitus / daily child = headache) complete / insight, resistce. much reduced. / 23/III. – Talks ⋆ about report that got / back. It was a beautiful Thursday when / was not tired. – Early in the morning after / getting up h̶a̶s̶ ̶i̶n̶s̶t̶ headache for a short while. / Thought about report that will

> at first about girl friend with whom formed secret group of / friends – does not give names / to anyone even aunt me / etc. at any / price etc.

p. 9e get back. – Has got 2 in / report; no mistakes but 13 punctuation / errors, commas wrong / etc. – can never understand – when / colon needed. – To colon / assocs. (at first long pause fierce resistce.) / – girl friend will collect her then wants / to stay at her house till evening. – Group of / friends – she gave her a pearl ring – / and she was given a red bow – which / they wear when they are togr. Also / gives the friend's name: little Liselotte Spreng-/er. – (Interpret mutl. wishes for masturbation & / voyeurism = exchange of ring [& bow][1] / therefore secret like masturbation hence also / resistce.) – Meanwhile she had suddenly / twisted [sth. crossed out] f̶i̶n̶g̶e̶r̶s̶ the 2 [index][1] fingers / together. – Fierce resistce. when asked for assoc. / Expresses great

scorn when I imitate / it – says when I ask for further assoc. / –
completely amazed that I am not annoyed / about her scorn, she
would get / very annoyed. – Assocs. then that they | always do this at   *p. 10e*
school ~~to her~~ when they / sang at school / ~~Also tho~~ That then the
wind / turns the mill – also that people also twiddle / their thumbs
like that, when they have / nothing better to do. – Interpret masturbation. / – Scorn & rage – because ask about it / indicates the wind &
mill herself / with her hands – hates Mummy because / forbade &
worried about it. – / 25/III. – Says half-mischievously has something
terrible / to report to me, makes me ask about this / for a long time
finally admits that she brought / the 7-yr.-old Liselotte about whom
she always talks / to my house & ~~in~~ young woman took her into the /
room. – Apparently had nowhere to leave / the little one & had
brought her on Grandmamma's advice. / – When ask her not to do
that / another time, she had repeatly. presented / this phant. – & the
reqt. [?] been / refused by me – fierce resistce. / In my place she would
make / nothing of it – Grandmamma will find | that very unmerciful   *p. 11e*
because an / orphan etc. – At school Fräul. / Stiewe [?] & schoolmaster would object / to that – but not the teacher. (Interpret / I bad
Mummy – who does not want / to be given ~~receive~~ made any child /
by her – father still friendly. – Interpret = further / love proposal – if
reject it / bad Mummy. – Says received 1 piece cake / from Lisel's
aunt that descs. / in terms of greatest delight. – / Espec. the yellow
cream that was in it / so thick etc. – Says about cake – / so ~~soft~~ &
white [& soft][1] when you bite into it / – assocs. to this her arm into
which (as / I could also already observe) so likes / to bite – also that
her cousin / always bites into her G's[5] arm. Assocs. / to this mother's
soft white breast about / which she says that recently told her /
children so much like to have in their / mouths. – Repts. then when
remind her pleasure | biting into apple – now in fact / she does not   *p. 12e*
like them – as after / apple & also after buttered bread rolls / if she has
them without drinking coffee – / gets headache. – (Interpret eats /
Mummy o. something from her & so receives / child = headache.)
Stuttering constly. / very little – sometimes 2 or 3. during the / whole
session & in the broken / form in which says to me 't-terrible'. – 28/
III. / Not very enthused about theatre prod.: 2 ladies / who argued
with each other because of 1 party / finally agreed with each other. –
Says has / 1 sentence to parse. Asks about / indirect speech. Aunt has
expld. it to her in a particular way / whether this is correct (definitely
always wants / to have advice!) – ~~Immediately afterwards has / dir~~

about dir. speech: 1. colon appears / directly = as if were / the right one {'die-rekt' = die rechte?} – or director – thinks of school director / Burg, whom finds sweet much / praises – had not so far had much /

p. 13e to do with him. — Immediately afterwards. | Had so little to eat at mid-day – / got nothing with it – stomach rumbles / is so hungry – would so much like / to have piece of buttered / bread – after resistce. admits / – would like to have this from me. – Says / they ate such big, round / loaf country bread, which gets from / milk woman – aunt gets headache / from other bread. – Curious / whether I get bread without coupons, have / the nice white bread. – Says she is / not so very partial to it [?] is so soft / not so filling – also not / so very fond of cake – has even recently / asked for bread inst. cake [from]¹ her friend. / – Ask what about sentence analysis assoc.: / says is difficult – you always have to ask / the right questions to get the [right]¹ answer / – parsing reminds of carving joint / that you have to cut into pieces /

p. 14e before you get into it. – (Remind roast rabbit | that had reminded her of my fur – that she once / liked, later not – interpret Mummy / = roast rabbit & roasting – eating her / – or getting something to eat from her – / white bread cake = breast – thick round / brown loaf, ~~with sth.~~ is stool that / asks me for – butter on it = stool / or sml. wish, milk. – ~~Has~~ Expld. / – she was crying the whole time suppsly. / from hunger & because [I]¹ [still]¹ gave her nothing) – the / real worry as previous refusal / – just like that time when did not bring her / glass of water – finally it was potty / with mother's urine that wanted. – 30/III. Says / was Liselotte's birthday, but was / not nice. She & Irmchen fell out / with her – now she is / not so fond of them any more. – Says had to / improve homework. When stuttered / at this (today much more heavily again) get / to assoc. ~~Says~~ ([One]¹ must improve mistakes, / e.g. in parish school children / make = mistakes such as: She goes [up]¹ to a house / – The wolf meets / him etc.ᵛⁱⁱⁱ

p. 15e Mistakes like this | are also made among them. They do not / usually correct such things / very much because it causes embarrassment. –) / 1 (Improving also makes her think of / improvement – yesterday they were playing / 1 game in which you had to say / words with 'ung' –

---

viii Translator's note: In both these examples that Grete gives, the wrong case is used: in the phrase 'to a house', the nominative form is used instead of the dative for the pronoun that follows the preposition *zu* – *ein Haus* instead of *einem Haus* – and, in the phrase 'the wolf meets him', the accusative case is used for the pronoun following the verb *begegnen*, which takes the dative *ihm* rather than *ihn*.

e.g. '*Verbesserung*' {improvement} [*Verlobung* {engagement}][1] / *Vermählung* [wedding]). – When she then begins / 1 sentence & wants to say: 'when I / began the sentence' – she does not immediately / rebuke herself here[ix] – is then very ashamed / says if aunt discovered that / from me, she would be very angry – / ~~say~~ she would immediately tell her proletar. / that is supposed to mean uneducated – she / thereby shows me however that she / is educated – but does not have to / say so at once because of minor detail – how that / would please her etc. – (Remind / sentence before comma take voice / down, voice up & down – colon / thing etc. – children come. | remind   *p. 16e* (private elocution lesson with / rich girl) – / it not yet right – making mistakes – / no correct children – because do not / yet have right pipi – Mummy arrogant / shows her that – rejects her. – Improving / = getting bigger more skilful better – / having children – getting engaged, marrying. / – Says that today for a short while / had headache: already on the way / in my street – warm took / snowball – held it to face / rubbed it in – then headache / went when she began to read / at my house. – About snowball: all children / do that. – Snow so lovely / white – would like to go / to artist with snowball / & have something done inside ~~it~~ – so that / the snowball does not melt / even in summer – e.g. oxygen / or have wax put around the / outside – then it does not matter / if inside disappears. – She would then / like to ~~have~~ it put into a cardboard box | & when she looks at it / to   *p. 17e* remember ~~that~~ how she / had the ball when she came to me. / About wax – it is yellowish like kind / with which lamps are smeared. / Admits is like butter = (Interpret / white ball = mother's breast – eats / like cotton-wool snow – has eaten / sth. from Mummy – gets headache. / – Also [after birthday][1] talked / a lot about Easter holiday / which dwells on as long as / possible – because wants to be with Mummy / a lot. – Came – despite last session / refusal of buttered bread – completely without / resistce. & is in very favourable state of mind. / – Calls me after birthday-/thing [with][1] Frau Sprenger. – 1/ IV. – ~~Has no headaches / either on Sunday or Monday.~~ / Talks about Easter eggs that would like to give / Mummy & aunt or 1 of them – / ~~eith.~~ eggs in a basket-nest with / paper. Great longing happiness, being / together with Mummy – happy not to be coming to me. | Says met Erich with young woman – Er. went / behind young   *p. 18e*

---

ix Translator's note: Instead of *als*, Grete used the world *wie* for 'when', which is a more colloquial usage.

283

woman play-acted probably to avoid / greeting her. – Saw bridal carriage / bridegroom & bride with myrtle headdress / phant. about the many myrtle flowers / – look like sml. half eggs – (Interpret wish / to give eggs aunt Mummy = to give / children and stool. – Not to me & hence wish to / get away from me – because I give nothing – have / 1 boy – whom favour: like mother brother / & father. – Wants to get married herself – myrtles / – get eggs children from father.) – / Immediately afterwards – question why flowers / in flat whether my bday. When confirm / very happy about knowing this, wants / to arrive next year with flowers / – very delicate lovely ones – phant. about my / birthday. – Asks if like / Jakobovitz (eleg. girl friend) I had 190 / guests – how many that was at most – whether 50 etc. / phant. about my bday. such a large table / that had to open sliding doors –

p. 19e
near / me right & left ladies, then gentlemen | thus alternating. – Coffee fine cakes – / vars. cold mousses; a roast in the evening / says stuffed goose & chicken – thinks / stuffed e.g. with apples – is served. – (Interpret many eleg. room(s) = mother / inside – the many guests = children who / feed from the mother – carved joint = / mother – abundance – apple = stool. – At the same time / many guests in me = father – who often – / (instead of with many) has coitus. She also still / to be in 'the company of many' – many little / girls = as well as wonderful mother. – / 4/IV. – Repts. that Sunday Monday had / no headaches at all. – Complains / was severely beaten / by aunt & grandmother – including on her head – because she / had been late back from friend. – Had to / ask their forgiveness – also wants to do this – asks me / for advice. – Not to bring up / aggression then – states still wants / to ask their forgiveness – as otherwise she will get no Easter eggs / from aunt. – Filled Easter eggs / or cardboard ones with cakes sweets / inside. (Interpret wish to be loved by mother |

p. 20e
and to receive stool & children. Therefore overcomes rage.) Says I had / kept silent when she told me about aunt's / beating – saw disapproval in this / will tell aunt that. – ★ Also complain / to her uncle's bride. (Interpret phant. / setting me against her aunt, also / her uncle's bride – then I will accept / her – has new good Mummy – that she / wanted when little & mother mistreated / her.) Agrees. 6/IV. – / Great joy & happiness going to stay / with Mummy. – Would like to stop eating and drinking / only sleep, so that it comes more quickly. / – Went to puppet theatre: laughs a lot – sings back / the song about Laatsch & / Bommel – descs. how the little puppets / kept raising their legs & feet alternly. / says – behind was of course a / grown-up

person – after all on its own / the puppet could not have moved like that. / Adults also did the speaking / and singing for them – they

Asks, if I would behave / like that towards my boy?

could not actually have done that on their own either. – / (She *p. 21e* stutters at the word 'puppet' – otherwise / hardly at all today). About puppet she says laughing / that her friend at school kept hiding behind / & taking out from behind her [the lid][1] of the small / oblong tin in which she keeps the / sponge. She pressed for so long / around her clothes until it came out / of there. – Does not want to work at all – explains / now it's time to have fun, laughs, sings / (repeated attempts at this in last few sessions) / puts her hands over her ears says will go / to sleep & constly. pleads – must tell / her funny story – thrashes around / at this – story of Laatsch & Bommel / & even funnier one. (Interpret puppets – moved / by grown-ups who also sing = / pipi that is moved by father & thus a noise / is made. – Lid above inside & out from / below = pipi, stool, that could also / go in above. Early inf. coitus observns. | that she found very funny & *p. 22e* strange / – then wish to try [she it with][1] mother – thrashes / etc. – & mother should tell / her funny stories = describe precisely what pipi / would have done in her.) – Also said / how glad she was to have / a cheaper seat. In the ~~better~~ [more expensive][1] seats they had to / strain their necks. (Interpret she had / (cs. mem.) her bed near her / parents' bed. – Brother elsewhere. She could watch / the coitus more easily & felt triumphant abt. it.) / – Holidays — missed the first meetg. / session after the holidays. Supposly. / misunderstg. I discover from aunt that / stuttering has got much worse since holidays – when / talks quickly – can hardly speak. / 22/IV. – Does not seem espec. happy to / see me again: repts (and, as often, boasts) about many / ~~presents~~ and sweets given by / Mummy & also aunt as presents. – Asks / if now the girl who was before her / (H. B.) is no longer / coming. – Immediately afterwards: / wants the session to end. – Repts. | happy *p. 23e* about cousin arriving. Would almost have / been in time to meet the train. – / So she met her when she was already / on the 10th step of the marble / staircase (staircase marble ~~not~~ etc. / polished 20 steps.) Hugged her so much / that they all nearly fell / down. – Says that now at her / Mummy's has practised so much – that can / jump down 6 ~~times~~ ~~ste~~ steps at once / she could also jump 9 – but / that would make too much noise. / Even so neighbour came out, when she /

greeted cousin like that. – (When asked / how she jumps then?) heavily: of course / with both feet rigid & in one go / should try to jump with / 1 foot! – (Remind how at aunt's / in Wannsee she jumped up and down on the mountain / – I meanwl. with [my][1] boy here in field. / Interpret steps – falling, jumping – / cousin [Mummy

p. 24e aunt][1] good Mummy – angry with me | because do not allow her – do not give choc / etc. – another ~~strange~~ girl comes / before her.) ~~Complain~~ 24/IV. – Very late, / complains about severe headaches. / After repeated questions: got them / when was cleaning her paint-box / in the afternoon. – Curious whether teacher allows / her to have it (she was given it by her cousin) / at school? – Repts. about dark / colours, black, brown, yellow – that does / not like – more of these already / used up – highly praises / light colours pink. – About dark colour: her / dress is not so very dark has 1 / ~~completely~~ black velvet dress with / green – is pretty altho. dark. – Talks [about][1] / mourning dress. That some ~~peo~~ people / when someone they know dies, have / no dark dress – have to wear / anoth. e.g. green dress. She would have her / black one. – To green assocs.: a / neighbour of her

p. 25e mother's, who when / another neighbour died – had to go | in a green dress. (Interpret, wish anoth. / neighbour = Mummy should die – she / already has mourning dress. – Dark dress = / dirt = just as with dark colours / from paint-box = stool – that Mummy / = teacher does not allow her – hence / hatred, death wishes. But therefore / towards me so much hatred or resistce.) / Agrees. – Complains hunger – / would like piece of bread & butter. – ~~Again interp~~. / brown bread, because white not / filling. (Interpret bread, white (cake / mother's breast) etc.). Says (when asked) / that after peeled or unpeeled apple – bread and butter without coffee gets / headache. – (Interpret with paint-box / = cleaning stool-apparatus – fear & / ~~m~~ hatred mother – at same time also already / child ~~in the h~~ stool in head – headaches) / about headaches says more a pressing ~~on~~ / on it – than outwards – indicates 1 / place on forehead – near temples more / to the front.

[B 2: A further notepad contains notes on Grete among other material]

p. 1F Grete[2] 27/IV. Resistce. / to arrangemt. [?] wants only / 2 × wkly. – finally / dawning pleasure – as allow / [sth. illegible] – flowers shoes / not watering etc. / aunt cousin [sth. illegible] / will about Weds.

arrangemt. / 29/IV. came so quickly / to me that really warm / – friend [sth. illegible][1] [sth. illegible] / wanted – her watch / she 2 – to wear later / what time — children / like to guess – | Cask without hoop [sth. crossed out] rooster / without comb – / flea – elephant – bringing / me flowers from journey / G. 3/V. – late – resistce. / to coming – stomach – / heavy ball – how to hold / away from me – light ball / made of cloth – bday. cow with / white and pink dress bow / (this new purple to white / & unkempt) *p. 2F*

[Again on another notepad]

Grete[2] 1/V. Happy esply. / Wednesday – ran so / quickly over there *p. 3F* etc. to me, warm – to tell / her what time. – Doing / what she wants – stay / a while longer – if / Liselotte sent away / – she also – Frau [?] earthy / path, high heels / slip [sth. illegible][1] zzz [?] / stockings pulling water / covering. V hungry / Fr. sentence Mozart 4 [sth. illegible] | 5/V. Grete[2] – resistce. because / I did not tell assoc. when *p. 4F* she / instructed me. Threat to betray / something indecent – stay away – / [sth. crossed out] / indicate about [sth. illegible][1] ball game / (heavy ball) again. – [Sth. crossed out] / my street / ugly – no / children. – 9/V. – At school / had 6 classes – likes new / biology teacher / singing teacher, kisses her / with head bowed & listens / to her, alto voice – / not like most girls / – try [sth. illegible][1] to sing / for myself – at first scorn / severity that Mel. wrote = / – I use coupon money / for my boy [sth. illegible] / – she needs enough money / not me – not only / coming 10 more times / no holiday – I go away / meanwl. statue, stone / sits there – listens question / does not answer – when / clock strikes goes – / stone – man with ball / ice cold – train doors / windows – half-glacier / – stone hard wood | man with no *p. 5F* sympathy when others ill / gives nothing – old lady / hard heart did not care / that cousin ill – / ice = man who neglects / town going to ruin / – woman who turns round / (thus [sth. illegible] observing 1 more time / town going to ruin / [7/V. Felix . . .] | Grete[2] 16. [? *p. 6F* overwritten] / V. Talks about Latin handwriting / curve of letter 'U' etc. – question if / came to me on time. / Walked very quickly / picked flowers. / Pen sharp / (very thirsty) long – other pen – / fountain pen – then wants / little dog from aunt. / Cousin says nice / to lie down at my house – she / thinks better to sit then / can see everything (Interpret / castratn. anxiety because / she fails (fountain pen / little dog makes child) – She when | She Grete[2] [pronounce: *p. 7F*

287

her]^1 eerie: / mixing up [sth. illegible] / woman & child. – / cold in my / room, street / friendlier more / children, nice

[B 2: On a further notepad, the first page contains the following]

<u>writing</u> / Grete^2: friend: [who writes like adult]^1 who holds pen / straight between two fingers – ~~holds~~ [writes]^1 / curve of letter 'U' backwards – can do / nothing else at all. She so / likes the letter D & Latin / script with curlicues according to / model by which children / wrote letter postcards as if were / rule – would like to / do it the same way. About curve of 'U': / the large curve that boys / make when urinating in the / street: – [Material follows concerning Felix and patient D]

[A single loose page] / Grete^2: Hansel & Gretl / angel so beautiful / & how witch in oven came / [Felix . . .]

9

Treatment notes on Rita

[B 9: The first treatment notes on Rita are recorded on a small notepad]

p. 1A   R.[3] – 6/III. — Bone Huckebein / twice 'poo' I / to climb chair / 8/III. – by mouth – at first not poo big one / ~~I scallywag~~ / – later, also wipes – orange = air. / Play phantasy repression / – Daddy duck, Mummy bear – she / is bears' Mummy – then retracts [that][1] [she Rita[2]] / (mother says: she Mummy, plays – [then][1] immediately no) / ~~9./III.~~ I say doll child – she / Mummy – she: no. – I threaten Suse / she anxious: is good again / ~~9./III. Peter shouts laughs~~ / should not do this – / I call {her} scallywag – she is pleased. / – [Doll][1] naked, goes away, hides / naughty – has her hide.

12. Ask [her][1] where [(toy)][1] dachshund, she eaten / it up = stomach = then immediately / no, does not [taste][1] nice – then is out of / stomach like water [spit, mouthfuls][1] drunk / then out at back – sticks for him / to build house. – [Busch:][1] monkey hat is / (holds in mouth) – She (= Peter) to put out / bathroom table. – Busch: / Dummy bee [asks][1] – I [mention][1] fear / of bees earlier she [held][1] piece of / paper = bee – no, no. – I am sting. / Interpret stick [bee (?) should give to Aunt Emma][1] – confirms Peter member

p. 2A   she would like to have stick – opening [Gerhard gave [?]][1] / she [is][1] not – everyone but her / – pleased I say: not women / not Frau Klein and I. – When / interpret father wish – she: no / that would hurt. – (less re- /pressed when anal) says not to explain [?] / when interpret Pepi's trousers.

9. – Peter cries – she laughs shouts that / not nice – she some-/ times also fun; / – stick – [mother][1] crying / I ask her: Mama bitten by / dachshund: – is [clever][1] wood-sprite – / duck eats bear's house, constantly / buying [new things][1] – from girl – / snowman only asks for something / from her – shows hip. / For building house. / (Anxiety dream [18 months][1] bee, stung cheek / crying throwing stick in hole) / only bathes and dresses and undresses doll / then only when encouraged. – poo

p. 3A   Mother R.[3]. Reports: sun, eats / bread roll – swallowing, 2 nights / sandman. – Bad / man hits horses

R.[3] 14/III. Crawls on ground / barks at doll's pram – I / should send dachshund away / like second session when I dachshund. When / ask if also bites Suse: / No, no – later bites / books. When I say she to send / away books – no does not also / bite books, is Rita[2] not

p. 4A   dachshund. – Bathes doll (not / poo) then brings for me to / put her

belt on – interpret / belt to her R.[3] like cobbler / = [stick][1] – member
– she suddenly / makes doll poo in (swing) / says: gives her stick looks
for / one, I should hold it out / and she thus makes her constantly /
do poo. – Crumples up / blanket – carefully wraps / doll in it for
quarter of an hour – / Suse, gives Peter's piece of leather / Suse looks
for [?] small stick (not everyone [something illegible] / 16/III. –
Greets me (laughing) / I once made trrr (lips / flatus) sound with /
her. – Peter doll and Suse / very thickly wrapped up / (as Aunt E.
wraps her when sledging) / – both have fever got chill / on excursion
– again R.[3] plays / dachshund – when I copy / her biting gestures –
pretends that / is biting both Suse and Peter / in leg – then / pram to
chest (into which | shoves throws everything / says she does not like   *p. 5A*
them. – / Later (after picture books) / etc. makes trr sound – I ask /
who wants to do poo? Quickly brings / Suse – makes her do poo /
looks for stick holds it out. / – I to dress her – first puts / doll's nappy
on bare body [making small triangle] / (like Peter's leather) and cobbler / belt (previously over clothes) / – when interpret small stick –
asks / to tie it in Suse's hair because / ruffled: then says is / now Peter.
Then to tie it into her own / hair. When / I say she Peter little stick
thing / identification dachshund – Peter etc., she: / yes but not to be
the bee / She does poo only play and takes [?] stick / – pushes swing
with foot / shows me – I: She father – / pushes mother, swing – doll /
well wrapped up there: I interpret / child in mother: I Frau Klein /
am father (put doll in) | When fear of bees – / bears gone away – Frau   *p. 6A*
Jerusa-/lem? – Since when book-thing? / – Since when phantasy
oppress-/ion – she Rita,[2] not / mother – / when she bites Peter. /
does [small][1] poo less often

[B 9: Treatment book on Tanja]
[Cover page:] Tanja[2] begun March 23rd

Continuing from previous page: / cart with small horse in which she   *p. 1*
& / Peter can then ride. Then / immediately tramples on stones as if
would / like to crush them – says once saw / car that crushed stones. –
(Interpret cart – car = member – her foot should / do the same, would
like to have.) – / At pile of stones fills / my pockets with stones –
ignores any / objection. Very negative. – Leads me / to drain, to throw
stones in – laughs / and points out to me how water / rushes. – When
I remind wish to / throw little stick there with Mummy, interpret /
little stick thing – she: no, no, little sticks / cannot be had, are too

expensive. / A man, without noticing us, / goes past – she: the gentleman said / 'well, well!' – Interpret father who does not want / to allow sticking member in Mummy, / more resistance: 'no, no!' – Has me lift her up & / show 1 pit {sandpit}. / Had allowed me to hold / her away like this from little girls / sandpit. Goes [?something overwritten] home with me & / is certainly in a more positive / state of mind. – Some dissolution of / resistance through interpretations

p. 2 un-/ mistakable. | 3/IV. – Had missed 2 weeks / because of illness and Easter. – R.[3] not asked after me at / all – tender contact with mother / soon back to contradiction & negative. / – Not very pleased to see me – but comes over. / Playing – but feel definite resistance. / Also asks me, if soon must go. / Wants to go for a walk with mother. / 4/IV. We play – she plays as recently / with dolls etc. – but not a word about poo, / little stick etc. [something crossed out]. / Changes game from one moment to next, / strong resistance. Suddenly explains / is going over to sand, little girls. – I / tell her story, 'Fritz and the raisins', / she listens reluctantly, explains / emphatically she is going over to sand. – I go with her & doll's pram / with doll inside – (at first also / played with bear again – more recent [sessions][1] no / longer) going for a walk. Will not / be led away (from little girls' sandpit / in park where she goes / with mother). – Says about doll's pram / doll inside – later

p. 3 would like a / continuation previous page | next page continues: / 6/IV. with an English girl. They read newspapers. / (When interpret father and mother in coitus) V contradiction / ~~also makes rep~~ Asks to go / for walk with me again – but is / fairly easily dissuaded. Building. Asks for / little watch-house. Immediately after my / interpretation: father puts little stick into mother – / takes doll out of bed, shows me / mattress and asks what is inside. (Interpret / curiosity about mother where father enters. / Remind had to lift her up last time / what inside pit = curiosity / what inside mother. – Makes a doll that / calls Fritz go to raisins – father says / has noticed how sensitive to criticism / floods of tears, when says 'well, well'. / – When mention aversion to bears – says has / read to her about bad bear and said / 'well, well'. – Also says noticed how for / 16–18 months tyrannical in that / he constantly has to read book / with her

~~V immediately afterwards, takes doll / out of cot, shows me mattress~~

p. 4 6/IV: Is friendlier, greets me although / still eating breakfast – takes

292

bread roll / and comes up to me. Says: old bears pour moo / from tails. When I get her to repeat / this (more willing): she repeats: / old bears pour moo from old tails / ★ Says that she does not like bears, are / bad – bite. – Winter also bad, bites. / Talks about Father Christmas, and beard / [something illegible] emphasises that very good – brought her some little / flowers and also Easter rabbit good. – Should tell her / story of 'Fritz and the raisins'. When I elaborate / say: she and I going somewhere, and visiting / Easter rabbit, as well as Father Christmas / – refuses: not Father Christmas – / (doubtless already object of anx- iety – when I asked / afterwards mother says – that she ~~anxious /~~ ~~before Christmas~~ recently disliked / hearing about Father Christmas.) – Ask / about dachshund. She: is gone, no / longer there, was made of chocolate, I have / eaten it. (At my remark that / child and where comes out – she points / at front below chest – previously her back / the next time anus – afterwards again below / chest – downward displacement: from above to / below and thus to the front.) – Immediately / afterwards: dachshund has gone away. / Gone to England. Works there / continues previous page

  ★ (When interpret tails~~)~~) she: ~~when~~ / how young woman – was there then Peter shouted / so and ~~with~~ in his hands / he had some paper and with this he did —— / this shows waving hands around / and that was such fun! Laughs very heartily

At first asks (never since illness) if / I am ill. She was ill, had a cold: / 9/ *p. 5* IV. – Very trusting. Ask her where are all the bears / that have moo that they pour out of tails. / She says does not want to talk about bears, are / bad. Only the one she got from Mummy is good. – / Interpret bear and tail. – She says saw birds / that had such pretty tails at the back. – Ask / her if she has dreamt or knows what that is. – / She says yes shows closed eyes, says dreamt / yesterday when Aunt U. and another aunt / were there. Then: I could not sleep / at night, the dolls disturbed me / (I: how so?) she: with their mouths (I / how then?) She: with talking. ~~They said / to Hans~~ (I, but what did they / say then?) She: they said to / Hans: 'Drive your underground / train up and down.' (Hans = a male doll / who sits on a device connected with 4 / wheels – she had shown him to me before / said he drives an underground train / and shown me – he holds that so well (on handlebars). Interpret that to her. She says no / just as with previous interpretations, but listens / to me with clearly interested facial /

293

expression. – Wants to build something, makes me / build a train, wants a chimney on it / to drive up to windmills. – Shows me | box of bricks – there with paper-covered / holes. Breaks through. – When I interpret – she / no, no: – (that she would like / a little stick like Papa and like Peter.) She: Peter does not / have one, nor do I. (Interpret that she would like / one, and therefore because angry says Peter does not have one / either.) She brings me tyre and stick should / constantly over to her but wants especially with / stick. – Then shows me a plastic ball / with a spiral that she pulls / says – it is a bonnet, will break / it – breaks it off [says = candlestick][1] – breaks pieces / off – bites it, throws it away. – / ~~Makes~~ me build little watch-house. / When asked if for bear – resistance / wants to go away, know nothing about it. / ~~Makes~~ Puts doll in box of bricks / interpret = in mother, hole in which stuck / finger. – Says it is an airship. / Makes me build an airship, says she / is Fritz and goes to raisins. / Then I should go in airship. – / Brings very small doll (whose feet she had first / once torn off) I am to undress her for bathing. Nothing more at all about |

p. 6

poo). I ask about washing hair. She: / doll will not allow this (a phobia of hers – / loud screaming when hair washed) because / so unpleasant. She gets a cold from this / becomes ill. Then shows me the doll's / hair says something sticking out – she has / a nail – she does not want a nail! – / Talking with parents I hear = that she / pretended to be Peter when she was / about 2¼ years old and wanted / in the tram to lie on her mother's breast / in order to suckle. – When 11 months old bit / mother so passionately on the lips / that caused injury | 10/ IV. – Comes in very trustingly without difficulty / from garden. – Says bears have gone away. Are / in the 'clock-wood' – had to go away, because watchman lives / in their little house. In the clock-wood also see overground / train running. – She also saw two overground trains / when she was driving with aunt etc. Enthralled. – / A gentleman gave her a lovely little book. / I should look at the lovely new shoes / she got. They also wanted to buy a new / hat – did not get one. – She went to the / zoo, saw such nice elephants – they sat / there on bench and ate chocolate – so good / – next time I should come too. / – shows me a piece of cotton wool – with which she / has to wash Fritz doll [supposed to be his sponge][1] – Tears it into tiny / pieces – that she throws on chair etc. / – points at small piece and says: that is a / bonnet [for 'a musician'][1]. The bonnet ~~from yesterday~~ that / is damaged – has already gone, [was][1] swept / away (smiles at this) (= the spiral of ball etc. / broken off yesterday): – Wants to hear / story about

p. 7

p. 8

294

Fritz and the raisins again. / – Then to build – sticks finger in hole of / box [of building bricks][1] and tells me that she is doing this. At interpretation / = little stick in mother's poo – and that she does not have / one – no contradiction at all. ★ Takes a / brick – column-like (capital) and ~~strikes~~ pushes / it at hole in box. Says 'that is a / hammer' – 'that (looks for a small [triangle made] / triangular brick' – (throws it

★ looks around her and says, wants to find / a little stick

right away from box) – 'is a / woman – who is frightened, when   *p. 9*
hammer strikes'. / At my interpretation: hole in box Mummy – / hammer Papa's little stick – [small][1] woman who / is lying far away – Rita[2] in cot – no / contradiction at all. She laughs, says: [something crossed out] / ~~was in my cot~~ when Daddy struck / hammer in Mummy – / I said in my cot: / 'Well, well'. (Threatens with finger.) She laughs / heartily at this repeatedly, later laughing / a few more times – at this expression.) She says / is taking her suitcase and travelling to / Jerusalem. There are 2 women there who talk / with her. 'Frau Jerusalem' (as she / then calls her) is sad – she wanted / to show her all her dolls – but she has / eaten them up. – When interpret eaten dachshund / = child – then comes out – she: Yes, 'there / near poo' where the big [at same time also (?) anus][1] pieces come / for first time [uses term][1] that I used as had / no word for stool herself). At

I remind her that the gentleman who went past / said 'well, well' – when we were throwing sticks / in the drain: [something crossed out], interpret that). – She no, we threw stones / in there, not sticks. – Also brings me / doll and a hat – I should see how it suits her.

my reply 'not there' – she points at front / below chest, no reply /   *p. 10*
when I call the place 'poo [in front]'[1]. – then: I / am Frau Storchin – she = Rita[2]. Comes to visit me / am to build watch-house / with bricks that Frau Holle[i] gave me she / repeatedly kicks it down. Tips all the bricks into my lap / then speaks as Frau Holle. – She makes / an

i Translator's note: 'Frau Storchin' literally means 'Mrs Stork' and 'Frau Holle' is a female character in a story of the same name by the Brothers Grimm; she is the guardian of domesticity, rewarding a hard-working girl and punishing a lazy one.

underground train from the bricks, rubbing / one brick against another and says, 'I'm rubbing, rubbing makes / (game) and runs underground train / under cupboard. (Interpret mother) – Then with bricks / sets out airship – in which I take seat with her / (she alone yesterday, then I alone). / Says she is Mummy, I Daddy. – Then / suddenly takes all the dolls children / animals lays them on our laps, gives them out / and phantasises us in sand raisins / explains raisins arrived, children / climb out. [Something crossed out] Afterwards makes children / travel alone in airship (Interpret coitus / children birth.) With 1 duck showed me / should blow air into it. Says is Daddy – / show her – has long bill – little / stick. – She [something crossed out] pulls bill – / puts it in her mouth – begins to / bite. – Asked if likes reading book / with Daddy. She: yes, but not about bad bear. / (has read her something about bad bear / and said: well, well!) Since then she has not wanted | to hear any more about bear). 12/IV. Very friendly. Wants / to go into garden with me, because chicks / are there immediately refrains when I call her / into room. Looks through my bag & says about / my key: there is the blue key. / Sees matches & sits down, smokes / using my key as a cigar / first one end in mouth, then the other. – Fetches / dolls, gives imaginary raisins to eat. Says / raisins blue and small pieces as / she reaches for anus. (When interpret raisins = stool) she / says, little sticks come out of there. – Again / airship, we travel to Russia eat raisins / there. Makes me build a little watch-house / immediately knocks it down. Says bears used to / live there now watchmen. (Mother / had told her that there was a bear / in the watch-house – later [mother][1] claims / bear gone – watchman lives there now.) (Interpret / duck constantly eats the bears' house, she / constantly knocks down bears' watch-house, she / [something crossed out] father who breaks into Mummy's poo = / collapses – has coitus. – She says: does not want / to see bear. Always pouring moo from tails / makes her – Rita[2] so tired. (When | asked where pouring moo = she / : on ground. – Tips / bricks into my lap – wants me / to put in an empty string-bag for her / Constantly repeats that. Say / that throws little stick in my poo = puts in – / I should do same to her. – To this she says (without / contradiction: I throw down poos again. / Then wants to wrap full string-bag around / herself. (Interpret hammer should also grow there) / Then airship again she Mummy I Daddy / Russia, raisins. Then sudden desire / to drink water runs into next room / (parents' bedroom) fetches glass of water / that is there and drinks from it, entreats / me to drink. – Then

p. 11

p. 12

suddenly / asks if I must go already (always / a sign of resistance). (Then interpret does / not like me now because I am Mummy / who does not give ~~enough~~ stool & milk. – / She suddenly wants a / glass of warm milk to drink & runs / down to ask for it & drinks it. (Mother / reports: still drinking from small bottle.) | Unusual to ask *p. 13* for a cup of milk.★ / 14/IV. Doll in pram carefully covered up, / ill. Says: bear has poured so much / moo from tail that has made doll ill / (Ask where bear poured out moo [something crossed out].) / She points at doll's pram and at / cushion that is on the doll's genital / area. (Interpret coitus through mother, mother / = bear.) She says no forcefully, but just very / loud (is otherwise very active) and not at / all angry, half joke – then immediately: I / have also had a cold. (Interpret cold / ill washing hair = also pouring out moo = / coitus. – Fetches bricks: am to build tall / watch-house. She sticks finger in hole in box of bricks / looking at me provocatively / (Interpret acting father again with mother.) She: no / no – Daddy Mummy going away. Says going away / for 2 days. When interpret she is indignant – she: no no / she is going to windmill. – Constantly with / interpretations – she does not want to see bear. – Takes

★ Runs underground train built from / bricks under toy cupboard. (never / before now)

raisins again journey airship, she and I / each take a doll with us / an *p. 14* elephant – leads him into the room / to walk around – says going away – (Interpret she is going away / with father leaving mother at home.) She strongly / disputes – goes to windmill. – Wants to play tyre game / with me, with little stick. Also fetches small / skittle, tries to open it wants me to / do this, wants to see what is inside: / Says sun moon and stars. Then bores / 1 small stopper constantly into it / then throws aside. Fetches mallet / begins to strike armchair in which am sitting / also hits me says I will get / very angry. Beats out cushions, mattresses / doll's pram. Bores into / doll's eyes and around, says she wants to take them. / Stands on my foot, does not want / to get down – very unruly. Interpret rage / because father mother going away and she acts / father sadistic view based on coitus / observations. Fighting. She no at first then / again: she is going to windmill. – She / takes a brick, strikes it on / the floor – spits on it, rubs 2 large / bricks together. Resistance, wants to get | away from me, but then just *p. 15* fetches new / books that she shows me. (Mother reports / about changes – she very tender (as was / before) but ~~with~~ less defiant. Rejects father [more]¹ / no longer wants to read with him. – Mother / struck by how she gave her some of her white / bread. – She had done this readily as a small / child mother had got her used to giving / a bigger piece – she did not seem to find this / difficult – but then at around {age of?} / stopped doing this. Now begins [that]¹ again. – Last / night severe anxiety attack. Called all the women / in the family to help, not the father / 17/IV.23. Shows me Easter rabbit, laughs a lot, / because a hole in it (made by her). When / it is shaken, all the wrapped sweets fall / into your hands and on to the floor. Shakes out / a [something crossed out] chocolate sweet wants / to give it to me. Says <u>blue</u> / sweet. Scratches at chocolate Easter / rabbit wants to give me some. / Says Easter rabbit = good, has no / beard.

p. 16 (Interpret no beard = castrated | like hole in Easter rabbit.) At first she / agrees laughing – then: she has not / taken the Easter rabbit's beard away. / Fetches bear and says will play with it / Says: is a good bear has no tail / from which can pour moo. Puts it on / couch and states her bear = tired / the small woman too because she has constantly / poured moo out of pots. – / Leaves doll Suse next to bear [on couch]¹ (otherwise / mother or Rita²) / When asked if that small woman / : 'No. Other doll that sits there on / chair = Peter-doll (small woman = / bear?) Wraps bear / carefully up in blanket takes care. – ~~Later~~ again / driving airship with various dolls / also dolls' house. Points at 'Lankit-age' {sic} [?] / = attached cord. – Makes / me build ship, but then puts

p. 17 / dolls in box of bricks and says / first we go in water ship | then in ship with no / water inside = in light-ship. – Hurts / her finger slightly wants big / bandage. Put it on and interpret she is / ill like the bear that also / well wrapped up. – She to finger = tail / = castration. She then takes / bear away wants me to make him / a compress shows genitals – then / immediately paw afterwards neck / says ~~has~~ moo [has]¹ also gone / through there – because yesterday evening / he drank cocoa. – Strokes / comforts bear 'poor little bear – / you'll soon be better' etc. Had / told me never wants to see / bear's tail again. (Interpret: recognises / nursing – but is no longer identifiable when she has torn out / bear's tail. – ~~Suddenly / asks me if I ever Ask~~ Looks

p. 18 for a / triangular brick but a big one | puts it down and says tall woman – / says 'bri ~~bri~~ puli' (etc. something / incomprehensible) – laughing a lot. Suddenly asks / if I must go now? – I (as / always when perceive resistance / immediately resolve it through interpretation.) – say tall / woman who talks like that is Mummy she / angry with

Mummy because she talked / so incomprehensibly & [Mummy][1] laughed / at her. She ~~says~~ Hans with the / underground train also talks like that (but / while making another sound / from lutes. (Notice that she has / put tall woman near Hans (underground train)[1] / and interpret: father, mother, talk / have coitus that she does not understand – / she finds it funny laughs at it.) She: / (imitating) You speak so / quietly (whispering – when friendly / trusting to me [?] – [she][1] always / whispers.) Fetches various books / and reads to me. – Says one is / torn – Mimi has torn / a piece off it. / – Told father: 'Frau Klein says bear / is Mummy. I don't want to see bear any more'. |

19/IV. – Very friendly – comes over immediately although was / looking on floor with aunt for [two][1] / washing vessels – ~~comes~~ brings basin with her, leaves / it though at my advice not to play with / water outside now. – Asks me to shake / sand out of shoes and insists / on it being shaken into box of bricks. / Afterwards no longer wants to put on shoes / stays in socks for whole session. / With great racket hits bricks / on floor (only big ones) thereby constantly drawing / my attention to this racket. / Says about brick = also screw-/driver, drill: strikes the floor with / large brick perpendicular / strikes another one horizontally on it V / (Interpret floor = Mummy – coitus.) She / strikes ever harder, fetches one-armed / doll Suse, cares for her tucks her up / in bed – pushes under her bed / says can always get her out / from there. – Shows me Hans with underground / train V asks if can take off his

p. 19

says has muzzle like dachshund.

V Since then after striking / has always rubbed bricks together

yellow jacket – does not like it. Immediately / after this if I have to go. – (Interpret: / Hans' jacket = erect penis – undressing / = castrating him – anger mother / about coitus with father.) – She tears / doll out of bed, throws around and beats it – / says laughing – I'm beating Mummy. – Then / [something crossed out] she puts doll back in bed / soon afterwards takes out and lays / down on the floor, very carefully puts blankets under her / says: Now I'm looking for a Daddy for her. – Looks around / in chest. I suggest Hans with the underground / train – she no, brings bear and says / that is Daddy. ~~So~~ Very tender with both / (When interpret they / are of her castrated parents / she loves) she brings them individually to me / and has compresses made

p. 20

299

for them / but several over each other V She herself / has hurt her finger / while hammering with brick (but since / interpretations much less sensitive / about such injuries) ~~and says / (when I tell her, in coitus her member / damaged) about the ribbon that she brings~~

Says they are ill, feverish. – ~~Has~~

p. 21 ~~to me as compress: there is a new hammer / from 'parents' (bear, doll) says afterwards: have / given them many new hammers.~~ ~~After~~ / [something crossed out] resistance (<u>still: 'Do you have to go?'</u>) / Remind about wash-tub in front of the door. / She fetches it, repeatedly tries to put tub / in box of bricks (not the other way round) and climbs / into tub. (Interpret into Mummy.) Suddenly demands / poo. (Interpret putting stool and urine into Mummy = / pouring sand into box) resistance gone / – Was very frightened [before][1] last night. Only / mother at night, wants to go to her in bed. – The evening / before had talked about bear clock-wood[ii] / – a lady said – there are also monkeys there / when the bears tease them, they throw / nuts at them'. In the evening half asleep / put on pot – she murmured: 'The / monkeys are throwing nuts'. – Unusually tender / with Mummy. – 21/IV. – Shows me Hans with under-/ground train, says: that is Mummy. – I ask / her – why did she cry in the night? At first / says – did not – then: 'Because I want to sleep / with my Mummy'. Brings bear, caresses / him tenderly, makes me give him / various compresses – her as well, when hurt / herself striking brick on / floor. When I interpret (her member hurt / by hammering) says – yes has a new V shows

Told mother: the bear / has come back to play

p. 22 ribbon that had brought as compress. Later / says – about compresses, has given bear many / new ~~compresses~~ [hammers].[1] – Wants to put / bear in small doll's cot: (regretfully): it is too small, / does not fit inside. (Interpret she is small / doll's cot – too small for big Mummy:) She / fetches very small doll puts it into bed / next to bear, carefully covers up tenderly / caresses – says: they sleep so beautifully / they must not be disturbed, they must / sleep like this all night and

ii Translator's note: The original is written here as 'U[h]^{1}r[en]wald' – which suggests *Urwald* or primeval wood.

day. – ~~Sugge~~ / Sits down right next to the sleepers. Then suggests / that she and I also sleep. Then suddenly / no I do not need to – she sleeps / with them. (Interpret she = small doll sleeps – / has coitus with Mummy – besides she sleeps / with her in person.) She caresses bear: / 'My lovely good, sweet, wonderful Mummy'. Lies / down right on top of bear in cot / and says: 'Please give me a dachshund'. / (Interpret asking to get child from mother) / States the ~~two had~~ small / doll has called, needs poo. – Holds / her over box of bricks, says [?] [she][1] does / not want to. ~~To d~~ {dachshund} Hits the doll because | she does not want to do it. Then she does it after all / Afterwards sits on chair, holds / small doll in lap, caresses her, feeds / her. States she must go back to Halberstadt / (mother's birthplace) so as / to fetch some balls. Peter-doll is / also next to her, her child. – (Interpret has received / child from mother [she][1] is Mummy but / better than her Mummy. She fetches more balls = stool and penis – ball with spiral – in order / to give daughter. – Hear from mother that / she is sleeping very badly, often wakes up screaming, wants / only to go to her mother – immediately completely reassured / when she caresses her – says at once = good / again now. – When taken into her mother's bed / early in morning snuggles in there / & gets bottle, then goes back to / her own bed. – Also called bear: Duh[iii] [?] / are a mill'. (Windmill – / mill from moo – perhaps Mummy?) – When I interpreted to her / dachshund = child that then comes out / she shows genitals as place of exit. – / Had wanted to build 2 watch-houses / 1 for herself, 1 for bear. | V (smiling at me / so approvingly – in aunt's / presence) / 23/ IV. – Sticks finger in box of / bricks V – shows me that this / destroyed by cracks along it / then climbs into box / afterwards goes into drawer so that / with 1 foot in drawer and 1 in box / and pushes them forward. – (Points at / broken lid of box of bricks.) – Tries to put long / stick into skittle / suddenly throws both angrily / aside as well as doll / asks if I do not want to go. V (Interpret / attempt at homosexual union) – Anger / because cannot) Immediately friendly / fetches stick and ball and plays. – Carves oblong piece off / from – broken box of bricks / and begins to stick / in [doll's][1] navel – then / in a hole in doll's foot – / here sticks wood in so deeply / that completely disappears. – (At same time / same time she also bites at the place where hole is

p. 23

p. 24

iii Translator's note: Rita is playing with words that have similar sounds in German – moving from *Duh*, like *Du* (you), to *Muhle*, to *Mühle* (mill), to *muh* (moo).

Later tries to attach this skittle / where the doll is missing an arm.
Comforts / herself that has hammer through compress

p. 25 sings loudly (generally becomes very / noisy and throws everything
with great / racket, strikes and visibly enjoys the noise.) / Asks what is
inside there, pointing / first to doll then to / herself (stomach area.)
Interpret / curiosity mother orientation / ~~Strikes~~ Throws large bricks
/ on floor with great racket / says wants to break floor / Places large
brick vertically / strikes another horizontally / on it, says is striking
into the devil / that is in the floor – afterwards / says the bear. – Devil
goes / into the bear's head and eats / a good lunch there. – Says /
directly about doll box of bricks / ground when hurls [?] [something
crossed out]: now I am / breaking Mummy. – Also, when she throws
p. 26 chair / around and sits | astride it: now I am breaking Mummy / –
Shows me [her][1] purse, takes banknote / out – says I should give it /
to my husband. Again: Must you go / now? – Interpret annoyance I
to my / husband = Mummy – Daddy – does not / give her poo [?]
[friendlier][1] ~~Takes doll lap~~ Takes / purse and says is going to Halber-
stadt / (mother's birthplace) to the theatre / Will drink tea there, eat
chocolate. / Will look at herself in mirror, listen to music / and stay
until the young woman from / theatre sends her away – fetches / long
chain, puts it on later also [gives][1] to me – then / hits floor with chain
– even says / is breaking floor and chain. Very / wild – also hits doll
with / chain and throws aside (Interpret / activity and sadistic coitus.)
Also treats / table chair etc. like this. Very nice / towards me. When
goes down into kitchen / hits out at aunt with chain. – / (Hear
generally that [something crossed out] very cheeky / high-spirited.
Practical joke – goes without hat and coat

Meanwhile also said: someone speaks ga / ga ga! – Interpret = duck
= father – coitus-talk thing / every time I mention incomprehensible talk-thing / she laughs very loudly and then veers into
anger. – Says repeatedly: 'Then I / said well, well – then they
laughed loudly. / Another time says: Then she laughed so loud /
that it woke me up.

p. 27 (impossible at the beginning of the treatment – / also could not
tolerate my going without / hat. – Also abandoned compulsively /
arranging – crumpled blankets in the doll's / pram – however she has
also / stopped clearing away the toys. – The / last few nights she slept

well, without anxiety. / 24/IV. – Goes away from me towards mother
– / not friendly, does not even want / to give me her hand – just
clings to mother. (I hear / that when talking about me day before she
/ said: Frau Klein – Kleen Kleene.) Cries on the way, wants to be
carried / by mother the whole way. – At home asks / to take off
apron because no fun for her. – Reluctance / to go with me – comes
immediately when I / suggest she searches through my / handbag. –
Tries to open clasp / gets me to explain. Looks at handkerchief / –
says it is like hers – stuffs it in small side / pocket, at first says does not
go – then / it does go. Looks at my key. / Says is a pretty colour – a
pretty / English colour. Takes it, tries to open every | available lock –   *p. 28*
(Interpret satisfaction / searching through mother – handkerchief =
hammer / can stuff into me – pretty English key / father's member. –
She ~~stuffs~~ shows me her / handkerchief stuffs it under her neckline /
into her chest – shows me her / small purse takes out key, says / is not
very pretty is green / it was prettier in the summer. Immediately /
afterwards: They went in underground / train, she saw a lot there, it
was / very nice, there was also an old gentleman there / he was very
nice, he kept / moving his head like this (shows shaking / head from
right to left) / (Interpret key-thing, also colour [= father's][1] She: / I
always take a stick. (I: / ~~Yes but i~~ interpret – but she would really like /
a grown-up hammer, hence apron = female / genitals = did not take
off cobbler's apron / furious with me because she is unable to / have
coitus mother) She: I go into a shop | [something crossed out] buy   *p. 29*
myself a pretty coloured stick (Interpret / colour, father's erect penis.)
She fetches large / stick and ball and begins to play / with them,
hitting ball with stick / and throwing it (Interpret.) ~~Brings~~ Looks for
an English / book, I am to read it to her. / She listens seriously and
attentively, (does not / understand anything). I interpret she is making
me / do mother-father talk-/coitus thing with her (When I mention
how father-mother talk incomprehensibly / laughs a lot again, but
again ends with / annoyance. – Takes big / bricks again – says screws,
screwdriver / drill hammer. Strikes 1 on floor / says = screw that goes
into / devil's head. Says devil is very pleased about this / devil = a nice
good worthy devil / Has no beard, does not bite. – Afterwards strikes
her small purse with brick / pushed the keys in too hard / strikes the
lock and shows me / strikes little button. Interpret clitoris | and   *p. 30*
masturbation. She: yes when on swing / (But afterwards does not
want to hear / any more [something crossed out] about it.) Going in
airship, I / Mummy she Rita[2] taking dolls. / 'Eats' raisins, [very

tenderly]¹ gives me all the dolls / wants me to give them to her. – Asks / poo. – Shows me bear, laughs when it / does moo and tells me – he ~~can~~ / is pouring moo from tail again. / – Overall resistance immediately / after pockets. – Interpret disappeared – but then still runs back around / chain – hits floor with it / puts it down near me. – (Mother reports: slept / without fear but moodier / again – Afraid of / maybugs but ate chocolate / maybug. – About devil: that when / she was not yet 2 years old Frau Rosenbaum / (charwoman she likes very much) called / her devil when she did not come over immediately. / – Towards brother Peter very tender / but now and then also very aggressive) / Had

p. 31 shown me bear that can | pour moo – when I say, but no / hammer, she took away – she: has / one again though (shows compresses). Also has / bear and Suse make themselves bandages / observed here that / deliberately struck herself first. Calls / doll Suse: Frau Holle, then / Haube {bonnet}, then 'Kaul'. – Had heard / about my son from mother – asks / how tall, whether he can come to see / her, hurt that already tall / whether she is not also that tall – name. – Says / does not like, why not called / Kaul, should be called that. When later / answer her question with right name – [something crossed out] / corrects is called Kaul. States / that Suse is also called that. 28/IV. – Shows / me boxes game (ever smaller ones placed inside / each other), I should do this. When interpret child in / Mummy – afterwards says, ~~should~~: I put it in Mummy's. / Before that showed me tennis racket hanging / on wall, am also to hang up another one. / Am to build her tower from boxes, leans on / tennis racket from both sides. – They are

> At talk of my (after several days / break) coming back, had {said} 'Dr Klein does not / need to come, she does not need to tell / us any more stories about the bear.

p. 32 ladders, looks for doll who is to climb on the / ladders, then takes them away – knocks tower / down – says am to build her train. At same time / however she begins to sing loudly and to strike things / so that I cannot hear what she is saying / (also never or only rarely repeats now when / I do not understand something). Meanwhile she / says [half scornfully]¹ why I am building train. – Come / over here, Herr Koks, Herr Schmutzfleck.ⁱᵛ / (Then interpret her incapacity

---

iv Translator's note: 'Herr Koks' literally means 'Mr Coke', and *Schmutzfleck* means a dirty mark.

active and because of / castration – father's member = simultaneously / also stool.) Shows me doll that previously / was to climb ladders and that she put / next to Suse in bed and is / ill. She has had oil poured down her / throat and this has given her stomach-ache. / (When asked who poured it down her): she (Rita[2])★ / Brings me doll ~~with~~ and some long / bricks. Puts them down [on my lap][1], says nothing. / When asked what I should then do with / her: Knock like Fräulein Dr Turnau / when she was ill. – Then she / suddenly takes one of the long bricks / says wants to make a phone call puts to [?] to

When asked why she poured oil down her throat / – she also did this to her

her ear – properly asks operator for Dr Klein and / calls him over   *p. 33* because her doll / is ill, has some oil in belly. – I then / answer and come as Dr Klein. She / puts a long brick / into my handbag and something sharp (metal / toy bell, wide at top and narrow at the bottom / at first makes me strike doll / with brick – then no, first with / sharp ends, then takes it herself and drills / in the stomach area (states = belly) / asks for my handkerchief, wipes. (When / I ask what she has drilled there, what / she is wiping there) 'something pretty, the Easter rabbit / comes out there'. She tries to perform these / actions herself but always immediately / makes me do them again. – Then she / puts doll into bed, gives her compresses / cares for her – is not yet well ★ (Interpret / birth – also memory of mother's deli-/very about which she was not told truth.) / Later she picks up tennis racket again / wants to fasten it with nail – asks if I / must go now (when I ask if I should): yes

Places a brick under doll's bed / says, it will grow there

Interpret anger – does not have member herself to fasten / not all   *p. 34* these things like Dr Klein – / can make active. – Then becomes very / friendly, very reluctant to leave me / when I have to go away shortly afterwards: the / short time very loud, sings a lot, loud noise / etc. – Afterwards she does not want to follow / mother's instruction to tie bow / falls over is laughed at by mother – / – cries, but then follows, lets herself / be guided by girl and when she comes back / asks mother very quietly: 'May / I no longer fall now?' (Mother / who is very irritated herself, treats her very / badly, accuses the little girl very rudely, spits / and hits, puts on an act, claims / afterwards did not mean to spit. – Is sleeping / very well, not been afraid since last / session, even in the afternoon / for very / long time more than half a year had not slept / in the afternoon. – Little girls' sandpit / likes very much hits them when they destroy / her cake. At mother's outrage: 'I *p. 35* / only hit the little girls though, | not the grandmother'. – 1/V. – In meantime / once at night [corrects to: one night] cried repeatedly. Said / Sandman scatters big pile of sand in / her eyes. According to mother in meantime hardly / better behaved hit boy with whom she was playing / in the back with sand trowel. Punishment. / Withdrawal of chocolate while others got some / in front of her. Afterwards she was very remorseful. With mother / very tender, especially needing affection / when knows parents going away. – Nice to father, / goes into garden etc. but no desire / to read books with him, prefers mother. – / Before session she says: Dr Klein should come / to talk with me. 'Greets me in especially / friendly way. Grinds coffee beans in coffee mill, / asks me to cut one up – looks / in my bag for implement, finds hair- / pin – asks me for paper and 1 stamp [that finds in it][1] / says: 'I am very sad because I have no / stamps'. – Says her Mummy is bringing her / a chocolate maybug, she will / eat it, will also let me have some. / Says she likes me – when I ask / if she *p. 36* believes I like her, says yes / smiling. – Wants to put her pencil in | my bag, says should take it with her but / gives back, says my key [pretty][1] English colour / wants to show me it hers. — Fetches me a paper / doll a small boy in green suit / I am to undress him, since that does not work, / she tries to smash him / with big brick then puts him in her / mouth in order to bite him – suggests this / to me – when I refuse: to bite / just once. (Interpret destruction / father's member, consuming / together with mother – satisfaction mother / whom she impregnates anally with chocolate maybug [(she also fetched [?] all from Halberstadt][1] / should give her stool, exchanging members.) / She draws on my black handbag / with pencil – [something crossed out] calls it Herr Koks – / sings a song in which 'dirt' also appears / that she does not however (most strictly forbidden by mother / to say it) repeat after-/wards. – Writes letter to my son with / pencil [just lines up and down][1] – says she has called him 'Kaul', / but we can also call him Erich. / Sticks stamp on it. Then writes / lines on table with *p. 37* pencil says / they are airships. – Strikes brick | very loudly on table – looks at me and asks / (seeking approval) how loudly she can / strike? Then she takes brick again / throws it forcefully on floor / asks me again – how she can make / racket? – and then spits on the floor. / (Interpret coitus with me, wants approval.) Then / strikes big brick on smaller one / then throws away, strikes on bigger one / [something crossed out] (When asked where devil now): / in the ground. (Interpret coitus with mother in which / she grants larger member to mother.) / [Other one than recently, the small one that always represented child in bear-thing][1] / Takes doll out of bed: says she is / ill, she still has a bit of oil inside / her. [Something crossed out]. She strikes (this time herself) / brick on and around her, says so that oil / comes out. Then puts her in bed, puts compress / on her belly. V (To my question / recently the Easter rabbit did come out there) / she: ~~but~~ is also inside her. Is the / Easter rabbit old or young? Why haven't you / brought your boy with you? (When / say he has to go to school) says / should collect him from school, pleads a lot

Wraps her up very tightly, says must / sweat as she (Rita[2]) did when she had / a cold and Dr T. came and she had to / sweat

V Then points at small (ill) doll / and says: 'there's a child now' /   *p. 38* therefore, says very movingly: 'I am very sad / because I don't have a boy.' (Interpret / shared child, to whom wants to give boy's name / member because is son.) V Has taken / doll out of bed, sits on chair, covers up / etc. – says is still ill. (When / I ask where is child then): 'is still / inside her'* Then she fetches eiderdown from / blanket she takes a small coloured handkerchief / sits down right next to me on / small bench pushes table up [close][1] / puts cushion on my lap so that it also / reaches the table, takes her handkerchief and begins / whisperingly and very affectionately to talk 'incomprehensibly' / with me. Many sounds with i or o in / lots of vowels. At same time calls / doll something else again, the last time 'Petschua' / also biribobo and suchlike. – (When I / interpret with her like father-mother talk-/ coitus scene same reaction of laughter and rage / as usual and remarks that she said / 'well, well' – parents then came to / her bed and said / 'well, well'. Then takes eiderdown

* ~~Later then again~~ – Later says: / but we do have a small boy / ~~little~~ our Peter!

on to her lap gives me handkerchief – / (when say exchanging mem-   *p. 39* ber with / mother) she really wants to give me large one / again. –

While striking bricks she / had deliberately struck her / wrist – asks for compress. – Finally / [also]¹ very affectionate does not want to / let me go. 3/V. – Greeting me not very / friendly, stays standing at the door, does not / let me in immediately, then shows no desire / to go with me. When I say look through bag / immediately goes with me★ – afterwards very friendly. / Searches through bag – about hair-pin says / mischievously: There you do have a little hammer / again. – Lays out on doll's bed 'little coal-black' / a black cat with very long bushy / tail, brings one-armed / Suse, shows has compress puts her into the bed / with little coal-black at first, does not find / much room, puts coal-black next to bed. Says: doll / ill still has a little oil in her / Dr Klein said, puts compress / on her belly. Has put tennis ball at / foot of bed. Tells Suse she cannot

at first asks me to take off her apron / because dirty – fetches ~~hammer~~ / long chain, puts it on. (Interpret is taking off / girl's genitals, putting on hammer)

p. 40 have the ball now, she is tired, is ill / must sweat, when well again / can have it ★ – when I ask ~~whether then / not like~~ [something crossed out] recently there with oil-thing / Easter rabbit – child – says: has ~~not~~ / not come yet. (Interpret mother who / gets child is at same time castrated / cannot get ball, member [?]) / she: Mummy has gone to England. / (since mother's departure which / took very calmly [two days ago]¹ has otherwise not spoken at all / about parents. Slept perfectly both nights, / according to aunt not naughty) / (When interpreted 'coal-black' = Herr Koks = tall / father Stuhlst. {stool street?} and also like hammer) / she: coal-black is ~~like~~ Mummy. Says / we must be quiet. Those two are sleeping. Now / is also going to sleep herself. Interpret / Suse is herself – coal-black Mummy. She / gets child from Mummy, they sleep / together. – Brings a tiny little / porcelain doll. Asks me if / head is made of glass, she thinks wood, is dis-/appointed when I say porcelain knocks it / repeatedly it on floor (but not / so hard as to smash it)

She is eating buttered bread at same time and shows / me how well she can bite. / Puts piece of buttered bread left over into / bed by Suse, later she takes it / back and eats it.

p. 41 says: but no – it is wooden. Brings / me this little doll and its clothes has / it dressed, takes special care of coat / with hood I pull over head, greatly / admires, puts it right next to Suse in the bed. (Interpret / child has come, boy to whom grants [?] / the wooden head with hood = member because / her son. – Hears below in garden / aunt who came back with little brother. / Asks if I must go now? (When ask / if I should – she: yes – then: no — / looking at me affectionately. (Interpret / aunt and brother = Mummy and child, envy / she has none; hence I bad. – Fetches / [something crossed out] rubs her hands with Vaseline / from tin, then brings it over, puts / it on my lap, rubs her hands / like that, puts lid on my dress: / When I then say with slight irritation: / But you should not put that / on my dress – she continues to rub for / 1 moment – but suddenly cries / screams violently – continues much more like / screaming) – [something crossed out] looks at me very afraid | runs to the door. I: want to show her / my bag – pick [?] it up – / this doesn't help – she goes out of the door [to][1] stairs / ~~dow~~ store-room [?] I say: Suse is calling – take / handkerchief out, give to small / doll – (whom she had previously taken out of / bed and undressed again.) / Compress from my handker-/chief V. She [really][1] comes back, still / howling, still looks anxious / constantly repeats: 'You have / become so angry' – and runs back / out through door to stairs. I take / tennis racket, pass her another one / suggest we might play. She says yes / calms down, is very pleased when / ball going back and forth between us (she is skilful / at this). (Interpret rubbing on Vaseline = / = pouring oil into me Mummy – my / refusal = threat anger mother / – playing tennis = continuation / with interrupted coitus earlier. – / Completely calmed down, brings me very / small doll, am to tie my handkerchief / around her body as a compress

p. 42

V I also say can rub grease on herself am / not angry

only then a skirt, shirt etc. – / goes to doll's cot – (only now takes / notice of my earlier requests) shouts / at Suse – why did she call before is / badly behaved, takes her out of bed, hurls / her at door, puts coal-black into bed. – / – Goes to window – sees girl hanging out / laundry – wants to help her and goes over to her / when session has finished. – 4.5/V. Receives me / in very unfriendly way, hardly greets me, also does / not want to go up with me – then indication / my handbag comes there. Most de-/lighted with pieces of paper and pencil there. Writes / lines all over every piece of paper, is letter / that

p. 43

309

she is writing to mother. Also father / also the chauffeur who drove her in / the car. One must constantly get / a new one to come from the garage. Asks if she can / keep all the letters, ~~also pencil~~ very / friendly when I let her. Later gives back / pencil that do not allow. / Fetches bear from cot where lay. Has me put / 2 compresses around |

p. 44 his neck. Pretty cap likes putting on head / admires, says has 2 hammers, shows / can do moo. (When asked if pouring / moo from tail again) – no: has / no tail. – Takes little basket / – eagerly takes out coloured bits of paper / from it, makes me put bear in it / (since little basket too small) covers / with big blanket, carries to veranda (corner by / window). Still ill, has some / oil in belly (When interpret child-thing / again – I ask if child has not yet / come, looks for a small doll / puts it next to bear. ~~Packs 2 small / suitcases someone is going away~~. Says / is looking for a woman to come to the / children, an old, no a nice / kind one. Says one will come soon / packs 2 suitcases with coloured bits of / paper, a pair of shoes and the / letters she has written. Goes to / Frau Jerusalim [~~Jerusalem~~][1], she will then come / to her children. Frau Jerusa-/lint (Jerusalem, raisins) lives in a / Russian street. She [added retrospectively] comforts children / she will soon come back – wonders – / whether she should take them with

p. 45 her on | journey. – Sits on small chair with suitcase / puffs, drives train. – Gives me oth-/er suitcase – I also drive in my / train. Then fetches bear, kisses caresses, / wants to put him on small chair with her / but then sits him separately; sits down / on (bigger bench) loads / it with all kinds of animals – (duck, little coal-black, / elephant, [billy goat][1], all father imagos) also little doll / ~~I interpret Says everyone has their ch~~ {chauffeur} Also / gives me and bear little doll. (Interpret / she allows mother children, when she / also has some, then satisfied with / mother.) Says: I also have my / chauffeur. (Interpret she father together / with mother, each has children – so / greatest agreement.) She puts / [the][1] bear and [(rubber)][1] duck down. Later / takes [duck][1] away again lets / air out of it – puts it [completely][1] aside and says / when it is broken like that, it is no / use and puts down bear / instead

p. 46 billy goat. – Talks / about a man on meadow (acquaintance) | who has a goat, hens that lay / eggs. – She also once swapped / my suitcase for hers / that was rather smaller! – Is movingly tender loving with bear, only [?] / children – perfectly satisfied / (agrees with my interpretation: Hans with under-/ground train thing; dolls say: just drive / back and forth with underground train = / father shared possession each children from / him). Otherwise for a few / hours (likely connection: / mother being stricter because of / bad habits that she is expressing / more freely) seems not to be listening / during interpretation always busy / very seldom commenting (when air / being let out of beak mouth had taken duck and sucked on it. Interpreted / sucking Mummy's breast, now father's / hammer – she: 'no' to this.) / When I want to go away – also during / the journey-thing once asks: must you / go away? (When asked if I should?) No! – / does not want to leave me, must first | just show all the wooden animals / that have letters on the back. / During journey-thing – she builds / tower with boxes from game, which she / constantly brings down, tries again, placing / 2 boxes so that opening / is accessible from side and says / something can be put into / this box there. (Aunt says: sleeping perfectly / completely well-behaved – no longer spitting. The screaming / in last session with me was like / what she did at other times only with me not as / loud. – While car was rocking / threw brother out of car, apparently / not violently – afterwards very frightened / and anxious.) 8/V. – Greets me very happily / looks through bag again, writes / several letters. Very happy when give her the / pieces of paper. [Gives me back pencil readily][1] writes to Mummy (has also now / in the mean time written to Mummy) / and Herr 'Schülke, who trod the wheel' / (Interpret Hans with underground train = father. / Brings back all the animals etc. puts my / suitcase on armchair takes bench

p. 47

Herr Schülke =

loads it with elephant, clown, goat / little coal-black duck monkey etc. – Then / puts them on their own chair that / she puts close to her own. Calls it / pram. Also gives me a child; / then puts her bench close to my / armchair. Pram thus between / two of us at the [head][1] end of bench. / Had stuffed letters in her suitcase / and a tennis ball, very grateful / when I tie it up for her with tennis net. / Generally charming with me. Constant / requests not to go away. Suddenly she / throws all the children etc. out of train compartment – / she gives them to Frau Jerusalint who / is standing outside – all the shoes – everything / toys, bricks, all the dolls / children. At same time she asks her just to / take. – Afterwards tells her: may I perhaps / take that one myself? – Takes / a doll, puts it back, looks around / takes monkey puts it aside. (Interpret / gives Mother everything children, father's member / if she is also allowed father's member = / monkey. – Later

p. 48

311

p. 49 she puts everything | back on bench. When asked / whether she is not leaving it for Frau Jer. – somewhat / angry – says but there are none there. V / Stuffs purse full of letters / and shows it to me. Suddenly asks if I don't want to go – says she wants to go to her / aunt now – goes out, completely refuses / to be persuaded to stay. When I / suggest to her stacking letters / in her small suitcase, comes back and plays / that. (Interpret anal resistance towards / mother who did not allow her / full purse = much stool. Forceful contra-/diction. – Takes my large black / bag tries to stuff it in / her small suitcase – becomes angry, runs down-/stairs. There (session already over anyway) / a young girl-friend has come to visit. / Brings her upstairs, is [ink stain] with her

V Looks at my patent leather shoes. Much / admires – wants to put on her own / patent leather shoes.

p. 50 admires her lovely green (in fact / black) shoes – dress belt / etc. thanks her for coming – brings / her all the dolls, toys. Asks the little one / if I should come back. When / she answers: no – tells me – am / not to come back. – 10/V. – Very friendly / although a ~~cousin~~ young cousin is visiting / happily goes with me. – Looks through bag / writes letters – but wants to keep / pencil and puts it in her small / suitcase. – Directs every possible animal / and things back to bench [shows Frau Jer./][1] and small chair – / puts bear on small chair, puts books / in front of him, gives me some as well. / (When interpret book = female genitals – father / reads books with English) she sud-denly asks / whether I must go? At first says I should – / then sud-denly smiling that I should stay after all / (interpret anger mother because of going away and coitus / father.) – Takes bricks says takes / hammer, screwdriver, drill – with this / smaller bricks and screws |

p. 51 strikes them hard on ground. V Ask if / devil inside. – She: no, no bear and / no devil. Have flown into the air / to birds. No in hell. A tailor / has cut off all the devils' / tails. – Sits on the chair – holds like / car. Doll in ~~hand~~ arm. She {looks at} me / laughingly and provocatively and says / 'incomprehensible'. Afterwards she makes / trr trr sound (as when anal material / first mentioned) IV (Interpret when tall woman spoke / incomprehensibly she furious, wanted to make / stool noises.) At this she makes / [-u][1] ch [-u] sound (as when children / squeeze) (Interpret that.) She [something crossed out] / fetches coffee mill wants to grind coffee / looks for fir cones breaks pieces / off makes me break some / off, lifts it up again, makes me / break it again etc. (Interpret anal / game and recent annoyance.) Has become / very friendly. Says / that Herr W. the cart-driver / no longer comes – he always

V Fetches skipping rope and beats forcefully / around her. Says is a hose and / waters the flowers all over with it. (Interpret / mother genitals) / IV when asked what she said: she (hypocritic-ally) / – I was mistaken – (Interpret has received answers / like this from adults.)

called her mouse. She liked that very / much. The new one is also *p. 52* nice. – 12/V. – Comes / although girl-friend visiting before, / fairly willingly, writes letters again: / to Herr Schülke, who trod the / Schülke-wheel. (Gives this information when I ask / what kind of wheel trod.) – Sits in large armchair / and says: she Dr Klein. – But then / stands up again. Does not fit in large / armchair.

[There are no notes available for the eight sessions from 15 May to 14 June 1923.]
[B 1: The bundle of papers at the back of Ernst's treatment book contains various things including a small notepad]

16/VI. Catching chicks / bird feathers imitating [?]-dress [also child][1] / remorse Jer – changing clothes / short socks – father / not with her naughtily / takes umbrella – billy goat / gives milk – little Peter – / small flower [?] Frau Jer. – / constantly {taking} small jacket – / cap on and off when / visiting and away (also / chain and away – men / who [something illegible] / – at this 'juh uj uj' and / 'ra ro' / – poo toilet Jer. floor / goes back J |

[On the back:] Devil Africa goes with / Engl. {England?} and Papa / – / never also before once / – Must you go – / not letting go coming / back. Saying you / never furiously throwing [?] / – / V jokes cutting [?] ribbon / cap – billy goat / ribbon bag – bag / tying flowers / – / – [something crossed out]

[There are no notes for the two sessions of 19 and 21 June 1922.]

[Folded portrait sheet of A4 paper, the first page is headed 'I']

313

At first poo – hole game / mother's slit / 23/VI. Rita²: again taking / with her twig / Frau Pestatores / – Jerusalist. Thinks / not changing clothes aunt Erna / angry (apparently only reduced compulsion) / – then does. Explains / socks clean – then changes anyway – completely / underwear – again at first still looking for / folded ironed dress – then shoes [?] / dress – tassel – tying well / – cap tassel at front / – especially black small jacket choice of / caps – gives me 1 – small suitcase / herself – skittle little doll (recently / cushion) at first puts cushion in, then / little monkey. – Changes socks [?] again / – 'blue English ones'. To [something crossed out] / question adds?: I can / go alone leaves. – Only takes 1 / doll with her completely changing clothes. / When I call her [doll]¹ Rita² – she also / speaks like this to [? Something overwritten] – [Something crossed out] ~~small jack~~ / With scissors cuts twig / smaller and smaller. – Reaches – me [?] / speaks to Frau Jer. – Very / timid shy corner of mouth / (always) turned down. – Passes twigs – / I say very small hammer / – before, already repeats – / there small jacket, tassel – straight |

[Next page:] fastens twig etc. interpret coitus / – she: not in there – to Mummy. / – Hardly arrived, as usual, immediately / going away. – Says completely / changing clothes – [something crossed out] first – Frau Jer. / I should get her train or tram / for journey back – then V [some time soon]¹ bad – / refuses to be dressed – twigs / all chopped to pieces – wants to cut up / her garter – cut off button – cut up sock – / cut off button – cut up / my jacket – cuts up / doll's dress – pinches me very hard – / despite expression of pain, even / more – ~~but wants~~ to press close [?] when / getting dressed – still wants me / to get her ready. At same time / also presses against me clearly lovingly / – When at pinching I say – not / next time repeatedly she need / not – runs away immediately – ~~after~~ / I quickly say soon coming back / only friendly – but does not / bother about me any more. / Runs into garden. –

V some time soon should stay with her again

Ask how bodice etc. / got dirty: Frau Holda with / stick. That dirty all round

[Next page:] bench arranged – so dirty / like inside cupboard. / – / Forgetting to clean teeth – ~~thus~~ / theatre ~~ta~~ woman puts on [?] / play concert. / 30. [Something crossed out] drinking tea / from cot. – little girl / [on]¹ picture ~~wanted to pinch tea~~ – / also to take to us. – then naughty / wanted to pinch tea. V – underwear yes, not – / finally not changes clothes shoes socks dress, / small jacket cap I also – again bag / and bear – wrapped in blanket. – She big chair – I / small one – house Frau Jer. – up the / steps upstairs – taking off jackets – little pi-hammer – ask where underwear dirty: shows / dark marks – Frau Pest. rubbed – / pulled – when interpret masturbation – hits: / forbidden. – I say broken. She: to fasten; / bear sad – she not cuddly / kitten – reaches Frau Jer. – wants to pull out / [does not matter that not mother's chain]¹ / mucky hairs from rabbit's beard. / V with shawl wiping dust / wrapping up in it.

[Some pencil-written lines follow that do not relate to Rita.]

[Next page:] less hypersensitive / buying me flowers – then little basket / from chest: buying eggs cannot find / but gets some. – Not changing clothes: then / happy I am still there. – / 5. drinking real tea V voracious / sugar back into big pot. – Frau Jerus. / I eaten children – she: yes – all of them, also / eaten cakes. Stomach out. 'Kause' {sic} [?] / mullion and transom – vertical nail – / Herr Pestatores [made dirty with stick]¹ knocked / not come in not done. / [Opened mouth so wide]¹ / trees Werderstrasse / Christmas trees on top of / each other – they help get themselves – / anxiety sock pressure pattern – also changing underwear / – arrived Jerusal. counts / to 15 – also shows ~~chair~~ / armchair marked with number shapes / am not to go away. – V big / mouthfuls gets big – I / to take small mouthfuls I / to get small – admired umbrella / hat dress – at / start of journey took doll / – then threw away – is naughty / takes goat with her (also repeatedly / called Peter) makes me / stroke him when arrived [at house of]¹ Frau Jer. / calls him Liese – says does not bite

[Another single sheet:] 25/VI: Changing clothes. When asked / why: underwear all dirty / Frau Holda (later Jerusalem also Pestatores) / she with Janastein (big Elisabeth / sings a song like this) she ~~mucky~~ / she dirty. – Knocked on wall – if may come in she yes – came like that / mucky at back also still / pieces poo then also points at front / belly stomach – shows small point – / also little skirt [something illegible] / later little button bodice. Shows / how rubbed at back and front / – again changed underwear etc. / – always valuing other dress – back and / forth and never the one I suggest. – Has taken / chain and says is 'little pi-hammer'. / – While getting dressed affectionately / kicks

315

both feet around bangs [against me][1] – shows foot in blue English /
sock – is pip-hammer – then says little pip-hammer / and shows
genitals there is pipi. Arrived at / Frau Jer.'s house – as usual soon
jumps up – asks for / needle material – wants to sew with machine /
should give her material cut out / etc. When I refuse, resistance (session / over) – runs into garden. Will not / have clothes changed. –
Had continuously / and said will sing for / Frau Jer. and little
pip-hammer / at first also did / but then soon jumped up

[On the back:] 28/VI. Again claim underwear / made dirty by Frau
Holda whose / stick was dirty because put / on bench. [Stick][1] was
dirty / all around like cupboard [something crossed out] / also
Janastein – as tall as her / Rita[2] – rubbed with it – again / sings little
Pi-hammer. States / wants to fetch Frau Jer. – at same time / in last
session says – sings / counts, drinking tea

[There are no notes for the two sessions of 3 July and 5 July 1923.]

[Another portrait sheet of A5 paper] II she naked Herr R will be /
pleased that she is naked / 7/VII. To take big piece of leather – hat /
[at first poo then washing foot soap. Now clean][1] / also undressing me
/ wants to see me – cold / that is under bottom. Has / dirty teeth –
she dresses / also underwear looks through my / bag – letter to
conductor / money – on floor doing poo / – before [?] [today and
also][1] last few times / quicker. Visit [even to][1] Jerus. always / very
short – not I, then / again yes. Jer. small jacket / [long ribbon fore-
head][1] / taking off cap when / reaches stairs / before with Frau Jer. –
hardly [?] / there with broom that when doing / poo took to
bathroom – / scrubs leather – Frau / Jer. to praise clean – counts /
again – restless – takes / hammer, hits ground – / poo, then says
immediately / poom claims did / not say poo. – Throws / down
hammer – does her / hair. Then looks

[On the back:] at me – am untidy / must do my hair. – Whether /
had finger below on bottom. / Hits me with comb. / – On Sundays
8/VII. visit so / does not want to come / anxiety gloomy [says Frau
Jer.'s house locked][1] looks through / bag [is not shut][1] – middle part /
ugly whether can / tear out – runs away after / interpretation tearing
out masturbation anxiety / – then drawing little box / and again
bigger one – runs away / to girl-friend goes to play in sand. / Bakes
cake brings me some. / At first poo – then washing feet soap, Jer.
cleanliness lied / 10/VII – looks through bag / writes letter to con-

316

ductor / not going to Jer. – then / [shortening shirt or sewing on it][1] / does go. Also all underwear / wishes for remark underwear not / dirty though was naked – / – Freckles on back / – woman sun hurt her / made dirty. – / Very anxious choice dress / back and forth – long blue / belt mother's long chain / – again Werderstrasse with / trees ~~cauffeur~~

[Single sheet that is headed 'A':] Rita[2]: 13/VII.23. – Is naked – also putting on / underwear, long socks etc. – [Something crossed out] Says Herr Petlatores / understood (Pestatores) was there. Had made her / dirty with 'Eiadum' and 'Fornenee' [?] / (purse).[v] Eiadum [Ei-dumm [?]][1] shows very big (she sits / on chair – shows up to her chest level (interpret [all that)][1] / is blue, yellow, black. Says is like / 'Ihnastem' {sic} [?]. – Again same anxiety, choosing clothes / indecision. – In fiercest heat / knitted jacket, cap – puts herself into / long knitted blanket. Says on journey to / Frau Jer. must sweat. – Also prepares / more quickly as in the last few sessions. Then in corner / takes off jacket etc. / puts on chest) wants to greet Frau / Jer. cannot find [her].[1] Points to electrical / contact there and says that is Frau Jer / States is sleeping – coming back / on Tuesday (analysis day) / Gives [over-written, Goes?] to chair / window, from there says that tomorrow no / time because going to doctor he will / examine her. When ask what is wrong [with her][1] – / says cold – then – it is nothing / to do with me, am not doctor. – Travels on / chair = underground train to doctor. Continues this / for whole session gets me to undress her says / should say nothing to Aunt E. [something crossed out] has changed clothes / – but although tolerated session is not positive. / – Tells [me][1] I am very thin – am stupid / – last but one session had also taken / very long blanket – ~~sleep-cerem~~

[Reverse side is headed 'B':] 14/VII. Again dressing from head to toe / – but this time not knitted jacket – (had constantly / interpreted – also why sweating on journey Jer.) / when dressing very tiresome [?] – I stupid crumpled / socks – cries because crumpled my (thick) cloth dress / with sleeves too big / creased – my fault. Looks for Frau Jer – says cannot / find. Goes to other room comes back / has not found. – In last few sessions / kept saying – collecting Jer. to us / – strong resistance – runs away from me not / to be restrained. In garden. Plays with dog / (mine) [?] does not want to tolerate crawls under my [?] /

v Translator's note: *Ei-dumm* (Eiadum) literally means 'egg-stupid' and 'Fornenee' is explained as *Portemonnaie*, i.e. 'purse'.

skirts. – Makes me take off / his collar – says – muzzle now / he can no
longer bite / – puts it in her small suitcase / then caresses dog a lot very
tenderly etc. / (interpret collar = hammer) castrated father – / did not
grant him to me = mother – Has / waddling duck pushed out by me
wants / to have dog up there – very concerned I / should not hurt
him! Comforts him for not / being able to come out waddling too – is
still small / little Purzel little child – can still only watch [?] / or only
waddle up to small duck. – Interpret turning back

> Before session stated going to Frau Jer. ill / cold because had had
> too many visits. / We visited too often.

> [Right at the back of the bundle of loose sheets is a sheet that is
> distinctly more yellowed/yellowish than the first sheet but is likely
> to be its continuation]

[Front page headed 'C'; torn-off corner] receives. Father to her when
she watched coitus / shows me that my nice ironed / collar has been
ruffled by wind – says better / I should have no collar than let it / be
ruffled by wind like that (interpret castration / clitoris – cut up shirt).
– Interpret / all that (father mother etc. garden) whispering / under
strong resistance. – She constantly / even before session – I am not to
/ speak – not to tell – Frau Pestat. / does not allow it. – I stay there
after / session over for a while so as to be able / to part in a friendly
way. – ~~Makes~~ Comes / very tearfully – father is causing a through
draught / – she does not want – mother should stop it / that harms
doll – she in garden. – / At interjection – put in room – also harms
her / there – she does not want the wind. – / But allows mother to
distract her / – according to mother distractible – before / then she
screaming crying. – Has / mother play her guitar – names the / songs
– sings and dances along – direct / lively enjoyment of music – leaves
me / anywhere then <u>not</u> hostile – but / ignores – e.g. despite request
– does not / show my chicks. With mother / exaggeratedly tender. –
Only pays / attention when say at my house play / piano – spontaneously happy journey
[Reverse side headed 'D'; top left-hand corner torn off, first two
lines incomplete:] – clearly very pleased that am going away [?] / –
then I won't visit her, she will / visit me. When interpreted duck
father / remind bear mother – she visibly relieved / I can talk <u>about</u>
<u>this</u> – beginning / session greeting [something crossed out] changing

underwear / (this time wearing) that made trousers / wet. When asked who – very angry / hits me: – not her – At Dr / G.'s house (neighbour) there she got wet / in the toilet. – Interpret she made / wet – wants to offload guilt / on mother – as with Frau Jer. / stick – instead of admitting own masturbation. / Hits me again. Forbids talking / etc. – Also interpreted journey Frau Jer. fruit-/less because no member – doctor examining / = allowing coitus (but meanwhile still / ambivalence mother [? something overwritten] oedipal wishes / repressed – but negative towards me / already comes out) – With mother steadily / nice – simply lets herself be covered / in blanket without ceremonial (not at aunt's house / only at mother's for about 4 weeks has wanted / this ceremonial – but now for / past year made to clean teeth etc. / in the evening – crumpled blanket doll / wrapping them up just as she / wanted now) – also recently asked / mother to change her clothes as with me.

[There is a further page, on which only the front is written, in which it is impossible to tell for certain whether it is headed 'III' or 'E', but which may be a continuation from above.]

Mention Christmas trees – she: has also / helped fetched hers. – Chauffeur / out of car drives over waits. – / ~~Arrived there   before~~ – doll wrapped / with blanket at same time my / bag that keeps opening / loses temper. Hits me as hard / as possible – then hits doll / flings away because its fault she cannot / keep bag shut. / Arrived: as always cannot keep jackets etc. shut / Arrived as always takes off / jackets etc. Acts all friendly – / but immediately asks if I must go / Counts up to 20 along / cot ~~as long as I am to stay many~~ / – I interpret despondent / satisfying Jer. Fetches skittle and ball – interpret / coitus attempt all the same – finally / hurls forcefully into corner. Then plays with / tennis ball with me. While / looking chest falls in / Very desperate. – At masturbation interpret / little button bodice [?] part bag / – resistance – also hits

[B 9: Treatment book 2]
[Cover page:] Exercise book 2, Rita² August 23

22/VIII. – result whole time unchanged / good. – Only once when   *p. 1a* cold coming on / scream crying [?] but only very quietly. Spoken about / me a few times; wished that / I was coming. – At aunt's house wanted to write / to apologise for constantly changing / her clothes with me. – Greets me / in a friendly way, but does not want to go room / but to little girls' sandpit / with me. Asks about my big piano / (I told her) wants to play it / Tells me: Sandpit boys make music / and little girls dance together / after that. – Wants to go into garden with doll's pram / then goes into garden corner of room. – / She is Mummy I Rita[2]. – Gives me shapes / I should sandpit – says cannot / take pram with bear, leaves / Peter at home as well. – Prepares table 'at home' / to eat on. Hairbrush = plums – a / small painted board = dog Suse that / is consumed – the comb = seed – / the hair slides spoon – someth a / brick = a sweet – others have

p. 2a incompre | -hensible names, like Loriam / etc. – Says wants to fetch / Frau Jer over. V At first said, aunt said / left 1 particular dress out / only for changing clothes – but then still / goes over to cupboard. Again has great / difficulty choosing – then changes dress / a few times – also shoes and socks / – goes away says Frau Jer no longer / lives in Wichernstrasse – goes / away, comes back – says is / ill, lying in bed has worked / too hard. – Thinks we had better / go to 1 <u>tradesman</u> soon, he / should make us a few new / rooms. – Asked for my / chain – at first tries on mother's. – V / But does not ask to change / underwear. – 27./VIII. Wants to go / away again. At my invitation / looks through bag – just at first / held back from my letting her / look through my bag. – Writes

V Also mother's belt – again / small jacket and cap. / V She looks everywhere – in various places / including bedroom cupboard / cannot find.

p. 3a [wavy line drawn] elephant – [shorter wavy line drawn] a little hen – / [2 short wavy lines drawn] a sweet [2 parallel lines drawn] 2 caterpillars – from / [wavy line drawn] also a train – runs / 2 [two long parallel lines] lines of paper over / whole table). Says – a car has driven / there. – Pencil wrapped in / paper. – As mother was very nice / to me – but also left me / at home because going to bank and too crowded / there! – 27 [overwritten: 25]/VIII. – Wants to go into garden again / but acts as if satisfied with bag – paper / stamp pencil. Writes a letter / to chauffeur Schülke to say we want / to go away. Then to some incomprehensible names / of 'tradesmen' that we want to / come over. Again plays / mother so resolutely that when / changing clothes V (not underwear – shoes, socks / and repeatedly dress – at this very / indecisive, anxious – changes / repeatedly.) Says tries one if too small / for her gives [it][1] to Peter. – Car (chair) arri-/ved, she sits on it, takes me / on lap. – Herr Schülke is no longer there / [something crossed out] car drives alone. – Getting out

accepts no help. Says: 'Can't your Mummy / do it well? – I: 'Yes, you are like clever Mummy'. / She: 'I am not a clever Mummy though – am a / big Mummy'. – I: 'yes, an old' – She – 'no, not / an old Mummy, a new one, but a big one'

takes pram – goes / on to balcony, there tradesman's / house. Said   *p. 4a*
beforehand – he / lives in Gloster. She wants him / to make some rooms / for us, we will live in one / each – the rooms will / have a lovely big pendant / lamp that hangs down. Had / {dressed} herself after difficult choice (although / easier than before – no underwear at all) / Thinks tradesman will be / surprised at how nicely dressed / she is. (Interpret indecision / choice – because looking for new not yet / masturbated slit with little hammer) / Put on little jacket again / tassels at front – then / into mother's cupboard – puts / a completely new jacket (her own) / over it. Also a cap. – Says cannot take / me with her to tradesman / too crowded there. – Then reports he will / then use space for a girl's room | V that is pressed / there he will also   *p. 5a*
fit / an alarm. V (Interpret tradesman, Gloster = father – / she mother goes to coitus – me – does not / take child with her. Chauffeur – father = engine, house / underground train = father – she drives alone / she has penis = tassel. – Girl's room / her lovely new genitals – pendant lamp / = member – also alarm (Frau Jerusalem / who was inside in the electric plug) / – V finally quickly changes / clothes again) – wants to keep jacket, cap / etc. on – resistance / runs into garden, does not / ~~accompany~~ lead me. – 25/VIII. Receives me in a / friendly way – stays there the whole session, although / mother meanwhile breaking promise / goes away alone and she guesses that. Writes / letter to Frau Jer. – then wants / me to draw her a very / big box with child inside – then garden / with pears and peaches and the child / standing in the garden. The child should / be a girl and have a skirt

I should stay longer – not go away yet. / I should stay much longer – 5, 7, eight – which / she indicates on the wall.

p. 6a   on. – She wants to go back to Frau / Jer. Whose mother (kind old face, / two years old) has told her / Frau Jer. well again we can / come. Was ill because / she had no money – money / is so expensive. – Again same preparations / changing clothes journey as before break. / Changes underwear – shoes socks / with dress even more indecisive / even tries several again / switches over. – Gets dressed and undressed as far as possible / on her own without me. Makes / me pick out my / favourite handkerchief, she takes / that – but very satisfied when I / like dress. Shows me end / of skirt, when asked where underwear / dirty (as she claimed.) – I / made it dirty with a / – later says with / a doll / the cuckoo is below on the cuckoo / clock and comes and calls.

p. 7a   – I have / put the cuckoo on her cuckoo clock | she had one in the night in the room / At my interpretation cuckoo = Jana [?] / stein – mother got dirty through / coitus father – she also cuckoo clock- / getting dirty = wants coitus through mother / but does herself – clock round = slit.) / She (forcefully) A kettledrum is also big / and round like that. I heard the men below / in the church playing drums, they / made a racket – I thought to myself / – [something crossed out] [what's this][1] what are they doing, will / they play drums when they have hung up / the kettledrum? Then shows how / they banged stick on kettledrum (= / table). Then also / talks about tying on the kettle-drum (Interpret / kettledrum etc. coitus, racket during this.) – / When taking off socks shows me / darned. She likes that, it is only holes / she cannot bear (Interpret again / damaged genitals) chooses shoes with great difficulty. / While putting them on had pulled over / doll's bedding and laid down Humpty Dumpty (like Punch, consist-

p. 8a   ing almost entirely of head), she wants | to go to him. Also calls him / Suse. (When remind Suse = dachs-/hund that bit Mummy = penis / – she remembers very well. / When she made trr sound and I say / doll did that, unfamiliar / to her – then <u>she</u> reminds / <u>me</u> that she [her-self][1] had made trr sound / (a few months earlier). Finally takes / my chain and mother's / brooch. – Says chain like sweets / wants to bite some off, hits / me when I do not allow it / and wants to send me away (anyway / session is over.) When realises / mother [something crossed out] secretly gone / away cries hard – but not act-/ual scream – crying. – Talks about / going to sleep, that she left her feet / free. 29/ VIII. – Says wants to go / to dentist with little rabbit. – / She (shows me) has ~~poo~~ completely / clean teeth – but rabbit's / are dirty. Wants to / change clothes also Aunt E. always / dresses nicely when going /

p. 9a   to dentist. Dentist has long drill, does not want to be drilled | with it herself only rabbit. When interpret / drill = screwdriver etc. big brick / struck floor = little hammer. / She: 'No, I don't want to be drilled / You only drill something when you / want to make it new' – wants to change clothes / also underwear – shows me a tiny mark ~~that~~ in / shirt that is not clean. – Then goes over to / chair ~~is~~ = car to dentist – says must / leave me, Rita², at home because train is / full. Chauffeur Schülke not yet there – has / come, cranks up – shows me place on chair where he sits. Says but has also already / seen that chauffeur drove with 2 women / to train. (Interpret house underground train / between 2 dolls = father, engine chauffeur / with her and mother.) – ~~Then again not when~~ / [something crossed out] when changing clothes cap again / every possible belt etc. – no / jacket. – When interpret also wants / little hammer, she: I have no little / hammer, only little rabbit. (Interpret = female – / genitals – teeth not clean = got dirty) / Then again not to ~~Frau~~ dentist / takes dolls – goes for a walk with her / children. – Then goes to a kind / woman who has 2 children – 1 boy / and 1 girl. Interpret = mother like | Frau Jer. She: *p. 10a* Frau Jer. had many / children (the ones who were eaten? – was / sad!) – ~~Fra~~ About Frau Jer. / had said – that she lives / somewhere incomprehensible name, where / there are small trees. She cut / them down because / they were not needed. She only left / 1 standing, 2 fruits were / growing on it. – Finally she / goes back to Frau Jer – / ~~To the~~ but just as little as / with dentist etc. – she / describes the stay and success / of the journey. – When I interpreted / chauffeur journey = coitus, ~~she~~ said / on this journey / father mother also did / not take her, as / she did not take me, she: 'When they went / to England they [also]¹ / did not take me. / ~~I./IX.~~ Only at very end of the / session some resistance. / I/IX. – Wants to cook – has small saucepan / etc. – we eat what is cooked, / I am Rita² again. Wants to / change clothes again – to go for | a walk with children. – Says ~~needs~~ underwear *p. 11a* cannot / change it, ~~is clean~~ because / window open – getting a cold. From wind coming / in. When shut window, still does / not change underwear, says is clean. No one / was there in the night. Goes to Frau Jer. who / lives in the window corner near heater. Shows / me lower pipe, says about this stick / you may not step on it, must step over it / – and then turn above where tap is (Interpret coitus / with mother so that penetrates / ~~ov~~ near mother's member.) Before we both had to / – when reached Frau Jer's house – we both / had to, before going inside – / put our caps on upper pipe. – When / changing clothes: shoes socks and / dress, this time more definite choice. / Then going in the car. – Duck swing-/cart with car duck = chauffeur. He / starts up, we both go with him (I / am Rita[2] again). We drive to / Gloster to Papa. – She has herself / drawn a huge box with a clothed little

p. 12a
girl / in it. – Says that you get | ill – about doll – if wind / comes in [something illegible][1]. A small / boy had also had / something like that in his hand. / Is so positive – that always runs / joyfully towards me when / comes – says / 'dear little Dr Klein' – leaves / playmates standing and comes over. / Towards end of session / repeated resistance. ~~This~~ / ~~time~~ Also she always changes / dress once again end of session / and not the original / one but another one from / the cupboard. This time / she says she wants an old / ugly one because she was / naughty has made herself wet. / (Interpret dirty below = / ugly old dress.) When we / had reached Frau

p. 13a
Jer.'s / house – she asks me if I | do not need poo. Then she goes herself / into corner of room and ~~mimes urinating~~ / makes as if she is about to urinate. – / Interpret: – coitus mother = also urinating / into. – 2/IX. Comes happily al-/though playmate is there. V – Changing / clothes wants to go to Frau Jer. – No / underwear. To my question if it is clean / if no one was there. Yes, Frau – / (incomprehensible name.) She rubbed it / with Frau Jer's stick. The underwear / is clean though not dirty. / (Then interpret Frau Jer = mother = she herself / her masturbation.) Temper tantrum. Hits / me, wants to throw armchair / at me – when she then bangs herself / on table also wants to throw table / at me. – Says (as often at other / times with resistance) I am not to / speak, I may not – her / mother said I may not speak. / Then interpret she herself mother who forbids

V When talk with father, she pulls me / away, asks if I like her?

p. 14a
me to speak. Recently / angry ~~but then given up resistance~~ / ~~Explains~~ ([something crossed out] A few times when I / Rita[2] she Mummy and I interpreted / [something crossed out] she tries in friendly way to / dissuade me: Recently / nevertheless I Rita[2] she Mummy – / then but I cannot speak / like that. – Or – now she has nevertheless / gone far away, I at home, / then I still cannot speak to her like / that. – Then puts on / some clothes (immediately succeeds in choosing / dress socks shoes, V / places great value on getting dressed / alone. Annoyed when has / to ask me for help. / Explains – I must stay / at home – she is going into big wide / world. – Then makes me take /

her over to balcony = station. / Must stay at home / she is going to Gloster/ When

also washing hands

comes back, says that she saw / horses at the station that were / so *p. 15a* wild that they smashed / people's windows and ate / them all up (Interpret also duck / watch-house bears = ate Mummies / = coitus damage horse = father / station = mother). – Makes me / wrap up small doll in / everything possible – more ribbons belts / etc. – (I also receive / a doll in my arm so we go / together to Frau Jer. – She / then tenderly pressing close / to me, also wants doll should press / close to me. V – Later she wants to go / into garden – I go with her, as / she [is][1] not to be restrained. She makes / me turn on tap water into / pail (said recently about water-tank / when noise after water flowing.) / But be quiet now, the tap / is already off and it is / no longer flowing, you should not

V Fetched Frau Jer. – states it / is 'Hans, with underground train' whom / she has put on chest of drawers. / (Interpret mother with penis.)

make such a racket) – / then wants secretly to take away / in front of *p. 16a* mother ~~pretty~~ [silver][1] spoon / – gives me from usual one / she – caught – also / gets one – stirring earth / in water. When she gets dress / dirty very anxious / immediately changes. Mother who / sees her (Rita[2] tries / to cover herself with curtain) / threatens half seriously half / joking – she laughs anxiously / at this – but as soon as we are / alone, hits ~~me~~ for it / Looks for dark little dress. / Interpret genitals made dirty. V./3/IX. – Tells me – greets most tenderly / we are going to a Frau Wespen / there we will buy wasps or bees. / We draw a picture of them – / then we go to Frau / Jer. – Then explains we are going / to a Herr 'Rote Grütze'.[vi] / He is a tradesman. Then ~~V~~

V no longer changing underwear. / Chooses dress fairly quickly / and in fact now for last few / days the same white one. / [written in the margin:] V has given up going away. Has a lot of work. Brings washboard and dolls, / wants to devote time to children

vi Translator's note: *Wespen* means 'wasps' and *Rote Grütze* means red fruit jelly or dessert.

p. 17a says dentist again V [– margin of previous page!][1] These destinations / constantly waver, are changed / while getting dressed etc. – Reluctant to / accept help from me – while I put / her shoes on she hits me. When / interpret aggression mother as switching / roles with her and did not want to let / her help me – strong aggression. IV / Says is going away, never coming back. / Goes to station Gloster – I / cannot come there with her / as Rita[2] as too stupid. – Then goes to duck-/ swing chauffeur is with her and steers. / Asks me to cover myself / with large cloth, not let it / hang out of the car because chauffeur / does not like that. Brings little rubber / doll and makes me dress it / in her / cap – then her little jacket – various / belts etc. Puts it in car and sets / off somewhere with it. – Terribly tender / with her – but very angry with me / as with naughty Rita[2] – does not / take me on journey with her etc. – Ask / what have done: I have smashed

> V. In journey preparations she packs / a cow bell – that she also needs when / driving to make a loud noise / She therefore packs it so that I / Rita[2] – am not to see it. (Interpret / mother who has hidden / father's member (he hers) inside her, does not let her see

> IV Says: – You should have been ill today and not / come (Her mother was ill that day

p. 18a a cup – she knows. – / Then again (Interpret genitals / broken by masturbation) / Then reconciled again, takes / me on journey with her. Has / bigger doll dressed in her / nightshirt and put in her bed. V / Blanket [at feet] turned down [rests][1] – so that / not she [nothing][1] does not fall out. / Also says doll has / rung bell. (Which she should not do / but does. Has also / called out for 2 weeks again now in evening / loudly although wakes up brother / also otherwise rather more mood / swings – but on / the whole, good kind / manageable, very lenient / and tender with little brother, / – distinctly 'good'. – Let / aunt wash her hair perfectly / well – not mother now.) / At end of session resistance / again.

> V (Interpret shows [something crossed out] in Rita[2] {wounded ?} / mother, how bad with her / true – but at same time is tender / towards little doll mother – as / good example – represents – gives / her own large genitals. / [written in margin:] V Also shows her the box with child inside that she made me draw. (Explanation that

326

she was denied) – In wrapping up doll places value (as previously) on her being able to look. (Interpret she wanted to watch father and mother herself.)

4/IX. – [Are][1] prevented from analysing / in child's room. – She says, *p. 19a* dirty there / cannot go. Makes me draw – / little box with child inside again – / brings books and postcards and points out / 1 boat to me. She would like to go to / Wertheim and buy 1 boat – then / she would travel to Herr / 'Rote Grütze'. – Later playing in sand. / Has prickled feet in grass. – / Will never walk on such horrible grass / again. Pricks like thorn. Thorn / that is on a cart. – (When interpret / thorn cart – bee phobia = penis / father's or mother's she / contradicts screaming, hitting me / as generally now expresses resistance very strongly and very / forcefully.) – Should go away should not / not speak. – Her little dress / had been dirty from playing in / sand; – she had told me this / when I came – but then | it does not matter, *p. 20a* can just / stay dirty. – After / thorn thing she explains / ~~must~~ wants to change little dress / becomes very anxious, cries / begs mother who because / brother ill cannot allow / her in the room, / only calms down when she promises / her to change dress again / before meal. – 5/IX. – Greets me / less happily. Looks through bag. / Changing clothes to Frau Jer. – / Wants to wash her feet. – / Does not change underwear again / although 'at night Frau Holda / was there'. This time chooses dress / with great difficulty, very indecisive. / Wants to get dressed alone – / do her hair. – Frau Jer. lives in / Lehmannstrasse not in / Stuhlstrasse {stool street}. She is not a / capable woman – no she | is very good at cooking. – I must / then dress the doll / in her *p. 21a* shoes socks dress, various / belts, she herself and doll. – At same time / secretly cuts up a ribbon / on one of her jackets in cupboard / states must sew herself a / new dress from this with needle. – / At beginning of session, had taken / a small picture off the wall / put in the bag and said / that is so she does not lose it. She / takes it to Frau Jer.'s house to a poor / little girl who has no / pictures. But also wants to take nail / out of wall in order to put / it up. (Interpret she herself at mother's house / poor girl that had no member / (drawing picture of wasps, taking it to / Frau Jer.) – she is good mother / who gives it. – Goes with doll / to car – I Rita[2] must stay / at home. – (Interpret nicely dressed doll | she herself her genitals. – Little rabbit should / go to *p. 22a* dentist. – I Rita[2] mother on / whom she takes revenge. – Lets me / go with her then too. – Then / goes on chair = car. Great / ceremonials.

327

Many blankets that / may not drag behind because / chauffeur does not like / that. – Has seatbelt done up / so that does not fall out / because car so fast. – (When interpret father fast in mother / with member – Hans underground / train – she confirms: Yes, the under- / ground train goes fast. / Immediately afterwards she / wants to draw little box / with child, brings extra / good pencil from father's writing / desk. Asks for big / box in which dog and / cat also inside (Interpret driving / car = coitus – drawing / – pencil = penis – is making child. |

p. 23a She confirms: 'Yes, I want to make a child'. / – Meanwhile when angry with me knocked / chair over says: naughty Doctor. / Keeps switching between chair and / table – in garden turns round / in circles – wonderfully. Tremendously / active and lively. – 6/IX. Very friendly / again. Goes to Dodenstrasse / to a Frau Dode. Then 'Frau tote'.[vii] / When I ask is that dead woman – she: / Yes she is dead – but she is not / yet buried. ~~Takes~~ Makes as if / to take shovel and spade / now I am burying you. A bit / later asks me if I am unwell / (mother had greeted me with this question / because looked bad) / Had said about Frau Dode = extremely / nice, has only 1 girl – (child) / cooks for herself. (Interpret death wishes / me, mother). Immediately afterwards wants / to urinate. Shows me

p. 24a underwear dirty / – (~~wet~~ rather mucky from stool) must | change. – When asked who / did this: she (evasively) at / Irene's house. Repeat question who did it [? she overwritten]. / She hesitates – 'The grandma'. – Interpret / is shifting guilt getting dirty / on to mother as with masturbation. – / Changes underwear but only undershirt / – ~~pulls it up~~ and puts on dress – / shoes and socks. Pulls up under- shirt / cuddles up to me – shows / her genitals – when I interpreted dirtied / genitals – therefore new undershirt, dress / wants to please mother. Interpret exhibitionism / and wants acknowledgement – is pleased however. – / Showers old one-armed doll with / tenderness gets me to dress her in / her clothes. – Goes with her / in the car, with Herr Schülke / driving them – I Rita[2] must stay / at home. – Says has brought / Frau Jer. with her. Quickly lays / table. – Puts 3 large bricks

immediately after shame looking at toilet / stool – she wants to put on / new velvet dress. (Interpret)

---

vii Translator's note: *Tote* means 'dead person'.

(before this struck hammer on floor) on table. / One contains *p. 25a*
salt – says always / falls over when salt came out – / second apple
jelly – third coke. – / People only think that coke does not taste /
good – in fact tastes very good. / Pours me some tea. (dirty / earthy
water from a toy saucepan / spills on cloth. Laughing bites when /
I say – done poo dirtied mother = / cloth – [something crossed
out] (Interpret content the / hammer – she has member – thus /
dirtied mother with semen urine, stool – / as thought father did. –
Had addressed / me as Frau Jer. but / put oilcloth on table for me –
so that / do not dirty cloth. (Interpret makes / mother the child,
revenge her / treatment.) – Then wants to change shoes / again. – At
same time while I help her / kicks both feet constantly / towards
my genitals. – | Speaks very quietly / to me. Is a bear and I should / *p. 26a*
be afraid. At same time kicks / her feet. – Says [she][1] was afraid of
bear / but it is also a friendly bear / and called her over. – (Interpret
father / who kicks foot = little / Pip-hammer – she wanted him to
have it done / to herself – but at same time afraid.} She / wants
father identification [?] to do it with / mother.) She then jumps /
constantly in and out of / the cupboard. When interpret = continu-/
ation – she said into the / cupboard – out of cupboard [two parallel
horizontal lines drawn] / into Mummy [letter crossed out] out of /
Mummy – she agrees and / then constantly sings [herself][1] – (also /
the next day in session / into Mummy – out of / Mummy. — She
tells mother / then she immediately / continued: into cupboard – /
out of cupboard – looks | at me with understanding at same *p. 27a*
time. Never told / a detail from analysis. – At end changes / dress and
shoes again. But chooses / more quickly. – 7./VIII.IX. Says we are
going to: 30 / balls. Wants to go to a department store and / buy
balls then she wants / to play ball with Frau Jer. so that she throws / it
and she rolls it back while / they sit on the floor rolling out from /
genitals shows. (Interpret ball V and remind ball with spiral / – she
called candlestick – bitten.) She / strongly agrees and remembers.
– She / goes to Wertheim and lady will give / her balls. – Brings
her doll clothes / in order to dress one-armed doll in them. / At
this she says she is a saleswoman. / (Interpret she mother – equips
small child / with large genitals, just as she / wants balls from
Wertheim.) She herself / only changes shoes and dress and / fairly
quickly. – Says, is taking her / 'pipi' (with her to doll) (Interpret =
little / pipi-hammer = genitals – leaves / me Rita[2] = child at home.)
Therefore

at first interpret as angry: throws shoe / after me. Interpret shoe = ball = penis

p. 28a carefully dressing doll. Passes her / dirty little dress to me as / Rita² – precise differentiation / between genitals and child.) / Yesterday she had taken / the little dog with her on journey / tied it up at gate once / she had arrived at / Frau Jer. – Today she / is taking cat with her – on / both days suitcase. Again / kicks feet towards my / genitals while swinging high / on chair and at same time / spits, spits at me. – / [When yesterday that]¹ behaved like bear = (When interpreted / seen father doing that – / she: she saw a / station with lots of trains.) / Then she was in Backerstrasse / there Frau Backer showed / her a

p. 29a dachshund made of / wood. She saw it very | deep in Grünewald.ᵛⁱⁱⁱ Interpret coitus / observations. – When ask Backerstrasse / was she also there? She: Yes she was / in there – then water sprite / came and helped her out of / there. (Interpret mother's womb and birth.) / Fetched Frau Jer. (again went / with chauffeur – had also written / her letter recently, wants / to go with me again.) – I am Frau / Jer. – thinks I had already eaten – / eats alone with doll. – Again picks up / hammer: jelly, coke – third is small town / when you pour from it = 'cake / comes out of there'. V – (When interpret / has coitus with little hammer and Mummy / also does poo = apple jelly in her) / She: 'But I don't have a little hammer / I: yes, but you would like to have one – / She: no I would not like one – a little / hammer bites. When I still had 1 old / little hammer yesterday, it bit. / (Interpret biting duck

p. 30a etc. and penis / wish. | After meal explains: we are going to / sleep together. Sits down / on a chair beside me to sleep. / Then resistance sets in [spits on me and hits]¹. – She sleeps / alone – sits down with chair by / her bed. – Afterwards stands up – / says must quickly darn sock / – because getting hole. Fetches needle / and thread and sews a sock. / Also changes dress. (Interpret / anger mother did not sleep with her and / have coitus. Masturbation – anxiety / damaged genitals. Hence sewing / sock and changing dress.) Fierce / resistance. – Also changes doll's clothes. / Puts on sewn sock / 8/IX. – At first eating – then changing / clothes – to Frau Jer. – changing / doll's dress because moths / got into it. Ask how: a / boy no lots of boys did

p. 31a / it. – Moths also got / into her dress: – from the coach | that came to them from Wertheim. / Brought coachman (Interpret moths = /

---

viii Grünewald is a district of Berlin.

wasps – picture thing.) Meanwhile she / takes picture from wall and [something crossed out] / puts into bag. – Changes shoes / socks dress. I should put / [her][1] ~~big~~ red knitted jacket on doll / underneath – over it some / nappies and ribbons that hold them in place. / Recently almost always sings / instead of speaking. – She keeps changing / shoes, socks. – 10/IX. – Wants to / go to a man to buy herself / a kite or a car. V The / man is a patient of Dr Gisell [?] – / (When interpret = father who has coitus with mother – car = / member = underground train). She emphatically (resistance / generally much reduced) Yes, I could really do with / an underground train. – Takes off / shoes and socks – shows me, she has / ~~leg there~~ – a small pimple that her

V in journey preparations suitcase etc. also puts / 3 small pictures from wall into my / bag

shoemaker who made her new shoes made / with his long needle.   *p. 32a*
(Interpret / father damage coitus) she runs to / her bed shows me that the bell / has broken off and says she was / so 'sad' in the mornings when she woke up / and saw that. (Interpret damage masturbation.) / Wants to change her clothes although has new velvet / dress and new shoes on for first time. – Kicks / feet towards me again so that / she also swings high [in the][1] chair / while holding armrest with her hands. / Spits at same time. (When interpret little pip / hammer = penis, spitting what comes / out of it) she says Frau H. told Aunt / E. her head is always taken up with money. / (Interpret something [coitus something [?]][1] comes out from head / mouth) She: yes, not at the back / – (points) – but there (genitals) / and there (anus) something / comes out. (When I ask what / then) she: 'But you know that'. / (Interpret stool, child and semen) / She changes dress (shoes, / socks) several times | ~~a few~~ – but chooses quickly. / Changing doll's   *p. 33a*
clothes – then undresses again / considers – says: 'Holes in those' – / next room, fetches a nail file / – at first tries a bit in children's room – / then goes with doll and file into / bedroom. When ask what doing there – slightly / embarrassed. Then murmurs 'going / to doctor'. – Eating again – I Frau Jer. – / 11/IX. – Says is going to a tower. / Then: going to visit me, tower is / at my house. – Undresses doll, must / change her clothes – showing me a small / injury to arm, then to foot, – / (when interpret damage little hammer) a / small hole hidden under hair – that / she got when she ran into wall. / (Interpret head

331

little hammer, – washing hair / – her anxiety coitus castration complex.) – / undresses doll so completely naked, shows / me has a proper bottom. When reply / but not proper slit, because there also / little

p. 34a button etc. – she begins to | play with purse – shows me how / can be opened and closed – there / is also 1 button and 1 small hole. / (Interpret shape genitals.) – ~~Gets / me {to put on her} shoes~~ Tells me doll was / naughty: made cake / got dirty with / poo and played with purse. / (Interpret her original ~~clock~~ crime[ix] – she = / doll, also mother.) – Says shoes / were naughty – have pinched something / wanted to take the clock away. / At same time begins to wind my / clock. – Quickly gets herself / dressed – chooses 1 blue and 1 / red sock. – Places most importance / on [dressing]^1 doll. – Puts into bed / 'naked' – at first on blanket, then / makes her stand up. – Also says meanwhile / that doll is ill. – / Then that she has slept / Then constantly sleeping / and getting dressed – especially carefully / early

p. 35a in the morning. Gets dressed – completely | clean etc. – also Peter's socks – (interpret / masturbation, afterwards getting dressed = changing damaged / dirtied genitals.) ~~Then~~ also herself. / Wanted to put on Peter's socks. – Takes / apron herself (refused for months / recently to mother's surprise / occasionally taken) and goes to cook. Takes / boxes etc. and looks for stirring / for a rubber ball with an extension / inside [?] and a bell. Says – fire / comes out of it – when stirs / (Interpret ball – ball with spiral = / penis – fire and at same time loud noise.) – Says immediately / – after she has dressed doll she is / taking her with her to tower – she puts her / on table, she should watch. – Points out to / me small wicker armchair – that is tower. / (When remind [something crossed out] knocked chair over = naughty / Dr Klein – laughs a lot, points at / other small chair (constantly switched / between that and table – at treatment / climbed

p. 36a hesitantly on to it) and says: that / is also Dr Klein. Then climbs | very carefully on to chair – looks / around – but is anxious soon / comes down, very quietly. – Says does / not want to climb up any more because / so high tower got tired. Saw / many houses there. – (Interpret climbing tower = / coitus.) Later puts chair / by cupboard, constantly climbs on to it / very skilfully – in recent sessions / generally still much more active / movements and more skilful. – / Makes me press my end of / chair = alarm – then immediately / goes to the

---

ix Translator's note: *Uhrverbrechen:* the German prefix 'Ur' means original but 'Uhr', as Klein first wrote it, means clock or watch.

door. – Had shown / me a few sessions earlier / scratched herself on this chair / in the session (nothing to see) / – and hit me for it. / Generally with injuries ~~blam~~ always blames and / then hits me. – Meanwhile / also drove car with duck- /cart. – While eating, when she | has put everything out and is putting / a brick to mouth – <u>ask</u> *p. 37a* <u>what she is eating</u>: / 'A shepherd boy'. – Another time / a lollipop-Suse. – (Interpret is eating penis – / small boy in hunting dress – picture / that bit.) 12/IX. Wants to go to Zehlendorf. She is Mummy – dog Purzel / is father – they travel together because in / Zehlend. a lovely bowl broke V / & she wants to repair it. To a Frau / Prech ('brechen' {break}!); following the name / as usual then much that completely in- / comprehensible (Prech instead of 'Brech' {break} like Dode instead of 'Tote' {dead person} / and further displacement then this completely incomprehensible) / Afterwards talks about her too as Frau / Dode – says that she was ill is / well again now, is very nice. – Wants to put on / secretly [something crossed out] one of her mother's forbidden / beautiful dresses that are in / bedroom – her own – chooses / a white one without thinking. – / Sits down in car with this and goes.

V Someone has pressed an alarm

Says does not need a chauffeur / moves cart back and forth herself / *p. 38a* 'can drive alone'. – Then / climbs on duck-cart moves / it, while constantly saying / 'gabi, gibi, gobi, gubi' – / generally lots of 'i', 'a' and 'o' sounds – talks / the whole session meanwhile constantly / completely eloquent / incomprehensible – but a kind of / fluent speech that / increases with it. Accompanied by activity / and I thus interpret – (speaking incomprehensibly / = at same time with coitus) / ~~Immediately~~ takes off dress, says / wants another one – but then undresses / so completely naked – / shows herself to me from every / side, cuddles up to me / wants to be admired like this / Explains does not need dress / wants to stay like that. – ~~Wants to~~ | Then looks for a *p. 39a* clothes-peg and a hair-/pin and goes naked – half / secretly with them into bedroom. – Admits / then with resistance – she sat / down there on father's bed and pulled at / her hair with the / peg (shows head). (Interpret secret / masturbation, exhibitionism in front of father and father masturbation / phantasies.) Lies down in bed says / is ill – then no only wants to sleep / wants to be completely naked – no night-shirt / no blanket. – Net for cot can stay / open – to shut later though. – After / getting up wants to be dressed carefully, tidied / hair – clean dress, socks / shoes – but only few underclothes, bodice / enough (exhibitionism still coming through here) / (Interpret that and also after masturbation and night phantasies / clean and pretty dress – repairs genitals.) / Repeats this procedure – sleeping / getting dressed – a few times, also ties / on girl's apron. (Interpret contented

p. 40a with female genitals. | 13/IX. – Drives to a Frau Pracht[x] – / agr [ees][1] = splendid – at her house / she gets poppy seed, they will / eat it together, then it / is embroidered on little dress. – / Then also talks about Frau / Wespen. Quickly takes / a very simple dress – but / also wants long white / stockings like mine. Does not want / to be helped with socks / and shoes although sees herself / that has put them on wrong. / Striking also how places / no importance on fastening / socks – although keep / falling down. – Changes / underwear – but only / puts on a bodice that she / brings down so that – shows me laughing / that her whole / stomach – (points at navel and genitals

p. 41a / is showing) and a dress over it. Suddenly wants | to take it off & be completely naked. Shows / herself to me seductively from every side. / Runs to balcony taking a / hair-slide, a manicure stick / on balcony puts it in / genitals, pressing and masturbating / at first opens genitals to / show it – shows me that / Peter has urinated on balcony & / urinates also in another / place. After masturbating / shouts over to neighbour Frau Dr G. / to come over to see, she is naked / also to seamstress in the room / is completely transformed as in / a frenzy. Keeps turning round / laughing etc. – Then with bricks / begins (after had masturbated / [with][1] hair-slide etc.) to build / builds a town – mountains etc. / Meanwhile grabs a brick

p. 42a puts / it between legs – shows me what | she has there. While building / sitting on floor she pushes a few / bricks against her genitals / presses them and says: If / they get broken, I have / some more. – She takes a long / brick pushes it under / genitals, rides on it – grabs / then suddenly dog, pushes / it between legs that she presses / very tightly together rides / on it and visibly has orgasm. / Makes dog / lick her body (unclear whether also [at other times][1] / on genitals?) At my wish / she sends dog away – follows / me albeit reluctantly also / with bricks into room. / There she builds houses again / shows

p. 43a me there must be | enough space between them for a person to / be

---

x Translator's note: *Pracht* means 'splendour, magnificence'.

able to get in there. Then moves with it all / into sun, at first enjoys the / warmth – suddenly explains too hot – / it burns. Interpret naked coitus with / father's burning member. She then wants / immediately to put on some play-trousers / – strong resistance (goes into the garden) / When came in from balcony shows / me 'little hammer' (foot) dirty / ~~wants~~ washes them, then rubs them a bit / with something, wants to tie on herself a long / strip of material with ribbons / to rub with – then explains must / dust herself down – dabs / her stomach and genital area with / feather duster lying there, also wipes / duster over them again. – 14/IX. Wants to go to Frau Jer. to fetch / picture-books that she wants to read out to me – / Rita[2]. Changing clothes for this. – Takes / long brown socks. When asked | why? – Because she will get so tired / from reading, then / her knee will hurt / is so sensitive there. Changes / only very quickly 1 ordinary dress – / then wants to change clothes / but takes all her clothes off. / As on day before runs naked / on to balcony, takes 1 safety- / pin (closed) 1 hair-pin / 1 nail-file out, puts file / between genitals, then a / brick between them – explains / now has something like Peter / below. When asked to come over, / immediately, – she only wants to do that / there. Calls over again / that she is naked. – Lets me / bring her into room sits / there continuing excited state. / Jumps up cheers spins around. – / Does poo on duck then up | Calls out at window to maid / to look at her, she is a naked little child. Then / calls dog Purzel to look at her / she is naked. [(Interpret exhibitionism father mother)][1] V asks to get / dressed only puts on / bodice, chooses very thin white one, / goes back to window / calls out again to both: she is already now a 'dressed little child' [?]. – (When I interpret / also exhibiting dressed – through thin / dress genitals are visible – asks / for apron over it and wants to run / away from me. When I remind wanted / to fetch books from Frau Jer. – brings / books. ~~Fet~~ Begins to read, fetches / scissors and at first wants to cut / shirt – then fetches goat / and trims his hair. Then / reads again, says goat = / Frau Jer. – Soon afterwards / resistance again – runs into / next room where seamstress – / wants to show me that can / use sewing machine – then / wants with needle and thread 1 piece

p. 44a

p. 45a

V Lies down on blanket again / in sun – says are sun-/faces there. Dr. Giesell [?] has sun-/flowers in garden. She is ill and / has a compress round her neck. / (Interpret sun-face = coitus – mother /

ill from this – therefore anxiety exhibitionism / constantly changes clothes after direct sunlight)

p. 46a material with pattern that says / = houses – to make a shirt. / But mainly snips with scissors / at material that has put around neck. / When cut goat's hair / also cut a small piece of book V / (Interpreted after exhibitionism anxiety / cannot have / coitus mother – cuts her / member.) – 16/IX. Greets very / happily. – Wants to go to market / and shop, so changing clothes / – From bedroom cupboard forbidden / dress – [something crossed out] pink ~~1 white~~ / sock. – While taking off shoes / goes to urinate in bathroom. – At same time / tells me: ~~tha el~~ the electric / switch broken, pulled / off, because the dachshund / pressed, bit the alarm and / broke it. At same time / she looks at me understandingly

Cuts her own nails / and manicures them – also recently / when wanted to cut so many / things, cut her nails then

p. 47a and says: 'But you know – the / dachshund!' (She repeatedly / refers now to results of earlier / sessions – her listening to / interpretations and understanding of these / also coming out now very clearly) / Adds to this: (again with this facial expression) / the duck has also kept / eating the bear's / watch-house. – Then asks for another dress / – very anxious when while undressing, which / she immediately asks for again, does / not go easily over head. – Goes to market and / brings in 1 box a small / wooden ball – hole [?]: that is red fruit – 1 little bottle / with cotton wool inside = milk. (When I interpret / buying member [something crossed out]) she very angry / wants to break something off small car / Then takes back down from wall / pictures that she bought. / At same time she says, she now has 8/3/5/ 17 – which she (as often already) / expresses with obvious / feeling of

p. 48a power – means something very | big. – Then hangs [them][1] 3 / (small) pictures on 1 nail – / states there should be a few / there – also at handle of Peter's / small clothes cupboard – then / on duck-cart [on the cross bar][1] so that they hang from / both sides of the head and beak / ~~on this as 1 cross-bar over~~ / – Then small / car cart – then / back with me and buys / milk there also – makes me / take cotton-wool out of it / (Interpret mother's breast – penis – / milk semen). – Undresses completely / naked – supposedly prettier / dress again, but then / stays naked. Jumps around / again, wants to go to balcony / but stays at my wish / in room. – Goes to sleep – completely / naked at first wants to put on / small apron but stays naked shows | me can get into bed by herself – / also put foot in chest (interpret / coitus). – Takes out her small monkey / caresses it tenderly – takes / her dear beloved little monkey with her / into bed – tells him: 'You can / hurt me'. When asked: how / then, she claps her hands / firmly on her belly and hips. (Interpret / father's genitals, naked coitus.) / She then throws little monkey aside, stands / up and puts on two unmatching / socks. Reason: wants to have one light / and 1 darker foot (interpret a non-aroused / and an aroused member). Then / without under-clothes, does not put on / pretty dress. Strong resistance, wants / to go into garden – as usual when / I clear away does not wait for me / (resistance to my clearing away.) / Father who has seen her naked, rather | curtly in her presence orders / her to get dressed because she might / get a cold. – She violent / scream crying and in fact not / because father displeased but / keeps shouting: Aunt Emma / will be angry, will not / love me. (When want / to interpret fear mother also father / because exhibits has coitus with / father in phantasy) very fearful rejects / am never to talk about little hammer / again. Flees to mother. – / On arrival she had / told me the doll Magare / ill. Must have her / examined by doctor. Allows / me (only reluctantly because cannot / do this alone) to undress her / at same time suddenly explains: [something crossed out] / you are a strange person / and thinks does not like me / can go. Ask what have | done: have not examined doll. / When asked why such lovely socks / because she can then examine / doll better with thermometer / (interpret foot = penis – doll / her – for her, I mother with whom in-/dignant because did not have coitus with her.) / Again resistance dissolved. Had / already shown me aversion to caterpillar / in garden. Did not want to / walk on steps, because caterpillar crawling on other / side. – While getting undressed showed / me with sign of disgust and fear / caterpil-lar on wall. Says that she / was stung in mouth by bee / while eating cake. When interpret caterpillar also / moves its sting like bee / she anxiously no caterpillar does not / move. (When interpret caterpillar = bee / = little hammer, wish fear / father coitus – movement) she goes / up to wall and watches | caterpillar moving. Afterwards / shows no disgust. – 18/IX. / In ~~eve~~ afternoon had said / to mother: Frau Klein always / talks to me about little hammer and / I find it unpleasant. / Made a second similar / remark. / In the evenings she asks for (last few / evenings has also usually / only let mother cover

p. 49a

p. 50a

p. 51a

p. 52a

her up without tucking her in – as with aunt / for several weeks now) mother to put her to bed again so / that blanket placed / under feet, completely folded in. / – She greeted me today much more quietly / not pleased at all but goes with / me without contradiction. Asks / me to take 'flower' / out of apple for her with knife (part that has / grown

p. 53a at the top) – Changing clothes | because wants to have small rabbit / (picture on wall). Wants to buy it from 1 / woman. For me, Rita[2] to play with. / But cannot give it to me because / needs herself. ~~To the~~ She needs it as / thermometer, also a knife / for taking 'the flower' / out of the apple and 1 needle / for crocheting mother's / belt (Interpret ~~picture~~ = small rabbit and picture = / all these toys = ~~genit~~ little / hammer remind wasps picture.) She happy: / yes, I want to go over to Frau Wespen. / Says wants to go to station into hospital / to fetch ill (operated) [something crossed out] cook. / States doll ill. When interpreting / she had gone off to naughty / – (doll) Magare. Hits / her and puts finger in her / navel. – Has an old electric plug / with lead. Says is her telephone receiver. Wants / to go with this and doll to another room – / but then hides in corner behind / cupboard – there

p. 54a puts on plug | was ill, now well. / Then she ill herself. Undressing / for bed. Little suitcase = hot-water bottle / puts it under legs. Wants / to stay naked, but then night- /shirt. – Explains: is sweating but / I may not look. Afterwards / getting up – goes to / small bench to radiator – turns heating device / = water tap and bath / rubs down – clean, gets dressed, but / no shirt only dress. + V Ill / again – [something crossed out] the same / [as before][1] only humming top under / legs. Says [top][1] cannot make such a good / noise because has no / string but does not want to have / string put on it. Shows me / at holes how can (from / bell) fill humming top with / water, then water comes / out of there warm. / (When interpret = father's member coitus) / obviously understands – shows me

[In left-hand margin is marked: + + next page / V (0)]

p. 55a a small red mark on chest: Papa did / that to me then. Asks me later / about spot on chest who poked / me there. Allows herself after bathing and drying (immediately {rubbed ?}) at my / encouragement to be fully dressed – socks / but not helped although sees wrong way round / says: 'There is one end at front – one end / at the back too only shoes. V (Sits down / on duck-cart [chauffeur there too][1] and rolls back and forth. Says / has got ill from lots of rolling. / Gets undressed again) previous page. / Sits down again, on duck-cart / takes out a vertical / board – expresses great pity / for poor duck, because she took the board / away from it and says – poor duck / is so sad because had to leave/ his lovely young woman in / Wertheim. – Then takes / her slippers says 1 = Papa / the other Mum – puts them on / duck-cart and makes them drive. | (Interpret castration father – *p. 56a* separates / father from mother when she / drives cart = having coitus – hence / remorse and union mother and father. – / – Interpret illness thing in reverse / order: at first exhibitionism – through this / coitus with father – made ill by this = / coitus quiet – then recently coitus / with birth Easter rabbit. – That [? something overwritten] while / sweating with hot-water bottle and spinning top / had to go away – as with treating doll / was not allowed to see, interpret secretly / masturbating in front of mother – having coitus / with father.) 18/IX. 2nd session on same / day. – Find her crying loudly because / mother not giving her sewing silk she / wanted. Comes although not / as happily as before / father incident. – Explains must first change / clothes for sewing. – Mainly / cuts out the material – then / also sews in between. – Goes away / – is Miss L. who is permitted to leave and / collects 1 girl friend. When while | driving on duck-cart she knocks *p. 57a* into / edge of cupboard – she / says I did that. Likewise when / near bed and table – every time / she moves more forcefully and knocks herself / she hits or scolds me. – / I did it (mother says as very / small child never spoke like this.) / Asks to do poo – wants it – had / said before going to Frau Jer. – / either on floor of / room or duck. At my request she / goes – but certainly thereby already / with resistance – with me into bath-/room, knocks into edge of table / and runs screaming loudly – that I / did that – to mother. Takes / rest of cup of milk to play with, ties on / apron – pours on to / saucer – stirs big brick / around inside it – throws in the pieces of material / that has cut – 1 garter | hair ribbon. Says ~~herself~~ [spontaneously]^{1} / about *p. 58a* [material]^{1} remnants etc. – it belongs to / Frau Dode. Recognises = dead woman V / V and says: the dead woman is now being / cooked and cut to pieces [and eaten]^{1} At same time / she washes small sock etc. / and winds it. Also says dead woman / is washed and wrung out. / At same time she drinks some dirty / water licks brick / and wet things – also 1 brick / that she then throws in too / Pulls socks and things out / and shows me on lower part / of sock that is the mouth / of ~~Frau~~ dead [? something overwritten] woman. – While sewing / [beginning of session]^{1} at first she had said – [she]^{1} is sewing / a 'cake-

339

bottle'. – Says herself / cake – also bites flask bottle / afterwards wants to cook. – [Something crossed out] / and changing clothes. – Goes with / me [as]¹ Rita² to Frau Jer. back into / corner 2 doors where / crouch down so that are covered

Frau Dode cannot cook as well / as she can. She does not cook it so that there is / so much meat in it. At same time / shows bow hair-ribbon etc. / as meat. Then spontaneously V

p. 59a by clothes. Then takes / cup of milk and begins to cook. / While stirring calls out from the / window: Purzel, I am cooking so / nicely for you and Dr Klein. / Also says while stirring and blowing. / 'It is really nice of me / to cook so well for you' – / wants at beginning of cooking / explains, needs something, runs / to bathroom and fetches loo / paper. Explains that loo-roll / holder (wooden device from / which you can pull out / loo paper) is a 'Frau Dowe'. / She is very sad because / the loo was sold to her. / She then mixes the loo paper / in as she stirs and / cooks. Bites and licks greedily / at all these things, drinks wa-/ter etc. – Afterwards when wrings / things out, she

p. 60a wants to throw them | out of window (leaving stool – guest-house [?] / witch at Erich's house window. Throws things / out.) (Interpret killing incorporating / mother – eating stool, member / milk, urine – milk cup mother's / breast – finally giving to / mother as child as stool) / – Later called to account / by aunt for wet dress / says: has been gargling. – / 19/IX. Still reserved / – but then goes away from / girl friend and over [? something overwritten] to me. / Goes to see a patient who / is rather ill. Wants to / cure him like doll (yester-day) / looks for electric milk-heater for this / – says, makes it so that / she [turns on and]¹ turns in front part. – / Changing clothes thin white / dress (from bedroom) two unmatching / shoes. Says Frau

p. 61a Jerus. | (Journey to patient immediately given up / when cannot find milk-heater at once.) / will say: but Rita,² you / are so elegant – have two unmatching / shoes on. Later asks: is / the shoe really a hammer. V / + Tonight I saw / Mummy's and Father's hammer. – / (When I interpret earlier – and she in bed / ft small woman fright-ened) she: / 'But I also laughed / a lot'. – Insists on putting / socks and shoes by herself; – lets / me dress her, but still / gets angry at this and hits. – / Asks me as chauffeur whether / will take her with me – whether still passenger. / When I say there is room – she says does not want to / maybe tomorrow – fetches from / next room big umbrella goes / like this to Frau Jer. – But is soon / tired of this, says ill, undresses – not

V Says she wants to go to cart [for milk][1], / barefoot – is better that way. (Then interpret bare / hammer – in Mummy-: +

in chest – then takes small / suitcase = hot-water bottle [?] – again / *p. 62a* rather secretively – says / sweated elegantly – then must / again wants to place / [red][1] leather (small piece) / on stomach. – Stands up / explains: 'very elegant' – but wants / to dress very elegantly to / go to lovely Frau Jer. / Has a bath – dries off. Shows me a / a ~~red~~ place on her chest: / 'Papa was rather clumsy / and put the little hammer in / so that the little end / of the hammer stayed / in there. When I ask where: 'He / has already taken it away again / – Also changes clothes again / [~~to Jer.~~][1] – indecisive, V then suddenly / wants to cook: 1 milk soup / with noodles in: again / ribbons, garter – / bodice – (tries small knitted jacket) – / Says spontaneously Frau Dode cooks

also urinating / V

Fierce resistance, ~~t~~ {then} runs / up the [? something overwritten] *p. 63a* stairs – asking to dress / doll – plans journey to Frau / Jer: ineffective. When asked / sewing – [but][1] comes back. But / tries to cut chair fabric with / scissors – to cut pieces from / dress mother is working on – desperate because / I cannot give her 1 piece / of material embroidered with flowers. / Wants to sew in garden, ~~w~~ {while} constantly / shredding material. Follow her into garden / and interpret [whispering][1] (electrician nearby / is adjusting bell) – that she is still cutting up / shredded cooked mother / but then makes her well again. / Resistance dissolved follows me into / room – sews and cuts. / Then asks to change / clothes again – hits me while / [putting on][1] socks – wants to go to / Frau Jer. – On way to Frau / Jer (beginning of session) she asks | me as conductor to keep / punching her ticket. – *p. 64a* Asks for / '2nd class, capitalist', – 2nd class / Europe, 2nd class Ora [?] – 2nd class Nuremberg. / Exhilarated by foreign words / like capitalist. – Constantly / speaks incomprehensibly – ~~but like this when~~ / and in fact also when she does not know / something. Recognises the colours white, / red, pink – confuses blue, green, / black. – With colours that she does not / know – often also gives incomprehensible / names. – Likewise with things to eat / that has put on table – / now

341

and then utters incomprehensible / numbers also with sense of power / – makes doll go down steps / counts 5, 7–8, 12, 15 – when cooked / today and says milk-noodle / soup says – is the [milk][1] cups / Mummy's breast? What / nonsense! – When cooking first milk-thing / began by pouring Laxol-powder [?] / into milk – wants to make / *p. 65a* Laxol-milk [?] Shouted that out from | window as well. – 20/IX. Changing clothes (makes do / as bedroom firmly locked / with 1 dress from own room) thin / white dress. Journey town to Frau / Jer: takes me Rita[2] with her / driving chairs – train – 1 man / made room for me. – Soon explains = ill / undressing —— is going to bed, looks / first in chest takes nothing out / explains is already well again / and has slept it off. She was not / at all ill and has also not / had hot-water bottle [?]. – She 'bathes' / on bench by hot air vent and tells / me: Papa was very nice. He / forgot to put the little / hammer into me. I did / not sweat at all. – While getting dressed / needs 'poo' – through on to floor / or duck – then makes me carry / her naked wrapped in towel ~~to~~ into / bathroom – does not want / to go to loo but children's *p. 66a* bath / with water inside. – Also to | carry her back again in my arms, says is / little Peter. – While putting on (until / now very affectionate) socks / she hits me. (Interpret does not / want to have Mummy's little slit / made again for her, wants to have another / one herself) V Then she asks for / my watch pleads / passionately. (Interpret wanted mother's / genitals from her – hence anger / when putting on socks.) showed / me 1 caterpillar on door, that / is moving. (When interpret little / hammer that moves in Mummy) – / she laughs goes closer and walks on without / sign of disgust. – Then / pulls out doll dressed as / her – takes her secretly / to chest and treats her / there with milk-heater. Then immediately / takes off apron and goes / 'to cook' H in picture-cube / (small box) water, puts / material etc. back in

V also furious because she small child / mother's help. – She – almost crying – 'I / am not a small child, now I am / sad'. 'H' At first says cooking me and Frau / Jer. – then cooking <u>for</u> me and / Frau Jer.

p. 67a ~~wants~~ stirs with toothbrush, puts on / tooth-powder, wants to pour things in / from various jugs and bowls. / With great passion / mixes, stirs and licks. – Asks me / as Rita[2] if I know why she always / {wears} cap when travelling: 'To keep / her head warm'. – Says: 'Give [me][1] dresses / underwear, bodices, vests!' 20/IX. – / Embraces and kisses me while combing. / But at mother's request may not / change clothes because has cold. – But wants / to do this as soon as we are alone. – / But then agrees puts on thin white dress / chosen [by her][1] over other one / (refusals now also more possible / in analysis – previously extreme resistance work / broken off. – In life according to mother / tolerates refusals very well) / Now changes socks shoes V chooses / because wants to cover / ink spot (recognises / little hammer poo) [on][1] leg / long socks. Says ink colour is / green, then black (in fact blueish) / Calls destination Udapuda (something like that / then Nollendorf. Takes me Rita[2]

V at first chooses sock with blueish border / says is taking socks with stripes, 4, 13

with her we go to see a man / 43. At first says is an old / gentleman,   *p. 68a* then no, is not old / Dr Simmel. He is a doctor for / calves [?] – he looks a bit [something crossed out] / ~~dr~~ doll has drunk ~~and why~~ / ~~it her~~ and what has harmed / her. – When dressed – and I ask / if we are going. No, we could / not, it would be too late – / conductor has been eating / supper so long, he had to and / then we could not go / any more. Supper salted / tea that took from picture / hanging on wall. – Also / ate something like what we / cooked. ~~Also ate Frau~~ (when / asked if also ate Frau Dode) / 'Yes, he ate dead woman. First / he killed her like this / (clenches teeth forcefully / together) then he cooked / and ate her up. (Interpret | eating (biting duck) = having   *p. 69a* coitus / father ate had coitus mother – there-/fore Dr. Simmel and conductor = father no / time for her and she dares not / go to him to have coitus. – / Gives money to me as Rita[2] I should / go to cart, take care / not to get run over / am to fetch milk from 'Herr / Gula' [?] / 'Herr Milch', 'Herr / Bolle'. Then says Herr Bolle / did not take any money for it. – Then / puts money in a little box with handle- /like extension – speaks to it as / 'Herr Hörer'[xi] and tells me to / go to Herr Hörer and give / him money for milk V – When little / chair falls on her – she explains / to me – ~~I m~~ Rita[2] I may / knock chair over, but to be / careful, not to turn it completely upside down, / or it will be damaged – Herr Bolle / would be angry then (Interpret coitus mother / careful – fear father's objection.) Sits

---

xi   Translator's note: 'Herr Milch' literally means 'Mr Milk' and *Hörer* means a telephone receiver; the name 'Bolle' may contain a reference to the cart (*Bollewagen*).

V Telephones a Frau 'Eia' about eggs / and Herr Bäck[xii] about milk

p. 70a down sideways on upturned chair, / states is a money-counting chair / because can count money so well / like this. – ~~Put~~ Suddenly explains / I must go begins putting / everything carefully back in its place (When / I interpret fear coitus mother anal / that she does not allow) she comes / back, explains ill tired / goes to bedroom ~~secretly~~ (I / not to go with her) lies down on mother's / bed – I should go out. – / Then looks for 1 stamp in / drawer stuffs it into key-hole / says that is where key belongs. / – Suddenly explains stomach pains / (also had these again / before.) does not let me take / her to loo, to aunt – has / no stool but tells her she / does not want to play with me. / But when invited comes to sew. / (When interpret afraid of mother

p. 71a because / bed in bedroom = coitus father | hence stomach-ache) resistance / lessens. – Also sews almost without cutting up / any material today. Makes / me show her how to use sewing / machine (Interpret needle, machine = / member – material is mother – cut up / cooked repaired.) Then looks / at sewing machine instructions – at first / I am not Rita,[2] then am. / (Interpret ~~after e~~ with coitus sight of / mother's genitals.) – When then looks / out of window with me / leans out too far, I say: / 'I must take care though that / Rita[2] does not fall out': She: / 'You don't need to do that / I am Mummy and / I am there too'. – When she has bumped into things / in last few days (much / less often, according to mother much less over-sensitive / more enterprising, more skilful) ~~she~~ / ~~says~~ repeatedly is not accusing me / 1 time even says: You did not / do that. – Says to cupboard when

p. 72a she | takes a pair of socks: 'Don't / shut yet, let me take the / socks first'. The cupboard / should – she says herself / Mummy – not shut the door. / Sees 1 postcard in my bag, / asks who I am writing to. Immediately / afterwards if that is my dog, / the big one that was by the gate. V / 21/IX. Friendly greeting – but not / as before period of resistance. – Makes do / while changing clothes again with pulling / dress over them. – Goes without me / Rita[2] – to incomprehensibly pronounced / country – then town Barslina [?] / Says herself bear lives there and Lina. / Says I should not speak, can / go. (Interpret resistance because going to / country = coitus mother and anxiety cannot / do it displeased with mother.) / Then friendlier again. – /

---

xii Translator's note: The name 'Eia' sounds like the German word for eggs (*Eier*) and 'Bäck' sounds like *bäcken* (to bake).

She takes her small bag with her / and shows me mysteriously has / beans in it and secretly taken / from father's bedside table. / 'Candlestick' (candle) (When interpret [something crossed out] taken father's little / hammer from Mummy

V. Before going away when I was still calling her / I have pencil you should come over. / In unfriendly tone: 'You don't need to / draw me a little box'.

hence fear of mother – ask if remembers / bitten candlestick [spiral])   *p. 73a*
forcefully confirms / says '[Yes:][1] Peter's candlestick'. – Goes on underground / train. – Wants to put on Peter's socks / does this although too small – says the corner / must only stick out at front (above). When / does have to let me put on her / socks or dress – then still moves them / around a bit herself, prefers to / put shoes on wrong than follow my advice. – / Fetches little monkey (secretly) from chest puts / it into my bag that she takes. / Suddenly asks when she is fetching something from / cupboard – whether I Rita[2] did not take something from her? / (Interpret she secretly steals from mother mother's or father's / member, she mother therefore suspects Rita[2].) – / Fetches mother's brooch from bedroom and hides / it under Peter's nappies. – Prepares meal / for me as well: big hammers / are meat, beans, soup – one for / her is soft, black meal – I get / green one. Very indignant when I take some / from other one. – Bakes new cake, but may / only eat my own [piece].[1] – Immediately afterwards / fierce resistance again, runs away, – / but comes back, to get me / to put long socks on her for garden. / – When I interpret fear mother from whom / she has stolen something member hammer / eaten whole mother – trusting / again.

[For the thirteen sessions from 22 September to 6 October 1923 there are no notes available.]

[B 1: Single piece of paper, undated]

/ Doll in there airship / finger in hole box / ball spiral bonnet / on chest dachshund

345

10

Treatment notes on Inge

[There are no notes for the twelve sessions from 18 September to 1 October 1923.]

[B 11: On the inside of the cover page] Inge[2] II / October 23

Much joy at so many bricks / – (newly bought small dominoes) / *p. 1*
Builds. Keeps saying does not know / herself what it will be – or know / what will build at next / moment. Builds: a racecourse with / 5 tracks running alongside / this [the coach-house &][1] the manor next to [that of][1] the / playground. – Builds a kind of rotunda / from small boxes, keeps saying / does not know what she is making. – Finally / above men are playing music below / the wedding room where the king / is dancing. Separate stand for wedding / coach – another wide crooked / path that leads to the wedding room. / Surprised that path so crooked / had not intended this herself. / (Interpret five paths = bodily orifices / she then counts them herself together / with me – path mother – father / noise & danced = coitus. – Interpret / also making me guess = revenge / parents who made her guess everything. / Point at book curious pictures. She / agrees smiling) | Goes to window [unfriendly][1] looks out, says watching / as *p. 2* workmen build a complete / house.) Interpret curiosity about how through coitus / child is made. – Becomes very / friendly – & (when interpret rotunda very like / shape of flowers on carpet, point to ball / games etc. there –) she: (happily) / we could play that again, shame / that no ball there. – 3/X. (At home / showed resistance – told mother at my house only such / small toys.) Brings box with her that / gives me as container for / toys – proudly shows me how to fit all the toys nicely in her / box. Has also brought little houses / from home. – Again builds something / does not know yet what it will be – ponders boxes / four steps – then makes one into the / longer staircase. Makes street from / smaller houses. – (Again interpret / mother's womb.) Takes 1 little chair, does gymnastics / with it holds it over head and someone / could sit on it – a doll | or (jokingly) I. – Then *p. 3* puts 2 / little chairs together so that with edges touching / they can hardly stay upright / (Interpret path into mother-coitus. She capable / of this – does gymnastics – can carry me – / but how do two members / meet.)

Then puts little chairs together / so that pushed into each other / they stay up (interpret member into / Mummy's; I point at train, which / was only toy asked for / today (apart from boxes / & bricks)

– held in / the air so that hanging down – then / asked how 1 carriage is hitched on to / other, as two hooks. Then placed / train next to building) Perhaps / would be fuller over session. – / She also less enthusiastic when sees me / clearing away, then hurries. / 4/X. Building secretly on window-sill away / from my view. But then calls me to

p. 4 staircase to / help. – Building made of boxes | wide staircase at front to which calls me over / to help. – Side staircase, both together / also linked with crooked path and / a road leads to – both. At first said / needs no car at all, no coach – / but then asks for old broken / car. [Something crossed out] Puts two cars next to house states / both are broken, just standing there, the path / may only now be used for coaches. / Small man is placed on the roof. / He is to keep an eye on house, can also shoot / if burglars. – Small woman drives away in / coach from back entrance, kitchen entrance / to the 'women's playground'. Has put swings / there – at first unsure whether / should put 2 swings front entrance / 2 back entrance. – Then in the evening / drives woman quickly home, because husband / is waiting. But always breaks back entrance / with coach driving along path. – A house / was put up specially, if the children / want to do gymnastics or play

p. 5 the violin – just | for the children to play. Interpret back entrance / anal intercourse homosexual – she herself burglar / at mother's house – destroys. Ask again if has / not played that with boys, she as / Mummy. She denies – but very cursorily / does not take in subject. – Shows me window / curtain is very prettily thin – they also have something / like that at home between {in?} a kitchen worktop whether that / is also sewn. (Interpret entrance vagina also / very easily torn. – Takes 1 chair sits / down on it and rocks singing to herself. / Am constantly to guess what she is doing. / Piles the cushions from the little chairs / on top of each other, sits down on them, puts / 1 foot between 1, other foot between / the other chair and rocks both / singing. – But previously after had rocked on them / all together – was under couch / had got me to look for her and ~~prob-~~

p. 6 ~~ably~~ / had yelled when I came near. | like that time as burglar. – When I ask if / burglar, she cheeky: I was in a flat / but I must be in a flat. / Interpret masturbation / alone small chairs / wish to break into / parents' bedroom, have coitus with both / 5/X. – No wish for toys. – Hiding. She always / wants [?] to look for me, hits me when has found me. / You are not hiding. – (Interpret she secretly watches at night / as father penetrates mother – wanted to catch and / prove.) To this she says just once she also [?] / wants to hide (Interpret imitation identification father) Once – / fear – often wanted.) Are to play like this. Shut both / eyes, go somewhere in the dark herself / to guess where standing – to ~~hit~~ catch the other. / Interpret she and father in the dark to see which / of them penetrates mother better – and who / catches the other.) She sits down in my / chair I am to try to get her out / of there by force. She defends herself at / first. Runs off laughing, couch is better place. – / But then comes back to my armchair – quic [sic] / sits – I am to fight with her. Falls to ground / and is dead. (I interpret fight father and she, she / loses). Continues: early in the morning mother | comes is very sad to find her dead, angry / with father; but when mother comes / home she is alive again. Then lies / on floor but is only sleeping. / Then goes when mother comes into her room [under green armchair][1] / (Interpret breaks into parents' bedroom – early in the morning / then she only sleeps there too – innocently – / breaks in at night etc.) Takes swings / into her room / green armchair and plays with them / singly at first – then makes one swing with the / other. Small car, overturns one swing / after another – then puts / swings in 1 row runs car at them / and pushes all four. – They could not / swing then though. The blue one / – she sings, 'blue = loyalty' – does / swing – it thus hits the others / and they swing too – the car / bumps it does not knock them / over, it just helps them to push / (Interpret with its help father's / pipi would have been able to have coitus / with her, mother and 2 sisters.) Says now wants / to build something secret. Using boxes / puts up 2 tall columns or towers | suddenly has to ~~masturbate~~ urinate / (when) [something overwritten] back keeps knocking, she herself out / says – wants to stay / in her flat / between 2 / doors; then from there / steals toys boxes and coaches / from small table. – Plays bing bongbing / signal = morning bing bong bing bong / bing bong signal night. – In the / night steals = burglar – in morning / cannot find. Then again night / where steals nothing. V – then she is once again as / now lies down as man who appears / good – puts on act – on couch / tells me: that these people come / from the wood – that they usually break / into 1 house for 1 year will / now probably ~~again~~ only a few more / weeks – then pass by again / after a while there. – Talks / very nicely to me comforts me / so innocently. Next night goes out into street / with expensive violin in order to chase / away burglars. They also want to come

p. 7

p. 8

even brings things back.

p. 9 to him. Has heard rustling / by my door. – Then shows me had / large and small toy violins / hidden there. Tells me I cannot / know – which one she played. / (Point to smaller / she agrees) – / only had small pipi also / wanted to steal father's big one from / mother in order to have coitus with her / 6/X. Fairly pensive unenthusiastic. / ~~sits do~~ lies on stomach on couch explains / no desire to play – bored asks / what we will actually do. – When / ask what she is thinking about: yes, if / there were 1 toy that I cannot / give her: 1 big real swing. / When then asked what we would do then – / we would take it in turns to swing – she / alone without help not sitting, standing / then is better much higher. (Interpret foot / – in both chairs = same car – path-thing / etc. rocking before session with other one / homo-

p. 10 sexual coitus; sitting on stool (lip [?] | anal – standing on feet = genital) Took hold / of thread hanging [?] from cushion / turns it round finger so that completely tangled then / unwinds again. Moves finger in circle / with it. – When asked what she is thinking about: / has a game, a ~~small~~ dwarf is running / around there, has to run into the middle (Interpret ball-thing / middle carpet = coitus. Her ~~little~~ finger = dwarf has / no real member, takes black wound one {the thread} / chair in between.) At same time she blows, head / down so that head almost stands on / carpet – needs to urinate. – (Interpret / standing on head is however attempt coitus – urinating / proof masculinity.) – Returns hesitantly / stays between door – ~~then~~ initially says / is no burglar. Then: but wants / to be [?]. Same as day before. – [Something crossed out] sometimes / does not steal, yes – then also gives / back at night. – (Interpret connection standing on head / [father identifica-tion][1] / urinating, breaking in. Creeps behind my chair / with stolen things. Yells / at me, wants to frighten me. (Interpret approach / to mother = loud coitus noises then lies down / on couch – frightens me

p. 11 when close | but then enters into conversation with me – 'He has / gone round [path][1] at the back of my house / – if I don't go into my flat / do nothing to him – then he is not so bad – / he also goes round to the front into my house / – but the others who come out of the wood / only they are bad – they only ever / come round from the back – he is / helpless against the others – actually / he never wanted to be a burglar, he / was 'a respectable person', had a / shop, they got him out of it / Tell me, some time my father should stand at night / with a proper gun in front of / the house and shoot at these bad men / then they will never come back. – Looks among / toys and takes out 2 small figures, puts / man back, stands little woman / in front of my

350

chair – she is my father / – (later says her [something overwritten] husband.) Throughout this / speaks in very soft, fairly quiet voice / – much as she does otherwise, even / continues when she begins to play more actively. / Seemingly coaxed out of this attitude?) / – Then says *p. 12* has gone back / into earlier shop = become / toy salesman. Am not to recognise her. – Only / sells toys for my children – and / explains to me – coaches cars are / much more expensive because rarer than boxes / then admits to me in conversation that used to be / burglar – but did not like it now good / again though – is in shop. – Also orders a / coach with wood a few hours later / first must have coffee with his mother / shop closed – only then gives away coach. (Interpret bad burglar round at the back / is father or someone else she has seen. / She is my husband, father watchman wanted / to protect mother from father – out of love / becomes burglar herself, violent remorse / wishes. – Bad man took her from lovely / shop = father who through birth took / out of mother. When penetrated mother's womb – through / coitus – stays there is good. – {some kind of} identification [?] / but better – sells / coaches to children. / Gives member). Such enthusiasm for play that / does not want to stop at all, says 'shame' / very pleased I am also going to Thielplatz. | I then see her hopping *p. 13* [further [?]]¹ on way home. / 8/X. Heard from mother, ~~th~~ fierce resistance – despairs / that is also to come when school. – Still [?] however very friendly though also rather serious / no enthusiasm for play – lies stomach down on couch / – reluctant to talk. I ask if was tired: She / 'very tired, did not want to come at all' – / through gentle questions I get her to say: / does not want to come when goes to school – only / every other day etc.! (Interpret tiredness reluctance – / and state cause – that we have recognised / 1 unpleasant fact – that does not want to / say. Reference path-thing at back – / ploughing policeman [?] etc. – states sexual act / occurs with her – in confidence please – relief / my – indication no one even parents / finds out.) She: Mummy asks always want to know / everything after session – stands firmly by this / (untrue) claim (Also exaggerates / with mother reluctance and resistance to analytic session) / – (At further encouragement and question who whether friend / D?) She no – intense resistance. – Then: at most / once. – Then standing and lying down – / later no only lying down. Does not know whether | garden *p. 14* or room. – Then admits. Little stick / denies any kind of pain, risk of harm / while sliding head down from couch. / ~~then takes~~ to table with toys / huddled. Takes car with various wooden things and at first

351

/ runs it back and forth on ~~longitud~~ cross-pole table / noisily. – Then
– am to drive towards / pile bricks – collect for building. – / Produces
building! – At first only fencing around it / with 2 different-shaped
car [? something overwritten] doesn't like / – one straight and smaller
– the other larger and curved – then the fencing becomes / 1 street
with houses in between. – The / garage has [children][1] entrance that
is closed / at night – in the day it opens automatically. / Puts locomo-
tive and car / in the 2 lay-bys – saying: locomotives / can in fact also
drive in very well [into the small straight one][1] / from behind. So she
puts them into / the lay-bys / first. – About chauffeur of wooden car:
'he has / a secret rank that he tells no one about / [something crossed
out] – then only her and me. (When I ask / whether has trust in us –
confirms – when asked / whether as she does in me confirms smiling.
/ ~~Makes~~ Has taken little women (loose / inside) out of houses (Erz

p. 15   mountains {?} little / rooms) – ~~can:~~ 'women can go calmly | away'.
Chauffeur drives up 1 in front of house / to drive lady out – is not
home drives / up in front of next one – is then to go alternately / to
one to other (4 rooms = mother, she and 2 / sisters) – then drives with
woman / who lives at No. 22. – Long journey across carpet / back
around chair and armchair. Lady / gets out, climbs on to armchair 4th
/ chair – there will also be No. 4 (domino / attached.) Chauffeur
comes back later / this time climbs on to chair – collects / her – she
climbs out after he has driven / around armchair – from couch ~~there~~ /
– tells herself at dentist – thus / going home. – Then suddenly wants
toy / shop – I come to buy something for my children / – she gives
me coaches etc. again very / cheaply – I buy for birthday. – (Interpret
the / whole representation anal coitus father – her / birthday she is
No. 4 [something crossed out] / 22 = also 2 + 2 [something crossed
out] / = since father / produced her like that – secret rank etc. / round
at back – she is also allowed with Wölfchen[i] – at same time woman
who not there chauffeur / who to various houses – wish father coitus
/ with her and sisters. – Father – and identification but / she is then
also good toy salesman / who gave them – genitals etc. – cheaply. |

p. 16   9/X. Brings me 1 postcard: (of train, 1 guard standing nearby 1
woman / an overturned tree, prettily gift-/wrapped. – Builds secretly
from me in / box: 1 dining room for many / guests – 1 reception
room. Drives / car on carpet – shows me / how when gives strong

---

i   Translator's note: 'Wölfchen' is a diminutive form of the name 'Wolf'.

impetus rolls / a lot further. – Then: I am to catch / the car [something crossed out] and send it on. Then back and forth between her and me. / Then a second I – and reciprocally – / then so that she sends them to me and I to her and each / attempts to take away from the other / and have both. – Then she runs her car / up to my armchair – thereby it / is noticeable again ~~how~~ makes / noise as when 1 car drives out. – I / am to drive my car after hers – / to look for hers – that is completely hidden / between cushion and armchair. – Then she ~~takes~~ / [fetches][1] 2 coaches standing by – takes / both cars away – these hide / and drive after our two coaches and / look for them. – They thereby struggle | against the cars – / previously the cars had fought / each *p. 17* other. When I lifted / mine up, she says, that is no good – they must / stay on ground. / Then she suddenly / lies down on ground her car in hand / sleeps – I Mummy am to think she is dead / call father – meanwhile she sits down at little table / and plays: then she is toy salesman: / I buy for my children like / yesterday – except even cheaper / end birthday snack-meal children to which / he also comes brings more cakes etc. / Interpret – car fight she I = coitus father / mother. – Taking away representation hiding giving / back member. – 2 coaches, camel thing / She herself seeking father's member to penetrate / mother to have coitus with her, fighting / with father – then plays dead – but / at same time also represents father after coitus – / then again during the day good father gives / children something to eat. – Gives life genitals etc. / Also interpret present = sign of trust / and admission Wölfchen-thing: – train, man woman / damage = overturned tree. – Both / yesterday and today longer – regrets is / over. Has also now repeatedly brought / knitted cap back into room with her – recently | little jacket as well. Was not cold – knows reason *p. 18* why / did not bring with her. – 10/X. – Again plays toy / salesman. – Like yesterday. Only in more detail / room more presents for children. Comes / on birthday brings cakes. – / And a party game: little toy birds / she and I and also children have – to throw / into box, each into his own so that lands inside / but when I have two inside – 1 / is closed she cannot get hers / through – (When remind sparrows fence – birds / is member and children – ball-thing – meet / in middle) she recognises similarity ball but / difference: when 2 already there – then great / skill and speed required / for 1 more bird to fly in (Interpret difficulty / production 3rd child.) Then: children not / to play with us – only us two. – Gets me / to describe in detail – how pleased children are with / presents what they say etc. – His wife / has also been invited to a birthday, also / goes away at 4 o'clock. But is to cook beforehand. / (Interpret I and wife = the same – but both [go]^1 to birthday / means [?] is my husband = father – good father. / Yesterday

p. 19 and today she had / got me to call her | Herr Glaser^{ii} there is something good / about him in primer. – When at request for / advice I suggested the name of her / chauffeur – that she took while driving / car – she rejects. (Interpret Glaser repairs / window broken (by him) = not / burglar-Papa – good Papa. Regrets / end of session today as well. / 11/X. – Immediately again very happily toy / salesman essentially as before. Diff-/ erences: no longer wants to be called Glaser – / but Grieshaber – the name of a fruit and / vegetable trader. Arranges table / thoroughly – keeps adding to it – beforehand / shuts shop – indicates that with / 'bing bing'. Bing = open. – I also come / repeatedly in vain to closed / shop ~~in vain~~ – at first very / low price no role – later becomes / more expensive. – Also prepares specific / real objects tins leather casket – exercise books / from bureau etc. for sale. / Then also her coat and gloves / – praising coat very highly – but / recommends caution, since easily gets marks / when it gets wet –

p. 20 must immediately | wipe dry with cloth (giving cue after / questions: how best to clean it at once / – then interpret genitals / made dirty by urinating and masturbation.) – When I (cue: ask whether Herr / Grieshaber also children – pensive does / not yet know for certain whether gets some / – had two daughters but they are no / longer there – gone away! (Interpret she her father whose elder / sisters died – uncertainty whether parents / get more children.) Tells me / (cue question whether I have 1 boy / and girl again) no, only a girl – / I can then give her all the birthday / presents (Interpret 2 sisters dead – she my only living / child.) Because I got everything so cheaply / I should then – also bring him / presents into shop – wants particularly / large violin – Then also brings to / birthday magnificent presents, pretty tin, / clock – but always makes a great fuss at / invitation: does not know whether can come / – later – sends me his wife – then: / can only manage if we come to him / has a magnificent flat with large

p. 21 / hall, gives ~~himself provides~~ cakes, | we must pass shop table that 'Ilse' (as she / called child) much admires. – Much / regrets end, endeavours to draw out. – 12/X. – / Has brought large pannier: inside – a / small scarf (for doll that she calls / velvet and also finds very

---

ii   Translator's note: The German word *Glaser* means 'glazier'.

beautiful) a little / horse and a small basket with Easter / eggs. – But I am not allowed to see everything secretly / arranges table – even now – keeps / shutting in order to restock. But also otherwise / I repeatedly come in vain because shop / closed. – Sets prices very high – (when I ask) supposedly / because the other gentlemen told him he / must ask that much – otherwise he / is booked by the police. Claims when / prices risen really high – hundreds / of billions – then goes back down again / also has very cheap days (to question: why / so cheap before then?) That was Herr Glaser. / (To my comment: then wants to buy more cheaply there) – / No, now he has another shop – vegetables / – no he only mends broken windows. / – Keeps buying – to celebrate / birthday. He no time – his ~~wife~~ mother / later refers to wife, comes brings / presents: tin, watch. – While | wife at my house   *p. 22* – rings at door must already come / home. – Repeatedly now – with me closed / shop – whispers with wife something I am not / to hear but I then see that she is receiving / exercise books for sale. – Expands stock further. / Covers – mat for feet from couch = tablecloth / scarf = blanket and for covering while / sleeping. – Apparently he cannot come to / birthday because too much loading to do – only / evenings and then wants to be with wife. I am called / Frau . . .[5]. (Interpret father who was good / at first – after break-in – more unfeeling again / gives things away: caresses dearer = rarer / – has not very easily given proper / genitals – mother – Frau Gr. who comes to birthday / but even more affectionate) – (She has [something crossed out] shut / when I interpret = shop closed. – Fairly im-/patient again keeps saying 'bing' – sign / shop open – stopping interpreting.) – Says we want / to have a really big birthday party he and / his wife should come beforehand / buy up whole shop – gives very cheaply – / setting previously bought things apart – also / I should only look at bought casket what / inside – Large distribution in which he and | his wife help. – Then portrays 'Ilse' / again, who is pleased. – Finally   *p. 23* she lets her go away / again – because also gives her knitted cap / as well as the large pannier. / (Agrees how Nikolaus with pannier = father / who not only takes care of everything in shop / = house – but also made children from / pannier and cap = member – given / bodily parts – mother only helps a little! further / enough does not possess own. Impatient interpreting / does not want to stop playing. – Way back / wants to take pannier on her back but then / not, because of unknown children. – Had / reported way here better; yesterday had / said how shoes wet and dirty, had to / stop at fence – a gentleman said

/ filthy path – shoes dirty all over / Interpreted = coitus mother –
dirtying also / for father.) 13/X. Brings the big old / bear that her
mother still had, / 'Bibi'. He is to represent child – many / consider
uglier than Seppel, she prefers / despite age. Ilse first – but then / boy
Bibi. – She is mother / I 'Frau Krish'. – Herr K is not / there. – Buys

p. 24 everything possible for 'Dieter' / then organises birthday coffee | in
which I and Frau K take part. Then / I am Fräulein, and hardly allows
/ me anywhere near the child for whom she cares most tenderly /
wraps in scarves, invites friends, sends me into kitchen / fairly
unfriendly criticises a lot. – She / is Frau Dr . . .[6] but also the child. /
As Frau K I have brought many / presents – sells cheaply shop always
/ open (Interpret exchanged roles mother – to / cook – cook = took
child to / builder = thus made into neglected child. / ~~thereby~~ Wanted
to take her child away / ~~her not to~~ father superfluous – but / then as
Ilse needing help has / Dieter back. Mother better, gets everything.) /
15/X. – She is Frau K – Claims has / saucepans so cannot be gentleman. – / Provides shop with basic items / scarves, blankets, cushions,
pictures, tins / exercise books etc. for '13-year-old' Ilse's birthday. /
My Frau Dr . . .[6] only daughter – / Frau K still sells cheaply / –

p. 25 manages – but does not come to birthday. | 13 girl-friends invited.
She herself then / portrays Ilse I Frau Dr . . .[6]. – Then she / is Fräulein
whose sister is / coming to visit and brings aspic. – Had / put 3 vases
on table, 1 cocoa, 1 / coffee, 1 piece of aspic. She keeps diluting them.
/ (When I ask what that is then) (somewhat / ashamed: there is no
such thing as diluted aspic / in reality only in play. Aspic / is bought
or made from meat / and other things in the shop / she does not like
eating it at all. / But in play the children eat so much / of it that we
cannot provide / enough – she then explains / her sister has brought
some taps / from Potsdam from which aspic, cocoa, / coffee flows – so
as to have / as much as want. Had first asked / permission to receive
her sister / who was supposed to arrive at a particular time. / Repeatedly gets Ilse to help her / is particularly lovable and willing to help /
– comes into room and asks / for some cake for herself and also for

p. 26 her | sister. – When previously she was still making / purchases for
shop as Frau Kr / and was to meet her in the street / she told me she
had bought some / pretty pictures. When I asked (<u>cue</u>: where then) /
she: from a gentleman who sells that / I – cue – whether I could not
then / buy that there myself? She – most / vehemently: No, that is
impossible – 3, no / 5, hours away, near Potsdam, very / bad road, lots
of puddles etc. / (Interpret Potsdam, path-thing = mother / pene-

trated there through coitus / she fetches member. She wants to play active / role with mother herself.) As always / recently regrets end of session / 16/X. – Comes rather pensively / stands in the room, also does not / immediately begin to play. – Then hear / that discovered intention analysis of her / sister. – Today she wants to be / Frau Dr . . .[6] – I am Frau K but shop-thing / recedes further and further – just / rather quickly buys – cushions, pictures | (that constantly stresses are especially valuable.) / tins etc. – Shows here that one / picture (received from Fräulein Wolffheim) fits / so well in leather casket and Ilse decides / it is best to leave it in there and / to keep the sewing things safe over there. – / Meal becomes the most important thing. I was / Frau K at first – am now Frau Dr / . . .[6] – she is alternately Ilse, who / is now already celebrating 14th birthday – is only / child – and Fräulein Berta, who is having / her sister Else (that is the name of her cook's / sister) to visit again. / Again question whether is already there at appointed time / may go to meet her. Sends me / and Ilse to second breakfast already / at which prettier plate with blue / rim (all imaginary: spoon etc. / paper – small vases the pots / box = cake.) Gives to Ilse – then / wants me to be Frau K in shop again because / wants to buy cushions for herself and / sister. – Then with sister cleans kitchen / very well and they go into her room. / First Ilse, then I look for them in kitchen / find them in room and praise for clean / kitchen. Meanwhile with sister she writes | letters to mother in kit- chen. Meanwhile I hear / them counting: 3 and 2 = 5 and 2 = seven (When / asked). They are counting together how many people / there are at home. – Prepares the meal / for 13. – this includes Dieter and another / boy. She puts down pieces of paper – the places must / follow a particular order. / When she cleaned kitchen she put vases (pots) the other way round on bureau – / then cleared away into drawer / for the meal she keeps the pots under / the knobs on bureau drawers / lowest [brown knob][1] = cocoa – second piece of aspic uppermost / coffee. Praises eggs highly – only / cannot let it flow so terribly – / only a thin stream – because otherwise you

At home a few days ago said / mother would like to drink at her / breast

cannot close it in time when / switching it off. – (When interpret mother's breast the white / knobs) – confirms smiling. (Interpret cocoa = / stool – aspic urine – coffee milk. – / She = only eldest

p. 27

p. 28

p. 29

daughter again – then / sister comes as younger) — had / spoken with sister about common / youngest. (Interpret the invited children / particular sequence = birth, the / many children whom suspected still in / mother, including 2 boys – / they then eat with mother = table has / changed birth order. she is eldest / – doing arithmetic writing letter sisters / mother = curiosity whether and how children / come) – Asks for cakes again / for herself and sister – constantly / brings some of each and explains – [something crossed out] [also very very]¹ / many cakes there. (At cue – where had / all this food they had already / eaten come from?) Yes, sister had / brought another screw, when you turn it a finished cake / in all colours falls out of opening / on to plate. Readily shows / operation of various [something crossed

p. 30   out] taps | and screws. – Wants children to / admire how many we have. – / – At the end more 'saucepan-beating' / ~~chil~~ in which children get presents / Dieter gets especially many – / including lots of penis symbols. – She then ~~rejects~~ gives away small / toy as no longer appropriate for her / when she wins in saucepan-beating / – Accords value to each person getting / one or 2 pieces of paper that state / what he has. – Had also given / for sale hat boa gloves cap – / treats especially carefully / generally very tidy – had found / picture from casket yesterday as Ilse in her room but / given back to Dieter who / was supposed to have it / to play with. – 17/X. – I / toy salesman Herr Kr. – Has brought / Seppl^iii along is only child has 12th birthday – / Takes offence I too expensive. – Invites / me and my wife birthday, but states / it is cancelled. – She Frau Dr . . .⁶ – I Miss / also have sister

p. 31   to visit | Gives me task of laying table. Couch that was the / shop = birthday table. How other differences / mustard should no longer be given / is unhealthy – moves away mustard tap / then: we had two – one = remained / Criticises me because while laying table I (supposedly!) / forget knives and spoons – altogether / rather sharp – keeps me constantly busy / does not let me have a rest – While laying / table gives me a knife (all pieces of paper) / that is the 'butcher's knife' – then / 'carving knife, which is also / for slaughtering'. – Again carefully / pieces of paper for table order – different children / coming from yesterday – criticises me / for not putting pieces of paper on the table in the right / order. – My sister must / come in good time – before / the other children get there. Am then given task

iii Translator's note: 'Seppl' is a diminutive form of Joseph.

/ together with sister / of inviting Marie to birthday as well / also at a specific time. / Then she is Miss – particularly skilful / and able – We also have a / tap for soup / between meals she | must go out / We can *p. 32* have soup in / various ~~times~~ colours according to how we / push or press tap or upwards. – I also / have a roasting device – and a / tap for gravy. As meal passes / whipped cream and points out to me bureau / drawers counted from top to bottom: topmost / whipped cream – then gravy, coffee / mustard, aspic, cocoa – for roast / and cake other side every other drawer / always down and screwing – over them = / then each opening roast and cake. – / As mother had taken / necklace off Seppl – I to keep safe in cupboard. / – Yesterday had put a round piece of wood / with hole in middle (coaster [from][1] small tree) / on the pot/vase of aspic / so that did not flow out so heavily. / (When interpreted parents away – she in mother's / place – at same time she also only child boy / the eldest – is indignant table order / = birth order – mother did / not give spoon = she did not become / boy – with sister calling sister [Marie][1] / shared path = shared coitus pro-creation | ~~chil~~ sister as child.) When interpreted she / wanted to be *p. 33* only eldest jealousy / sisters – she: whether . . .[9] also came / to me on time – (I interpret jealousy / also with me = jealousy mother) 18/X. – / Buys [in][1] unknown shops V – pushes aside / shop-thing – has already bought / ~~in~~ birthday table – I mother / prepare couch – but [birthday][1] entered / background. – Only 4 children visiting / including 2 Inges – 1 Inge = Inge castle / association castle – she believes 1 castle / is very tall stands in water. 2 / boys – Dieter and Wölfchen. / While laying table she looks for representing / roast – the 'long paper / with holes in' (sick note) / the two top drawer knobs on bureau / are both whipped cream – later / only 1 again – near me serving / table she gives it to me – I pass it on / – cuts roast back and forth / with butcher's knife into smaller pieces / (only does this with paper), saying '<u>those</u> / holes were already in there'. Whispers

V does not want shop-owners to be / invited – are strangers

secretly with Inge. [Has taken cap from pencil and sucked it][1] – *p. 34* (Interpret holes are / maternal orifices = mother's breast – slaughtering / cutting up mother.) At first had still / said brings goose – then chicken / roast. – ~~About slaughtering~~ Says animal was / already slaughtered in our screw / beforehand Miss slaughtered it / and cut off head. No special resistance / interpretation.) Also her sister comes at appointed / time. Telephones Sweden / with her. – Will also come to us / in service later. – (When I explain children / still very hungry at end what / she could still do, very pensive. / – Fruit no more garden – compote / our screw-device is very / laborious must be prepared beforehand / (Confirms interpretation urine and fluids quick / – stool slow.) Has accorded especially great / value to her room. Takes tassel / there (Rolett {sic}-cord in there – that / she would like to adjust somehow / so that it would have a door – calls me / to tele-

p. 35 phone – a Herr Backer is calling. – Shows | me as she puts knitting-needle in / telephone socket – but does not want to give me / anything to say. – When I only say vaguely 'yes, yes / certainly etc.' – she impatient: I would have done / that completely differently, a moment later becomes / Frau Dr – cheerfully discusses approaching visit / with Herr B. – talks about last / theatre trip together. – Immediately afterwards / goes into her room lies down with sister / to sleep in her room – one [into][1] bed other / sofa. From there I must call her out to lay / the table. V. (When interpret telephone / theatre / coitus parents – as a result she masturbated / with sister) – she crawls / away – without denying or confirming – behind my armchair corner – (exactly where when made me / guess with ball what was doing / with fingers [which I interpret][1] (Also interpret: without parents, ~~sis~~ / are unknown – sisters having / coitus together, making children: – was / altogether more depressed, less eager / cheerful. – Afternoon at home I hear – / irritated cried easily – but did not / express reluctance to go to analysis as strongly / as before

V Finally more children raffle-presents / at same time pulls the remaining paper strips / back out of my tear-off calendar – counts and / orders them.

p. 36 Begins very pensively – stands / in room – does not want to sit down / constantly looks at me – certainly / more pensively than unwillingly. – / I thus ask in passing if knows story how / negroes arose? I tell it. During / story she took brick-domino / boxes from little table – at first / secretly rearranges one – then keeps / trying to empty box on to carpet / so that the contents stay together. [Emptying][1] / on hand says does not want to, anyhow / it is easier that way. – First scattered these / little heaps – then arranges them / all in a long row. – From these / a 'builder' – she – fetches bricks / makes from them 1 courtyard with 3 houses / and at the end a playground with

2 swings / (Interpret: large screw compote – / cake = stool – likewise bricks from / box – interpret anal game – she / from excrement makes imitation father children.) / She has left 1 piece behind – arranges / them by numbers – counts how many of | each number *p. 37* – at 'two' she says is / main thing – at 'three': 'three always goes / in front' – at 'four' she says / repeatedly: 'Four again – that is / mean' (Interpret 2 = parents = coitus. 3 parents / and 1 child she Inge[2] as Alberto and boy / – four is mean – when another / child comes. – Interpret ordering, counting = / counting stool and also children in / mother – is identical – when going / away she tells me – goes other way / to Thielplatz [?] – ~~so out at back~~ / is fun to keep finding / a new way.

[For the next period of the treatment – first up to 5 July 1924 and then again from 3 February 1925 to 1 May 1926 – there are only some isolated notes.]

[B 3: These include some 'children's dreams' on a notepad]

Inge[7] 20/VI. 1924 She has sold the schoolhouse – / because schoolhouses always burn down after all. – For the / 90 marks money (later 90 pfennigs) – she bought lots of / balls – clothes / and went to eat in the restaurant / with her girl friends. Association [something crossed out] burning schoolhouses: fire / in mountain [?] barn burnt down – thought the house / opposite will burn down too. Evening burnt fiercely / more terrible at night – stopped early – probably set alight by / some badly-behaved boys. 5 boys, who played / there with matches – house opposite – / in her game where house available and for gentleman (father) / to sell – it is near Frau Dr . . .[6]'s house . . . / is just as pretty. – Ball penis in her games – where / must meet in middle of [something illegible] carpet – then hides / with ball behind my armchair I am / to guess what she is doing there – masturbation – new dress / coat-thing repaired at tailor's – [something crossed out] / cuffs are hanging down should be upright. / Restaurant repeated games – where small figures / – also little men – [Dream. Inge[7] 2][1] eating together / at same time. – Mother breast and father penis. / At the time of this dream. – Gentleman who shops in the / office is to go away without her theatre restaurant – she / (Frau Dr . . .[6]) goes with Frau Klein. About 90 marks – / 90 pfennigs – has girl friend who will soon be 9 years old. Writes / price in marks on swing (as shopkeeper) – on / the other that is not worth much (in reality the same) just as

361

much / in pfennigs – clear at same time is her sense of inferiority / on account of genitals damaged by masturbation. – About 5 boys – / next session theatre game – 'Travelling in clouds, then / giants appeared, frightening the audience' slowly lets / one finger after the other appear out from under the table / over edge until all 5 on top. In this theatre-thing she is to portray / – refuses to watch – refusal voyeurism in connection flight Oedipus. – / In same theatre production / 1 play: coaches collide (everything collapses – / first of all a person where woman waits. 1 chauffeur arrives / but has been waiting for someone else and goes / away with that person by train. – About travelling in clouds – / the cloud the giants are in clouds – / we do not know exactly.

[B 11: There are a few more separate pieces of paper in the file]

[1. A sheet of paper, front page]

30/X. [1925] theatre (says everything [always]¹ belongs together.) 'The pretty apple / and the funny lady'. I must look away / sets up room, camp – [something crossed out] first bites into / hidden apple she has brought – then reflects / amusement: 1 hour of gymnastics – then: 'too tired' / would rather read. – Looks for little book that father- / admiration also fear: boy who is not to / look with big eyes in bird's nest. – Fox that / stole goose – lion and slave: comparison / peasant and king – then 2 prayers is to be good / ~~night~~ while reading these – leg movements that / indicate thighs pressed together – / – Then gymnastics after all: at same time song: 'Zion's / daughter rejoice' – then pit-foreman {song} – then / Softly passing through my mind^iv the sourpuss / when you pull its tail it makes a horrible face / – ~~Again masculine voic~~ gymnastics in which / very lively and in fact with arms and legs that throws / together meet in genital area = masturbation [? overwritten] / pressing together thighs and [something crossed out] rubbing hand. / Then again masculine voice gramophone / again sun that burns out little eyes. Quiet / here – only rhythmic leg movements / then again gymnastics [to]¹ pit-foreman song – at same time / also bangs stomach head beats with / fists,

---

iv The *Steigerlied* is a well-known old German mining song and 'Softly passing through my mind' (Leise zieht durch mein Gemüt) is the first line of Heine's poem *Frühlingsbotschaft*, which was set to music by Mendelssohn-Bartholdi.

chest – keeps noise going – then / with fists at back – says then also striking / sideways.

[Back page:] Female masculinity complex / Inge[2] material – about waiter-thing – lady who / has also been waiting long – (sitting in her place) / comes too early in the morning [waiter lying asleep][1] – [must][1] wait / lady whom receives as final guest in the evening / [bad egg cook's fault – comforts: doesn't matter][1] / – then cushion-thing: Frau Riehl – then / waiter game again – but without making / wait and details of refusal. – Then gym club / swimming club – does everything on little table. / Theatre: young gymnast – then lady on / magic blanket – (cushions underneath sometimes soft sometimes / hard.) – Then theatre: the funny lady / has eaten supper (connection with evening of / catering puts towel-rack on cushions on / table waves back and forth – goes / to sleep 'less funny' – looks for key – little stick / wood – opens cupboard – then pencil paper / writes to gentleman – [something crossed out] to sell her flat – no, exchange / – his bigger, nicer – no – hers – enough for her / alone – counts numbers bank notes – meanwhile / I do not look whether thought plays with toys – / (depressed) – play gramophone, dance / to it – then [something crossed out] no longer dancing listening / masculine voice gramophone: song pit-foreman / light climbs in. Digs [?] mine – deeply tanned girls love second song. Power of storm – princes / of the earth, ship raises red flag [like blood][1] V – again / gramophone to which she dances / lady when she gets up: cleaning / makes – coffee table – sausage jam eggs coffee / thinks about what did in the evening – when was funny / gramophone – dance ~~various~~ gymnastics / of various kinds – takes off clothing, shows trousers. – Every record different – [something crossed out] moving thighs and legs / then arms again – whole body / stands head – lays back belly (admits various / kinds masturbation) – then sings again 'masculine' / voice – listens to 'sun rides around earth – burns / out your little eyes' – then settles back down to sleep.

2nd song: the most powerful king in the realm of the skies – little birds / start quivering. 2nd verse – the lion roars in the wilderness – animals start to quiver / 3rd verse blood-red flag raised on mast / comes too early in the morning [waiter lying asleep][1] – [must][1] wait / lady whom receives in evening as final guest / bad egg cook's fault – comforts: doesn't matter / – then cushion-thing: Frau Riehl – / waiter game again – but without making wait / and details of refusal. – Then gym club

[2.) 4 sheets of paper (typewritten) headed] 'Female masculinity complex. Continuation of Inge work':

Beginning of November
Very unenthusiastic, playing indecisively, draws rather aimlessly. Then explains [it]¹ [as]¹ timetable of a rollercoaster [I], is a man who sells me timetable and explains. Drives between mountains and hills. It turns out that timetable is also a creature – animal's head with woman's body. (Again masculine role, flight from feminine because of masturbation – see last session 30 October. Continues this masculine attitude as follows:) ~~Draws little man and makes him dance from a cord to which he attached. Then two more, a boy, man, woman~~. Makes a bag, scrawls on it and is surprised to see the name of a girl who was at her house five years earlier and is the screen-figure for the governess on whose experiences she eavesdropped. Man tips bag on me, bits of paper. Claims afterwards the boy did it. (Boy allusion to sexual experience with boys).

4 November
Theatre, concert again. 'The funny lady'. Before lying down. Wants to be funny, do gymnastics. Sees that <u>gramophone needle broken off, so would rather not do gymnastics</u>. (Freud: female aversion to masturbation, reminds lack of penis.) Sits down, sings: 'Fox you have stolen the goose'.ᵛ Repeats: would rather not do gymnastics after all. Writes out an arithmetics exercise, small multiplication table, without working out. Sends it in letter to Frau X. (reminiscent mother's name). A child is to do the calculation (similar to maid who should explain the lion-thing. In both cases actually meant lady.) Calculation is question from where to take member stolen by the fox, how to put it together, general question about explanation, connections with incomprehensible coitus = and birth. <u>Article on school inhibition</u>.
[p. 2:] Afterwards calculation of larger sum, which I am to solve. (Meaning of arithmetic, schoolwork). Very listless, bad-tempered. Draws a little house from which smoke is emerging, cuts it up. A little house with a pond in front, some people are going past, getting fish out of the pond, the whole thing turns into a goose or a duck (familiar children's drawing!) Afterwards less definite shapes that she calls biscuit, over it a cap with hanging tassels (latter clearly penis). Shows me

v   This is a well-known German children's song.

in address that I had written for her that my 'r' is much more compli-
cated than hers; hers is a straight line with two curlicues. (Struggle for
phantasised penis; cap simple 'r' in contrast to existing goose, little
house, biscuit etc.)

3 November. Funny lady does not play gramophone concert. From
bigger book with children's songs and stories chooses the following:
1. song about sky and earth, which hold on to each other. 2. Sun rode
around the earth, the little stars that wanted to come too and would
burn out little eyes. 3. Sledging at night, wolves that hunt there. 4.
Klein = little Irma, who must hold on to her little parasol and gets a
little sunshine. 5. Little sheep, to which a good man gives a his coat
instead of a new fur coat. [6.][1] Animals that are paired together in
stable, dachshunds, hares, oxen, mice, while the animal that tells story
is alone. (Sadness, coitus observations and own abandonment and lack
of penis.) At the end sings 'Fox you have stolen the goose' and goes to
sleep. While singing like this, she lies on her stomach or back, with
thighs pressed together. Clearly visible. ~~Again wants~~

6 November
Wants to play funny lady again, but cheekily plays funny man. Clown.
Tips the bag on me again. Accuses other people at first. Then ceases all
denial and becomes terribly cheeky. Does what he wants. Is stronger
than me. I am to ask him for shopping bag. He refuses at first, then

[p. 3:] 6 November
Listless again, reluctant to play. Draws aimlessly. It becomes a little
man attached to a cord. Then draws three that are dangling from the
cord. Wants to add many more to this. Representing: small clown,
father, mother. Then makes a bench for one of the little men, places
him in a standing position and wants to give that to little boy cousin.
(Identification of small boy with herself, as often. The present of
member along with female genitals – the bench, that was initially to
become a little bed – as well as many additional children, whereby
parents become child. Replacement of penis by the child.)

9 November
At first wants to play funny lady, but plays funny man. Clown.
Extremely cheeky. Tips bag on me again. Blames other people at first.
Then ceases all denial. Does what he wants. Is stronger than me. I am

to ask him for shopping bag. At first he refuses, then sells it in exchange for brightly coloured pencils. Then steals bag from me again. Also steals from me a letter that a lady – with name clearly reminiscent of mother's – wrote to me. Then I have to complain because the clown has made large spots in the letter that 'ruined the letters with tails'. (Article on school inhibition). Then steals all the cushions from me, explaining that she needs something soft to sit on (now female genitals). Then goes with Frau X (mother) into cinema, pretending to think that she is me, Frau Wett (association with running a race [*Wettlaufen*]). Clown lives in 'Know-All Street' [*Alles-Wissenstrasse*]; they know him at the post office and give him my letters. Gets a letter with cinema tickets from Frau X, which I am to receive and goes with her without her noticing. Then again, and he sends her a forged ticket and she has to pay later. Before the cinema he is very sweet to her, afterwards rude and unfriendly and leaves her standing there. Has also taken money that Frau X gave to Frau Wett (governess's present [p. 4] in return for discretion). Frau Wett has to watch as the two of them drive away in the car, cannot help it. This continues with the clown standing between the two of them and there is nothing she can do about it.

10 November
Continuation from 9. The same game. At the theatre a song is sung, made up by Inge, that she will now go to sleep and receive something good, a present. Then: she comes back from the long walk home and receives something pretty and sweet, although it is not Christmas or a birthday. More details about clown's friendliness before theatre. Rudeness afterwards. Asks Frau X for money. Also quarrel about wrong tickets. Clown very cheekily says, good, what he wants. Mistake here that clown writes to Frau Wett and goes into theatre with her.

13 November
Continuation and repetition of previous. Clown paints a pretty picture: it looks as if it is about to burn. The sun is shining. Everything is reddish. Shows it to Frau Wett, sneers at her, does not give it to her, under her gaze keeps going with Frau X theatre, cinema. Friendly beforehand, then cheeky. She complains, keeps being deceived. Inge admits: must finally know after all that it is clown and not her. Clown brings the red sheet of paper Frau X into theatre, gives it to her, afterwards takes it away. Some singing, while an instrument is beaten

on box: sun around the earth – wayfarer on high mountain, looks down on little house (she herself) [bachelor – added in handwriting][1] – cheerful gypsy life etc. Finally made up herself: she goes to bed at home, looks further under the bed first and goes to sleep. Then denies having said 'under bed'. Strong resistance. Finally admits still very afraid at 6 years old. Has always searched under bed and corners. This fear and fear of open window dates back to this period.

[3.) Single sheet of paper]

Tips 'Ela' {sic} bag – denies. – Boy somewhere / still has no bag / Inge[2] – 11 [overwritten 12?]/XI – funny man – Frau Ho / very. Frau Wett – clown steals ticket / and letter (Know-All Street) – ~~goes~~ theatre / with Frau Ho. 2nd song she has made up: / goes to sleep – / received present from somewhere not Christmas or / New Year) – [clown][1] friendly beforehand – not afterwards / asks her for money – had bought / wrong ticket – completely irresponsible / quarrel / Frau Ho had sent Frau Wett money – / clown took – ~~as well as bag that~~ / previously / clown tips bag boy – who still / has none blames – my request bag / sells in exchange for pencils steals back / also keeps pencils – steals letters / post office bribed – letter damaged / letters with tails [?]. / [Steals cushions / soft/hard to sit on][1] / hides steals my letter / Frau [Ho][1] in cinema – alternately / so that she / sends ticket and then goes or he forged / and thus pays later. – Ho and Wett / have so little to do with each other. Kept apart / by clown

[Back page:] previously: / funny woman:

[4.) Single sheet of paper] ~~Inge[2]~~ Inge material 14/XI.25 / 14.) Wett visits clown. Apparently / reproaches cinema with Frau Hops – admiration / picture sun. – Clown sneers at her / does drawing – Frau Hops and Frau Wett / under every clown. – Then attaches / it with cap – box lid / on stomach on which stands: Frau Hop [sic] / and Frau W are daft – bangs and jumps / around (clear wish for / clown and same bad treatment) / shows Frau W his tricks / 17. – Again Frau W visiting / clown. He has also painted / sky [blue hand scrawled][1] / (picture 17.XI) – does not / find as pretty as sun. Tells song / about Daddy Sun, Mummy Earth / clown paints me sells me / picture. – ~~Takes cap back~~ / But cuts out pieces of paper – wanted to cut up picture / and writes on the back: daft (makes / cut up and daft) – then again / cap – box etc. as on 14th / and takes me – despite being an unknown / child – to play ball with him

[Back page]: also into cinema (without mother / knowing beforehand, to whom lied: 'just going to the park!') with me, who am from Bavaria, very nice, / ~~since~~ he also comes from there. 'I'm sick / of adults, they / get more annoyed by that'. We grumble [?] / together about Frau Hops and Frau / Wett whom I also know / [meanwhile unwell headache, slightly sore throat][1] / 18. At first dressed ~~like~~ like clown. Cap / lid with inscription, scarf, but not pinned to trousers, hanging free. Is / Frau Ho who is lying ill. – Is completely / covered under large blanket – moves / rocking back and forth – complains / sore throat, thinks, perhaps of last / visit to cinema (rocking movements coitus – / blanket lion cap etc. artificial penis / her throat infection) – Frau Wett / visits her in bed – then she quickly gets / well. Draws pictures 18/XI 25 (Inge[3+6]) / where ~~only~~ 1 cabin on steamer which / abbreviates to 'lady'[vi] only half / 2 chimneys in between (member / coitus) then 2) 1 bigger and smaller cabin / as well (meaning: she also joins in with / coitus!) then 1 entrance ticket into cinema / – on 1 side mess of lines / (female genitals) that is torn up in / cinema (throat infection)

[5.) An A4 sheet that only has writing at the top]

Inge work
[1925] Clown friendly again with girl – plays / game – messy numbers on sheet of paper to be / connected by lines that do not touch others!) / Very friendly interested – meets her in park, then / sends home (play [sheet of paper][1] finally looks 'like hedgehogs or moles under the earth'), then Frau / Wett keeps visiting him – every possible / pretext – ticket picture of suns and sky. – Gives it away / steals it in the night – breaks in with Dietrich – / – tips out bag – at same time Frau W's throat sore / (police say – clown <u>may</u> be cheeky and do anything) / (throat infection!) – but Frau W keeps going over! / [spontaneously][1] tells about memory of 'Asser' {sic} [?] only [knows][1] now that once existed.

[6.) Single A5 sheet of paper]

---

vi   Translator's note: The German word for steamer is *Dampfer*, which is abbreviated to *Dam* (Dame), meaning lady.

Inge[2]

4/XII.25 – Flat again / arranges it with curtains / cloth etc. – so that I (Frau Wett / again) have a room / next to clown – he has found ~~himself~~ / 3 books (of many / received on birthday & / brought to session.) Reads / from these. – Var. [?] adventures / fire burns dog bites / beats stick etc. other / man climbs ladder falls & an / ogre appears etc. / Makes enormous noise / with the 3 books moans / sings disturbs. Makes me / keep coming to / complain – mocks – I / keep asking (is / very cheeky scornful direct / coarse! – Reversal of role in which / she had to watch – / recognises identification 3 mountains / 3 books = 3 sisters) / – Has rented a shop / & deceives me & other [Back page:] women by selling: sugar / that is just scraps of paper – vegetables / just scraps of paper – sausage / just scraps of paper (disgust / fatty sausage) Takes money / from me. – [Something crossed out] Cheeky – does / not give money back – police / (mostly identified with him) agree / with him – a clown may / do anything he wants (from coitus / observations: semen, stool – member – / that not the right one though – / (comfort from frightening / away and denigration) – in the night breaks / into my house tweaks / my hair – throws his cushions / on to my stomach – (~~admits~~ [says why][1] / initially I think [?] – father through / castration mother obtains his / member) – in night again / robs me steals letter / & cuts hole in it

[7.) Single sheet of paper:] 5/XII. Inge[2] clown for (Inge) / she writes – mother may / not know – school lies / praise there teacher / [previous teacher][1] does somersault [?] / [on][1] chaise-longue and head down / slides letter of praise home. / Her dog run away. Dogs / [always go after cats . . .][1] / ~~dog cat~~ (* here begins assoc-/iations to mistakes – '<u>doc</u> and <u>cal</u>'[vii] – in the exercise / written by in dog = clown

Wrote 't' instead of 'd' = dumplings / with little sausages inside – / in 1 is nose, confirms member / S Z[viii] = sugar lumps big / fat – suddenly feels hunger desire / s = salt asks for salty / S not pretty = curved / not straight like Z = [continuation][1] next page / 8.) – Comes too late, reluctance to play / then gives me some of her nuts / – sets up a house for herself under bed / Am to phone her from there to / arrange a visit. – She reports / her nice dog that ran away from her / came back with Frau Dr [next* page][1]

---

vii Translator's note: *Hunt* instead of *Hund* (dog) and *Kalse* instead of *Katze* (cat).
viii Translator's note: *Zuckerstücke*, meaning sugar lumps.

[Back page:] she = Inge[2] cries – I mother. – We / visit each other, show each other / flats (remind Frau Holzst.-thing / homosexuality as result of flight from oedipal phantasy / material last session hence / resistance. – Draws a child that / thought would ride alone / on a sledge run – (it was / naked when it thought th{at}) but / there were already many / other children there

Continuation from 5/VIII. [sic] = thus distant / from father = dog – that takes / dumpling little sausage – thus / mother's genitals, gives him / the straight member, tulip – / takes cat from mother – that / Z the ~~straight~~ sugar lumps / (sudden greediness) and gives her / bad things for it – to same / badly curved member (stool / probably instead of it)

⋆ on 8/XII. previous page: at same time a hiding / place under blanket from fear of deceived / mother – must be pacified by my / friendliness telephone . . . invitation.

[8.) Small single sheet of paper] Inge[2]

Constantly under / bed lives – alone paints sings / to me bed telephones – / make little boxes / together – next / session would prefer / little boxes with boys

11

Treatment notes on Erna

[B 13: Treatment book, cover page]

Erna[8] Jan. 1924. 6 years old

p. 1 Begins 1st session: Runs small carriage / towards me = (aiming at genital region) / says is fetching me – continues with small / woman (figure). – She climbs with man / on to a carriage – another man comes / up to carriage, runs them over – are dead / were eaten up. – I am a lute-/ player am run over by a man / with carriage because am in the way. – Another / time builds house. Man is on the / ground, catches mice, roasts he – [something crossed out] says / – her favourite meal potato fritter. / – The people burst, burn up / house collapses. – Another time house / is protected against burglars / on all sides. – A small man / (again the 3rd one – who still runs over / with carriage – but who also comes / to visit man and woman & woman bites / off nose in 1st session.) wants to / [In first session she also wants to bite off my nose][1] / creep in there. – Stops playing. After / interpretation – she small man who ident. {identification} / father wants mother – continues / to play. – Many games of this kind. – / Thereby as school: teacher shows children / how plays lute with head. Then / throws lute away and dances with / schoolgirl (interpret also here her / head-banging) – eight days long / day & night, in which terribly

p. 2 aggressive | Another time schoolmaster and schoolmistress / are with children – whom they were teaching / how to bow etc. abe – at first very / obedient & polite – then attack / schoolmaster & school-mistress – kill, roast them / – the children are devils & are happy / – while constantly trampling etc. / – then they are both in heaven / – the former devils are angels – 'but are / not former devils at all, know nothing / about them so cannot be them'. God the Father / (formerly the man) kisses the woman passionately / all well. – When school-master dances with schoolgirl – / tenderest embrace kisses – asks me / if I allow marriage – dances to loud / noise 8 days & nights long, with / her. – Thereby terribly aggressive & scornful / towards me – shouts me down / when I want to speak (interpret in order not to listen / which she had to with mother) – Another time shows / how man reads a book / while standing on his head (bumping / his head!) – Immediately in 1st session interpret her / running over carriage – running over / lute-beater – man with carriage who runs / over man & woman – running over woman / as coitus wish & coitus observation / & imitation. Also that the fear / of robbers that stops as long as /

she | bumps her head – is why the head-bump-/ing compulsive. – When in playing first | session constant faltering and / resistance – *p. 3* interpreted: result removal / of resistance expansion in desire to play. – / – Showed me that catkin (plant)[i] / in vase at my house so lovely – licks & kisses it wants / to bite it. Very soon (3rd session) she acts / Frau Dr Klein; interprets to me. – When I set up man / and woman. Both read – woman asks / man something because of his book: she: / She tells him: now put your pipi right into me. – In one game in 2nd session / man had wanted to climb into post-van / tried various entrances – then / stuck head in at window. Then had / told car: but come right inside / to me (Interpreted mother who draws father's / pipi and him completely into herself.) – She / brings me this interpretation / now. – When she / wants to interpret to me again – I interpret she plays / mother and child – then really plays / mother & child: I still small, not / speaking – put everything in mouth – first / thing I put in mouth: engine with / 2 lamps, suck on it. (She had / much admired engine – said / 2 gilded round parts / – lamps – were: so beautiful, / so red & burning. Thereby stuck / in mouth – just as when talks / about little collar, catkin – also when / woman run over by man – afterwards cooking / eating and puts man or woman in / mouth – sucks, bites.) She then constantly / says 'ugh' – I put away again put / to mouth – also carriage or man / (Then also interpret engine with 2 lamps = mother's breasts & penis) | (following her *p. 4* instruction.) Divides up bricks / so – that she always has more than me – / overcompensation – then again too many to me / – back and forth – counts, begins compulsively / to divide up repeatedly. Forces me / to build as well. – Then makes ever bigger / garden or house – pushes at my / building – knocks over bricks, throws down / wants to make me pick up. – Here / especially strong sadism emerges. – Must / explain when silent, be silent when / want to speak. Makes me build so as / constantly to prove hers prettier, bigger. (Interpret / her competitive envy – house, garden / [into][1] which puts man = body, genitals.) / In the garden makes fountain. As first from this: / woman drinks. Then drinks / glass of water from my tap – then / goes to loo. Drinks water in every session. – / With building-thing talks about 'pieces' – / that I threw around & other material / as stool-thing. – When interpret is stool – anger / with mother about stool-control – /

---

i Translator's note: The German word *Kätzchen* means both 'kitten' and 'catkin', the plant.

she puts brick in mouth, sucks / & bites – says: it is even nicer now / when is wet – more appetising. – (Interpret / at same time with stool also making wet & thereby / putting in mouth.) – Here also penis meaning of / bricks clear. E.g. cries and begs / because small man has no feet and cannot / stand – wants me to stick | brick on him – therefore cries. (I interpret small man / she – repeatedly the 3rd – burglar – who bites / off nose – the brother, the guest.) Br- /ick = penis – she begs me for this.) One / of her games in 1st session. Man and woman / caress, kiss each other – drive in cart. / Small man on other cart goes towards / them – runs over, kills them – re-/peatedly runs over particular force. – / ~~When~~ In fight small man's cart / is also thrown around – woman helps him to / stand up – comforts, kisses him – says no / longer needs old man had enough / – marries small one kisses passionately / loves him. – Is herself small man who / in 1 session also bites off nose – (as / she wanted to do to me) when comes as guest / – runs cart against woman as she / against me etc. – With building-things plays / that in this built house / man woman live, who burst, burn up / house collapses etc. – Wants to make / me give present, takes brick with her / terrible despair when want to refuse / interpret stool-frustration. While dividing up / bricks etc. – recognises envious / aggressive impulse, admits – also play-/acts supposedly dividing equally – destroys house / pretending 'by chance', throws / bricks down etc. – Only admits with difficulty / – but then recognises, exercises aggression etc. / [something crossed out] (overcoming ego-resistances / – at home and kindergarten becomes / wildly aggressive but also much less anxious, more pleased) / – Paper games – begins to cut out | blankets – serrated, fringed. Gives / to me – but wants to make me give her / 5 pfennigs for the paper. – Gives me strips of / coloured paper – 'no child brings me so many / presents'. – Then asks me again what / least pretty of the cut-out material / – that she gives me – along with strips of black / paper because least likes – even mentions / great wish – this colour. – Thereby / tells how – while cutting out is making / minced meat – blood must then also / come out – 'trembles, should not speak / about it – because feels very ill then'. / – Then says are fringes that she cuts / in my nose – thereby repeated / ~~praye~~ wish & also attempt to bite off / my nose. – Then gives me blanket / cut into several pieces – says she / can put them together again for me [something crossed out] / agrees interpretation that wants to put / together reshape my cut-up genitals in overcompensation. / Wants to force me / to keep giving her lots of new paper to /

p. 5

p. 6

[sth crossed out] cut up while taking special / pleasure in using up for me as much / as possible to destroy. When I want to reject / compulsion – terrible despair. Forgets / loses prepared paper from home – after / a while and interpretation of her will for power / and destruction she readily brings paper / to cut up with her. – Folds, makes / 'puff-star' that she can blow up | herself recognises penis that   *p. 7* expands. – At same time / and during building-things – draws. / – Drawings at end of exercise book. {Figures 1 and 2} Laughs / at drawing with house below / [(interpret mother dies)][1] because woman above it. Heaven comes / – then house is scrawled / all over with black / lines – beginning to / understand anal material! Says knows that / would like to smear herself with / small and large – that she / would really like to do that in bed – / she even knows that very well herself. – / Against wanting to eat stool urine at first / resistance – but then admits / from material. – That fountain [the rest illegible because of mark] / also breast-milk – also original [rest illegible because of mark] mother / licked off bricks [rest illegible because of mark] / asks for pot with [water][1] / [rest illegible because of mark] [wants][1] to make / little ship swim [rest illegible because of mark] wash-stand / added to this [rest illegible because of mark] number / of sessions the following water games: – / cuts out little pieces of paper – doubts / whether girl – or boy captain: previously / had asked for Erich. – Makes captain / swim – ship goes down saves herself / wreck – swims on. – States / cannot sink (although keeps ducking / him) has something long, golden, / that holds him up – tears his head / off – is drowned. – [something crossed out] Washes underclothes / pieces of paper. Is a washerwoman. I mother / child has underclothes with stool and urine keeps / dirtying herself. Then I child again | *p. 8* keeps giving me clean nappies. – This game / in ever new variations: – dashes up to me, to splash and dirty me / – pours from glass and flower-vase – points / to big stream of water. Also asks for brushes / – all three penis from which would like to / splash. – Asks for big piece of soap / when does not get afterwards / we play 'Emperor and King' [soap = pipi][1] by throwing / each other wet towel from wash-stand. / – About wet towel she had asked me if she could / throw it at the wall and leave it lying / where it fell. – Wet towel, wet little cloth / repeatedly also penis as also / wet nappy and alternately she washerwoman / I mother – then I child. – Here she advises / as washerwoman beating child / in order to cure uncleanliness [?], beating / on buttocks with stick [represented on armchair][1] under a small piece /

375

Figure 1 The above-mentioned drawing is dated 16 January 1924; on the front page appears the drawing interpreted above: the upper half is headed 'In heaven', and next to each other are 'Angel – the mother – angel'. Underneath is 'the laughing house' (because the mother is in heaven) that is covered over in black'. On the back is: 'The wind – a tree – [underneath] earth – the wind'.

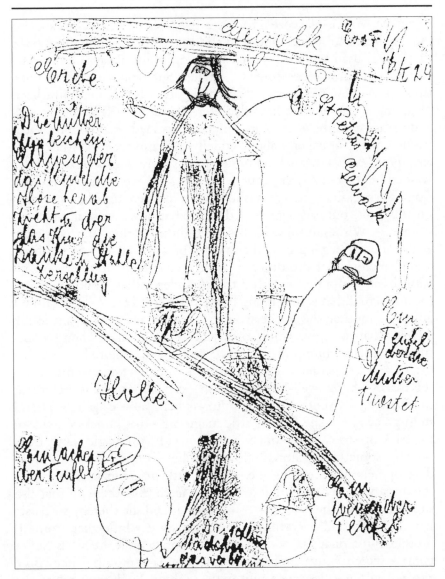

Figure 2 A second drawing is also dated 16 January 1924. It is subdivided into clouds, earth and hell. At the top left is 'The mother (also a Chinese man) whose trousers are being pulled down by the child and whose benches and chairs the child was smashing', next to that 'St Peter clouds' and 'A devil that comforts the mother'. In hell is 'The bad girl who was banished'. On her left is 'A laughing devil', and on her right 'A crying devil'.

of cotton wool is placed. – From this the child / becomes clean, also quickly learns to speak / and read and everything. – Sometimes plays that / it is used but mainly that beating / must <u>always</u> be done by father / who must ~~repeatedly~~ be / fetched. She is often tender mother, thinks it / doesn't matter at all if child gets / dirty, should just keep changing / trousers that has filled etc. – Then she / feeds me as well and in fact with the water / in which she washed and also with the /

p. 9 washed pieces of paper – about which | she also says well stuck on – also spoke / stool so stuck on underclothes – says / also what we have washed or cooked / is the same. – She herself keeps / drinking water from wash-basin – the / washed paper pressed together / chews greedily spits out eats again – / delighted at how fine, will not be / stopped. – Wishes to fill wash-basin / right up to the outermost edge – here / pours from glass and also once breaks / glass in doing this – also phantasises / that is doing it in me – clear that / mother's womb wash-basin – also that not [?] / to me underclothes – but paper also means / child that is thus being treated and cared for. / – One time I am to be mother, she washerwoman / who is also doctor, am to ask advice what to / give child, so that becomes clean. – Then recommends / me a white powder mixed with / red. The red is rose that grows / in her garden – crushed mixed with / white given to eat – this makes / her so well-behaved, clean – can talk / speak is as clever as mother etc. / – Another time I am to ask her / advice again. – Then I must go away / – she fetches little magician – that knocks / twice at the back on stool-hole – once / on the head with magic wand, from

p. 10 which / something yellowish flows into her – from this | miraculous development like previous one. – This / little magic man also shouts – she must quickly / carry that to school – fetch from there / – that also shows here that she can cook / for mother and she thereby surpasses her / in this and everything. – At this [when little man comes][1] mother must disappear / however. Interpret: [little man][1] is father penis – which / gives nourishment in vagina = mouth – likewise / also red-white – destroyed pipi with / semen. Stick with white the same. – Long-/ ing incorporation as seen by mother / then still surpasses mother. – One time / explains wants to play water games while sitting on chair. / Then had doubts because makes everything too wet / great resistance. – Then proves to me / was right that way. – Sitting on chair turns out / later to be lavatory, pot – meant prohibition / cleanliness training. – After once / spoken about doing poo and pee-pee presses / against me shows me bottom – suggests to me /

to dance to show me – Then dances / doing poo – so that bottom sticking backwards / legs stretched but not ungracefully / – a completely different position – also agile – / dances doing pee-pee. – Thereby also for me and / also besides wish to see me – phantasises / repeatedly mother also father bathroom / listening. – The countless changes in these / water games always follow / interpretations, details return until / cleared up. – Repeatedly also phantasy / that I as mother dirty myself – | – thereby she calls father one time, shows how / mother dirty trousers – calls police- / man who leads mother away gives / her only bread and water. – She then informs / policeman has found much / more filth of mother's – after that he / leaves her to starve. – She lives with / father ~~must first from~~ that is me – / who is completely in agreement with this / explains that mother dead – cleans all / mother's filth away and it becomes clear that / everything touched in room / filth – table chairs floor pile / – all food and drink full of it – / then must call for help / to a Frau 'Dreckparadi'[ii] who also does not / immediately get ready – by her / self portrayed – says later / that she herself also 'Dreckparadi' / – then cooks for father and gives him / something to eat, while scolding / mother and he constantly / recognises her superiority. – / Next session strongly inhibited, no / wish for any water games – says does / not want to think about that mother starves. / – Meanwhile again sessions in which / folds. Teaches me this – / continually indicates – badly made, / star torn in wrong places / – recognises herself: damaged / little slit – keeps making / herself new ones – superiority | also proves how after Emperor King / throwing wet cloth – teaches / me gymnastics – shows how not / good stretching arms straight out – can / shake hand loose – interpret superiority / sexual intercourse with also masculine / mother – she better pipi. – At beginning / anal material appears – asks me / for a new pfennigs for folding paper from / Fräulein W. – explains father mother never / give her that – tries to win me over / with presents but only / cuts off strips of coloured paper that gives / to me, more and more in order to assert / will. (Interpret remembers black paper – / stool-presents.) Then cut-out little blankets / frayed into pieces etc. that I can / put back together myself – minced / meat making cut-up genitals / good again. – But thereby always takes / what is prettier and bigger. Also crowns / that places on head. – After

p. 11

p. 12

ii   Translator's note: The name 'Dreckparadi' connotes 'filth' (*Dreck*) and 'paradise' (*Paradies*).

a few / hours after beginning, in which licked and bit / – catkin = little collar – frantically / straightens hair – says slide will not stay in / – [something crossed out] hair so untidy could / also sleep so badly at night because / slide held so badly. – Speaks to slide / as she fastens – with 'You monkey, Frank, you should / stay in place'. Frank = neigh-

p. 13 bour, gentleman / in same house. – Tells girl friend, he | is so funny, is like monkey in zoo. – / Interpret father's member – that is in her / hair = holding genitals still – also own / pipi – that she disturbs at night through / wishes. – She then puts slide / in mouth, also keeps doing that / later – just as when with / wishes to damage I indicate / castration – this man or woman / etc. often puts in mouth sucks / bites. – When notices change / in my hairstyle – was hairdresser – immediately scornful / remarks – ugly hairstyle or / changed. – In playing mother and child reproaches / me for untidy hairstyle, combs / – clearly – my damaged genitals. / – Between water games and afterwards / constantly theatre. A large / part of the mentioned games with figures / is theatre – then I must always / first shut my eyes and suddenly / see (interpret perceived coitus parents / from sleep.) ⊖ At theatre she / speaks mainly verse rhymes usually even / meaningfully. – Once also among other things a / policeman says to the little woman / has bit of white fluff at the back that / must remove from her. – Says herself / at interpretation father – for whom that is Mummy she / looks at what is behind = stool / says [?] to me, when I

p. 14 say: let us have a look | at it – always gets frightened and thinks / – looking at bottom. – During water games / also one repeatedly for a while asks / whether I angry or I sad – until after / interpretations fear of mother because of dirtying / from stool – again other details. / – At theatre also once 1 man who / cuts out a pleat from a woman's dress / at the back – says then not entirely at / back thus in between – whereby again shows / that for her everything was bottom – the pleat / is pipi. – Woman then runs / over this man – roasts – smashes etc. / – One time woman wants to put the man / with whom she has quarrelled in oven / and roast him – but he roasts her, she was / a witch – then he is released, is king's / son – marries king's daughter – / another little woman – passionate / kisses – wedding lasting for days – Right / at beginning had talked about fear of / robbers. Comes with stick or rifle / or something else long, to hit / them with it – when she bangs head / no anxiety – but only as long as / she – lying on stomach bangs head against / cushion. Interpret she is hitting herself / head = stick – both pipi – accepts / and says also defending herself this

way. – | Another time: robber has a green / suit on and white shoes p. 15
[something crossed out] / and socks Mummy has white shoes and
socks. / – Later after policeman-thing – / I suggest robber also
Mummy = police-/man, green suit. – At theatre / after sessions that
are productive – / – [something crossed out] sometimes stronger
inhib-/ition especially at beginning. – Then says / this woman = now
not Mummy though or / and she will not play theatre with / people.
– Only with carts or cars. / When then in enthusiasm carts / drive
over each other, entirely the same / complex-driven things as with
people. | 13/II. – Receiving new purse. – At first [something crossed p. 16
out] / begging for gift of money – soon – much red-/uced passion –
question whether I again find / better to explain as giving present –
that also a present. / – Theatre: at first father, daughter, bridegroom fly
/ on plane = purse. – Daughter does not want / to marry bridegroom
at first. (Recently in play / also such refusal – makes a fuss – then she /
takes good giant comes [?] later, flies away with her – then / she is
satisfied and marries – the one intended for her / (interpretation:
father) After the flying – she steered – / purse belongs to her – she is
satisfied with bridegroom / – marrying – father then says ~~are~~ was fun
/ are brother and sister. – Father teaches / them how should do in
trousers. Shows positions / constantly changing trousers, dirtying /
changing. V [Looks at children underneath whether stool good]★ /
he calls mother who also agrees with / lesson on dirtying ★ – father
also looks / under mother's skirt. She also dirtied – / etc. – but is
killed / by father with children. – Filth-orgy follows / constant dirtying – eating – / <u>own stool and others' – drinking</u> / V Purse = lavatory
is there. – Interpret purse / and my money gift = stool-/ thing. –
Afterwards continues: (intensified / pleasure): father calls mother –
asks me what / she says: I: I believe angry – she then:

[ ]★ Indicated with a line that it belongs two lines below]

urine – doing on purse – immediately eating / fresh – children throw- p. 17
ing father in toilet – / putting on dirty-fellow suit fetching / out
again – [something crossed out] Thereby putting in purse. – Then /
rolling around in dirt. Explains: table chairs / walls house – everything
filth whole world / filth. – Phantasises greatest passion. – Presses /
herself on to my lap – I am a / large bottom she also – when we are /
together – her stomach gets fatter and fatter. – / Then in rage throws
all figures on to / floor. Previously also told: often licks / ~~licks~~ finger

that rubbed on genitals / – lets urine run over finger and licks it / also with finger dirtied by / stool-paper. – After rage throwing away. She Frau / Klein I her. – She sitting in my chair interprets / my game anally. – Thereby increasingly forcefully / jumps (up and down in chair – compulsion with / her.) – Tells me – that she masturbating / – calls masturbation – when she crosses legs / and thereby presses herself against chair – such a / nice feeling. That she wants not only to play / cupboard. Explain = is rubbing clitoris. – Would / like to bore a hole and pull out / something very long from there. – Clitoris. – / Does not want to know any more about / masturbating, is ugly after all, not healthy. / Asks me. – I conciliatory answer. – Whether / [something crossed out] it is not that she is to not to masturbate –

p. 18 Interpretation game was: / 2 women driving in car – men | walking along behind – women in their / beds doing – man pushes them – pushes / pipi into them. Thereby jumps more and more / furious wants to stop session. – Interpret coitus observation / mother dirtying – father coitus. – She / identification rage because does / not have pipi or father not to / dirty. – Suddenly pleased – would / like to play some more. – 14/II. More inhibited, play / less enthusiastic. – At first mother – then gym- / mistress. Humiliates me because do / not stretch arms out well – can / shake hand loose – turn head round / well. – 'Emperor and King' – with throwing towel / (the days before – throwing wet towel / after pouring glass of water in curve, / – asking if she can throw wet towel / at wall, leaving it lying where / falls.) – Interpret she father I mother with / pipi = king – but she teaches / – Then hiding from each other and she / chooses corners by stove etc. – watches me / when I hide. Says / sees although does not want to. – (Interpret / plays mother and child – creeping away path / coitus – making me creep away – / thereby voyeurism about what father did to / mother. – Yesterday also made clear / to her everything was bottom – what bottom – little slit / little collar. – Told me wants

p. 19 to take out / eyes make eye-salad | In her ecstasy yesterday also addressed: You / eye-salad – cut-up nose – cut- / up little slit feet legs etc. – / 18/II. – Strong aggression beginning forcing to / come to her, take off coat. – I take off – / she treading on me kicking wants to / smash everything. Then I leave it to her to go – but interpret / rage mother – cuts out more quietly: may-bug / with 2 feet – 'all bugs with 2 feet' – Then / doll's dress – meanwhile inflatable doll' – ~~too~~ / 'Szani' – has only one bad tooth – my / good tooth – is bad, relieves / herself, – no is well behaved. – Constantly calls / me also recent

sessions 'bottom, pee-pee / poo' ~~Szani has no fir-tree~~ / ~~moves fir-tree~~.
From Szani / associates: rainbow and fir-tree / tall one. Constantly
does poo and pee-pee – / and rainbow rains on it. (After interpretation / all pipis castrated = also men – / she only bad pipi – Papa
rainbow / Mama fir-tree – envy rage dirtying / each other) suddenly
asks why / she so pleased. – Throws chairs little table / around – sets
up dining-room several / lavatories – little chairs – at same time /
steps also turned into lavatory. – / Cooks for me – is daughter – I
father / mother dead we annoyed to death. / Brings me 'shit coffee' –
again | very forceful and agonising demands statement / she cooks   *p. 20*
better than mother. – I interpret = again / relaxation. – Then I place
lavatory / she brings me food – soup / – says is what is at back and
came / out at front. – Whether I want to eat / the same for myself that
I make – she also. – / Then: I her from mine she wants / to give hers
to me. – Full of enjoyment – / asks me why such fun? / – Has
surprised me on lavatory / listened to me – unlocked key – / locked
again – so that no one / else comes. – Then portrays / looking
underneath me observing / stool, stool-hole. – Request not always /
lavatory, dirtying trousers watching / each other. – With key drills /
around my thigh looks / at lavatory – interpret penetrating looking
/ into intestine. – At farewell / again – as usual – concealed rage. –
/ [Something crossed out] wish to undress me in front of her / [some-
thing crossed out] repeatedly after phantasises giant / and interpretation large pipi – ask whether / she if she marries big father – / then
her husband will also have / large pipi. Happiness, will be able / to
look at it while getting dressed. – Here / puts a figure into mouth,
biting / – I interpret biting off. 19/II. Intense jealousy | of Felix[2]   *p. 21*
whom she encountered. – Whether my chair / stands like that because
he wanted – why 2 little / chairs close together – furiously demands /
paper to dirty. Disappointed because / I give this and ~~paper~~ pencil –
wanted to torment / annoy me. – After interpretation – scrawling
rage / jealousy because suspects father and mother / secretly dirtying
each other. – Relaxation / wants to sit near her when scrawls. / By
rocking chair eagerly / masturbates 'sculpting'. Here presses underneath / and also stool-hole. Describes / and shows me – jumping –
with feet / jumping around on the bed – rocking / = 'sculpting' –
cupboard games = / tugging clitoris – banging head and / then going
to sleep while sucking thumb. – / Uninterruptedly to orgasm / masturbates in front of me – meanwhile / stands up in order to stand with
/ legs uncrossed. – / Sits down in corner – I to play / water games, she

watches masturbates. – ~~Mo~~ / She as mother says, doesn't matter if / child dirty – I washerwoman / wash underclothes. – Then Emperor / King, throwing towel. – Finally / only now masturbates – stands up / masturbates etc. – at request / now refrains, telling thoughts. | (in strikingly raised prettily / performing tone – very pretty selected / expressions. – Both also other times – but / this time particularly successful). A king's / son rides on horse. Whip cheerful / queen rides on horse, also king's / daughter. Both wonderful crowns. – / King lights large stove. Stove / leaps on to horse – horse on to stove – / queen on it – King's daughter / on her. – Interpret masturbation phantasises: / she getting dirty together with mother / (following coitus or dirtying / phantasy of parents) – masturbating in front of mother / dirtying herself – dirtying child / allowed – washing paper with soap = / care of the body – soap also pipi – this / followed by coitus (Emperor, King – / throwing towel – once asked to throw / wet towel – but I must leave / there on wall where falls down.) – Then / phantasy coitus together mother father / according to observation. Noises – whip – / and looking – stove etc. – 15 and 16/II. / Very greedily eats oblong yellow / sweets – says like 'egg' – then 'cherry / with glycerine hands – theatre / small woman little man and mother / – father dead – everyone to receive half a sweet | all the same. – Then / everyone 1 whole one. Child went into the / shop to buy. – Then puts sweet / in mouth, sucks on then playing / Emperor King – then just imaginary / children – at our call playing as well / – just girls. – Interpret sweet = pipi / red – eaten with semen – she father / Emperor – with mother also man / producing children. 20/II. – Cautiously / asks what and how Peter[2] played [we spoke][1]. Lurking. / Says no desire play I am to tell / stories. Passionately asks for and orders paper – / dissatisfied with what is given. – Then writes letter / does not want to reveal contents. Then asks me to write letter father dictates I only / pretend do not really help – closes tenderly. / Threatens to show father letter. – (Interpret fear of / masturbating etc. observation mother – will / report father = Peter[2] – play-acting – / forcing mother to admit unlovingness father.) / – Am to play theatre. She interprets. – I play / little man and little woman go for a walk – ~~policeman~~ / [something crossed out] visiting gentleman in house – going away / from there – he comes after them. – / She interprets: father, policeman brother / sister forbids to do pipi-thing. – / Asks whether all adults know what / they thus (means 'unconsciously') think – whether / she when big that will / also know about herself and others. – Interpret observing /

mother's thoughts – detecting something offensive | to her. – Builds *p. 24*
flat again – / overturned table dining-room – asks / why always so
pleased when / sits down in it – little chair lavatory – anal / phantasies
– eating stool etc. – Meanwhile / again threat – to show father letter. /
– Interpret requirement mother they to dirty each other / etc. – 21/
II. ~~Shows me picture~~ Goes as / usual first to lavatory and 'magics' – so
that / 2nd little chair that stands in front of table is put / away and toys
cleared away from / little table. When coming in ordered / me to do
that – then asked, I am to do it, the magic / works. (Little chair, toys –
jealousy / previous patient.) – Game: [she has a][1] pig ~~is~~ slaughtered / –
each chooses a piece, may only / answer with this word. – Shows me /
a picture she painted. God on a / throne says looks like animal associates / pig. – Interpret slaughtering pig = / cutting up father's pipi –
always only / that 1 word – Juli (invented name). / Pig slaughtered =
mother has slaughtered / pipi, she also wants a piece. – Then / asks for
water games. I always have / to wash children's filthy underclothes, /
does nothing – but then washes herself / asks me for a wet cloth /
when cannot give – fit of rage. / Will take something herself – the
broken / little men – whom I do not need / anyway – otherwise takes
uninjured / little bird – also puts it in her pocket | Then takes little *p. 25*
calendar- / book from desk – keeps it – looks for middle / where
divided – licks it. Interpret still / denial father's wet pipi – least /
damaged – in her opinion after coitus inside / remained damaged –
robs mother's / genitals. – She wants to hit pinch / push asks to
tolerate it since she cannot / bear it otherwise, rages and wreaks havoc.
/ ~~Something flows away after interpretations~~ / 22./II – then writes
me letter with / tenderest birthday wishes / – Interpret hiding rage
hatred behind love. / – Previously had also ~~on~~ from cart that covered /
with {synthetic material} wanting to take / this down could not
further fit of rage. / Interpret licking father's semen down / from
mother's genitals. – After letter / further fit of rage – treading hitting
etc. / that after interpretations somewhat diminished. / 22/II.
Immediately begins again to masturbate / intensively. V. Ask her to
refrain / to tell thoughts, after a few resistances / obeys: – mouth,
strawberries – knight Georg / squire. – Tells about knight G. – bold
knight, could

Sucking as well.

travel a lot riding vicious horse: before / 1 front-door stands poor *p. 26* man – laughed at / by brothers – because they prettier coats and hats, / knight G. gives him his 2nd horse – had / ridden on 2, takes him as squire. – / Come to witch who has magic wand / take it from her and book (in which formula / smearing soles with grease, becomes / sprinter) – with miraculous hand / squire has smeared her chair with grease so that / she can never get down from it again. – / Freeing king's daughter – killing / big snake – knight G. marries her / – squire himself becomes knight. – (Interpret she / squire – envy ~~genitals~~ penis, men. / G. rides 2 horses = she and mother – she / also king's daughter – but also / father with mother. – Masturbates again. / Thoughts. Beefsteak gets annoyed about / roll-cutlet because has so / much roll on it. – Baby puts / on black cutlet-trousers. Beefsteak is like goose, roast stupid / goose. – Roll-mama tells / children – they may not laugh – then / they can keep so much roll / on them. – (Interpret: stupid goose to me day / before repeatedly said = mother – is also / to be roasted eaten. ~~On~~ roll / on her = stool. May let / it stick on her – but must pretend – not / show how likes it. Black trousers =

p. 27 | dirtying. – Break in masturbation / starts afresh. Interrupts [further] thoughts: / a little girl called shit-bottom / mother says may go into next village. / Filling trousers there. – But she then / notices she can do it immediately in next / room. Fills trousers so that gleams / wonderfully like silver and gold. – With / G's suit of armour she also spoke of / little golden masturbation-thing. – Again / in especially dreamy tone and pretty / words. – Interpret everything as masturba- tion / phantasies. – 23/II. – ~~Wants songs~~ speaks / scornfully about question of Peter[2] in encounter. / Then she wants to sing me a song. / Takes my chair. Concealed rage / because little stools next to each other. – Needs / lavatory lingers outside with girl / forceful resistance. Sings song about 2 little / rabbits grazing between mountain and valley / shot by huntsman – but they still / escape. – Previously asked until comes / from lavatory supposed to be enchanted – moved a little / chair away. – Does not want to get out of / my chair. – Interpret rage – little chairs next to each other / the one with boy = jealousy. Parents bed / next to each other. Forcing me beds / apart – to give up / my place for her = double bed [beaming][1] has really / once, because

p. 28 her bed broken, slept in mother's | bed next to father, mother only / on chaise-longue. Dicky-bird and starl-/ing. – So that ~~who~~ starling quickly / occupying space when standing up. – Thereby / she forces me like her to sit / on little chair. – Interpret again / fight in double bed. – Constantly / meanwhile forces wants father writing letter /

386

that I only pretend, do not help. – / Masturbates again, does not want / to bring thoughts, states my fault that masturbates / so much I ~~explain because~~ because I have explained / to her. – Associates ~~earl~~ then from wreath / on the wall (carpet, little rose in the middle) / has glycerine hands. – Then sets phantasy / as play production – A witch = a car / drags wreath away – her witch-children / help her – they put wreath in stove / cook, roast it in order to eat – 1 / witch-child has sympathy – she also wants / to roast it – but then comes scolding [?] / in her – harms her wreath, take it / out – poor person becomes well / again. – Has 1 completely red face nose / etc. like devil and white hands. Interpret / mother lets her eat member with her and / semen, then well again. – / To little rabbit associates: bad conscience / pee-pee, poo, bottom – king's son, inn / place to sleep. – I interpret. – Meanwhile con-/stantly masturbation – and fiercest resistance. | – Finally more play [with figures][1] between masturbation. / Girl sleeps as if dead. Father wakes her / says does not need to be like angel – may / take wood from wood-van climbing / on to cart – making trousers – but / then looks over and chases her away. / – Interpret uncertainty in behaviour parents / refusing and satisfaction, also reproaches me. / – Also interpret always after masturbation session / anxiety about betrayal – therefore my accusation / to father – resistance towards [analytic][1] work / that I do not discover anything from it – at first wanted / to play pig-slaughter head etc. / again whole session / – ~~Then~~ session / of 20th still plays – she brings father / food – says herself 'shit-coffee' / and – intensely aggressive and threatening / forces me to praise that cooked even / better than Mummy – says 'made'. / – At my question where is / Mummy then in fact: 'but we have annoyed her / to death, don't you know'. – / She forces more and more to / praise the food – immense rage comes out / here. – 25/ II. More approachable. / Begins masturbation again – but very soon / brings thoughts when encouraged and thus / refrains from masturbation. – [sucks thumb and refrains when asked][1] A black dog / wears glasses. She has diamonds / ~~that shine like rainbow~~ dog / comes into a small shop – shows | cupped hands joined together – there / he receives something from a bag – that is brown / outside black inside. Inside eggs that / black with white mark. – About glasses: / Mummy wears – then also father wears / glasses. – (Interpret mother who receives from / father in coitus – eggs = penis, stool – / semen. – Resumes masturbation / sucking – again thoughts: 'pee-pee, poo / bottom – cupboard, picture, whip. / King's son. – He wears glasses.

p. 29

p. 30

~~Otherwise~~ / ~~w~~ He rides horse again. – The glasses / also have diamonds: they shine like rainbow. Has all colours. – It / received them from colours on which it placed / itself in order to suck out honey there / – the colours were on clothes as we / 'also wear them'. ~~Interpret~~ (With honey-sucking / – again thumb-sucking.) (Interpret / pipi coloured like mother's genitals / there receives mother's secret – / sucking that!) – Again masturbation – / but this time desire to play instead of / speaking. Puts track together. / Calls girl 'Merda' – associates / murderer – engine with 1 coach = girl / murderer – another part of train is called [?] / Krummellinda. – These separate / and unite, fall over – / 1 piece of one or another / always remains – that stands

p. 31 up the other. – | 'Linda' = linden – a tree that / sticks tongue out. – (Interpret / Krummellinda[iii] = father's member – / shattered in pieces eaten like 'Krummel' by mother = murderer. / Also thumb-sucking again here / – In general was very much more / obedient. – 26/II. – Reports was at dentist / her tooth pulled out – she also pulled her own / tooth out – string tied to door / pulled and torn out like that. – Shows / finger ring (too big for adults). Has / an invisible hook that / holds it (interpret loss member through / father – claims is really dent-/ist – but also through masturbation. Then / wants mother's genitals with invisible / penis.) Then again emerging known / menacing aggression (asking but threatening / and tormenting). Immediately giving paper – / but ~~the kind on which~~ writing-paper / (repeatedly refused.) Takes ~~paper~~ / pencil and rubber, scrawls over it / also table although forbidden. – Again / attempt to kick feet – (but which also / like pinching etc. through energetic prohibition / can generally prevent.) / Wants to force me to write to father, cannot / help her. V At first draws ring but then out of this a small

Wants to take little calendar, licks / at it, taking paper-knife with her

p. 32 princess {Figure 3} – other side tall / princess – and tells about conductor who / drives train and has red cheeks. (Interpret / rage she alone – parents' coitus.) / ~~3~~. Then tall princess in thin / dress says herself nightshirt and / small. – [something crossed out] Then Father Christmas / with bag with gifts, toys – / things to eat. – On other side

---

iii Translator's note: 'Krummellinda' sounds similar to 'crooked lime tree', which would be *krumme Linde*.

Figure 3 The drawing presented on 26 February is dated 27 February 24. On the front is a 'little princess' 'at first ring clowning [?] removed.' On the back a 'tall princess towards whom train is driving with conductor'. / On a second page – also from 27 February 24 – is a 'tall princess in thin dress', next to her a 'little prince'.

tall / princess who constantly eats / from bowl on birthday table. {Figure 4} (Interpret rage / mother from father in genitals food.) / She should be together with her / in night. – ~~Before beginning drawing when / so maliciously furious.~~ – Wants calendar / and licks it – (also father's semen / in mother's genitals) etc. taking to herself. / Interpret either having or enjoying pipi = / taking mother's genitals. / [While drawing – meanwhile constantly sucks thumb but does not masturbate.][1] / 27/II. Sits down immediately in my chair / – asks (in

Figure 4 The drawing presented on 26 February is dated 27 February. On the front page appears 'Father Christmas with presents, the princess feeds (other side)'. On the back 'tall princess who constantly feeds from table'.

this usual insistent / way) for a sip of water to be brought over / is so tired, has not slept at all / there was a masked ball. – Then I am to / take off her coat for the same / reason. – Ask about masked ball. / Great rage. Tries to hit / push – but finally regains her self-/control. – Despairing requests for / my seat – when I bring her / other armchair in the meantime takes / my footrest scornful angry does / not want to *p. 33* give back – to share the least. | ~~27/II. States very tired, then / immediately back into my~~ Then satisfied with / small chair and association to foot-/rest: nothing, nothing, nothing – keeps / repeat-ing. – A mermaid. – Has caught a / little man and a little woman. They / escape to the coast. Little woman throws / a mirror-mountain behind her – does not / mind when mermaid smashes with / ham-mer. – Mirror-mountain so beautiful must / always be scrubbed smooth. / (Interpret she mother, who with Erna's[2] father / coitus is prevented. – Erna[2] mermaid who / has nothing = no pipi = footrest / and takes it from mother = mirror-mountain that / wants to smash to pieces in rage.) – Plays game idea masked ball: a car / and an engine run into each other. / She has a magic lute – (wanted to represent / that by a little man) – then / says it is herself. She plays on it / so that 2 can separate again. / They keep driving together. / – ~~she plays~~ they dance – that is the / ball. She is a musician and plays music / to it. – The engine is called 'Schabramänn'[iv] / Then starts sucking thumb again / – often at same time also picking nose. / About 'Schab' = [1 sweet brother no an old one][1] – knocking, something white – / makes bubbling movements as / with 'flower-food'. – So that / is completely scraped to pieces. ~~Is a sweet~~ / Ra = (Rahel) her favourite friend – no / she is stupid – in reality nice. | Man is an old man. – Interpret / 'Schabramänn' = father's pipi makes / sweet semen in Rahel = mother and belongs / a man. – She sucks thumb and masturbates with / these phantasies. – She anxious, I should / not remind her of mas-turbating / ([something crossed out] second session no attempt at this) / otherwise she must do it. – Interpret anxiety as a result of / mother's example coitus induces to / masturbation. – Tiredness = not sleeping / because observing parents' coitus. That's why / also rage especially me from oral / envy. – Climbs on to little table and does gymnastics. / Has me admire muscles. From table / constantly full (~~seemingly~~ not really / apparent overcompensation) tenderness / in armchair falls into my lap and / arms – then as I gently refuse / portrays it on other armchair. Thereby / strokes, kisses. You Sweetie etc. – Meanwhile / though wants to push and pinch again / to open bottom with key – look at / what is inside. – Interpret longing during coitus / observations and masturbation phantasy [something crossed out] replacing father / for mother. – 29. – Building / hospital from bricks. A completely injured / man in one bed – a less injured one /

p. 34

iv Translator's note: This sounds similar to *Schabrameng*, which is later explained as 'cream butter'.

in second bed. As doctor she says to injured one / that he is beyond help, to second that she will / help him. – Injured man goes / to hell also one woman. – | She herself – the doctor – but also dies – / goes to heaven – she is / put in a bed covered in roses, that / have been picked in the garden. She / is received by dear God – / kissed – followed again as usual by dancing / and wedding. (Interpret – has mother double bed – / in which father was castrated – repressed – / also killed father – but then double / bed = heaven united with father / roses = pipi.) Strong resistance. / Pushes table towards me – in order / to annex my chair at all costs. – / At story of roses begins to suck / then also to masturbate plays it to end / says afterwards – such a bad conscience. | 1/III. – As usual beginning of session rage / and jealousy of previous patient. – Demands / struggle for my chair / insisting on beautiful writing-paper – / Draws star that fastens to sky / with hook. – A star that is filled / with pee-pee and poo and on which it comes out at the back. Many stars / like this. No only one. The others / fine – there the finest cake comes / out. – Smells me and states / I stink. – Wants to caress me – and / jabs pencil at me; – harasses in every / possible way pushes table at me – too / close pushes too close with feet. – Then / stabs star all over with pencil. / – ~~Lies on floor cushions under~~ / Arranges flat again an over-/turned table = dining room – little chair = / loo. – I must go to loo / press there – afterwards if piece / has gone through be 'happy' like / her. – Must then on my / chair fill trousers and throw / stool over into the loo, for which / she gives me small cushions. – I have / difficulty in subduing the aggression / constantly directed at me / – every day problem in the session – / also tenderness behind which aggression / immediately reappears – and inducing / other aggression. | Lies on floor, cushions under / head – position as in bed and aims / small cushion – previously stool / at a small chair – says against / 1 woman – also repeatedly against / 2 little chairs [that placed next to each other][1] – finally hurls them / apart – says with satisfaction now calmer. / Is tired would like to sleep! – Thereby / sucks thumb and masturbates. (Interpret masturbation phantasy / separating killing parents with / stool-missiles.) ~~3.III~~ Afterwards tries to take / with her or damage every possible / object in the room. – ~~A~~ 3./III. / Again struggle for my armchair / and footrest. – Finally obeys / but demands other large armchair / and places legs on small table. Scrawls / pencil all over table and tremendously / happy when want to forbid. – / Has talked about 'eye-salad' – / suddenly while scrawling hurls / {Figures 5 and 6} pencil at my

p. 35

p. 36

p. 37

Figure 5 The drawing mentioned on 3 March appears on a sheet of paper on which 2 March 1924 is indicated (probably mistakenly as 2 March was a Sunday). On the front page appears a 'girl who shuts her coat against the wind'. On the left is 'A negro whose head shows a "quitsche" ', next to him by the girl is noted 'pipi below'. On the right, 'fiercely blowing wind'.

eye so that / the eyelid hurts. – Draws – / ~~after~~ – at first as usual difficulties / because of paper – girl who ~~is ashamed~~ / and closes coat against wind. – / On the right the wind blows hard. – Other / side girl – who constantly does poo / and pee-pee. – Tells me when / I say poo she is always ashamed / another occasion repeats: better to say / urine and stool = more attractive. – | ~~Also mother~~ Meanwhile /   *p. 38* begins to suck thumb masturbate. / Associations: eye-salad – tooth- /

393

Figure 6 The drawing mentioned on p. 38 is on another sheet of paper from 2 March 1924. On the left is a 'pot with "quitsche"', underneath 'girl who does wee-wee and poo. Next to her is the mother who at first had no eyes and nose'. At the top right appears 'Mouth!', underneath is 'Mother without eye, nose at first, then at top right and left finally as it is'.

nose powder. – Then draws mother / who comes to look no / eyes and nose at first – only hair / reinforces – but then does draw / nose and eyes (interpret tearing off / mother's eyes nose – hatred / because of supervision masturbation.) – Ask / about eye-salad. She draws . . .

[represented wavy line] Drawing of / 2/III.24.1) always one below the other; these are / components of salad. – Added to this / are: tooth-nose-powder / crushed – tooth-nose salad soft, mild / quitscham-salad.[v] Flour salad, 'einwuschpeng',[vi] something sweet / (Interpret: sweet brother, hit / scraped etc. = semen) 'cell-potatoes', / glasses from behind. – About 'quitscham' / = 1 'quitsche' – draws completely black / round one ~~that~~ on p. 1 in pot – / / p. 2 then becomes the head of / the negro. That is brought close / to the fire – also the eyes – / earlier spoke about juice coming from / eyes – are / at first (said with hesitant / tone and facial expression) gently / and softly cooked – then the | the other things go in. – (Interpret / negro *p. 39* = 'quitsche' in pot = stool / and stool noises – flame = penis / anal coitus.} = ~~She~~ salad = eyes / nose teeth crushed ground / etc. mixed with stool). With / this salad / spoke constantly sucked / thumbs. – At interpretation stool-thing / draws in girl who closed coat against / wind, but underneath also / pipi – draws small one but not large. / 4/III. Already yesterday showed new watch, compared / with mine – like operation [?] – / if not the same – hers better, prettier / – becoming as usual and in everything / increasingly spiteful. – Today similar. / Builds watch-clock from bricks; – but then / makes stairs and small hut / from them. – Inhabited by woodcutter / poor – who has little horse with / broken legs. – Makes him / mat – the hut changes / into a palace, ~~so~~ throne on which wood-/cutter sits as king. Lives happily / with his beautiful daughter – / must go into garden pick a / rose, he kisses her on both cheeks / which he should not have done, only on the right – / then everything changes back into | hut. – Daughter *p. 40* pleads with little horse for / a clock, brings it to her – then it becomes / a pretty garden and a palace and then they live / happily (Interpret: legless horse = castrated mother / or she herself. Mother allows her father – ~~thus becomes~~ / – gives her genitals to her, so everything / pretty). — Father daughter then go into river / swim together in 1 very big / rose and come out of it / in completely changed form and are very happy. / Immediately afterwards lies down on couch, says / has very bad conscience, depressed. / (Interpret wishes mother repression – together / giving back with father.) – Jumps on / my bed with both feet looks / at everything – pictures. – Says tired sleeping. / Is

v 'Quitsche' and 'quitscham' are invented words of Erna's that may be connected with *quietschen*, meaning 'to squeal or squeak'.

vi An invented word of Erna's.

surprised at what she is from – ~~how~~ / whether she is there. / ~~Sue~~ Sucks thumb, masturbates / (Interpret coitus observations night – tired – cur-/iosity how all that went on – tired, / sucks thumb, masturbates) Stops that at / my request. Thoughts: poo, pee-pee, bottom / Papa, Mama, North pole. A train with / North pole drivers. A father with daughter / engine always goes away from carriage / [without them noticing it. V][1] / A strange man watches them. He / is a lute-player. The curve is / a woman – the other is a whip. / Throws the lute away and then they dance / both women dance together

V The coal carriage falls over and covers / everything in grease.

p. 41 5/III. – Offers sweet. – Plays theatre / and I am not to look [until prepared][1]. – A train / ~~like~~ North pole driver. – The engine / keeps moving off – a woman drives in it / with her ~~daught~~ husband no with her / daughter; – the carriages run over / each other – also the 2 are run over / by the engine – then / they are no more they were / run over. The 2 dance together / and caress each other. – Suddenly emerg-/ing aggression. Sucks thumb. / ~~Begin~~ eats sweets enthusiastically / [bites little man and trains][1] / – playing Emperor King – passionate here / her place always Emperor – she wants to / force me to serve, bend to pick things up etc. / – throws cloth too far – associates to / cloth that we throw to each other – tiger / lion – that pulls in one corner / of cloth. ~~Because~~ is not like / balcony parapet that so thick / crust the cold does not blow through / – has only thin crust (recognises / interpretation cloth = pipi, semen ejaculation = / something cold. – Rage and playing Emperor etc. = / fact has no pipi – cannot / take father's place and have / wedding with mother /. –

p. 42 6/III. Theatre again. / Not to look at preparations. – Train | that does not ~~go~~ [falls apart][1] mother daughter – daughter / drives in own special stable / fast train to shop [man [?] with shop][1], buys sponge there. / – Then (emerging aggression) – / again to shop – beats man to death / now the shop belongs to her and mother. / At first she had negotiated with man, / what does the shop cost. – He had understood 'big wish-shop' / quarrel – beating him to death. – Suddenly reluctance / to play – perhaps with water [playing?][1] – / begins to put her feet close to me. / Then we will make / our own flat (now she enters the game again / in person) into which rain never comes – / also now have own shop. – / Turns table round = dining room / setting up little chair = loo / my footrest stairs. – She / lives with father – no with mother / cooks for her demands key / larder. – Asks what shall / we cook? – I ask for potato fritter / (her ~~favou.~~ 'favourite dish'.) – She suddenly / asks for toilet – says in game / let's say goes to baker – / in reality great wish. – / Comes back and passes me (phantasy / potato fritter – then goes to / little chair loo – says does not want / to think about stool (interpreted) at meal | ~~then stacks footrest~~ *p. 43* ~~on it~~ / ~~small cha~~ bakes something oven / ~~sta~~ {stacks} That is little chair on which places footrest / sits on it. – Pushes bright-coloured little / cushions under it = fine cake / baked. (Interpret star that makes cake – / poo = stool). – At first she – then I / 2 days unwell. 12/III. – Hardly greets / me – asks if I am ill. – Then / why not several children also once as / with Frl. Wolffheim – ~~whether~~ where my / little boy – she ~~sm~~ {small} may also / say pee-pee poo with Mummy. – Here / suppresses rage aggression, does not take / off coat – looks hostile. – Then asks together with this / also whether was ill. – (Interpret resistance that / was not allowed to come – disbelief that or why / ill – what possible thing / I am doing with boy = man or / also child. ~~Several~~ / children and mother pee-pee poo = resistance / to my knowledge of her looking at bottom / Mummy – masturbating knowing {?} in morning.) – Agrees / asks if my husband tonight put / pipi into me – how often – when – / whether I also masturbated as child. – / (Interpret original curiosity.) – Resistance / much reduced – abandons – wants to play – / friendly. Tells said at home / does not want to come. ~~Sorrow~~ Meanwhile / eats at 'deusch' [?] sweet – drinks water. | Takes cigarette packet from ~~bust~~ – chest – / calls her bust – *p. 44* fills it / with sweets. – Puts little man in bus / [partly with head][1] – then goes on playing with woman. – She / drives bus – runs over / man by mistake – regrets, comforts him – / leads him into bookshop and cures him / with cream that is inside book. / ~~Here puts violently~~ ~~(Here viole~~ – They / caress each then fly high in sky / bookshop (also called teacher): is / on their heads. In sky it / is then a completely different shop – they / also know nothing more about earlier – / God kisses them are very well-behaved. (Interpret / coitus observation: first father in mother – / then mother on father. – Gives him from her / genitals in coitus secretion – that she / recognises.) – Suddenly strong resistance. Takes / her little wind-turbine (bright feathers) that / brought with her, goes with it on to balcony / [lets it turn in the wind][1] / leaves door open – (which repeatedly forbade), / scorns me, does not come – then / explains how usually in such cases when encouraged [?] / 'is sensible again'. – (Interpret rage / parents gifts to

each other – she alone / pipi. Turning wind = masturbation.~~) G~~[vii] / [something crossed out] Drinks water greedily – sucks / sweets. (Interpret observation together – coitus / masturbation sucking) – (Interpret sky – / high – movements coitus. – Sky / changes God = repression being well-behaved. – / Makes engine drive with carriage
p. 45 and then | alone: engine is called 'Schnettereng' [?]. – / Drives constantly round the table. / Is red at first – then yellowish like dots / on engine – then white like pieces / of paper – that tears off and throws down. – The / white is then like whipped cream / – the engine then takes it / in and gets very fat from it. / About 'Schnetter': eyebrow-<u>cutter</u>. / then contains salad: ~~eyebrows~~ zalla-powder / love teeth – eye cut-outs – nose- / powder – brooch-powder – something red-eyed – / apple-brows-vanilla – 'stink-plom' – / hand cut-out (shows cut-away middle / and index fingers) – railway – purple-pully – / monastery – poo, pee-pee – pencil – tooth-powder / 'billbill', little key-axe – lily-salad / rose-oxen. – About 'reng.' = ring, cigarette / (at interpretation – coitus again 'gifts' – semen / etc. – Engine that gets fat = / mother.) – Again fiercest resistance gets / dressed – (end of session) takes sweets / again – puts down little woman too makes mistake. – / into packet with sweets – / at which says – bust and what comes out / of it. – (Interpret oral envy, reduced / resistance.) – Also asks 5/III. – [something crossed out] / about [something crossed out] better-behaved and worse-behaved Erna.[2] / (After emphasis wild and anxious – conciliation compromise) Question whether one then / also
p. 46 may be somewhat wild. – Answer | wishing thoughts uninhibited / – reconciliation compromise) She beaming / 'That is a wonderful story / that you are telling me'. 13/III. – / 3 little men come to ~~bo~~ shop. / Bookseller has poison for sale. How they / touch the book that he passes to them / fall down dead. – Bookseller / also is then killed. Little / men come alive then jump / around with 2 women so that – 1 / stands in the middle – 1 on the right [something crossed out] over / her, she over him and he jumps the other way round / – likewise the other. – ~~Another game~~ – / (Interpret 3 little men = penis. – She: 'The / pipi and [something crossed out] poo and pee-pee at the back! – / Book bookshop mother – penis / broken – returns to life – mother / dead. – Shared between her and mother / [~~A~~ 2nd) car keeps hooting although / woman is not in front of it but always / running after it at the back. – From 4 corners carts cars hoot – / always – towards middle

vii 'G' may stand for 'gift' or 'God' (*Gabe, Gott*).

– so that / woman finally lies between / immured and dead. – Then woman / comes alive – cars are her toy-carts. / After that she drives. Has a magic / and also enchanted – that small / woman is there and dances with her. / Also charms carriages completely away / then back again. – They hear that / her magic is over [?] hoot again | and drive – but she charms again / so that belong to her. Puts 2 away that had / only persuaded the 'other children'. / – Here when speaking about charming woman / – says 'I'. (Interpret identification with mother – / battle between mother and father for / penis – at same time also children – that / feared possible. – Mother keeps / only 2 – she and father.) – Thereby she becomes / more furious scrawls table demands paper: / draws broad tall man [?] – / in which everything very muddled. / Then explains where legs = head – / those are arms and everything the other way round / (Interpret standing on her head = father / in coitus – hence rage – because she did not / have any of it) – Drops pencil / pleads with me / passionately to give it to her. – Then as I bend down – / light blow on the bottom, to me – I / am so pretty and stink. – Takes / my place – interprets game to me – / scornful – clearly all nonsense / points at me. – Still wants to learn / from me to play – rages – pushes me / feet. (~~Interpret rage, mother suspects / her~~ talk about / dirtying from this and I describe her / fear of being caught masturbating / dirtying – wish herself / to catch. – ~~Resistance~~. / States has never even / as very small child never dirtied | herself – asks my / daughter's name. (Interpret fear withdrawal of love / – other daughter) – reduced resistance. / – ~~With rage, that~~ 14/III. – Had forgotten handkerchief / yesterday – by pestering / got me to lend her a handkerchief. – Today / process repeated – asks, pleads – / when does not achieve – uses apron – ostensibly / fear of mother about lost handkerchief / – should give her another one – 3 little men / each one an animal. ~~Woman none~~ with her / (cow, dog, sheep) Woman none – moans / movingly. Suddenly recognises herself in / pipi moans – woman struggles with / 1 man tears his away – rejoices. / Later wins man back again. / Then all with animals against woman who is killed in the middle. Goes / into 1 bed with barbed wire. Little men / jump around with animals, ~~go~~ / also dead – go to heaven in / bed with roses – God loves them. – / When woman had taken away animal / – the shop also belonged to her and in fact / – the shop-keeper – was / her. – More furious, demands paper, / scrawls table. – Draws: 'pretty' / girl, dressed up for a wedding / – next to her bride-groom. (Big buttons / in the middle – long beard – long / black

p. 47

p. 48

p. 49   (drawn like beard) / ears. – Other side: – a small girl / then 'another one comes along – they | also go to wedding. – (Interpret – children who at coitus / thereby – intra- extra-uterine – and come / through coitus) draws another child / = boy – but trousers are ruined. ★ / (Again begging for my armchair. Then / other one. – Sits down in it. Is child whom / I Mummy allow any urinating / stool shovel out with hands / eat some of it, give her some. At same time also allow / sucking (otherwise in session, like / masturbating very much reduced.) – Then I / am father who also allows the same. – / 20/III. – Visiting thanks new figures, carts. / Game: – Woman secretly lies down on cart – / keeps {Figures 7 and 8} climbing down so that coachman / does not see. – Then 2 women lie / on each other in cart, so that even heavier. / Coachman – represented by small / man who climbs down from other / cart, is seized by women / goes to hell. – Scorned by devils / locked in loo where is to be / roasted. – Flees into night, caught / by watchman – keeps all awake in night – / is put to sleep by / magic, only woken to feel that / is burning. Is burned / in loo. Description moaning etc. / The two women – about them mistakenly says / little men arrive in heaven / ask modestly want to work.

p. 50 | God receives them. / etc. in order only to be tolerated. At first / were mistakenly Hell there / wings that devils or robbers tore off / attached, with which they could fly. / (Interpret struggle with father for penis / coitus with mother: – carts, wings.} / Hatred sadistic phantasies father – describes / moaning etc. – at same time theory / of anal birth. But finally father = / God wishes. – conscience anxiety: / hell, heaven.) – 21/III. – ~~drawing~~ / ask what Rolf – more tense furious. / Facial expression – at my house / broken. (Interpret jealousy father coitus.) – / Drawing: copying little pig. / Discouraged V (~~Interpret~~ then cart – / little man so that imitates. / 'Will be able to go home immediately / for man has pipi, will not / be sad any more! – Suddenly anger / sets in, scrawls table, throws pencil / at me: asks, when hits eye – / am I blind? – (Interpret rage dissatisfied / cannot produce penis). Mean- / while says – will eat / restaurant – serves you right – I not. (Interpret / rage – wants to remember! Also not to suck father's penis III

    V Interpret imitating penis = producing / – does not work. /
    III These 2 pages / after the next 2 pages/
    ★ Continuation to this / follows page after page after next

Figure 7 For 20 March 1924, there is a sheet annotated with '1. The old lady who goes to heaven'.

19/III. Affectedly friendly. – Goes to toilet / Meanwhile I am to *p. 51* magic away / 1 chair – and to magic up paper. – Draws: / 'beautiful' girl, bride / full dancing skirt – next to it thinner / and shorter man = bridegroom. / Other side small girl – also / very big dancing skirt (with both / as usual down skirt-hem pee-pee / poo; – drawn in

401

Figure 8 '2. The house is so happy that the old lady is coming to heaven that it makes itself all dirty (the lines underneath)'.

completely black and thick / also buttons) next to this the / much taller bridegroom. – / Other page: queen with crown / wrong checked skirt is / wrong has stolen crown / princess in cradle (other side drawn). / Next to her at first policeman who / caught her – then figure is / – also in checked skirt like / false princess next to her =

mother. – / Has a large eye at side with / which sees everything – below a large / pipi – then father had put / pipi in – she quickly stood ⋆ / up to catch false princess, / – then the pipi stayed inside. – (When I begin to interpret – strong aggress-/ ion. Scrawls table – and / pretends – states – must draw / cross on table because it is | appropri- *p. 52* ate – takes some writing-paper / despite being forbidden – and draws on it the / real 'beautiful princess' / with hands of gold and silver / etc. (highly exaggerated praise beauty) / next to bridegroom. At the side train- / bearer (interpretation: dethroned mother / policeman = mother – when she / steals Erna^2 crown = dignity and pipi) / she envious and gets annoyed. – Immediately / afterwards battle for my / chair. Then makes do with / armchair moved close to mine / into which she falls from little table / with glowing declarations of love / 'Dearest, Beloved, Sweetheart' – while / actually wanting to fall on me / like that and also does once. – / Lead away to armchair / demonstrations of love. – But thereby seizes / little chair and hurls it away / full of rage. – At interpretation is hiding / aggression behind love – furious / hammers on armchair. Then / 'tired and bad mood'. / ⋆ Cont. from fourth to last page: pleats – | Cutting out – rage – tears *p. 53* to pieces / scatters earth. – 16/III. Shop: 3 shopping / 3 animals for gentleman – little fool = the smallest / the dog – takes all away, also / shop, animals pictures that belong to him / then the biggest of the 3 is the little fool / who takes all that away from others. / Mother makes sure that all / march exactly on middle / strip table. 17/III. Invited / – states to wedding. Will be / whipped cream – she is marrying Georg / no Dieter – she has put on jewellery has / train-bearers – 5 women, 3 little men / march around corners. Wedding / – 2 mocking nothing. Demands / my chair – to swap roles / demands footrest – complains / bad conscience – wants to / swap jewellery with me, has mother's / ribbon. | Continuation from 21/III. – Had also copied / little man in *p. 54* larger size, with 'more buttons / prettier, taller – sneers but has suc- ceeded / then rage – smears little man ostensibly / corrects nose ear – breaks off little man's arm. / – Rage V [something crossed out] She to play theatre – I / to shut eyes. – At first driving / cart, furiously hurls away. – Rocks / little chair in hand – terribly heavy / can throw (with great force) / then dance, to which I am to sing. – / Teaches corrects me – again / rage – throws little table around – / footrest goes in = is car into which / I climb – she chauffeur – pushes / up large armchair. – At first / little table – pushed / in front of and behind her – praises / something for track / again rage discouragement. – I am to /

comment – whether better ~~bottom~~ little table / in front or behind (Interpret despairing / attempts penis – father role – from / behind = producing stool. – After

V Draws me apparently really / beautiful with pointed cap on head / Interpret – father's pipi.

p. 55 interpretation – unsatisfied. – whether she then when / I explain – still gets pipi? – Then / whether she will be more comforted, none. / But will get that man has / but belongs in fact to both with Mummy did / not at all know – her or father. – In / chauffeur game I must pay her / (Interpret exchange mother stool – cream / from book for flower-food pipi.) / At rage eyes casting paper at me / on that ~~when~~ drawn me – / cuts up with pencil into nothing but / strips. – Scornful: / can be put together. Gives to / cut-up mother and little slit / [Strong resistance because of rescheduling of session.][1] / 22/III. – Does not want to see rocking cannot / bear – likewise little women with / mouldy red faces. – / Asks because 'ostensibly' dark, little toy table / little chair my armchair window. – / Seemingly very pleased – I put up there. – Passionately demands / that I bring her a glass of water / Greatest despair (strikingly = not / rage) because I refuse. – I have never / yet in life done given her something – / no more wishes if I allow her / being well-behaved – etc. – When I bring – de-/mands

p. 56 passionately footrest 'just for a few | moments. – Again greatest / despair refusal. – Leaves / room {Figures 9 and 10} (for first time) wants drawing-room expecting / father, never coming again! – I allow / and interpret! (From the dark my bed = armchair / brought to hers = moves from bedroom / to her child's room. – Then [despair-ing][1] attempt also / to [still to][1] receive chest and pipi-fluid.) / – Puts my hat on – draws / me with pointed cap. – (Interpret = father's pipi / put on woman – likewise always the / crown that has grown.) She: yes, is there too / so that both together have / the pipi when Papi puts it in Mummy / then not known to whom it belongs / (Interpret wish to give her mother / fluid from ~~fa~~ pipi) – Ask whether will / be comforted has no pipi, if / then will get pipi from her / husband? – Resistance again / dissolved – very warm. – 24/III. – Again / sad, anxious rather than furious. / Tries to be friendly. – Immediately / categorical – moving window so / that I only see door and only she sees / the beautiful sun. – ~~chopped up~~. Damaged / little man cannot endure among things / – puts away. – Then also other / toys away,

404

Figure 9 The drawing mentioned on p. 54 appears on a sheet of paper from 21 March 1924. On the front page there is a 'little man copied, enlarged'. On the back is a 'cloud [?]', under it a 'little man', next to it on the right 'I! With pointed cap'.

draws. – A / boy who comes saying with / hand gesture 'Jule has / | slaughtered a pig. – Then it was / not a boy but a woman. – / Then only wants to play Jule slaughtered / pig – which 'part do / you want to have?' She 'little tail' – / wants to say that the whole time. – /   *p. 57*

405

Figure 10 Annotated with 22 March 1924 are two sheets of paper with drawings; on the front page of one on the left appears the 'Furious old lady or train-bearer', next to her 'the bride' and next to her 'the bridegroom'. On the back is the 'The "old lady"'. On the other sheet of paper is 'The furious train-bearer' on the left, 'The charming bride' in the middle and next to her 'bridegroom'. On the back appears 'The "old lady" is furious'.

~~Interpret~~ For time being, before drew 'Jule' / – attempt to copy little man / little woman, cart – then again fury / scrawls table – then Jule – / thing. (Interpret failed attempt / – she had been very scornful – / drawn cart prettier than / reality etc.) – copying pipi mother's / little slit – requires / mother who slaughters pipi in / coitus to give up her part. Here / had taken pencil mouth / bitten – again I interpret oral / envy, sorrow. – {Figure 11} 26/III. Brought me / flower, very friendly. = Takes off sandals – ask whether / pins not going into her feet / will not prick her foot. / Draws small sledge on which / Mummy sits – tiny little 'baby-like' / – The sledge is pulled by a charming / blonde girl with fat | belly. – Next to her 1.) {Figure 12}   *p. 58* The girl in the workday apron and her crown. – / At first had drawn on her notebook / with her pencil – then book / shame – 'pencil breaks too easily / to use with hard pad / not soft one. Continues with my / pencil. – Other page charming / bride who has 1 pipi herself though – / bridegroom also has one {Figure 13} – next to them / old lady – but she receiving her (Erna's[2]) bad little / pipi become very small and / stupid. (Interpret she blonde girl pulls sledge / mother = child – she become mother.) / 'The old lady' so furious because she has / bridegroom who will kill old lady. / Other page: she sits corner [below in her][1] room / because wants to hear nothing about it {Figure 14}. – Above she and her bridegroom who / rub their hands. 3.) The bridegroom / makes his eyes so big to / {Figure 15} [something crossed out] frighten kill the old / lady – kills her with saw that keeps / sticking into body: other page: / she has such a lot of long hair / plaits, longer than bridegroom {Figure 16} – / also a pipi. Are very happy. / 4.) {Figure 17} A dangerous crocodile. / Underneath it bride and groom. | ~~Other page: she is also lying in grave / dead,~~   *p. 59* ~~next to her crown.~~ – Says really / wants to die, lies on couch, – ~~I~~ / is dead, I bridegroom weep over her / doctor fetched: first doctor shakes, taps / her – dead. – Second doctor – / gives hope prescribes tea–water / with soup, shakes her. She cannot / speak – bridegroom calls / doctor again – finally dead. – Repeated / death wishes. Draws: other / side: she in the grave {Figure 18} next to her crown / (interpret dying = having coitus – but / also real expectation of death / guilt feeling death wishes / mother in observation parents' coitus. / Big eyes father = erect / penis – saw = member. – Anxious / expectation after mother's death – / father has coitus with her – at same time also / fear guilt feeling. Also fear / mother with penis: – [I][1] she with my / shoe treading bare foot – pins / – her weak pencil. – /

407

Figure 11

408

Excessive friendliness / tenderness from sense of guilt | 29/III. *p. 60*
Woman in middle – 2 corners cars – / other corners little men –
world belongs to / her. Cars drive her order – two / little men come –
finally / conjures away cars. – 2 couples with animals / and cars –
separately stands little fool / who has nothing. He then collapses
everything / mixes it up – then he / has everything, others nothing. –
Strong / aggression towards me and ob-/jects room. 31/III. Water
games. / How lovely clean the underclothes. Not / to talk about poo
– wants to know / nothing about it. – Before Easter – / ~~por~~ repeated
portrayals / theatre. – Terrible rage because / wants stage bed and I do
not allow / to walk on it and play there. – Finally / satisfied with
couch. – Represents / curtain there – I may only look when / it has
gone up. Until then must / sleep. – Dances around there stamps / feet
sings along. – Is mother / who cooks, makes something soft by cook-
ing. | Fruit – plums, – pears. Another / day father cooks, but makes *p. 61*
her buy fruit for it with / little basket. – Afterwards at theatre production / always rage. I. – Easter break (3 weeks) / fairly good. At first
more difficult – / then quieter and again more / excessively tender
with mother. – When resumes again / extraordinarily polite affected
/ inhibited. – Already end of ~~next~~ session / again aggression and rage
outside / in time May and June – draws / woman man child –
together / are in meadow. – This followed by enormous / rage. – No
not together. Again / draws charming woman & bridegroom / child
herself has husband. – Then / plays – I her husband. – ~~Went~~ / ~~away~~ At
first affectedly tender / – then I went away – / not back on time,
fetches police-/man in rage: should lock up / her husband who does
not want to / come to her 'to put in pipi'. Husband

I. Very frequently then also lying down – / masturbating, sucking
thumb [after report softly cooked fruit][1] – putting to sleep / (representation her participation in nocturnal / coitus observation.

Figure 11 There are three sheets of paper dated 25 March 1924. On the front page of
one on the left appears 'The furious train-bearer', next to it 'The princess with crown'
and on the right 'Bridegroom', with a particularly pronounced 'pipi'. On the back
appears 'The princess' and next to her 'Bridegroom'. On a further sheet at the front
again next to each other are 'The old lady', 'Princess', 'Bridegroom'. On the back are
'Furious old lady', 'Princess', 'Bridegroom'. On a further sheet at the front it is noted
'The charming girl', on the right it says 'about the murder'. On the back again there
are 'The old lady', 'The charming girl', 'Bridegroom'.

[B 26: A sheet of paper with drawing from 28/V.24] *On the front Erna's first name and the first letter of her surname are indicated, as well as the date 28/V.24. On the back is written 'A female clown' and 'A male clown'.*

[A page with drawing from 2/VI.24:] *On the front Erna's first name and the first letter of her surname are again indicated, as well as the date 2/VI.24. There is also the following comment: 'A cow (this is how she thinks her 3½-year-old Peter[2] predecessor in the analytic session would have drawn it)'. Further annotated in each case are then 'udder', 'person', 'bucket'. On the back it states 'A cow (as she can beautifully draw it)'. The 'udder' is also annotated {Figure 19}.*

In addition to this, there appears a cut-out figure, in which Erna's first name and the first letter of her surname are again noted on the back, as well as the date 20/VI.24.

[For the four sessions from 1 June to 4 July 1924 and the ten sessions from 3 September to 13 September 1924, there are no notes available.]

[A sheet of paper with drawing from 6 September 1924:] *Again Erna's first name and the first letter of her surname. On one page it states 'The breakfast table for mother and child'. On the other side are indicated from left to right 'door – breakfast table [underneath it] cup – coffee [underneath it] coffee pot – cup – door'.*

[A sheet of paper with a drawing with Erna's first name and the first letter of her surname, the date is smudged over the day, but it is legible that it originates from 24 September:] *'At first: girl – then it is mother with night-cap. Wakes child up to have breakfast.' On the back again from left to right: 'Cushion – [underneath it] child – bed-curtain*

Figures 12–14 The drawing mentioned at 1. appears on a sheet from 26 March 1924. On the front page on the left is 'little blonde girl with fat belly pulls sledge'; on the right, 'The little blonde girl with workday apron', with the word 'crown' over her head. Below in the middle is noted 'Sledge with Mummy inside'. On the back 'Bridegroom' appears on the right, 'the pipi' is again especially pronounced. Next to them is 'the charming girl', and to her left, 'The old lady has received her little child's pipi'. In the second picture appear on one side from left to right next to each other: 'Furious old lady – princess – bridegroom'. On the other side appears at the top 'The charming girl', next to her 'The bridegroom'. In the lower right-hand corner, 'She sits in her room to avoid knowing anything about the murder'.

Figure 12

Figure 13

412

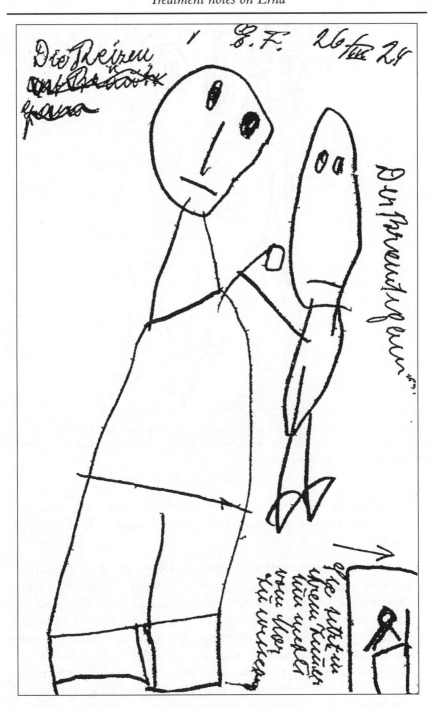

Figure 14

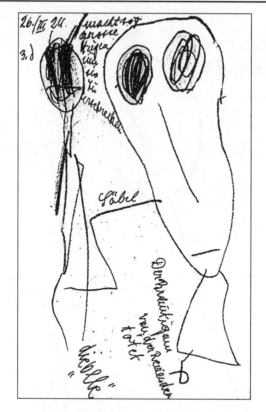

Figure 15 The picture described at 3 is inscribed at the front 'makes such big eyes to frighten her', then a 'saw' is marked. Below it states 'The bridegroom of the charming girl kills the "old lady"'.

— *[underneath it] chair on top of which the small girl's clothes — quilt — night-cap — [underneath it] mother — door — [underneath it] handle'.*

[B 13: Single sheet of paper] Erna[8] 15/IX. – Lining up carriages / looks for engine – chair / bathroom – Washing. / Washerwoman – I supposedly: / clean – trousers thick / with blood dirt! / (Exercise book! Schoolmistress!) / from dirt. Laundry / fishes – [counting][1] [?] money also / for that [something crossed out] – chair / – water representation / paper tap – sack / t. {then?} stares sacrament / – lake – fishes () / – very cheap / by policeman made / expensive – policeman / arm movements [?] / pastry cook – whipped cream / nut cake – same / water – paper [something illegible] /

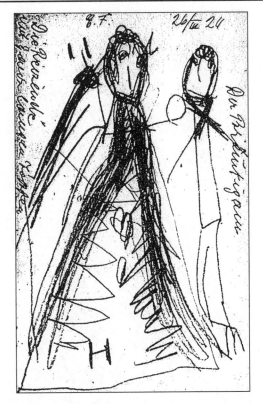

Figure 16 On the back appears 'The charming girl with very long plaits' and next to her 'The bridegroom'.

spit – with pencil / hitting – dirtying / [something illegible] sheet /

[Back page:] takes away – makes / pay – rage spitting [?] / hitting.

[On a notepad with three pages, on which the writing is fairly faded, are the following treatment notes:]

[Sheet 1, front page:] 16/ How she chair (speaks / sings) / glass water ink – / pencil pen – floor / exercise book – sponge – wheels / – washbasin also / ink: – crowns 1 with [?] / 'Emperor-ink' – only for / her: – water in glass / spit with it – with / thermometer like mine [something illegible][1] / hot ink – this glass / [I bad schoolmistress – holes paper][1] / with spit on thermo-/meter =

415

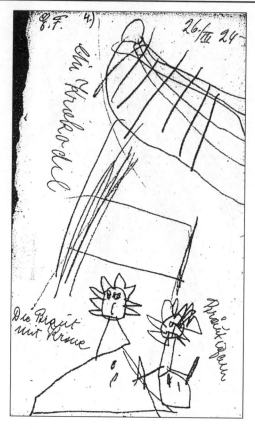

Figure 17 The picture mentioned at 4 from 26 March 1924 portrays 'a crocodile', 'the bride with crown', 'bridegroom'.

Papa's fatness – / = 'Schabrameng' / no 'schlaben', sleeping![viii] / – representing water / represent 'Schanka'. – / ballet girls / dancing at same time = to / waterbed drinks

[Sheet 1, reverse side:] whole night – still / calling out – like a / flower together / chews the water fl. [something illegible] / – cook cooks. / Soup – tastes very nice. / – Spit in – / accusing father – / cook away – Erna / who cleans = not as / well as they think – / after previous [?] cleans / kitchen clean – also / spit – takes care of

---

viii Translator's note: This is a progression of similar-sounding words from *Schabrameng* to *Schlaben* and then to *Schlafen*, which means 'to sleep'.

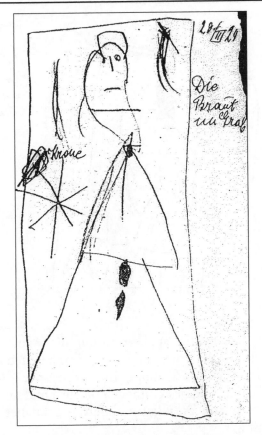

Figure 18 On the back appears 'The bride in the grave', next to her the 'crown'.

me / intestinal catarrh – pears / she me well / my pretty dress / to her. – Erna's husband / the child – at washba . . . [?]

[Sheet 2, front page:] grasps – hits, pinches / bites – induces / father to hit – away – / goes. – /

[17.9 on individual sheet of paper, see below]

18/IX.24 / Erna[8] / mother: pretty bow / ties on I to take off/ rings. Friendly / wakes: school. – There / am to make some holes in exercise book / and stick it – / others me therefore / and I write badly. / – She ashamed this / excuses me. / Only small hole corrects / mistakes: at home:

[Sheet 2, back page:] not eating with father. – / She Dr Schranka

417

Figure 19

~~sou~~ / milk I and maid / apple soup but also / fine. – At request allows / to sleep with father and her / coitus here red / belt reaches in [?] / genitals – child wakes up / asks for pee-pee – / she pretends in front of child / denies coitus – / keeps child away – / but is friendly / early still breakfast / different from her / only very slightly sadistic.

[Sheet 3, front page:] Erna[8] 19/IX. / Mother: early school / lady gentleman writing. Always / A1, O wrong, paper / E1, Q has holes in it I move [?] / places – mother father / shows + relatively / less strict – gives / new exercise book. – Midday / powerful again / feeds extra food. / – I am biting / her arm – wild animal – / ill – ~~forg~~. operates / – forgives – bites / again – father comb / throws kills – previously / beating and reproaches / (broken foot mother

[Back page: one more line follows about another patient]

[Single sheet: front page:] 17/IX.24 / Erna[8]: dresses up / my belt V – ribbon / [I jewellery off][1] / – domineering child to / serve her. – Puts / child to bed. – / ~~With~~ scorn 'theatregoing' / with husband theatre. / Many spectators / dance recit.! – tailor / her new dress / [cut out][1] (from middle of paper) / she received bracelet / – [both][1] greatest joy world / – little angel with / watering can. / Sleeping with husband / coitus – 'buttering' / child watches / Husband beats it / <u>mother lies to it 'nothing happened'</u> / At first: 'parting / hair – mother 'boy's- / head' – supports hair / then belt head / small bow – long / ribbons.

[Reverse side:] Mornings husband / quickly sends away / without breakfast / – child forceful / gives breakfast / supposedly Dr Schanka / milk and bad / cake. (Coitus only / to torment child!) / She boss – dictates to me / previously [specific words][1] punctuation / man as servant / choice of husband (kings / schoolmistress 'Renée' / 'pretty station' / 'white track'. / Gives child food / parents other / child bad semolina / parents cream semolina / child – earth, sand / instead of compote

[B 13: Continuation in treatment book after many blank pages] | 20/IX. – Bathroom: imperious / I am to bring little chair. She *p. 1a* schoolmistress / ink in washbasin. – In the glass water / into which spits is bad ink. Will / become good in Emperor-ink. – Wipes / and cleans what we made dirty. / ~~Then theatre from~~ Meanwhile shows / us children: paper around water-tap / water flows – she leans over catches / – says afterwards = that was theatre / production – she dancer – who catches / water. – Takes paper that was / around tap tears it up is now / fisherwoman who extols merchandise – / Has flounders, eels, caterpillars [new 'caterpillar-fishes'][1] – / 1 [fat][1] pig that only shows / does not sell because she herself/ she and her husband eat some of it / every day. – Has 'Gai' – fishes and 'Ga' fishes / association – parrot[ix] – fishes – 'Ga', 'ga' / – here makes incomprehensible sounds / in which 'ducks' also features / – praises as cheap – then again / forced to make payment of 1000 Marks with which / policeman helps her. – The money that / I give her becomes again to be fished. / Especially valuable extols 'dry / fishes in the glass' – because they are not yet / as soft as the wet / fish but are completely hard.

[B 3: Two sheets of paper] *1. Erna[8] 20/IX.24 / The exercise book that as / a schoolgirl I should / scrawl on, tear up and then / on the hole . . . [?] stick. / (That repeatedly / the case.) – With the other / I had to decorate and smudge letters /*

---

ix Translator's note: *Papagei* is the German word for 'parrot'.

[Reverse side of folded sheet: a kind of fence created with irregular horizontal and vertical lines into which individual letters, mainly As, are painted.]

2. Small piece of paper with row of letters from A and the comment 'Erna's writing on 20/IX.24. As schoolmistress she wrote that as well as she could'

At this required shopping still / gives back to me wrongly. – Then I / must 'steal fishes' from her from basket / while she is not looking – says herself / = stealing = caterpillar[x] fishes. – At first / she had only falsely / accused me of theft. – Also I / must give her false money and will / be locked up for this. – Asks with 'stealing / fishes' – whether washbasin porcelain – / fragile. – Gathers papers torn / wet into balls, blocks washbasin / throws them loo – takes hairpin / throws loo – hopes to block / it with that – throws pencil tub / – strong aggression. – 22/IX. – Again / schoolmistress at washbasin. – Strict: / we are to take care. – Water flowing / leaves tap with paper wound / around it: Quiet! Children must / behave as quietly as mice. – Priest / who puts on production. – Dancer / who (drinking from tap joins in / thereby sings: Mummy takes the moth / with her. Then: no that Cinderella. |

p. 2a

Then song about the queen of / England, who gets / divorced: sudden desire / to play mother and child with me / [something crossed out] – she child. – I early morning / tender – discover she has / dirtied herself. She scornful – previously / acts friendly – then / breakfast I force ~~br~~ semolina / – she deliberately brings it up. / I complain father. He scolds / at first – then her side. – / Gets divorced, marries her / Dr makes me / child with magic wand. – Badly / treated alone eating / differently from parents – scolded by father / beaten behind her, who puts back 'the chairs / cleaner', etc. in school schoolmistress says 'Du'[xi] to me [?] / treated as bad pupil / am beaten by schoolmistress. / – At home last few days again / much more aggressive more difficult | also depressive – over-tender / mother – complains I do not help / her: 'I don't know what it should / mean that I am so sad / don't like life – sometimes / she loves, she bad – Abraham / suggests. 23/IX. Schoolmistress – / as pupil at first I am bad / laughed at by another schoolgirl / because of scrawling & holes in exercise book – / Then am praised by teachers again, / the other

p. 3a

p. 4a

x   Translator's note: The word for caterpillar (*Raupe*) sounds similar to *rauben* (to steal).
xi Translator's note: *Du* is the familiar form of 'you' in German.

schoolgirl ~~praised~~ / [humiliated][1]. (Repeatedly as with / sisters: mother who has a good / & 1 bad child. – Thinks praise of / better pupil is to humiliate worse one) / Then she model pupil – she / as example can do everything / at theatre, or best-behaved – hands always / nicely folded over table. – Yesterday / after phantasies mother bad treat-/ment – exhibits – wants to make / me masturbate her genitals / (dubious experience with / little girl. – Bedroom door | locked – had undressed / alone with her – very embarrassed when *p. 5a* mother / knocked. Although no reproach / repeatedly returned to it with / evident bad conscience / {Figure 20} 25/IX. Reports deep depressions (heartache / so sad, guilt feelings – no one / loves her)

Figure 20 A drawing, on the front of which: Erna[7] 23/IX.24 / The bigger 6-year-old girl with long hair / a tulip and below it a pipi / On the back: letters (Erna's writing?) / 'The smaller girl (4 years old) who / only a stone belt'

keeps asking if I / love her. – Here ~~cuts up~~ cuts corners / off note 'don't / need those' – chews them – shreds to pieces / rubber – asks if I have / allowed? – Interpret connection / guilt feelings mother – phantasies / of last few days – castration and / biting to pieces [something crossed out] – reports me experience small / girl – states but only / tickled! By schoolmistress finally / admitted (what always denied – / some difficulties at school.) – States / schoolmistress very nice, she just badly / behaved. – I then pupil / while she scrawls paper / with dark lines – I make / trousers. – Then I schoolmistress | tell children who scrawl [on paper][1] – should / not make themselves trousers. All make / trousers – but are not shamed / as I am by father, mother – but / mother listens in on schoolmistress sees / how nastily scolds and badly / deals with children – insults them / states schoolmistress to blame, did not / pay enough attention earlier – informs / other mothers – children all taken / away from her – she may / no longer teach anyone is laughed / at by children etc. (analogy / phantasy [?] several months ago – / robber woman, mother who eats out / her children – guilt feeling: castra-/tion – eating up penis, children.) / Phantasy of mother child – / again so that father on mother's / side – mistreats child – / in which she herself is child this time. / (Guilt feelings). – About school thing | had once brought in her / real school-books and exercise books / and shown to me. – Always / in game with schoolmistress – mother who / accuses schoolmistress or vice versa / and [?] father. When I interpret / guilt feelings depression – she pensively: 'Perhaps / don't like it in world / that Daddy & Mummy do / pipi thing? – 27/IX. – Annexes my / shawl – red belt head / – she queen I child – but / only peasant child. – Servant cheeky / with her on telephone grumbled / about her – she very domineering – / proud, conceited king constantly / throwing out servant on her / orders & slapping his face. / New servant who is only to bring / her hat – immediately puts it on / her, she outraged, because hair / tousled, boxes ears again – dismisses. / At pleas for forgiveness, she scornfully / refuses (also still scornful towards mother | play in such cases – but / entirely peacefully considers like adult) / Asks king to find / her a lady-in-waiting – dismisses all the servants – / only keeps 'tender [?] servants' 2 little / dwarfs who dress her and get her ready. / Lady-in-waiting = train-bearer / satisfied praises. – Asks king / to send to Lipos/ Kurfürstendamm where two boxed together. / Then wedding with king. – / Complaining about child, that wants / to have everything like her but is only / peasant

p. 6a (margin)

p. 7a (margin)

p. 8a (margin)

422

child. – Father constantly / beats. – At the beginning of session / tore hooks off eng/-ines – extreme aggression towards toys / 29/IX. – She child but has belt / ribbon head, represents / long hair. – I observe her / enviously – wants to make / cut hair – so / (to persuade her) have | *p. 9a* my own hair cut with intense / pain caused by hairdresser. / – She mocks me, is doing nothing. / Puts on lipstick, make-up – I / furiously complain to father – who {takes} her / side: I become very ill / 'illness: God has spoken / to me' – conscience pangs / was so bad to daughter. – Then / I well, she taken ill. Ill-/ness 'maternal excitement'. V / Doctor taps – very concerned. / Father incessantly torments / me reproaches – she expels / me from room – does not forgive. / – dies. – [Father in despair][1] – father beats me up / throws comb. – Then again / pulls out dead child to show / kills me again. – She loud / noise = life has returned / comes to, has cancer that got / from 'maternal excitement'.

Here her head gets very red, / hot:

Then school, at first throws / all bricks on floor. – On 'Exercise book' *p. 10a* / begins to write 't'. – (Interpret / stool.) – I – schoolmistress – write 't's / badly – she cheeky with me teaches / me scorns – her mother her / side – all decide she becomes / schoolmistress, I pupil – magic-/ ian with magic wand makes / me small – I am scorned / shamed – in vain look for / previous role – I write badly – squiggle / instead of straight lines 'bows' / [something crossed out] holes, smudges. – / She cuts off straight stripes, / cuts them out, eats them up. – I keep / starting 'fresh' exercise book / – likewise. – She makes small cloth / out of stripes, cuts out, spreads / with spit furiously. – Ties me / with belt so that grade / cannot be seen – then keeps / tying round neck – says herself | is 'strangling me'. Would like / to hurl teacher at me – *p. 11a* hurls / cushion. – Before this latest / aggression – again wanted to go / away very downcast.

[Individual sheet of paper, front page:] Erna[8] 30/IX. [1924] / school t [?, A] A – fury / holidays. – She child whimpers [?] / lovely kissing – father / forgives mother furious / pulls out chair / makes it dirty – spit-covered paper towards me (: poo / with pee-pee.) – Forgetting poo / school: repeatedly / new exercise book – scrawling / torn apart, hole covered / torn – Pretty / [exercise book][1] cover – pretty / dress – table – smears / everything – going

423

away / − shawl for me, I / queen − she sets up / throne − angels around

[Reverse side:] me kneeling − / next moment / tears away my / collar − my / chair, footrest

[For the three sessions from 1 October to 3 October 1924 there are no notes.]

[Individual sheet of paper, front page:] 6/X [1924]: Erna[8] − schoolmistress − / I always 'misunderstand / write something else' − she / (articulates unclearly) − / she then always cuts / something away 'for me' / (exercise book) about pencil: / 'some skin still sticks out on it / in front of = wood, not completely / sharpened. She mother / puts on make-up powder [veil-belt][1] = / most beautiful woman world. / I child am to / go to sleep − enviously watch / − father comes − complains [about][1] / child. − More tender / with [?] waking child / (fewer affects − especially less conflicting / love hate) − child

[Reverse side:] gets dressed − mush garden / = water sand, plays / eats − punishment no / lunch − then / gives semolina after all / − reserves 'Schlagmia' soup / for herself and father − / Again father complains / 'eating mush'. − / Decision child children's / home − God-sou [?] / (soul? [?])

[B 13: Continuation in treatment book after three blank pages and a few obviously torn-out pages]

p. 1b from 7–10th. − Schoolmistress − lenient / tries − but then again from exercise book / when (on her instructions I write badly) / cuts away more and more / pieces from exercise book − in corners and / places − but then directly in / form of hole out of the middle. / Finally forces me to write / on tiny pieces − until cuts that up too. / While doing so [once][1]: 'I'm cutting that away from you'. − / ~~Meanwhile after~~ for days this cutting / up. − Meanwhile repeatedly attempts / leniency. Then fury and following phantasy. − / Is 35 years old − I, 40. − Rebels / against me in every way − / annoys me by secretly getting / herself a bridegroom − I only / discover by chance. − is a famous writer / a Dr − who has made / her famous − by writing / about her. Afterwards story father really wrote / in newsp. [?] about her. Very / famous.

424

Most famous in world. Grandiose / phantasies. – ~~from 14–18~~th These last few / days – guilt feelings – depression / suicidal comments (falling | out of window – because not allowed to see / mother because of throat infection – in analysis / she herself got this illness as / mother – and also as child made / mother ill. – Remarks – / heartache, so sad – will never / be able to live inconspicuously among / people. – Repeatedly / cut something up, also crunched – / chewed. – Time [?] such severe depression / as never before. – On 9th again / alleviation – from 14–19th. – / Again cutting up exercise book – / repeatedly gives new one – / warns child to do well now / cuts up again. Here states / I had cut up myself. – / Then cuts out 'pretty cover' / for parents keeps back – after to / child promised, shown, not / given. – Again decorating / with ribbons and veils. Child / must go to sleep. – Pleads / with maid – who carries / ribbons etc. to mother – to have one [?] 1 | is turned away. Maid receives / veil as present from mother wants / it does not want / to lend to me ~~to her not~~ / as child. – Am constantly to urinate / and release stool. Always watching / maids. Servants / with ribbons wave at this. Release urine / on walk – I deny / to mother claim sweat – / had urgently <u>required veil</u> / <u>maid</u> – because had urinated / should not be seen. – Also / defend myself against it – that only / maid takes out pipi / while urinating. – Am boy, have / pipi. – Defend myself because perhaps / takes away. – At interpretation fear mother / by touching child-care – / damages pipi – who cut up / the cover the exercise book – guilt feelings / mastur- bation – displacement on to mother – / – objection: likes so much when mother / rubs in dabs – wants to have / it again immediately in the evening. – 17. – Christmas | plays. Good mother who directs giving / of Christmas presents – I meanwhile play garden . – / But no longer do poo pee-pee trousers / also no longer eat mush (sand / with poo and pee-pee) garden (as always / last few days) eating – am well behaved. – / Mother reports all kinds of toys cart / little woman, ball etc. / and meal in evening together / with parents – various little / bottles, ointments etc. from washstand / At first gives me some from all – all / bottles around my glass – previously / likewise decorated with ribbons / like herself – may even keep / rings. – With such fine Vaseline that / I fall over because cannot / hold out at all. At masked ball and / theatre may not only watch / but dance and play / together with parents – and she / teaches me. – Only at / very end belt around neck / am hanged up because wanted / to masked ball. – That (for the first / time) phantasy almost without ambivalence.

p. 2b

p. 3b

p. 4b

Dresses herself and me up alternately with

p. 5b ~~me~~ – previously resentment / guilt feelings masturbation damage / – here also were complaints again with / father – eaten mush / dirtied – arranging with / father – stabbing child with sabre / all kinds of tormenting – constantly / giving water to drink – otherwise / letting starve cellar. – / Good sister Lotte – at first / laments René's death – then / joy. – Followed by remorse – resistance / wanted to cut short session. – / – Meanwhile last few sessions / sought out undamaged carts – / making verbal slip – / we have new ones Christmas. / (Masturbation damage: new / genitals.) – On the following 17th / determined solution. – Session / begun with happiness repaired / toys – 18/IX. Again only / she mother giving out birthday presents / she

p. 6b birthday and Christmas / 1 day ~~always togeth~~ after each other. | Again similar to yesterday, even more / presents – meal again – / I fall over – because ointment so / fine. Here layered – less / pretty, sticky brilliantine / at first (stool). – About round bowl with water says = German / – oblong France. – Enemies / we eat both up. – Says / Frank = always a man (Frank the monkey) / = mother father we consume. – / Previously had dressed me up / like herself again – long / ribbons as plaits. – As ambivalence / clear again following: I / play with neighbour child [until mother directs distribution of presents]^{1} – this / through ribbons toilet – rings / dazzle (but without making fuss – / as I naturally do – am / dressed up by mother. Lips / [also show off with gold possessions [?]]^{1} red – eyebrows.) Neighbour child / that does not have from her mother / constantly does poo pee-pee – is /

p. 7b scorned by me, accuse her to / schoolmistress. (Interpret: Lotte ~~good~~ well-behaved / sister – I in relation / neighbour child = feared / approaching well-behaved sister – an image / of mother – neighbour child again / mother made into child. – / This time distribution of presents says / once – without father – we alone. / Also in dancing and masked ball / [at first only she and I]^{1} / – he dances with men. Then / though I do dance with parents three / together. – Constantly swapping / ribbons. – Finally / again as on 17th I fall over / (interpret: also dying = having coitus, / mother saw.) Friendly without / rage closes. 20/X. – 'No longer / Christmas'. I am to take off rings / again. – She mother – adorned with all kinds of / ribbons – I full envy – receive / nothing. Again watching / her and husband (I) having coitus. Buttering / etc. she has taken off ugly / skin, put on pretty one

p. 8b I listen / to that – immense envy. – Then | no – the husband has ugly skin / burnt so that she always wears a / prettier one. – ~~thus~~ child sees her in / prettier – next night husband / again burns reserve ugly / skin so that child now always sees / her like this admires – therefore immense / envy and apparently fear mother of / child. – She leaves husband – remains / scornful, coldly leaves child ~~there~~ with / husband (Interpret: father mother separate – she / alone father.). – Says wants punishment / husband to first best beggar man / to go away. Desperate husband plays beggar / she sees through leaves him. – Goes / with minstrel who is then 1 / king – but in kingdom only small / king – she orders him – he / her servant – treats him arrogantly / (reason – arrived too late / father = man). – 21 / X. – School again / am to write badly – schoolmistress / scrawls thick lines over / my exercise book – says I make | my trousers just as full – / ~~afterwards terrib~~ Gives me   *p. 9b* new / exercise book, scrawls again – cuts / out – afterwards terrible fit of / rage. Throws cushions at me – / spits at me, pinches etc. – / Wants to play war with me. – / After forbidden – so: that I am little / chair – against which cushions – she / chooses black [(stool-dirtying – missiles)]¹ gives me less pretty / one – the missile with which we / alternately throw – when she hits / 1 little chair – I fall down dead / – other little chair placed next / to it father, also shoots around him – / – Repeatedly makes me (little chair) / alive, so that she can kill it / again. Then explains cuts out / mother a chair saws her up / etc. and then sits on it / – says I am to wail as if / I were in a lot of pain. – Sits on ~~little table~~ / little chair by table – wobbles / falls so that armrest strikes her / neck (though only very lightly) | Terrible shouting and crying. Deathly pale / ostensibly severe pain but this / immediately passes when I interpret fear from sense of / guilt (cut up mother – little chair – cuts / off her head.) Previously – when missiles / thrown – suddenly falls on couch – / she has been shot. Reluctance to play (interpret guilt / feelings – fear). Continued to play. – Association / I.-p poo, pee-pee, sun moon stars / hunter. Hunter has – shot sun / moon and stars sad – stars are / child. – ~~No~~ – 1 deer in wood is / also received as child to the / stars above. – The hunter shoots / deer. (Interpret shoots mother identific. {identification} / with father –   *p. 10b* guilt feelings – she is shot) / 22. Mother – I child – driving zeppelin / to America – at first: father gone away / – said need none. – Then driving / to him in America – there bananas / and other fruit grow on bushes / – all ~~wea~~ naked, wear only 1 cloth / also father exactly the same as us | In journey across ocean I must be / afraid, might fall in –   *p. 11b* she comforts / me puts me to bed. Meeting / father. In America again

427

round / trip. – Am to pick flowers – no, / bananas that makes into soup / (gets me to cut them reduced guilt feelings / and allows child) – afterwards fried / pineapple. In evening may go to / masked ball and theatre. – Am to ring at door / of neighbour's child – mock – tell / what I eat, no more school – all only / cloth may do poo, pee-pee. Am / dressed up by mother like her. Child / asks to come too – I mock – / 23. – Again zeppelin America / at first that yesterday's only dreamt / – now real journey. – Must be / afraid during crossing. She shows / me – how during journey / jumps up and down – fetches / bananas for me. How I jump off half-dead / and fall down crushed, come /

p. 12b back to life, learn it from her. – | May – as naked – do pee-pee any way / I like all may – she, too elegant, does not / do. When I then – then I also [something crossed out] / not – furious: I am to be well behaved and / only do pee-pee. (Mother's superiority / in cleanliness is driving-force!) Telephoning / neighbour's child – merits – also / extolling masked ball and pee-pee etc. / – saying when ill to eat / bananas – immediately cured. Neighbour's child / begs to come – I refuse: she: mother / says: we don't need another child. / – I then telephone mother before neighbour's / child I scold – pig, goose etc. / – mother also comes over – have / her eaten up by cannibals / does nothing to us. (She thereby bites / pencil, paper etc. also with / banana soup!). – 24/X. P̶h̶a̶n̶t̶a̶s̶y̶ / Again relapse rage etc. / Interpret disappointment phantasies un-/fulfillable. – Following interpretation

p. 13b / birth, mother's womb etc. | Countless questions – where child / comes out – whether anus etc. – sucking / and pulling at curtain-cord – / she can now never go away / from it when swallows – i̶n̶t̶e̶r̶p̶r̶e̶t̶ s̶e̶x̶u̶a̶l̶ / t̶h̶ at most when vomits again. / Interpret sexual theory incorporating / penis – birth by vomiting. – / 25/X. – Phantasies (but tells this phantasy / very often as true) was in Frankfurt / at grand-parents' house – made flight / in the zeppelin ordered / by mother.) Recently as true, that / because of short-sightedness to eye specialist / must go (made up). – About 1 / week then a̶l̶s̶o̶ phantasies / has shop. At first toys / then soon fashion boutique. – t̶h̶e̶r̶e̶b̶y̶ / at first 'normal phantasy appear-/ing. – Soon she does not / sell individual things – as soon as I ask / for them – then terribly expensive / keeps the prettiest for herself – then / as a salesperson I must give things / back to her for

p. 14b free. | Finally force is also used. / Ties garter to me – / belt around me does not take it / off again although this displeases / me. – I go to Dr to various / girl friends – who all scornfully ask / me with whom I was before – I complain / that is too hard and thick for me (at front /

428

over genitals 2 garters / wound together) – / they say would have to / cut through it for me – too hard. / Repeatedly undo and do it up / for me.

[B 25: There is a pad with six pages of writing; the remainder is blank. It is headed '25/X.–25/XI'. No year is indicated, but it might be 1924, cf. notes 25/X.1924 'Fashion boutique'.] *p. 15b*

Eva / fashion boutique / undoing doing up belt – hard thick / cutting *p. 1* in two – scorn girl / friends, Dr – unhappy when missing. – / – Keeps silent: Mama Papa speaking. / Giving nothing away fashion boutique – / cheaply back. – Saleswoman – / phantasies – wet things – / sausage, potatoes etc. – / I woman scolds: too expensive – then / again excessive money: finest / pork world – I not / envious – on account of sweets [something crossed out] buy / beggar woman – court-beggar (sympathy) / – Meanwhile schoolmistress new phantasy / mainly furious. – Again schoolmistress / scrawls a lot over exercise book – she rebukes / shames – looks at bottom / place – all children special / good Lotte – hitting bottom / – punished at home – then pee-pee / was blood – poo – 1 piece meat / came out at front or back / 'Le perateon' [?] – all also forgiving | schoolmistress on bended *p. 2* knees. – King / hears: she Rapunzel – princess / chooses again – prince from / behind – chooses one of earlier / old acquaintants, sends away – gets / child – very affectionate. / – Once: only mother child / – father away. – Then to negotiation / widow. – Is killed because / children behaved badly – previously / she loo. – (phantasy fetched little silver / pot – says electric chair / leads in electric current / out again – dying. / – With man [something crossed out] coitus – / again complaining child. – / – Sale [something crossed out] / shop – counter repeatedly / at loo – pulls cord / always wet merchandise – slices of sausage / scrubbed. / Potatoes more expensive than sausage / This: [something crossed out] pig or ox / – potatoes field. – All | want. – I out, she defaecates. / Then again extols potato / merchan- *p. 3* dise – more valuable than sausage / – whereby everything always has to be / wet – repeatedly shopkeeper / – only too expensive – I no money – / meanwhile attempts wanting / to give away cheaply or for free – when / happens – considers and still / scorns it. – Shop – where it lasts / until I get / sausage or stick of / rock. – From 1 counter / to another – 'that is the same in every / shop'. – Meanwhile also still / plays strict schoolmistress and indeed / so that pronounces things unclearly / I must understand – then scolds / 22. [something crossed out] meanwhile also as mother / French –21/ – At first selling / (everything so difficult to obtain!) – then / schoolmistress – here only dirties and / promises pretty lines exercise book – / but does not then give – finally fashion boutique / where sells me things / cheaply. – At cruel / schoolmistress game – must always / give new exercise book –

p. 4 but she then | scrawls and tears – then / asks whether not trousers poo and / mocks – hitting well-behaved children / with bottom. – / Sells – I must work out / what I must be (also refuses information / Lieschen.) – Wet eel – then also / greenish sausage – bites and listens in / so difficult to get. – Then / special wrapping [?] counter (wet / paper perfectly folded – takes long time. / Police otherwise get lost to death – / (guilt feelings displaced chewing – / very liberating interpretation) – otherwise no / elegant people come to buy. – / – then also schoolmistress – / rebuking but much less / cruel. |

p. 5 Remorse – the ever-punished = little / sister – also she herself – big / Lotte, who can do everything better – big / sisters. – On 22. – phantasy – / only mother and child – father gone away. / – She already big – bridegroom writ-/er etc. – I satisfied – she / lovely villa – next-door for me and / my husband who still alive all / together (happy feeling of relief) / [something crossed out] next day continues – / finally though I die – big / sister who went away no longer dying / I see – bequeath little sister to her. / Here already little sister opposite / looks again and ashamed stool-thing / in front of people. – (Alleviation) Previously / wanted to play – I to give out Christmas presents / I receive – but stops. / Must see how mother puts on make-up. / Furious. (Altogether milder but / for this – often stops – because becomes / reluctant. – Bigger sister / pupil / also dances better – I praise myself / at first – I everything better – but / then girl friend admits / everything – stool dirty-ing etc. but / [something crossed out] asks me and whispers some-

p. 6 thing: am to say everything – / also that wanted to bite off pipi | here though girl friend then laughs at me / killing mother etc. – In last / few days often greater insight / into things – question whether was / happy when boy – or little slit / with pipi and some hairs on it. – / – Says when pulls in then very small: father song / little podge something in little trousers / displeased her so much – with school-mistresses – / game: 'Lutschi – ka – t'. / Makes me present school-mistress all guilt feelings and / phantasies etc. hers from recent time. Then / scorn

[For the 175 sessions from 25 November 1924 to 4 November 1925 there are no notes.]

[B 26: Individual sheet of paper, commentary on the drawings attached to it]

5/XI.25 / 1. Queen has short hair – / none at all – just wig / draws flowers (genitals) / with special care – but then / covers in red, supposedly prettier / (Interpret steals & tears genitals to pieces / tears out pubic hair.) / Same with lines over face / – damage. Criticises fat / legs, left heel twisted / foot sprained – mother's / foot disease!) / 2. Begins to draw / more beautiful princess. Does not / succeed, gives up. / 3. Meant to be a beautiful / princess but finds this / not worked, legs / thin. 4. Thunderbolt princess / has become bald & ugly / behind only poo – reluctance / to play, / depression, remorse / then school lessons

[For the seven sessions from 6 November to 13 November 1925 there are no notes.]

[B 25: In each case individual sheets of paper, to which drawings are attached]

14/XI.25 At first I ~~want~~ strict schoolmistress. {Figure 21} Writes out / B., which I am to copy / badly. Associates: B lower part of bottom / & stomach; red line (she made) / cut up, bloody. + in middle body / whole person that she constructs from B / (In reverse, she strict mother, punishes / me [her] for cutting up & taking out / stomach. Reluctance / to play school, draws {Figure 22}. / 1. X = 1 beautiful girl / under spell from witch; black / hair poo'. _|_ Witch herself also under / spell so must do evil; cries / bloody tears (recognises red / body etc. bloodily cut to pieces, by / her.) {Figure 23} 2. Witch is released = more beautiful {Figure 24} / 3. Princess is freed by / prince, who wants to marry her. / Suddenly explains will not marry / her, princess ugly, bad / & wants to cut her into pieces while / draws thick lines from other / side. On other page 8 stomach also / filled with stool.

[Front page:] 16/XI.25 / Furious; mother had visit from Herr H / she had to go out. / {Figure 25} 1.) Strict schoolmistress. Crosses out my / 'l', bad mark. Reluctant to play / {Figure 26} 2.) Beautiful

431

Figure 21

432

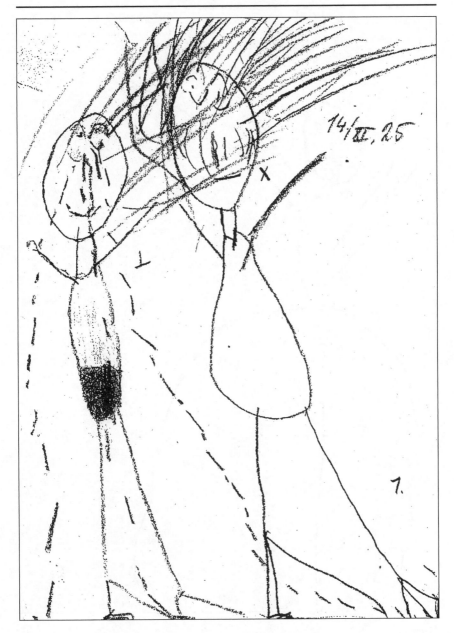

Figure 22

Figure 23

Figure 24

Figure 25

436

Figure 26

princess (all the mother's attributes / familiar from the material: crinoline = / belly with children – ribbon immaculate. / Female genitals – neck & heels on shoes = member – still: mother robbed / hence guilt feelings later in play). / {Figure 27} 3.) a = an ugly, bad no very /

Figure 27

good-looking and kind man. A 'police-/ruler' – then king. – Hairs / sticking out at first – then through / thunderbolt flat. High / collar – ~~drawings~~ stripes uniform / heels eyes etc. penis symbols. / b = beautiful princess. King / strict with her at first, then kind / gives her arm. Allows her / to go to her bridegroom.

[Reverse side:] {Figure 28} 4. b) = she has suddenly become very / ugly. Elves have put a spell / on her. Bridegroom a mocks her / no longer wants her; and has made / himself so [something crossed out] that / she is no longer to want to have him and / gets frightened. – Hair, arms, legs / body everything coils up. / c. elves. Recognises elf / d. as woman, for whom she has forgotten / to make arms. (Castrated / by her, in picture 1 the mother / deprived of attributes, from whom she wants / to take father (3) & has sex with him ~~wants~~ / (to stretch arms) takes revenge. Picture 4. / Belly missing again, defaecating / ~~all~~ thus child & bad! All attrib-/utes gone. Is only anxious & wishes / for father with erect penis. / About coiling suddenly explains / they are in fact like 1 and e und like b / like all letters turned round and / coiled; the whole thing / association to school thing / and over-strict schoolmistress (superego) / who punishes her phantasies about the / schoolmaster.

[Front page:] 17/XI.25. / 1. Beautiful princess (at first just / ordinary girl) the king wants / to give a husband. Refuses, goes to her / old lover (1 equipped with all / maternal attributes: crinoline = pregnant belly / neck = member – likewise high / heels and crown + bow = female genitals, long / hair = pubic hairs and stool; [something crossed out] / 2. Princess on way to lover / (states has become ugly). Cannot / find his palace; ~~in front of~~ [in] 1 cave ugly / old man who became small / like Rumpelstiltskin. + she must release him / but / ~~3)~~ as ~~she~~ draws [princess][1] realises / 3. that she looks dead and drawing / does not succeed. / II (Depression, spits, pushes at / carpet with feet (but very gent-/ly) – wants to pull scab off her lip / had spattered picture 1 again with water / 'tears' & wanted to destroy it) – I after / ~~plays with water~~ breaking off / drawing first plays with rest of colour pencil /

[Reverse side:] & water – scrawls then energetically / cleans [table][1] proves to me table, chair / were dirty. – From the beginning today / competitiveness her colours – my pencils – / writes exercise against my will / asks during drawing 1 if her yellow / (pencil) is not prettier than mine. / (Competitiveness stool cleanliness – gives / cause [uncleanliness][1] competitive struggle with mother / for father defeated. – During drawing of / 1 intense guilt feelings – afterwards /

Figure 28

440

repeatedly wants to destroy – that's why / 2 ugly, 3 dead. She steals everything / from mother wants to rescue father from cave (mother's: / genitals) in which evil witch / turned him into Rumpelstiltskin (castra-/tion member in coitus) – / incapacity competitiveness because of / guilt & inferiority feelings from / cleanliness anxiety & Oedipal guilt / dies herself – scab falls off / self-harm – also in that / wants to destroy 1.

Erna[8]

[Front page:] 18/XI.25. {Figure 29} ~~Countess~~ / 1 charming princess, who carries / a small prince completely hidden / in her pretty bow: 4 years. When mother / tells her to change / bows, puts him back in / carefully hidden – about green neck: 1 / poor, [sth. crossed out] pestered, beaten / neck – green marks. In the dress / precious stones 6 (association later with / picture 4) under ~~it~~ 1 red one from which / shining and light – urine – emerges / checked dress – as with vein and where / blood goes through / 2. {Figure 30} Is at grandmother's house. She wants / her to marry 1 prince. Asks / 8 days time and talks with / prince in bow. – Meanwhile bow / is very thick (erect penis) – neck / red 'says bloody' – mouth bigger / oral view coitus) – dress / green and blue 'says beaten / green and blue' – (coitus = occurs – / alleviation [something crossed out] guilt feeling: grandmother / wanted wedding) / 3) ~~wedding: all p. at first~~. [Then][1] is prince / who was under a spell had been released because / she had carried him with her for so

[Reverse side:] long. He had bathed / in 1 lake, had & got rid of his things / there – 'pipi'. – Then came 1 witch / & made him small. (Rumpelstiltskin / a few days before!) – (castrated during coitus with / mother – she wanted to help father!) / 3.) {Figure 31} wedding – 'all lamps [(previously penis, shining)][1] shine / on them both – other couples hardly / to be seen (coitus observation reversal!) small / pair birth children and reversal: parents / small. – + prince says furiously in / drawing: 'Doesn't have brown hair like / princess or 'has just something else / – just bananas' (penis envy – / he also more in the background!) O = the / lovely red curtain where prince comes in. / {Figure 32} 4. ~~1 spirit~~ this 1 good spirit from heaven / which brought o an angel from heaven / with it but because is ashamed has turned / into 1 lamp. – Explains the squiggles / around the head etc. as sixes. They appear / when he is embarrassed – when / he is not

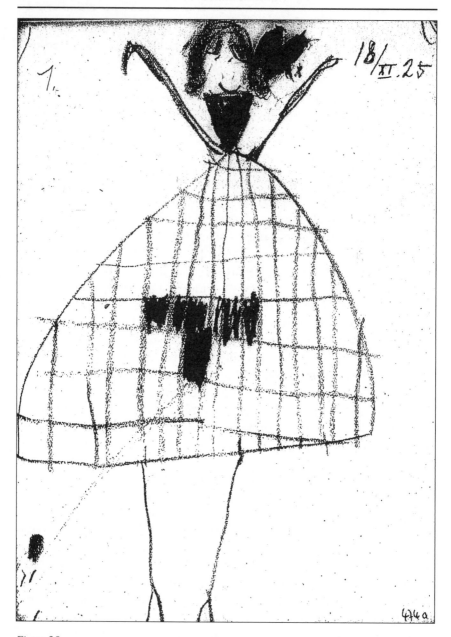

Figure 29

Figure 30

Figure 31

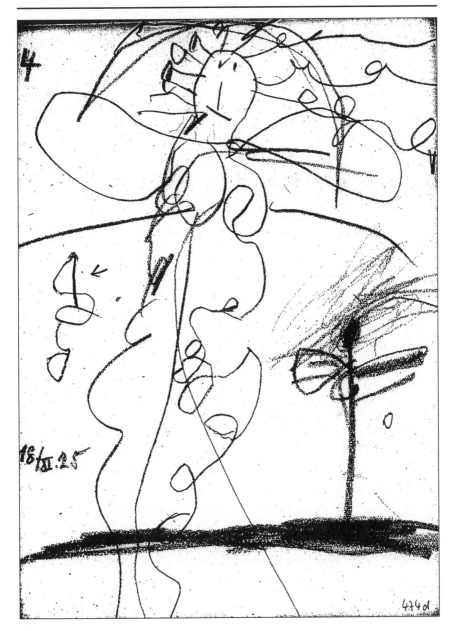

Figure 32

embarrassed, then they are / embarrassed. Explains 6 as a collaps-/ed thing. Shows – is thus upright / alive – 6 is so dead – and collaps-/ed (penis changed after ~~erection~~ / coitus – impression coitus observation) / the 6 stones on dress are just (castration) / says all figures and letters are / squiggled like that, the same – so are / hairs

[2nd sheet:] 18/XI.25 / 5. Has spat between lines – mixed / together & produces with great resistance / following story that received / as advert for cream butter (*Schabrameng*): / 1. 1 little man chased by / robbers wants to go into house. At window / beautiful dead woman who cannot / or will not let him in. Masturbates (again / since long ago) during this story. / Masturbation during coitus observation. Fear / of mother who castrates father (robbers) / but gets killed herself – / explains lines in 5 as blood poo / wee-wee, '*Schabrameng*' (butter) – that / imagines in coitus.

[Front page:] 19/XI.25 / 1 b = ~~princess~~ countess no princess / ([something crossed out] modest, adjusting more to reality) – / nearby a the younger less pretty / but still very pretty sister. b has only / brown bobbed hair – small – makes for herself with / paper (stool instead of member) long legs – but / feels very well (yellow bow – pipi – / few pubic hairs in). Here depression / set in – association with O: = ~~is so b~~ / blue neck blue bow – because <u>one</u> (severe / resistance) she so beaten. – Empty stomach / because on page X brown bow comes / out. Younger sister pulls her out with / hand. ★ brown red etc. stool blood / children (theft from the mother) – ground red with / blood. O big mouth: eating up the mother / 2. Now younger sister has become so beautiful / (stolen contents of stomach!) 'but yet more / completely full – because in bow so much' (member / father as castrator) neck blue because / beaten blue. Also body blue and / green. – She is very beautiful but ~~bad~~ / mother wants to have her bobbed hair / all cut. – No hairdresser / can be found – all refuse because they / so admire child and hair. Finally / though one specified by mother – does it / 3. Hairdresser allows her to sit on golden throne / while having hair cut – as long

[Reverse side:] hair falls – wonderful new locks immediately / grow on her. – She disappears and / 4. is a choir of children who emerge / from their golden locks / under each other completely tied by / bows because love each other so (~~question~~ / they sing where mother stands and walks. / Songs of reproach – hundreds of times / (why daughter's hair cut – / how sees again etc. / also green / on body because beaten. – King / throws mother prison – she may / remain with king. (Coitus with father / hairdresser (says afraid of dentist and likes / going why so often toothache?) Already / in picture 2 after had robbed / mother – thick bow! – similarly 3 where / anal coitus and birth at the same time / coitus with father (fear and guilt feelings) / becomes punishment, castration / that mother arranges. – Striking that / thus brings pictures and phantasy / to end – previously always breaking off / 5.= only a mess in Mummy's stomach – admits she / cut up.

[On the last drawing is noted the date 20/XI.25, which is missing from the written page but relates in terms of content to the corresponding drawings.]

[Front page:] 1. Woman who became so fat because ate / so much & who urinates & does / poo. Grabs with hands ↓ urine & / poo. – O in dress = collapsed / pipi – (fat stomach = pregnant, / yellow bow brown hair is stool / & urine. / 2. Beautiful lady – has so bent / back behind (bottom!) – also arms / because modern ladies stand like that. / Such a red dress – bloody – someone must / have done that to her. ↓ = floor / of king – beautifully lacquered but also / blood with it – perhaps because she stepped / on it (castration of father.) Contrast [?] / 2 to 1 – nobly behaving hypocritical / mother – eats up stool, castrates father / etc. – Excuse for her that she / cuts up and mutilates. / 3. Beautiful princess. Has only / a few red lines in otherwise empty / stomach. Blood that discharges (fear / question mother whether she does not have discharge? / + bust and + stomach – has appropriated / all that from / 2 mother. / Reluctance to draw still does / 4. Is nothing left of princess only / cut up stomach / lies on chaise-longue again

[Reverse side:] masturbates with severe resistance tells / queen – has ugly dirt grey / daughter – beautiful good stepdaughter / as kitchen maid – prince (question: king / always married, prince unmarried?') takes, releases her (Interpret guilt feelings / because of poo – accuses 1.) mother of same / desires simultaneously theory to eat stool, produce / children – this makes her evil ugly, / good father releases her and makes good. / – She tells of memory (still concealed) / where in children's home (not at home) / repeatedly dirtied at night. / Defaecated in trousers when saw / another child defaecating. Constant / masturbation here: 'Question why always / pulls up trousers – father says / moves stomach up (Interpret: desire and / fear losing stool, pulling up / trousers.

447

[Front page:] 21/XI.25 / 1.) A princess who is very fat subsequently / – (associates almost everything when drawings / finished) – fat but stomach empty. Cuts / her finger, ~~because blood~~ while cutting / bread red line through chin and / chest, thinks has cut off her; also / in lower body something bloody. / 2.) Beautiful elder sister 'bows / colours: 'blood and beaten blue. / In stomach: little green leaves chil-dren / tulips pipi: the inner triangle / is so crooked – something crooked in her / – mother has womb crooked / wrong way round; blue neck – beaten blue. / Looks angry because scolded / with sister; she beaten her again / (– damage – cutting bread – cutting / out from her stomach stool / children – at same time shows large red / crown, damage wishes during / parental coitus – erect penis – at same time / also damage from father in coitus) / 1 = prince, she – so growing insight that / she herself bad feels wishes projected / on to mother. – 1). = combination of her and / mother – ~~robs~~ 1 comes to 2 [something crossed out]

[Reverse side:] Ghost – then at midnight all / flower spirits wake up including lily of the valley / that was awake till 12. / 3.) + = ghost. It is itself all bloody / – blood drips and it also makes bloody. / King O goes to see who is there – / ghost tears his nose off. Blood flows / down and back again because he / does not really want to be useless on earth / (Interpret she herself 'tearing off nose' during / coitus mother damaged wanted to castrate father. / At association about bloody ghost / question whether can tear off scab / on lip) – self-punishment. / 4.) 2 other ghosts (father and mother / in coitus.) – very severe resist-/ances – a part of the association masturb-/ating – again rage (although for long time / not as originally) spitting – dirtying / scrawling.

[Front page:] 23/XI.25 25 2 S / Has such ~~sad thing~~ played cinema with girl friend; she has made up the following: – queen / bad has taken good people, / men women children prisoner; / prisoners had to cry – were freed / by empress. There was no king. / The queen then moved into the / empress's castle. / 1. Here has begun to draw / (connection prisoners = children / birth with following) / ~~then draws~~ and only recognises later / that has not drawn a woman / with body and legs but a / mermaid that crawls on sea. ★ = 1 arm / (only one) + + legs O = blood that mean-/while runs out o = body/ – All / the rest bloody tears and blood / that black top left 1 piece / stool (mermaid where prince / who bathed pipi-less = mother giving birth – blood / stool flows out, castration by coitus and birth) / 2. Then / depression, reluctance to play. – Tells / with resistance has told once / before kindergarten girl friend / story about giants that come to / Berlin and Charlottenburg; of which she / is afraid. Girl friend is not to tell her / mother that though or they would / die. – Collects spit foaming / in mouth: would like to spit it out / but also not. Association does not / want to forgive; rather to receive / (Interpret father's, giants' spit. Question / whether also in reality I would still / now such things as eating spit

[Reverse side:] urine etc.: (explanation: tall strict / Erna[2], nausea reaction etc.) She: but / she would never like to have children. / Fear – damage child crawls / out of her, she is torn / by this. (Crawling bloody / mermaid – bleeding mother damaged / by coitus and birth – prince / who had 'bathed pipi-less' in / sea). – Interpret revival theory. / – Fear of return. By her / bloody – mother with torn womb / – who tears and damages her. – / Intense relief and amusement / says cheerfully: besides child has / after all such a small / head (everything that mother said) and with / which it stretches its way out / does not therefore have to damage mother / (later question – whether she at mother's / delivery wanted to tear / her?) – To all these associations / masturbation (masturbation phantasy at / listening in to coitus!)

[Front page:] 24/XI.25 / 1.) Tries princess, which rep-/eatedly fails. / 2. bad ~~queen~~ woman (strikingly thin / body = stolen from her) blue / bow = beaten blue – / bloody below. / 3.) bad ugly stepdaughter / she has a double mouth / upper lip pulled down over lower / lip and double chin / the contours of a pregnant / belly (contrast 2) thin / empty mother). – 2. has found 3 / and taken with (bowing) / birth.) – About double mouth: / association: cigar hole burnt. / (Fear of damage from coitus / at same time masturbation with these / thoughts) – 3 was mermaid / (6) has turned into human being / but could only into ugly one! / 4.) Princess at first with long / hair – that later cuts off / 4b should become like beautiful / puff sleeves but only became / 1 stain poo. (Genitals damage / only stool – wants 'to remove this / yellow hairs – in order to become perfect / – egg-white [?] head – so also / (masturbation here too) protecting

[Reverse side:] again 'failure'. Can / wants to be beautiful princess but / feels is ugly bad stepdaughter. / – 2 has stolen princess / from emperor's castle; but then / states princess purple bow / and skirt because king beaten her / because ran away to woman (brown / upper part – yet stool when / also wanted to eliminate!) / 5. = princess as she now / very beautiful and with bad woman / red bow

449

red neck; is beaten bloody by father aggr. [?] after / coitus. Pushes pictures 2 and 3 / with heads against each other: 'they do / pipi-thing'. Then 5 and 3 do / it as well. – But then 5 / goes home to father emperor's castle / empress none there, already / dead. V illustrates her repression-. / Development – because of sadistic / wishes towards mother and therefore fear / of punishment (also coitus as / punishment) – flight to homosexuality / – return love father) / 6. Mermaid with tail / from which 3 changes.

[Front page:] 25/XI.25/ 1.) Furious schoolmistress strict / corrects my 1 so that adds / pieces ★ association = z – this a / proud not beaten / pipi – the straight lines on / sheet O – exclamation marks! – are / also pipi straight. – On 2 draws / associating to this 'straight pipi' / curved 'm' and hairs – squiggles / hairs. 3.) Just 'straight' / 4.) = 5. = fat stomach Mummy. / (Mother corrects damage genitals / = adds = at same time homosexual / coitus.) – Suddenly she is big / sister and takes me to dentist / talks about daughter there. – / Dentist torments – threatens to take out tooth / pulls out – but after anaesthesia / by syringe very nice, I / ask for more tooth extraction / – But beforehand she cuts off / hair with scissors on carpet / wants before to me dentist / pulls tooth – steals mother / genitals and hairs etc. / for coitus hence guilt / feelings, therefore wants to / turn coitus into

[Reverse side:] punishment. Desire comes through.

[Front page:] 26/XI.25 / Tears up after she has drawn it / 1.) At first wants to draw / a princess, then she explains as / old and stupid woman Mummy-Brown = poos / I – hairs and she also cries poo / as tears. The squiggles O that / remind her of 6s are only / beaten pipi. / The thick short straight lines / hard thick poos – like pipi (stool = member) / so old that although will / soon die and her life is no fun. / 2). Is the stupid old woman (mother / recognisable from eyes; supervises / stool). – Cries tears because / has nothing (also no body) / only very thin little skirt / that (~~she~~ Erna² rubs with water so long / till paper tears) / breaks. Has no house, must be / outside in cold –. / 3.) She has become more and more / beautiful. Has made herself new [?] little / skirt from foliage. – At first has / a foliage hut – was only / enchanted – then a real / lovely house with warm / stove and pretty garden and / suitor. Longs very much for / child. Cuts her finger and / a little bone off puts it in / cart a child comes out of it. (Here

[Reverse side:] has drawn little skirt / red – bloody and rubbed / hole in it – castration and birth, guilt feelings. / (Masturbation here wish for children!) / 'Neck beaten blue – also / crown, bloody and blue – by / father – but for no reason, has / done nothing. V other sheet. – ★ she would now so / like 1 new little skirt for / a prince is to come who / wants to marry her. – She goes to / her old cupboard (always takes / ribbons from mine!) / Sees 30 wonderful golden and / silver garments inside – but it says / above this, she may not / take them – the cupboard = / made from an old oak / that is the mother of all trees / with exception 1 Christmas tree / that was already there before. – The / old lady (2) was so shrunken / that she died and became 1 tree. / 4. despite prohibition has / taken a dress – but says is / empty inside! – Superego! – only bloody / and marries prince. – Begins / to tear up and chew up picture / (guilt feeling!) – 1). (She and mother at same time / – She recognises herself earlier as bad / projected mother. – About 3 – are many / unknown suitors: – father who beats / has coitus from which child. From / fear and / guilt feelings–: castration etc. here.

[2nd sheet of paper:] 26/XI.25 / Throws herself couch be-/gins to bang head / lying on stomach. / Then 'we have / not played swimmer-man for long / time (~~could~~ / father identification from / fear damaged / genitals and flight / Oedipus complex.) Then / after interpretation continues / ★

[Front page:] ~~27~~/XI 25 / Ugly woman – just poo and / collapsed pipi / meanwhile also 'straight pipi' but / are from poo. Tells about Frau Kloss / in her dream. Real: the bag / with 30 Marks was stolen. Is / a bad woman who always scolds / beats her young woman pushes in corners (admits / beating and pushing her idea). Dream: / Frau Kloss ~~notices her bag~~ climbs / out through window. A little [red][1] man / still stands at the window. – Frau Kl. hears / noises in the flat & goes back / again. Then no longer there. Then something / is stolen at the back (in the flat). – Probably her / bag. – She herself, Erna,[2] looks out / through the window & watches everything. / She says to the little man (very tenderly) / Nice little man will you / break into my house too? He: No, I / only do that to bad people. – Association: / to the window: that was modern before / through the window, was also such an / enormous one that you could go out / as with a door & only had to jump / a bit. – Little man was actually very nice / (Rumpelstiltskin, little cream-butter man / immediately recognises member) and her contrary request / to break into her house. – Becomes afraid

[Reverse side:] of coitus. Is punishment only for bad / people. – To little man: following story. – Once was a very good kind king. He /

451

was very fond of his daughter. Then he / went & stole things from people, for his / daughter's sake who ordered him to steal / very beautiful bags, gold & silver ones / (he brought them to her – analogy silver and gold dress / stolen from the cupboard) – Then / he stole a bag that was not / so beautiful & had little in it. But / he became very rich anyway and had / everything. – Much less depression and almost / no masturbation – only in story chewing and / sucking little man and king / paper etc. – about 2: numbers – everything / wound round squiggled (drawn / during association to little man

[Front page:] 27.28 [unclear] / Nov. 1925 / 27. – I am to play with cart. / Dreams just that everything alive and / according to my wish. Cart up to / me – coachman/only with majesty / says reluctance to play – interrupts. Then: / she friendly big sister, mother / dead. – She talks with big girl friend. / Friend is persecuted by mother, must have / her hair cut. (Short hair / unmodern!) She advice of girl friend: / she herself independent dancer – / bridegroom with beautiful villa etc. / no already married – but with it / more certain celebrating 2nd wedding – no / every year, every day. – Advises me / also to get married – bridegroom / is to protect me from / hair-cutting mother – reluctance to play. / Lies on couch; unwell – it also / hurts her a bit. Association pipi / wee-wee poo. / – Imagines wonderful bird with / completely straight outspread wings / great tenderness admiration bird / then wants to tell me about king / was always in his wonderful / castle so that people could not / see him. – At request shows himself / wonderful silver dressed servant / in front. – Children all towards him

[Reverse side:] – he rejects her – says if / comes so close must die. All / close to him – he dies. – Almost no / masturbation at all with association. – / At beginning – as sister – tells: Lies-/chen tells on her – she furious / but still embraces her next / morning. – Repeatedly forgets rage. / Here has – begun to smash / wheels of (little cart) – wants to take / middle out, which looks like cream. / During story what happy / marriage she has – constantly cuts up / also cardboard etc. / Then suddenly her finger hurts – / then unwell. – At story / of handsome dying king / chews brown strips of cardboard / into small pieces (kills castrates / father because she not – Later / dissatisfied voyeurism because no / longer coitus observation – before going / away only that she would still like / to chew me.

[Front page:] 30/XI.25 / While drawing dream association – beautiful child / full bag, little suitcase, <u>Lieschen laughs</u> – old gentle

man / admired – dressed-up king, getting to know / poverty misery
– cries and is happy – rusty / ring, rusty knife – virgin appears. /
Mermaids stolen – people happy / long for her – at first tiny [onn [?]
finger instead of [?] ring]¹ then / ever larger. – At association little
suitcase – furiously / scrawls table – makes bricks / wipes shoe
[cleaning everything with spit cleaning conflict]¹ constantly chewing
– blowing dry [?] / ball games – fury stealing bag king's I remind / –
aggression towards me – Lieschen laughing admits / – stresses child
and yet such a lovely little suitcase.

[Reverse side:] ~~about woman~~ – / at first game, mother / and father
without wound / stroking door – she / Lieschen Iza, Iar. Heldb. [?] / –
driving up in cart / then she and father / running everyone over, man
/ so difficult, finally / does run over / and kills him. – Suddenly / says
at the front she and / father – so not / mother

[Front page:] 1/XII.25 / 1.) Am to become 1 beautiful princess –
with / special care eyes, eyebrows etc. / In drawing gives her double
chin / explains when flesh is cut apart / there – is double: a large piece
/ inside that she calls husband. (Supposedly / Prof. H explained to
her). – Afterwards: it is not / princess after all but mother (mechanism:
the ugly / – has coitus sadistically – (cutting up / mother) = intolerable is changed into / mother – as driving force also quarrelsome for /
narcissism – refusal: of reality – 'holding to / dream. – The body
empty. – At first stated / in the beautiful hair lovely dark / stones –
poo – then aversion / 2.) Now to be princess after all. The / bright
streaks are hair – at the end / is small head'. O = bent body / stomach
sticking out – also 1 arm. – / had made very deep incision in / genitals
later when finished – in rage / torn off leg and cut everything up. /
The princess sat in large hall on / wonderful throne x = of bright-
coloured stones / illuminates o – then cuts up / (anger poo after all!).
– The cutting up / begins when the expected prince / explains –
does not want her because: head / small – hair bright, incision large

[Reverse side:] Body bent. – Seeks advice from / beautiful lady-in-
waiting (similar to her but / beautiful). – She wants to lend her / her
clothes prince who does not recognise her / takes her home feels like
false / bride. – Later with most violent / fits of rage – chewing toys /
and paper, claims never said: / but other way round lady-in-waiting
takes / clothes from princess and so prince drives her / home. – (Next
day concedes) / rage and despair – cutting off / her buttons from
garter / cuts up rubber – and cuts up / 2 entirely (quarrelsome her
theft / and sadism towards mother: 'driving-force' / – at prince

refuses because of small / head says 'Z'. – At question / then draws sheet 3 (both sides) / ZN and all such letters / when far out another O = are / 'proud upright' pipi. When / pushed together. S. 4 are ugly like / little boxes = female genitals.

[Front page:] 2/XII.25 / Wants to draw a girl; does not yet / know if will be princess. If not / this must do as well. With uncertain care / & patience repeatedly slowly / attempts heads, erases etc. / Always fails at mouth. Then / draws 1. – Herself completely satisfied / (unusual – (actually not exaggerated / holds on to it: gloriously wonderful / hair etc. then anger & tearing up.) / but with calm criticism: pretty etc. / – mouth not pretty, 'then that's / exactly how it must be' – once attempt = / mother – but immediately again – no is / the girl herself after all! – linen-basket ★ on / both sides = wonderful silver blue / handle that is sewn on to dress at / back. – But she still wants to make something beautiful / 2. – 'has after all no simple bow / (1 not) but for it very big mouth'; / mouth despite all efforts fails / dress 'again beaten blue – big / mouth' = genitals eating up penis / – with 1 penetrates at back – with 2 at front / – (bow) and big mouth. – / – Quietly ends the session / without masturbation. The cutting up

[Reverse side:] does not happen till next day, when looks at / pictures again.

[There are no notes from 3 December 1925.]

[Front page:] 4/XII.25 / Erna[2] / Very angry: (mother evening before / went out very dressed up / as usual suspicion with boy friend.) / ~~Was~~ on toilet [at my house must 1][1] man [have been][1] because / [(abnormal gift for observation or rather spying)][1] / bowl back, 2 drops there / – no stocking damaged / who bit into new red pencil / (phantasy!). – Again in everything / exaggerated way about wonderful / princess while drawing / begins – after mouth states / is not princess 'but / the – mistakenly called 'terrible' / lover of the knight. – She has cut into the finger of the / red hand arm. Blood / runs back again. – ~~Why~~ Says / bow mouth – dress below = / everything the same. – Why so / red – bloody because knight / beat her blue and bloody / 2 princesses ([great][1] adjustment to reality / short hairs (as usual pubic hairs) / and a child as she states / as child. Then through

[Reverse side:] cheeks, mouth – this previously / really established impression / changes. x chain of rubies / originally forgetting arms – then / stump (left!). – While / decorating the dress / terrible rage and aggression – / begins to cut thick card-/board – fringes and pieces / – from paper – when one of rejected / suitors in / blue suit (yesterday /

sailor = member!) speaks / cutting out from paper / clearly penis shapes. – play, or rather / reluctance to draw – cuts wood / with knife – / story that tells while / drawing 1 or 2 tells as follows: beautiful / princess suitors come. A / knight who loves his fertile / lover (meant to say) loves lover terribly)[xii] / and was always faithful to her cannot / resist when he sees / princess. – She is arro-/gant, rejects them all / – at first the one with black / velvet jacket (Jarrek) then / blue suit. – Breaks off and

[2nd sheet of paper:] previously described associations / and behaviour. – Then to drawing / associates – 2 should be a / child – only dress does not suit / her – is like that of a lady. / – Association while cutting up: / father goes with pipi stairs / or down and out again / he hits there below (stripes / edge) in all colours. – / Mouth bow cheeks = bloody / genitals. – ~~Fierce resist-/ance~~ Here falls from couch / on to floor, hits herself / on little chair and roars from / fear (not pain). Immediately / afterwards bumps head (unintentionally) / against mine. – Fierce / resistance when aggression / and theft not only mother's / 'old cardboard' wood etc. – / but bloody genitals / through cutting up chewing / father's penis, when she has coitus. / – After fierce resistance great / relief (flight into homo- / sexuality also on account of this aggression)

[Reverse side:] changes into mother / (projects – from injured narciss- / ism – inferior etc. more distant / sadism towards mother – but / also towards father, this apparently / in this connection (with / longed-for coitus) very deeply repressed / – With all these latest asso- / ciations again masturbation / and banging / Erna[8] 5/XII.25 / Fury, quarrel Lieschen / man she shames her / [something crossed out] cheeky wanted (tells while / I explain reasons castration / to father.) – To become / handsome prince – after mouth / explains is not her. – / Commands me, snatches / pencil away – rage – neck bloody / beaten – ~~everything~~ – ringlets hair / that blue = pipi brown poo / = everything bloody from angry father / in bulge – in hollow in flesh (meanwhile cutting up paper, rubber / scratches out – long knife – scrapes blood out – / leaves something inside otherwise / dies – also blood keeps / coming back. – (Everything bloody / because castrates father = man) / – indicates from below

[Reverse side:] how she cuts it up / through the middle – makes / cry, enjoys this. / (Coitus bloodbath – she / sadistic here.)

---

xii Translator's note: Erna uses the word *fruchtbar* (fertile) instead of *furchtbar* (terrible).

[Front page:] 7/XII.25 Erna[8] / [something crossed out] [Day before falls off / couch – head together][1] / nose mouth, child, something yellow / from nose, – something curled up – arm / no other side, hair, above / below – does not know what woman / below = woman lying down / 2. [something crossed out] body like inside / blood from inside – no / digs out, bends down / licks chest. / 3. again = all bloody / also eaten up below – / I am to sharpen pencil – / uncertain – my hands wet / red – big sister / lipstick red. Plait – small – then / again same on same / Erich together – then / others away, jealous / parents agreed. / – Depression (weak) – bangs (homosexual / beautiful girl (Mel.) wishes for / curls like that, old / mother – association husband ding dong

[Reverse side:] big sponge – wet, big / barrel – too big – Frenchman – / too small – furious – at / last part since depression masturbation / God old stupid / – 4 = letter to bride parents / are agreed.

[Front page:] 8/XII.25 / wants to draw 'beautiful princess'. – / 1.) At first hair – when face (I) line) / drawn – explains is not princess / = a wonderful chandelier. / (When asked 'face was too fat' – then / draws another double-chin line on it / – otherwise mostly after mouth obstruction [?]. / 2.) Beautiful princess from the side. Above / the wonderful chandelier only shines / on her. The rays on her / head. Crown consists in little boxes / (pipi and little slit at same time). – Has drawn with / special care in middle of dress / 1 forget-me-not and 1 red / tulip. – Severe resistance at question / about this. Then draws red over it / and then blue on that. – Princess had / many suitors – (lists names of all / mother's friends) but wants Hellmut = father / Gets 1 suitor to bring him to her / He loves her too and explains that to her. / Says [something crossed out] already seen 1 other / also with such flowers and / dress. She is so pure sweet though / But how she princess was very / good, prayed to God every day.

[Reverse side:] (Immediately expresses doubt – / comment from yesterday!) – blasphemous prince / gives her 1 kiss (here draws / dress red and then blue.) During / conversation suddenly makes prince / (bottom of drawing) big and small / [something crossed out] – at first prince had still / admired beautiful stones in shoes / that shone up to the chandelier / – Then after poo – amazement departure of / prince. – princess accuses lady-/in-waiting of having done that. / Prince orders her out of kingdom. / Then they marry. – She had forgotten / to draw arms – then / adds. Previously had spoken / about 'praying': praying uplifted arms. / o = the red curtain through which prince /

walked – talks (with great difficulty) about flowers / forget-me-not
went walking in woods / and / then found it the tulip sat / on it – it
was his little horse / rode home

[Front page:] 8. [not completely certain whether 9 painted over it]/
XII.25 / Almost no depression – no masturbation / – When I interpret sending away lady-in-waiting and remind / games how she was
thrown / out as a child, she quietly smiling: / 'from the window, even
now that / all seems so strange to me – I / was so sad and furious /
then.) – Greatest resistance / when interpret castration of / father in
sexual intercourse. (Chandelier / = member – father otherwise hardly
to / be seen only indicated / behind curtain. – Forget-me-not =
female genitals / tulip member destroyed by her in / coitus – therefore red dress that covers / flower – blue = at same time something
happens / to her in coitus. – She defaecates / and urinates in coitus –
anal representation of / coitus – at same time (rushing ahead of / ego
development. Very ashamed). Disparages / mother with anal accus-
ation / how she her (representation thus / denigrates to father.) – Has
also / fat stomach of mother, receives / in coitus anal children (previous / phantasy: has been wrongly / accused by mother of / having
wet [?] and dirtied / herself. – Doctor diagnoses – ill-/ness: at back 1
piece of flesh / and at front blood comes out. Cinderella

[Reverse side:] turns into princess – father / = doctor mother kills
or sends away) – / – identification with mother from same / wish in
coitus observations – / then in order to shift sadistic theft / from
mother's body on to her / – But especially (since now most severe /
resistance) – because in coitus wants / to castrate and destroyed
beloved / father. – Doubt about her capacity / to love – thereby
doubt about / that of others and general / doubt

[Front page:] 10/XII.25 / 1.) The bad woman (by mermaids so /
injured without / belly, leg on neck / 2.) The beautiful one banished
/ count's daughter fetches / another bucket coal and may / go home
(little suitcase – cut diamonds / drilled in – man last page / 3.) little
suitcase with shirts inside / when closed: cut diamonds. / 4.) Count's
daughter finds / mourning mother in garden / Changes count's
daughter from picture 2 / in beginning in bad scornful laughing /
mother (lack of attributes – 2 cut off / pipi, belly etc. – because
become / older, small shrivelled 'when you are 100 years old' – / 5.)
– the rather prettier and better old / woman (everything bloody gone
– pipi / to below = coitus without destruction of member.

[Reverse side:] 6 = the dress that so loves / like mother / – at first

457

drills flower then cut diamonds / 4 b = mermaids in water – the / woman round nose – mouth / crooked position of eyes – / cuts away. Body – and / drilling around, after sweet / 'Schabram'. – 1 little mermaid sleeps.

[There are no notes for 11 and 12 December; at 14 December 1925 is noted 'missed'.]

Erna[2] 15/XII.25 / 1.) pot, potato broth, stove / steam (man from back toilet / 2.) Steam-princess / 3.) Father pays no attention, not / nice, because only steam – her / face with slit eyes / becomes Chinese – father / loves and also steam (to her!) / 4.) Slit eyes and / propeller – usually eyes / round.

[There are no notes for 16 December 1925.]

[Front page:] 17/XII.25 / 1.) The bad woman who / is to bring princess 2 / the lost ring / from the fountain – but / falls and dies. / 2.) 1 bow was in fountain / was brought by old / woman – from it come / so many [children pipi etc.][1] – pipi green / (punched because red too / clear. – Phantasy / where all in castle / friendly – one furious punches / all, therefore green. – / From where father so many pipi / – the attached pipi / 1 on right – 2 the golden / hair – stolen creams / rays – that more beautiful / and less beautiful standing / Chinese lantern. – About punching / phantasy where theatre / is played at her house / she principal dancer dances

[Reverse side:] with gentleman – no only / minor role (rage) – again / unctuously with 'wonderful / sun-rays – laughing / 'pinched' – kicking feet me / blanket; with punching discussing / phantasy about mother in bed / or killing her being with / father, the latter. Interpret wish / am to give ring. / 18/XII.25 / Fury shoving me / game: cobbler-prince-officer / policeman does not order 2 – / but 3–4 etc. 9 to place chairs. / Princess appears rejects / princess – without arms, cape / 'other dress – no bigger / sister: queen: suitor / appears officer – prince loves / queen refuses. – Prince takes / then sends away – queen / loves – (meanwhile questions – whether / princess likes dress / ~~and~~ brown stripes etc.?) – / suddenly wants to cut up king / – In comparison with king – / immediately gives princess / arms: attributes compares / mother everything

[For the eighteen sessions from 4 January to 29 January 1926 there are no notes; there is a folded sheet of paper in which cut-out painted figures are placed. On the outside it reads '5/I.26 ghosts'.]

['Packet' of 1/II.26]

1st sheet: [front page drawing of a princess] / back page: Erna[8] / lady-in-waiting ('leirb.' [?]) / mother / showing / just as / ugly / (lady-in-waiting = 3 / assuaging / guilt feelings / praise mother

2nd sheet: [front page: drawing of a princess or similar] 1/II/26 / [back page:] / 2 princesses / 2 strips from / mouth – shoe = / 2 pipis father's and mother's (who stole) / yellowish buttons children and stool

3rd sheet front page: 1/II.26

[Back page:] Ugly lady-in-waiting / (even thinner) / pseudologia: lovely / pointed shoes receiving / from aunt. / Goes to children's / party: her kitchen full / less [?] gives [?] with little bottle of / petrol

4th sheet: / Compares and wants / to have praise about / various colours / (her and my / pens; comparison / value her and my / chair.

[For the forty-nine sessions from 2 February to 15 March 1926 there are no notes.]

459

Bibliography

Abraham, H. (1976). *Karl Abraham: Sein Leben für die Psychoanalyse*. Munich: Kindler.

Abraham, K. (1913a). Mental after-effects produced in a nine-year-old child by the observation of sexual intercourse between its parents. In *Selected Papers of Karl Abraham, M.D.* Ed. E. Jones. Trans. D. Bryan and A. Strachey. London: Hogarth, 1957, pp. 164–168.

—— (1913b). A constitutional basis of locomotor anxiety. In *Selected Papers of Karl Abraham, M.D.* Ed. E. Jones. Trans. D. Bryan and A. Strachey. London: Hogarth, 1957, pp. 235–243.

—— (1913c). Restrictions and transformations of scopophilia in psycho-neurotics. In *Selected Papers of Karl Abraham, M.D.* Ed. E. Jones. Trans. D. Bryan and A. Strachey. London: Hogarth, 1957, Chapter IX.

—— (1917). Some illustrations on the emotional relationship of little girls to their parents. In *Clinical Papers and Essays on Psycho-Analysis*, Vol. 2. London: Hogarth, 1955, pp. 52–54.

—— (1919a). Observations on Ferenczi's paper on 'Sunday neuroses'. In R. Fliess (ed.) *The Psychoanalytic Reader: An Anthology of Essential Papers with Critical Introductions*. London: Hogarth, pp. 312–315.

—— (1919b). A particular form of neurotic resistance against the psycho-analytic method. In *Selected Papers of Karl Abraham, M.D.* Ed. E. Jones. Trans. D. Bryan and A. Strachey. London: Hogarth, 1957, pp. 303–311.

—— (1920). Manifestations of the female castration complex. In *Selected Papers of Karl Abraham, M.D.* Ed. E. Jones. Trans. D. Bryan and A. Strachey. London: Hogarth, 1957, pp. 338–369.

—— (1921). Contribution to a discussion on tic. In *Selected Papers of Karl Abraham, M.D.* Ed. E. Jones. Trans. D. Bryan and A. Strachey. London: Hogarth, 1957, pp. 323–325.

—— (1922). On parapraxes with an overcompensating tendency. In R. Fliess (ed.) *The Psychoanalytic Reader: An Anthology of Essential Papers with Critical*

Introductions. London: Hogarth, pp. 294–298. Also in *Clinical Papers and Essays on Psychoanalysis*. London: Hogarth, 1955, pp. 76–80.

—— (1924). A short study of the development of the libido, viewed in the light of mental disorders. In *Selected Papers of Karl Abraham, M.D.* Ed. E. Jones. Trans. D. Bryan and A. Strachey. London: Hogarth, 1957, pp. 418–501.

—— (1974). Little Hilda: daydreams and a symptom in a seven-year-old girl. *International Review of Psychoanalysis*, 1, 5–14.

Aguayo, J. (1997). Historicising the origins of Kleinian psychoanalysis: Klein's analytic and patronal relationships with Ferenczi, Abraham and Jones 1914–1927. *International Journal of Psychoanalysis*, 78, 1165–1182.

Anderson, R. (1988). Interpretations in child analysis. Weekend Conference, London, 14–16 October 1988.

—— (1993). Die Krise hinsichtlich der Frequenz in der Kinderanalyse. *EPF Bulletin*, 41, 60–64.

Anthony, J. (1986). The contributions of child psychoanalysis to psychoanalysis. *The Psychoanalytic Study of the Child*, 41, 61–87.

Anzieu, D. (1985). Jeunesse de Melanie Klein. In *Melanie Klein aujourd'hui*. Lyon: Cesura Lyon, pp. 11–35.

Argelander, H. (1970). *Das Ersteinterview in der Psychotherapie*. Darmstadt: Wissenschaftliche Buchgesellschaft.

Bannach, H.-J. (1971). Die wissenschaftliche Bedeutung des alten Berliner Psychoanalytischen Instituts. In *Psychoanalyse in Berlin: 50-Jahr-Gedenkfeier des Berliner Psychoanalytischen Instituts (Karl-Abraham-Institut)*. Meisenheim: Anton Hain, pp. 31–39.

Bateman, A. (1996). Thick- and thin-skinned organisations and enactment in borderline and narcissistic disorders. Weekend Conference, London, 4–6 October 1996.

Begoin-Guignard, F. (1987). Die Erfahrungen des Psychoanalytikers mit Kindern und Erwachsenen. *EPF Bulletin*, 29, 45–61.

Beland, H. (1981). Hinterm Berg, hinterm Berg brennt's: Ein Beitrag zur Interpretation von Mörikes Feuerreiter. In U. Ehebald and F.-W. Eickhoff (eds) *Humanität und Technik in der Psychoanalyse*. Bern: Huber, pp. 217–237.

—— (1991). Der Lehranalytiker, der gut genug ist. In U. Streeck and H. V. Wertmann (eds) *Lehranalyse und psychoanalytische Ausbildung*. Göttingen: Vandenhoeck & Ruprecht, pp. 11–26.

—— (1992). 'Erraten der Übertragung' (Freud) durch 'Vorahnungen' (Bion). *DPV-Informationen*, 12, 2–6.

—— (1995). Thesen zur psychoanalytischen Methode, zur Subjektivität und zur Verifizierung psychoanalytischer Forschungsergebnisse. In F. Berger (ed.) *Hundert Jahre psychoanalytischer Methode*. Autumn Conference of the German Psychoanalytical Association. Frankfurt: Kongreßorganisation, Geber & Reusch, pp. 61–73.

Berberich, E. (1993). Some comments on the crisis around frequency in child analysis. *EPF Bulletin*, 41, 64–67.

—— (1994). Der Beitrag der Kinderanalyse in Theorie und Praxis zur Analyse von Erwachsenen. In V. Friedrich and H. Peters (eds) *Wege und Irrwege zur Psychoanalyse: Standpunkte und Streitpunkte der Gegenwart. Arbeitstagung der DPV 1994*. Frankfurt: Kongreßorganisation, Geber & Reusch, pp. 239–250.

Berna-Glantz, R. (1987). First standing conference on child and adolescent analysis. *EPF Bulletin*, 29, 37–44.

Berna-Simons, L. (1989). Die Anfänge der Kinder-Psychoanalyse. *Arbeitshefte Kinderpsychoanalyse* 10, Gesamthochschule Kassel, pp. 99–110.

Bick, E. (1962). Child analysis today. In E. Bott Spillius (ed.) *Melanie Klein Today: Developments in Theory and Practice. Vol. 2: Mainly Practice*. London: Routledge, 1988, pp. 168–176.

Biermann, G. (1968). Zur Geschichte der analytischen Kinderpsychotherapie. *Monatsschrift für Kinderheilkunde*, 116, 41–49.

Bion, W. R. (1959). Attacks on linking. *International Journal of Psychoanalysis*, 40, 308–315; reprinted in *Second Thoughts*, London: Heinemann, 1967; reprinted London: Karnac, 1984; also in E. Bott Spillius (ed.) *Melanie Klein Today: Developments in Theory and Practice. Vol. 1: Mainly Theory*. London: Routledge, 1988.

—— (1962). *Learning from Experience*. London: Heinemann.

—— (1963). *Elements of Psychoanalysis*. New York: Basic Books.

—— (1965). *Transformations*. London: Heinemann.

—— (1970). *Attention and Interpretation*. London: Tavistock.

Birksted-Breen, D. (1996). Phallus, penis and mental space. *International Journal of Psychoanalysis*, 77, 649–657.

Bittner, G. and Heller, P. (eds) (1983). *Eine Kinderanalyse bei Anna Freud (1929–1932)*. Würzburg: Königshausen & Neumann.

Blarer, A. von (1994). Gegenübertragung in der psychoanalytischen Supervision. *Psyche*, 48, 425–452.

Bornstein, B. (1948). Emotional barriers in the understanding and treatment of young children. *American Journal of Orthopsychiatry*, 18, 691–697.

Brede, C. (1993). Der Berufsstand der analytischen Kinder- und Jugendlichen-Psychotherapeuten in der 'FOGS-Studie'. *Psyche*, 47, 71–81.

Brenman-Pick, I. (1985). Working through in the counter-transference. In E. Bott Spillius (ed.) *Melanie Klein Today: Developments in Theory and Practice. Vol. 2: Mainly Practice*. London: Routledge, 1988, pp. 34–47.

Britton, R., Feldman, M. and O'Shaughnessy, E. (1989). *The Oedipus Complex Today: Clinical Implications*. London: Karnac.

—— (1995). Wirklichkeit und Unwirklichkeit in Phantasie und Dichtung. *Jahrbuch der Psychoanalyse*, 35, 9–33.

—— (1997). Diskussion. In C. Frank and H. Weiss (eds) *Groll und Rache in der ödipalen Situation*. Tübingen: Diskord.

Bruns, G. (1996). Freuds Herzneurose und das identifikatorische Prinzip in der Psychoanalyse: Klinische und theoretische Überlegung. *Jahrbuch der Psychoanalyse*, 37, 47–84.

Campbell, D. (1992). Introducing a discussion of frequency in child and adolescent analysis. *EPF Bulletin*, 38, 118–128.

—— (1993). Notes from an informal meeting on frequency in child and adolescent analysis. *EPF Bulletin*, 41, 76–82.

Canestri, J. (1994). Psychoanalytische Heuristik. In I. Behrens, F. Berger and T. Plänkers (eds) *Der Widerstand gegen die Psychoanalyse*. Autumn Conference of the German Psychoanalytical Association. Frankfurt: Geber & Reusch, pp. 97–115.

—— (1995). Einige Überlegungen zur Supervision in der psychoanalytischen Ausbildung. In F. Berger (ed.) *Hundert Jahre psychoanalytischer Methode*. Autumn Conference of the German Psychoanalytical Association. Frankfurt: Kongreßorganisation, Geber & Reusch, pp. 239–263.

Chadwick, M. (1925). Über die Wurzel des Wißtriebs. *Internationale Zeitschrift für Psychoanalyse*, 11, 54–68.

Cycon, R. (1995). Preface to the German edition of the Collected Writings. In M. Klein, *Gesammelte Schriften*, Vol. 1. Ed. R. Cycon with assistance from H. Erb. Stuttgart: Frommann-Holzboog, pp. ix–xvi

Danckwardt, J. (1989). Eine frühe, im Spannungsfeld zwischen Traum und Übertragung unbewußt gebliebene Phantasie Freuds über die psychoanalytische Situation (1898). Ein Beitrag zur psychoanalytischen Kreativität. *Psyche*, 43, 849–883.

—— (1994). Veränderungsangst und mediale Normierung der inneren Realität. In I. Behrens, F., Berger and T. Plänkers (eds) *Der Widerstand gegen die Psychoanalyse*. Autumn Conference of the German Psychoanalytical Association. Frankfurt: Geber & Reusch, pp. 251–253.

—— (1995). Introduction to 'Hundert Jahre psychoanalytischer Methode'. In F. Berger (ed.) *Hundert Jahre psychoanalytischer Methode*. Autumn Conference of the German Psychoanalytical Association. Frankfurt: Kongreßorganisation, Geber & Reusch, pp. 37–45.

Danckwardt, J. & Gattig, E. (1996). *Die Indikation zur hochfrequenten analytischen Psychotherapie in der vertragsärztlichen Versorgung: Ein Manual*. Stuttgart: Frommann-Holzboog.

Dantlgraber, J. (1982). Bemerkungen zur subjektiven Indikation für Psychoanalyse. *Psyche*, 36, 193–225.

De Clerck, R. (1994). 'Der Traum von einer bess'ren Welt'. Psychoanalyse und Kultur in der Mitte der zwanziger Jahre: Berlin und London. *Luzifer-Amor*, 13, 41–70.

Deutsch, H. (1942). Some forms of emotional disturbance and their relationship to schizophrenia. *Psychoanalytic Quarterly*, 11, 301–321.

Devereux, G. (1967). *From Anxiety to Method in the Behavioural Sciences*. The Hague: Mouton.

Diatkine, R. (1972). Preliminary remarks on the present state of psychoanalysis of children. *International Journal of Psychoanalysis*, 53, 141–150.

Diatkine, R. and Simon, J. (1972). *La Psychanalyse précoce: Le Processus analytique chez l'enfant*. Paris: Presses Universitaires de France (revised 2nd edition, 1993).

Donaldson, G. (1996). Between practice and theory: Melanie Klein, Anna Freud and the development of child analysis. *Journal of the History of the Behavioural Sciences*, 32, 160–176.

Dornes, M. (1993). *Der kompetente Säugling*. Frankfurt: Fischer.

Eckstaedt, A. (1991). *Die Kunst des Anfangs*. Frankfurt: Suhrkamp.

Eitingon, M. (1923 [1922]). Report of the Berlin Psycho-Analytical Policlinic (March–June 1922). *Bulletin of the International Psycho-Analytical Association*, 4, 254–269.

—— (1924). Bericht über die Berliner Psychoanalytische Poliklinik in der Zeit von Juni 1922-März 1924. *Internationale Zeitschrift für Psychoanalyse*, 10, 229–240.

Ellenberger, H. F. (1994). *The Discovery of the Unconscious: The History and Evolution of Dynamic Psychiatry*. London: Fontana.

Esslinger, H. (1972). Überlegungen zur Ausbildung und Tätigkeit des Psychagogen. *Psyche*, 26, 716–719.

Etchegoyen, R. H. (1991). *The Fundamentals of Psychoanalytic Technique*. London: Karnac.

Feigelson, C. (1974). A comparison between adult and child psychoanalysis. *Journal of the American Psychoanalytic Association*, 22, 603–611.

Fenichel, O. (1979). Statistische Bericht über die therapeutische Tätigkeit 1920–1930. In *Zehn Jahre Berliner Psychoanalytisches Institut (Poliklinic und Lehranstalt) 1920–1930*. Meisenheim: Anton Hain, pp. 13–19.

Ferenczi, S. (1909). Introjection and transference. In *First Contributions to Psycho-analysis*. Trans. E. Jones. London: Maresfield, 1952, pp. 35–93.

—— (1913a). Stages in the development of a sense of reality. In *First Contributions to Psychoanalysis*. Trans. E. Jones. London: Maresfield, 1952, pp. 213–239.

—— (1913b). A little chanticleer. In *First Contributions to Psychoanalysis*. Trans. E. Jones. London: Maresfield, 1952, pp. 240–252.

—— (1913c). The cause of reserve in a child. In *Further Contributions to Psycho-Analysis*. Trans. J. I. Suttie et al. London: Maresfield, 1926, p. 327.

—— (1919). Sunday neuroses. In *Further Contributions to Psycho-Analysis*. Trans. J. I. Suttie et al. London: Maresfield, 1926, pp. 174–176.

—— (1920). The further development of an active therapy in psycho-analysis. In *Further Contributions to the Theory and Technique of Psycho-Analysis*. London: Maresfield, 1950, pp. 198–217.

—— (1924). On forced fantasies activity in the association-technique. In *Selected Writings*. London: Penguin, pp. 222–230.

—— (1931). Child-analysis in the analysis of adults. In *Final Contributions to the Theory and Technique of Psycho-Analysis*. Trans. E. Mosbacher et al. London: Maresfield, 1955, pp. 126–142.

—— (1934). Thalassa: a theory of genitality. *Psychoanalytic Quarterly*, 3: 200–222.

Ferenczi, S. and Rank, O. (1925). *The Development of Psychoanalysis*. Trans. C. Newton. New York: Nervous and Mental Disease Publishing.

Fichtner, G. (1989). Freuds Briefe als historische Quelle. *Psyche*, 43, 803–849.

—— (1994). Die ärztliche Schweigepflicht, der Analytiker und der Historiker: eine notwendige Stellungnahme zur Edition des Freud/Ferenczi Briefwechsels. *Psyche*, 48, 738–745.

—— (1997). Professional secrecy and the case history: a problem for psychoanalytic research. *Scandinavian Psychoanalytic Review*, 20, 97–106.

Fischer, G. (1995). Möglichkeiten und Probleme der psychoanalytischen Prozeßforschung am Beispiel des dialektischen Veränderungsmodells. Vortrag bei der Arbeitsgemeinschaft für wissenschaftlichen Austausch am 25.2.1995 in Frankfurt am Main.

—— (1996). Die beziehungstheoretische Revolution. In J. Cremerius et al. (eds) *Methoden in der Diskussion: Freiburger Literaturpsychologische Gespräche*, Vol. 15. Würzburg: Königshausen & Neumann, pp. 11–31.

Folch, T. E. de and Folch, P. (1988). Die negative Übertragung: von der Spaltung zur Integration. *Psyche*, 42, 689–708.

—— (1996). Psychic reality and external reality in the analysis of children. *EPF Bulletin*, 46, 5–20.

Franch, N. J. P. (1996). Transference and countertransference in the analysis of a child with autistic nuclei. *International Journal of Psychoanalysis*, 71, 773–786.

Frank, C. (1994). Überlegungen zu 'Durcharbeiten in der Gegenübertragung'. In *Wege zur Deutung*. Opladen: Westdeutscher, pp. 72–89.

—— (1995). 'Weder Mensch noch Gebein': Annäherung an eine 'Erfindung', die 'Antigone' des Sophokles. In J.-H. Haas and G. Jappe (eds) *Deutungsoptionen*. Tübingen: Diskord, pp. 344–381.

—— (1999). The discovery of the child as an object *sui generis* of cure and research by Melanie Klein as reflected in the notes of her first child analyses in Berlin 1921–1926. *Psychoanalysis and History*, 1: 155–174.

Frank, C. and Weiss, H. (1996a). The origins of disquieting discoveries by Melanie Klein: the possible significance of the case of Erna. *International Journal of Psychoanalysis*, 77, 1101–1126.

—— (1996b). Der Beginn einer Kinderanalyse im Spiegel der handschriftichen Notizen Melanie Kleins. *Luzifer-Amor*, 17, 7–31.

Freud, A. (1927a). The role of the transference in the analysis of children. In *Introduction to Psychoanalysis: Lectures for Child Analysts and Teachers, 1922–1935*. London: Hogarth, 1974, pp. 36–49.

—— (1927b). Preparation for child analysis. In *Introduction to Psychoanalysis: Lectures for Child Analysts and Teachers, 1922–1935*. London: Hogarth, 1974, pp. 3–18.

—— (1927c). The methods of child analysis. In *Introduction to Psychoanalysis: Lectures for Child Analysts and Teachers, 1922–1935*. London: Hogarth, 1974, pp. 19–35.

—— (1927d). Child analysis and the upbringing of children. In *Introduction to Psychoanalysis: Lectures for Child Analysts and Teachers, 1922–1935*. London: Hogarth, 1974, pp. 50–69.

—— (1968). *The Ego and Mechanisms of Defence*. Trans. C. Baines. London: Hogarth.

—— (1972). Child-analysis as a sub-specialty of psychoanalysis. *International Journal of Psychoanalysis*, 53, 151–156.

—— (1974). Introduction. In *Introduction to Psychoanalysis: Lectures for Child Analysts and Teachers, 1922–1935*. London: Hogarth, pp. vii–xiii.

Freud, S. (1900). *The Interpretation of Dreams*. S.E. 4–5.

—— (1901a). *On Dreams. S.E. 5*.

—— (1901b). *The Psychopathology of Everyday Life. S.E. 6*.

—— (1905a). *Three Essays on the Theory of Sexuality. S.E. 7*.

—— (1905b). Fragment of an analysis of a case of hysteria. *S.E. 7*.

—— (1907a). Delusions and dreams in Jensen's *Gradiva. S.E. 9*.

—— (1907b). The sexual enlightenment of children. *S.E. 9*.

—— (1908). On the sexual theories of children. *S.E. 9*.

—— (1909a). Analysis of a phobia in a five-year-old boy. *S.E. 10*.

—— (1909b). Notes upon a case of obsessional neurosis. *S.E. 10*.

—— (1910). The future prospects of psycho-analytic therapy. *S.E. 11*.

—— (1911). *Psycho-Analytic Notes on an Autobiographical Account of a Case of Paranoia (Dementia Paranoides). S.E. 12*.

—— (1912a). The dynamics of transference. *S.E. 12*.

—— (1912b). Recommendations to physicians practising psycho-analysis. *S.E. 12*.

—— (1912–1913). *Totem and Taboo. S.E. 13*.

—— (1914a). On the history of the psychoanalytic movement. *S.E. 14*.

—— (1914b). Remembering, repeating and working-through (further recommendations on the technique of psycho-analysis, II). *S.E. 12*.

—— (1915a). Observations on transference-love. *S.E. 12*.

—— (1915b). A case of paranoia running counter to the psycho-analytic theory of the disease. *S.E. 14*.

—— (1916–1917). *Introductory Lectures on Psycho-Analysis. S.E. 15–16*.

—— (1918). From the history of an infantile neurosis. *S.E. 17*.

—— (1920a). The psychogenesis of a case of homosexuality in a woman. *S.E. 18*.

—— (1920b). *Beyond the Pleasure Principle. S.E. 18*.

466

—— (1922). Some neurotic mechanisms in jealousy, paranoia and homosexuality. *S.E.* 18.

—— (1933). *New Introductory Lectures on Psycho-Analysis. S.E.* 22.

—— (1955). Original record of the case (Notes upon a case of obsessional neurosis). *S.E.* 10.

Freud, S. and Abraham, K. (2002). *The Complete Correspondence of Sigmund Freud and Karl Abraham, 1907–1926.* Ed. E. Falzeder. London: Karnac.

Freud, S. and Ferenczi, S. (1993). *The Correspondence of Sigmund Freud and Sándor Ferenczi, 1908–1933, Vols 1–3.* Ed. E. Falzeder and E. Brabant. Cambridge, MA: Harvard University Press.

Freud, S. and Fliess, W. (1985). *The Complete Letters of Sigmund Freud to Wilhelm Fliess, 1887–1904.* Trans. and ed. J. M. Masson. Cambridge, MA: Belknap Press of Harvard University Press.

Freud, S. and Jones, E. (1993). *The Complete Correspondence of Sigmund Freud and Ernest Jones 1908–1939.* Cambridge, MA: Belknap Press of Harvard University Press.

Freud, S. and Jung, C. (1974). *The Correspondence between Sigmund Freud and C. G. Jung.* Ed. W. McGuire. Trans. R. Manheim and R. F. C. Hull. London: Routledge.

Friedrich, V. (1988). Briefe einer Emigrantin. Die Psychoanalytikerin Clara Happel an ihrem Sohn Peter (1936–1945). *Psyche*, 42, 193–215.

Frier, I. (1986). Begegnungen mit Fremdem: Produktion und Rezeption in der Beziehung zwischen Text und Leser. In J. Cremerius et al. (eds) *Methoden in der Diskussion. Freiburger Literaturpsychologische Gespräche*, Vol. 5. Würzburg: Königshausen & Neumann, pp. 43–58.

Gammill, J. (1992). Introduction to the panel on the question of frequency in child and adolescent analysis. *EPF Bulletin*, 38, 109–117.

Geissmann, C. & Geissmann, P. (1998). *A History of Child Psychoanalysis.* London: Routledge.

Gesing, F. (1989). *Die Psychoanalyse der literarischen Form: 'Stiller' von Max Frisch.* Würzburg: Königshausen & Neumann.

Gibeault, A. (1996). Scientific and professional developments in psychoanalysis in Europe: introduction by the President. *EPF Bulletin*, 47, 69–94.

Gillespie, W. (1987). Book review of P. Grosskurth's *Melanie Klein: Her World and Her Work. International Journal of Psychoanalysis*, 68, 138–142.

Goeppert, H. and Goeppert, S. (1981). Zum Verständnis von Sprache und Übertragung in Becketts 'Endspiel'. In B. Urban and W. Kudzus (eds) *Psychoanalytische und Psychopathologische Literaturinterpretation.* Darmstadt: Wissenschaftliche Buchgesellschaft, pp. 72–86.

Graf-Nold, A. (1988). *Der Fall Hermine Hug-Hellmuth: Eine Geschichte der frühen Kinder-Psychoanalyse.* Munich: Verlag Internationale Psychoanalyse.

Grosskurth, P. (1986). *Melanie Klein: Her World and Her Work.* Northvale, NJ: Jason Aronson.

Gutwinski-Jeggle, J. (1995). Zum Verhältnis von Gegenübertragung und projektiver Identifikation. *Luzifer-Amor*, 15, 61–83.

Hamann, P. (1993). *Kinderanalyse: Zur Theorie und Technik*. Frankfurt: Fischer.

Heimann, P. (1950). On counter-transference. *International Journal of Psychoanalysis*, 31, 81–84.

Hellmuth, H. (1911). Analyse eines Traumes eines 5¾ jährigen Knaben. *Zentralblatt für Psychoanalyse*, 2, 122–127.

Henningsen, H. (1964). Die Entwicklung der analytischen Kinderpsychotherapie. *Psyche*, 18, 59–80.

Henseler, H. and Wegner, P. (1991). Die Anfangsszene im Prisma einer Analytikergruppe. *Forum der Psychoanalyse*, 7, 214–224.

Hermanns, L. M. (1992, 1994). *Psychoanalyse in Selbstdarstellungen*. Vols 1–2. Tübingen: Diskord.

Hinshelwood, R. D. (1989a). Little Hans' transference. *Journal of Child Psychotherapy*, 15, 63–78.

—— (1989b). *A Dictionary of Kleinian Thought*. London: Free Association Books.

—— (1991). Psychoanalytic formulation in assessment for psychotherapy. *British Journal of Psychotherapy*, 8, 166–174.

—— (1994). *Clinical Klein*. London: Free Association Books.

Hinz, H. (1991). Gleichschwebende Aufmerksamkeit und die Logik der Abduktion. *Jahrbuch der Psychoanalyse*, 24, 146–175.

Hirschmüller, A. (1989). Freuds 'Mathilde': Ein weiterer Tagesrest zum Irma-Traum. *Jahrbuch der Psychoanalyse*, 24, 128–159.

—— (1991). *Freuds Begegnung mit der Psychiatrie: Von der Hirnmythologie zur Neurosenlehre*. Tübingen: Diskord.

—— (1996). Introduction. In S. Freud, *Schriften über Kokain*. Frankfurt: Fischer, pp. 9–39.

Hitschmann, E. (1913). Gesteigertes Triebleben und Zwangsneurose bei einem Kinde. *Internationale Zeitschrift für ärztliche Psychoanalyse*, 1, 61–68.

Holder, A. (1991). Kinderanalyse und analytische Kindertherapie. *Zeitschrift für psychoanalytische Theorie und Praxis*, 6, 407–419.

Horney, K. (1936). The problem of the negative therapeutic reaction. *Psychoanalytic Quarterly*, 5, 29–44.

Huber, W. (1980). Die erste Kinderanalytikerin. In H. Gastager, W. Huber, A. Rubner, E. Rubner and S. Schindler (eds) *Psychoanalyse als Herausforderung: Festschrift Caruso*. Vienna Verlag Verb. d. wissenschaftlicher Gesellschaft Österreichs, pp. 125–134.

Hug-Hellmuth, H. (1921a). On the technique of child-analysis. *International Journal of Psychoanalysis*, 2, 287–305.

—— (1921b). Vom 'mittleren' Kinde. *Imago*, 7, 84–94.

Hughes, J. M. (1989). *Reshaping the Psychoanalytic Domain*. Berkeley, CA: University of California Press.

Isaksson, A. (1992). Summary report about the standing conference on child and adolescent analysis, 1991. *EPF Bulletin*, 38, 128–136.

Jappe, G. (1991). Tradition – Identifikation – Imitation: Versuch über psycho-analytische Identität in der Bundesrepublik Deutschland. In J. Haas and G. Jappe, *Deutungsoptionen*. Tübingen: Diskord, pp. 408–436.

Jones, E. (1953–1957). *The Life and Work of Sigmund Freud, Vols 1–3*. London: Hogarth.

Joseph, B. (1985). Transference: the total situation. *International Journal of Psycho-analysis*, 66: 447–454. Reprinted in M. Feldman and E. Bott Spillius (eds) *Psychic Equilibrium and Psychic Change*. London: Routledge, 1989; also in E. Bott Spillius (ed.) *Melanie Klein Today: Developments in Theory and Practice. Vol. 2: Mainly Practice*. London: Routledge, 1988.

—— (1989). *Psychic Equilibrium and Psychic Change: Selected Papers of Betty Joseph*. Ed. M. Feldman and E. Spillius. London: Routledge.

Jung, C. G. (1910). Experiences concerning the psychic life of the child. In *Collected Works*, Vol. 17. Trans. R. F. C. Hull. London: Routledge & Kegan Paul.

—— (1954). *Collected Works*, Vol. 17. Trans. R. F. C. Hull. London: Routledge & Kegan Paul.

—— (1961). A case of neurosis in a child. In *Collected Works*, Vol. 4. Trans. R. F. C. Hull. London: Routledge & Kegan Paul.

King, V. (1995). *Die Urszene von Psychoanalyse: Adoleszenz und Geschlechterspannung im Fall Dora*. Stuttgart: Verlag Internationale Psychoanalyse.

Klein, M. (1921). The development of a child. WMK I, pp. 1–53.

—— (1922). Inhibitions and difficulties at puberty. WMK I, pp. 54–58.

—— (1923a). The rôle of the school in the libidinal development of the child. WMK I, pp. 59–76.

—— (1923b). Early analysis. WMK I, pp. 77–105.

—— (1925). A contribution to the psychogenesis of tics. WMK I, pp. 106–127.

—— (1926). The psychological principles of early analysis. WMK I, pp. 128–138.

—— (1927a). Symposium on child-analysis. WMK I, pp. 139–169.

—— (1927b). Criminal tendencies in normal children. WMK I, pp. 170–185.

—— (1927c). The importance of words in early analysis. WMK III, p. 314.

—— (1928). Early stages of the Oedipus conflict. WMK I, pp. 186–196.

—— (1929). Personification in the play of children. WMK I, pp. 199–209.

—— (1930a). The importance of symbol-formation in the development of the ego. WMK I, pp. 219–232.

—— (1930b). The psychotherapy of the psychoses. WMK I, pp. 233–235.

—— (1931). A contribution to the theory of intellectual inhibition. WMK I, pp. 236–247.

—— (1932). *The Psycho-Analysis of Children*. WMK II. London: Hogarth.

—— (1933). The early development of conscience in the child. WMK I, pp. 248–257.

—— (1935). A contribution to the psychogenesis of manic-depressive states. WMK I, pp. 262–289.

—— (1936). Weaning. WMK I, pp. 290–305.

—— (1940). Mourning and its relation to manic-depressive states. WMK I, pp. 344–369.

—— (1943). Memorandum on her technique. In P. King and R. Steiner (eds) *The Freud-Klein Controversies: 1941 to 1945*. London: Tavistock-Routledge, 1991, pp. 635–638.

—— (1945). The Oedipus complex in the light of early anxieties. WMK I, pp. 370–419.

—— (1946). Notes on some schizoid mechanisms. WMK III, pp. 1–24.

—— (1948). On the theory of anxiety and guilt. WMK III, pp. 25–42.

—— (1952). The origins of transference. WMK III, pp. 48–56.

—— (1955). The psycho-analytic play technique: its history and significance. WMK III, pp. 122–140.

—— (1957). Envy and gratitude. WMK III, pp. 176–235.

—— (1960). A note on depression in the schizophrenic. WMK III, pp. 264–267.

—— (1961). *Narrative of a Child Analysis*. London: Hogarth.

—— (1995). Der Familienroman in statu nascendi. In *Gesammelte Schriften*, Vol. 1. Ed. R. Cycon in collaboration with H. Erb. Stuttgart: Frommann Holzboog, pp. 1–9.

Knöll, H. (1985a). Auschnitt zur Entwicklung der analytischen Kinder- und Jugendlichenpsychotherapie in der Bundesrepublik Deutschland und Westberlin. *Praxis der Kinderpsychologie und Kinderpsychiatrie*, 34, 320–323.

—— (1985b). Zur Entwicklung der analytischen Kinder- und Jugendlichenpsychotherapie in der Bundesrepublik Deutschland und Westberlin. In *Arbeitskreis DGPPT/VKJP für analytische Therapie bei Kindern und Jugendlichen*, Vol. 1, pp. 8–17.

—— (1987). Zur Entwicklung der analytischen Kinder- und Jugendlichenpsychotherapie – Rück und Ausblick. In *Arbeitskreis DGPPT/VKJP für analytische Therapie bei Kindern und Jugendlichen*, Vol. 2, pp. 1–12.

Köhler, T. (1996). Anti-Freud Literatur von ihren Anfängen bis heute. Stuttgart: Kohlhammer.

Kraft, H. (1990). Ein Beitrag zur inhaltsbezogenen Formanalyse von Romananfängen. In *Zur Psychoanalyse der literarischen Form (N). Freiburger Literaturpsychologie Gespräche*, Vol. 9. Würzburg: Königshausen & Neumann, pp. 135–152.

Kutter, P. (1971). Über die Tätigkeit der Psychagogin in der Erziehungsberatung. *Psyche*, 25, 775–790.

Laplanche, J. and Pontalis, J.-B. (1973). *The Language of Psycho-Analysis*. Trans. D. Nicholson-Smith. New York: Norton.

Leuzinger-Bohleber, M. (1996). Psychoanalytische Überlegungen zu Elfriede Jelineks Lust (1989). In J. Cremerius et al. (eds) *Methode in der Diskussion:*

Freiburger Literaturpsychologie Gespräche, Vol. 15. Würzburg: Königshausen & Neumann, pp. 211–230.

Levita, D. de (1993). A few notes on frequency. *EPF Bulletin*, 41, 67–70.

Likierman, M. (2001). *Melanie Klein: Her Work in Context*. London: Continuum.

Loch, W. (1965). Übertragung und Gegenübertragung. *Psyche*, 19, 1–23.

Loch, W. and Jappe, G. (1974). Die Konstruktion in der Wirklichkeit und die Phantasien. Anmerkungen zu Freuds Krankengeschichten des 'kleinen Hans'. *Psyche*, 28, 1–31.

—— (1976). Psychoanalyse und Wahrheit. *Psyche*, 30, 865–898.

—— (1995). Psychische Realität – Materielle Realität. Genese – Differenzierung – Synthese. *Jahrbuch der Psychoanalyse*, 34, 103–141.

Lockot, R. (1985). *Erinnern und Durcharbeiten: Zur Geschichte der Psychoanalyse und Psychotherapie im Nationalsozialismus*. Frankfurt: Fischer.

Lorenzer, A. (1981). Zum Beispiel 'Der Maltese Falke': Analyse der psychoanalytischen Untersuchung literarischer Texte. In B. Urban and W. Kudzus (eds) *Psychoanalytische und psychopathologische Literaturinterpretation*. Darmstadt: Wissenschaftliche Buchgesellschaft, pp. 23–46.

—— (1986). Tiefenhermeneutische Kulturanalyse. In *Kulturanalysen*. Frankfurt: Fischer Taschenbuch, pp. 11–98.

Mächtlinger, V. (1995). Einleitung. In S. Freud, *Analyse der Phobie eines fünfjährigen Knaben*. Frankfurt: Fischer Taschenbuch, pp. 7–38.

MacLean, G. and Rappen, U. (1991). *Hermine Hug-Hellmuth*. New York: Routledge.

Maeder, T. (1989). *Children of Psychiatrists and Other Psychotherapists*. New York: Harper & Row.

Mahler, M. (1968). *On Human Symbiosis and the Vicissitudes of Individuation*. New York: International Universities Press.

Mahony, P. (1986). *Freud and the Rat Man*. New Haven, CT: Yale University Press.

Matte-Blanco, I. (1988). *Thinking, Feeling and Being*. London: Routledge.

Meisel, P. and Kendrick, W. (eds) (1986). *Bloomsbury/Freud: The Letters of James and Alix Strachey 1924–1925*. London: Chatto & Windus.

Meltzer, D. (1967). *The Psycho-Analytical Process*. London: Heinemann Medical.

—— (1978). *The Kleinian Development. Part II: Richard Week-by-Week*. Perthshire: Clunie Press.

Money-Kyrle, R. E. (1956). Normal counter-transference and some of its deviations. In E. Bott Spillius (ed.) *Melanie Klein Today: Developments in Theory and Practice. Vol. 2: Mainly Practice*. London: Routledge, 1988, pp. 22–33.

—— (1978). *The Collected Papers of Roger Money-Kyrle*. Perthshire: Clunie Press.

Müller-Braunschweig, C. (1970). Historische Übersicht über das Lehrwesen, seine Organisation und Verwaltung. In *Zehn Jahre Berliner Psychoanalytisches Institut (Poliklinic und Lehranstalt) 1920–1930*. Meisenheim: Anton Hain, pp. 20–44.

Müller-Brühn, E. (1996). Geschichte und Entwicklung des Instituts für analytische Kinder- und Jugendlichen-Psychotherapie in Frankfurt am Main. In
T. Plänkers et al. (eds) *Psychoanalyse in Frankfurt am Main*. Tübingen: Diskord,
pp. 654–702.

Müller-Küppers, M. (1992). Aus den Anfängen der Kinderanalyse. *Praxis der
Kinderpsychologie und Kinderpsychiatrie*, 41, 200–206.

Neidhardt, W. (1990). Von der Psychagogik zur Kinderanalyse: Darstellung
einer Entwicklungslinie aus dem Bereich der Stuttgarter Akademie für
Tiefenpsychologie und analytische Psychotherapie. In *Arbeitskreis DGPPT/
VKJP für analytische Therapie bei Kindern und Jugendlichen*, Vol. 3, pp. 1–28.

—— (1995). An diese Kinderanalysen knüpfen sich mancherlei Interessen.
DPV-Informationen, 17, 21–28.

Nerenz, K. (1997). Bemerkungen zur Geschichte des Gegenübertragungs-
begriffs. *Psyche*, 51, 143–155.

Norman, J. (1993). Frequency in child and adolescent analysis. *EPF Bulletin*, 41,
56–59.

Nunberg, H. and Federn, E. (eds) (1962–1975). *Minutes of the Vienna
Psychoanalytic Society*, Vols 1–4. New York: International Universities Press.

Oberborbeck, K. W. (1994). Kinderanalyse im Umfeld des Berliner Psychoanalytischen Instituts 1920 bis 1933. *Luzifer-Amor*, 7, 71–120.

—— (1995). Zur Geschichte der Psychagogik und 'Erziehungshilfe': Psychotherapie bei Kindern und Jugendlichen am 'Deutschen Institut' Berlin
1936 bis 1945. In *Analytische Kinder- und Jugendlichen-Psychotherapie*, Vol. 87,
pp. 177–244.

Ogden, T. (1989). On the concept of an autistic–contiguous position. *International
Journal of Psychoanalysis*, 70, 127–140.

Ophuijsen, J. H. W. van (1920). Über die Quelle der Empfindung des Verfolgt-
werdens. *Internationale Zeitschrift für Psychoanalyse*, 6, 68–72.

O'Shaughnessy, E. (1981). W. R. Bion's theory of thinking and new techniques
in child analysis. In E. Bott Spillius (ed.) *Melanie Klein Today: Developments
in Theory and Practice. Vol. 2: Mainly Practice*. London: Routledge, 1988,
pp. 177–190.

—— (1987). Book review of P. Grosskurth's *Melanie Klein: Her World and Her
Work*. *International Journal of Psychoanalysis*, 14, 132–136.

—— (1994). What is a clinical fact? *International Journal of Psychoanalysis*, 75,
939–947.

—— (1998). Wenn Wissen schädlich ist – Bions Konzept Minus K. In C. Frank
and H. Weiss (eds) *Kann ein Lügner analysiert werden?* Tübingen: Diskord,
pp. 126–143.

Overbeck, G. (1993). Die Fallnovelle als literarische Verständigungs- und
Untersuchungsmethode: ein Beitrag zur Subjektivierung. In U. Stuhr and
F.-W. Deneke (eds) *Die Fallgeschichte: Beiträge zur ihrer Bedeutung als For-
schungsinstrument*. Heidelberg: Asanger, pp. 43–60.

Peters, U. (1985). *Anna Freud: A Life Dedicated to Children*. London: Weidenfeld & Nicolson.

Petot, J.-M. (1990). *Melanie Klein. Vol. 1: First Discoveries and First System 1919–1932*. Madison, CT: International Universities Press.

Pfeiffer, S. (1919). Äußerungen infantile-erotischer Triebe im Spiel. *Imago*, 5, 243–282.

Pick, I. and Segal, H. (1978). Melanie Klein's contribution to child analysis: theory and technique. In J. Glenn (ed.) *Child Analysis and Therapy*. New York: Jason Aronson, pp. 427–449.

Pietzcker, C. (1992). *Lesend interpretieren: Zur psychoanalytischen Deutung literarischer Texte*. Würzburg: Königshausen & Neumann.

Racker, J. (1968). *Transference and Countertransference*. New York: International Universities Press.

Raguse, H. (1991). Leserlenkung und Übertragungsentwicklung: hermeneutische Erwägungen zur psychoanalytischen Interpretation von Texten. *Zeitschrift für psychoanalytische Theorie und Praxis*, 6, 106–120.

Rehm, W. (1968). *Die psychoanalytische Erziehungslehre: Anfänge und Entwicklung*. Munich: R. Piper.

Rey, J. H. (1979). Schizoid phenomena in the borderline. In E. Bott Spillius (ed.) *Melanie Klein Today: Developments in Theory and Practice. Vol. 1: Mainly Theory*. London: Routledge, 1988, pp. 203–229.

Riesenberg, R. (1977). *Das Werk von Melanie Klein: Psychologie des 20. Jahrhunderts*. Zurich: Kindler-Verlag, Vol. 3., pp. 210–249.

Riesenberg-Malcolm, R. (1990). As if: the phenomenon of not learning. *International Journal of Psychoanalysis*, 71, 385–392.

—— (1994). Conceptualisation of clinical facts in the analytic process. *International Journal of Psychoanalysis*, 75, 1031–1040.

Riviere, J. (1927). Symposium on child analysis. *International Journal of Psychoanalysis*, 8, 370–377.

—— (1936). A contribution to the analysis of the negative therapeutic reaction. *International Journal of Psychoanalysis*, 17, 304–320.

Rosenfeld, H. (1975). Negative therapeutic reaction. In P. Giovacchini (ed.) *Tactics and Techniques in Psychoanalytic Therapy*. Vol. 2, pp. 217–228.

—— (1987). *Impasse and Interpretation*. London: Tavistock.

Rubins, J. (1978). *Karen Horney*. New York: Dial Press.

Sandler, J., Dare, C. and Holder, A. (1973). *The Patient and the Analyst: The Basis of the Psychoanalytic Process*. New York: International Universities Press.

Sayers, J. (1991). Karen Horney. In *Mütterlichkeit in der Psychoanalyse: Helene Deutsch, Karen Horney, Anna Freud, Melanie Klein*. Stuttgart: Kohlhammer, pp. 73–119.

Schoenhals, H. (1994). Kleinian supervision in Germany: a clinical example. *Psychoanalytic Inquiry*, 14, 451–461.

Schönau, W. (1995). Literarische Kommunikation in psychoanalytischer Sicht.

In R. Holm-Hadulla (ed.) *Vom Gebrauch der Psychoanalyse heute und morgen: Arbeitstagung der DPV.* Frankfurt: Geber & Reusch, pp. 143–152.

Segal, H. (1964). *Introduction to the Work of Melanie Klein.* New York: Basic Books.

—— (1972). Melanie Klein's technique of child analysis. In *The Work of Hanna Segal.* New York: Jason Aronson, 1981, pp. 207–216.

—— (1979). *Klein.* London: Karnac.

—— (1997). The uses and abuses of counter-transference. In H. Segal, *Psychoanalysis, Literature and War: Papers 1972–1995.* Ed. J Steiner. London: Routledge, pp. 111–119.

Sharpe, E. (1927). Symposium on child-analysis. *International Journal of Psychoanalysis,* 8, 380–384.

Simmel, E. (1993). Zur Geschichte und sozialen Beduetung des Berliner Psychoanalytischen Instituts. In E. Simmel, *Psychoanalyse und ihre Anwendungen. Ausgewählte Schriften.* Ed. L. M. Hermanns and U. Schultz-Venrath. Frankfurt: Fischer, pp. 132–138.

Sokolnicka, E. (1920). Analyse einer infantilen Zwangsneurose. *Internationale Zeitschrift für Psychoanalyse,* 6, 228–241.

Spielrein, S. (1987). Schnellanalyse einer kindlichen Phobie. In S. Spielrein, *Sämtliche Schriften.* Freiburg i. Br.: Kore, pp. 225–228.

Spillius, E. Bott (1983). Some developments from the work of Melanie Klein. *International Journal of Psychoanalysis,* 64, 321–332.

—— (1988). Introduction to 'Developments in technique' and Introduction to 'The analysis of children'. In E. Bott Spillius (ed.) *Melanie Klein Today: Developments in Theory and Practice. Vol. 2: Mainly Practice.* London: Routledge, 1988, pp. 5–16, 155–157.

—— (1993). Book review of J. Petot: *Melanie Klein: Vol. I, First Discoveries and First System. 1919–1932* and *Vol. II, The Ego and the Good Object. 1932–1960. International Journal of Psychoanalysis,* 74, 1274–1280.

—— (1994). Developments in Kleinian thought: overview and personal view. *Psychoanalytic Inquiry,* 14, 324–364.

Spitz, R. with Cobliner, W. G. (1965). *The First Year of Life: A Psychoanalytic Study of Normal and Deviant Development of Object Relations.* New York: International Universities Press.

Steiner, J. (1984). Some reflections on the analysis of transference: a Kleinian view. *Psychoanalytic Inquiry,* 4, 443–463.

—— (1985). Some thoughts about tradition and change arising from an examination of the British Psycho-Analytical Society's Controversial Discussions 1943–1944. *International Review of Psychoanalysis,* 12, 27–71.

—— (1993). *Psychic Retreats: Pathological Organizations in Psychotic, Neurotic and Borderline Patients.* London: Routledge.

Stekel, W. (1908). Die Angstneurose der Kinder. In W. Stekel, *Nervöse Angstzustände und ihre Behandlung.* Berlin: Urban & Schwarzenberg, pp. 100–116.

Sterba, R. (1927). Über latente negative Übertragung. *Internationale Zeitschrift für Psychoanalyse*, 13, 160–165.

Stern, D. (1985). *The Interpersonal World of the Infant*. New York: Basic Books.

Strachey, J. (1934). The nature of the therapeutic action of psycho-analysis. *International Journal of Psychoanalysis*, 15, 127–159.

Stuhr, U. (1995). Die Fallgeschichte als Forschungsmittel im psychoanalytischen Diskurs: ein Beitrag zum Verstehen also Methode. In E. Kaiser (ed.) *Psycho-analytisches Wissen*. Opladen: Westdeutscher, pp. 188–204.

Stuhr, U. and Deneke, F.-W. (eds) (1993). *Die Fallgeschichte: Beiträge zur ihrer Bedeutung als Forschungsinstrument*. Heidelberg: Asanger.

Tausk, M. (1983). Wer war Viktor Tausk? Ein biographischer Versuch von seinem Sohn. In V. Tausk, *Gesammelte psychoanalytische und literarische Schriften*. Ed. H.-J. Metzger. Vienna: Medusa, pp. 92–111.

Tausk, V. (1924). A contribution to the psychology of child-sexuality. *International Journal of Psychoanalysis*, 5, 343–357.

Taylor, D. (1996). Über einige Aspekte von Melanie Kleins Einfluß auf die British Psychoanalytical Society. *Luzifer-Amor*, 17, 113–123.

Teising, M. (1994). Die Bedeutung der Säuglingsbeobachtung für die Psycho-analyse am Beispiel von D. Stern: Die Lebenserfahrung des Säuglings. In C. Frank (ed.) *Wege zur Deutung: Verstehensprozesse in der Psychoanalyse*. Opladen: Westdeutscher, pp. 17–31.

Thorner, H. (1983). Vorwort. In M. Klein, *Das Seelenleben des Kleinkindes*. Stuttgart: Klett-Cotta, pp. 7–11.

Torok, M., Sylwan, B. and Covello, A. (1998). Melanie Mell by herself. In L. Stonebridge and J. Phillips (eds) *Reading Melanie Klein*. London: Routledge, pp. 51–80.

Viner, R. (1996). Melanie Klein and Anna Freud: the discourse of the early dispute. *Journal of the History of the Behavioral Sciences*, 32, 4–15.

Wegner, P. (1988). Die Bedeutung der Anfangszene im psychoanalytischen Erstinterview. Dissertation. Tübingen.

—— (1994). Von der freien Assoziation zur Gegenübertragung. In C. Frank (ed.) *Wege zur Deutung*. Opladen: Westdeutscher, pp. 54–71.

Weiss, H. and Frank, C. (1995). Rekonstruktion des Würzburger Falles 'Erna' von Melanie Klein: Seine Bedeutung für die Entwicklung von Kleins theoretischen Konzepten zwischen ihren Berliner und Londoner Jahren. In H. Weiss and H. Lang (eds) *Psychoanalyse heute und vor 70 Jahren*. Tübingen: Diskord, pp. 120–137.

Winnicott, D. W. (1947). Hate in the countertransference. In *Collected Papers: Through Paediatrics to Psycho-Analysis*. New York: Basic Books, 1958, pp. 194–203.

—— (1977). *The Piggle: An Account of the Psychoanalytic Treatment of a Little Girl*. New York: International Universities Press.

Wittenberger, G. (1995). *Das 'geheime Komitee' Sigmund Freuds*. Tübingen: Diskord.

Wolffheim, N. (1973). Psychoanalyse und Kindergarten. In N. Wolffheim, *Psychoanalyse und Kindergarten und andere Arbeiten zur Kinderpsychologie*. Munich: Ernst Reinhardt, pp. 103–154. [*Psychology in the Nursery School*. Trans. C. Hannam. London: Duckworth, 1953].

—— (1974). Erinnerungen an Melanie Klein. In G. Biermann (ed.) *Jahrbuch der Psychohygiene*, Vol. 2. Munich: Reinhardt, pp. 294–304.

Wulff, M. (1912). Beiträge zur infantilen Sexualität. *Zentralblatt für Psychoanalyse*, 2, 6–17.

Young-Bruehl, E. (1988). *Anna Freud: A Biography*. London: Macmillan.

Zwiebel, R. (1994). Das Protokoll von Analysesitzungen. *Zeitschrift für analytische Theorie und Praxis*, 9, 192–203.

Index

Abraham, Hilda 22, 24
Abraham, Karl 12, 49n2, 71, 227; 'A
    constitutional basis of locomotor
    anxiety' 74; analysis of Klein 11, 33;
    beginnings of child analysis 22–3, 24;
    homosexuality 98–9; intellectual
    displacement of infantile sucking
    pleasure 232n25; minus K 232n25;
    negative transference 34–6; object-
    hostile tendencies 231; 'Observations
    concerning Ferenczi's paper on
    "Sunday neuroses"' 81; 'On
    parapraxes with an overcompensating
    tendency' 74–5; support and
    reassurance from 4, 55
absence and return 121, 122, 124
acting: 'acting in' 87; acting out by
    Klein 125, 130; 'Erna' and the
    significance of acting out in child
    analysis 169, 172–3, 224; play-acting
    see enactment; role play; role play see
    role play; toy use for acting out 159
    see also toys, as part of child analytic
    setting; transference and acting out
    224–6 see also transference
aggression: aggressive impulses at root of
    anxiety 135; attacks on the object's
    perceptual capacity ('Erna') 184–99,
    207; based on fear and a need for
    punishment 171–2; explained
    through play 202–3; interpretation of

envious–aggressive impulses 223,
    231–2; see also destructiveness
Aguayo, J. 26
Alexander, F. 69, 80
ambition 170–1
analysis see child analysis
analytic relationship: anxiety about 144;
    'Erna' case 183, 199–200; negative
    transference in 99–102 see also
    negative transference
anxiety: about feelings of exclusion and
    abandonment 86; about the analytic
    relationship 144; aggressive impulses
    at root of 135; castration see castration
    anxiety/complex; depressive 209;
    eased through interpretation 43, 143,
    144; guilt-derived 209; intellectual
    inhibition and 4; learning inhibition
    and 174; objects 124; recognition of
    importance of 12, 47, 124, 135; and
    the superego 4; systems of defence
    and 9; wish and anxiety
    interpretations of resistance 83
'as-if' personality disorder 141, 147

bad breast 125
Bannach, H.-J. 54
Berlin Psychoanalytic Polyclinic 49–55
Berlin Psychoanalytical Society 36, 55,
    68, 69, 70
Berna-Simons, L. 23

477